FADLALLAH

Jamal Sankari

FADLALLAH

The Making of a Radical Shi'ite Leader

SAQI

British Library Cataloguing-in-Publication Data
A catalogue record for this book is available from the British Library

ISBN 0 86356 596 4
EAN 9-780863-565960

This edition published 2005

SAQI
26 Westbourne Grove
London W2 5RH
www.saqibooks.com

Contents

Introduction

On 5 March 1985, a large explosive device was detonated in a car parked outside a high rise apartment in the densely populated quarter of Bi'r al-Abd in Beirut's southern Shi'i suburbs. It left a huge casualty toll, with nearly 100 dead and over 200 injured, all of them civilians, with a disproportionate number of women and children. Though the remote-controlled explosion caused massive destruction to the whole neighbourhood, the attempted assassination missed its target: Sayyid Muhammad Hussein Fadlallah, who was not in his residence at the time of the explosion.

Since the late 1980s, Fadlallah has been barred from entering the United States, demonised in the wake of 11 September as a terrorist leader, and ostracised and maligned by powerful conservative Shi'i clerics in Iran and the Arab world for his openness and rationalism.[1]

Who is Fadlallah? Why is he such a controversial figure? How influential is he? Is he the so-called 'spiritual leader' of Hizbullah in Lebanon? What is the true nature of his relationship with the 'Party of God' and other Islamist groups? Is he a theologian of liberation or a Muslim terrorist? Is he a scholar-activist or an anti-imperialist agitator? How has he risen to become the influential figure that he is? Where does he stand on the crucial issues that have dominated the recent political landscape of the Midldle East, the Palestinian Intifada and the Arab-Israeli peace process, the American-led invasion and occupation of Iraq, and the global 'war on terror'? What role will he has played in shaping the future of the Middle East, and charting the trajectory of the Shi'i Islamist movement in Lebanon and the Arab world? These are some of the key questions that will be addressed in this study of Fadlallah, his career, views and programme, which will attempt to provide an account of Fadlallah's thought and activism.

The many faces of contemporary Islamism are encapsulated in Fadlallah's personality: his pragmatic radicalism in activist politics; his radical reformism in the spheres of religious jurisprudence, Shi'i doctrine and historical narrative; his rationalism in intellectual inquiry and the reading of classical texts; and his trenchant anti-imperialism and anti-zionism.

Fadlallah is the pre-eminent Islamic religious scholar (*'alim*) in Lebanon, one of the Shi'i world's premier jurisconsults (*maraje'*), and one of the foremost Islamist intellectuals in the Muslim world today. How has he been able to rise to such prominence, and gain such wide recognition in each of these leading roles? What is the extent of his influence, and how does he exert his authority?

Rejecting the fundamentalist tag, with its negative connotations of intolerance, irrationalism and militancy, Fadlallah depicts himself as an activist Islamist, preferring it over confessionalist portrayal of Shi'i leader, and a rationalist and humanist thinker. Fadlallah's status transcends the confessional identity of his Shi'i community, and the narrow parameters of his ancestral homeland, Lebanon.

Fadlallah was one of the first Muslim scholars to publicly denounce the attacks of 11 September 2001. He justified his position on the basis that he does not sanction aggression against the American people [*Newsweek*, March 2004]. Yet, three years on, and nearly three years into President George W. Bush's so-called war on terror, with American and allied invasion troops in Afghanistan and Iraq, there has been a discernible shift in Fadlallah's perspective on the 9/11 attacks. Writing in the London-based *al-Sharq al-Awsat*, Fadlallah asks the following probing questions: who was behind those events? And who has been the beneficiary? [*al-Sharq al-Awsat*, 11 September 2004.] Fadlallah expresses the now commonly held view, among Arabs and Muslims in general, that Israelis had foreknowledge of the impending attacks but withheld that intelligence from their American friends, and that the US has since 9/11 taken advantage of favourable world sentiment to pursue its own 'neo-imperial' interests and ambitions, behind the smokescreen of the global war on terror.

Assuming multifarious roles, Fadlallah has kept up a very rigorous schedule. Delivering his Friday religious–political sermon before leading congregational prayers at the sprawling Masjid al-Imamayn in the heart of Beirut's densely populated southern suburbs, he gives a *mawitha* (a general exhortatory speech) on Thursday evenings at the same venue. He conducts twice-weekly courses on *al-fiqh wa usouluhu* (jurisprudence and its principles) for advanced students on Tuesdays in Beirut, and on Saturdays in Damascus, and supervises from afar a study circle in the Iranian holy scholastic city of Qom. Outside his teaching and lecturing hours, Fadlallah is engaged in responding to the numerous queries relating to religious, legal and social matters sent to him by religious laypeople; receiving guests, including dignitaries such as senior government ministers, parliamentary deputies, ambassadors, scholars and political activists; providing interviews at least once a week for print and electronic media; and as a guest speaker at various functions. He issues he covers range from the Islamic perspective on human cloning to globalisation and post-modernity, the rights of women, and the questions of Palestine and Iraq.

Fadlallah is also an accomplished poet, who began seriously composing quite early in his teenage years. Several compilations of his poetry composed throughout his activist and intellectual career have been published in recent years. The subject-matter of Fadlallah's poetry varies, but the predominant theme is Islam, Islamic culture and religiosity, and issues germane to the Islamic *umma*, such as Palestine, Muslim solidarity and brotherhood.

Side by side with Fadlallah's political and intellectual activity and teaching commitments are his philanthropic interests. Since founding al-Mabarrat in 1978 Fadlallah has overseen the development of an extensive network of elaborate social welfare institutions in Lebanon, providing specialist care and shelter for the disadvantaged in society – namely orphans, the poor and destitute, and those with disabilities. Spread throughout the country, al-Mabarrat has become a household name, and is the largest of its kind after that administered by Hizbullah. But whereas Fadlallah's Mabarrat is not state-funded, relying instead on donations and tithes of the Shi'i faithful in Lebanon, the Arab world, and in the West, Hizbullah's charitable and welfare institutions are sponsored in part by Iran.

Since the early 1990s Fadlallah has become a television celebrity – a regular guest on prime-time interview programmes on Lebanon's commercial stations, such as MBC; NBN, LBC and al-Mustaqbal. He has appeared at least once on practically every Arab satellite channel, including al-Jazeera, al-Arabiyya, Kuwait, Emirates, Dubai, Orbit, ART and Iqra', among others.

In Western media, academic and political circles, Fadlallah is widely (and simplistically) regarded as the paramount 'ideological mentor' of Hizbullah, or the 'Party of God', the premier Islamist movement and political party in Lebanon.[2] Less well known are other aspects of Fadlallah's leadership, which has transcended the ideological and organisational parameters of Hizbullah:

he is the pre-eminent theoretician of Lebanon's contemporary Islamist movements; he is one of the most influential Islamist intellectuals in the Arab world today; as one of the Shi'i world's foremost *maraje'*, he has a large number of followers in Lebanon, Iraq, and the Gulf Arab states, as well as amongst Muslim communities in Western countries. In addition, Fadlallah is a prolific writer of prose and poetry, a leading Shi'i religious scholar, an astute political analyst and principled activist, a potent orator, a media celebrity, and a popular philanthropist. Combining Islamic tradition with modernity, Fadlallah was among the first Muslim 'ulama to embrace the Internet, establishing his homepage in 1996.[3]

This book will analyse Fadlallah's professional and activist career, study his intellectual and political thought, and examine his plans and modes of action. Its framework of analysis is the dynamic nexus between Fadlallah's thought and action, and between his textual interpretation, reading of contemporary and historical contextual reality, and Islamist vision. This book evaluates Fadlallah's influence on the basis of what he has articulated in his lectures, writings, interviews, speeches and sermons, as well as the attitudes and activities he has taken as a politically engaged Shi'i public figure in Lebanon. His religious–political thought is studied within the context of contemporary Shi'i Islamist discourse and praxis in Lebanon and Iraq, to which he has made a significant contribution. The study of Fadlallah's career and thought will provide insight into the Shi'i Islamist movements in Iraq and Lebanon, and a basis for understanding his broader social and political influence amongst Shi'i and Sunni activists in Lebanon and the wider Arab world.

The book will also demonstrate that Fadlallah's intellectual thought and political ideology were shaped by forces specific to the contemporary Middle East – that is to say, his ideological orientation and political behaviour were constituted and defined by the interplay of local and regional forces that have operated, and in some cases still operate, in the modern Shi'i milieux of Iraq, Iran and Lebanon. It is thus against the background of the socio-cultural, political and economic transformations that have taken place in modern Iraq (1920–1966), contemporary Lebanon (mid-1960s to early 1990s), and revolutionary Iran (from 1979), that my endeavour to trace Fadlallah's origins and examine his scholarly and political career will be undertaken.

The principal question that will be addressed in this book is: can a valid case be made for identifying Fadlallah as a pragmatic radical Islamist? The secondary questions are as follows:

1. What was the nature of Fadlallah's links with the radical Islamist party, Hizb al-Da'wa al-Islamiyya [The Islamic Call Party], and how important was his early experience in political activism and Islamist ideology in shaping his future political behaviour, intellectual discourse and world-view?

2. What impact did the Islamic Revolution in Iran and Imam Khomeini's assertive political ideology have on Fadlallah, who, at the time, maintained close ties with his renowned and staunchly apolitical mentor, Ayatollah Sayyid al-Kho'ie, of the Iraqi holy city of Najaf?

3. Can we regard Fadlallah merely as an articulate disseminator of Khomeini's revolutionary ideology, with particular reference to the agents and processes of radical change and the structure of modern Islamic rulership; or should he be viewed as an innovative thinker in his own right?

4. How can we account for Fadlallah's strident opposition to US foreign policy in the Middle East, and his publicly expressed abhorrence for the very existence of the state of Israel?

5. How significant was the sudden disappearance of Musa al-Sadr in 1978 to the rise of Fadlallah, who ultimately became one of the foremost (and perhaps the most pre-eminent) Shi'i scholarly figures and activist leaders in Lebanon?

6. How did Fadlallah emerge as the pre-eminent theoretician, within Hizbullah or any other Islamist groups? What were the sources of influence among Shi'i scholars and Islamic intellectuals in Lebanon, and the Middle East as a whole? To what extent does he owe his current stature and influence to those roles?

7. As a proponent of empowerment and salvation of the disenfranchised and downtrodden, to what extent can Fadlallah be regarded as a theologian of liberation?

8. As an orator, Fadlallah has been able to project Islam as a vibrant and comprehensive faith with direct relevance to the issues of the day. To what degree were Fadlallah's oratorical skills relevant to his significant and expanding role in contemporary Lebanese society?

This book is organised around a number of propositions. First and foremost, it will be argued that Fadlallah is a pragmatic, radical Islamist. Fadlallah describes his discourse and praxis as both revolutionary and rationalist. For Fadlallah, the former denotes the employment of a coherent long-term strategic plan for the radical transformation of society.[4] In Fadlallah's conception, a true and successful revolutionary is necessarily rational, since he employs his intellect both to formulate and refine the means and to establish and revise the timeframe for attaining such major goals.[5]

Thus, Fadlallah is a radical in the sense that he presents a major reinterpretation of a number of accepted juridical and conceptual formulations extrapolated from Islamic canonical sources. He provides a thorough analysis of traditional Shi'i and Islamic institutions and rituals, the modern-day significance of which is thus made immediate and central to the lives of the Muslim faithful; he offers an incisive reading of current political events and developments at the local, regional and international levels, with a view to furthering the Islamist cause by assuming a practical and assertive role in political affairs; and finally, he ardently espouses the universal ideals of Islamically conceived global justice and freedom, and sustains long-term revolutionary goals. To the extent that Fadlallah actively aspires to the realisation of a restructured Islamic socio-economic and political order in the sprawling Muslim world, and ultimately to the gradual Islamisation of the non-Muslim world, he is unquestionably a radical.

Despite the radical underpinnings of his thinking, and the revolutionary nature of his goals, the views that Fadlallah holds on a variety of major issues are, by contrast, thoroughly pragmatic. A cursory look at Fadlallah's pragmatism on a number of topical issues will justify this assertion. He regards the quest for an Islamic state in modern Lebanon as an impracticable venture, at least for the foreseeable future; he considers the unilateral 'liberation' of Palestine, as actively pursued until recently by Hizbullah from its paramilitary bases in South Lebanon, as unfeasible; he assumed a favourable disposition towards the Lebanese parliamentary elections of 1992, actively encouraging the country's Islamist groups to participate; he was a prominent, seminal contributor to, and an influential proponent of, Sunni–Shi'i juridico-doctrinal concord and political solidarity; and finally, Fadlallah has been a leading and consistent advocate of sustained and substantive dialogue between Lebanon's Muslim and Christian communities as a necessary prelude to peaceful coexistence and national reconciliation.

Secondly, it will be argued that Fadlallah is a theologian of psychological empowerment and political liberation. This claim is grounded on his Qur'anic theory of justice, empowerment and liberation – a theory which envisions the enfeebled and oppressed ultimately inheriting the earth. The practical implication of this view is that, to the extent that one is religiously devoted, he is empathetic towards the pauper and underprivileged and committed to the invigoration and liberation of the disenfranchised and downtrodden from regime iniquity and foreign hegemony.

Thirdly, it will be demonstrated that the ascent of Fadlallah, in the wake of the mysterious disappearance of Musa al-Sadr, was critical to the twin processes of the religious revitalisation and political radicalism of the Shi'a in Lebanon, whose adherents constitute the country's largest confessional community. A corollary of that claim is that the recent ascendancy of the radical Shi'i Islamist movement in Lebanon can be attributed, to a large extent, to Fadlallah's recognised religious–juridical scholarship and political Islamist leadership. It will be argued, further, that Fadlallah's Islamist intellectual discourse provided ideological and juridical guidance to the cadres of Hizb al-Da'wa, while his writings and sermons provided the ideological foundation for the formation of Hizbullah.

Fourthly, it will be argued that, among its manifold political, military, religious, social and cultural functions, Hizbullah has served as an important and potent conduit for the dissemination of Fadlallah's Islamist views among Lebanon's politically disaffected, economically deprived and socially alienated Shi'i citizens. Furthermore, Fadlallah has adroitly utilised his autonomous relationship with Hizbullah to project his influence through the agency of the party's offices, as well as through his own elaborate independent channels. In this way, he has been able to extend his considerable influence beyond merely that of providing ideological guidance to the cadres and leaders of Hizbullah and Hizb al-Da'wa, to one of directly appealing to the sizeable but amorphous body of disaffected, primarily devout, Lebanese Shi'a, as well as to Sunni Islamist intellectuals and activists. Moreover, I will argue that Fadlallah's crucial premeditated unofficial ideological role in relation to Hizbullah and Hizb al-Da'wa al-Islamiyya has served to complement the substantial authority he currently wields – in his capacity as a leading religious scholar and Shi'i jurisconsult – among the Shi'i faithful in Lebanon and, to a lesser extent, Iraq and the Arab Gulf states.

While there is little doubt that the rise of Fadlallah as an influential public figure of regional significance was closely analogous to the ascent of Hizbullah, it would be wrong to assume that the nexus between the 'theoretician' and the movement was the determinant of that emergence. Nevertheless, the speed of his ascent was largely the outcome of his being associated (regardless of the extent to which that association is accurately perceived by political commentators) with Hizbullah – a potent and successful militant movement which he helped to inspire and nurture. Yet, given his independence of thought, his international scholarly authority and juridical eminence, it can be argued that Fadlallah's emergence as one of the world's pre-eminent figures of Islamist discourse would have taken place even without his relationship with Hizbullah.

At the time of writing, no book-length study of Fadlallah has been written in any Western language – although two substantial academic articles examining Fadlallah's thought, by the French scholar Olivier Carré, have appeared.[6] Two studies have been published in English since 1995, both in the form of book chapters. The first of these – an analytical account of Fadlallah's thought – is by Ibrahim Abu Rabi; and the second, the most detailed Western account of Fadlallah's career, is by Martin Kramer.[7] Preceding these two English-language studies was a forty-page booklet examining the thought of three influential Lebanese Shi'i 'ulama: Shaykh Muhammad Jawad Mughniyya (d. 1979), Shaykh Muhammad Mahdi Shams al-Din (d. 2001), and Sayyid Muhammad Hussein Fadlallah.[8] In general, but to varying degrees, the Western works on Fadlallah have glaring deficiencies in the area of accounting for the forces that shaped his childhood and early life, the development of his Islamist thought and scholarly career in Iraq, and his role in relation to Shi'i Islamist movements in Lebanon.

Western and Arabic academic studies tend to focus disproportionately on his controversial and ambiguous links with – and putative 'spiritual' leadership of – Hizbullah. Much less scholarly attention is given either to Fadlallah's role in the nascent Iraqi Shi'i Islamist movement of the late 1950s and 1960s, or to his relationship with the largest and most important organisation within that movement: Hizb al-Da'wa al-Islamiyya. Despite the undeniably important relationship between Fadlallah and Lebanon's premier Shi'i Islamist movement, its contours have, since the early 1980s, been amorphous and fluid. Fadlallah and Hizbullah's leadership may have coalesced at times, in some areas of mutually benefit, but the relationship has not always been one of concord, or immune from frostiness and uneasiness, and has never become binding and permanently symbiotic. It is the implications of this complexity and fluidity underlying the Fadlallah–Hizbullah relationship that will be examined in the following pages.

Omitted from the current literature on Fadlallah – or at least not treated adequately or systematically – are the Iraqi and Lebanese milieux, which are indispensable to any inquiry aimed at reaching a full understanding of his significance. If one is to gain insight into Fadlallah's Islamist world-view and activist agenda, and discern the complex development of a sophisticated intellectual, a radical visionary and ideologist, and a committed and pragmatic activist, an inquiry into the origins and development of his intellectual and ideological thought in Iraq is imperative. That country was his birthplace, the centre of traditional Shi'i scholasticism, and at once the cradle and crucible of Shi'i Arab Islamist discourse and activism. It was against this background that Fadlallah's thought was shaped, and his career evolved. Furthermore, given that his informal association with Hizb al-Da'wa pre-dated the relationship with Hizbullah, the formation and rapid development of the Lebanese Shi'i Islamist movement, along with the swift ascent of Fadlallah, cannot be fully understood without a close examination of Hizb al-Da'wa and of his role with respect to it.

As for Lebanon – Fadlallah's ancestral home during the years 1966–96 (the period under examination) – the relevant literature, to varying degrees in terms of emphasis and detail, surveys his activities and attitudes within the narrow and misconceived framework of the Hizbullah–Fadlallah nexus. For a more profound understanding of Fadlallah's public views, behaviour and relationships in Lebanon, it is necessary to move beyond those confines and analyse these matters in relation to the interplay of thought and praxis, the dialectical dynamics of ideology and changing reality, and the interface between radicalism and pragmatism.

Though the book draws heavily on primary Arabic source materials – and principally on Fadlallah's copious monographic and periodical writings, his numerous speeches and sermons, and his numerous interviews (including my personal interview and correspondence) – it does not provide a comprehensive and systematic account of Fadlallah's prolific literature. Given the inescapable thematic limitations of this book, Fadlallah's voluminous works, including a 24-volume Qur'anic exegesis, leave ample opportunity for scholars in the future to embark upon a series of accounts of his thought, or on detailed studies of the influence and origins of his ideological and political views, in comparison with those of other prominent Islamist figures.

ONE

The Formation of Modern Iraq, 1914–1932

A Geographical and Historical Outline

Situated on its southeastern periphery, the territories contained within modern Iraq constituted an important possession of the sprawling Ottoman Empire. From its conquest, accomplished between 1517 and 1534 AD, through two short intervals of Persian domination, to its final loss to Great Britain in 1917/18, the geopolitical area of Iraq (which did not historically form a single territorial entity) was internally divided into three separate provinces: Baghdad, Basra and Mosul. Representing the coalescence of these three distinct administrative units, the modern state of Iraq was essentially the creation of the British imperial government, formed in the immediate aftermath of the dismemberment of the Ottoman Empire at the end of World War I.[1]

The conspicuous lack of historical cohesion or organic unity among the three disparate parts of modern Iraq can be attributed, to a large extent, to preponderant aspects of physical and human geography. Iraq is a land of considerable contrasts. The rugged, mountainous terrain of the extreme north is delineated sharply from the alluvial, agricultural plains of central and north-central Mesopotamia, while the isolated marsh region of the lower Tigris–Euphrates basin contrasts markedly with the expansive arid and semi-arid zones of the south and west.[2]

Iraq's human geography was and remains populated by a multiplicity of confessional and ethnic communities. According to the official 1919 British census on Iraq, Shi'i Muslims constituted the largest confessional community in the country, comprising between 53 and 55 per cent of its total population. The overwhelming majority of Shi'i Mulsims were Arab, who comprised some 80 per cent of Iraq's ethnic composition. Sunni Arabs, though less numerous than their Shi'i counterparts, comprising roughly 20 to 22 per cent of Iraq's population, had traditionally dominated key government bureaucratic and military posts. Among the non-Arab ethnic minorities, the Kurds – who represented at that time between 16 and 18 per cent of the national population and were predominantly Sunni – formed the third-largest distinct community, followed by the significantly less numerous Turkomans, Assyrians, Chaldeans and Armenians.[3]

The three largest communities were distinguished further by their particular distribution; the bulk of the members of each of the three major communities were and remain concentrated in three corresponding geographical regions. The area to the south and southeast of Baghdad, encompassing the fertile territory between the Tigris and Euphrates, is populated predominantly by Shi'i Arabs; while the regions to the immediate north, the upper Mesopotamian plains of the northwest, and the western arid zone, are dominated by Sunni Arab populations. Finally, the extreme northern and northeastern mountain region occupied mainly by Sunni Kurds. Superimposed on this pronounced tripartite religious–ethnic division in early-twentieth-century Iraq was a discrete cleavage between the inhabitants of the major urban centres and the rural majority, most of whom were sedentary and semi-nomadic tribal people, which comprised nearly 80 per cent of the total population.[4]

Analogous to these intricate divisions in early modern Iraqi society was a marked socio-economic disparity between Sunni and Shi'a Arabs. Though constituting a slight majority of Iraq's population, the Shi'a living under Ottoman rule were prevented from assuming a role proportionate to their numerical weight. By virtue of their fervently Sunni persuasion, the Ottoman sultans and their provincial subordinates displayed a profound sense of mistrust towards their Shi'i subjects, and towards the Shi'i 'ulama in particular. The latter, owing to their confessional ties to their co-religionists in Iran, were sympathetic to the Shi'i Safavid dynasty that ruled Iraq's eastern neighbour and was the Ottoman Empire's regional nemesis. Thus, under the Ottomans, the Shi'a of Iraq were systematically excluded from the province's key government, educational, and military institutions. Admittedly, this process was to some extent facilitated by the Shi'a themselves, who refused to enrol their children in government schools where only Sunni teachers were employed. Similarly, since only Sunni judges were appointed to the shari'ah courts, the Shi'a boycotted them. This state of affairs was perpetuated under the British Mandate, to which reference will be made later; suffice to say here that this factor represented one of the seeds that spawned social alienation and political disaffection among the Shi'a.[5]

From Ottoman to British Domination

A major outcome of the 'Great War' was the eclipse of Ottoman hegemony and the ascendancy of British suzerainty in the Arab Near East in general, and Iraq in particular. In his capacity as paramount custodian of Sunni Islam, and by virtue of his being sovereign of the only remaining Islamic regional power, the Ottoman Sultan, Mehmet V, on 1 November 1914, declared war on the Triple Entente powers (Britain, France and Russia), and consequently entered World War I on the side of Germany and Austria-Hungary. That decision was to have far-reaching consequences, leading directly to the dissolution of the ailing Ottoman Empire in the Balkans and the Middle East and the emergence of a new political order in the region.[6]

Given their geo-strategic location, the provinces that came to constitute modern Iraq were destined to play a pivotal role in the overall course of military operations conducted by the Ottoman Turks and the British in the Middle Eastern theatre of war. Britain prosecuted a protracted and debilitating military campaign in Mesopotamia in the face of stiff resistance from regular Ottoman military garrisons stationed in Iraq, operating in concert with bellicose Shi'i Arab tribesmen. It was indicative of the intensity of the struggle for supremacy over Iraq that approximately twenty-eight months elapsed, following their initial marine landings in southern Iraq in November 1914, before the British expeditionary force was able to enter Baghdad in triumph.[7]

For Britain, Iraq was important, firstly, because its territory straddled the air route between its Mediterranean possessions – particularly Egypt – and India, and extended across the maritime route to India.[8] Secondly, British strategists took into consideration the proximity of Iraq, with its rich natural resources and potentially extensive oil deposits, to the British-controlled oilfields in southwestern Persia, and the Anglo-Persian Oil Company, centred on the vital port of Abadan.[9]

Central to British strategic thinking was the need to co-opt those influential Arab leaders who opposed Ottoman rule, and to cultivate their active participation in the Allied war effort. That need became all the more urgent in the light of the Ottoman Sultan's call, on 11 November 1914, for Muslims worldwide to wage a jihad against the adversaries of the Ottoman Empire. To Britain's dismay, among the segments of Iraqi society that heeded that call were the fiercely independent Shi'i Arab tribes of the middle and lower Euphrates basin.[10] The powerful tribal shaikhs had been exhorted by the influential Shi'i mujtahids to repulse the British invaders. The celebrated Shi'i 'ulama, residing in the four holy cities of Iraq (Najaf, Karbala, Samarra and Kazimayn), with their vehement dislike of 'infidels' and foreigners, had issued in late November 1914 fatwas, affirming a Muslim obligation to wage jihad in support of the Ottoman state.[11] Despite its evidently ailing condition and traditionally strained relations with the Shi'i religious establishment, the Ottoman Sultanate was regarded by the 'ulama as the last sovereign Islamic power with a potential to act as a bulwark against European encroachment and domination.[12]

It was thus with a view to understanding the patent utility and legitimacy of the primarily anti-British jihad that Herbert Lord Kitchener, the British Secretary of State for War, corresponded with the discontented Arab tribal chieftains of the Hashemite lineage, headed by Sharif Hussein, the custodian of Islam's holiest city of Mecca, hoping to elicit their active support against the Turks.[13] The success of the exploratory communication induced Sir Henry McMahon, the British High Commissioner in Egypt, to enter into correspondence with Sharif Hussein.[14] Though he had been appointed as Emir of Mecca, in 1908, by Sultan Abdul Hamid II, relations between him and the central authorities in Istanbul began to deteriorate following the seizure of power by the Young Turks, who pursued the twin policies of administrative centralization and Turkification.[15]

It was against this background that in February 1914 – some six months prior to the outbreak of World War I – the Hashemites of the Hejaz commenced confidential diplomatic negotiations with the British. Accordingly, at the behest of Sharif Hussein, his second son, Abdullah, proceeded to Cairo and conducted talks with Lord Kitchener with a view to exploring the possibility of obtaining British military aid should his father initiate an armed insurrection against the Turkish garrison in the Hejaz.[16] Since the Ottoman Empire was regarded in the pre-war period as a friendly power by Britain, Kitchener's reply was non-committal. However, with the outbreak of hostilities in August 1914, which saw the alignment of the Ottoman Empire with Germany, Britain promptly reviewed its position vis-à-vis Sharif Hussein.[17]

It was in these radically changed circumstances that the Hussein–McMahon correspondence, as it was later known, took place. It entailed the secret exchange of letters in July 1915, October 1915 and January 1916 between

Sharif Hussein and Sir Henry McMahon, in which the latter pledged in vague terms to grant, in the post-war era, political independence to the Arabs of the Arabian Peninsula and the Fertile Crescent, in return for their active support for the Allies.[18] The precise boundaries of the territories in question, however, were left undefined by the British – a subject of intense controversy in the immediate aftermath of the war. One of the key disputes revolved around the zone ambiguously designated as 'west of the district of Damascus', which was excluded from the territory of the prospective independent Arab state as pledged by McMahon.[19] According to official British and Jewish interpretations, this ill-defined area was Palestine. The Arabs, on the other hand, maintained that the excluded area was Lebanon, and that Palestine fell within the designated zone that was guaranteed independence.[20]

With respect to the Mesopotamian provinces of Basra and Baghdad, McMahon had stated in one of his classified letters to Sharif Hussein that, in view of Britain's vital strategic interests in the region, she would have to set up 'special administrative arrangements', thereby omitting altogether to recognise the intrinsic interests and aspirations of the indigenous Arab inhabitants. For his part, Sharif Hussein believed that those arrangements would be only transitory contingency structures, in no way acting as a hindrance in the long term to the establishment of the future pan-Arab kingdom.[21]

These disagreements aside, it was on the basis of this correspondence, which Sharif Hussein had deemed to be a definite understanding but which was never ratified as a legally binding accord, that he raised the banner of revolt against the Ottoman Turks on 5 June 1916.[22] Some five months later, in what was believed by his followers to be the dawn of a glorious new era, Sharif Hussein proclaimed himself 'King of the Arabs', though Britain subsequently recognized him as King of the Hejaz only. Command of the Arab Bedouin force was entrusted to Emir Faisal, Sharif Hussein's third son, who later became King of Syria (1918–20), and later still King of Iraq (1921–33). Acting in close consultation with British military advisers, Faisal's mounted irregulars gradually advanced northwards by evicting the Ottoman army stationed in the Hejaz, and wresting control of south and central Syria. Damascus was captured on 1 October 1918 by a joint British–Arab military force.[23]

Britain's military campaign in Iraq, which commenced with sea landings at Fao on the southern Iraqi Gulf coast on 1 November 1914, oscillated widely between success and failure. The British took the port of Basra in December 1914, but further north, in April 1916, Major General Townshend's army was encircled by Ottoman forces at the village of Kut on the Tigris. After a debilitating siege lasting 146 days, the beleaguered British army capitulated to the Turkish commander, Khalil Pasha. Notwithstanding Britain's setback in Iraq, its military fortunes were decisively reversed with the occupation of Baghdad by a new British expeditionary force in March 1917, under the command of Stanley Maude.[24]

The Sykes–Picot Agreement, the British Mandate and Iraqi Response

While the correspondence between Hussein and McMahon was seen by the Hashemites as a major concession to Arab nationalist demands, a separate treaty, known as the Sykes–Picot Agreement, was concluded without the knowledge, much less the consultation, of the nationalist leaders of Iraq and Syria, and at the expense of their fundamental political aspirations. Four months after the undertaking given by McMahon to Sharif Hussein, and three weeks prior to the commencement of the 'Arab Revolt', senior British officials entered into serious negotiations with their French counterparts over the political future of the Arab Near East. Following extensive correspondence, involving the exchange of eleven confidential letters between Sir Edward Grey, the British Foreign Secretary, Paul Cambon, the French Ambassador in London, and Sir Mark Sykes, a renowned Orientalist in the British Foreign Office, a secret agreement was concluded with Charles Georges-Picot, formerly French Consul-General in Beirut, whereby the Ottoman territories in the Arab Near East (excluding the Hejaz and Yemen) would be divided into respective British and French zones of direct control and spheres of influence.[25]

As a consequence of that arrangement, Britain would administer the Mesopotamian provinces of Basra and Baghdad (which together with the northern disputed province of Mosul later coalesced under the Mandate to form the modern territorial entity of Iraq), the geographical area that became known as Transjordan, and the Palestinian ports of Haifa and Acre. The greater part of Palestine, including Jerusalem, with its special religious status, was reserved as an area for which an 'international administration' would be established, while Syria and Lebanon were to constitute the French sphere of influence.[26]

The Sykes–Picot Agreement caused a furore in intellectual, political and religious circles in Iraq, and elsewhere in the Arab world, when in October 1917 the revolutionary Bolshevik regime in Russia publicised the confidential accord with a view to driving a wedge between the 'colonised' Arab Middle East and the capitalist, imperialist European powers.[27] This momentous agreement, which was subsequently ratified in April 1920 by the Supreme Council of the San Remo Conference, determined the territorial parameters and political structures of the separate politically defined territories that were to comprise the post-war Arab Middle East, foreshadowing the emergence in Iraq, as elsewhere in the region, of nationalist and Islamic opposition movements. The implications and consequences of the accord will be discussed below.

The Rise of Proto-nationalist and Islamic Opposition to British Occupation

The earliest religious–political formations during this period were Jam'iyyat al-Nahdah al-Islamiyya (the Islamic Renaissance Society) and Hizb al-Najaf al-Sirri (the Clandestine Party of al-Najaf). The two organizations were founded in the Shi'i holy city of Najaf, in late 1917 and early 1918, respectively, by a group of activist Shi'i 'ulama.[28] The former was the first organised Islamic group to incite armed uprising against the British military administration in Iraq, and to work openly towards establishing a regime committed to governing in accordance with the shari'ah. In pursuit of that goal, the organization played an instrumental role in March 1918 in initiating and prosecuting the armed insurrection in al-Najaf against the British, whose reaction was swift and ruthless; ringleaders of the revolt were executed or deported. With this depletion of its rank-and-file membership, the party soon faded into oblivion. But Hizb al-Najafi al-Sirri, as we shall see, was to play a central role in the 1920 Uprising, which engulfed the whole country. Yet not unlike the Jam'iyyat al-Nahdah, the organization disappeared from the Iraqi political scene following the suppression of the major revolt.[29]

Despite the short-lived experience of the two organizations, it should be noted that the leadership role played by the Shi'i 'ulama in the mass urban-based resistance to British occupation represented the continuation of their earlier anti-British activity during World War I. Their discernibly enhanced role and stature – arising from the militant pursuits of their peers during the war – was perpetuated and further strengthened by their assertive role in the political agitation during the six-year period that followed World War I.

In evident contrast to the parochial character of the nascent Islamic parties, whose activities were restricted primarily to the city of Najaf and its environs, the proto-nationalist Hizb al-'Ahd al-'Iraqi (Iraqi Covenant Party) and Hizb Haras al-Istiqlal (Guards of Independence Party) operated on a national scale. Both organisations were active in Iraq's three largest cities, Baghdad, Basra and Mosul. Founded in late 1918 or early 1919, Hizb al-'Ahd al-'Iraqi, as the name suggests, was the Iraqi splinter formation of the veteran pre-war

Hizb al-'Ahd, which came into existence in Istanbul in October 1913, with branches established in the major cities of the Fertile Crescent. Party members accounted for a significant number of Arab officers who had graduated from the Ottoman military academy in Istanbul.[30]

During World War I, many former Ottoman military officers from Iraq participated in the Sharifian-led Arab revolt against the Turks.[31] This coterie of ex-officers was later joined by former civil servants in the Ottoman bureaucracy. Both groups were overwhelmingly Sunni and Arab nationalist in composition. Crucially, the bulk of the government and bureaucratic officials who were to serve under King Faisal and the Mandatory administration were prominent members of the al-'Ahd group.[32]

Although Hizb al-'Ahd's platform advocated national independence, its charter nonetheless made a provision for the acquisition of British economic and technical assistance. This 'compromise' became a source of perennial tension between al-'Ahd and its stridently nationalist rival, Hizb Haras al-Istiqlal. In common with other short-lived nationalist and Islamic organisations of the period, Hizb al-'Ahd al-'Iraqi had, by the end of 1920 or the early part of 1921, ceased to operate as an effective political force.[33]

Formed in Baghdad in February 1919, Hizb Haras al-Istiqlal strove vigorously for the complete independence of Iraq, preferably under the rule of the Hashemite dynasty. In contrast to al-'Ahd, members of al-Istiqlal comprised both Sunni and Shi'i activists, with the former constituting a slight majority. al-Istiqlal's first elected president was Sayyid Muhammad al-Sadr, a renowned Shi'i scholar from the holy city of Kazimayn. This, and the fact that the son of the grand Shi'i jurisconsult, Muhammad Taqi al-Shirazi, was a leading activist, enabled the party to have 'special relations with Shi'i mujtahids'. This nexus would later prove to be a crucial factor in the process of radicalising the hitherto apolitical quiescence of the eminent Shi'i jurists, as well as providing the religious–juridical justification for the launching of the 1920 revolt. The party was at the forefront of the mass anti-British demonstrations that preceded the outbreak of the 1920 insurrection, in which its members played an important part, and which led directly to a major British crackdown on party affiliates, resulting ultimately in its dissolution in late 1920.[34]

The political geography against which these various political groups were formed was delineated by momentous and interrelated developments that unfolded between 1918 and 1921. One week after the Mudros Armistice, signed on 30 October 1918, which signalled the official end of World War I, the British and French governments issued a joint proclamation. It enunciated the common goal of Britain and France with regard to the Fertile Crescent: namely, 'the complete and final liberation' of the Arab people, who had been subjected to a prolonged period of Ottoman Turkish oppression, and the establishment of 'national governments and administrators that shall derive their authority from the free exercise of initiative and choice of the indigenous populations'.[35]

Significantly, the Anglo-French Declaration of 7 November 1918, designed to allay Arab nationalist apprehension regarding British and French designs on Arab territories, was followed by the referendum of December 1918–January 1919, the timing of which was clearly aimed at manufacturing congenial public opinion. Initiated by Arnold Wilson, the Civil Commissioner in Iraq, the plebiscite sought to gauge public opinion as to the delineation of Iraq's borders, and the extent of national support for the nominal rule, under British tutelage, of a leading Arab figure with Hashemite lineage. While the overwhelming majority of Iraqis voted for a single, unified state encompassing the former Ottoman provinces of Baghdad, Mosul and Basra, the distribution of votes in respect to the second issue was not as decisive. The leading tribal chieftains, merchants and notables, and some Shi'i 'ulama – whose status, prestige and economic well-being were enhanced by the British presence – favoured direct British rule.[36]

Hashemite Monarchy, British Policy and 'Ulama Response

Opposing this pro-British group were members and sympathizers of the underground nationalist parties, namely urban intellectuals and the majority of the Shi'i 'ulama and their novices, who called outright for an independent Sharifian-ruled Iraq. The stridently anti-British 'ulama demanded unequivocally the establishment of a unified, independent constitutional Islamic state, governed by a Sharifian or Hashimite leader. Among such proponents was the supreme mujtahid Imam Mirza Muhammad Taqi al-Shirazi, who had issued an influential fatwa prohibiting the election or installation of a non-Muslim ruler over a Muslim country like Iraq.[37]

The Arab tribes of southern Iraq were to play important but conflicting roles – the anti-British shaykhs being the key propellent of the 1920 Revolt and the pro-British chieftains acting as a solid mainstay for the Mandatory authorities. As a fundamental component of its colonial strategy of divide-and-rule, Britain exploited the primordial cleavage between the tribes of the countryside and the urban population. The Ottoman policy was essentially to emasculate the traditionally unruly chieftains of the powerful Arab, predominantly Shi'i, tribal confederations by attempting to bring the tribes under the sway of the central authorities. Instead, the British embarked on a systematic policy of empowering those tribes, who virtually ruled the hinterland. This radical change in official approach was motivated by a persistent need to economise, avoiding unnecessary the employment of highly-paid British officials posted in rural Iraq. To that end, the British Mandatory authorities, in a move that became an enduring legacy of the British in Iraq, officially recognised the paramount tribal shaykhs' authority to act as arbitrators and upholders of law and order, which involved the settlement of tribal disputes through recourse to tribal customary law in their particular domains.[38]

As a result of this calculated policy, the leading tribal chiefs became the recipients of government arms and subsidies, and the sanctioned collectors of tax revenue from agricultural produce and livestock, and in the process became staunchly loyal to the British. Furthermore, a British Mandatory law enshrined the ownership rights of tribal shaykhs to land in their domains; an ordinance that acted to the detriment of petty landholders and landless cultivators. Finally, the bolstering of the power of the major tribal shaykhs had the effect of alienating the tribal chiefs of lesser stature and influence from the central government. That profound disaffection among the lesser tribal shaykhs of the middle and lower Euphrates basin was to prove a potent factor in persuading those tribesmen to play a pivotal role, in conjunction with a militant segment of the Shi'i 'ulama, in the major armed uprising against the British administration in Iraq[39] – a pivotal event in the modern political history of Iraq that will now be examined.

The 1920 Uprising

The educated Iraqi populace had entertained high hopes of achieving complete and immediate independence. In the light of the undertaking given by McMahon to Sharif Hussein during the war years, and in view of the subsequent Anglo-French Declaration of November 1918, many Iraqis genuinely believed that Britain's military occupation and subsequent civil administration would be a brief, transitory phase between the eclipse of Ottoman rule and the dawn of Arab national independence. Much to their dismay, such expectations were shattered by the ratification of the Sykes–Picot Agreement at the San Remo Conference of 25 April 1920, whereby Britain was assigned a League of Nations' Mandate over Iraq. The perceived duplicity in Britain's plans vis-à-vis Iraq caused profound indignation and deep resentment, which in turn fuelled subsequent political agitation against the British, who were soon confronted with a full-scale armed uprising. The

Revolt engulfed half the country, and involved four British divisions in six months of intense fighting before it was suppressed.[40]

The British administration viewed the 1920 uprising as a tribal insurgency incited by the Hashemite Arab nationalists based in Syria. Batatu and other historians of modern Iraq identify the revolt as both archaic – in so far as the discontented Arab Shi'i tribes of the middle and lower Euphrates represented the core belligerents in the uprising – and also proto-nationalist, by virtue of the active involvement of urban-based nationalists affiliated to al-Istiqlal and al-'Ahd parties.[41] Indeed, it can be argued that in so far as the Revolt galvanized, albeit temporarily, the otherwise disparate segments of the nascent Iraqi society in a common, overarching cause of ousting the British, it was 'nationalist' in character.

Nursing a loathing for the foreign 'infidel' occupier. and aspiring to establish an Islamic regime in Iraq, the Shi'i 'ulama played a pivotal role both in the prelude to the 1920 uprising and during its course.[42] They were crucial in exhorting the disgruntled Shi'i tribesmen of the Euphrates basin to rise up against the British, in some cases fighting alongside them. The issuing of a fatwa in March 1920 by the pre-eminent Shi'i mujtahid, Sayyid Mirza Taqi al-Shirazi, was illustrative of the influence of the Shi'i 'ulama over those disaffected tribesmen. The edict, which stipulated that holding government office was contrary to the injunctions and precepts of the Shari'ah, precipitated widespread resignations in the tribal region. In ruling the election or acceptance of a non-Islamic government impermissible, the grand mujtahid provided the juridical basis for the subsequent insurrection.[43]

The process that facilitated the expression of proto-nationalist sentiment – in which the Shi'i 'ulama and several notable political activists (Ja'far Abu Timmam and Muhammad al-Sadr) were instrumental – was the unprecedented rapprochement, in the period prior to and during the 1920 Revolt, between the Sunnis and Shi'a of Iraq. The concord involved joint *mawlid* celebrations, by Sunni and Shi'a religious leaders in southern Iraq, of the birthday of the Prophet Muhammad, and *ta'ziyya* mournings commemorating the martyrdom of Imam Hussein. Since the Sunni–Shi'i reconciliation was dictated by the overriding political concern of launching and sustaining a war of popular resistance against the British, the eventual quelling of the Revolt allowed temporarily submerged particularistic interests, and denominational traits with their own inherent tensions, to resurface.[44]

The important roles played by the 'ulama and tribal shaykhs in the uprising revealed the extent of power and influence they wielded over Iraqi society. As a consequence, the British Mandatory administration and its installed monarchy embarked on a set of measures aimed at curtailing the capacity of the 'ulama to challenge seriously the authority of the central government. This policy led directly to a discernible decline in the status and influence of the Shi'i mujtahids, as traditional foci of power.[45] A consequence of the 1920 Revolt – and here it can be associated with the emergence and activity of contemporary Islamist movements of Iraqi Shi'i activists – is that the assertive oppositional role of the Shi'i 'ulama provided inspiration for radical Islamic political activism.

While the 1920 Revolt was ultimately crushed, albeit at a high human and material cost, it did have some important direct effects: first, the replacement of the acting Civil Commissioner, Arnold Wilson, with the more pliable Sir Percy Cox – a change that was coupled with a shift from direct to indirect rule; and second, the hastening of the British decision, in 1921, to install Amir Faisal as King of Iraq. That decision was based on several considerations: Faisal's Sharifian credentials were held in high esteem by both the Sunnis and the Shi'a; his role as commander of the Bedouin forces that fought the Turks made him a proven Arab patriot, and the most revered of Sharif Hussein's sons; his close ties to the British made him the best candidate through whom the latter could exercise indirect rule; and finally, his eviction from Syria by the French had left him without a domain or throne.[46]

Upon his accession to the throne on 27 August 1921, and his immediate appointment of *Sunni* Arab loyalists to senior posts in the embryonic government, civil service and army – and mindful of his recent, short-lived political experience in Damascus – Faisal embarked on a carefully balanced course with a view to legitimizing his recently conferred authority as monarch. This in turn provided a focus of loyalty for the disparate segments of Iraq's population; Faisal's advocacy of the gradual movement of Iraq towards independence combined simultaneously with 'maintaining close and cordial relations with the British Mandatory authority'. It was precisely those intimate and friendly relations between Faisal and the British that led to the emergence, in the wake of the promulgation of the 'Law of Association' in July 1922, of opposition parties. Among the newly formed political organizations were Hizb al-Watani al-'Iraqi (Iraqi Nationalist Party) and the reconstituted Hizb al-Nahdah (Renaissance Party), both of which had been predominantly Shi'i and sharply nationalist.[47]

The opposition of the nationalist movement became increasingly strident with the unfolding of the Anglo-Iraqi Treaty negotiations in mid-1922, designed to ratify British control over Iraq. Thus, on 23 August 1922, the two political parties issued a strongly worded joint communiqué, which included demands for the suspension of the treaty negotiations and the appointment of the prominent Shi'i nationalist, Sayyid Muhammad al-Sadr, as Prime Minister.

Refusing to yield to those demands, and exploiting the opportunity arising from King Faisal's sudden illness, the British High Commissioner instituted draconian measures against the leaders of the opposition. He clamped down on the anti-British movement by apprehending and deporting its leaders, banning the parties, censoring the press and ordering the aerial bombardment of insurgent tribes in southern Iraq.[48]

The Anglo-Iraqi Treaty and Popular Reaction

On 2 November 1922, the British High Commissioner, at the behest of Winston Churchill, induced a pro-Mandate Iraqi politician, al-Naqib, to form a 'moderate' government, which subsequently endorsed the controversial Anglo-Iraqi treaty. Although officially ratified on 13 October, and followed eight days later by a royal decree, providing for the holding of elections on 24 October for the Constituent Assembly, the treaty remained until the termination of the Mandate in 1932 the principal cause of anti-British sentiment and activity on the part of Iraqi nationalists and Shi'i 'ulama. That the treaty became anathema to the nationalist and Islamic opposition movements can be attributed to the fact that it served to safeguard British strategic and economic interests in the country by rearticulating the terms of the Mandate as a treaty with the fledgling state of Iraq. Specifically, the treaty stipulated the appointment to key posts of British officials, to act as advisers and inspectors, and required the monarch to be guided by the High Commissioner's advice on all matters pertaining to British interests.[49]

Closely interrelated with the ratification of the treaty was the promulgation of the 1922 Constitution, which aimed at applying the British imperial system of indirect rule and maintaining Iraq as a dependency of the British Empire. The Constitution was designed to provide the monarch and the High Commissioner with adequate executive powers to govern effectively and uphold the constitutive provisions of the treaty. Endorsed with a few minor modifications by the Constituent Assembly in 1924, the Constitution invested in the bi-cameral parliament the power to dismiss a cabinet. This prerogative, however, was 'counter-balanced by granting the King the right to [validate] all laws, to call for general elections, and to [dissolve] parliament'.[50] Moreover, the right was conferred upon him to formulate decrees for the fulfilment of treaty stipulations without parliamentary approval.

The Opposition of the 'Ulama to the 1922 Treaty and Elections

Though student objections to the ratification of the October 1922 Treaty were voiced by urban-based Sunni Arab nationalists, the staunchest objections came from the Shi'i 'ulama, whose power was still significant, though diminished in the aftermath of the 1920 Revolt. Spearheading the circle of activist Shi'i religious scholars was the eminent mujtahid, Shaykh Mahdi al-Khalisi, who rose to prominence in April 1922 when he played a key role in convening the Karbala Conference, attended by some 200 mostly Shi'i dignitaries and tribal elders. The declared objective of the forum was to marshal dissent against the prospective Anglo-Iraqi Treaty. al-Khalisi had set a precedent for other senior Shi'i 'ulama by issuing a fatwa forbidding the faithful from taking part in the elections for the Constituent Assembly, on the grounds that they were contrary to the interests and aspirations of the populace. The majority of Iraqi Shi'a heeded the edict, resulting in the abrupt halting of the election process.[51]

Failure to yield to government demands to call off the boycott prompted the British authorities to take action against leading figures in the opposition. The central authorities clamped down on those 'ulama who were deemed intransigent and recalcitrant. Among those militant 'ulama targeted and eventually deported to Iran on the pretext of being foreigners, and hence of posing a potential threat, was Shaykh al-Khalisi, who was at the forefront of both the movement of opposition against the treaty and the British administration, and of the campaign to institute a polity governed by the Shari'ah. Nine leading Shi'i mujtahids residing in the holy cities of al-Najaf and Karbala reacted to the deportation by organizing and leading a voluntary migration of many 'ulama, together with their followers, to Iran. With the exception of Shaykh al-Khalisi, these protesting 'ulama were, significantly, permitted to return to Iraq upon pledging not to resume religious–political dissent. The immediate result of this – the gradual marginalization of the Shi'i 'ulama as a potent voice of opposition – led indirectly to a discernible decline in their religious–political influence.[52]

The 'ulama-led protest against the 1922–23 election campaign and the Anglo-Iraqi Treaty induced Faisal to initiate a process of reconciliation, which led to a political crisis between the king and the prime minister, who along with his cabinet had orchestrated a campaign of suppression against the militants. Thus, in a purposeful move aimed at appeasing the Shi'i national and religious opposition, the prime minister was forced to resign, and a new government was formed incorporating two Shi'i cabinet ministers, and presided over by the prominent Shi'i nationalist Ja'far al-'Askari.[53]

'Ulama Decline and Nationalist Ascendancy

The marked decline in the incidence and influence of 'ulama-instigated political agitation in the immediate wake of the protest movement against the ratification of the treaty was accompanied by an similarly pronounced rise in the oppositional activism of the nationalist movement. Drawn from the urban middle classes, the nationalists, both Sunni and Shi'i, were as much averse to the continuing and pervasive British influence as to the growing concentration of power in the hands of Faisal and his pro-British cohorts. In particular, the nationalists objected strongly to the domination – by pro-British ministers and parliamentarians – of cabinet and parliament, which were viewed as mechanisms of foreign manipulation.[54]

Notwithstanding that common anti-British sentiment, the nationalist movement was beset by Sunni–Shi'i dissension arising from conflicting positions and divergent grievances. The Shi'i politicians were acutely dissatisfied with Sunni domination of all the levels of state apparatus. The real sense of injustice and inequity felt and lived by Shi'i citizens was accentuated by the espousal of quasi-secular Arabism and pan-Arabism by the preponderantly Sunni ruling elite. Shi'i intellectuals and politicians were traditionally lukewarm towards pan-Arabism as an ideology, fearing that it would submerge their Shi'i Arab particularism. Likewise, from the Sunni perspective, the Shi'a were suspect for their deep-seated historical and religious ties to Iran.[55]

The confessional factor apart, the nascent nationalist movement was plagued by deep political division. The Iraqi political scene in the mid-1920s was dominated by three principal single-issue opposition parties: Hizb al-Watani (Nationalist Party), formed in 1922 by Ja'far Abu Timman; Hizb al-Taqaddum (Progressive Party), founded in 1925 by Abdul Muhsin Sa'dun; and Hizb al-Sha'ab (People's Party), established in 1925 by Yasin al-Hashemi. All three political organizations were singularly concerned with terminating the Anglo-Iraqi Treaty. Unfamiliar with the operational mechanisms and structural organization of modern political parties, politicians formed fragile parliamentary blocs and shifting political alliances, determined by personal ambitions, parochial interests and nepotism. This incapacity to build broadly-based political institutions, to formulate policies related to major socio-economic issues, or to attract a mass following, constituted a major debilitating factor that consistently undermined the unity and effectiveness of the nationalist movement during the 1920s and early 1930s. The British Mandatory government was thus able to manipulate the various contending political forces, playing one off against another, in conformity with their strategic plans and interests.[56]

Negotiated by the newly appointed Prime Minister, Nuri al-Sa'id, and ratified in June 1930 by parliament, the Anglo-Iraqi Treaty, which enabled Iraq to become a member of the League of Nations by October 1932, stipulated mutual assistance in times of crisis, close consultation on external affairs, and open access for the RAF to two major airfields in Iraq. The renegotiated treaty led to the formation of new political parties and alliances. Opposing Nuri al-Sa'id's pro-British government were the leaders of the People's and Nationalist parties, which coalesced to form Hizb al-'ikha' al-Watani (National Brotherhood Party). The newly created group agitated against the granting of oil concessions and access to the country's military bases for the British. Due to their exclusive preoccupation with the 1930 treaty, the attainment of independence by Iraq in 1932 rendered the existing political parties redundant. Among the key events that ensued from this important development were the king's dismissal of the al-Nuri government and the creation of new political organizations to address the new issues arising from the country's recently won independence.[57]

British Land Tenure Policies and Their Consequences

The British Mandatory authorities sought, largely with success, to simplify the complicated land tenure structure that existed under the Ottoman regime, with a view to augmenting the position of the big landlords and tribal leaders. The growing accumulation of land in the hands of these two groups had the effect of gradually excluding the petty rural producers and landless cultivators (fellahin) from participating in the market economy. The fellahin were compelled to rely increasingly on borrowing from their landlords, who – mindful of the peasant's financial vulnerability – would lend money at an exorbitant rate of interest, resulting in widespread indebtedness and acute poverty. By the end of the 1920s, the severe plight of the peasantry, the majority of whom were Shi'a, had therefore forced increasing numbers peasants to abandon the countryside in search of a more secure livelihood in the major cities, particularly Baghdad.[58]

The promulgation towards the end of the Mandatory period of the Law Governing the Rights and Duties of Cultivators deepened the peasantry's plight and accelerated the process of rural-to-urban drift. Among the most significant articles of the law was the stipulation that cultivators who were indebted to landholders would not be permitted to cease employment and abandon the land until the designated debts were settled. However, as the vast majority of the fellahin were in serious debt, the only means by which to break out of this cycle of debt-bondage was to abandon the land altogether. Compounding the cultivators' predicament was another legal clause which stipulated that the peasant's failure to demonstrate the land's sustained productivity would automatically invalidate his land title, thus rendering the bulk of the petty landholding *fellahin* landless.[59]

The influx of the impoverished, predominantly Shi'i peasants into the cities produced extensive slum quarters inhabited by largely unskilled, unemployed, disgruntled rural immigrants. It was this ever-expanding reservoir of poor Shi'i malcontents that provided radical political parties in the 1940s and 1950s – and in particular the Iraqi Communist Party – with the most fertile ground for recruiting party cadres.[60]

It was against this turbulent social-economic background – superimposed upon a milieu of chronic political instability whose landmarks between 1933 and 1935 included the death of King Faisal and the succession of his son Ghazi, the formation and collapse of some eight different governments, followed by a five-year period of coups d'état – that Sayyid Fadlallah was born and lived his childhood.

Two

Fadlallah's Social Origins and Early Political Formation, 1935–1957

In order to understand the genesis and evolution of Fadlallah's thought and activism, the distinctive milieu of Najaf must be taken into account. The city provided not only fertile ground for the 'ulama-led armed and civil agitation against British imperial encroachment between 1914 and 1924, but also a spawning ground for both scholastic reformist and radical Islamist activities. A cursory view of the most eminent figures of contemporary Shi'i Islamist movements in Iraq, Iran and Lebanon will show that most of those leaders had studied or taught in Najaf.[1] It was in Najaf that Fadlallah had made a major contribution to the evolving radical Islamist discourse, and where his colleague, Sayyid Baqir al-Sadr, had founded in 1957 or 1958 the first revolutionary Shi'i Islamist political party (Hizb al-Da'wa al-Islamiyya). It was here, too, that a young group of dedicated Lebanese Shi'i students of Sayyid al-Sadr, who would subsequently constitute the nucleus of Lebanon's Hizbullah movement, had lived and studied in the 1970s. Finally, among the more renowned figures who made Najaf their home between the mid-1960s and the late 1970s was Imam Khomeini, the paramount leader of Iran's 1978–79 Revolution and founder of the Islamic Republic.

Najaf: its Character and Function

Located approximately 160km southwest of Baghdad, Najaf is situated on a plateau at the southeastern fringe of the flat, arid dune plain that forms the eastern extension of the Syrian Desert. Contributing to the desolate nature of Najaf's hinterland is the city's torrid climate, with intensely hot summers and stifling sandstorms. Notwithstanding its relatively small size, inhospitable climate and scant natural resources, Najaf was, until very recently, the premier sacred scholastic city of the Shi'i Muslim world.[2] Apart from being – according to popular belief – the burial site of Imam Ali bin Abu Talib, the Shi'as' first Imam and the Sunnis' fourth 'rightly-guided' *khalifa*, what distinguishes Najaf from the other three Shi'i holy cities –Karbala, Kazimayn and Samarra – is the concentration of the Shi'i world's most famous traditional religious seminaries.[3] Furthermore, Najaf has traditionally served as the seat of the Twelver Shi'i Marja'iyya (the supreme Shi'i authority for religious–juridical emulation). It was on account of its renowned religious colleges that Najaf became the principal residence of Shi'i students of diverse ethnic and social backgrounds. During the first two decades of the twentieth century, foreign students in the holy city (predominantly Iranian and Indian) outnumbered their Iraqi brethren.[4]

Najaf's burial grounds, especially the sprawling site of Wadi al-Salam (the Valley of Peace), are regarded as the most sanctified in the Shi'i world. For here – according to popular lore and traditional Shi'i sources – lies the body of the first Imam, Ali bin Abu Talib, the cousin and son-in-law of the Prophet Muhammad, who, in death, Shi'i Muslims believe to be the second most influential intercessor on behalf of the Shi'i faithful before God on the Day of Resurrection.[5] That belief has ensured that Najaf has become, over the centuries, the most popular destination of Shi'i pilgrims from all over the world.

The rise of the modern state of Iraq in 1921, and the establishment of Pahlavi dynastic rule in Iran in the same year, saw the governments of both states implement a number of measures that led directly to a marked reduction in the volume of traffic of pilgrims and corpses. Apart from the obvious sanitary problems associated with the otherwise unregulated traffic, the Iranian regime, under Reza Shah, was for its part motivated largely by the desire to elevate, at the expense of Najaf, the status of Iran's holy cities, Qom and Mashhad, as viable alternative centres for religious pilgrimage and burial.[6]

Najaf's pre-eminence is also owed to it being the oldest seat of Shi'i religious learning. Although historians of Iraq and the scholars of Shi'ism differ as to the precise date on which Najaf assumed the role of a centre for religious and theological learning, it seems that the shrine town of Ali only took on its central teaching function with the arrival of the celebrated jurist–theologian, Shaykh Abu Ja'far Muhammad al-Tusi (965–1067 AD). Regarded as the foremost Shi'i authority of his time, Shaykh al-Tusi is credited with establishing an informal religious study circle, known as *al- hawza.*[7]

The central figure in the *hawza* system was the *mujtahid* (a jurist who undertakes *ijtihad* – independent reasoning based on accepted principles of Islamic jurisprudence), who taught either in the shrine of Imam Ali, one of the city's courtyard mosques, or in a private dwelling. The *mujtahid* gave his lesson by sitting on the floor with his students around him, with his back to the wall. Unlike modern universities in the West and modernised Islamic institutions of higher learning, such as Egypt's al-Azhar, the traditional seminaries of Najaf were remarkably open. An aspiring student of the religious and legal sciences could freely affiliate himself with anyone of the numerous study circles that were active in Najaf during this period. There were no legal, administrative, financial or even age restrictions for the would-be student. There were no preconditions for admission, no student enrolments or 'on-campus' student rules and regulations to abide by, no tuition fees to pay, no annual exams to pass; nor was there a prescribed period in which to complete a particular course of study. Furthermore, since their mentors were not salaried functionaries, they were compelled to rely on the generosity of the faithful, who paid *al-khums* (a religious tithe calculated at one-fifth of one's annual income).[8]

Traditionally collected by the personal local or regional representative (*wakil*) of the *Marja'al-Taqlid*, the *khums* was conventionally divided into two special categories: *Sahm al-Imam* and *Sahm al-Sadah*. The former, forming half of *al-khums,* constituted the designated share of the handful of elderly *maraje'* (sing. *marja'*), who, in their individual capacities as recognised vicegerents of the Hidden Imam, are believed to have been invested with the authority to exercise substantial discretion in relation to the distribution of *al-khums* for a wide range of purposes.[9] The *Sahm al-Sadah* portion, on the other hand, which accounted for the other half of *al-khums*, has traditionally been the exclusive share of the family members of the Prophet and their Hashemite descendants (distinguished by the Sayyid title). Besides *al-khums*, the senior-ranked 'ulama assumed the role of collecting and distributing *zakat* (alms tax) to those who qualified as legal recipients, most notably the poor and destitute. In addition, the 'ulama received a considerable portion of their income from voluntary pious donations (or *sadaqat*, sing. *sadaqah*).[10]

The Shi'i *mujtahid*'s diverse sources of income had significant socio-economic and political implications, in that they rendered the 'ulama financially, and therefore juridically and intellectually, independent, and virtually immune to political manipulation by the ruling elites.[11] The financial independence of the Shi'i 'ulama contrasts sharply with the government patronage, in modern times, of the Sunni 'ulama establishments in Egypt, Saudi Arabia, and throughout the Arab world.

The scholastic education traditionally undertaken in Najaf's seminaries was, and still is, divided into three sequential stages. The first level, *al-Muqadimat* (literally, the introductory stage), conventionally lasts for three or five years, and commonly commences with the novice choosing his own teacher. During this intensive phase of learning, students are taught, from classical and rather abstruse texts, the subjects of Arabic syntax and grammar, prose, rhetoric and logic.[12] Theology, Arabic literature and mathematics may also be added.

The second and intermediate phase, *al-Sutuh* (literally, 'the surfaces'), consumes between three and six years. This stage involves the close study of the classical works of Imami Shi'i jurisprudence and its principles (*al-fiqh wa usuluhu*), the principles of deductive jurisprudence (*al-fiqh al-istidlali*), dialectic theology (*'ilm al-kalam*), *hadith* sciences, Qur'anic exegesis (*al-tafsir*), and philosophy (*al-falsafa*). As with the previous level, students are at liberty to select their own mentor, but with one significant difference: students concur with their teachers on an itemised reading list for their subjects. Students' progress is judged on the basis of their regular attendance of *hawza* classes and dedication to their studies.[13]

The third, final and most demanding level is known as *Bahth al-Kharej* – literally 'external research' – and entails extended research and critical analysis of more advanced literature, above and beyond the 'undergraduate' textbooks. This stage involves active student participation in large discussion groups which congregate around a senior *mujtahid* or *marja'*. The students of *al-hawza* listen attentively to their lecturer's commentary on a particular aspect of jurisprudence, its principles and practical application. Students invariably take notes on that commentary, which commonly expounds the divergent legal positions of the foremost Shi'i jurisconsults, and concludes with the lecturer stating his own legal opinion. Finally, students are invited to debate the principal issues raised in their mentor's lecture, such as methodology and sources of interpretation. Occasionally, a *mujtahid* might be challenged by one or more of his students on specific points relating to the line of reasoning underpinning his theory or judgement, and its practical ramifications.[14] After devoting anywhere between fifteen and twenty-five years to mastering the expansive subject-matter and various methodologies, successful students are awarded an advanced certificate – not by the *hawza* seminary per se, but from their mentor – qualifying them to exercise *ijtihad*.[15] Thus, by virtue of his being recognised as a *mujtahid*, the Shi'i jurist is entitled to be emulated (*taqlid*) in religious–legal matters by the faithful.

The rigorous nature of student life in Najaf's religious seminaries often means, for the overwhelming majority of would-be 'graduates', a life of financial hardship, poor health and religious asceticism. The most assiduous and promising of these students survives by means of a small monthly stipend paid by their teachers.[16]

Najaf Between Continuity and Change

Notwithstanding the attractive features of Najaf's lax administrative structure and open learning character, student numbers estimated at 10,000 prior to 1914 began to drop appreciably during the 1930s and 1940s, so that by 1957 there were fewer than 2,000 students in the holy city. The significant fall in student numbers was analogous to the general decline of Najaf as the premier seat of Shi'i learning. Several factors coalesced after the mid-1920s to contribute to this trend. Politically, the downward trend in Najaf's role paralleled a discernible decline in the city as a major centre of political ferment. The downturn in oppositional activism can be attributed to the suppression of the 'ulama-led anti-colonial uprising of 1920, and, in the immediate aftermath, to the curtailment of the political assertiveness of the 'ulama by the British Mandatory administration. Symptomatic of this decline was the fact that the Shi'i 'ulama of Najaf had disengaged as a whole from overt political activity between the mid-1920s and the early 1950s, when the spectre of communism impelled a major change in their posture. Finally, the steady waning of Najaf corresponded to the emergence of the Iranian holy city of Qom, which was promoted by the Shah as a serious contender for the mantle of pre-eminent Shi'i centre of learning.[17]

Furthermore, the foundation of the modern state of Iraq in 1921 was followed by the emergence in earnest of a national network of state-funded and administered modern schools. The emerging public school system came to present a steady challenge to Najaf's seminaries as a destination for young Shi'i aspirants. These students were lured by the secular education and professional career paths offered by the burgeoning public education sector. They were dissatisfied with the preponderance of religious instruction in traditional curricula, with the predominance of archaic textbooks, and the use of abstruse language and terminology.[18] Student discontent was also fuelled, on the one hand, by the inadequacy, and in some cases absence, of student stipends, and, on the other, by the prolonged duration and intensity of *al-hawza* education, which compared unfavourably with the security of government financial support, as well as with the existence of mechanisms to monitor and assess academic progress, with due consideration given to standardised courses and time-frames for completion.[19] Coupled with this general grievance among the religious students of Najaf was frustration arising from the belated realisation of the difficulty (upon completing the *Sutuh* level of *al-hawza* education) of alleviating their socio-economic plight, or of competing for employment with their modern state-educated counterparts.

It was to arrest this alarming trend that a group of reform-minded Shi'i 'ulama and intellectuals, led by Shaykh Muhammad Rida al-Muzaffar, convened a secret meeting in 1924 to establish the foundations of a new religious educational society in Najaf: Jam'iyyat al-Muntada al-Nashr. In 1935, the founding members of the society submitted a successful application to the Ministry of the Interior for the registration of al-Muntada. Despite the staunch opposition of the conservative 'ulama, the first state-registered modern Islamic primary (and later intermediate-level) school was opened in Najaf in 1938. Pupils were taught Arabic syntax and grammar, Arabic literature and religious jurisprudence, as well as foreign languages (principally English) and modern sciences (such as psychology and sociology).[20]

In establishing a new type of religious school, the founding fathers of al-Muntada envisaged that the institution would provide Shi'i Muslims with a viable alternative both to government secular schools and traditional religious seminaries. It was envisaged that this reformist school would produce a new generation of modern-educated Shi'i *mujtahids* and preachers, who would be receptive to the changing needs of modern-day society. Modelled on the modern state school system, the Muntada society recruited modern qualified teachers, who received a monthly salary. Its students were paid a reasonable allowance, while periodic examinations were set to assess students' progress. Although the society was able to expand its network of schools and steadily increase student enrolments, nevertheless student numbers were too few to have a substantial impact on either traditional religious or secular educational systems. Strong opposition by the Shi'i 'ulama ensured that the reformed religious schools would not supplant the traditional *hawza* seminaries. Nevertheless, a number of prominent Shi'i intellectuals and young would-be 'ulama, including Fadlallah, had studied, for varying periods, in one of the society's reformist schools.[21]

Besides being the focal point of clerical–legal learning in Iraq, and the Shi'i world in general, Najaf flourished during the first four decades of the twentieth century as a centre of literary and poetic activity.[22] The memorisation and public recital of poems were deep-rooted and authentic facets of Najafi popular culture. Illustrative of this distinction was the fact that, of Iraq's leading literary and poetic elite of that period, several had studied in one of the city's traditional colleges. Although the content and form of poetic literature varied considerably within this eminent group of poets, a common thread pervaded their writings: concern for current political and social issues.[23]

Despite its significance as the traditional centre of poetic literature, during the course of the emergence of the Iraqi state in the 1920s and 1930s, Najaf was gradually overshadowed by the rapidly growing capital city, to which the vast majority of Iraqi poets and writers of regional backgrounds had migrated in search of government employment. The fact that several of Iraq's leading contemporary romantic-turned realist poets – namely Badr Shakir al-Sayyab (1926–64), Nazik al-Mala'ika (1923–) and Abdul Wahhab al-Bayyati (1926–) – were either born or were based in Baghdad, demonstrated Baghdad's ascendancy in the cultural–literary field.[24] Although it lost its pre-eminence, Najaf nevertheless remained an important centre of poetic and literary output. Significantly, all of the above-mentioned poets, who rose to prominence in the early 1950s, influenced (to varying degrees) the development of Fadlallah's own poetic œuvre.

In the 1930s Najaf experienced decline in several important areas, for a number of reasons. Firstly, with the rise of the Iranian holy city of Qom, Najaf no longer held a monopoly over traditional Shi'i learning. Secondly, the emergence of modern Iraq in 1921 and the rise of Pahlavi dynastic rule in 1926 set in motion the process of state centralisation, which adversely affected Najaf's vibrant local economy. The resulting economic recession and concomitant social change led in turn to a drastic reduction in the volume of, and revenue from, the traditional transnational traffic in religious pilgrims to Imam Ali's shrine, as well as the flow of Shi'i corpses to the city's sacred burial precincts.[25]

In an attempt to curtail the self-flagellation rituals performed by Shi'i devotees in the holy month of lunar *Muharram*, the British-backed Iraqi administration issued a decree in 1935 that prohibited the public *'Ashoura* celebrations. This led to a sharp drop in the number of foreign pilgrims arriving in the twin shrine cities of Najaf and Karbala. Those foreign Shi'a allowed to visit Najaf were obliged to obtain a travel visa and to comply with restrictions imposed on all but personal provisions, and on the duration of temporary residency.[26] The decline in the incidence of self-flagellation at *'Ashoura* celebrations was a result not only of stern government measures, but also of the expressed displeasure of a number of prominent Shi'i 'ulama, of whom the most vocal was Sayyid Muhsin al-Amin, a Syrian reformist *mujtahid*.[27] The reformists strove successfully to foster the development of a new generation of well-educated *Muharram* rostrum speakers.[28]

Symptomatic of Najaf's general decline was the progressively diminishing role played by the city's senior 'ulama in the major political events and developments that unfolded in the predominantly Shi'i south. Whereas in the 1920 uprising the Shi'i *mujtahids* of Najaf had played a central role, the 1935 revolt saw the powerful Arab Shi'i tribal chieftains of the southern hinterland come to greater prominence.[29]

Sayyid Fadlallah's Upbringing and Early Intellectual Life

It was against this background that Sayyid Muhammad Hussein Fadlallah was born in 1935, into a family steeped in religiosity and scholasticism. His father, Abdul Ra'uf Fadlallah, a Sayyid (a title denoting descent from the Prophet Muhammad, and in Fadlallah's case through his elder grandson, Hassan) and a recognised Ayatollah, was born in 1907 in the southern Lebanese village of 'Aynata. Fadlallah's mother, al-Hajja Ra'ufa, also hailed from the far south – specifically Bint Jbail, a traditional centre of religious learning in the area. Muhammad Hussein's mother came from an influential family; she was the daughter of al-Hajj Hassan Bazzi, a renowned Lebanese political activist. In sharp contrast to his erudite father, Fadlallah's mother had received a modest education – one that was dictated by her religiously conservative and traditionally rural upbringing.[30]

Sayyid Abdul Ra'uf was reared by his father, Ayatollah Sayyid Najib (1863–1916/17), an eminent *mujtahid* in Jabal 'Amil (an upland Shi'i district in Lebanon's south), who was a dominant figure in his home town of Bint Jbail, and the founder and director of a well-established religious school, from which a number of 'ulama had graduated.[31] Losing his father at the age of ten, Sayyid Abdul Ra'uf began his elementary religious education at a school in Bint Jbail, where he studied the Qur'an, the Hadith, and *Nahj al-Balagha* (authored by Imam Ali), and apparently memorised the contents of the first and last of these. In 1927, at the age of twenty-eight, Sayyid Abdul Ra'uf journeyed, like many 'ulama aspirants before him, from south Lebanon to Najaf, where he remained until 1955, having successfully embarked on a course of traditional Shi'i higher learning.[32]

Sayyid Muhammad Hussein's father began his standard introductory (*al-Muqadimat*) and intermediate (*al-Sutuh*) studies under the patronage of his distinguished elder brother, Ayatollah Muhammad Sa'id Fadlallah

(1898–1954). Upon completing the first two stages of his education, Sayyid Abdul Ra'uf moved on to the advanced, specialised stage of *al-Bahth al-Kharij*. He attended the senior-level study circles and lectures conducted by some of the most eminent Shi'i *maraje'* of their time – namely Sayyid Abul Hassan al-Isfahani (1860–1945), Sayyid Mahmud al-Shahrudi (1882–1974), and Sayyid Abdul Hadi al-Shirazi (1887–1962). After mastering the Shi'i religious sciences and excelling in the skills of scholastic research, critique, and philosophical dialectics, Sayyid Abdul Ra'uf attained the rank of *mujtahid*, entitling him both to exercise *ijtihad* and to teach advanced religious studies. According to biographical sources on Sayyid Abdul Ra'uf, at least twelve Shi'i students either received part or all of their traditional religious education from the newly recognised Ayatollah, and were to graduate later as 'ulama and *fuqaha'*. Among this group of graduates were Sayyid Fadlallah and his two brothers, Muhammad Jawad (1938–75) and Muhammad Ali (1939–), as well as his colleague Shaykh Muhammad Shams al-Din (1936–2001), the late Chairman of the Higher Islamic Shi'i Council of Lebanon.[33]

The oldest male member of a family that comprised five brothers and five sisters, Sayyid Muhammad Hussein Fadlallah's childhood was conditioned by a climate of religious asceticism and erudition, a background of financial hardship, and by the harshness of the physical environment. Reminiscing on those years, Fadlallah recalled how the hot seasonal sand-laden desert winds regularly forced the city's inhabitants to seek shelter in specially constructed tunnels and subterranean chambers. He also recounted his family's ordeal in the face of severe economic hardship; a plight that was experienced by most religious students in Najaf. He described, graphically, how poverty virtually drove his parents to the brink of starvation. He attributed his family's predicament to the spartan and pious character of his father, Sayyid Abdul Ra'uf, who had shown a genuine reluctance to compromise his personal pride and his family's dignity by approaching the wealthy for financial relief.[34]

That experience left an indelible imprint on Fadlallah's psyche in two respects: firstly, it spawned in his personality an intense distaste for opulence, and a pronounced dislike for the contemptuous and extravagant lifestyle of the wealthy; and secondly, the rigorous religious and intellectual climate and economic adversity in which Fadlallah was reared had the effect of depriving him of those pleasures that are inherently associated with childhood. Conversely, the experience of deprivation and impoverishment had a major, long-term effect on Fadlallah's disposition towards the poor; it instilled in him a particular attachment to, and genuine empathy for, the wretched and underprivileged.[35]

Born and reared in the holy city of Najaf, the young Sayyid, not unlike other Shi'i children, was moved by the general religious atmosphere that traditionally envelopes the Shi'i populace, and which reaches a passionate climax during the annual ritual mourning (*ta'ziyya*) for Imam Hussein, the slain younger son of Imam Ali. The intense collective outpouring of grief and lamentation exhibited by the procession mourners on *'Ashoura* on the tenth day of *Muharram* (the first month in the Islamic lunar calendar) had a profound influence on Sayyid Fadlallah. The rite of collective self-flagellation performed by the most zealous among the devotees was for the young Sayyid a clearly reprehensible manifestation of the observance. He recalled how he was dismayed by the relentless gushing of human blood from the heads and backs of frenzied devotees, arising from the sometimes fatal, self-inflicted wounds caused by the repeated chain lashings and sword lacerations. Strongly objecting to the sanguine nature of the *ta'ziyya* rite, Fadlallah regarded ritualistic blood-letting as an inappropriate means by which to convey the emotional import of grief, and felt that such a display could not conceivably be a civilised form of expression.[36] Fadlallah's oppositional stance later became a central plank in the reformist agenda of the group of Shi'i *mujtahids* and intellectuals referred to earlier, who sought to purify the customary religious observance from what was viewed as illegitimate historical accretions and cultural traditions.

The distinctive Shi'i rituals of *'Ashoura* aside, Fadlallah's upbringing, particularly his education, was doubtless determined by the immediate context of his parents' home environment. His poor, religious – yet scholastic – background dictated the nature of his education, and ultimately his career. For both financial and religious reasons, Fadlallah, unlike most aspiring Shi'i 'ulama, was not sent by his parents to a modern government school. Instead, he began his rudimentary education in a *kuttab* (a traditional Qur'anic school organised in the form of study circles, or *halaqat*), which was located in the Kashif al-Ghita' mosque. Whilst there, the young Sayyid, we are told, was taught by a stern shaykh with a limited educational background, basic reading, writing and Qur'anic recitation. He was subsequently transferred to another *kuttab*, where an appreciably more congenial and competent Qur'anic teacher taught pupils in the shrine of Imam Ali, which dominated Najaf's skyline.[37]

It was not long before the Sayyid was again shifted, but on this occasion it was to one of Najaf's newly established modern religious schools, a network founded by a group of reform-minded Shi'i ulama affiliated to Jam'iyyat Muntada al-Nashr. As stated earlier, the society was formed to bridge the rift between the teaching curricula and methodology employed in modern government schools, on the one hand, and that of the traditional *hawziyya*, on the other. Being a gifted pupil, who was now ten years old, Fadlallah was placed in the school's grade-three classroom. He apparently performed exceptionally well in his class, and was elevated to grade four. However, for reasons unknown to him at the time, Fadlallah did not continue his education at this modern school. It is worth mentioning here that the schools affiliated to al-Muntada Society had attracted some of the brightest religious students in the Shi'i holy cities. Of this distinguished coterie of Islamic activists and eminent intellectuals, unquestionably the most renowned figure was Sayyid Muhammad Baqir al-Sadr (1935–80). Al-Sadr had studied at the society's school in his home town of Kazimayn, and became a close colleague and friend of Fadlallah. Although he was destined to embark on a traditional *hawziyya* career path, from as early as 1946, Fadlallah would often visit Jam'iyyat al-Muntada, showing a keen interest in the society's cultural and literary activity.[38]

During the same period, Fadlallah had contemplated becoming a journalist, and so co-operated with his cousin and intimate friend, Sayyid Muhammad Mahdi al-Hakim (the son of the illustrious *marja'*, Ayatollah al-'Uzma Sayyid Muhammad Muhsin al-Hakim), in the writing of a periodical manuscript, *Majallat al-Adab* ('The Literature Magazine').[39] In all, four or five issues were put out in 1945–46, or according to other sources, 1949–50.[40] Remarkably for his age (of twelve or thirteen), Fadlallah was widely read in all the major Arab literary and cultural magazines published in Egypt and the Fertile Crescent in the 1940s and 1950s. He followed with zest the periodic issues of *al-Risalah* ('The Epistle'), edited by the prominent Egyptian writer, Ahmad Hassan al-Ziyyat (1855–1968), and of the *al-Thaqafah* ('Culture') and *al-Musawwur* ('The Illustrated') magazines, as well as *al-Kitab* ('The Book') by 'Ali Ghadban, and *Kitab al-Misri* ('The Egyptian Book') and *Adab al-Kitab* ('The Book of Refinement'), both wriiten by Taha Hussein (1889–1973). A leading Egyptian literary critic, Taha Hussein was regarded by Fadlallah to have had considerable influence on his own literary development.[41]

At the time of the launching of the short-lived *al-Adab* magazine, the ten-year-old Sayyid discovered his extraordinary potential in the writing of poetry. The first verses he composed articulated a maturing world-view – a rejection of aristocratic opulence and arrogance, and a resolve to tread the rigorous path of righteousness and self-exertion.[42] Thus began the ascent of Sayyid Fadlallah, the poet, long before his rise as an influential religious scholar–jurist and renowned political activist. Finding himself naturally attracted to the writing of poetry – which he described as having been a spontaneous production – Fadlallah began to participate in the religious and social festivals that regularly took place in Najaf.[43] Consequently, in frequenting the city's public forums and social gatherings to exhibit his poetic talent, Fadlallah won acclaim despite his young age. The young Sayyid's early fame was not restricted to the locality of Najaf, for he travelled to a number of small towns situated in the southern province of al-Nasiriyya, where he participated in two Islamic festivals with a view to publicising his poems.[44]

Encouraged by his success in the literary sphere, Fadlallah founded, in collaboration with a number of his friends, Usrat al-Adab al-Yaqaz [The Society for Animated Literature]. In adopting free verse, the society introduced a radical style of poetic composition. Facing significant opposition on the part of the those who belonged to the traditional Najafi school of poetry, Fadlallah and his colleagues elected to use pseudonyms in order to publish their radical work in Iraqi newspapers. In this context, it should be noted that three poets (all Iraqis from Baghdad) – Badr Shakir al-Sayyab (1926–64), 'Abdul Wahhab al-Bayyati (1926–), Nazik al-Mala'iki (1923–) – were credited with originating incorporating the radical free verse and incorporating it into modern Arab poetry, thereby revolutionising traditional poetry in the Arab world. It was during the 1950s that Fadlallah began to acquaint himself with the modern poetry that appeared in successive issues of *al-Adab*, a newly established and widely read magazine. Of those poets, Fadlallah was influenced most by al-Sayyab, who was himself influenced by modern trends in English poetry. An admirer of Taha Hussein and the Lebanese poet, Ilyas Abu Shabaka (1903–47), al-Sayyab won widespread acclaim as an accomplished writer of socially and politically committed poems. He skilfully managed to diagnose the malaise in Arab society by interweaving the anguish and lamentation of the poet with his commitment to social and political ideals.[45]

During the 1940s, Fadlallah had delved into the poetic writings of the principal Arab neo-classicists of the period – namely Ahmad Shawqi and Hafiz Ibrahim from Egypt, Muhammad Mahdi al-Jawahiri from Najaf, and Ilyas Abu Shabaka and Khalil Mutran from Lebanon. Fadlallah stated that he was influenced considerably by Muhammad Mahdi al-Jawahiri (1901–), Ahmad Shawqi (1868–1932), recognised as the 'Prince of Poets' in the Arab world, and, to a lesser extent, by al-Akhtal al-Saghir and Ilyas Abu Shabaka. An accomplished neo-classicist, Shawqi wrote long, patriotic and religious poems which addressed major political developments of the day, and which evoked a pronounced sense of lamentation. A great admirer of Shawqi, al-Jawahiri was regarded as the most passionate of all neo-classical Arab poets. His political verse was strikingly emotive, captivating his readers through his scathing critique of prevailing social, economic and political conditions in Iraq and the Arab world in general. [46]

Concerned with Fadlallah's increasing preoccupation with poetry to the perceived detriment of his formal seminarial education, a group of senior 'ulama from Najaf advised the young Sayyid to abandon poetry altogether.

Perturbed by the dilemma he now faced, between continuing with his poetic pursuits and disregarding the expressed displeasure of the clerical establishment, or conforming with their wishes, Sayyid Fadlallah chose the former option. Convinced of his ability to pursue satisfactorily his religious–legal studies and poetic compositions concurrently, Fadlallah elicited the support of his respected uncle, Ayatollah Sayyid Muhammad Sa'id Fadlallah, as well as the approval of Ayatollah al-'Uzma Sayyid Abdul Hadi al-Shirazi, the mentor of Fadlallah's father. Thus, with their backing, Fadlallah was able to resume poetry writing, albeit with circumspection, having decided to attach the pseudonym of Abu Ali to the end of each poetic piece which, in the late 1950s and 60s, would be published in the forthcoming *Majallat al-Adwa' al-Islamiyya* ['The Journal of Islamic Illuminations'].[47]

Fadlallah did not, however, limit his extra-curricular pursuits to poetic writing; he discovered in himself, during a series of correspondences on literary developments with some of his relatives in South Lebanon, a talent for writing creatively and critically. It was when he was elected in the 1950s as a delegate to the Majama' al-Thaqafi li Muntada al-Nashr [the Cultural Convention of the Dissemination Club], which commissioned Fadlallah to write an exposé on the problems of traditional Najafi Arabic literature, that the Sayyid became recognised in the holy city's literary circles as a distinguished writer.[48]

Vindicating his exuberance and self-confidence in his intellectual abilities, Fadlallah's literary and poetic activities do not seem to have impacted adversely on his formal scholastic career. Tutored by his father, Ayatollah Abdul Ra'uf Fadlallah, the young Sayyid had managed to complete his *al-Muqadimmat* and *al-Sutuh* stages of the traditional *hawza* education. He studied classical texts on Arabic grammar, syntax, rhetoric, logic, Islamic jurisprudence, Qur'anic exegesis and Hadith literature. Fadlallah thereafter attended the advanced-level study-discussion circles (*al-Bahth al-Khariji*) of the most erudite and revered Shi'i *mujtahids* of his time: Ayatollah al-'Uzma Sayyid Abu al-Qasim al-Kho'ie (1899–1992), Ayatollah al-'Uzma Sayyid Muhsin al-Hakim (1889–1970), Ayatollah al-'Uzma Mahmoud Shahrudi (1882–1974), Shaykh Hussein al-Hilli, and Mulla Sadr al-Badkubi.[49]

Even while embarking on *al-Bahth al-Kharij*, Fadlallah began to tutor beginning and intermediate level students, a common practice among the seminary's advanced students and would-be 'ulama. Finally, after twenty-two years of religious scholarly learning, Fadlallah was accredited, in 1965 by his premier mentor, Sayyid al-Kho'ie, with a certificate of *ijtihad*. It was al-Kho'ie who would later designate the accomplished Fadlallah as his personal *wakil* (representative) in Lebanon.[50]

Evolving Political Consciousness and Experience

While it is difficult to ascertain the year in which Fadlallah embarked on the course of Islamic political activism, it can nevertheless be established that even while he was pursuing his advanced religious–legal studies that the Sayyid began to give serious thought to the means of rejuvenating modern Iraqi society. Fadlallah's formative political awareness was shaped by a turbulent political scene, whose character had undergone major change, thanks to the transformative forces that operated at the local and regional levels during that period. On 29 October 1936, the first *coup d'état* in modern Iraqi history was mounted, which led directly to a four-year period of military dominance of the country's politics. Moreover, the political ascendancy of the military – a development that paralleled the burgeoning nationalist sentiment – had eventually paved the way for the rise of the virulently anti-British but short-lived Rashid Ali al-Gaylani regime.[51]

It was the salient political developments that unfolded in the post-war era that impacted most profoundly on the young Sayyid's maturing political awareness and evolving world-view. On 15 January 1948 the Portsmouth Treaty was concluded. It proved to be deeply unpopular because it amended the earlier Anglo-Iraqi Treaty of 1930 to the effect that it reaffirmed British authority over the fledgling state, particularly in relation to the crucial spheres of military and foreign affairs. The treaty enraged an already embittered intelligentsia and educated urban middle class, who, propelled by a fervent nationalist sentiment, saw it as a fatal compromise of Iraq's political sovereignty and national dignity. Popular resentment and indignation gave rise to mass uprisings that centred on Iraq's major cities. While the disturbances were predominantly carried out by Arab nationalists, activists belonging to the nascent Islamist and Marxist movements played a minor role. In his own recollections of the period, while Fadlallah relates how he observed closely the political oppositional currents (the nationalist, democrat, and Marxist) that were active in the late 1940s, he makes no specific reference to the urban unrest arising from the above treaty.[52] On the basis of this omission one can plausibly infer that Fadlallah did not actively participate in the street protests and riots that occurred in the wake of the treaty.

Facing the most formidable mass upheaval in the history of the Iraqi monarchy, the government, headed by Salih Jaber, reacted by violently quelling the disturbances, leaving a large number of casualties.[53] The net effect of those events was the galvanisation of the otherwise disparate political opposition, which forced the resignation of the government, the dissolution of the national parliament, and finally the abrogation of the detested treaty.[54]

Important as these political events were for Iraqis, they were soon overshadowed by the cataclysm of the Palestine War of May 1948–January 1949, which convulsed the country and the Middle East in general. Indicative of the importance of the conflict were, firstly, the dispatch of Iraqi military units to the Transjordanian front; secondly, growing pan-Arab nationalist sentiment; and thirdly, the intensifying animosity towards Britain's over its pivotal role in the establishment of a national homeland for Jews in Palestine. Popular indignation and consternation over the future of the Holy Land were translated into mass strikes and demonstrations against the United Nations resolution on 27 November 1947 to partition Palestine into two separate states – one Arab and one Jewish.[55]

For Fadlallah, the disastrous war for Palestine became a central religious and pan-Islamic cause that implanted itself deeply in his psyche, and constituted an integral part of his political and religious consciousness. At the age of twelve – symptomatic of the importance he attached to Palestine – Fadlallah composed a short poem, from which he recollected the following lines: 'Defend our usurped rights in Palestine with our sharpened swords, and remember Salah al-Din [Saladin's] era, when he proceeded to evict the foreigner.'[56] Fadlallah also reminisced on a lengthy editorial article he wrote in an unnamed Islamic magazine at that time, in which he forcefully argued that

> The issue of Palestine may sometimes be presented as Palestinian, other times as Arab nationalist, and still other times as Islamic; [and yet because or in spite of these diverse identities] we ought to refrain from entering into vindictive quarrels so that all three distinctive currents may complement each other in a common struggle for Palestine.[57]

This tendency towards pragmatism was to become a constitutive theme in Fadlallah's evolving realist–radical praxis.

Besides Jordan, the Arab state most directly affected by the Palestine War was Syria. The immediate aftermath of the 1948–49 disaster in Palestine heralded a period of acute political instability in Syria, which became the focus of intense inter-Arab rivalry, as Iraq, Egypt and Jordan tried separately to influence the direction of events in that country. Thus, between 30 March 1949 and 3 December 1952, Syria underwent three military *coups d'état*. Fadlallah was among those young Iraqis who followed the rapid developments in Syria with interest.[58]

In 1952, a year that coincided with widespread student riots in Iraq, at the age of sixteen, Fadlallah accompanied his father on his first trip to

Lebanon, apparently with a view to visiting his relatives in the south of the country. During his stay in Beirut, Fadlallah attended a major honorary gathering held in the Lebanese capital to commemorate the passing of the fortieth day since the death of the late Ayatollah Sayyid Muhsin al-Amin, a reformist Lebanese Shi'i *mujtahid.* According to Fadlallah, the congregation was attended by eminent political, scholarly and journalistic figures. Among the renowned dignitaries was Shaykh Mustapha al-Siba'i, the General Guide of the Syrian Muslim Brethren, who, as the Sayyid later reminisced, delivered an impassioned speech. As for the seventeen-year-old Fadlallah, he was, by his own account, able to attract the attention of the dignitaries when he recited a poem that revolved around Islamic political solidarity and religious unity, and touched on the question of French imperialism in the Levant, as well as on pressing social issues in Lebanon.[59]

Remaining several months in his parents' district in Lebanon's 'deep south', Fadlallah was to spend considerable time engaged in vigorous ideological debates with ardent secularists (socialists, Arab nationalists, communists, and Ba'thists) on the role of Islam in modern society. Fadlallah's enthusiasm for and competence in the arts of dialectics and polemics can be traced to his seminarian background and his wide reading. Fadlallah believes that his training as a religious scholar made him receptive to diverse intellectual and ideological trends. Yet out of this openness to engage with the proponents of modern secular ideologies, Fadlallah began to acquaint himself especially with Marxism, and with dialectical materialism in particular. The Sayyid also read, unsystematically, the works of Jean-Jacques Rousseau, Frantz Fanon and Paolo Freire.[60]

Fadlallah's political perspective and intellectual orientation were further enriched by the extended discussions that took place between himself and a local group of Arab nationalists and Marxists during subsequent trips to South Lebanon. The most notable of these was on 15 July 1955, when the young Sayyid again accompanied his father, Abdul Ra'uf, who left Najaf after a period of approximately thirty years of intense study and teaching for permanent residency in his country of birth. Remaining in Lebanon for eighteen months, Fadlallah travelled widely and engaged in intellectual discussions and political debates. The successive trips to Lebanon provided Fadlallah with an invaluable opportunity to survey at first-hand the highly complex confessional composition of Lebanese society.[61] Fadlallah also noted the prevailing political situation in Lebanon, shaped as he perceived it to be by the intense and polarised positions rivalry between Britain and France, on the one hand, and between Britain and the United States, on the other, with the latter actively seeking to establish a foothold in Lebanon.[62]

This perspective on the interventionist foreign policies of the Western powers vis-à-vis Lebanon, and the region at large, was vindicated in the eyes of Fadlallah by the Baghdad Pact. The alliance, which came into official existence on 24 February 1955, tied Iraq, together with Turkey, Iran and Pakistan, to Britain and the Western powers. The pact proved highly controversial domestically, and deeply divisive regionally. Specifically directed at stemming the rising tide of Arab nationalism, the pact led directly to an intense cold war between the conservative Hashemite monarchic states of Iraq and Jordan, and the republican and assertively pan-Arab regime in Egypt, which pursued a policy of containing and ultimately unravelling the influence of what was perceived to be an imperialist–reactionary axis, and Hashemite-ruled Iraq. The latter became the target of incessant disparagement by military strongman Gamal Abdul Nasser, through his radio mouthpiece, 'Voice of the Arabs'.[63]

It should be stressed here that the 1952 Egyptian Revolution became the focus of considerable interest for Fadlallah, as it was for all young educated Arabs of his generation. Fadlallah states that he and his colleagues had 'interacted' with the Revolution, notwithstanding its pronounced Arab nationalist character.[64] That interest turned into profound concern and populist pan-Arab support for President Nasser with the outbreak of the 1956 Suez War, which was precipitated by the Egyptian leader's nationalisation of the Suez Canal. This unilateral but domestically popular action brought about the ensuing invasion of Egypt by Britain, France and Israel. For the Iraqis, in common with other Arabs, the tripartite invasion was regarded as an act of perfidy. Consequently, public fury was translated into a tide of protests and demonstrations which swept the country, resulting in violent clashes with state security forces. Nur al-Sa'id's government took draconian measures, in a desperate attempt to stem the mass uproar. Martial law was subsequently imposed, but having failed to curtail the spreading clashes between students and the police, the authorities closed all colleges and secondary schools in Baghdad indefinitely. The popular unrest subsequently spread to engulf all of Iraq's cities and major towns.[65]

In southern Iraq, the disturbances were centred on Najaf, where the ubiquitous network of subterranean chambers and passages served as ideal spawning grounds for dissident activity. That Najaf, a bastion of traditional Shi'i religiosity and erudition and a renowned focal point of periodic political ferment, became a major arena for mass strikes and demonstrations fomented and organised by members of the local branch of the Iraqi Communist Party, was totally unexpected, and for the custodians of Shi'i Islam – the 'ulama – a deeply disturbing development. Moreover, what was particularly alarming for Najaf's 'ulama, in regard to the magnitude and depth of communist influence in this centre of Shi'ism, was that the Shi'i malcontents failed to heed the recurrent, strident exhortations and supposedly binding decrees of their *mujtahids* to terminate their militant activities and association with an 'ungodly' and politically subversive organisation. Instead the unrest continued for another week, during which cities in northern Iraq were swept by mass protests, expressing solidarity with Najaf.[66]

Important as the regional repercussions of the political events centred on Egypt were for the national and local milieux of Iraq, of more immediate concern, as far as a small circle political activists and reformist Shi'i 'ulama was concerned, was the vitality and rapid expansion of the Iraqi Communist Party into the Shi'i heartland. Fadlallah was one of those intellectual activists who was dismayed at the pivotal role played by the communists in the unrest in Najaf. Facing what was perceived to be a crucible, Fadlallah and his dedicated Islamist colleagues were propelled into formulating a new line of Islamist discourse and organised political activity, or in the words of Fadlallah, 'a dynamic Islam', which would be capable of meeting the challenges of 'shifting political realities'.[67]

THREE

Shi'i Islamism in Revolutionary Iraq: Genesis and Development, 1958–1966

Beginning with the formation of Hizb al-Da'wa al-Islamiyya and ending with the departure of Fadlallah from Iraq, the years 1958 to 1966, saw major political and ideological developments. It was a period of political upheaval – revolution, military coups and counter-coups – and ideological ferment and struggle, witnessing, on the one hand, the emergence of the premier Shi'i Islamist organisation, and the rapid spread of the Iraqi Communist Party, and radical secular ideology in general, on the other.

The July 1958 Revolution: Causes, Catalysts and Consequences

The collapse of the Old Regime of the Hashemite royal family was not a sudden, spontaneous event, but the outcome of a meticulously planned and well-organised military coup staged by a group of senior and middle-ranking army officers. Headed by the future president, Staff Brigadier Abdul Karim Qasem, commander of the 19th Infantry Brigade, and his lieutenant, Colonel Abdul Salam 'Aref, commander of the 20th Infantry Brigade, the leading elements that comprised the circle of dissident military officers, named their formation the Supreme Committee of the Free Officers.[1]

As a 'local manifestation of a larger revolutionary movement' that was anchored in Egypt and inspired by President Gamal Abdel Nasser's Pan-Arab nationalism, the first rudimentary clandestine cells were formed in the immediate wake of the Egyptian Revolution of 1952. But it was the 1956 Suez War that precipitated the coalescence of radical elements within the upper echelons of the military with the Iraqi Free Officers, who later, upon their ascension to power, were to organise themselves into a Revolutionary Command Council on the Egyptian model. Although the Free Officers did not comprise a cohesive body that subscribed to an elaborated set of principles and or programme of action, nevertheless they shared a loose notion of Pan-Arabism, a longing for Arab unity through a common struggle against western imperialism and feudalism, and an aspiration to socioeconomic justice and republican rule.[2]

The dissident military officers belonged to a generation that, with the exception of Abdul Karim Qasem and Abdul Salam 'Aref, was drawn from the middle or lower-middle classes, to which the majority of modern Iraqi professionals and intellectuals belonged. By virtue of his senior rank, Qasem became in 1957 the recognised head of the fourteen-member, predominantly Sunni Central Committee, the supreme body representing the Free Officers, who, at the time, numbered between 170 and 200. The grievances that propelled the Free Officers to insurrection against the monarchy were deep-seated and manifold, but can be broadly divided into internally and externally induced factors. As members of an educated, modernising class of Iraqis, their aspirations to upward mobility were blocked by the sluggish pace of social and economic reforms instituted by the conservative ruling elite, who represented the older generation of established Iraqi politicians. Essentially comprising the national leaders of the post-World War I struggle for independence, the ruling clique represented an alliance between two traditionally conservative segments of Iraqi society – namely the large tribal landholding and the merchant classes.[3]

Politically, too, those frustrations were exacerbated by what was perceived to be the abject failure of the established British parliamentary system of government in terms of political openness, including freedom of political affiliation and party organisation, and political justice in the form of genuine power-sharing with the major modernising political and social groups in society.[4]

Externally, the ruling elite became the source of nationalist disaffection and popular indignation on account of its foreign policy. As we saw in the previous chapter, the old regime had instituted a series of foreign policy decisions based on the preservation of British strategic interests – namely the 1955 Baghdad

Pact, which tied Iraq to the Western powers, and the 1956 tripartite invasion of Egypt. In February 1958, Prime Minister Nur al-Sa'eed, a conservative stalwart, established a union between Britain's two neighbouring Hashemite-ruled Arab states of Iraq and Jordan. This alliance came as a direct response to the creation on 1 February 1958 of the United Arab Republic, which unified Nasser's Egypt and Ba'thist Syria. Designed to contain the rising tide of Arab nationalism emanating from Egypt, and more recently from Syria, the Iraqi-Jordanian union was a belated and counter-productive scheme. It totally disregarded the extent and depth of Pan-Arab sentiment among Iraq's predominantly Arab citizens, and, in particular, it collided with the profound influence of Nasser's radical political ideology among important segments of the Iraqi officer corps. In this way, the old regime's domestic and foreign policies deepened national resentment and antipathy towards the monarchy and the government.[5]

Consistently deprived of the right to play any meaningful role in the country's political and social affairs, the Iraqi national opposition, which encompassed the Iraqi Communist Party, the Ba'th Party, the National Democrats and the Independence Party, formed the United National Front (al-Jabha al-Wataniyyah al-Muttahidah), in the wake of the rejection of a formal application for registration submitted by the two latter, relatively moderate, parties in 1957. The Front, headed by the Supreme National Committee, comprised four oppositional leaders, each representing one of the four principal political parties opposed to the Government. The Front's platform called for the resignation of the Prime Minister, the withdrawal of Iraq from the Baghdad Pact, the abolition of martial law, and the enshrining of political and constitutional freedoms.[6]

Although the Free Officers shared the political ideas and values of their young civilian compatriots affiliated to the national opposition parties, and indeed had forged links with the Supreme National Committee, the disaffected military officers progressed from a state of frustration and yearning to one of organised revolutionary action. The catalyst for the coup ultimately came in the form of an Arab nationalist uprising in Lebanon against the pro-Western Government of President Chamoun. The mass outpouring of Pan-Arab sentiment among Lebanon's influential Sunni community led to civil strife in mid-1958, and caused trepidation in conservative government circles in Baghdad and Amman. In a move aimed at containing the fall-out, Prime Minister Nuri al-Sa'eed ordered the despatch of Iraqi military units to Amman to bolster the regime of King Hussein. For Brigadier Qasem and Colonel 'Aref, who commanded the Iraqi expeditionary force and secretly opposed the deployment, the mission provided the pretext to activate their long-awaited plot.[7]

The ensuing sequence of events included a march on Baghdad by Qasem's troops, the seizure on 14 July of the government's broadcasting station, the occupation of the royal palace and the summary execution of the royal family and the prime minister. No sooner had the newly installed revolutionary regime announced the demise of the monarchy and the establishment of a republic than the streets of Baghdad became swollen with raging mobs who took to spontaneous lynching of suspected officials of the old regime, wanton looting and the destruction of property. As a result of the havoc and carnage wrought by street mobs, a curfew was imposed by the military regime.[8]

In view of the deep unpopularity of the old regime, it is not surprising that the fall of the monarchy was received with mass euphoria. During his first few months in power, General Qasem was hailed as a national hero and patriotic revolutionary. The fact that Qasem was able to ride on a wave of mass support was largely due to the initiation of an independent foreign policy and the overturning of the defunct regime's controversial foreign policies.[9]

Among the young Iraqi citizens who shared the euphoria of the early days of the revolution was the twenty-two-year-old Sayyid Fadlallah. In common with many of his compatriots, he saw in the revolution the dawning of a new era of political freedom, economic progress and social justice. In an impassioned poem that was published by the official Iraqi Republican Newspaper in 1958, the young Sayyid captured the popular mood and general attitude of those days of ferment. In his emotive free verse, Fadlallah praised the architects of the Revolution, viewing it as the fulfilment of his nation's long-suppressed national and patriotic aspirations. He expressed confidence in the return of a just and popular regime in Iraq, and the hope of preserving its national neutrality between the rival Western powers and the Eastern Bloc. In another poem, entitled 'Which Revolution?', also composed in Najaf in 1958, Sayyid Fadlulah vividly captured the prevailing patriotic sentiment and outlined the significance of the Revolution. For him, as for most Iraqis, the event symbolised the avid national quest for self-identity, crystallised national consciousness, and finally, signified and engendered the reawakening of an ethos of nationalism.[10]

While Fadlallah was a keen observer of the Revolution, there is no evidence to indicate that he had taken part in mass the demonstrations in support of General Qasem. That position seems to be congruent with the posture adopted by his fellow young Islamists and his mentors, chief among them being the pre-eminent Iraqi Shi'i *marja'* (source of religio-juridical 'emulation'), Ayatollah Sayyid Muhsin al-Hakim, who in the first months of General Qasem's ascension to power expressed his qualified support for the new regime, expecting the incumbent administration to fulfil the aspirations of its citizens and govern in accordance with the precepts and ordinances of the shari'ah.[11]

The favourable disposition of the Islamists towards the revolutionary regime was soon to change, as General Qasem began to pursue policies that they saw as being in conflict with their values and detrimental to their interests. It is on the most important development to unfold in the immediate wake of the revolution – namely, the rapid expansion in the membership and influence of the Iraqi Communist Party, with the tacit patronage of the President – that our attention will now focus; for this provides the crucial background to understanding the formative phase of Hizb al-Da'wa's development and relations with the republican regime.

General Qasem, the Defeat of the Arab Nationalists and the Ascent of the Iraqi Communists

No sooner had the Free Officers seized political power than serious difficulties began to arise, centring on the pace, mode and nature of social and economic change, and on political union with the United Arab Republic. The fact that those complications did emerge was not surprising, as the single overriding factor that solidified the disparate elements that constituted the revolutionary officer corps, whose members came from a variety of backgrounds and held a diversity of views, was the aspiration to overthrow an unpopular monarchy. Those divergent views cystallised around the two prime movers of the revolution, General Qasem and his lieutenant, Colonel 'Aref. The former favoured a reformist mode of change and upheld *al-Wataniyya*, or local (Iraqi) patriotism, as distinct from *a-Qawmiyya*, or Pan-Arab nationalism, with the immediate and sweeping social and economic change advocated by the latter. Specifically, the two leaders of the revolutuion held opposing views over the crucial question of union with Egypt and Syria. Colonel 'Aref, an avid admirer of President Nasser and a strident proponent of Arab unity, called for Iraq's immediate merger with the United Arab Republic. General Qasem, on the other hand, was lukewarm towards the unity scheme, and favoured a federation instead. Whereas Colonel 'Aref cultivated discreet personal contacts with President Nasser (during the latter's visit to Syria) with a view to unseating General Qasem from his presidency, the latter began in earnest to forge strategic links with the influential Iraqi communist movement.[12] The president, lacking both the support of the military's upper echelons and a firm and independent support base among the key organised political parties in the country, found a willing and potent ally in the Iraqi Communist Party (ICP). This symbiotic relationship was, as we shall see, to have far-reaching implicationsfor the ensuing rift and polarisation between the secular nationalist and Islamist movements, on the one hand, and the regime and its communist allies, on the other.

A number of interrelated factors had contributed to the impressive expansion of the ICP during the 1940s and 1950s.[13] The first of these was the marked socioeconomic disparity and growing rift between the labouring lower classes and the salaried middle classes, on the one hand, and the enrichment of the privileged minority comprising the 'large landholders, prominent merchants, speculators, politicians', among others, on the other.[14] Communism's class-based analysis of society was perceived by many of Iraq's poor citizens as directly and immediately relevant to their plight. What is particularly relevant to our discussion is that class cleavage in Iraqi society was superimposed over confessional demarcations, as manifested in the systematic discrimination of Sunni-dominated administrations against the economically deprived and politically marginalised Shi'i community. The alienation of the Shi'a provided the single largest reservoir of potential recruits for the ICP.

The second reason for the appeal of communism was the inability of impoverished and discontented citizens to voice their grievances collectively and publicly, much less redress their plight in the legal arena. Thus, disillusioned and resentful, the dispossessed constituted a turbulent reservoir receptive to calls for change made by such a radical organisation as the ICP. Thirdly, and closely related to the spread of communist influence, was the suppression of Arab nationalist groups under the monarchy during the 1940s, which created a substantial political void that was eventually filled by the ICP. Finally, to the disaffected among the educated lower-middle class, the ICP surpassed the other oppositional parties by virtue of its tight and elaborate organisational structure and its extensive political experience, as the oldest secular political party in modern Iraq. In sharp contrast to the vague idealism of the Iraqi nationalists, the ICP advocated a detailed programme for social and economic change, reinforced by its proven record of active hostility towards Western imperialism.[15]

An important question, which provides an invaluable insight into the formation of the Iraqi Islamist Shi'i movement, is how to explain the mass attraction of Shi'i Muslims to the ICP. The mere fact that the overwhelming majority of Shi'i activists and intellectuals were attracted to secular ideologies and political organisations would indicate, as will be shown, that Islam as a divinely regulated way of life was losing its allure for the young and modern, educated generation of Iraqis. Although Islam traditionally constituted the foundation of Iraq's society and way of life, for an increasing number of the country's Muslim citizens their identity, affiliation and observance of Islam was merely nominal. To many Iraqis, Islam was at variance with modernity; the faith was in a state of stagnation, as it was viewed as having lost its modern relevance and innate vitality.[16]

Contributing to this decline in Islamic religiosity was the marked decrease in the number of students of religion who resided in the Shi'i holy cities. In 1918, for instance, there were some 6,000 Shi'i religious students enrolled in Najaf's scholastic seminaries. This number had fallen by 1957 to 1,954, of whom only 326 were Iraqis. Furthermore, in view of the fact that the Shi'i religious seminaries were traditional havens for young Iraqi males who sought to avoid compulsory military conscription, many of those enrolled were doubtless not bona fide students. Another important indicator in this trend was the decline in the number of Shi'i 'ulama and religious functionaries, and their concomitant diminution in status and influence. The grossly disproportionate number of 'ulama and religious functionaries in comparison with the size of the Shi'i constituency in Iraq was an another important indicator here. Thus, in the late 1950s there were a paltry 'five 'ulama and fifty lower-level religious functionaries' in Baghdad's al-Thawra district, which had more than a million residents but only 100 mosques. A similar situation existed in Iraq's second-largest city, Basra, whose population of one million was served by a similar number of mosques, but represented by only fifteen 'ulama.[17]

Although the reasons for the ebbing of Islam in modern Iraqi society were manifold, two factors can be identified as fundamental, both of which have were treated in detail in the preceding chapter; but a further brief reference is warranted. The first is related to the gradual withdrawal – since 1914–24, when they were at the forefront of the religio-political struggle against British colonial domination and Hashemite-installed monarchy – of the Shi'i 'ulama from political activism. With the exception of one prominent Shi'i *mujtahid*, Shaykh Muhammad Hussein Kashif al-Ghita', the leading Shi'i 'ulama of Najaf and Karbala henceforth devoted their energies to religious and juridical teaching, undertaking traditional apolitical activities such as furnishing legal advice and religious guidance, and dispensing welfare funds to the needy. Yet it was precisely during those crucial years between the 1930s and 1950s, when the majority of the Shi'i 'ulama had eschewed involvement in political affairs, that a number of secular opposition parties and movements emerged – namely the ICP, the Independence Party and the Ba'thists. Whereas, following the suppression of the 1920–21 uprising, the Shi'i 'ulama publicly renounced their Islamist struggle against British imperial designs in Iraq, thereby forfeiting their erstwhile role as foci of political activism in the country, the nationalists and communists during the became 1940s and 1950s almost the only effective elements in the struggle against the British and the Hashemite monarchy.[18]

The second major factor accounting for the ebbing of Islamic consciousness was the spread, during the 1930s and 1940s, of modern public schools. Viewing the new European-modelled educational system as a British-inspired scheme aimed at weakening the influence of the traditional Shi'i *hawza* learning institution, the Iraqi *Marja'iyya* issued a decree prohibiting Shi'i citizens from entering and enrolling in these schools.[19]

Yet the 'ulama – with the exception of a minority of reformist religious scholars and intellectuals – took no practical steps towards the establishment of a network of modern Islamic schools, effectively driving the young Shi'a into the government schools. As prospective graduates and would-be professionals and employees, the growing body of young, educated Iraqis became secular-orientated, and thus increasingly estranged from their Islamic heritage and culture. Many of these students, attracted to nationalist and Marxist ideologies, were to comprise the rank-and-file of the Communist and, to a lesser extent, Ba'thist parties.[20]

The marked decline in the number of religious students not only signified a substantial loss of young and otherwise promising souls to 'ungodly' ideologies, but also had adverse financial effects. Since the financial well-being and influence of the 'ulama were largely predicated on the continuous flow of religious tithes (*zakat* and *khums)* and *sadaqah* (voluntary donations) from the Shi'i faithful, the religious scholars lost considerable financial resources and clout, as an increasing number of formerly generous and devout laymen became newly recruited comrades of the ICP.[21]

A description of the lamentable state of affairs given in 1953 by one of Iraq's pre-eminent *mujtahids*, Shaykh Muhammad al-Hussein Kashif al-Ghita' (1876–1954) illsutrated the extent of the impact of communism on the Shi'i community. He relates how, in bygone days, the people and tribal leaders were virtuous and generous, showed reverence to the 'ulama and came to their assistance. The renowned religious scholastic seminaries of the Shi'i holy cities survived on their generous donations and gifts. The changing times had seen the shrivelling of benevolence and the spread of the corruption of wealth, leading to the decay of the religious schools.[22]

For Shaykh al-Ghita', a virulent opponent of communism, the principal agent of this radical change in attitudes of the Shi'i youth towards the 'ulama was unquestionably the ICP. It was on account of his strident hostility towards communism that Shaykh al-Ghita' became the focus of diplomatic activity by both the British and the Americans, who, in 1953 and 1954 respectively, had despatched special envoys to negotiate and co-opt the services of the *mujtahid* in the struggle against the communist menace. Thus, in early October 1953, the British ambassador to Iraq, Sir John Troutbeck, travelled to Najaf and held talks with Shaykh al-Ghita'. The two discussed the pressing issue of communism, regarded as the common enemy whose 'dark propaganda' had diffused so extensively that 'numerous cells, embracing spirited and ardent young men' flourished in the very midst of the Shi'i world's holiest city. Shaykh al-Ghita' declined to co-operate with Britain or the United States, lest he unwittingly contribute to the preservation of the imperial interests of the Western powers in the region.[23] Ironically, it was a small, discreet group of young activist Shi'i 'ulama who, less than four years on, were inadvertently to give practical expression to the British Ambassador's vision for a politically active body of 'ulama commited to combatting the communist 'peril'. This development found its crystallisation in the creation of Hizb al-Da'wa.

Before examining the circumstances that led to the formation of Hizb al-Da'wa, it is useful to explore the processes that facilitated the appeal of communism among the Shi'i citizens of Iraq. During the last decade of the monarchy, two momentous socioeconomic changes took place: a mass movement of the rural poor to the major towns and cities, and the ascendancy of the urban Shi'i middle class. Between 1947 and 1957, the increasing poverty among the peasantry, owing to the oppressive taxes exacted by the powerful tribal shaykhs, precipitated a mass drift of predominantly Shi'i peasants and labourers to the capital and the major regional urban centres, where they formed a reservoir of impoverished semi-proletariat.[24] By escaping the burdensome living conditions of the rural south, the Shi'i peasantry had severed their ties – precarious as they had been – with the tribal shaykhs.

The second important factor that facilitated the diffusion of communism among the Shi'i community was related to the fact that the Shi'i politicians and intellectuals were of urban origin, and their character, social consciousness and world-view were thus shaped by an urban cultural setting, rather than forged a relationship with the tribal shaykhs in the countryside, whom they traditionally despised. As a natural consequence, those politicians were not in the least interested in ameliorating the plight of their poor co-religionists – whether in the countryside or in the makeshift slum dwellings of Baghdad – lest they be accused of confessional bias. The Shi'i secular, westernising elite belonged to the educated middle class, and drew their support from the social mobility of the Shi'i merchants and traders, who after the flight of Iraqi Jewry became the country's dominant commercial and financial group. It is not surprising, therefore, that the neglect of the underprivileged and wretched

Shi'a by their politicians produced a disaffected mass that became receptive to communist propaganda. Specifically, many Shi'a were attracted to the ICP's revolutionary position on the British and their dependent feudal ruling elite, and its radical social and economic programme – namely, demanding agrarian reform, emancipation of the peasantry from the perpetual dependence on feudal landlords and unscrupulous urban-based creditors, and exemption of the *fellahin* from paying their grinding taxes.[25]

The large number of Shi'a who joined the ICP ultimately had the effect of altering the confessional complexion of the party. Thus, whereas, during the 1930s, Sunni Arabs had dominated the upper echelons of the party (forming some 60 per cent of the Central Committee's membership), mirroring the community's traditionally ascendant position in Iraqi social and political life, by the 1940s their primacy in the party's senior positions had gradually been eroded. They came to comprise only 40 per cent in 1941–42, and 31.3 per cent in 1945–47. Conversely, the Shi'i members of the Central Committee, comprising students, teachers and lawyers, increased from 20.5 per cent before 1949 to 46.9 per cent after 1949. On the other hand, the Shi'a within the party, constituted the largest proportion of the party's rank-and-file, comprising 36.6 per cent of the middle-ranking and 33.3 per cent of the lower-ranking positions.[26]

Important as these figures may be in revealing the extent of communist influence among the country's largest confessional community during this period, what was most revealing – and disconcerting for the 'ulama – was that the communists had succeeded in making significant inroads into the insular heartland of Shi'ism, the holy city of Najaf. The success of the ICP's recruiting drive in this ultra-conservative locale can be gauged by the data available on the Shi'i composition of the ICP leadership between 1955 and 1963, which reveal that one third of the party's Central Committee were either sons or close relatives of the city's prominent 'ulama and Sayyid (noble) families. The Communist Party's first Secretary General, Hussein Ahmad al-Radi, for instance, was a Sayyid and son of an eminent Najafi *'alim*. The vulnerability of Najaf to infiltration by the communists demonstrated especially to the young Shi'i 'ulama and political activists like Sayyid Fadlallah just how imperative it was at this critical juncture to mount an organised political and ideological effort to stem the seemingly inexorable 'red tide'.[27]

The reform-minded and radical among the 'ulama saw the sacred milieu bedevilled by a deep-seated malaise, characterised by intellectual ossification, cultural stagnation, religious decadence and intolerance, ideological disorientation and political marginalisation. Attributing those maladies, in large measure, to the aloofness of religious scholars and jurists from pressing social issues, and to their avoidance of political affairs, the Shi'i Iraqi Islamists turned to the radical option – indeed prescription – in the form of Hizb al-Da'wa al-Islamiyya.

Before examining the formation and development of Hizb al-Da'wa, it will be necessary to inquire into its intellectual and ideological antecedents. In the previous chapter, we saw how the inadequacies of the traditional Shi'i Islamic institution (*al-Hawza al-'Ilmiyya*) in the face of an ascendant modern school educational system had prompted an eminent religious scholar, Shaykh Muhammad Rida al-Muzzafar, to advocate the systematic reform of existing teaching methods and curricula. In pioneering the modern intellectual reform movement, Shaykh al-Muzzafar encountered intense opposition from the conservative Shi'i establishment, which viewed the idea of reform with apprehension, seeing it as detrimental to the very survival of the traditional *hawza* institution. After several failed attempts, the reformist shaykh finally succeeded in founding Jami'yyat Muntada al-Nashr in Najaf in 1935, with its own modern Islamic school. Three years later the school was upgraded to a college of jurisprudence.[28]

One salient development associated with the society's reformist educational institution was that a small but significant number of young Islamists (including Fadlallah and Sayyid al-Sadr) had either studied at or graduated from one of its schools, and would together form the nucleus of a new generation of religious scholars, intellectuals and political activists, committed to radically reforming society at large. This small group of individuals was to play an instrumental role in revitalising Islamist sentiment, which had been dormant since the 'ulama-led civil agitation of the early 1920s. The shift to renewed political activism by the young Islamists, beginning in the mid-1950s, was a slow and gradual process, due to political inertia and the opposition of conservatives associated with traditional *hawza* circles.[29]

Hizb al-Da'wa: Shi'i and Sunni Antecedents

Many Shi'i Islamists joined those Islamic political and cultural groups (both Shi'i and Sunni) that were active prior to the formation of Hizb al-Da'wa. A handful of the Shi'i groups came into existence during the early and mid-1950s – namely, Hizb al-Ja'fari (Ja'fari Party), Harakat Shabab al-Muslim (Muslim Youth Movement), Munazzamat al-'Aqaidin al-Muslim (Muslim Credal Organisation) and Shabab al-'Aqidah wal-Iman (Youth of Creed and Faith).

Hizb al-Ja'fari, named after Ja'far al-Sadiq, who is venerated by the Twelver

Shi'a as their sixth Imam, was founded in 1952 in Najaf by three Islamists: Abdul Sahib Dakhil, Hasan Shubbur and Sadiq al-Qamousi. All three had received their primary education at Najaf's recently established reformist school of Muntada al-Nashr, where two of them (Shubbur and Dakhil) became colleagues of Fadlallah and were later among the earliest members of Hizb al-Da'wa.[30]

To escape detection and harassment by government intelligence agencies and security forces, weekly meetings were convened secretly at either the private residence of one of the founders or at Muntada al-Nashr's school. Meetings were attended by trusted friends, who would exchange views and discuss local issues. During its short-lived existence, the party's activities focused on the nurturing of spirituality and religious observance among local Muslims. To that end, limited copies of the Party's views and goals were covertly circulated among selected individuals. The Party sought unsuccessfully to create a popular base of support among the Iraqi populace. One major reason for its failure was the vigorous opposition of the senior conservative 'ulama, who accused its members of being pro-Sunni, or even Wahhabi – the traditional implacable foes of the Shi'a. It was in their attempt to dispel such allegations that the founders belatedly chose an unambiguously Shi'i appellation. However, despite the best efforts of its leaders, the Party was never able to free itself completely – in the minds of the Shi'i populace – of the Wahhabi or Sunni stigma. This factor, coupled with the hostile political environment of the old regime in which it operated, as well as its limited finances, led inevitably to its gradual weakening and eventual dissolution during the course of the following year.[31]

The second, comparatively more successful, organisation was Harakat Shabab al-Muslim. The Muslim Mens' Youth Movement was founded in Najaf in 1953 by Izziddin al-Jaza'iri, the son of an eminent *'alim*, Shaykh Muhammad Jawad al-Jaza'iri. The movement drew its most active support from secondary school students in Karbala and Najaf.[32] Apolitical in orientation, the movement focused on inculcating Shi'i youth with Islamic tenets, and by means of its periodical publication *Majallat al-Zikra* (Remembrance Magazine) and a series of instructive booklets, entitled *Min Wahy al-Islam* (From the Revelation of Islam), it sought to raise their religious consciousness.[33] What began purely as a religious educational venture subsequently expanded into the political sphere as well. Based at Karbala Secondary College, the movement organised street demonstrations against the imposition of martial law by the government of Nuri al-Din Muhammad.[34] The movement was thereafter subjected to harassment by Arab nationalists, who prevented its founders from convening their weekly meetings in Karbala, thereby precipitating its gradual emasculation, and eventual dissolution in 1954.[35] With its demise, the majority of the movement's affiliates subsequently either joined Hizb al-Da'wa, or abandoned political activism altogether.

The third Shi'i group, Shabab al-'Aqidah wal-Iman, was founded in Najaf in 1957. Its members, drawn from Najaf's merchant class, focused on religious and cultural education. To that end, weekly group discussion meetings were held, and lectures delivered at a number of mosques and private residences of members. Like the other formations of the period, the society was forced to dissolve itself soon after its inception, due to government harassment and internal splits.[36]

The fact that these Shi'i groups were short-lived can be attributed to a combination of factors, including a hostile political environment and inherent weakness, which pervaded all three organisations. They lacked structural cohesion, ideological rigour, and broad membership. In sum, although they proved to be ineffectual political actors and insignificant mediums of religious dissemination, nevertheless, for those Shi'i Islamists who were involved in their founding and functioning, they represented the first tentative steps in rudimentary organisational activity, and their shortcomings were to provide valuable experience for the architects of Hizb al-Da'wa.

Predating the founding of these localised Shi'i groups were two transnational Sunni Islamist movements – Jama'at al-Ikhwan al-Muslimun (Society of Muslim Brothers) and Hizb al-Tahrir al-Islami (Islamic Liberation Party). The former organisation – the oldest and most influential Islamist movement in the Middle East and North Africa – was founded in 1928 in the Egyptian city of Isma'iliyya by Shaykh Hasan al-Banna, a schoolteacher; while the latter was established in 1952 in the holy city of Jerusalem (al-Quds) by Shaykh Taqi al-Din al-Nabahani, a Palestinian religious judge and former schoolteacher. In view of the fact that a significant number of Shi'i Islamic activists had, at various stages, been affiliated to, or influenced by, either al-Ikhwan al-Muslimun or Hizb al-Tahrir, it is helpful to look briefly at the emergence, growth dynamics, and socio-religious and ideological character of both groups in the Iraqi context, as important antecedents to the rise of Hizb al-Da'wa.

Emerging in the early 1940s and operating under the name al-Ukhuwa al-Islamiyya (Islamic Brotherhood), the Iraqi branch of al-Ikhwan al-Muslimun was formally established in 1947 or 1948 (twenty years after the founding of its parent organisation in Egypt) in the northern, predominantly, Sunni Iraqi city of Mosul, by Sunni scholar-activist Shaykh Muhammad Mahmoud al-Sawwaf. Shaykh al-Sawwaf, who was born in Mosul in 1912, had met Shaykh al-Banna in 1939, during the former's brief stay as graduate student at Cairo's al-Azhar University, and became deeply impressed by the founder and the 'General-Guide' of al-Ikhwan al-Muslimun.[37]

While al-Ikhwan al-Muslimun underscored the central importance of religious awareness programmes and social welfare activities for the reformation of the individual, and ultimately of society, from its inception in Iraq, al-Ikhwan assumed an assertive role in the country's political affairs. In particular, the society voiced its opposition to key controversial foreign policies pursued by the government. Thus, al-Ikhwan played a prominent role during the popular uprising of 1948 against the terms of the Portsmouth Treaty, which was concluded between Britain and Prime Minister Salih Jaber. Members and sympathisers of al-Ikhwan also actively participated in mass street protests over the partition of Palestine in 1948.

Jam'iyyat Inqath Filistin (Palestine Salvation Society) was set up by al-Ikhwan to serve as a front for the marshalling and channelling of funds and volunteer fighters to Palestine. In 1952, al-Ikhwan published a periodical, al-Ukhuwa al-Islamiyya. Regarded by Islamists as the first religios–political publication of its kind in Iraq, it was geared, among other things, towards the dissemination of the society's critical views of the policies of Prime Minister Nuri al-Sa'eed. Prompted by what they deemed open dissent, the authorities censured the publication and clamped down on those activists who were associated with it.[38]

Notwithstanding the government-imposed restrictions on the society's activities, al-Ikhwan managed to diffuse its influence significantly, a fact which left the mistaken impression in government circles that virtually all politically oriented, devout Muslims were members. The fact that, until the early 1950s, the society was the only Islamist movement doubtless contributed to that perception. During the early and mid-1950s the society underwent a rapid expansion in membership and influence. That growth was the direct outcome of al-Ikhwan's intensive recruitment campaign, which focused on most of Iraq's major urban centres – Baghdad, Mosul, Kirkuk, Arbil, Suleymaniyya, Rumadi, Basra, Tikrit and Samarra. With the exception of Baghdad and Basra, all of those towns and cities were, and remain, predominantly Sunni. A concerted effort was mounted by the society to infiltrate the country's major professional associations and trade unions. The success of that drive was evidenced by the fact that, by the early 1950s, the majority of the society's members were high-school and college students, lawyers, engineers, physicians, and lower and middle-level bureaucrats.[39]

Although the membership of al-Ikhwan al-Muslimun was predominantly Sunni, the society had a small but significant number of Shi'i activists who were attracted to the group's openness and international *Weltanschauung*.

This ecumenical orientation was initiated by the chief mentor of the Iraqi branch of al-Ikhwan al-Muslimun, Shaykh al-Sawwaf, who, as a gesture of good will, embarked on a tour of Najaf and Karbala, where he visited the leading *mujtahids*. But beyond the relatively small number of Shi'i members of al-Ikhwan al-Muslimun, the society exerted significant influence on other Shi'i activists, most of whom would later join Hizb al-Da'wa. That influence can be explained by the fact that, prior to the founding of Hizb al-Da'wa and the subsequent rise of Sayyid Baqer al-Sadr and the influence of his works, Shi'i Islamists, lacking their own corpus of contemporary ideological and intellectual writings, relied almost exclusively on the commentaries of such prominent Sunni Islamist intellectuals and ideologues as Shaykh Hasan al-Banna, Maulana Abul Ala al-Mawdudi, Shaykh Taqi al-Din al-Nabahani, and Sayyid Qutb. In particular, it was the intellectual writings of Shaykh al-Banna and Sayyid Qutb that served as a major source of indoctrination and discussion for the Shi'i Islamists, and it was their ideas that contributed substantially to shaping their vision and world-view, and which were later refined by Sayyid al-Sadr, Sayyid Fadlallah and others.[40]

Two years after the founding of Hizb al-Tahrir by Shaykh al-Nabahani, in Jerusalem in 1952, a branch of the party was set up in Iraq, where all of its earliest members and the majority of its cadres were drawn from the country's principal Sunni-inhabited cities and urban quarters – Baghdad, Mosul, Ramadi and Basra. As a genuinely Islamic political party that was founded on a coherent set of Islamic tenets, Hizb al-Tahrir's avowed goal was the seizure of political power with the view to restoring the long-defunct *khilafa*, whose sovereignty and territorial expanse would transcend the multiplicity of present-day Muslim nation-states and comprise a super-state that would ultimately encompass the entire world.[41]

Arriving comparatively late on the Iraqi political scene – some six years after the advent of al-Ikhwan – Hizb al-Tahrir was smaller in membership and wielded less influence in society at large than its counterpart. Two other factors also had the effect of limiting its size and impact. Of the two, the most important was the party's rigid and arguably incomplete programme of action, which entailed three sequential phases. These began with the intellectual and political indoctrination of its cadres for the purpose of creating an enlightened and dedicated vanguard, then moving on to the public dissemination of its ideology, and ending with the establishment of an Islamic caliphate, in place of secular and 'illegitimate' polities, following the pursuit of a politically nonviolent but subversive struggle against the incumbent regimes in the Muslim world.[42]

One pronounced outcome of that strategy was that the party remained essentially an elitist organisation, as it made no attempt to engender, like al-Ikhwan, a mass base of support through *Da'wa*. Furthermore, again unlike al-Ikhwan, because it remained singularly focused on realising that one grand goal – the restoration of the *khilafa* –the party was patently indifferent to socio-economic issues and, consequently, became detached from the wider community of believers, with their much more immediate and temporal concerns. The second factor which limited the party's expansion was its relentless hostility towards the government of Nuri al-Sa'eed and its practices – particularly its controversial policy of assuming a pivotal position in establishing the Baghdad Pact of 1955. The virulence of Hizb al-Tahrir prompted the regime to suppress the party and imprison its principal affiliates, weakening it significantly and forcing it to operate clandestinely.[43]

In spite of those limitations, and the decidedly Sunni persuasion of its leading members in Iraq, information provided by Fadlallah and other Islamists indicates that a sizeable number of Shi'i Islamists, originating from Baghdad and Basra, joined Hizb al-Tahrir.[44] On account of Hizb al-Tahrir's greater stress on the importance of ideology for the transformation of society and polity, according to Fadlallah the party was able to attract a greater number of Shi'i Islamists. However, owing to the subsequent emergence of disagreements between the party leadership and Shi'i cadres over specific ideological and methodological details, as a group they were to leave the party between 1958 and 1960.[45]

These former Shi'i affiliates of Hizb al-Tahrir and al-Ikhwan al-Muslimun were to bring with them their respective theoretical constructs, schematic programmes of action, and practical experiences in organisational and political activism into the al-Da'wa party, where such matters became the subject of debate among senior members.[46] While the Shi'i Islamists shared with their Sunni brethren in Hizb al-Tahrir and al-Ikhwan al-Muslimun the axiomatic notion of Islam as inherently embodying a both religion and state – creed and law together – they differed with the former over the specific character of the ideal Islamic polity, the most feasible strategy by which to achieve set goals, and the priority that should be accorded to a myriad of issues relevant to the Islamisation venture. Hizb al-Tahrir, for instance, unequivocally called for the reinstitution of the political structure and administrative mechanisms of the *Khilafa al-Rashida* (the four Rightly Guided vicegerents who followed the Prophet Muhammad). This unambiguously Sunni political paradigm, with its concomitant juridical implications and doctrinal underpinnings, varies from the Shi'i ideal, as embodied by the Twelve infallible Imams, who developed a distinct system of theology, jurisprudence and political thought, and whose divinely conferred authority the Shi'a believed to have been usurped by successive Sunni rulers.

It should be stressed that the influence of Hizb al-Tahrir and al-Ikhwan al-Muslimun on Shi'i political activists did not cease with their withdrawal from those movements. On the contrary, according to one Islamist source close to Hizb al-Da'wa, some members became profoundly influenced in the 1960s by the revolutionary Islamist thought of Sayyid Qutb (d. 1966), the pre-eminent radical theoretician of al-Ikhwan al-Muslimun.[47] Following the ascension of the Ba'th party to power in 1968, a group of Hizb al-Da'wa affiliates fervently espoused some of his key radical notions, namely *inqilabiyya* (revolutionism), *jahiliyya* (pagan ignorance) and *hakimiyya* (divine sovereignty); concepts which, in the light of the repressive milieu in which Islamic activists then had to operate, served to propel Shi'i political activists towards an ideological and political confrontation with the new regime. Important as that struggle for supremacy may have been, in view of the fact that the confrontation unfolded during the course of the 1970s, and that Fadlallah had left Iraq for Lebanon in 1966, an account of the course and outcome of the ensuing events is beyond the scope of this book.

Notwithstanding the influence borne by the former Shi'i affiliates of Hizb al-Tahrir and al-Ikhwan al-Muslimun, the fact is that, as far as those activists were concerned, the vast majority of the Iraqi Shi'a populace were either ignorant of or oblivious to the existence of these two parties. Moreover, the powerful conservative Shi'i religious establishment, with its extensive religious–juridical authority and staunchly apolitical orientation, constituted a major factor militating against the appeal of organised modern religious–political formations among the Shi'i faithful. It was anathema to the majority of Shi'i *mujtahids* to establish or join modern political parties with their separate structural organisation, distinct mode of activity and partisan loyalty, as it was not only regarded as an unprecedented and inauthentic innovation, but a serious departure from the traditional *mujtahid*-laymen network, and undermined the undisputed authority of the grand juriconsults.[48]

As far as the *Shi'i* Islamists were concerned, Hizb al-Tahrir and al-Ikhwan al-Muslimun, owing to the fact that their centre of gravity was the Sunni urban centres of Iraq, while their presence in the Shi'i south was marginal and tenuous, were incapable of significantly heightening the religious awareness of the Shi'a or posing a credible ideological force capable of warding off the threat of communism. Indeed, in surveying this lamentable state of affairs, the Shi'i Islamists arrived at the conclusion that the lack of a coherent set of philosophical and political Islamic ideas in modern Islamist discourse had created an ideological vacuum, which to a large degree had facilitated the expansion of communism in Iraqi society.[49] The patent inability on the part of the 'ulama and the Islamic activists to address the social, ideological and political threat of the ICP – much less stem the rapid advances made by the party, and, to a lesser extent, the nationalists, even in supposedly traditionally conservative religious bastions of Shi'ism centred on Najaf and Karbala – coupled with the emasculation of the Islamists groups (Hizb al-Tahrir in particular) and the eventual dissolution of the Shi'i religious movements, engendered a new line of thought among Shi'i Islamist circles.

Among the nucleus of young, committed Islamists who discussed, in closed meetings in Najaf and Karbala, the urgency of devising the most effective means for projecting a sophisticated and appealing Islamist discourse and revitalising organised Islamic political activism, was a close colleague of Fadlallah, Sayyid Baqer al-Sadr. According to his most authoritative biographer, his student Sayyid Kazem al-Haeri, al-Sadr was born on 1 March 1935, in the north-central town of al-Kazimiyya, into a traditionally pious and renowned scholarly family, which claimed descent from the Prophet Muhammad through the seventh Imam Musa al-Kazim.[50]

In common with Fadlallah, al-Sadr's family originated from Jabal Amil, in south Lebanon, whence his great-grandfather (Sadr al-Din al-'Amili) had emigrated. Like Fadlallah, al-Sadr was only an infant when his father, Sayyid Haydar, died in 1937, at the age of forty-six, and he lived his childhood in poverty. Like Fadlallah, he acquired his primary education at one of the schools set up by the reformist Islamic society, Muntada al-Nashr. At the age of eleven or twelve, Sayyid al-Sadr moved to Najaf to embark on formal religious scholarship. While there, together with Fadlallah, he attended the lessons of the leading Shi'i luminaries of his day, including Sayyid Muhsin al-Hakim and Sayyid Abul Qasem al-Kho'ie. Remarkably, by the time he was in his early or mid-twenties, Sayyid al-Sadr had, according to informed Arabic sources, attained the rank of *mujtahid*, thus entitling him to give advanced lessons on *fiqh* and *ijtihad*. Finally, like Fadlallah, al-Sadr's inquisitive mind and Islamist world-view had motivated him to complement his religious studies with close reading of political events and developments in Iraq and the region. Thus, with his exceptional intellect, Sayyid al-Sadr rose quickly to prominence, attracting around him a small group of young 'ulama (like Fadlallah) and educated Shi'i faithful.[51]

For al-Sadr and his colleagues, contemporary Iraqi Muslim society was debilitated by the decline in the perceived relevance of Islamic values and institutions, the diffusion of non-Islamic customs and traditions, the ascendancy of materialist and atheist thought, and the subjugation of Muslim countries to imperialist powers. The cure for the present multi-faceted and deep-seated malaise was radical, yet peaceful, transformation of the *Umma*, beginning with Iraq. It was on the basis of that grim diagnosis, which consequently called for a drastic prescription, that al-Sadr began seriously to contemplate, and indeed devise, the ideological and political formula for bringing about the necessary revolutionary change in society.[52] Thus was a radical Islamist organisation founded, in the form of Hizb al-Da'wa, that would bring an end to inertia and atrophy and set in motion the process of recovery and transformation.

However, the advocates of radical Islamic activism were compelled, during the preparatory stage that preceded the formation of Hizb al-Da'wa, to discuss their views and organise the rudimentary structure of the party with vigilance and circumspection. That discretion a calculated response to two imposing factors: a political regime, in the form of the British-installed Hashemite monarchy, that was hostile to radical political organisation, and the apolitical position of the senior 'ulama, who held that political organisation and activity was contrary to the precepts of the shari'ah, and constituted an heretical innovation.[53]

The Formation and Character of Hizb al-Da'wa al-Islamiyya

Iraqi and Western scholars, as well as Islamic activists close to the party, have cited various dates for the founding of Hizb al-Da'wa. Internal party sources are even in disagreement as to when precisely the party was established. One group, comprising the majority of the party's founding members and senior affiliates, cite early October 1957, which coincided with the birth date of the Prophet Muhammad, as the date of its foundation. According to the minority of early party affiliates, chief among whom was Talib al-Rifa'i, the party was founded several months after the revolution of July 1958.[54]

As far as Western scholarship on the Iraqi Islamist movement is concerned, the research findings based on reliable party sources by two leading specialists, Amatzia Baram and Joyce Wiley, have supported the version provided by the former group. On the other hand, drawing on government sources, Hanna Batatu and Farouk Sluglett, renowned historians of modern Iraq, erroneously trace the emergence of Hizb al-Da'wa to the late 1960s, following the seizure of power by the Ba'th Party.[55]

Disagreement as to the precise date of Hizb al-Da'wa's formation can be attributed to the semi-clandestine nature of the party's leadership and, until 1968, the denial of its existence by the Qasem and 'Aref governments. While the party's formation precedes the July 1958 Revolution, its political activity began in the immediate wake of that Revolution. The advent of the second phase was precipitated, as will be shown, by General Qasem's openness towards a multiplicity of competing political organisations and movements, espousing a multitude of ideologies, of which the most prominent and dynamic was communism.[56]

There is little variation between the majority of party affiliates in relation to the date and location of the informal foundational convention and the identity of its participants, but there is some disagreement as to who took the initiative in bringing together the founding members of the party. A small nucleus, of no more than eight individuals, comprising junior 'ulama, political activists and religious laymen had attended the founding meeting of what was later named Hizb al-Da'wa, at the private residence of al-Marja' Ayatullah Sayyid Muhsin al-Hakim. That such a meeting took place in the home of Sayyid al-Hakim implied that the founders had at least the countenance of Iraq's foremost Shi'i juriconsult (as well as the tacit approval of other senior Shi'i *mujtahids*, like Ayatollah Shaykh Murtada al-Yasin and Ayatullah Sayyid Isma'il al-Sadr, the maternal uncle and brother, respectively, of Sayyid al-Sadr), which proved to be crucial, in the face of the generally apolitical orientation of the elder 'ulama, in conferring legitimacy on the embryonic organisation.[57]

The party's inaugural meeting was the culmination of a series of clandestine gatherings of activists and young 'ulama, which commenced in 1956. The secret informal meetings that preceded the founding of Hizb al-Da'wa were convened by Sayyid Mahdi al-Hakim (a young *'alim* and elder son of the Marja' Sayyid Muhsin al-Hakim) and two laymen, Talib al-Rifa'i and Abdul Sahib Dakhil, as well as an unknown fourth person, possibly Sayyid Murtada al-Askari, an *'alim*. The cell tentatively discussed ways in which to draw up plans to establish an Islamist party with a radical program. The first major issue that was addressed was the question of the legitimacy of an Islamic government during the occultation of the Twelfth Imam. Following a request from the activist group, Sayyid Baqer al-Sadr delivered a detailed legalistic paper, in which he furnished evidence in support of the legality and necessity of establishing a contemporary Islamic polity in the absence of the Hidden Imam. This seminal study was to become the first internal ideological publication of Hizb al-Da'wa, and its key elements were to constitute the central plank of its manifesto.[58]

The first concrete step taken towards the founding of Hizb al-Da'wa came in a meeting between Talib al-Rifa'i and Sayyid al-Sadr, during which the former briefed the latter on the proposal to establish an Islamist party, to which al-Sadr gave his assent. In turn, al-Sadr suggested and secured the co-optation of Sayyid Murtada al-Askari, who came from the latter's home town of al-Kazimiyya.[59] As for the complete list of names of those who formed the foundational coterie of the party, the matter is subject to disagreement among Islamists and scholars.[60]

On the pertinent question of who took the initiative in founding Hizb al-Da'wa, the prevalent view based on internal party testimonies and Islamist sources is that Sayyid al-Sadr was the founder and architect of the party.[61] With the exception of H. Batatu and T. M. Aziz, who, basing their investigations on the statements of Sayyid Baqer al-Hakim and Talib al-Rifa'i, respectively, deny that Sayyid al-Sadr played a direct and instrumental role in establishing the party, Islamist writers close to Hizb al-Da'wa affirm that Sayyid al-Sadr assumed a pioneering role in founding the organisation.[62] They refer to a number of supporting circumstances: that at least one of the series of preliminary secret meetings took place in the residence of Sayyid al-Sadr; that during one of those gatherings, he moved a resolution to embark upon 'a comprehensive study of the constitutions of the major political parties in Iraq and the world at large, with a view to devising a preamble or guiding principles for the constitution of the [prospective] party'; and that he was from the outset the party's jurisconsult, ideological mentor, strategist and political organiser.[63]

In reflecting on the revolutionary contribution of al-Sadr, Fadlallah describes his late colleague as being more than just 'a puritan theoretician, formulating abstract revolutionary thought'; for he had devised a 'practicable comprehensive scheme for revolutionary action', and, more specifically, he had laid the basis for the establishment of an Islamic political organisation founded on a revolutionary interpretation of the Islamic world-view and ideology, predicated on and bound by an established body of jurisprudential precepts.[64]

It was al-Sadr who persuaded a number of activist 'ulama, namely Sayyid Mahdi al-Hakim, Sayyid Murtada al-Askari and Shaykh Baqer al-Nasiri to join the Hizb during its embryonic phase.[65] In his endeavour to elicit the approval of the leading *mujtahids*, al-Sadr notified his mentors, Ayatollah Sayyid Abu al-Qasem al-Kho'ie and Ayatullah Shaykh Murtada al-Yasin, and gave each a copy of the party's manifesto, entitled *al-Usus*, written by him. He also distributed copies of *al-Usus* to Shaykh Hussein al-Huli, who was antipathetic towards the Hizb, as well as Shaykh Hadi al-M'arafa.[66] Outside Iraq, Sayyid al-Sadr strove to use his contacts in Iran to acquaint a number of senior 'ulama with the goals and programme of the party. Although it is difficult, in the absence of adequate information, to gauge the success of al-Sadr's quest in Iran, what is nevertheless certain is that he was able to brief a certain eminent *mujtahid*, Sayyid Sultani, who had close ties to the Shi'i world's pre-eminent *marja'*, the apolitical al-Sayyid Hussein al-Burujurdi.

Unlike al-Sadr, and although he had lived through the crucial evolutionary phase of the Hizb al-Da'wa and maintained close links with its senior members, Fadlallah decided against becoming a formal member of the party. While lauding the outstanding achievements of al-Sadr, Fadlallah reveals that there were differences of opinion on certain undisclosed details, most probably relating to the method of approach in advancing the Islamist cause, and the merits of members of the 'ulama affiliating themselves to a political organisation.[67]

In a sympathetic and detailed account of the course of the Islamist movement in Iraq, whose preface was written by Sayyid Fadlallah, al-Mu'min cites the name of Fadlallah among the list of fourteen Shi'i 'ulama and laymen whom he identifies as founding members, or activists affiliated in varying degrees, of Hizb al-Da'wa. In several interviews, Fadlallah has stated consistently that although he played no direct part in founding Hizb al-Da'wa, nor had ever been a member of the party, he was one of the pioneers of modern Shi'i Islamist discourse, and as such had a significant intellectual role in spawning Islamist activism and in contributing indirectly to the formation of Hizb al-Da'wa. This account of his role in, and association with, Hizb al-Da'wa is corroborated by internal party annals and reliable sources close to Fadlallah.[68]

As to the reason why Fadlallah, a political activist, should refrain from assuming a direct or central role in Hizb al-Da'wa's organisational and political activities, he gives no explicit answer, beyond stating that 'there were no realistic circumstances' at the time that would have propelled him into such a role. Nevertheless, it would be plausible to speculate that Fadlallah, in adopting such a position, had made the assessment that he would be more able to serve Islamist ends by remaining formally unconnected to the organisational body of Hizb al-Da'wa. He may have calculated that in such an arrangement he would able to work effectively towards rejuvenating Islam intellectually and revitalising it politically, without being hamstrung by the organisational strictures and binding resolutions that invariably characterise political parties, while, simultaneously, maintaining cordial relations with individual senior party figures, al-Sadr in particular. Fadlallah rules out the posibility that he may have been pressured or influenced in his decision by either of his mentors, Ayatollah Sayyid Muhsin al-Hakim and Ayatollah Sayyid Abu al-Qasem al-Kho'ie, stating, without elaboration, that there were personal circumstances militating against joining Hizb al-Da'wa.[69]

It is instructive that al-Hakim, unlike al-Kho'ie, had, as mentioned earlier, supported the founding of Hizb al-Da'wa and encouraged two of his sons to join the party – although he himself deemed it inappropriate to be the chief oracle of an Islamist political formation, which was characterised by its clandestine nature and limited membership; traits which would have been detrimental to his status and patriarchal role as Iraq's pre-eminent Shi'i religious jurisconsult.[70]

This analysis of Fadlallah's association with Hizb al-Da'wa enables us to discern a correlation in his position on formal affiliation to contemporary Islamic political parties, such as Hizb al-Da'wa and Lebanon's Hizbullah. This nexus provides an indispensable basis for understanding the background to the continuity in Fadlallah's links with those Islamist organisations. This issue, however, will form the subject of analysis in a later chapter.

Both al-Sadr and Fadlallah were impelled by perceived need to develop an organised political Islamist movement capable of revitalising Islam, and moving it centre-stage in the political, social, economic and cultural affairs of contemporary Iraq. Inextricably linked to the rejuvenation of Islam as a sustained local, regional and global power, was the reinvigoration and transformation of the 'ulama, as a corporate body, into a politically assertive force and agent of social and cultural change.[71] But beyond sharing this fundamental outlook, the positions of the two young 'ulama diverged; for while both were at one as to the legitimacy of, and need for, a radical Islamist party, they differed over the desirability of assuming a formal position in Hizb al-Da'wa.

As to the rationale for setting up a radical political organisation, Sayyid al-Sadr argued that Hizb al-Da'wa was the most effective means by which to propagate Islam – as creed, ideology and law – to the largest body of nominal and devout members of Iraq's Muslim community, so that, in time, they may be impulsively committed to 'living in conformity with the Will of God'. Herein lay the reason for the adoption of the appellation 'Hizb al-Da'wa al-Islamiyya' – literally, the Party of Islamic Call. Religiously, the term *Da'wa* is employed to denote the mechanism of invitation or call to the public to embrace or adhere to Islam. Specifically, *al-Da'wa*, as a distinct and integral peaceful mode of spreading the Word of God, has its historical origins in the proselytising paradigm of the Prophet Muhammad, whose incumbent exemplar underscored the paramount importance of evangelical work for human enlightenment and salvation. For al-Sadr, the justification for naming the organisation al-Da'wa al-Islamiyya was that it is the natural name for our activity, the legal expression of our obligation to invite the populace to Islam; as there is nothing that prevents us from regarding ourselves as a party, movement or organisation, for we are *hizbullah* [the party of God] the supporters of God, and the supporters of Islam; for we are a movement in society, an organisation in activity, and in all circumstances we are *du'at* [callers] to Islam and our activity is [essentially] *Da'wa* to Islam.[72]

> It was in view of what was perceived to be an alarming contemporary trend among the disenchanted Shi'i youth to turn away from Islam and espouse godless, and secular values and 'decadent' Western culture, and in the light of the vitality of the ICP, that the launching of a party committed to the *Da'wa* ethos and Islamic political activism was deemed crucial. Contrary to the prevailing opinion of the majority of the Shi'i 'ulama, al-Sadr forcefully argued that 'given that the Shari'ah does not enjoin the pursuit of a designated mode for Islamic dissemination and transformation, then it would be legally permissible to pursue any [feasible] course for the propagation of the tenets of Islam and its precepts, and for the transformation of society through that medium, so long as that method does not involve a course of action deemed from the shari'ah standpoint to be unlawful.' [I have added quotation marks to the above sentence.]

He further adds that

> marshalling of endeavours for the sake of Islam and its co-ordination with prudence, and selecting the best course for organising [those efforts] is not merely a legitimate issue in our age, but is obligatory, provided that the [envisaged] transformation of society [into that which is in the state of] servitude to God, and in confrontation with unbelief are contingent on them.

Furthermore, according to al-Sadr, with the diffusion of

> anti-Islamic parties with their multitudinous sects, divergent motivations and disparate ends, that have collectively competed to pervert the human race, it becomes incumbent on the 'ulama of Islam to espouse organised party-based activism in order to confront these [secular] parties with their own effective means.

Sayyid al-Sadr concludes by stating that 'the experience of the various international organisations has demonstrated that [action based on party] formation is a successful medium by which to transform society towards good or evil'.[73]

From these passages it is evident that al-Sadr, not unlike many other Islamist theoreticians, presents a melancholic diagnosis of modern Muslim society as one which is in the process of gradual disintegration. He attributes that plight to the 'dissolution of the Islamic [Ottoman] state [in the aftermath of World War One], which signified the collapse of the Muslim civilisation and the concomitant termination of Islam's role as the pre-eminent force in the international arena'. As a corollary to the above sombre analysis, the panacea that is prescribed by al-Sadr is the reinstitution of the Islamic state, which is viewed not merely as a legal requirement and a necessity, but also as a civilisational imperative, as it is the only organisational entity that ensures the marshalling and channeling of the potent human energies and vast natural resources of the sprawling Muslim world. Thus, by virtue of its self-righteous mission and formidable power, the Islamic state would recapture its erstwhile position of ascendancy and world leadership of human civilisation, thereby ensuring the 'salvation of the [imperilled] Muslim *Umma* from all those [conditions] that are besetting it, as manifested in the forms of dispersion, dependency and perdition'.[74] The two above passages were articulated by al-Sadr a considerable number of years after the founding of Hizb al-Da'wa, but his forthright diagnosis of societal malaise, and his vision for an Islamic polity with a civilisational mission, had been encapsulated earlier in the ideology of the party.

Having set forth the philosophy behind the establishment of Hizb al-Da'wa, it would be fitting at this stage to examine the party's ideology, goals and strategies, organisational structure and social composition, and the background of its members. Although Fadlallah was to play a major contributing role alongside al-Sadr and others in the Islamist discourse that evolved in the period two years after the July 1958 revolution, he did not directly contribute to the formulation of the party's ideology or programme of action. Fadlallah correctly praises al-Sadr for devising *al-Usus*, the philosophical and jurisprudential underpinnings of *al-Da'wa*, the contents of which will be examined later.[75]

To the extent that it is committed to instituting profound change in the existing society, Hizb al-Da'wa is radical. It espouses an equally radical programme as a means of disseminating Islamic political consciousness among Iraqi citizens, with a view to engendering the necessary conditions that would eventually lead to seizure of power, thereby enabling the fulfilment of its ultimate objective, the founding of an independent Islamic state with a vigorous evangelical mission. That revolutionary quest was articulated in an internally circulated memo, dated 1962: 'We are revolutionary *du'at* [those who impart the Faith] striving for the transformation of society from its roots and altering all the foundations on which the political, economic, social, ideological, spiritual and philosophical conditions are based.' This self-portrayal of the party's revolutionary mission is predicated on the assumption of a revolutionary conceptualisation that would give rise to a new *weltanschauung* that would bring about the overturning of the prevailing traditional outlook, consisting of inherited 'ideas, concepts, customs, traditions and individual and collective behaviours'.[76] The party's goal was the comprehensive transformation of human society by the fundamental alteration of existing patterns of social relationships and behaviour, cultural values and religious beliefs, economic systems and political regimes.

In its view of the Muslim individual and of society, Hizb al-Da'wa holds two contrasting positions. On the one hand, in common with Sunni Islamist groups like al-Ikhwan al-Muslimun and Hizb al-Tahrir, it deems individuals who constitute the Islamic *Umma* to be Muslims, and treats them accordingly. This standpoint is upheld irrespective of the extreme variations betwen individual Muslims, in relation to the extent of normative adherence to, and faith in, Islam. On the other hand, in assessing the permeation of Muslim societies by Western secular values, Hizb al-Da'wa arrives at the conclusion that the current alienated and Westernised society is not Islamic in the maximalist, ideal sense. But in contrast to the view held by the radical Egyptian ideologue of al-Ikhwan al-Muslimun, Sayyid Qutb, contemporary Muslim society is not regarded as *jahili* (the modern equivalent of the state of paganistic ignorance and backwardness that prevailed in pre-Islamic Arabia).[77]

In contradistinction to Hizb al-Da'wa's view of society as being only nominally Muslim (in form not substance), the party deems the existing political regimes in the Muslim world as *jahili*, and thus unambiguously un-Islamic secular entities. Representative of the general Islamist view is the assertion, made by one of the earliest members of the party, Abdul al-Sahib Dakhil, that those 'political regimes that govern Muslim societies today are *jahili* entities implanted by the imperialist invaders, on their terms, prior to World War One and its aftermath in order to serve their ideology and preserve their economic and social interests'.[78]

In the light of what Hizb al-Da'wa, in common with other Islamist groups, perceives to be the inauthenticity and juridical illegitimacy of the existing regimes in the Muslim world, what strategy has the party devised in order to bring about change in the political status quo? In other words, does the party espouse a revolutionary or reformist course of action? Al-Sadr answers that central question by stating that

> if Islam represents the axiomatic foundation on which the current mode or system of existence is based, then Hizb al-Da'wa al-Islamiyya ought to assume a reformist orientation. But when Islam loses its centrality in relation to the axiomatic foundation [of existence] and is supplanted by antithetical paradigms, then in such a situation, [Hizb] al-Da'wa al-Islamiyya ought to be revolutionary, as this is the reality that the *Umma* has been experiencing since the First World War. The actual state of affairs that is beyond doubt is that the replacement of one system of rule with another does not merely signify a changing of one law for another, nor does it designate ... a casual [ad hoc] event in the *Umma*'s entity; rather, it denotes the replacement of all the fundamental views and notions of life and the cosmos on which the previous systems of government and societal structures were founded, with the views and concepts on which the new regimes are currently based. Thus, the pertinent issue in regard to the state of Islam in [current] circumstances is not that of reform but of revolution.[79]

It is in response to the challenge of what are perceived to be illegitimate political regimes that Hizb al-Da'wa actively advocates the pursuit of a 'comprehensive' revolutionary strategy, aimed at demolishing those polities and supplanting them with a regional Islamic state. From the party's perspective, given the pivotal importance of the Islamic state, every Muslim is religiously obliged and impelled by necessity to give serious contemplation to, if not actively strive for, the realisation of the Islamic political scheme. In common with the doctrinal views of Hizb al-Tahrir, it is deemed – in the absence of an Islamic state – a cardinal sin for a Muslim citizen to remain indifferent and apathetic.[80]

According to a *hadith* cited by al-Sadr and attributed to the Prophet,

> *al-hukm* [sovereignty or authority to the Islamists; juridical judgement to the traditionalists and modernists] is of two types: the *Hukm* of God or the *hukm* of *al-jahiliyya*. Whosoever errs in regard to the *Hukm* of God would [by default] have exercised *al-hukm* on the basis of *al-jahiliyya*.

The implication of this ruling, together with the often-cited Qur'anic verse, 'And whosoever does not exercise *al-hukm* by that which God has revealed, then they are the unbelievers', for al-Sadr, Fadlallah, and indeed other Islamists, is that where the state is deemed to be un-Islamic, by virtue of its legislation and ideology being at variance with the creed and laws of Islam, then the ruler of that regime forfeits the right of allegiance on the part of the citizens. With his rule declared illegitimate, it becomes an incumbent duty on the Muslim faithful to challenge their head of state through civil disobedience, or even by rebelling against his rule, commensurate with the divinely ordained dictum, 'The enjoining of that which is acceptable and interdicting that which is objectionable', with a view to bringing about his resignation or, if practicable, his overthrow.[81]

Sayyid al-Sadr elaborated on this issue by stipulating that the duty to overturn such an un-Islamic government ought not to entail any action that would expose the revolutionary activists to peril, nor preclude the likelihood of a favourable outcome. In other words, the specific strategy pursued must be devised so that the envisaged degree of revolutionary force be appropriate to the prevailing conditions and proportionate to the countervailing forces.[82]

In relation to the character and function of the Islamic polity envisioned by Hizb al-Da'wa activists, al-Sadr, unlike Fadlallah (who did not write an ideological tract on the Islamic state in this period), in his short indoctrinatory treatise, *al-Usus al-Islamiyya*, identified two variations of the Islamic polity. The first and highest form is the ideal Islamic religious–political paradigm, represented by the divinely designated and inspired rule of the Prophet Muhammad, and for the Shi'a by his cousin and son-in-law, Imam Ali, to whom – by virtue of their alleged infallibility and divine authority – unquestionable obedience was owed. The second and more applicable type of Islamic state in the period of the occultation of the Twelfth Imam is a government headed by an adhering and just Islamic leader. But being fallible, such a ruler is naturally prone to err in his judgement or edicts, and consequently it is the obligation of the religious jurists and of educated citizens to advise him.[83]

What differentiates the two models is that, whereas in the former case the head of state is designated by God and his authority to rule is derived from his Lord, and thus precludes public opinion or resolution on the question of the incumbent's tenure, in the latter case the Muslim citizens exercise the inalienable right to elect or nominate the most suitable candidate to govern the state. The second distinguishing trait of the Islamic state is the mechanism of *shura*, or consultation. The process obliges the incumbent to enter into deliberations with informed public representatives, who would comprise a cross-sectional consultative assembly, on the specific form of government to be exercised.[84]

It is revealing that – aside from accountability, justice and rule by the *shari'ah* – neither al-Sadr nor Fadlallah, in this period, designated a specific form of Islamic rulership; that is, they neither advocated the classical *khilafa*, as upheld by Hizb al-Tahrir, nor *Wilayat al-Faqih* (governance of the jurisconsult), which was propounded in the early 1970s by the Iranian revolutionary leader Ayatollah Khomeini. However, with the triumph of the 1979 Iranian Islamic Revolution, al-Sadr shifted his position and espoused the principle of *Wilayat al-Faqih*, which became the system of government for the newly instituted Islamic Republic of Iran.

Briefly, as far as the functions of the Islamic state are concerned, al-Sadr reaffirms the conventional responsibilities of the ideal Islamic state as elucidated by classical theorists and jurists such as al-Mawardi (d. 1058), and modern Islamist theoreticians like Shaykh Taqi al-Din al-Nabahani – namely, that the Islamic state is required to proclaim the injunctions and precepts of the shari'ah as the law of the land; to devise a legal code of reference for the implementation of shari'ah ordinances and provisions; and to arbitrate in disputes between the ruler and his subjects, and between the subjects themselves.[85]

However, before the ultimate goal of establishing an Islamic state can be attained, a number of lesser, but crucial and interconnected objectives must be achieved. Those objectives collectively entail the transformation of society, particularly in regard to the powerful secularising trend and its concomitant influential institutions, with a view to transforming the condition and outlook of the individual.[86] In committing itself to effecting radical change in the Muslim *Umma*, Hizb al-Da'wa conceives that process as necessarily entailing four sequential phases.

The first phase focused on the formation of an 'enlightened' and dedicated vanguard of Islamist activists, selected because of their resourcefulness and unswerving commitment to bringing about comprehensive change in the Muslim community. In the process, it is assumed that the public would be favourably disposed towards the activists and their cause, and would eventually constitute the envisaged mass following of the party. Upon the fulfilment of this phase, a sustained political struggle with the regime would ensue, which would involve the use of all available methods. The third and decisive stage, representing the culmination of the envisioned conflict with the regime, would result in the seizure of power – perhaps involving the use of violence – by the *hizb*, and the subsequent establishment of an Islamic polity. The final phase involves the total application of the *shari'ah*, the implementation of which would be closely monitored by a special committee. Upon the consolidation of the Islamic regime in Iraq, a peaceful world-wide proselytisation campaign will be launched, as will be the quest for global Islamic rule.[87]

The party sought to 'enlighten' and mobilise the faithful was through the publication and distribution of pamphlets and booklets, participation in the organisation of popular religious and cultural festivals, the delivery of instructive religious–political sermons from the mosque pulpit to the faithful prior to Friday congregational prayers, and the setting up of religious and ideological study circles administered by 'ulama associated with the party. To ensure the secrecy of its embryonic organisational fabric and activity, and hence the safety of its operatives, Sayyid al-Sadr devised the party's structure in the form of semi-independent cellular entities, organised in a pyramid structure. Such a calculated design provided for a discrete separation between the various organs, since mutual knowledge of members affiliated to different cells was precluded.[88]

The organisation of Hizb al-Da'wa was divided into four hierarchical tiers. The first and highest level was the Council of Jurists, headed by al-Sadr, whose functions included the devising of general policies, the issuing of guiding principles, the resolving of legal issues and the dispensing of legal advice. Below them was the Leadership Council, which managed day-to-day affairs – namely providing guidance and outlining and supervising the responsibilities of lower bodies. The third tier comprised Executive Committees, which were in charge of party organisation and activities on a national level, as well as executing the instructions of the senior bodies. The lowest level consisted of local committees, which comprised five to seven members known as *halaqah* (pl. *halaqat* – literally, 'rings'), each of which was answerable to the local committees (*lajna*) set up in urban quarters and national subregions.[89]

In the eighteen months prior to the July 1958 Revolution, the party leadership gave particular attention to the creation of an elaborate cellular network, restricted principally to Najaf. Public dissemination of the party's platform began soon after the Revolution. However, it was not until 1962 that the *hizb* launched an intensive public recruitment drive. That, in the intervening years, the party witnessed a slow growth in membership, is borne out by the figures provided by Sayyid Bahr al-Uloum, an *'alim* who had close contacts with the *hizb*. According to al-Uloum, the number of affiliates at the end of 1959 was a mere twenty individuals, while party supporters numbered less than 100. As stated earlier, the majority of the earliest members of Hizb al-Da'wa were young Shi'i 'ulama, the remainder being either religious students or Islamist intellectuals. Later, with the overt recruitment drive of the early 1960s, which targeted the educated stratum of society (mainly religious and secular university students and academics), a growing number of Iraqis (which in absolute terms remained small) was drawn from the urban trading and professional middle and lower-middle classes. Confessionally, given the existence of well established Sunni Islamist movements pre-dating Hizb al-Da'wa, Sunnis comprised a mere 5 per cent of all party affiliates.[90]

In a systematic bid to appeal to educated Iraqis, the party began establishing a network of Islamic bookrooms and libraries, which were located throughout most of the country's Shi'i-inhabited towns and cities. The party also continued the process of modernisation of the traditional Shi'i system of education that was started by Shaykh Muhammad Rida al-Muzzafar, which focused on reforming established teaching methods and school curricula. To that end, the party played an important part in founding a number of modern institutions of higher learning, namely Kulliyat al-Fiqh (College of Jurisprudence) in Najaf, and Kulliyat Usul al-Din (College of the fundamentals of Religion) in Baghdad.[91]

It is revealing that the these modern colleges had their origins in the reformist cultural educational society known as Muntada al-Nashr (a publishing club), whose first reformist religious school modelled on modern secular institutions was referred to in an earlier chapter, was founded in the mid-1930s by Shaykh al-Muzzaffar. Furthermore, it is instructive that Fadlallah's colleagues, who were either founding or early members of Hizb al-Da'wa – namely al-Sadr, Hasan Shubbur, Abdul-Sahib Dakhil, Shaykh 'Aref al-Basri, Shaykh Muhammad Mahdi al-'Asafi, Sayyid Abdul Rahim al-Shawki, and Fadlallah himself – had at one time or another studied at, or graduated from, one of the society's schools established in the Shi'i holy cities.[92]

As regards the ideological background of Hizb al-Da'wa members, available data, including information provided by Fadlallah, reveals that, prior to the founding of the party, some of its founders and early members had been affiliates of various Shi'i and Sunni Islamist groups. Two of Ayatollah Muhsin al-Hakim's elder sons, Sayyid Mahdi and Sayyid Baqer, for instance, who were among the founding cell of the party, had been at one stage affiliates of the predominantly Sunni Hizb al-Tahrir, as was Shaykh 'Aref al-Basri. Abdul-Sahib Dakhil, one of the founders of Hizb al-Ja'fari, likewise became one of the earliest and most senior members of Hizb al-Da'wa, while most of his colleagues also later joined the party. Another founding member of the party, Sayyid Murtada al-Askari, had previously established close ties with both al-Ikhwan al-Muslimun and Hizb al-Tahrir. Finally, a majority of the members of Harakat Shabab al-Muslim had joined Hizb al-Da'wa soon after its dissolution. As observed earlier, to the dissatisfied Shi'i activists affiliated to either of the two Sunni Islamist movements, Hizb al-Da'wa was perceived to be capable of filling the ideological void created by the marginal presence of al-Ikhwan al-Muslimun and Hizb al-Tahrir in the Shi'i south, in the face of the rapid inroads made by the Iraqi Communist Party (ICP), and well adapted to addressing the particularistic interests, grievances and aspirations of the Shi'i community in a way no Sunni Islamist movement could hope to achieve.[93]

Before examining the activities of Hizb al-Da'wa and aligned groups under General Qasem, it will be necessary to outline the processes of recruitment and indoctrination pursued by the party. As previously mentioned, the party, in its recruitment drive, targeted pious college students who had no organisational affiliation to rival groups, as they were considered to be suitable cadres for ideological propagation among student colleagues. Aside from its significant representation of affiliates drawn from the middle and lower-middle classes, a large segment of ordinary party cadres came, during the 1960s, from the pauperised urban lower class, who were viewedas a possible reservoir of mass support for the party, and a powerful buttress against any potential government crackdown. Although new recruits were not required to attend any initiation ceremony or to be issued with a party membership card, they nevertheless underwent a mandatory probationary period, during which the candidate's preparedness, devotion, fortitude and self-sacrifice were tested.[94]

The inculcation of party cadres during the 1950s and 1960s was divided into three sequential phases. The first, basic level of indoctrination consisted of several components: the recitation, comprehension and memorisation of selected passages of the Qur'an; sound understanding of the Islamic creed and other faiths; familiarity with the Prophet's career, the life of his companions and household as well as a general knowledge of Islamic history; acquaintance with principal Islamic legal rulings, principles of jurisprudence and philosophy; and familiarity with the party's constitutional articles, conventions and publications. The second level entailed a heightened understanding of the above subjects and the nurturing of sound intuition; an ability to structure and present ideas coherently; and an ability to ascertain whether a particular thought is authentic or innovative on the basis of the Islamic criteria. The third and final stage was attained by the most dedicated and accomplished senior party members. This advanced specialisation phase was divided into four categories: generic thought, essentially encompassing the world-view of Islam; organisational thought, which pertains to the nature and dynamics of the cadre-leadership relationship; political thought, which embodies a multiplicity of political ideas, trends and issues in the world at large, and the Muslim world in particular; and finally, religious thought, which aims at rectifying and enhancing the religious behaviour both of individual cadres and of nominal, unaffiliated Muslims.[95]

Islamism and the Struggle Between Communism and Nationalism

Having analysed the formation and character of Hizb al-Da'wa, it will be necessary to survey its political and ideological activity and that of other Islamist groups, and to examine the dynamics of the vacillating relationship between the Islamists, the 'ulama establishment, the Qasem regime, and the ICP. Such a survey will provide an insightful background for understanding the nature and development of Fadlallah's Islamist – albeit organisationally unaffiliated – career path, which was devoted to advanced religious–juridical study, scholastic teaching, and intellectual and ideological discourse.

The political activity of Hizb al-Da'wa following the 1958 Revolution can be divided into two phases. The first six months were characterised by cordial relations with the republican regime. The second and longer period encompassed the years 1959–62. The amicable nature of that relationship during the first period was dictated by, firstly, the then incomplete evolution of the party's vital cell formations; secondly, by the party's recognition of General Qasem's widespread popularity among the majority of Iraq's citizens; and thirdly, by the revolutionary regime's non-aligned foreign policy. The new regime, at this early stage, had not instituted domestic measures deemed by the Islamists to be contrary to their goals and interests. Indeed, it was in appreciation of the loyalty of Hizb al-Da'wa and the closely aligned Jam'at al-'Ulama ('Ulama Society), that the Government gave permission for the society to broadcast its views weekly over the state radio, from a transcript overseen by Sayyid al-Sadr.[96] Similarly, as has already been mentioned, the emotive political poems of the young Sayyid Fadlallah – which, reflecting the popular mood of patriotic euphoria, warmly praised General Qasem and the revolution – were published in the official republican newspaper.

While all the Islamists, including those affiliated to al-Ikhwan al-Muslimun and Hizb al-Tahrir, initially welcomed the radical changes that accompanied the change of regime, their favourable posture towards General Qasem and his foreign policies subsequently underwent a gradual shift. Thus, at the beginning of 1959 Hizb al-Da'wa held its first convention in Karbala, during which the conferees addressed current political developments in Iraq, and discussed means by which to deal with the challenge of the 'un-Islamic parties' – a reference to the Communists and the Ba'thists. During the course of 1959, relations between the republican regime and the Islamists deteriorated on account of the tacit strategic alliance forged between General Qasem and their common nemesis, the ICP. Although the undeclared pact was ostensibly aimed at undercutting the increasingly strident Pan-Arab nationalists, who longed for Iraq's merger with the United Arab Republic, the Islamists saw

General Qasem's overt tilt to the ICP as a sinister scheme to undermine the Islamists and Islam in general.[97]

According to Fadlallah's recollections, General Qasem was not regarded by the Islamists as a man of ideological conviction, but rather as an opportunist leader employing contradictory themes and symbols in order to appeal to the widest cross-section of Iraqi society, with a view to consolidating his grip on power. This perception of General Qasem is accurate to the extent that, as will be shown, he had at first actively encouraged the expansion of the ICP against his Arab nationalist opponents, who were led by the president's erstwhile comrade, Colonel Abdul Salam 'Aref, but thereafter began to curb their power, lest the Communists induce a popular backlash and undermine his rule. Again for the same ends of ensuring a popular backing for his regime, General Qasem at various times attempted to woo the influential Shi'i religious establishment to his side by portraying himself as an earnest friend of the 'ulama and the devout.[98]

Given the central the role of the ICP in the struggle for ascendancy between General Qasem and the Pan-Arabist opposition, it is necessary to give a brief account of the pertinent events that had a significant bearing on the political attitude and activities of the Islamists in relation to the regime, and its principal contending political forces. General Qasem and his fellow military dissidents among the Iraqi officer corps belonged to the clandestine Free Officers organisation. While he and his comrades were inspired by President Nasser's Egyptian Revolution of 1952, General Qasem remained, at heart, an Iraqi patriot, who, as an advocate of reformist change, was lukewarm about unifying republican Iraq with the newly formed United Arab Republic (UAR), which united Egypt and Syria; an arrangement which, if effected, would have inevitably ended his political primacy and subordinated him to President Nasser's pre-eminent authority.

Viewing the Arab nationalists led by Colonel 'Aref – who repeatedly called on the president to unite Iraq with its republican neighbours – as a serious threat to his nascent authority and tenuous political base, General Qasem turned to a cogent and reliable countervailing political and ideological force, namely the Iraqi Communist movement. Being unquestionably the largest and most influential political and social movement in modern Iraq, the ICP served as an important strategic ally of the president. That the ICP was a natural counterweight to, and an implacable foe of, the Arab nationalists, can be attributed to three factors. Politically, the Communists were opposed to the proposal of Iraq merging with the UAR on account of the bitter experience of their comrades in Syria, where the Communist Party was forced to disband. Consequently, if the advocated union was allowed, the ICP would face the prospect of extinction. Ideologically, in accordance with the priorities of the Communist Party, Arab unity was subordinated to the struggle against imperialism and feudalism in Arab countries. Finally, the ICP's Central Committee adopted the controversial policy of the Soviet Communist Party, which supported the United Nations resolution that called for the bi-national partition of Palestine, which, together with the Soviet Communist Party's recognition of the State of Israel, placed the ICP at loggerheads with the Arab nationalists, and with the Islamic sentiment of the Muslim populace at large.[99]

The ICP had been severely repressed under the monarchy; members were executed, imprisoned, or forced to flee abroad. Thus, the ascension to power of General Qasem, who ordered the release of incarcerated Communists and allowed activists abroad to return, was a welcome respite for the party. Though the new regime was far from being a proletarian polity, nevertheless the Communist Party leadership believed that it was possible to exploit the internal class conflicts in Iraqi society. The Central Committee of the ICP sought to induce General Qasem to include Communists in his cabinet as a first step towards achieving Communist domination. However, in anchoring his power base in the formidable social niche created by the ICP, the president rendered himself open to scathing criticism from Arab nationalists and Islamists that he was being subservient to the Communist Party, and a traitor to Pan-Arabism.[100]

During the first months of the Revolution, General Qasem attempted to stem the rising tide of Pan-Arab sentiment in Iraq by encouraging mass rallies organised by the ICP, whose participants chanted pro-Qasem slogans and called for federation, instead of union, with Egypt. The patriotic rallies were orchestrated to demonstrate the extent of influence wielded by the ICP, and the scale of support for the president. Consequently, the president accorded almost total freedom of activity to the Communist Party. As part of his methodical strategy of bolstering his position and containing the Pan-Arabists, in early August 1958 General Qasem authorised the organisation of a mass militia loyal to the regime, named al-Muqawamah al-Sha'biyya (People's Resistance). This Communist front formation, which was controlled by the president but trained by military officers, consisted of 11,000 young male and female members, growing to 25,000 by May 1959.[101]

The arrest, trial and imprisonment in October 1958 of Colonel Abdul Salam 'Aref, General Qasem's lieutenant during the revolution, on account of his discreet liaisons with – and pledge of loyalty to – President Nasser, signalled the onset of the regime's crackdown on Arab nationalists in senior government positions. General Qasem tightened his grip on power by purging the Cabinet of 'Aref supporters, replacing them with Communists, while in the army pro-'Aref officers were transferred or demoted.[102]

Despite the control of the military, the Communists dominated the Departments of Defence, Education and Guidance. Among the major newspapers controlled by the ICP were Baghdad's *al-Bilad* and *Sawt al-Ahrar*, and Najaf's *al-Ayyam*. Trade unions, outlawed in the mid-1950s and reconstituted following the Revolution, came under the influence of the Communists, as did the Student Association and the Peasant Bureau. The party dominated the country's professional organisations – namely the Teachers', Engineers', Medical, Lawyers', and Journalists' Associations – as well as the Youth and Women's groups.[103]

Alarmed by the pervasive influence of Communism in Iraqi society, the Islamists sensed a growing drift away, among the Muslim populace, from religious faith and observance, a phenomenon which was discerned to be directly related to the inexorable expansion of the ICP. To their dismay, they discovered 'scepticism and even disdain for traditional rites ... rife among the educated Shi'is'. Furthermore, tens of thousands of impoverished, newly arrived drifters from the countryside, who subsequently settled in Baghdad's al-Thawrah district, became for the Communists a prime target of a concerted and largely successful propaganda campaign, which portrayed the Shi'i 'ulama as reactionary, and religious thought as ossified and anachronistic. Most importantly, the Islamists attributed the above malaise to the apolitical and conservative orientation of the Shi'i 'ulama, who were generally perceived to have been relinquishing strategic ideological turf and socio-religious space to the Communists, thereby contributing, inadvertently, to the undermining of their own status and influence among their traditional constituency.[104] The upshot of this, in the eyes of the Islamists, is that the traditional 'ulama had, by default, unofficially but practically forfeited their crucial role as the effective custodians of Islam.

It was against this backdrop that a significant segment of the 'ulama acted, shunning the apolitical stance and intellectual inertia of the traditional religious scholars and jurists, and giving engaging practically in political affairs and ideological discourse. This circle of activist middle-ranking 'ulama organised themselves into Jama'at al-'Ulama (The 'Ulama Group), with the aim of disseminating Islam as a comprehensive and practical mode of existence with a distinct and coherent ideology.[105] As in the case of Hizb al-Da'wa, the precise date on which the society was founded is subject to disagreement among Islamist writers and Western academics. Nevertheless, the prevailing view is that the society, unlike Hizb al-Da'wa, came into existence after the 1958 Revolution. The most informed and credible sources indicate that the society had emerged either in late 1958 or early 1959.[106]

The 'Ulama Society, which constituted less a well structured and cohesive organisation than a loose grouping of like-minded scholars committed to the intellectual and cultural renaissance of Islam, comprised a circle of middle-ranking Shi'i 'ulama and *mujtahids*, representing the second echelon below the grand *mujtahids* or *maraje'*. Headed by Sayyid Baqer al-Sadr's maternal uncle, Shaykh Murtada al-Yasin, the society comprised fourteen Arab and Iranian members, and had two separate administrative committees. Jama'at al-'Ulama not only received the approval of the foremost Shi'i Marja', Sayyid Muhsin al-Hakim, who had earlier given his active support for the founding of Hizb al-Da'wa, but also the unequivocal backing of two other leading *mujtahids*, Shaykh Abul Qasem al-Kho'ie (Fadlallah's mentor) and Abdul Hadi al-Shirazi.[107]

Two junior 'ulama were conspicuous by their absence from the membership of Jama'at al-'Ulama – namely Sayyid al-Sadr and Sayyid Fadlallah. Both Islamists, together with others like Shaykh Muhammad Mahdi Shams al-Din, were not members of the society due to their comparatively young age; al-Sadr was twenty-four, and Fadlallah twenty-two.[108] Informed sources are unanimous, however, in depicting al-Sadr as the architect and real driving force of the society. He assumed the role of adviser to his uncle, Shaykh al-Yasin, the society's General Director, and wrote most of the society's proclamations and statements.[109] In addition – as will be observed later – he collaborated with Fadlallah in writing the first and second editorial articles of the society's Islamic intellectual periodical, *al-Adwa'*.

Fadlallah was among a circle of junior activist 'ulama who were at the forefront of disseminating Islam among the Shi'i community, and with whom the scholastic members of the society had close links. These young 'ulama, who included Shaykh Shams al-Din and Sayyids Mahdi and Baqer al-Hakim, collaborated in writing a series of ideological booklets on a wide range of religious and socio-cultural issues. It is significant that all thirteen or so participants were either colleagues or students of al-Sadr, and had direct or indirect ties to Hizb al-Da'wa, whose members – by virtue of the pivotal nexus of al-Sadr, and to a lesser extent al-Fadlallah – had close links with the affiliates of Jama'at al 'Ulama in Najaf. Its sister association, Baghdad's Jama'at al-'Ulama, and Kazimayn, which was established in February 1964 (several years after the founding of the original society), had maintained even closer ties to Hizb al-Da'wa. Compared to its parent society in Najaf, the Baghdad-based group had a young clerical membership, and some of its affiliates were also members of Hizb al-Da'wa.[110]

To the extent that Jama'at al-'Ulama sought to reaffirm the primacy of

Islam as a coherent ideology and practical system, the society was as much political as it was religious. During the first months of its existence, it prudently avoided attacking General Qasem; indeed, it gave him its qualified support. Owing to the president's popularity and favourable foreign policy initiatives, the society focused its political campaign on disparaging and warding off the Communist challenge, and promoting Islamic cultural, philanthropic and educational activities. In return, General Qasem allowed the Islamist association to publicise its views via state-run radio, and gave permission to publish *al-Adwa' al-Islamiyya* (The Islamic Lights), the society's principal mouthpiece. To broaden the scope of its anti-Communist strategy, the society engaged in a variety of activities, including the organisation of cultural festivals, intellectual forums and religious gatherings, as well as issuing proclamations and distributing pamphlets. It also formed special committees charged with establishing hospitals and clinics, religious schools, orphanages, infirmaries, and centres to assist the poor and needy.[111]

However, in the absence of detailed information on these institutions, it is difficult to ascertain the extent to which they fulfilled the needs of the Shi'i community, on the one hand, and stemmed the tide of Communism, on the other. What is clear from the response of the 'ulama establishment, and of Islamist intellectuals and political activists, is that their reactions to the Communist threat were uncoordinated, even discordant. While some activists readily organised anti-Communist forums at Islamic Eid festivities, conferences and *'Ashoura* processions, at which young 'ulama such as Fadlallah, with a gift for oratory, delivered sermons and lectures, and read out poems, other more senior *'ulama* devoted their efforts to reforming existing educational institutions or establishing new ones. The most influential of these was the College of Jurisprudence, which was founded in 1958 in Najaf by Shaykh al-Muzzaffar, a reformist scholar and member of Jama'at al-'Ulama.[112]

For their part, the leading Shi'i *mujtahids* embarked upon a major building programme, which included the founding of a significant number of mosques and *huseiniyyat* (sing. *huseiniyyah*: place where Imam Hussein is mourned), in a number of cities and towns, as well as the sponsoring of libraries. These became venues for congregation, study, debate, indoctrination, recruitment and mobilisation. As part of Ayatollah Sayyid al-Hakim's strategy to contain the spread of Communist influence, he despatched his official representatives to major urban centres in southern Iraq with the objective of raising Islamic consciousness and enhancing religious observance. Among Sayyid al-Hakim's chief representatives were Sayyid Isma'il al-Sadr (Sayyid Baqir al-Sadr's elder brother), Shaykh Muhammad Mahdi Shams al-Din (the late colleague of Fadlallah and former head of Lebanon's Supreme Shi'i Muslim Council),

Sayyid Mahdi al-Hakim, Sayyid Murtada al-Askari, and Shaykh 'Aref al-Basri.[113]

Motivated by a real sense of urgency arising from the marginalisation of Islam in contemporary society, due to the ascendancy of secular ideologies and 'materialist' culture, a small group of young activist 'ulama committed themselves to producing a coherent and comprehensive system of thought, predicated on the Islamic world-view and on religious precepts capable of demolishing the sophisticated ideology of Communism, with its elaborate philosophical underpinnings. It was Sayyid al-Sadr who proved to be the most outstanding figure among this group of emerging 'ulama, contending directly with that Communist challenge. Hence his seminal and lucid treatise entitled *Falsafatuna* ('Our Philosophy'). Completed in 1959, while al-Sadr was in his mid-twenties, this widely acclaimed monograph served as a detailed and critical study of the premises of Marxist thought, with particular reference to dialectical materialism.[114]

Employing Islamic and Marxist terminology, and showing a sound grasp of the salient concepts of Communism, al-Sadr tried to demonstrate what he perceived to be fallacies in the postulates of Marxism.[115] In particular, he attempted to demonstrate the flaws inherent in the philosophical underpinnings of dialectical materialism, and in the materialist conception of history.[116] He concluded that Communism, as an ideology, was fundamentally flawed, and thus could not logically represent a cure for humankind's many and complex problems. In completing his monograph, al-Sadr expressed the hope that Muslim students and intellectuals would acquire a profound understanding of the true – 'misleading' – nature of Marxist thought, and thereby contribute to the curtailment of its influence in society.[117]

It is revealing that this text was hastily written to address the deep-seated anxiety of his co-religionists over the ascendancy of the Communist movement in key state and civil institutions. The Islamists and Arab nationalists were, moreover, alarmed by the unbridled and provocative militant activities of the Communists during the course of 1959. In particular, those apprehensions and animosities crystallised in the wake of two major events in that year: the Mosul insurrection in March, and the Kirkuk massacres in July.

The Mosul revolt was initiated by a group of disgruntled members of the Free Officers, who were stationed in that northern, and predominantly Sunni city. As former comrades of General Qasem, and as vehement anti-Communists and Arab nationalists, led by Colonel Abdul Wahhab al-Shawwaf (commander of the Fifth Brigade), these insurgent officers were alienated by their exclusion by the president from the central revolutionary ruling body, and by his close links with the ICP. The rebels were supported by the Ba'thists and al-Ikhwan al-Muslimun, whose stronghold was Mosul. In retaliation for their open challenge to his authority, General Qasem unleashed the ICP's militia, the Peoples' Resistance Force, and the pro-Communist Kurdish irregulars, resulting in the deaths of hundreds of rebel officers and sympathetic civilians. Arab nationalists and Sunni Islamists belonging to al-Ikhwan in the city were subjected to indiscriminate mob lynchings, beatings, detention and torture. As testimony to the ferocity of the carnage and destruction wrought by the merciless Communist witch-hunt, bodies of suspected members or sympathisers of al-Ikhwan were disfigured, corpses dragged through the streets, families of Islamic activists and nationalists intimidated, offices of the Brethren ransacked, radio stations shut down, and property confiscated. Among the major figures of the Muslim Brethren who were detained and imprisoned was the society's leader, Shaykh Muhammad Mahmud al-Sawwaf. Released in 1959, he left Iraq, initially for the northern Lebanese city of Tripoli, followed by Saudi Arabia, before finally settling in Syria, where he resumed his open opposition to General Qasem.[118]

Although the upheaval in Mosul remained geographically restricted to the far north, the Shi'i 'ulama in the south of the country were not oblivious to those disturbances. On the contrary, the chief Marja, Ayatollah Muhsin al-Hakim, expressed sympathy and solidarity with the Muslim victims of Mosul. He condemned the outrages perpetrated by the Communists in the wake of the abortive al-Shawwaf revolt, and deplored the president's inaction to prevent, or at least put a halt to, the wanton killings.[119]

Even before the events in Mosul, Najaf's *mujtahids* had – between December 1958 and February 1959 – exhorted the faithful to be vigilant against the provocations and 'machinations' of the Communists. Since December 1959, when the controversial Personal Status Law was promulgated, relations between the Shi'i 'ulama and the regime had soured. The main provisions of the new code, to which the 'ulama objected, were gender equality in respect to inheritance, which conflicted with specific injunctions of the Qur'an; the abolition of polygamy; the raising of the legal age of marriage to eighteen; and compulsory marriage contracts allowing for divorce proceedings by the wife. Despite the strident remonstrations of the religious scholars and jurists, and the organisation of street protests by Hizb al-Da'wa, the president did not yield to their demands for abrogation.[120]

Relations between the Islamists, religious conservatives, and Arab nationalists, on the one hand, and the regime and the ICP, on the other, reached their nadir folllowing the sanguine events in Kirkuk, in July 1959. Fuelled by class disparities between the generally less well-to-do Kurds and their traditional rivals, the affluent Turkoman minority, three days of riots left a death toll of 100, mostly Turkomans massacred by communist Kurds. The incident aroused widespread revulsion and indignation, and moreover it brought the Communist Party into disrepute, prompting a public recantation from the party's Central Committee in August 1959. The excesses caused a drastic fall in the number of recruits to the Party's front organisations, and led to a straining of relations between General Qasem and the ICP.[121]

Sensing the groundswell of popular outrage against his Communist allies, the president began to distance himself from the ICP. To maintain his grip on power, General Qasem proceeded to enfeeble – significantly but not critically – the formidable power-base of the ICP, lest it become an independent organisation with a capacity to challenge his authority seriously. Thus, branding the Communists as anarchists and even fascists, General Qasem launched a major clampdown on the party. He purged Communist officers from the armed forces, disbanded ICP front formations and trade unions, and closed down communist newspapers.[122]

The response of the regime to the challenge of the Communist Party was aimed at wooing the estranged and embittered nationalists and, to a lesser extent, the religious leaders and Islamists.[123] However, the concessions were not enough to allay the fears of the anti-communist constellation of forces, and as a result relations remained strained. The continued opposition of the Islamic activists and senior 'ulama to the Qasem regime can be ascribed to the still dominant influence of the ICP, and the implementation of the Personal Status Law, widely perceived as obnoxious.

But the Islamists were too fractured to challenge the regime, either openly or covertly. In the wake of the Mosul uprising, the principal Sunni Islamist group, al-Ikhwan al-Muslimun, was decimated by the arrest of its members and the flight of its leaders, while the recently founded Hizb al-Da'wa lacked the organisational capacity or popular base to mount a sustained and effective campaign against General Qasem. For it was not until 1962–63 – late in General Qasem's reign, when support for the regime was tangibly diminishing, and indeed all strata of Iraqi society had become alienated from the government – that Hizb al-Da'wa's leadership seized the opportunity to launch an open and intensive recruitment drive, targeting university and college students and teachers, as well as the devout urban poor of Baghdad's densely inhabited slums.[124]

In contrast to the Islamists, the Ba'thists were not only far from placated by General Qasem's tough policy on the Communists, but were committed to toppling the Iraqi leader. The Ba'th Party was founded in Syria in 1940–41 by three French-educated school teachers: Michel 'Aflaq (a Greek Orthodox Christian), Salah al-Din al-Bitar (a Sunni Muslim) and Zaki al-Arsuzi (an

Alawi). Michel 'Aflaq was recognised as the ideologue of the party. His ideas, however, were not systematically formulated, showing a lack of coherence attributable to his romantic style and 'undisciplined eclecticism'.[125] The party platform comprised a syncretic combination of three cardinal tenets: unity (of the Arab people), freedom (from imperialism) and socialism.

The Iraqi branch of the Syrian parent body was established in 1951 by Fu'ad al-Rikabi, a Shi'i graduate of the Engineering College of the southern city of al-Nasiriyya. Alongside the remarkable growth in the party's membership – which increased from a mere 150 in 1952 to around 15,000 by 1963 – was the confessional complexion of the Iraqi Ba'th Command Committees, of which, between 1952 and 1963, 53.8 per cent were Shi'a. Appalled by the Communist Party's support for the partition of Palestine, many Shi'i activists became attracted to the Ba'th Party on account of its political and socio-economic radicalism.[126]

In the immediate wake of the Kirkuk massacres in July 1959, the Ba'th high command in Baghdad had come to the realisation that General Qasem had to be removed from power so as to bring about the demise of the ICP. To that end, secret preparations were made to assassinate General Qasem. The plot, which was carried out on 7 October 1959 by a group of young Ba'thist operatives who included Saddam Hussein, resulted in Qasem being seriously wounded. Recovering from his wounds after a few months in hospital, General Qasem promptly ordered the arrest and trial of senior Ba'thists. Fu'ad al-Rikabi, however, managed to escape to Syria. Paradoxically, a direct outcome of the abortive assassination attempt was a dramatic improvement in the fortunes of the ICP, which was revitalised by the expansion of its base of support.[127]

In a move calculated to appease his political opponents, the president opened a new chapter in the political history of Republican Iraq by embarking on a brief experiment in political pluralism. Thus, in January 1960, he promulgated the Associations Law (*Qanun al-Jami'yyat*), which finally reversed the ban on political parties, enforced since September 1954 by Prime Minister Nuri al-Sa'id. Taking advantage of this political openness, several parties applied for registration – including, in addition to the three secular organisations (two Communist groups and the National Democratic Party) two Islamist parties, Hizb al-Tahrir al-Islami (Islamic Liberation Party) and the hitherto unknown Hizb al-Islami al Iraq (the Iraqi Islamic Party). The leadership of the former group made two unsuccessful applications for an official licence in 1960, the first on 2 February and the second on 27 March. The refusal of the authorities to grant permission was apparently on the grounds that the organisation had links with a parent organisation operating from abroad – namely Jordan; and that it was a clandestine revolutionary party, whose platform was deemed to be diametrically opposed to the country's constitution, the foundations of the regime, and the nation-state of Iraq. At the same time as the formal application submitted by Hizb al-Tahrir was made, the newly established Iraqi Islamic Party submitted a similar request for registration, which met the same fate. However, the party's second application, lodged with the Court of Cessation, was approved on 26 April 1960.[128]

Western sources – namely Joyce Wiley and Majid Khadduri – differ as to the respective roles of al-Ikhwan al-Muslimun and Hizb al-Da'wa in the formation of Hizb al-Islami al-Iraqi. For, while Khadduri maintains that the party was formed by al-Ikhwan, Wiley contends that it was established by Hizb al-Da'wa. Islamist sources do not indicate, however, that the party represented a merger between al-Ikhwan al-Muslimun and Hizb al-Da'wa, as contended by Wiley, although it is established that the party's operational founders were two Sunni activists, Ibrahim Abdullah Shihab and Nu'man Abdul Razzaq al-Samirra'i, while Sayyid Muhsin al-Hakim assumed the role of unofficial patron of the Iraqi Islamic Party. Furthermore, it is known that Hizb al-Islami al-Iraqi had an ecumenical memberbership, which comprised both Sunni and Shi'i Muslims, reflecting a common perception of the need for joint action by activists of both denominations.[129]

Notwithstanding the court's ruling in its favour, the Iraqi Islamic Party – which, in the first few months of its existence, had cordial relations with the regime – encountered considerable restrictions on its political activity. Those restrictions – manifested in the government's refusal to permit the publication of the party's mouthpiece, *al-Jihad*, as well as its program – were due to its strident hostility towards the Communist movement. On 12 February 1960, less than six weeks after the application of the Iraqi Islamic Party for official registration, Sayyid Muhsin al-Hakim, patron of the party, issued a fatwa in which he denounced Communism for its atheism, affirming that it was contrary to Islamic persuasion to join the ICP. Due to his stature and influence, the fatwa had the direct effect of inducing other Shi'i *mujtahids* to issue similar religious–juridical edicts, including Sayyid al-Kho'ie and Sayyid al-Shahrudi.[130]

An imposing backdrop to al-Hakim's fatwa against Communism was provided by the various forms of pressure exerted by the ICP on the pre-eminent *mujtahid* and his colleagues. During the course of 1959, al-Hakim saw the Communist Party wage against him a systematic campaign of intimidation, harassment and denigration. In Najaf itself, the Communists regularly aroused the religious sensitivities of the pious inhabitants by chanting slogans deemed to be blasphemous, violated the sanctity of mosques, and in the process created an emotionally charged atmosphere punctuated by frequent violent street clashes between Shi'i devotees and Communist acivists.[131]

The fatwas issued by the country's top ten *mujtahids* had the net effect of tangibly arresting the continued expansion of Communism, by inducing many potential and wavering Shi'is to refrain from joining the ICP. While Hanna Batatu, an acclaimed scholar of Iraq, contends that the fatwas left the status quo essentially intact, another specialist scholar, Farhad Ibrahim, argues that the issuing of the edicts led to a rift within the Communist Party hierarchy regarding policy. Copies of the fatwas, explicitly prohibiting any form of association with the ICP, were made, distributed, and posted on government buildings in Shi'i-inhabited districts, including Baghdad, by both Islamists and Arab nationalists.[132]

As an indication of the seriousness with which the regime viewed the impact of the anti-Communist edicts, the state authorities placed al-Hakim under house arrest. The detention caused widespread indignation, and motivated his followers to despatch petitions to General Qasem calling for his immediate release, as well as that of the prominent Sunni activist-*'alim*, Shaykh Abdul-'Aziz al-Badri. Faced with the large following of al-Hakim, who was depicted during an interview in early 1961 as 'the strongest popular personality in Iraq', General Qasem was compelled to yield to public demand in order to avert an impending crisis. As a gesture of good will, General Qasem visited al-Hakim in hospital, and instructed his Interior Minister to censure several Marxist publications considered scandalous by many religious people. Although the impact of the edicts, and subsequent fall-out from al-Hakim's detention, had the effect of inducing General Qasem to distance himself from the ICP, the shift was not accompanied by a rapprochement with al-Hakim. The latter had steadfastly declined the former's overtures of appeasement, demanding instead the abrogation of the controversial Personal Status Law.[133]

Concurrent with the issuing of a series of religious edicts prohibiting membership of the ICP was the overt virulence manifested by the Iraqi Islamic party towards the Communists and its oppositional stance towards the regime. This was borne out in a series of political memoranda, issued by the party, attacking the policies of the government. Beginning at the end of May 1960, the Iraqi Islamic Party submitted a memorandum to General Qasem, requesting laws of the state to be reformulated in congruence with the precepts and ordinances of the shari'ah. This was followed in June by another petition, addressed to the president, demanding that he take prompt measures to curtail the ICP. It rebuked the government for encouraging godless ideology and neglecting Islamic teaching. The petition also called on the president to release two prominent religious scholars and political activists, Shaykh

Muhammad al-Khalisi (a Shi'i) and Shaykh Abdul-'Aziz al-Badri (a Sunni), who had been languishing in prison for over five months. On 5 July 1960, the party issued a proclamation 'denouncing the Communists', while at its convention, held on 29 July 1960, among the several resolutions adopted was the decision to launch a 'war on heresy and atheism'.[134]

The vitriolic assault by the Iraqi Islamic Party on the ICP and the regime culminated in a detailed public petition that was put out by the party and published on 15 October 1960 in the sympathetic weekly newspaper, *al-Fayha'*. In what became a turning-point in the party's short-lived history, the Islamist organisation launched its last and, as yet, most scathing denunciation of the government and its public record. The party accused the authorities of negligence in regard to realising social equality, and attacked General Qasem for spurning the Islamic creed and stifling political dissent. The regime was severely reproached for having established an unholy alliance with the Communists, and provided patronage to the ICP in its campaign to undermine the party. It further berated General Qasem for what it perceived to be the 'appalling' state of the economy, with much of the citizenry starving. Responsibility for this wretched state of affairs was attached unequivocally with the head of state. Finally, the petition demanded that the government immediately terminate its liaison with the Communists, put their leaders on trial, proscribe the ICP, and suppress all party publications.[135]

Predictably, the regime's response was swift and stern. In October 1960, eleven senior members of the Iraqi Islamic Party were apprehended, its offices in Baghdad and Mosul were shut down, and the party's licence was revoked. After serving five months of imprisonment, the party's leaders were released on 15 March 1961, following public appeals for the freedom of the detained activists by party affiliates, the 'ulama and sympathetic journalists. Contrary to widespread fears, the release of party leaders did not lead to the regeneration of the outlawed organisation, or resumption of political activity; instead, the party, at the behest of the authorities, was disbanded. A government proposal that its leaders apply as a group to register as an association was rejected, and nothing more was heard of the party.[136]

Such was the tumultuous course of political events, and the shifting shape of the struggle for survival and supremacy among the principal contending political factions – namely Communism, nationalism and Islamism – between late 1958 and early 1961. The foregoing discussion provides the context in which to undertake an inquiry into the nature and development of Sayyid Fadlallah's intellectual thought, and to assess the significance of his contribution to the emerging Shi'i Islamist discourse of the late 1950s and 1960s.

The Islamist Writings of Sayyid Fadlallah

Although, as observed earlier, Fadlallah was a member of neither Hizb al-Da'wa nor Hizb al-Islami al-Iraqi, he enjoyed a prominent role as a young Islamist writer, and his contribution to the evolving Islamist discourse of the early and mid-1960s was discernible.

As important as the sequence of anti-Communist edicts may have been in limiting the extent of Communist influence among the Shi'i faithful, al-Sadr and Fadlallah were of the view that those edicts were inadequate to face down the challenge of Communism. For the small circle of dedicated intellectual Islamists, the interdictions issued by the senior *mujtahids* needed to be complemented, if not buttressed, by the articulation of a systematic theory of Islam. Accordingly, Islam is presented as a total and vibrant system of – and a natural and vital panacea for – present-day and future human existence, and for its myriad and complex problems. Shaped by this distinctive world-view, and impelled by their religious convictions and the exigencies of their times, al-Sadr, Fadlallah and Shaykh Shams al-Din, among others, pioneered a new genre of modern Islamist writing with a subtle Shi'i nuance.[137]

Rising anew to address the challenge of the Marxist ideological paradigm directly, along with the concomitant political and social dominance of the ICP, was Sayyid Baqer al-Sadr who, as mentioned earlier, had authored in 1959 the influential treatise, *Falsafatuna.* In 1961, al-Sadr wrote a sequel, *Iqtisaduna* ('Our Economic System'). In the 700-page study, the author presents an analytical critique of capitalist and, in particular, Communist economic theories, and a sophisticated exposition of the ideological foundations and jurisprudential bases of the ideal Islamic economic system. Fadlallah regarded the work of his senior colleague as a seminal masterpiece, which rendered him the first Islamic intellectual and religious scholar to extrapolate from the classical texts of Islamic jurisprudence a schema for the construction of a distinct and comprehensive school of modern Islamic economic theory.[138]

More modest in size (totalling 133 pages) and scope, and less influential than *Iqtisaduna*, was an important work written in 1960 by Fadlallah, when he was twenty five, *Usloub al-Da'wa fi al-Qur'an* (The Mode of Calling [or inviting non-Muslims] in the Qur'an). Whereas in *Iqtisaduna* al-Sadr was primarily concerned with demonstrating the 'bankruptcy' of Communist ideology, in *Uslub al-Da'wa fi al-Qur'an*, Fadlallah attempted to reveal the fallacy inherent in the orientalist interpretation of the Qur'an, and in particular to demonstrate the invalid and misleading correlation made by Western proponents of that school between jihad and the supposed natural proclivity for violence, and between *Da'wa* and coercion.[139]

Defining *Da'wa* as a distinct form of 'activity that Islamic callers perform outside the sphere of Islamic [community] life with a view to attracting others [non-Muslims] to Islam', Fadlallah divides his work into two parts. The first section inquires into the nature, characteristics and method of *al-Da'wa*, through a close study of pertinent Qur'anic verses and the exemplary career of the Prophet Muhammad. He forcefully argues that *Da'wa* is an essential prelude, following the formation of an Islamic society, to the establishment of an Islamic polity, whose goal is to further the cause of Islam by giving the process of *Da'wa* a vital impetus, and expanding its capacity to undertake the peaceful mission of global Islamisation.[140]

Fadlallah was not the first Muslim scholar or ideologue to determine the existence of an intrinsic connection between *din* (religion) and *dawla* (state), having been preceded some three decades earlier by Shaykh Hasan al-Banna, but he can be credited as being among the first Shi'i 'ulama to have expounded on this cardinal principal of Islamist thought.

In the second part of his treatise, Fadlallah presents a detailed critique of the orientalist conception of *Da'wa* in Islam. Citing the Irish-born critic and dramatist George Bernard Shaw as epitomising the misconceived orientalist perception of the Islamic process of proselytisation as fundamentally coercive, and the instrument of *jihad* as invariably violent, Fadlallah analysed seemingly irreconcilable Qur'anic verses – such as that in which God enjoins the faithful to 'Fight them [the unbelievers] till there is no more sedition', on the one hand, and the verse in which God affirms that 'There is no compulsion in religion', on the other.[141] Juxtaposed with this attempt at synthesis in Qur'anic exegesis is an historical outline of the venture of early Islam, as manifested in the religious and political career of the Prophet, and in particular his record in statecraft, diplomacy and war with the adversaries of Islam.

While dismissing out of hand the distorted view of Islam as a faith impelling fanaticism, xenophobia and bellicosity, he argues that Islam enjoins its believers to be both vigorous and steadfast in the defence of their faith and community (if necessary, through the medium of jihad), as well as tolerant, compassionate and humane towards non-Muslims. For Fadlallah, the Qur'an delineates the exemplary character of the *da'i* (the caller) – namely morality, spirituality, understanding and flexibility.[142] The implication is that these very features inevitably propel the Muslim proselytiser to a higher moral ground in the battle for minds and hearts between Islam and unbelief.

Fadlallah addressed the use of force in jihad, pointing out that, while it is a divinely sanctioned, and in certain cases mandated act, it is in the final analysis an exception to the normative conduct of affairs for adherent Muslim individuals, societies and states. Drawing on the extensive body of legal work on jihad by classical and modern Muslim jurists and scholars, Fadlallah affirms that jihad, when invoked as physical or collective armed struggle for the sake of God, is employed either to ward off real or impending danger to the Muslim society or as a last resort in order to remove any insurmountable impediment put in place by a power or powers hostile to Islam, to inhibit or halt its otherwise peaceful diffusion by *Da'wa*. In other words, jihad is a defensive struggle resorted to when there are no longer any avenues for the continued propagation of Islam.[143]

Fadlallah's explanation of the historically momentous shift from the original, peaceful course pursued by the Prophet and his companions in Mecca, to that of jihad following the historic migration to Medina, differs fundamentally from the interpretation of orientalist historians. For the latter, the originally meek character of the early devotees of Islam a masquerade lasting for as long as they were a fledgling and beleaguered community; but with the establishment of an independent power base in Medina, the benign and gentle posture of Muslims was, in a Machiavellian way, abandoned for bellicose jihad, in keeping with the innately intolerant and pugnacious Muslim character. Rejecting this view out of hand, Fadlallah justifies the Prophet's recourse to jihad in terms of the incessant persecution of weak, downtrodden Muslims in Medina, who – far from being unscrupulous – were fervently and earnestly committed to spreading the Word of God through peaceful means, only to be ostracised, harassed, and finally forced to leave their belongings and place of origin. Thus, it was in the face of such torment that jihad was divinely sanctioned, as it was believed to be the only means by which the nascent Muslim community might gradually erode the superiority in manpower and equipment held by the pagan Quraysh tribe and its allies, and thus create the necessary conditions of freedom for the propagation of Islam and the eventual return of the dispossessed Muslims to Mecca.[144]

Fadlallah's principal aim in writing his first monograph was to establish the legitimate procedure employed in the conduct of *Da'wa,* together with its ethical and moral dimensions, and to demonstrate the immediate relevance of the Qur'anic and Prophetic paradigms to the needs and aspirations of Muslim activists, and in contemporary Iraq, in particular.

A striking feature of Fadlallah's treatise is its manifest absence of specifically Shi'i themes and idioms. The thrust of his discussion, and the nature of his language and tone, leave the impression of a work that was written by an objective Islamic writer, rather than by a Shi'i in the particularistic sense. The only indication that the author is a Shi'i derives is from the sources cited in the footnotes, which total twenty (excluding references to the Korean), of which twelve are attributed to several Shi'i religious authorities, while five are attributed to two Sunni writers, of whom the most prominent is Sayyid Qutb.[145] The fact that the work is an atypical ecumenical Islamic treatise indicates that Fadlallah, even at this early phase in his evolution as an Islamist writer, was consciously formulating and articulating his thought so as to transcend the traditional parochial and confessional parameters. It could also be perceived as an integral part of the overall strategy of the Islamists, articulated in their discourse, whereby universal commonalities of Islam were defined and elaborated, and under which references to divisive, particularistic dogma were omitted or diluted.

Similarly, al-Sadr's two most outstanding scholarly works, *Falsafatuna* and *Iqtisaduna*, do not manifest the conventional aspects of the writings of a Shi'i *'alim*. Both he and Fadlallah were mainly concerned with developing a coherent and sophisticated Islamic ideology, drawn from both Shi'i and Sunni texts. Accordingly, the ecumenical outlook, and the anti-Communist activism, of Fadlallah and al-Sadr necessitated avoiding Sunni–Shi'i doctrinal polemics and historical controversies.[146]

However, whereas al-Sadr was to shift his focus to preponderantly Shi'i themes during the 1960s and 1970s, as the threat of Communism receded, Fadlallah's major writings during the 1970s and 1980s betrayed a pronounced continuity of orientation, which reflected his ecumenical world-view.[147] Fadlallah's works manifest no significant signs of Shi'i bias, except for the traditional Shi'i narration of the historical schism in early Islam, and the upholding of what is believed to be the usurping of the inherited right of the Prophet's progeny to rulership.

However, even this central issue is carefully expounded in a manner that does not arouse confessional sensitivities. This is a reflection, no doubt, of both Fadlallah's rationalism and his pragmatism – traits apparent in his ability to select and re-interpret – at times, radically – the constitutive elements in Shi'i dogma. It is reasonable to assume that Fadlallah's analysis is firmly based on a deep-seated conviction of the soundness of this theory, rather than on any transient interpretation conditioned by political convenience, necessity, or personal utility. Indeed, over time the transcendant Islamic orientation of his writings, and the principled approach in his discourse, have not undergone any substantative shift with changing political conditions. In other words, as the threat of Communism in Iraq receded, and no other comparable ideological or political challenge was encountered by Fadlallah and Lebanon's Shi'i community during the 1960s and 1970s, there was no discernible shift from his unmistakably de-confessionalised message of the 1950s and early 1960s to the Shi'i particularism that came to characterise the later writings of al-Sadr.

The completion of Fadlulah's book, *Usloub al-Da'wa*, coincided approximately with the launching of *Majallat al-Adwa' al-Islamiyya* (Islamic Lights Magazine), the most influential Shi'i Islamist periodical of the period; a project in which, together with al-Sadr, he was to play a pivotal role.[148] The periodical was the product of some of the most talented young Muslim intellectual minds of that period. Among the distinguished contributors were Sayyid Baqer al-Sadr (editor-in-chief), Sayyid Fadlallah, Shaykh Muhammad Mahdi Shams al-Din, Shaykh Muhammad Mahdi al-Asafi and Sayyid Isma'il al-Sadr. Sayyid Baqer al-Sadr wrote, under the title *Risalatuna* ('Our Message') the journal's leading editorial, until the sixth issue, after which the leading article was written by Shaykh Shamsiddin.[149] The second editorial of *al-Adwa'*, entitled *Kalimatun'a* ('Our Word') was written by Fadlallah over a period of six years.[150] Fadlulah's editorials in *al-Adwa'*s first year of circulation were subsequently collected to comprise part of a book which was published in late 1960, under the title *Qadayana 'ala Daw' al-Islam* ('Our Affairs in the Light of Islam').[151] Although the full series of articles which originally appeared in *al-Adwa'* is unavailable, the periodical's first editorials, written by al-Sadr, and later Shaykh Shams al-Din, were later compiled into a booklet, entitled *Risalatuna* ('Our Message'), which was prefaced by Sayyid Fadlallah and published in Beirut in 1981.[152]

The contributors to *al-Adwa'* sought to bring about the cultural transformation of Muslim society through the reformation of the individual. To that end, they focused on modernising the classical science of Islamic jurisprudence and reinterpreting key aspects of Shi'i historical and doctrinal tradition. The content of *al-Adwa'* differed radically from the traditional approach and subject-matter of the Shi'i religious seminaries. From the outset, the editors of the Islamist magazine eschewed direct criticism of the incumbent president or the policies of his government; instead, they focused on diagnosing what they perceived as the current malaise, by addressing the values of modernity, namely: justice, individual freedom, national liberation, economic development and social progress.[153]

The editorial articles that Fadlallah wrote for *al-Adwa'* in its third and fifth years were compiled in a separate book, entitled *Afaq Islamiyya wa Mawadi Ukhra* ('Islamic Horizons and other Matters'). The articles deal with such diverse issues as positive mental attitude, indifference, method of approach and mode of thought. He also addressed issues commonly encountered by the Shi'i faithful, particularly the activists among them: the problem of confessionalism, the state of Muslim education, the cleavage between parochial and universal Muslim consciousness, and the problems caused by the divergent tactics of different Islamist groups.[154]

In an article entiltled 'The Crisis of the Muslim Individual in the Shadow of non-Islamic Legislation', Fadlallah outlines the problem facing the contemporary Muslim citizen, torn between complying with the religious and legal obligations of his faith, on the one hand, and emulating Western culture and adopting secular values, on the other. Perturbed and alienated from their own society, many Muslims feel that there is a vital need to bring about an Islamic way of life and an Islamic order. Fadlallah castigates those Muslim modernists who, captivated by the scientific, technological and organisational advances attained by Western nations, seek to emulate modern Western legal institutions and systems of thought, with the aim of assimilating reactionary, backward and passive Muslims into the civil and progressive culture of the West. In the view of Fadlallah, the modernists are unmindful of the fact there is a large chasm between the nature and historical evolution of Muslims, on one hand, and Western societies, on the other.[155]

To underscore the gravity of adopting Western civil law in Muslim countries, Fadlallah cited the often-quoted Qur'anic verse, 'And whosoever does not rule by that which God has revealed, then they are the unbelievers', maintaining that the 'essence of our creed and religion rejects any code of law that is at variance with the law of religion, its shari'ah, and is deemed to be tantamount to iniquity, unbelief, deviation and rebellion against the Will of God'. He adds, accordingly, that 'no person has the right to legislate vis-à-vis the legislation of God, and no one has the right to govern vis-à-vis the rule of God'. Fadlallah affirms that the Muslim individual is not obliged to abide by secular laws; indeed, not only is he entitled to defy such un-Islamic laws, but it becomes incumbent on him to rebel against the authority of the state, with a view to bringing about the abrogation of detestable laws, in accordance with the precept of 'enjoining the good and forbidding the reprehensible'.[156]

As a result of the impact of Western civil legal codes, there emerged in Muslim societies, in the view of Fadlallah, a hybridised intellectual approach. According to Fadlallah, this trend stemmed from a view of Islam as an inherently pliable, all-inclusive religion that has the natural capacity of accommodating virtually any concept or theory, irrespective of the incompatibility in its foundation and character. In attempting to propound a syncretic or eclectic version of Islam, the Westernising, secular elites had posited the inevitable separation of religious precepts and values from political affairs. Islam is thereby reduced primarily to a uni-dimensional function of providing ethical values and devotional–spiritual bonds between the creator and his worshipping servant.[157]

The implication of this erroneous conception, according to Fadlallah, is that Islam is considered merely to embody certain broad principles that relate to socio-economic justice, and consequently lacks those elements crucial for extrapolating a distinct and coherent economic theory that would represent an authentic and viable alternative to the Marxist and capitalist economic systems. It follows from this line of thought that nothing in Islam prevents a person from concurrently being a Muslim believer and a communist or capitalist. As a direct consequence of what Fadlallah considered to be a gross misconceptualisation of Islam, many Iraqi Muslims, predominantly Shi'i, had naively adopted this notion. He concludes by affirming the Islamist tenet that Islam, as a divinely revealed and organic system of existence, does not need to borrow, much less incorporate, alien terminology and foreign concepts, tenets and theories.[158]

Besides writing critically on the influence of Western secular legal and intellectual 'accretions' on Islamic juridical and doctrinal thought, Fadlallah examines, in another article, the various courses of action pursued by Islamists in Iraq. He distinguishes three methods for the Islamisation of contemporary life. The first is the educational–indoctrinatory approach, which targets nominal or wavering Muslim individuals with the aim of creating or bringing about an organic body of pious and conscientous believers, whose quest is not the establishment of an Islamic state but the preservation of Islam for the next generation. The second constitutes a corporate action in the context of creating an 'an Islamic society that is unified and cohesive in every country and generation'. The third and most politicised approach represents organised 'action geared towards resurrecting the Islamic state that would institute the process of societal Islamisation … and bringing into existence a formidable Islamic political entity that would ultimately govern the world'.[159]

Fadlallah did not perceive in the three forms of action any necessary clash; on the contrary, each of the above modes of action represented in reality a preparatory phase for the next. The complementary sequential phases can be explained as follows: the engendering of conscious and committed Muslim individuals in society would constitute the first phase in creating a true Islamic society, through the nurturing of fraternal Islamic ties and the insemination in the collective psyche of Islamic precepts and values, such as social justice, equality and solidarity. Similarly, 'the existence of the [envisaged] Islamic society that is unified in sentiment, doctrine, outlook and purpose would represent a fundamental pre-requisite for the establishment of the … Islamic state; for, it goes without saying that a state that was founded without a popular following that professes its creed and espouses its ideas would be destined to being ephemeral'.[160]

Fadlallah states that 'any group that espouses one of these three courses of action ought to be capable of proceeding without being at loggerheads with the other two groups'. Hence, each of the Islamist groups would be able to benefit from the experience and accomplishments of the other two. In urging the various Islamist groups active in Iraq (an oblique reference to Hizb al-Da'wa, al-Ikhwan al-Muslimun and Hizb al-Tahrir) to harmonise their interim goals and strategies through the consensual distribution of roles and labour, so that they may correspond to these complementary phases, Fadlallah was consciously assuming that these groups would be capable of subordinating their particular differences to the overriding goal of invigorating Islam into a dynamic force, and a civilisational paradigm in contemporary life.[161]

In his first leading editorial for *al-Adwa'*, under the title, 'The Fundamental Pre-condition to the Renaissance of the *Umma*', Sayyid al-Sadr stipulated three factors deemed to be indispensable to the renaissance of Islamic civilisation. The first was the existence of the authentic and righteous creed or doctrine, *al-Mabda' al-Salih*, that would define the *Umma*'s *weltanschauung*, determine its goals and ideals, and set its course. This was to be followed by a sound Muslim understanding of, and ultimately profound faith in, the veracity, soundness and practicability of the Islamic creed.[162]

Sayyid al-Sadr posited a direct link between the lack of a proper understanding of Islam and the dearth of religious fervour. The result, according to al-Sadr, while not a society exactly comparable to *jahiliyya* society (a reference to pre-Islamic Pagan Arabia), is nevertheless one whose Islamic identity is characterised by a patently superficial belief in Islam. He concludes by stating that what is urgently needed is a general and proper understanding of Islam as a sound and coherent ideology, and a valid and complete way of life. Without setting forth in detail the way in which it would be achieved, al-Sadr is emphatic in his assertion that the fulfilment of such a crucial prerequisite would suffice in bringing about the renaissance of the *Umma*.[163] Five other topical editorials were written by al-Sadr; each dealt, briefly, with one aspect of Islam's world-view or mission.[164]

Fadlallah did not restrict his intellectual contribution to *al-Adwa'* to the writing of prose; he also composed a number of poems in this period, which were published as two monographs. The first, *Ya Zilal al-Islam*: *Rubai'yyat* ('O' the Shadows of Islam: Quartets'), was first published in Beirut in 1977, and subsequently reprinted in 1985, while the second work, *Qasa'id lil Islam wal Hayat* ('Poetic Verses for Islam and Life'), was published in Beirut in 1984. Besides these two works, a third book, *'Ala Shati' al- Wujdan* ('On the Shores of Passion') contains poems written by Fadlallah before the revolution of 4 July 1958, and thus before the existence of *al-Adwa'*.[165]

The foregoing excerpts from articles appearing in *al-Adwa'* are illustrative of the general thrust of the emerging intellectual Islamist discourse. To the extent that these articles engage in a critique of both the traditional religious establishment and modern legal institutional, intellectual and cultural trends, and call for the transformation of society and culture, they are radical. The advocacy of radical ideological and intellectual reformism by the young generation of Islamic scholars was evidently in disharmony with traditional religious and legal scholasticism, and with the placid political acquiescence of the conservative 'ulama. Furthermore, thanks to the size ble readership it was able to acquire in only two years, *al-Adwa'* was perceived as a threat to the conservative heritage and principled apolitical position of the majority of senior Shi'i 'ulama.[166]

The Conservative Backlash Against al-Adwa' *and Hizb al-Da'wa*

The open hostility of the conservative 'ulama to their ideas meant that al-Sadr and Fadlallah and their colleagues now had to fight a battle on two fronts: against the Communist Party, and against the the insular religious conservatives.[167] However, it is revealing that there is no indication that Fadlallah was targeted by the powerful apolitical clerical establishment. Their focus on al-Sadr stemmed from his pre-eminent position in *al-Adwa*'s editorial board, and from his likely prospective nomination as *Marja'* for the Shi'i faithful.

The establishment's pretext for launching a campaign of denigration against al-Sadr in early 1960 was his use of the appellation Jama'at al-'Ulama, of which he was not a member due to his relatively young age, on the grounds that he wrote his editorials under the name of the society without the prior knowledge or consent of its members.[168] That al-Sadr had in reality supervised *al-Adwa'* and written its leading article, with the support and encouragement of the society's members, and with the enthusiastic assent of the supreme *Marja'*, Sayyid Muhsin al-Hakim, was disregarded by his detractors.[169]

The continuing opposition of the anti-*al-Adwa'* 'ulama eventually became too serious to overcome. As a direct consequence of this unabating opposition, the grand *Marja'*, *Sayyid* al-Hakim, who had from the outset given patronage to *al-Adwa'*, persuaded al-Sadr to terminate his association with the periodical. The Islamists viewed the campaign mounted by the religious conservatives as primarily aimed at bringing al-Sadr into disrepute, thereby jeopardising his assumption of the mantle of the *Marja'iyya*. Fadlallah recounts how his colleague was forced to cease writing for the journal on account of the 'stern measures employed by some influential circles in the powerful *hawza al-'Ilmiyya* (the traditional learned establishment) so as to propel him away from an orientation towards an organised Islamic political formation on the Muslim scene'.[170]

Thus, it is evident that al-Sadr's resignation from the position of editor-in-chief of *al-Adwa'* was made under duress, in order to forestall or contain any serious damage to his credibility, and thus harm his future prospects as a candidate for the *Marja'iyya*. Although the editorials for the seventh issue onwards were authored by Shaykh Shams al-Din, they were written with the explicit approval and encouragement of al-Sadr, who continued to liaise with the editors.[171]

If the conservative religious scholastic establishment frowned on clerical engagement in Islamic ideological discourse, then al-Sadr's role in founding and leading an organised political party, with an avowedly radical agenda, was seen as an unprecedented and unpalatable aberration. As mentioned earlier, Shi'i convention dictates that no *mujtahid* with an aspiration to be a leading religious–juridical authority can involve himself in ideological discourse or political affairs, much less be an affiliate or leader of a political organisation.[172] As with the controversy over his association with *al-Adwa'*, pressure was exerted by the conservative 'ulama on al-Sadr over his pivotal role in Hizb al-Da'wa.

Pressure was also brought to bear on Sayyid al-Hakim to persuade his three politically active sons, as well as al-Sadr, to withdraw from Hizb al-Da'wa, which he succeeded in doing in 1962. Although al-Sadr reluctantly complied with the request of his superior by severing his formal ties to the party, he nevertheless continued to maintain close indirect links with the party's leadership, providing advice and guidance and resolving contentious issues. However, according to two Muslim academics, al-Sadr began to devote the bulk of his time to scholastic research, and to teaching students of the religious seminary from a reformed curriculum.[173]

The official withdrawal of the foremost Islamist intellectual activist in Iraq saw effective leadership of the party pass to al-Sadr's confidant and operational lieutenant, Abdul Sahib Dakhil. An agronomist by profession, and one of the earliest members of Hizb al-Da'wa, he was a devout layman and a diligent political organiser. According to a former affiliate of Hizb al-Da'wa, Sayyid Muhammad Bahr al-Uloum, the withdrawal of al-Sadr and the al-Hakim brothers led to the suspension of the party's activities. This, however, can be disputed on two counts: firstly, the ascent of Abdul Sahib Dakhil to the leadership of the party in 1962/3, together with the prominent role played by the junior-ranked 'ulama and personal representatives of Sayyid al-Hakim – like Sayyid Murtada al-Askari and Shaykh 'Aref al-Basri – coincided with the launching of an open and vigorous recruitment drive by the party. Secondly, as we shall see later, until the seizure of power by the Iraqi Ba'th Party in 1968,

Hizb al-Da'wa, though never legalised, was at no stage subjected to a systematic campaign of repression, the absence of which provided Islamists with the incentive to expand rather than reduce their organisational activities.[174]

The Fall of General Qasem, the Ba'thist Coup, and the First 'Aref Regime

General Qasem's decision to curtail the seemingly inexorable expansion of the Communist Party – which, in the wake of the sanguinary events in Mosul and Kirkuk in March and July of 1959, had become increasingly unruly – led to three years of continuous waning in its influence. A major factor in the party's decisive decline in membership and influence was the government's disbanding of the People's Revolutionary Front militia, and the dissolution of the ICP's mass auxiliary organisations – namely the youth and women's movements, and labour unions. Weakened appreciably by those government measures, the Communists, who had hitherto enjoyed virtually undisputed control of major city streets, began to see their extent of their dominance gradually fall, as emboldened Arab nationalists and Islamists went about reclaiming lost turf from their opponents. In their passion for vengeance for the Mosul and Kirkuk massacres, the anti-Communists carried out frequent violent attacks on Communist cadres, and ransacked ICP offices.[175]

Like the Nasserites, the Ba'thists were suppressed in the immediate wake of the abortive assassination attempt on the president in November 1959. However, unlike their nationalist counterparts, and particularly after enduring a serious split in their ranks from the years 1959–62, as well as the flight and arrest of many of their member, the Ba'thists were better organised and more cohesive, and espoused a radical ideological platform geared towards socio-economic transformation. Moreover, in the wake of the collapse of the United Arab Republic, the Ba'thists had begun by 1962 to recover, covertly rebuilding their organisation and devising plans for a coup against General Qasem. When the coup did take place, on 8 February 1963, effected by Ba'thist and Nasserite military officers and allied militiamen under the overall command of the pardoned Colonel Abdul Salam 'Aref, it took three days of fierce fighting with loyalist troops, backed by thousands of Communist cadres and supporters, before resistance was quashed and the government capitulated.[176]

It is telling that a large proportion of those civilian communists who rushed to the defence of the beleaguered regime were Shi'a, coming from the impoverished and densely populated districts of Baghdad, particularly Madinat al-Thawrah. Owing to its elaborate organisational network and social welfare programmes, the ICP under General Qasem had become a magnet for these paupers and malcontents, who perceived the party as the natural champion of the underdog, committed to alleviating their conditions of poverty and deprivation.[177]

Motivated by the impulse to settle scores with their ideological opponents, the Revolutionary Command Council, the Ba'thist ruling body that seized power embarked on a systematic and ruthless campaign of repression against the ICP. Between February and Novermber 1963, the regime's recently formed Republican Guard proceeded to detain thousands of Communist Party members and sympathisers. Incarcerated without trial, they were routinely subjected to torture, while hundreds of others were either executed or lynched by Ba'thist militiamen.[178]

While the Nasserites and the Islamists welcomed the suppression of the detested ICP, they were disaffected with the autocratic, one-party rule of the Ba'thists. Prior to the overthrow of General Qasem, the latter had, reportedly, won the support of al-Hakim against the old regime in return for a pledge from the nationalist leaders to repeal the Personal Status Law and clamp down on the Communists. Upon seizing power, however, the Ba'thist ruling clique reneged on their pledge, and refused to allow the Islamists to operate freely.[179]

The regime in fact went one step further, launching a partial crackdown on the Islamists and followers of Sayyid al-Hakim, who, contrary to the claims of the authorities, did not constitute a revolutionary threat to the stability of the regime. In the end, scores of Islamic activists were apprehended, imprisoned without trial and tortured. Sayyid al-Hakim deplored the serious violations of human rights, and demanded an immediate end to the violent episode of state repression. In an attempt to arouse public antipathy to the regime, al-Hakim embarked on a three-week trip to Karbala, al-Kazimiyya and Samarra, where he attracted large Shi'a crowds, who paid homage to their *Marja'* and denounced the regime. Although tension between rival supporters of the regime and al-Hakim produced occasional street clashes, the Islamists never posed a major threat to the status quo.[180]

One organised political formation that did pose a serious threat to the ruling Ba'thist Party was that of the Nasserites, who, alienated by their exclusion from power, began to gather strength as a movement. Led by the renowned Arab nationalist Colonel 'Aref, who acted as a figurehead of the Ba'thist regime, the Nasserites had exploited the dissension within the ruling party elite – between the military and civilian factions of the party, on the one hand, and between the rightists headed by Michel Aflaq and the leftists led by Ali Salih al-Sa'di, on the other.[181] It was in the midst of the Ba'th Party's self-destruction that Colonel 'Aref, with his power-base in the military, seized the opportunity to effect a bloodless coup, on 18 November 1963.[182]

An avowed Pan-Arabist inspired by President Gamal Abdul Nasser's strand of Arab Socialism, Colonel 'Aref instituted a series of measures aimed at emulating and co-ordinating with Egypt in the military, economic, political, social, and cultural spheres. The ultimate goal was the unification of the two countries, to be ruled by a single political party, Egypt's Arab Socialist Union, and with a nationalised and centralised socialist economy.[183]

Under Colonel 'Aref, military rule was reasserted: his grip on power was consolidated by the formation of a professional and feared Republican Guard, existing political parties were banned, and public dissent was suppressed. In line with his espousal of Arab Socialism, a provisional constitution was promulgated on 3 March 1964. Deemed to be the first crucial step towards eventual union with Egypt, the constitution led directly to the issuing of socialist decrees announcing the nationalisation of banks and industries, the regulation of administrative councils of industries, and the establishment of an Economic Organisation for the implementation and control of a socialist economy.[184]

Combined with Colonel 'Aref's pronounced Pan-Arabism and socialist orientation was his overt Sunni particularism. During his rule, a number of general religious edicts were issued – namely, a ban on the serving of alcoholic drinks at state functions, the enforcement of fasting during the holy month of Ramadan, and the mandatory swearing of fidelity by would-be government officials. But in projecting himself as a staunch Sunni, and outwardly exhibiting a genuine devotion to the faith, he showed a patent Sunni bias, which was translated into open discrimination against Shi'i government employees, and in the allocation of state funds for the development of services in their communities. Although the Islamists and religious conservatives had genuine grievances against socialist economic policies, which were held to be in fundamental conflict with the principles of private ownership and individual commercial enterprise that are enshrined in Islam, as well as against overt Sunni confessional bias, nevertheless, they did not precipitate street protests or violent militancy.[185]

While the Shi'i Islamist movement was spared the repression it had endured under the Ba'th regime, during Colonel 'Aref's reign Hizb al-Da'wa was kept under close surveillance, and was subjected to occasional harassment and arrests by the security forces. By marked contrast, Colonel 'Aref, as an ostentatious Sunni, granted almost total freedom of political activity to the

Sunni Islamists, and in particular the Iraqi branch of al-Ikhwan al-Muslimun, even while its parent organisation in Egypt was being mercilessly suppressed by President Nasser.[186]

Deeming socialism to be anathema, Islamist 'ulama – both Sunni and Shi'i – responded by condemning the government's economic policies. Shaykh 'Abdul Aziz al-Badri, the most outspoken Sunni scholar-activist, wrote an influential treatise, *Hukm al-Islam fi al-Ishtirakiyya* (The Ruling of Islam on Socialism), in which he repudiated socialism's premises and rationale, and denounced it as being the first phase of communism. For their part, the senior Shi'i 'ulama sent petitions to the government, remonstrating against the expropriation of private property, the imposition of a levy on hitherto tax-exempt *waqf* property, and open discrimination against the Shi'a in employment (Colonel 'Aref had reversed General Qasem's policy of opening up the military to Shi'i applicants).[187]

The president pursued a dual strategy towards the Shi'i Islamists. On the one hand, he sought to contain the influence of the Shi'i *Marja'iyya* and marginalise the role of the Islamists in society; but on the other, he attempted unsuccessfully to co-opt Sayyid al-Hakim, despatching senior government officials with a view to effecting a rapprochement with the *Marja'*. Alienated by the regime's controversial policies, al-Hakim declined to give the official envoy an audience, and he refused Colonel 'Aref's offer of a meeting between the two leaders, demanding instead the annulment of the Personal Status Code, as well as of the regime's socialist decrees and its confessional discriminatory policies.[188]

It is evident that, since the withdrawal of al-Sadr and other key 'ulama activists in the early 1960s, Hizb al-Da'wa had been politically overshadowed by the assertive leadership of Sayyid al-Hakim. That the premier Shi'i Islamist party had kept a low political profile under the Ba'thist and 'Aref regimes was due to the Hizb's focus on organisation, propagation and recruitment. In return for refraining from openly berating Colonel 'Aref – an activity that was vigorously pursued by Sayyid al-Hakim on behalf of his religious followers and Islamist associates – Hizb al-Da'wa did not experience any systematic attempts by the regime to curb its activities.[189]

The party, headed by Abdul Sahib Dakhil, launched a major effort to enhance religious observance and heighten political awareness among the Shi'i population of Madinat al-Thawrah – the poor, densely settled suburb of Baghdad built by General Qasem. Despite the re-establishment of a special government surveillance and intelligence agency (the Special Branch), to monitor the activities of Hizb al-Da'wa closely, the party was able to make significant headway, both increasing its membership and augmenting its support base, particularly among university students and intellectuals.[190]

The party's expansion was indicated by the wide circulation of its official mouthpiece, *Sawt al-Da'wa* (Voice of *al-Da'wa*), of which 1,500 copies were distributed among members and sympathisers at Baghdad University alone. In a sign of the party's vitality, affiliated students commemorated *'Ashoura* by conducting street procession in support support of the movement. This period also saw a significant increase in the number of religious students attending the traditional seminaries of learning – a trend that was accompanied by the founding of religious colleges, Islamic centres, and public libraries. Sponsored by Sayyid al-Hakim, the colleges – namely Kulliyat Usul al-Din (The College of the Fundamentals of Religion), founded in Baghdad in the early 1960s and modelled on Cairo's al-Azhar University, and Madrasat al-'Uloum al-Islamiyya (The School of Religious Sciences), established in Najaf in 1963 – were set up as modern educational institutions committed to reforming and systematising their curricula.[191]

Sayyid al-Sadr played a major role in devising modernised courses, and in overseeing a reformed administrative structure. His influential studies on the Qur'an, on sources of religious jurisprudence, and on philosophy and economics became textbooks for college students. Alongside the teaching of traditional religious and juridical subjects, al-Sadr recommended the offering of secular courses, and proposed the setting up of a stringent and organised course assessment structure, whereby students would be required to attend classes regularly and participate in group discussions. He also recommended that satisfactory completion of research and written work, and the passing of regular, formal exams should be crucial components of student graduation.[192]

Fadlallah and the Confluence of Sunni and Shi'i Islamist Movements

The early 1960s also witnessed important moves among the Islamists of both denominations to work together in adopting uniform positions on major issues, issuing joint resolutions, and embarking on mutual projects. For instance, the prominent Sunni *'alim*, Shaykh al-Badri, had, since the late 1950s, established close ties with Sayyid al-Hakim. Moreover, since 1962 Hizb al-Da'wa had opened its publications to the writings of Shaykh al-Badri, as well as to another Sunni activist, Shaykh Amjad al-Zahawi, and it proceeded to forge cordial relations with al-Ikhwan al-Muslimun and Hizb al-Tahrir, all three of which saw a need to close ranks in the face of common threats, and co-ordinate their otherwise disparate activities towards accepted goals.[193]

One young *'alim* who was a consistent proponent of inter-denominational dialogue and co-operation among Islamists, and who welcomed Hizb al-Da'wa's openness and receptiveness towards Sunni Islamists, was Fadlallah. In early 1964 he wrote an article for *al-Adwa'*, entitled 'Positivity and Our Confessional Reality'. In it, he identified confessionalism as a preponderant factor in defining contemporary ideological and political configurations. He alluded to the Sunni ruling elite, headed by Colonel 'Aref, who, he said, had espoused socialism rather than communism, which was seen as the prefered ideological persuasion of the Shi'i masses. As far as Fadlallah was concerned, both ideologies were anathema, since their tenets and premises were fundamentally antithetical to Islam.[194]

In the view of Fadlallah, the existence of distinct and separate Islamic denominations is not in itself an objectionable reality, as religious plurality can be enriching. The crux of the confessional problem can be attributed not to the prevailing confessional division of Islam, but rather to the lack of profound religious consciousness and political awareness among Muslims of 'the sinister machinations and diabolic schemes of the imperialist unbelievers, aimed at driving a wedge [between Muslims of different persuasions], thereby destroying their religious, social and political entity'.[195]

In proposing a solution to the problem, Fadlallah called for mutual respect, recognition and openness by the denominations towards each other's views, interpretations and practices, since both Sunnis and Shi'a professed the same faith. On the vexed issue of the distinctive traits of Sunnism and Shi'ism, Fadlallah argued that they should be the subject of a substantative and objective inquiry by scholars of both denominations. He expressed the hope that the momentous fatwa of Shaykh Mahmud Shaltut (the rector of al-Azhar University, who had, in February 1959, officially recognised Imami Shi'ism as a legitimate Islamic school of religious thought and law) would inaugurate a new era of religious unity and political solidarity.[196]

Consistent with his non-partisan intellectual approach to Islamic activism, Fadlallah refrained from citing the names of individuals or groups (particularly those whose views and actions he objected to) in his writings. Thus, in an article, published in *al-Adwa'* in August 1964, entitled 'Min Mashakal al-Amal lil Islam' (Some of the Problems Encountered in the Cause of Islam), which is illustrative of this objectivity, Fadlallah set forth his observations on some of the most common problems experienced by Islamic activists. While not prepared to become an organisational member of the existing Islamist groups, Fadlallah registered several points in defence of the validity and utility of the various Islamist movements. Among the most significant of these is his exhortation that Muslims ought not impugn these Islamist movements and raise doubts over the legitimacy and practicability of their goals and programmes. Furthermore, he stressed that any errors of judgement or imperfections in their activities should not detract from the manifold positive elements that they embodied. Islamic activists, he said, whether in their theory or praxis, should not be the subject of hasty or crude or criticism, as this would be tantamount to the unjust indictment of the majority for what was perceived as the unjustified or misguided behaviour of a minority of activists.[197]

The Emergence of New Islamist Groups

These articles were written by Fadlallah against a backdrop that included the formation of new Islamic political groups and intellectual institutions. Among the intellectual Islamic societies that emerged in the early or mid-1960s was Jama'at al-'Ulama, in Baghdad and al-Kazimiyya, modelled on Najaf's Jama'at al-'Ulama. That the society's activities were not restricted to intellectual, cultural and religious spheres was evident from its social composition. Its members comprised senior and middle-ranking Shi'i 'ulama, such as Sayyid Murtada al-Askari, Sayyid Mahdi al-Hakim, and Shaykh 'Aref al-Basri, among others; all of them were political activists and either current or former members of Hizb al-Da'wa. The society, which was headed by Sayyid Hadi al-Hakim and Sayyid al-Askari, played a major role in disseminating Islam in Baghdad through print and electronic media, as well as from the pulpit at Friday prayers and during religious festivities. It also provided important welfare and educational services to members of the Shi'i community.[198]

Sometime between 1961 and 1965 a small group of young Islamist 'ulama based in Karbala fell out with the leaders of Hizb al-Da'wa over strategy, and founded a separate, clandestine and more militant Shi'i Islamic organisation.[199] Headed by Sayyid Muhammad al-Shirazi, Munazzamat al-'Amal al-Islami (The Islamic Action Organisation) included as its senior members the founder's brother, Sayyid Hasan al-Shirazi, and his nephew, Sayyid Muhammad Taqi al-Muddarisi.[200]

Roughly simultaneous with the evolution of Munazzamat al-'Amal al-Islami was the emergence of al-Kutla al-Islamiyya (The Islamic Bloc). Although the internal sources of this Islamist group cite 1963 as the date of its foundation, other Islamist and academic sources make no mention at all of its existence in the 1960s. This conspicuous absence from scholarly and Islamist accounts suggests that if, as its founders claim, the Islamic Bloc did exist in that period, it would have been as a rudimentary and ill-defined coterie of individuals representing an entity in an embryonic phase of development. According to a senior figure in the group today, its founding members included Shaykh Abdul 'Aziz al-Badri (a prominent Sunni 'alim), Muhammad Faraj al-Jasim (a military general), and Abdul Ghani Sinwalah (an engineer), while its cadres reportedly represented both Sunni and Shi'i persuasions.[201]

Notwithstanding its composite membership, and in spite of the close ties forged between Shaykh al-Badri and Sayyid al-Hakim, the Islamic Bloc was and remains unquestionably Sunni in its political and ideological perspective. Specifically, thinking of al-Kutla al-Islamiyya was influenced heavily by Hizb al-Tahrir al-Islami, of which Shaykh al-Badri was an erstwhile senior member. Both groups aspire to the utopian realisation of a unitary Islamic state that would encompass the entire Muslim world. From Hizb al-Tahrir it borrowed the strategy of *inqilab*, or military coup, as the most effective means for overthrowing a political regime deemed illegitimate or iniquitous; while from Sayyid Qutb it borrowed the conceptual term of *al-jahiliyya*, applied to supposedly Muslim countries that are not governed totally in accordance with the shari'ah.[202]

As well as articulating the pressing need for mutual recognition and strategic co-operation between existing Islamist movements, in 1964 Fadlallah delineated the most pressing issues confronting the Muslim world.[203] He cited political apathy, religious ignorance, intellectual and scientific inertia, cultural backwardness, socio-economic inequality and civil strife as pervasive maladies besetting the contemporary Muslim *umma*. In common with other Islamists, he viewed the Muslim world as being divided between the rival hegemonic powers of Western imperialism and communism. As far as he was concerned, the position of Islam on these two dominant powers was unambiguous: they must be viewed by all Muslims for what they were – 'implacable foes of Islam'. Thus, Western imperialism was denounced, because it invariably entailed systematic oppression, exploitation and the monopolisation of indigenous resources, labour and markets, as well as the deprivation of liberty and independence.[204] Likewise, communism was condemned for its avowed atheism and materialist world-view, and socialist socio-economic system.

Fadlallah exhorted his fellow Muslims to show genuine empathy with the plight of Muslim peoples world-wide, particularly Muslim countries symbolising vital causes. Among the issues deemed to be of paramount importance was Palestine, whose identity was quintessentially Islamic. The crux of the problem, as perceived by Fadlallah, was the unmistakably grave Zionist–Jewish threat to the preservation of the Islamic identity and heritage of Palestine, and to the continuity of its indigenous, predominantly Muslim inhabitants. While Fadlallah conceded that Palestine was a pivotal issue in the

Arab nationalist cause, he saw no reason why Islamist and Arab nationalist movements, in each of their separate spheres, could not pursue the same struggle.[205]

The Impact of Ayatollah Khomeini in Najaf

It is telling that while Fadlallah expressed concern over major political issues in the Muslim world, this did not extend to the oppositional campaign against the Shah of Iran mounted by Ayatollah Khomeini. In order to understand why Fadlallah did not publicly express his support for Khomeini's militancy against the Shah in the early 1960s, it will be necessary briefly to survey the background of the Iranian cleric's oppositional movement against his country's absolute monarch, his subsequent deportation to Turkey and eventual migration to Iraq, and the specific conditions that impinged on him in Najaf.

Khomeini's confrontation with the Shah stemmed from a number of interrelated grievances pertaining to the domestic and foreign policies pursued by the government. He began his campaign against the Shah in March 1963 by publicly attacking what was perceived to be the monarch's increasingly autocratic rule, the diffusion of Western cultural 'decadence', and the Shah's land reform legislation.[206] Arrested for his strident dissidence, Khomeini was soon released, only to resume his assault on the regime, focusing his anger on the extent of American influence in Iran, and on the close political and strategic links between Iran and Israel. Khomeini's struggle with the Shah reached a climax on 13 October 1964, when the Iranian Parliament approved a bill granting full diplomatic immunity to American military servicemen and their dependents in Iran, castigated as the 'Capitulations Agreement' by the country's opposition. Khomeini fiercely berated the Shah and the regime for what was viewed as a flagrant and ignonimious sell-out of Iranian sovereignty to the United States, and a blatant affront to national dignity. As a direct result of his excoriating speech, Khomeini was seized by the state authorities and deported to Turkey on 4 Novermber 1964, where he would languish, isolated from his supporters, for the following eleven months.[207]

In October 1965, President 'Aref gave his consent for Khomeini to migrate to Iraq and settle in Najaf. On 14 November 1965 – that is, six weeks after settling in Najaf – Khomeini delivered a sermon that made no direct reference to Iran, and instead focused on reaffirming Islam as the supreme paradigm for regulating all aspects of human existence.[208] Interestingly, besides this sermon and an open letter written in 1967 to the Iranian government, in which he criticised Iran's strategic ties with Israel and the United States, public political statements by Khomeini were a rarity until the death of Sayyid al-Hakim in 1970.[209]

A number of interrelated circumstances seem to have determined Khomeini's political posture. From the outset, Khomeini tentatively explored the possibility of gaining the support of Najaf's foremost *mujtahids* for a programme of major change in Iran. On 19 October 1965, a meeting took place between Sayyid al-Hakim and Khomeini, during which the latter raised the feasibility of initiating a popular uprising against the Shah, arguing that his Iraqi counterpart wielded an extensive base of support in Iraq and in the region generally. Sayyid al-Hakim refused to be persuaded by his colleague's reasoning, pointing out to his guest that his numerous followers would not heed his call for revolt due to their supposedly wavering faith and political apathy.[210]

Al-Hakim's lack of receptiveness to the call of his colleague can be explained in terms of his cordial relationship with the Shah, who had backed his candidature for the *Marja'iyya*, following the death in 1961 of the Grand Ayatollah Sayyid al-Burujirdi. He had no inclination to jeopardise those ties by forging links with the Iranian opposition movement. Furthermore, in his assessment of the possible political scenarios that might unfold in Iran, al-Hakim was apprehensive of any major change in the political status quo lest it ensue in a leftist takeover of power in Teheran. For his part, Khomeini, aware of the fact that he was being kept under constant surveillance by both Iranian and Iraqi intelligence and security organisations, realised that it would be imprudent to resume his anti-Shah activities unilaterally, and thus resigned himself, during the course of the 1960s, to that which 'God had ordained'.[211]

It is not surprising, therefore, that Khomeini's interaction with Iraqi Islamist 'ulama in Najaf during the 1960s was limited. According to Ali al-Mu'min, Hizb al-Da'wa had closely followed the course of political events in Iran that culminated in the expulsion of Khomeini, and had expressed its support for the revolutionary *mujtahid* by distributing his sermons and proclamations, and sent a delegation offering him the services of the party. While welcoming the offer, he was understandably circumspect about establishing substantative links with the Iraqi Shi'i Islamist oppositional movement, for fear of arousing the displeasure of President 'Aref, and thereby provoking his expulsion from his host country.[212]

The foremost Shi'i Islamist *'alim*, Sayyid al-Sadr, clearly sympathised with Khomeini's militant campaign against the Shah and his subsequent banishment to Turkey, and was among the faithful who greeted him on his arrival in Najaf. Yet it would be some two years before al-Sadr paid a personal visit to Khomeini. The meeting, which apparently took place at the request of Khomeini, came in the immediate wake of the Arab military disaster of June 1967, inflicted by Israel. The two radical 'ulama discussed the implications of the Six Day War and the fate of the Muslim world, the appropriate means by which to disseminate and revitalise Islam, with particular attention to the role of the 'ulama in politics, and to propel the faith to the centre of world affairs, thus enabling it to become the preponderant political, ideological and cultural force in the international arena. It may have been more than coincidental that al-Sadr's meeting with Khomeini had taken place during the politically relatively tolerant rule of General Abdul Rahman 'Aref, who had succeeded his brother Abdul Salam 'Aref, following the latter's death in a helicopter crash on 13 April 1966, at the end of a political tour of southern Iraq.[213]

Significantly, although Fadlallah was still in Najaf when Khomeini arrived in late 1965, the liaison between al-Sadr and Khomeini took place nearly eighteen months after Fadlallah had left Iraq for Lebanon, in early 1966. Although he was to be inspired fifteen years on by Ayatollah Khomeini's triumphant return to Iran, and was to visit the Imam on several occasions following the Islamic Revolution, Fadlallah justifies the fact that there were no meetings between Khomeini and himself in Iraq on the grounds that he did not remain long in Iraq after Khomeini had arrived in Najaf.[214]

For the short period prior to the departure of Fadlallah from Iraq, two considerations seem to have come into play. First, Fadlallah was aware that, in sharp contrast to Khomeini's prominent role in leading the anti-Shah movement in Iran, since settling in Najaf he had decided not to renew his public struggle against the Shah or forge direct links with Iraqi Shi'i Islamists, so as to deny the Iraqi regime a pretext to exile him.[215] Second, in 1965, after twenty years' study, Fadlallah attained the rank of *mujtihad*. To pursue what would be perceived as dangerous liaisons with Khomeini would have aroused the ire of his revered religious scholar colleagues, and jeopardised his future as the agent (*wakil*) of Sayyid al-Hakim in Lebanon.

As to the reason why Fadlallah decided to return to Lebanon, Martin Kramer speculates that he might have been motivated by the success of Sayyid Musa al-Sadr, the Iranian-born Shi'i 'alim who had become the leading reformist spokesman for Lebanon's discontented Shi'i community. It will be recalled that Sayyid Musa al-Sadr and Fadlallah had studied together in Najaf under Sayyid al-Hakim and Sayyid al-Kho'ie. After completing four years of advanced study, Sayyid al-Sadr, at the behest of Sayyid al-Hakim, had migrated in 1959 to Lebanon to assume leadership of the Shi'i community in Tyre. Three years later, according to his own account, Fadlallah paid a visit to his colleague in the southern Lebanese port city, where they reportedly collaborated in drafting a petition to the Shah of Iran.[216]

Without substantiating his assertion, Martin Kramer surmises that Fadlallah was motivated by a personal ambition to emulate al-Sadr, or perhaps surpass his exploits. Also unsubstantiated is the speculation that Fadlallah's move to Lebanon may have been encouraged by his maternal relatives, the powerful landed Bazzi clan of the Bint Jbail district in Lebanon's far south, who, supposedly holding a personal grudge against al-Sadr due to his meteoric rise and land reform policies, sought to counter-balance his reformist influence with one of their own.[217]

Fadlallah cites two factors as having induced him to leave Iraq for Lebanon. First, a delegation of Lebanese Shi'a, who were affiliated to a cultural society named Usrat al-Ta'akhi (The Family of Fraternity), visited the residence of al-Hakim, to ask him to invite Fadlallah formally to settle in Lebanon. Furthermore, having been both awarded the rank of *mujtahid* and appointed *wakil* by al-Hakim, Fadlallah had a natural longing for his ancestral country. During his his periodic visits to Lebanon during the 1950s and 1960s, Fadlallah had also established close ties with Usrat al-Ta'akhi, and developed personal friendships with its leaders.[218] He knew and accepted the fact that he would be expected to assume a pivotal role in meeting the religious–juridical needs of the local Shi'i community.

The second reason cited by Fadlallah for his move to Lebanon relates to the 'complicated conditions' that existed in Iraq under Colonel Abdul Salam 'Aref, compelling him to emigrate to Lebanon.[219] Little did he know that those unpropitious circumstances were soon to give way to more favourable ones. For, ironically, Fadlallah was to leave Iraq only a few months prior to the demise of Colonel 'Aref.[220]

Fadlallah had lived through a tumultuous era, which saw the unfolding of the Qasem-led Revolution, the Ba'thist seizure of power, and the Nasserite coup, as well as recurrent outbreaks of social unrest and political insurrection. He experienced the political and ideological ferment of the period and the struggle for survival and supremacy between the Communist, Arab nationalist and Islamist movements. Of the three trends, the Islamist movement was the smallest in size, as it was younger than its ideological rivals. The Shi'i Islamist wing – as represented principally, but not exclusively, by Hizb al-Da'wa and patronised by Sayyid al-Hakim – differed on the question of strategy from the Arab nationalist and Communist organisations, in that, before 1968, it advocated and pursued radical social and political change through peaceful and methodical reform, rather than mass revolutionary action, or the military or paramilitary seizure of power.

There are three important aspects of Fadlallah's Islamist discourse and activities during this period. First, his radicalism was shown in his denunciation of the status quo and his call for radical change. Second, his pragmatism was evident from his appeal to rival Iraqi Islamist groups to harmonise their agendas and resources, and to work towards a collective strategy, as well as from his advocacy of Islamist co-operation with activists affiliated to secular leftist and nationalist movements. Third, his intellectual rationalism was evident in his commitment to ecumenism, and his emphasis on objectivity and independent reasoning, and their application to the re-interpretation of Shi'i religious and legal traditions.

Although Fadlallah was not as influential a figure as Sayyid Baqer al-Sadr, nevertheless he did play a significant role in formulating Islamist discourse in Iraq during its crucial formative phase of intellectual and political formation. Whereas he took no part in developing the organisational structure of Hizb al-Da'wa, nor did he become a member of the party, Fadlallah's vision and ideas were important enough to inform the world-view and ethos of the Shi'i Islamist movement; while in his intellectual and literary writings he made a major contribution in defending the legitimaticy and necessary role of the Islamist movement. Owing to his principled stand in not affiliating to any one organisation, Fadlallah held the conviction that he was well positioned intellectually to contribute objectively to the evolving Islamist discourse in contemporary Iraq.

In the end, the thirty-year-old Fadlallah was to leave Iraq for the last time in early 1966, having undergone the scholastic rigours of completing advanced religious–juridical study and research, engaged in the discursive philosophical debates and intricate ideological polemics of the period, and closely observed the momentous events and developments that unfolded in a milieu characterised by political ferment, ideological conflict and social change. He was to come away with the axiomatic theory of Islam as a coherent and distinct ideology and total organic system of human existence. His challenge in Lebanon was to mould this Islamist credo, with all its radical implications, to fit the complex confessional landscape that characterises that country.

FOUR

Lebanon, 1966–1976: from Consolidation to Dislocation

The Shi'i Community Between Continuity and Change

Throughout the modern history of Lebanon, and in particular the 1960s and 1970s, its Shi'i citizens, despite representing the country's largest single confessional group, have constituted the most politically disenfranchised, economically disinherited, and socially alienated of the country's confessional communities.[1] Until the 1970s the Shi'a generally lived on the margins of Lebanese society and on the geographical periphery of the state.[2] Indeed, until the late 1960s when Sayyid Musa al-Sadr launched his public campaign for communal awakening, the marginalisation of the Shi'i community was, in large part, perpetuated by the acquiescence of the 'ulama and the traditional communal leaders.

Until the arrival of Sayyid al-Sadr in 1959, Shi'i 'ulama in Lebanon had been, with the exception of one of the country's leading *mujtahids*, Sayyid Abdul-Hussein Sharaf al-Din of the Southern port of Tyre, politically subservient to the *zu'ama*, (singular, *za'im*) or traditional feudal bosses.[3] It is revealing that in the period prior to the Shi'i political activism of the 1970s, the Shi'i 'ulama of Lebanon, unlike many of their peers in Iran, were more akin to their Sunni counterparts, and were more dependent on government funding than on the generous donations and religious tithes provided by the faithful. This general dependency, along with deference to the traditional political bosses, was crucial in forestalling the emergence during the 1950s and 1960s, of an autonomous and assertive Shi'i 'ulama-led movement.

Closely associated with the general state of poverty, and with the apolitical passiveness of the majority of the 'ulama in Lebanon, was a perceptible decline in their status and authority among the lay population. This trend had the effect of discouraging young Shi'a belonging to prominent religious scholarly families (such as Sharaf al-Din and al-Amin) from otherwise emulating their erudite fathers in religious scholasticism.[4] This shift away from a traditional religious career to modern secular professions was analogous to the pattern of behaviour among young Iraqi Shi'a during the 1940s and 1950s, described in the previous chapter.

That the power of the Shi'i *zu'ama*, the most prominent being the As'ad, al-Khalil, Hamdani, Haydar and al-Zayn clans, had overshadowed the influence of the Shi'i 'ulama in Lebanese society can be attributed to the fact that they were the mainstay of the traditional semi-feudal order of the countryside. They were the recognised power-brokers, arbitrators, owners of land and wealth, and upholders of order in rural areas. Drawing on their traditional clan authority and large landed wealth, the *zu'ama* were able to exercise and maintain their power through a combination of coercion, intimidation, manipulation and consent. Specifically, their sway was maintained through the existence of an extensive clientele, drawn from dependent local families and minor clans, as well as the through the allegiance of a body of aspiring local politicians, enabling them to secure, during the 1950s and 1960s, a large bloc of parliamentary seats, and in turn acquire government patronage.[5] Not surprisingly, then, the *zu'ama* were, until the ascent of al-Sadr and the transformation on the land during the mid to late 1960s, able effectively to subvert all attempts at substantive reform. As a result, social advancement and mobility were very limited and selective, with nepotism and cronyism firmly entrenched.

But the traditional *zu'ama* ultimately could not deflect the winds of change, which, since the mid-1960s, had began to erode their base of power. Three forces of change can be identified: first, the decline of the agricultural sector, the mainstay of the livelihood of the poor peasantry and petty landholders, leading to mass rural migration to the major urban centres, principally Beirut; second, the deteriorating security situation in the south of the country, arising since the late 1960s from the escalating military conflict between the Israeli Defence Force and the armed Palestinian resistance movement;[6] third, the rise of the largely expatriate and politically ambitious Shi'i Lebanese bourgeoisie.

From the late 1950s, traditional land tenure in South Lebanon and the Bekaa valley underwent a major transformation arising from the development of a capitalist market economy. The commercial development of agriculture saw the gradual supplanting of traditional crops and animal produce by export-oriented cash crops. This was made possible by the purchase of large tracts of arable land by an emerging class of urban entrepreneurs and Shi'i emigrés. The changes to land use caused a drastic decline in the income of small landholders, rendering them acutely vulnerable to indebtedness, exploitation and dislocation.[7] The increasing hardship compelled an increasing number of Shi'i peasants to leave their villages and drift, principally but not exclusively, to Beirut, where they formed a burgeoning and alienated underclass.

Disenchanted with the absolutist control of the *zu'ama*, wealthy Shi'i expatriates returning to Lebanon in the 1960s from West Africa, the Americas and the Gulf began to invest in real estate and commerce, develop a cash economy and build much-needed infrastructure in Shi'i-inhabited backwater areas and rural peripheries.[8] Excluded from the country's political hierarchy by the entrenched interests of the Maronite and Sunni Muslim establishment, this educated, aspirational entrepreneurial class publicly advocated a reformed political and administrative system more equitable and open to qualified candidates from the Shi'i community. Sharing the quest for reform of the confessional system of government and the traditional feudal order was the charismatic and the rapidly popular Sayyid Musa al-Sadr, at whose disposal they now placed their considerable talent and financial resources.

The Advent of Sayyid Musa al-Sadr

Sayyid al-Sadr was born in March 1928, in Qom, the premier city of higher Shi'i religious learning in Iran. Like Fadlallah, al-Sadr traced his lineage to the Prophet Muhammad, but whereas the former claimed descent through the Prophet's grandson, Imam Hasan bin Ali (the second Imam for the Twelver Shi'a), the latter claimed descent through the seventh Imam, Musa al-Kazim. Again like Sayyid Fadlallah, he was the son of an eminent *mujtahid* – in this case Ayatollah Sadr al-Din (1882–1952), and belonged to a family containing a distinguished line of 'ulama.[9] Like Fadlallah's, al-Sadr's forefathers hailed from the Lebanese village of Shahour, in the district of Tyre.[10]

Sayyid al-Sadr was initially taught at home by his father, and subsequently completed his secondary school education, which was complemented by religious studies at the College of Jurisprudence in Qom. He thereafter moved to Teheran and enrolled in the city's premier university (a modern secular tertiary institution), to study law. After four years, he graduated with a degree in law, and began to teach jurisprudence and logic at one of Qom's seminaries, where he also assisted in the founding of a religious journal – *Maktab-i Islam* (the Islamic School). In 1954, al-Sadr moved to Najaf to pursue advanced learning in *fiqh wa usuluhu* (religious jurisprudence and its principles). Upon successfully completing his four years of advanced legal studies at the relatively young age of 30, al-Sadr was certified by his mentors to exercise *ijtihad*.[11]

During his student years in Najaf, al-Sadr came into contact with a young would-be *'alim*, Sayyid Fadlallah. The two studied under the same luminaries, Ayatollah Sayyid Muhsin al-Hakim and Ayatollah Sayyid Abul Qasim al-Kho'ie, and, according to Fadlallah's recollections, they forged 'a very close' relationship.[12] The bonds of the student years were to weaken during the subsequent years in Lebanon, but the relationship remained amicable.

al-Sadr made his first visit to Lebanon in 1955, at the invitation of the aging Sayyid Abdul Hussein Sharaf al-Din (1873–1957), the mufti of the port city of Tyre and a leading Lebanese *mujtahid*, religious reformist and anti-French activist. The 82-year-old Ayatollah had invited the young *mujtahid* to his ancestral home with a view to arousing his interest in becoming a permanent resident. Sayyid Sharaf al-Din was apparently so impressed by the talents of his young relative and guest that he considered him to be his worthy successor. Thus, upon the death of the mufti of Tyre in December 1957, the deceased's family (according to some sources) or the leading residents of the city (according to others) extended a formal invitation to al-Sadr to settle in Lebanon and assume the vacant leadership post. Initially hesitant, al-Sadr waited until the end of the Lebanese civil war (May–July 1958) before embarking on a brief exploratory trip to Tyre prior to deciding his future. After consulting with his mentor, Sayyid Muhsin al-Hakim, al-Sadr accepted the invitation. Yet it was not until late 1959 that al-Sadr actually moved to Tyre, where he took up residence in his predecessor's house.[13]

As to why al-Din would favour a 31-year-old Iranian-born distant relative over senior, more learned local potential contenders for the position, Gharbieh reveals that as an independent-minded reformist, al-Din was at odds with his more conservative peers, and more importantly, strongly objected to their deference to the *zu'ama*.[14] Thus, it was not merely his religious scholarly credentials, but also social and cultural views that determined the selection of the young Sayyid, much to the dislike of the senior 'ulama.

al-Sadr's arrival in Lebanon in late 1959 came about eighteen months after the end of the 1958 civil war, and during the first year of the presidency of General Fu'ad Shihab. The two figures were to develop a cordial working relationship based on mutual interests and a common outlook. The new president sought to invigorate the central authority of the state, reform the existing inefficient fiscal system, and reverse his predecessor's policy of unequal regional development by means of increased government investment in the neglected infrastructure of provinces of the south and the Bekaa, the undermining of the power of the feudal lords, and the elimination of institutionalised corruption and nepotism.[15]

As a newcomer, al-Sadr needed to slowly put down his roots in his country of origin, gradually gain the acceptance of the Shiʿi community at large, and realise his agenda through the political establishment. As a reformer, he called for the establishment of much-needed vocational schools and clinics, proportional representation of qualified Shiʿis in the government and civil service, and a substantial increase in public works expenditure for the underdeveloped, largely Shiʿi-populated provinces of the country.[16] As important as these shared concerns were, what had above all brought the modernising elite of the state and the reformist leadership of al-Sadr together was the quest to break the oligarchic power and exploitative feudal order of the traditional lords – particularly Kamel al-Asʿad.

Although mindful of the widespread suffering of the majority of Shiʿis, stemming from inadequate or non-existent ancillary services, al-Sadr began his quest for the amelioration of the plight of the Shiʿi population by focusing on the pressing needs of his host community in Tyre. In 1961 he assumed the leadership of a local benevolent society (Jamiʿiyyat al-Bir wal-Ihsan), which was founded in 1948 by Sayyid Sharaf al-Din. He set about reorganising the society, transforming its role from one of merely dispensing charity to the needy members of the Shiʿi community to one of providing a wide range of social welfare programs, irrespective of denominational persuasion.[17]

Having secured an appreciable increase in the amount of donations to the society and a substantial enlargement and diversification of its members, al-Sadr now set about providing work training for the city's unemployed and poor residents.[18] In 1962, he established al-Muʿassasah al-Ijtimaʿiyyah (The Social Institute) to cater for the needs of the community's destitute and orphans. This was followed in 1963 by the founding of Bayt al-Fatat (The Girl's Home), which functioned as a boarding school, providing training in nursing and sewing for young girls.[19]

In addition to these philanthropic projects, al-Sadr was also involved in educational and intellectual activities. In the early 1960s, in Tyre, he founded Maʿhad al-Dirasat al-Islamiyyah (The Institute for Islamic Studies), where he frequently lectured to religious students. He also taught at the ʿAmiliyya school in Beirut. Intelligent, well-read, and with an ecumenical vision, al-Sadr, participated in numerous inter-religious symposia and conferences, where he lectured on Islamic culture and history. In a move that reflected his religious ecumenicalism as much as his commitment to social activism, al-Sadr joined al-Harakah al-Ijtima'iyyah (The Social Movement), a multi-confessional movement dedicated to development of the country's peripheral regions.[20] The movement was founded and headed by a Greek Orthodox metropolitan, Monsignor Gregoire Haddad.

While al-Sadr was involved in these activities in the South, the capital Beirut, and in the Bekaa, Fadlallah was contributing to the social and intellectual scene in Nab'a, the southern quarter of Bourj Hammoud. However, before examining Fadlallah's pursuits, it would be useful to provide a historical overview of that eastern suburb of Beirut, where Fadlallah resided from 1966 to 1976.

The Evolution of Bourj Hammoud/Nab'a

Prior to 1975 there were an estimated 319,000 Shi'i residents in the municipality of Beirut and its suburbs; of those who inhabited the localities outside Beirut proper, some 93 per cent were concentrated in three urban sectors: Ghubairi (78 per cent Shi'i), Bourj al-Barajneh (85 per cent Shi'i), and Bourj Hammoud (50 per cent Shi'i).[21] While the first two localities form a large part of Beirut's southern suburbs, Bourj Hammoud (which includes the southern quarter of Nab'a) is located in the north-western sector of Beirut's eastern suburbs.[22]

In the eastern suburbs of the capital, the Shi'a constituted the largest single community, numbering close to 100,000, or 33 per cent of the area's total population.[23] Before the mass displacement of its Shi'i populace in 1976, Bourj Hammoud was the most populous, and arguably (owing to its geo-strategic location) most important, of the eastern suburbs.[24] Moreover, it held the distinction of being the oldest inhabited locality in Beirut's eastern suburban sector, having been settled in the early 1920s by Armenian migrants and refugees fleeing persecution in wartime Ottoman Turkey.[25] Numbering some 200,000, the Armenians who arrived in Lebanon, settling predominantly in Beirut and being granted Lebanese citizenship in 1924, were ethnically and linguistically distinct from the Arab-speaking Lebanese, but as overwhelmingly Christian Orthodox they shared a common religious heritage with the country's Greek Orthodox community.[26]

Bourj Hammoud was also differentiated from the surrounding suburbs by the highly heterogeneous composition of its inhabitants, who represented a microcosm of Lebanon's confessional and ethnic mosaic. Within its parameters lived Lebanese Shi'a, Armenian Christians, Syrian Kurds and Alawites, and Palestinians (the majority of whom were Sunnis). The Shi'a formed the largest single community, numbering in 1974 close to 60,000, or just under 50 per cent of the suburb's population.[27]

Finally, in the pre-1976 period Bourj Hammoud was the most populous urban locale among the suburbs of east Beirut, accounting for some 41 per cent of the area's total population. Indeed, by the 1960s it had the highest suburban population density in Greater Beirut, with 55,392 persons/km^2, which was more than double that of Beirut proper.[28] It was the slum quarter of Nab'a – in the southern sector of Bourj Hammoud, where Shi'a predominated – that included the highest concentration of make-shift dwellings.[29]

The history of Shi'i settlement in Bourj Hammoud can be traced to the first wave of rural migrants during the late 1940s, in the wake of the 1948 war for Palestine. Although they were the first Muslim citizens to settle in the suburb, the Shi'a were soon joined by a significant but unknown number of displaced Palestinians. The Shi'i newcomers found most of the district dominated, socially and politically, by the well- to-do and highly organized Armenians. Consequently, the majority of the Shi'i migrants settled in the area's less urbanised southern district of Nab'a. The second influx of Shi'a occurred in the wake of the 1967 Arab- Israeli War, and continued during the early 1970s, when southern Lebanon became the only remaining active military front against Israel, following the expulsion of the PLO from Jordan. As a result of the arrival in Bourj Hammoud of thousands of new Shi'i migrants and refugees, joining the existing Palestinian refugee population, and of Syrian itinerant labourers, the demographic preponderance of Armenians came to an end.[30]

However, the Armenians of Bourj Hammoud have held on to their economic dominance, thanks to a vibrant and enterprising communal ethos, sustained by a deep sense of separate and cohesive national identity. Seizing, in the absence of public services, on the imperative of establishing independent institutions that specifically catered for the wide-ranging needs of the community, and beginning gin the 1920s, they set up their own schools, clinics, sports and cultural clubs, and boy and girl scout associations, as well as philanthropic and welfare establishments for the elderly, the infirm, blind and deaf people, and the mentally disabled.[31]

By sharp contrast, the Shi'i residents of Bourj Hammoud and, in particular, of Nab'a, were overwhelmingly poor, mostly young, and of rural semi-skilled or unskilled backgrounds. Shi'i migrants from the south, or from the eastern Bekaa valley, who belonged to the same village, extended family or clan resided in their own distinct neighbourhood. In this way, traditional village identity, with its regional and parochial nuances – and not communal or confessional identity – was transplanted and preserved in an urbanised, yet fragmentary environment. Superimposed on this plethora of neighbourhood clusters inside each quarter was a marked segregation between densely, mostly Shi'i-inhabited slums and interwoven middle and upper-middle class Armenian residential areas.[32]

The Shi'i-inhabited areas of Bourj Hammoud, particularly Nab'a, comprised part of what was known as the 'belt of misery', which enveloped the depressed, heavily populated areas of outer Beirut, which extended from the Palestinian refugee camps of Sabra, Shatila, and Bourj al-Barajnah in the south, through to the portside slum quarters of al-Maslakh and Karantina in the north, to Nab'a, and the Palestinian refugee compounds of Jisr al-Pasha and Tal al-Za'tar in the east. The wretchedness and hardship which the pauperised or lower-class unskilled residents of those areas experienced were compounded by a lack of public infrastructure and government welfare agencies. Like many of their underprivileged counterparts, namely Syrian seasonal stevedore labourers and impoverished Palestinian refugees, the destitute and newly urbanised Shi'a migrants had as young men left their villages to settle in Beirut in search of employment, social security and a dignified life. Instead, many found themselves jobless, frustrated and alienated, while others were able to find insecure, low-income menial work, provided by well-to-do Armenian traders and manufacturers.[33]

Thus, while some Shi'i lower or lower-middle class residents of Bour Hammoud owned and operated small-scale confectionary outlets, fruit and vegetable stores, and butcheries, and although there was a small emerging class of Shi'i entrepreneurs (many being former expatriates) who began to contribute in a limited way to the country's economy, the impoverished majority genuinely felt that they were excluded from benefiting from the burgeoning prosperity of Beirut, and of Lebanon as a whole.[34] Unprecedented exposure to the forces of modernity in cosmopolitan Beirut (most notably education, the mass media, and political organisations, still combined with class disparity and discrimination) produced a large reservoir of young, politically conscious Shi'i malcontents, who, in their yearning to have their deep-seated grievances addressed, developed a pronounced radicalism. Hence, during the 1960s and early 1970s, it was to the secular Lebanese leftist parties and radical Palestinian organisations that disaffected Shi'a turned in Bourj Hammoud, as elsewhere in Beirut.

Fadlallah in Nab'a and Beyond

One young, educated Shi'i migrant to Nab'a who also espoused radicalism – albeit of a gradualist and decidedly Islamist complexion – was Sayyid Fadlallah. It was in early 1966 that the thirty-year-old *mujtahid* arrived in Lebanon to settle in the Nab'a quarter of Bourj Hammoud, at the invitation of a certain al-Haj Khalil al-Huwali, a wealthy Shi'i entrepreneur from Nab'a. The slum quarter was not unfamiliar territory to Fadlallah; as he since the early 1950s had been an occasional visitor to the locale. (Fadlallah, NBN Television interview, Part 2, 18 April 2004. Fadlallah informs us that during his visits to Nab'a, he would tour the most impoverished areas of the quarter, intermingling with the underprivileged youth who were affiliated to secular or leftist organisations.) In conjunction with a group of former Shi'i business expatriates, al-Huwali had set up Jami'yyat Usrat al-Ta'akhi (Society of the Family of Fraternity) in the early 1960s, with the aim of fostering religious and cultural awareness among the local alienated youth.[35] As there were deemed to be no suitably qualified local *'alim* capable of providing services such as advanced religious education and juridical guidance on specific issues encountered by the local faithful, the quest for the right candidate was shifted from Nab'a, and Lebanon in general, to al-Najaf.

Thus, in 1964, al-Huwali travelled to Iraq's premier Shi'i holy city and held talks with the pre-eminent *Marja'*, Sayyid Muhsin al-Hakim, from whom he was able to extract a fatwa that exhorted the faithful to contribute financially towards the construction of the society's *husayniyyah* (Shi'i religious centre). It was while he was there that he met Fadlallah and extended an invitation for him to return to the homeland of his forefathers and settle in Nab'a. According to Fadlallah's recollections, it was in 1966 that he received a formal invitation from Jamiyyat Usrat al-Ta'akhi, with which he had had an earlier acquaintance.[36] In more recent interview Fadlallah mentions Usrat al-Ta'akhi's invitation to In any case, Fadlallah accepted the invitation, but only after apparently rejecting a salary offer of 500 Lebanese pounds (the equivalent of a secondary school teacher), insisting that his income could only consist of his legitimate share of *al-khums* (religious annual 20 per cent net income tax paid by Shi'i laymen to the senior *mujtahids* or their local representatives).[37] In an another more recent interview Fadlallah mentions that the leaders of Jam'iyyat Usrat al-Ta'akhi had approached Abdul Ra'uf with a request to have his son, Muhammad Husayn, relocate to Nab'a. Baulking at first, Fadlallah subsequently accepted the invitation, compelled we are told by Fadlallah's dramatically changed family circumstances; Fadlallah, NBN Television interview, Part 2, 18 April 2004. He arrived in Beirut early that year, and set up his living quarters in the building of the host society.[38]

From the outset, Fadlallah's stay – not unlike that of his colleague, al-Sadr – was characterised by vigorous activity and systematic institution-building. Soon after his arrival, he embarked on an exploratory tour of Nab'a and its environs. He found a society beset by serious problems, including the fragmentation of the Shi'i-populated quarter into splintered neighbourhoods and a resultant lack of communal identity, the lack of government services, and the marginalisation of religion in the daily life of residents.[39] Specifically, he would have noticed that there were too few religious institutions to cater for the needs of the Shi'i locals. In 1966, for instance, there was only one mosque (Masjid al-Imam Ali bin Abu Talib) to serve the 60,000 Shi'i residents of Bourj Hammoud. This contrasted, in the same period, with the eight existing Armenian Orthodox churches. In addition, there were few communal-based educational establishments. Again, in contrast to the Armenians, who were served primarily by community-owned schools, all 20 schools in Shi'i areas were privately owned, and therefore expensive. Finally, there were no hospitals or orphanages, and too few clinics.[40]

One explanation for such a lack of community-based institutions is that the majority of the Shi'i residents of Bourj Hammoud did not see the depressed urban area as their permanent home. Strong ties still bound the newly urbanised residents to their villages of origin, whence many periodically returned to visit friends and relatives, and – in the case of young males – to marry.[41] Thus, prior to the communal-based political activism of al-Sadr's populist Shi'i movement of the late 1960s and 1970s, for most Shi'a the village represented the locus of traditional authority, and the fount of an immutable sense of identity and sentimental attachment.

It was against this background that Sayyid Fadlallah established a number of religious, educational and social institutions in Nab'a and its environs. They were heavily geared towards cultural education and legal guidance, both along Islamic lines, rather than the provision of welfare services and vocational training programmes. In expanding the institutions of Usrat al-Ta'akhi Society, Fadlallah established a *musallah* (prayer hall) and a *husayniyyah* as centres of religious gathering, discussion, worship and sermonising. To foster cultural interest among the local youth, he founded an Islamic library; and to boost the female contribution to Islamist programmes, he set up a cultural club for women, which also became affiliated to Usrat al-Ta'akhi. Finally, to meet the basic health needs of his deprived constituency, a medical clinic was established.[42]

From the outset, the building that housed Jami'yyat Usrat al-Ta'akhi became a major forum for Fadlallah's lectures, as well as various intellectual debates and symposia that dealt with cultural, religious, social and political issues. The society, and particularly its affiliated *husayniyyah*, also became a regular venue for the traditional *'Ashoura* ceremony. For ten days, beginning from the first day of the lunar month of *Muharram* and climaxing in the day of *'Ashoura*, the Shi'a traditionally commemorate – with emotive speeches and poems and passionate dramas – the slaying of Prophet Muhammad's grandson, Imam Husayn bin Abu Talib, on the Southern Iraqi plain of Karbala in 680 C.E. Lecturing to these special gatherings, Fadlallah sought to heighten religious awareness and enhance general understanding of the modern-day significance of the Imam's martyrdom. Moreover, as a reflection of his ecumenical outlook and endeavour to open up its traditionally exclusively Shi'i audience, the *'Ashoura* ceremony provided Fadlallah with an opportunity to forge inter-confessional ties, as Sunni and Christian religious dignitaries were invited to actively participate.[43]

Although Fadlallah's sermons and lectures touched on political as well as religious affairs, there is no evidence – in sharp contrast to al-Sadr's populist socio-political activist movement – that he engaged in political or militant activism. Indeed, Fadlallah justified this abstinence on the grounds that the prevailing conditions at the time were not conducive to organised public activism and, consequently, confined himself to the formulation and inculcation of Islamist ideology.[44] To this another explanation can be added: Fadlallah was discreetly nurturing an indigenous Islamist movement that was passing through an embryonic stage of development.

According to one informed source, the premises of Usrat al-Ta'akhi served as a venue where Shi'i religious and activist students were systematically indoctrinated in an Islamist ideology that posited Islam as a complete and eternally valid system of human existence. The principal source materials comprised Sayyid Baqer al-Sadr's influential intellectual works – notably *Iqtisaduna* and *Falsafatuna* – and classical jurisprudential literature produced by the foremost Shi'i authorities, as well as Fadlallah's own series of lecture notes and writings (both monograph and periodical).[45]

One of the first, and arguably most enduring, of Fadlallah's institutional achievements was the establishment of al-Ma'had al-Shari' al-Islami (The Islamic Legal Institute) in 1966. Located in Nab'a and modelled on Najaf's religious scholastic circles, the institution was unique in Lebanon. Under Fadlallah's stewardship it offered advanced Shi'i juristic studies to young 'ulama aspirants. The Institute was designed, in large measure, to meet the higher shari'ah-learning needs of local students, who were drawn from various parts of the country. Nevertheless, some of the more outstanding and ambitious graduates of the Institute still travelled to Najaf or Qom to pursue several years of further specialised studies, before returning to Lebanon to take up teaching positions in al-Ma'had.[46]

While many of these students or graduates were later to form the nucleus of the Shi'i Islamist movement, others rose to become prominent activist 'ulama. Among the more renowned young 'ulama graduates was Shaykh Raghib Harb. After spending a short period of time in Najaf, he returned to Lebanon, where he became a mosque Imam with a popular Islamist following in the South Lebanese village of Jibshit. Captured and interrogated for his vehement anti-Israeli diatribes, he was assassinated in 1984 by an Israeli army unit for his role in the emerging armed local resistance movement against Israel's military occupation of South Lebanon.[47]

As part of the strategy to attract the educated youth to the Islamist fold, especially those from Beirut's secular universities, Fadlallah offered a reformed and systematic teaching curriculum. Although relevant data are unavailable, according to one scholar, Fadlallah managed to induce a small but, in the context of the recently founded establishment, significant number of university students of applied science and Arabic literature to enrol in the Islamic Institute. That young Shi'a pursuing modern secular careers, rather than traditional students of religion, were targeted was a studied response to what was commonly perceived among 'ulama circles to be an alarming trend among the educated Shi'i youth, including those from a traditional 'ulama background, to shun religious scholasticism in favour of a professional, secular career. Fadlallah was all too aware of the ebbing status of Lebanon's 'ulama. The prevalent view of the 'ulama as a group out of touch with modern reality, and too traditional and even anachronistic in their outlook, was a major concern to young reformist-minded religious scholars like Fadlallah and al-Sadr.[48]

What distinguished Fadlallah from al-Sadr was that his commitment to change saw its practical manifestation in the establishment of a distinct and successful institution. By attracting students with diverse career paths, and who were mindful of the challenges of modernity and committed to social and cultural change, Fadlallah believed he had found the means of restoring the former status of the 'ulama. As a means of giving impetus to that process, Fadlallah encouraged a group of Islamist students from the Arab University of Beirut in their formation, in 1966, of al-Ittihad al-Lubnani lil Talabah al-Muslimeen (Lebanese Federation of Muslim Students). Since September 1977 the Federation has produced a bimonthly journal (*al-Muntalaq*), to which Fadlallah has regularly contributed leading articles.[49]

No sooner had Fadlallah settled in Nab'a than he found himself at loggerheads with an older, but less learned, conservative '*alim*, Shaykh Rida

Farhat. As a long-time resident of the quarter, who had served as Imam of the Imam Ali bin Abu Talib Mosque, and later, in 1969, as general director of al-Majlis al-Islami al- Shi'i a al-'Ala (the Higher Islamic Shi'i Council), Shaykh Farhat was an influential local figure. Although no mention of Farhat is made by Fadlallah in his authorised biography or personal recollections of the period, according to the respected Lebanese Shi'i-born American author, Fouad Ajami, the two were estranged from one another for the duration of their residency in Nab'a. Ajami asserts that the discord between the two clerics was the outcome of conflicting personalities and diametrically opposing views. Whereas Shaykh Farhat craved worldly pleasures and indulged in ostentatious luxuries, he claims Fadlallah was a much more morally disciplined and religiously devoted man. Furthermore, whereas Fadlallah personally admired and publicly supported Imam Khomeini's campaign against the Shah of Iran during the early 1960s, Farhat 'courted the Shah's regime and received some subsidies from the Shah's operatives in Lebanon'.[50] Despite the rift between the two, there is no evidence to suggest that either Fadlallah's personal status and authority or the scope and influence of his activities were significantly impaired.

Fadlallah's religious–cultural and social activities, and his institutional projects, were by no means confined to Nab'a or Bourj Hammoud; he expanded the geographical scope of his Islamist mission and the distribution of new mosques and *husainiyyat* to encompass other eastern suburbs of Beirut.[51] Although those localities (with the exception of the far eastern districts of al-Fanar and Tall al-Za'tar – until August 1976 the largest Palestinian refugee camp in Lebanon) had a definite Christian majority, there were also a large number of Shi'i residents. In Tall al-Za'tar, for example, 43 per cent of the camps' total estimated 1974 population of 30,000 were Shi'a, while in al-Fanar, 75 per cent were Shi'a.[52]

Combined with these activities, Fadlallah embarked on a regular programme of *Da'wa*-related activities in the country's south – particularly the villages and small towns of Bint Jbail and al-Nabatiyyeh. He devoted a day or two of every week to touring rural areas and preaching to Shi'i villagers, many of whom had relatives in Bourj Hammoud. During those weekly visits, he readily organised or participated in local social and religious festivities, which not only focused on disseminating Islamic values and heightening religious consciousness but also dealt with pressing socio-economic and topical political issues.[53]

Although, in the absence of independent research in this field, it is difficult to gauge the impact of these newly introduced Islamic programmes, according to Fadlallah they aroused much interest among the villagers, and hostility from activists of the well-established secular leftist parties. Fadlallah frequently organised ideological debates with activists affiliated to various leftist political organisations, most notably the Lebanese Communist Party. According to Fadlallah, these gatherings proved to be very popular among the locals. Nevertheless, we are informed that the apparent success of these lectures and polemic discussions as a regular feature of village events was only achieved when Fadlallah overcame the staunch opposition of the local Communists, for whom the Bint Jbail district had effectively become a stronghold. In the view of the Communists, the Islamists were reactionaries, tied to regional powers of Western imperialism, who were not only encroaching on their turf, but making inroads in this strategic zone bordering Israel.[54]

It was not at all incidental that Fadlallah sought to focus his Islamic dissemination in the south, on the town of Bint Jbail and its satellite villages, which included his ancestral village of 'Aynata. The town itself, the home of the powerful landed Bazzi clan, to whom Fadlallah's mother belonged, was a major source of migrants to Nab'a. Besides the obvious sentimental and social significance of the town, Bint Jbail was and remains the largest population centre in the central sector of South Lebanon. It was due to its strategic location, demographic weight and administrative function that Bint Jbail became during the 1960s the focal point of political and ideological activities in the region. Moreover, as the prime town in a rural district that is contiguous with the northern Israeli border, Bint Jbail's strategic importance was heightened from the late 1960s onwards, as the zone became a frontline in an escalating cross-border military conflict between Palestinian guerrillas and Israel's armed forces.[55]

To his credit, Fadlallah was able to contain the otherwise damaging propaganda put out by the Communists and Ba'thists. With resolve and open-mindedness, he managed, apparently, to outmanoeuvre his leftist rivals by inviting them to an open and forthright discussion, in which any tenet, no matter how sacrosanct, and any issue, no matter how controversial, was open to scrutiny and debate. To demonstrate unequivocally his commitment to open dialogue, Fadlallah declared: 'There is no frivolous or perplexing question [that is unworthy of consideration], as truth is the crux of any dialogue'; and that '[f]or every question there is an answer'.[56]

The stated purpose of Fadlallah's open lecture programmes in Beirut and the South was to bridge the gulf between religion and the youth. He attributed this chasm to the traditional 'ulama's detachment from the daily affairs and contemporary concerns of their constituency. This aloofness and shirking of social responsibility generated a common perception that religion was devoid of any real relevance to the institutions and issues of modern society. In his diagnosis of the problem of youth alienation, Fadlallah ascertained that the young were not in fact antagonistic towards religion as such, but were repelled by what was seen as the backward and traditional mode by which Islam was interpreted and conveyed.[57] With a view to redressing this problem, he delivered a regular series of roving lectures on topical issues, which were conventionally followed by open question-and-answer sessions. The aim was to enlighten and advise in a forum of uninhibited inquiry and debate, thereby stimulating genuine interaction between the young Sayyid and his audience, providing him with the opportunity to deepen his own understanding of the concerns and aspirations of young people.

While it is difficult to ascertain the extent to which Fadlallah's claim that the venture he initiated was a success, nevertheless there are indications that these forums, as observed by their pioneer, provided the basis for a new mode of thinking and debate. To the extent that he was able to fortify links with local Shi'i youth, and thus restore somewhat the blemished image of the 'ulama, his experience had borne fruit.[58] Moreover, he managed to rejuvenate their wavering faith in Islam's validity and modern-day practicability, thereby creating the necessary conditions for engendering a young generation of future Islamists. Finally, it is a testament to the success of Fadlallah's lecture and discussion programme that it has ever since become a popular and integral part of his weekly agenda.

Fadlallah's Public Discourse in the 1960s and 1970s

A complete collection of Fadlallah's lectures for the period 1966–76 is unavailable. However, some of his earliest lectures, including those delivered in 1966, have been compiled and appended to an enlarged Beirut edition of his book, *Qadayana 'ala Daw' al-Islam*, (Our Issues in the light of Islam) which was published in Iraq in 1960. Moreover, the bulk of the available public lectures – delivered in South Lebanon, principally in the district of Bint Jbail, in 1972 – were compiled in *Mafahim Islamiyyah 'Ammah* (General Islamic Concepts). Since a detailed survey of Fadlallah's published work is beyond the scope of this chapter, what follows is a selected sample of his more important lectures on a variety of themes, but linked by a common underlying conceptual thread.

It was on the occasion of the birthday of the Prophet Muhammad, in July 1966 in the village of 'Aitaroun in the district of Bint Jbail in South Lebanon, that Fadlallah delivered his first lecture. Stressing the importance of a proper understanding of the prophecy, and extolling the virtues of God's final Apostle, he underscored the continuing relevance of both the Prophet's exemplary character and exploits, as well as the general Islamic paradigm of existence, to contemporary Muslim lives.[59] He proceeded to highlight what he perceived to be an alarming discrepancy in the role of religion in the ideal sense, and the actuality of present-day Muslim character and way of life.

Graphically illustrating the marked incongruity between theory and practice, he made the observation that

> we are religious, yet we do not genuinely understand the faith; we are pious … yet we pursue all the paths of unbelief; we are religious … yet we follow, intimately, the footsteps of the oppressors; we are religious … yet we bear in our hearts rancour, malice and enmity towards our brethren in faith; we are religious … yet we backbite, slander, lie, fornicate, drink alcohol, cheat and deceive.

He moved on to ascribe the lamentable state of religion to the role played by unscrupulous political leaders. He stated emphatically that the tragedy of religion in the modern age was that it has readily been subjected to manipulation by what he called the 'entrepreneurs of politics' who, by hypocritically raising attractive religious banners and slogans, had callously exploited the Islamic sentiment of the masses, with a view to furthering their self-centred interests and narrow ambitions. In concluding, he called on Muslims to be vigilant in order to foil all those diabolic, exploitative schemes aimed at undermining the faith.[60]

In his first lecture, entitled 'Social Refinement in Islam' delivered in Bint Jbail under the auspices of the Young Believing Mens' Club (*Nadwat al-Shabab al-Mu'min*) on 27 May 1972, Fadlallah presented a portrait of the diverse social and ethical maladies that were plaguing current Muslim society. He pointed to the marked disparity between Muslim reality and Islamic norms with respect to individual character and social behaviour. Reminding his audience that modern Western societies did not represent the only model for social civility, he stressed that Islam, by virtue of its divine and comprehensive legal system, embodied an unsurpassed normative code and practical set of values, which together provided the basis for refining individual behaviour and reforming social relations.[61]

At the end of the lecture, a number of questions were addressed to Fadlallah, including the following: 'Why are youth repelled by religion?' and 'Does Islam restrict the working role of a woman to the home?' In relation to the first query, he attributed the alienation to a long list of factors, including: the ossified mentality of the traditional 'ulama; the historical legacy of Muslim despotism and iniquity; the stifling dissent and suppression of individual freedoms by many Muslim rulers; the ascendancy of secular modern western culture, with its historical aversion to the public role of the Christian churches; and finally, the ascendancy of modern Western civilisation, whose pervasive materialist-orientated culture had accorded primacy to matter over spirit, and individual freedom and cultural rebellion over social welfare and harmony.[62]

On the second question, Fadlallah advanced a view that fell mid-way between liberal and classical conservative interpretations of the issue. Differentiating between the unmarried and married status of a woman, he stated that no one had the authority to coerce the former into performing housework. He maintained that, although it is seldom exercised, unmarried women had the right to receive remuneration commensurate with their domestic service. Similarly, not only is household work not obligatory for married women, and not only is it within her legal right to ask for recompense for work, but as a mother she is entitled to a specific allowance from her husband for weaning an infant. Furthermore, provided that the income requested is within reason, the husband has no right to object.[63]

Mindful of the fact that this interpretation was not espoused, publicly at least, by the majority of contemporary Islamic scholars and jurists, he stressed that the above exposition fell purely into the theoretical domain, and that in practice the norm for the wife was to perform essential domestic chores voluntarily. In Fadlallah's view, the philosophy behind the theoretical status of those legal entitlements served to enhance the status of the wife in the eyes of her husband, discouraging her treatment as a servant, in favour of her role as a dignified, equal partner in marital life. This, he added, served to heighten the husband's sense of appreciation, and thereby assisted in fortifying the marital relationship. As to whether the woman is entitled to work outside the home, his response was in the affirmative, but that such entitlement was contingent (unless explicitly stated otherwise in the marital covenant) on such factors as the consent of the husband and type of employment. In the final analysis, Fadlallah believed that the public working mother had more to lose (in terms of motherly attention to her children) than to gain.[64] He was in no doubt that the most dignified and rewarding type of work for mothers was that related to the rearing of children.

On related social issues, such as the female dress code in Islam, Fadlallah held the conventional religious view, as stipulated by the Sharia, that a loose dress should cover all body parts except the face and hands. The conventional rationale for this is that it serves to preserve the woman's chastity and highlight her essence as an honourable human being, rather than as a tool of seduction and sexual desire. As regards polygamy, here too Fadlallah did not dissent from his peers. As it was explicitly sanctioned in the Qur'an, he could not but be expected to uphold the practice, but with the important provision that the husband is obliged, in financial terms, to treat his wives equitably.[65]

One customary practice to which Fadlallah was, in contrast to other more reticent 'ulama, stridently opposed, was the slaying of promiscuous Muslim females by male family members. Denouncing the practice as a manifestation of ignorance emanating from a primitive pagan tribal mentality, he asked why the woman alleged to have engaged in an illicit sexual relationship should bear sole responsibility for 'stigmatising' the family when it is the man who most probably initiated the encounter. What is more, such killings, in the name of preserving the family's honour, are strictly forbidden in Islam, since according to Islamic law the designated punishment for fornication is a hundred lashings, while that for adultery is public stoning to death. In both cases, however, sentencing, which can only be passed by a shari'ah judge, is dependent on the unlikely circumstance that testimonies are provided by four witnesses, or on the perpetrator admitting the offence.[66]

On 24 June 1972, against a background of escalating conflict in the south, Fadlallah delivered a lecture in which he analysed the current state of the Muslim world in the context of Western and Eastern global hegemony, and of the dependence of the Third World. This perspective on international relations, while not original to Fadlallah, has informed his political world-view ever since his experience in Iraq under late monarchic, then republican, rule, during the twilight of British imperialism and the apogee of the American-established, anti-communist regional alliance.

Entitled 'The Question of Pride and Ignominy in Islam', Fadlallah's lecture sought to highlight what were perceived to be the serious challenges confronting present-day Muslim societies arising from the political, military, economic and cultural dominance of Western and Eastern powers. The neo-imperialists, according to Fadlallah, had pursued a long-term, malign strategy that had seen the 'dissolution of their [transnational Islamic] identity, and the throttling of their deep-rooted sentiment of pride and dignity, thereby creating the impression of the necessity of submitting to the status quo imposed by these powers, and acquiescing to their domineering agendas … so as to preserve their presence and interests'. Consequently, Muslim countries have been lulled into the false belief that their state security and national interests are fundamentally dependent on the great powers, and that this dependency is perpetuated by propaganda to the effect that foreign patronage is imperative in the face of the persistent threat posed by the adversarial power.[67]

To illustrate the state of Muslim subordination and dependency, he refers to big power politics played out during World War II by Great Britain and France, who, in order to realise their strategic interests in the Middle

East, projected themselves as liberators of the Arabs from the Turkish yoke, thereby succeeding in driving a wedge between the Ottoman Empire and its Arab subjects. Reneging on their pledge to grant independence to the newly liberated Arab-populated provinces of the defunct Empire, Britain and France proceeded to divide the region between themselves, bringing it under their political and economic domination. In the post-war era, the political and economic hegemony of the old colonial powers was inherited by the United States, against which the Soviet Union strove to cast itself as the champion of the decolonised, less-developed Third World countries, against the control of Western capitalism and imperialism.[68]

In diagnosing the lamentable state of affairs in the modern Muslim world, Fadlallah was particularly perturbed to see that, as a result of decades of Western dominance, a once proud and redoubtable *umma* had been transformed into a constellation of disunited and dispirited nation-states, subservient to the major powers. He regarded the domestic problems, and in some cases serious internal conflicts, that had plagued the newly independent Muslim countries as being the indirect outcome of the Cold War, in which client state leaders 'struggle not for the welfare of their countries and citizens but on behalf of the interests of this or that superpower'. For Fadlallah, and indeed other Islamists, the processes of fragmentation and subjugation had severely enfeebled the sense of a common Muslim identity and mission, leading to 'our current disorientation and vacillation in the face of political reality. This, in turn, has paved the way for our continued subservience and ignominy to this power, on account of its infusing us with pride and dignity vis-à-vis the rival power.'[69]

Having outlined the nature and severity of the disease, Fadlallah proceeds to lay the basis for a remedy. Affirming that pride and dignity are the quintessence of Islamic individual and collective identity, he states that 'those who bless the treaties of imperialism in all its forms, or sympathise or collaborate with it, or proceed in a manner that consecrates submission, servitude and ignominy, cannot be [deemed to be true Muslim] believers'. In this context he poses the question: 'Can feebleness be a sufficient justification for acquiescence to this or that power?' Quoting from the Qur'an, he replies that the downtrodden masses, incapable of resisting, much less overcoming, their oppressors, and who thus have no effective means for ameliorating their plight, nevertheless have no licence to live a life of humiliation and passivity.[70] What is required of those who are subjugated is not to accept the status quo, but, where possible, to migrate to a new location free of tyranny and persecution. By contrast, Fadlallah refrained, either deliberately or otherwise, from providing advice to those politically disaffected Muslims who are committed to forceful change or militant activism.

Fadlallah held the firm view that there was no real benefit to be derived, in terms of pride or dignity, from the alliance of a Muslim country with an adversarial power. Citing specific Qur'anic verses to support his case, Fadlallah maintained that Muslims would be deluding themselves if they thought that by entering into friendship ties with the 'enemies of God' they would regain their pride.[71] He stressed to his audience that this should not be construed as advocating an isolationist stance vis-à-vis the international powers, as this, would contribute only to the marginalisation of the Muslim countries. On the contrary, Muslim societies could not afford to seclude themselves from world affairs, but ought to partake actively in the momentous developments of the contemporary world, with respect both to social and scientific–technological progress.[72]

In the view of Fadlallah, in order to regain its pride and glory, the *umma* must marshal and activate its formidable human and material resources, and then, in a coordinated fashion, channel them towards pivotal causes and vital interests. But in order to solidify and sustain the pooling and propulsion of those resources, it was imperative that Muslims nurture their spiritual power, by being neither dependent on nor subordinate to the transient powers of the West and East, but on God, the Omnipotent. Only when the currently fragmented power of the *umma* had reached the threshold of inexorable dynamism would any form of 'cooperation with a non-Muslim power be anchored in a position of strength not weakness, a position of pride not ignominy'.[73] In the conventional calculus of power politics, which Fadlallah would regularly invoke as a framework of analysis, the attainment of strategic parity would necessarily diminish, if not preclude, the possibility of undisputed domination by either party.

In order to illustrate the broad spectrum of Fadlallah's intellectual and ideological work during this period, it will be useful, given the extent of communist influence in the locality, to present his attempted refutation of Marx's famous dictum: 'Religion is the opium of the people.'[74] He provided a critique of the fundamental premise that posited thought as a product of matter, and, in particular, the derivative postulate that conceives religion as the creation of false human consciousness. The logical implication of this theory, he said, is that religious decadence is a direct reflection of societal malaise, of social wretchedness. As a corollary, religion functions as an inherently conservative force, perpetuating an undesirable status quo rather than bringing about change.[75]

Fadlallah sets out to contest the validity of the Marxist thesis on the origin of religious thought – that is, that it had essentially evolved from man's ignorance and innate deficiency; conditions which induced him to contemplate and believe in the existence of an unseen supernatural deity who possesses the unique power to regulate the awesome forces of nature, thereby invoking vital spiritual solace in the face of worldly hardship and suffering.[76] Dismissing the above scientific-positivist conception as a flawed hypothesis, Fadlallah attempted to demonstrate, through selective references to Qur'anic verses, that God had elevated the status of man over nature. In bestowing upon man His vicegerency on earth, God has delegated to man the essentially important right and responsibility to subject nature to his will, by harnessing its energies and developing its resources for the welfare and progress of humankind. As regards the supposed correlation between the role of religion and the perpetuation of the status quo, Fadlallah, once again citing relevant verses of the Qur'an to substantiate his view, stressed that Islam, when interpreted correctly, eschews human inertia and resignation, and that the doctrine of divine foreknowledge, fate and predestination does not necessarily negate the existence of individual volition and human-induced change. Indeed, for Fadlallah, the true believer is not only a responsible organic member of society, but an active agent of individual and collective change.[77]

The Higher Islamic Shi'i Council: Background and Fallout

Having presented a selective analysis of Fadlallah's ideas, it would be useful to survey those major developments that unfolded after 1966, impacting on the Shi'i community at large. The first and most contentious was the formation of the Higher Islamic Shi'i Council. As significant as the Council was, it was overshadowed from the outset by deep controversy within 'ulama circles, between proponents, led by Sayyid Musa al-Sadr, and opponents, including Sayyid Fadlallah, whose relationship with his former student colleague was tested soon after his settlement in Nab'a. However, even prior to the fallout that preceded the Council's creation, Fadlallah was drawn into assuming a mediatory role in an acrimonious dispute between al-Sadr and an elder Lebanese scholarly friend, Shaykh Muhammad Jawwad Mughniyya (d. 1979).[78]

The altercation between the two 'ulama had its origin in 1959, when al-Sadr, as mentioned earlier, was invited to the port city of Tyre to assume the vacant role of the country's principal religious–juridical Shi'i leader. As a well-known, respected senior *'alim*, Shaykh Mughniyya – who regarded himself as the best candidate for the job – was naturally disappointed at being overlooked in favour of a newcomer of junior rank. Independent-minded and forthright in his views, Mughniyya apparently lost the bid due to his open contempt for the traditional patronage system of the feudal lords, and his defiance of the will of the political establishment. Indeed, during the 1950s and 1960s, he built a reputation as an ardent advocate of social justice and equity, who showed genuine empathy for the rural poor, championed the cause of the downtrodden, and stridently supported popular Third World liberation movements against Western imperialism. For these tendencies he became endeared to the country's leftist parties, and was dubbed 'the red shaykh'. It is not surprising, then, that Fadlallah – considering his ideological 'liberationism', his impoverished background, and his natural affinity for the poor, living in the underprivileged quarter of Nab'a – had expressed his admiration for the shaykh.[79]

Mughniyyah's resentment at al-Sadr's appointment soon turned to overt hostility and public denigration – so much so that the foremost Shi'i *marja'*, Ayatollah Sayyid Muhsin al-Hakim, was forced to intervene by despatching a delegation charged with the task of reconciling the two estranged clerics.[80] However, this, along with subsequent attempts at settlement, was unsuccessful, mainly because Mughniyyah continued throughout the 1960s to express his ill feelings towards al-Sadr.[81] This virulence led him to write a disparaging manuscript on his rival. Entitled *al-Jasus al-Mu'ammam* ('The Turbaned Spy'), the polemic was never published, thanks to Fadlallah. He told his close friend that it was not befitting for a senior respected *'alim* like Shaykh Mughniyya, or the 'ulama in general, to engage in public recriminations.[82] However, although Fadlallah managed to put an end to the bickering, the two scholars never reconciled.

Sayyid al-Sadr's decision to set up the Higher Islamic Shi'i Council in 1966 not only rekindled old tensions, but engendered new ones, polarising a large segment of the Shi'i 'ulama community. During his extensive tours of predominantly Shi'i-inhabited regions of Lebanon, al-Sadr noticed the extent of government neglect of, and systematic discrimination against, the residents of those areas (namely the South, Bekaa, and suburbs of Beirut), who felt that they were treated as second-class citizens in their own country. His solution was the creation of an autonomous administrative institution that would cater for the Shi'i community's religious, legal, and social affairs. Thus, on 15 August 1966, al-Sadr convened a news conference during which he highlighted the plight of his coreligionists, and articulated what he saw as the pressing need for an institutional body that would redress the deep-seated grievances that stemmed from deprivation and marginalisation. In doing so, he argued that he was not advocating a novel or revolutionary change to the prevailing system, but rather was following the precedent set by the Sunnis and Druze, who had set up their own bodies in 1955 and 1962, respectively.[83]

Since 1959, Shi'i affairs had been administered by the mufti of the republic, the most senior government-appointed Sunni juridical functionary.[84] As the country's largest and most disenfranchised community, al-Sadr argued that it was time that the Shi'a had their own separate institution. To justify the split, al-Sadr referred to what he viewed as the uncompromising stance of the Sunni mufti himself, who was apparently declining all suggestions of reform to the existing structure, whereby the Shi'a would share equal status with Sunnis, and religious leaders from both denominations would alternate in assuming the presidency.[85]

The Sunnis objected to the initiative as they feared it would seriously undermine Muslim unity, encourage foreign manipulation, and entrench Maronite supremacy in Lebanon. To this can be added the private concerns of Sunni religious officialdom, that a Shi'i council would end its traditional dominance. Among the Shi'a, the 'ulama and political leaders opposed the council for varying reasons. The traditional feudal lords (*zu'ama*) were concerned about the extensive authority such a national body would wield, as well as the momentum it would give to the political ascendancy of al-Sadr. As regards the Shi'i 'ulama, more than half of them were against the proposed institution.[86] The more conservative of them objected because, in their view, it was an illegitimate innovation. But for the bulk of the 'ulama, opposition was based on the fact that the council, once established through an act of parliament, would function as an organ of the state, thereby inviting government interference, and with it the erosion of the traditional autonomous authority of the 'ulama.[87]

Islamists like Fadlallah objected to the very essence of the Council, deeming it fundamentally divisive, on the grounds that it would inevitably foster a distinct confessional identity and institutionalise a separate communal entity for the Shi'a, which, in time, might eclipse their original and fundamental Muslim identity. For Fadlallah – whose outlook was shaped by Islamic universalism rather than Shi'i communalism, and whose overriding concern was to maintain cohesion between the two communities which professed the same faith – primary allegiance was owed to the global *umma*. Hence, he espoused the view that there ought to be one unifying body, as represented by the existing Higher Islamic Council, managing the affairs of a single indivisible community of believers.[88]

Fadlallah argued his case to al-Sadr, but failed to persuade him. Recognising that his plea for unity lacked substantial support among the Shi'i 'ulama, he announced that he had ruled himself out from assuming any role in the prospective Council.[89] Thus, when the elections took place on 23 May 1969, two years after the proposal was passed by parliament and subsequently endorsed by the government, Fadlallah was conspicuously absent. He was not alone; in fact, more than half of his clerical colleagues had boycotted the election.[90] Yet, having demonstrated his disapproval of the Council, Fadlallah, realising the deep divisions and serious infighting that had beset the 'ulama community during and following the elections, joined with Shaykh Muhammad Mahdi Shams al-Din (a former student colleague in al-Najaf and future Vice-President of the Council) in attempting to reconcile the opposing camps.[91] Though there was a reduction in tension, however, complete rapprochement was not achieved.[92]

As expected, al-Sadr was elected president of the Council for a six-year term.[93] He presided over a hierarchically structured organisation whose executive committee comprised forty-three seats, nineteen of which were reserved for Shi'i parliamentarians, while twenty-four were evenly divided between the 'ulama and religious laymen (professionals and entrepreneurs). By virtue of being the head of the Council, al-Sadr was catapulted from being the foremost religious leader in Tyre, and a leading Shi'i in the country, into the position of official head and undisputed religious–political spokesman of the national Shi'i community.[94] Emblematic of al-Sadr's meteoric ascent was that, henceforth, his followers would address him as 'the Imam'.[95]

In spite of their differences, Fadlallah had always maintained that his personal relationship with his colleague was not adversely affected, and that he continued to have a good rapport with the 'ulama members of the Council.[96] The common background and set of contemporary challenges shared by Fadlallah and al- Sadr meant that the interests and endeavours of the two men converged on major issues. Both were publicly committed to redressing the conditions besetting the Shi'i community – of economic backwardness, social deprivation and political marginalisation. As 'ulama who saw themselves as agents of social change and political action, they were committed to bringing about an end to their community's prolonged political quiescence. Both strove to combat the influence of modern secular ideologies among the disillusioned Shi'i youth by engaging in a modernist Islamic discourse that expounded the civilisational and humanist nature of Islam, stressed its compatibility with the technological and scientific dimensions of Western modernity, and underscored the dynamic nexus between religion, social justice and political activism. With regard to the latter, it can be argued that, in terms of its orientation, this Islamic discourse is comparable with Christian liberation theology, though not with its socialist or Marxist analytical and philosophical framework.

Both men were political pragmatists. Both had shown a propensity to enter into working interim relationships with non-Islamic organisations, be they leftist or Arab nationalist, to fight common enemies ranging from local feudal lords to Israel and Western 'neo-imperialism'. It will be recalled from the last chapter how Fadlallah, in an article in which he exhorted his fellow Islamists to cooperate with Arab nationalists in the common strategic struggle for Palestine, revealed a pragmatism dictated by strategic goals and governed by Islamic principles. Notwithstanding the firm Islamist anchorage of the two Sayyids, the difference between them was one of nuance; al-Sadr's pragmatism tended to manifest itself in vacillating positions and revolving tactical alliances, to a point where 'several well-informed Lebanese ... have commented that nobody knew where the Imam stood'.[97]

Furthermore, while both men were tolerant towards Christians, preaching religious openness, dialogue and peaceful coexistence, and regularly meeting with Christian religious leaders, al-Sadr was more bold and controversial in his gestures. Thus, 'when he appeared in a church to deliver a sermon, his conservative rivals in the clerical establishment circulated a photograph of him under a cross.' In these actions, al-Sadr was motivated by a genuine desire to allay the fears of Christians relating to the political reawakening of the Shi'i populace, and to demonstrate his commitment to Lebanon's religious pluralism. But for his opponents, such an unprecedented act from a *mujtahid* was not only unthinkable but abominable.[98] Fadlallah, on the other hand, abstaining (in keeping with protocol) from publicly criticising his 'errant' colleague, showed no inclination to emulate him.

The point where the two clerics fundamentally diverged revolved around their respective visions and strategies. Whereas al-Sadr sought to mobilise the latent power of the Shi'i masses so as to further the neglected interests of his community per se, Fadlallah strove to utilise that revitalised power for global causes, principally freedom from Western political hegemony and economic exploitation. In this way, the parochial interests of the Shi'i community of Lebanon were subordinated to the grand interests of the *umma*.

This variation in outlook was reflected in strategy. Fadlallah was (and remains) an Islamist committed to radical change in society through gradual means. His strategy has always been based on cadre indoctrination in Islamist ideology, cohesive organisation, careful and long-term planning, and the peaceful dissemination of Islam – in other words, on bringing about a metamorphosis 'from below'. al-Sadr, by contrast, was a Shi'i confessional-minded reformist, who actively sought rapid but not revolutionary change, and employed mass rallies and strikes; a strategy that necessarily downplayed the importance of the lengthy process of indoctrination of selected individuals.[99] Thus, in conformity with the strategy of effecting change 'from above', he favoured the mobilisation of Shi'i malcontents as a means to pressure the government into yielding to his demands for state-instituted reform.

Al-Sadr, Fadlallah and the Palestinian–Israeli Conflict

One of the first major issues addressed by Sayyid al-Sadr as President of the Supreme Islamic Shi'i Council was the issue of South Lebanon. Since 1968, when Palestinian guerrilla groups based in the country's south began their armed struggle against Israel, al-Sadr had been a vocal supporter of the Palestinian cause. He began actively to support the Palestinian resistance movement following the promulgation in early June 1968 of a momentous fatwa, by Sayyid Muhsin al-Hakim, the Shi'i world's pre-eminent jurisconsult.[100]

In 1969–70 two major events took place that had adverse consequences for the citizens of the south, and serious implications for al-Sadr in particular. The first was the Cairo Accord of 13 November 1969. Signed, under the auspices of President Nasser, between the PLO and the Lebanese military high command, the main articles of the agreement meant that the PLO was not subject to the laws of the host country, and had jurisdiction over Palestinian refugee camps throughout Lebanon, and explicitly enshrined the organisation's right to pursue armed struggle against Israel. As a consequence, Palestinian guerrillas intensified their attacks on Israeli targets.[101] The second major development was the military defeat in September 1970 of the mainly PFLP-led resistance in Jordan by the Hashemite royal army. The evicted Palestinian leadership, along with thousands of fighters, were forced to relocate first to Syria, then to Lebanon. Henceforth, Beirut would be the political headquarters of the PLO, and South Lebanon the Arab world's remaining active military front facing Israel.[102] The net result was a marked increase in the frequency and magnitude of cross-border guerrilla raids and Israeli retaliatory military strikes; repeatedly the Shi'i residents of the south bore the brunt of the incursions and bombardments.[103]

With the deterioration of the security situation in the south, it became difficult for al-Sadr to maintain his earlier unqualified support for the PLO. He told an American political official that, though he sympathised with the plight and cause of the Palestinians, that sympathy 'no longer extends to [support for] actions which expose our people to additional misery and deprivation'. However, while he criticised the Palestinian leadership for being oblivious to the welfare of his Shi'i constituency, he continued to castigate the government for continuing to neglect South Lebanon and its defenceless residents.[104] Caught in a bind between the obligation to protect the vulnerable Shi'i residents of the region and the increasingly untenable moral duty of supporting the Palestinian resistance – with which the majority of Shi'a still identified – al-Sadr effectively resolved the predicament by reproaching the government for its inaction.[105]

Beginning in mid-1969, he presented the government with a list of demands, including the introduction of military conscription, the fortification of the south, and the training of a civil militia.[106] Seeing that none of his demands were met, al-Sadr initiated a campaign of civil agitation. On 26 May 1970 he called a one-day general strike to demonstrate solidarity with the south.[107] The nationwide strike successfully pressured the government into convening an urgent session of parliament, leading to the establishment of a public institution (Majlis al-Janub, or Assembly of the South) to meet the special needs of Southern residents. [108]

Although both al-Sadr and Fadlallah regarded the Palestinian armed struggle as a legitimate cause, and the liberation of Palestine as a sacred duty, they approached the issue from different viewpoints. From the regional Arab perspective of Fadlallah, the south is an integral part of the Palestine question, and thus its resolution lies in the hands of regional and international powers.[109] While he shared with his colleague the view that the liberation of Palestine is essentially an Islamic cause, Fadlallah went further than al-Sadr in according the holy struggle precedence over the communal interests of Lebanon's Shi'a. Moreover, while both viewed Israel as an alien, abominable and expansionist entity, Fadlallah did not regard the Palestinian resistance movement in Lebanon as a burden that the Shi'i residents of the south could do without.[110] As far as he was concerned, given the strategic territorial ambitions of Israel, South Lebanon would remain unstable, regardless of the extent of activity of the Palestinian guerrillas.[111] For, according to the Islamist and Arab nationalist view, Israel has, ever since its establishment, coveted south Lebanon, and has thus moved gradually closer to attaining it through a systematic strategy of destroying the local armed resistance.[112]

On 24 June 1972, as part of a lecture and question-and-answer session in the southern town of Bint Jbail, Fadlallah gave a revealing analysis of the South Lebanon–Palestinian problem.[113] In response to a question relating to Islam's position vis-à-vis Arab resignation in the face of Israeli might, Fadlallah asserted that while the Arabs ought to eschew the position of passivity and apathy, they should also give serious contemplation to the crucial question of what could be realistically accomplished. Emotionalism per se, he added, was not the solution. Before giving his prescription for the crisis, Fadlallah presented a diagnosis of the problem.

Among the several intertwined factors that he identified as having contributed to the malaise was, first, the historical legacy in Lebanon of social backwardness and economic underdevelopment, stemming from prolonged periods of 'iniquity, persecution, impoverishment and ignorance'. He accused the central government of perpetuating these conditions through systematic neglect of the south, and through its traditional policy of 'consecrating' the authority of the feudal bosses. He accused the Lebanese government of 'having pursued a systematic policy of perpetuating the underdevelopment of the South so as to justify its occupation by the enemy'. In common with al-Sadr, he exhorted the central authorities to establish sustainable agricultural and manufacturing projects in the south, aimed at attaining self-reliance that would serve as an incentive for the rural populace to remain in their villages, rather than migrating to the cities. The third factor related to the role played by the international and local political media in projecting an image of Arab defeat and subjugation at the hands of Israel, which was strategically buttressed by the United States, to the extent that the latter's commitment created the impression that it was prepared to wage a third world war for the sake of Israel. In stark contrast to the common vital interests that underlie the strategic alliance between Western imperialism and the Zionist state, Arabs and Muslims, in general, lacked the support of a countervailing military and economic power with the capacity to preserve and advance their interests.[114]

This lamentable state of affairs was aggravated by simmering intra-Arab disputes between conservatives and radicals, and their respective offshoots, behind which the 'sinister hands of imperialism and Zionism have unquestionably played an abetting role'. The symptoms of these maladies were ideological disorientation and intellectual paralysis. They were manifested in part by the perplexity of the ordinary Arab citizen when attempting to distinguish clearly between patriotic and 'perfidious' political leaders, and in part by the realisation that the plethora of ideological and political movements that had emerged on the Arab scene since the 1950s had not brought about political change of any consequence. [115]

From the standpoint of the above diagnosis, Fadlallah concluded that it would be difficult in the present local environment, particularly with Israel endeavouring to spread 'terror, carnage and destruction everywhere and by any pretext it deems fit', for the individual to feel proud and dignified. Fadlallah outlined his prescription in rather general terms: 'To replace our existing naive crude perception of the enemy's programme with a profound view that seeks to unveil the future agenda by considering its past and present experiences. It is on this basis that we then plan our political, economic and military life.' He illustrated this by referring to the experience of the Zionist movement which, thanks to its long-term strategic planning, saw the transformation of a cherished dream into reality, with the creation of Israel in 1948, and asked why the Arabs could not pursue a similar strategy.[116]

For Fadlallah, the first and most important step in the long path to recovery consists of nurturing religious faith, instilling moral fortitude, and enhancing political consciousness.[117] In his theory of change and theology of liberation, the transformation of an individual's faith and character were the vital precursors to the formation of a righteous leadership that would bring about divine deliverance and worldly triumph.

Harakat al-Mahrumin: Background and Formation

Although both Fadlallah and al-Sadr persistently criticised the central authorities over their neglect of the pressing security needs and socio-economic conditions of the residents of the south, the latter was by 1974 firmly committed to populist political action to attain his public goals. Evoking and redefining the traditional Shi'i tenets of martyrdom and rebellion against injustice, al-Sadr turned to mass activism as an effective means of energising the politically dormant Shi'i community and instilling his constituency with a sense of communal identity, pride and purpose.[118]

On 17 March 1974, the fortieth day after *'Ashoura*, al-Sadr addressed a huge crowd (estimated at 75,000 people) in the town of Baalbeck.[119] He attacked the government's incompetence, corruption and discrimination, and enumerated the deep-seated grievances of his constituency. He extracted from his followers a pledge to 'fight for our rights to our last drop of our blood'.[120] The Baalbek rally was followed on 5 May by another mass procession of 80,000 people, this time in al-Sadr's host town of Tyre. He again reproached the authorities for their ineptitude and apathy, berating them for rendering Shi'i citizens the 'most deprived of all communities'. As in the previous assembly, he extracted a collective oath from his supporters to struggle together until the country was liberated from 'deprivation' and 'disinheritance'.[121]

It was at the March rally that al-Sadr, at the height of his career, announced the formation of Harakat al-Mahrumin (Movement of the Deprived). According to the movement's preliminary charter, it was 'a movement of the deprived that believes in God's and Man's complete freedom and dignity, that rejects social injustice and the confessional political order, and that struggles relentlessly against authoritarianism and feudalism. It is a patriotic movement that upholds [Lebanon's] national sovereignty and territorial integrity.' Though intended by al-Sadr to represent the grievances and aspirations of the underprivileged, irrespective of religious persuasion, the fact that the Shi'a comprised the most disadvantaged and marginalised community predetermined that the movement would be mostly Shi'i in membership.[122] But the movement did not betray a sectarian world-view or political programme. As one prominent political editor observed, the object of the 'Shi'i revolt' was not to establish Shi'i governance, but to end government injustice.[123] The Harakah functioned essentially as a nationwide communal movement, whose membership encompassed nearly the entire ideological spectrum.[124]

To the extent that the movement sought not to overturn the Lebanese political system, but to secure for the disenfranchised Shi'i community a proportionate share in that order, it was reformist. However, while being a movement of social protest and a vehicle of socio-economic change and political reform, Harakat al-Mahrumin, did not have a detailed programme of action. The onset of the civil war one year after its founding saw the stalling of al-Sadr's momentum towards communal reform, and eventually the marginalisation of his movement by the chaotic maelstrom of the conflict.

The Lebanese Civil War, al-Sadr and the Emergence of Amal

An analysis of the causes and shape of the first phase of the civil war (April 1975–October 1976) is beyond the scope of this chapter. Instead, an attempt will be made to establish the extent and role of Shi'i involvement in the fighting, and the impact of the conflict on Shi'i residents of Beirut (particularly Nab'a), with particular attention given to the activities and positions of Sayyid al-Sadr.

When the war erupted officially in April 1975 – thanks to the now infamous 'Ayn al-Rummana incident – Lebanon's newly politicised Shi'is entered the conflict on the side of the Lebanese National Movement.[125] However, because of his misgivings about the secular, radical leftist orientation of the LNM and its leader, Kamal Jumblatt, on the one hand, and his opposition to the continuation of the war on the other, al-Sadr's alliance to the movement was in reality only nominal. More important as factors accounting for the involvement of young Shi'i activists in the fighting were, first, that the majority of Shi'i combatants who had fought against the militias of the Maronite right were not affiliates of Harakat al-Mahrumin under the leadership of al-Sadr, but members of the leftist parties and recruits of the Palestinian organisations. Second, the bulk of Shi'a who participated in the war dwelt in localities, like Nab'a and Shiyyah, which, due to their proximity to both the militarised Palestinian camps and hostile Maronite urban districts, were transformed into frontline battle zones throughout the war.[126]

It was in protest against the escalating nationwide conflict that al-Sadr embarked on his much-publicised hunger strike on 27 June 1975, in a mosque in Beirut's southern suburb of Ghubayri. He declared his resolve to continue the fast until a government of national unity was formed and fighting brought to a halt. Concerned that a continuation of the conflict would lead to the disintegration and partition of the country, he declared that 'non-violence is our way … our weapons are the words of God'. Visited by a constant stream of political and religious dignitaries and militia leaders, al-Sadr ended his fast five days into the vigil, following assurances from the newly formed government that his demands for national reconciliation and reform would be implemented.[127] But no sooner had he broken his fast than fighting resumed with greater intensity and scope, spreading to Christian and Muslim areas of the Bekaa.[128]

Only five days after the end of al-Sadr's fast, an incident took place in the Bekaa valley which revealed the existence of a hitherto clandestine paramilitary organisation, Harakat Amal ('Movement of Hope', whose Arabic name was an acronym of Afwaj al-Muqawamah al-Lubnaniyyah, or 'Lebanese Resistance Detachments').[129] At a press conference the same day, al-Sadr was forced to confirm the existence of the hitherto secret organisation, acknowledging that Amal was trained by the PLO, and was intended to be the paramilitary wing of the Movement of the Deprived. He attempted to justify the movement by arguing that it was set up as an auxiliary militia of the regular army, solely to engage the Israelis in the south, with strict instructions not to become embroiled in the country's internecine civil conflict.[130] Be that as it may, the fact that Amal was an armed militia founded and headed by Sayyid al-Sadr served only to cast doubt on the sincerity of his earlier unequivocal denunciation of the conflict, and on his public campaign against the proliferation of paramilitary formations.

A fact not disclosed by al-Sadr at that news conference was that Amal's covert military ties to the PLO were founded on a secret pact, concluded on 24 June 1975, between the two organisations, as well as pro-Khomeini Iranian revolutionaries.[131] The active presence of Iranian dissidents made it all the more important for al-Sadr to maintain the alliance's strict secrecy. Furthermore, according to the same source, among the signatories to the pact were Sayyid al-Sadr and Sayyid Fadlallah.[132]

Mirroring the composite membership of the Movement of the Deprived, Amal attracted mostly young urbanised Shi'a of diverse political orientations and ideological persuasions – from the secular left to the religious right, from reformers to radicals, and from Shi'i confessionalists to Islamic ecumenists. Many of its recruits were former Shi'i members of radical leftist and Palestinian organisations, who were disillusioned with their secular non-confessional character, and yearned 'to belong to a movement of their own sect'. Indeed, one of the reasons why al-Sadr had founded Amal was to stop the prolonged haemorrhage of Shi'i youth to the secular left through the establishment of an effective and distinctly Shi'i organisational alternative.[133] While Amal espoused the charter of Harakat al-Mahrumin, the latter's agenda of social and political reform was soon eclipsed by the war, and by the militancy of the former group. During the war, the two movements became synonymous with each other, with Amal in effect superseding its parent movement.

Yet, for all its significance, Amal played only a peripheral role in the civil war. Essentially, three factors determined the movement's limited military contribution. First, the bulk of young Shi'i fighters participated in the war on the side of the leftist multi-confessional radical parties and the PLO.[134] Second, at the time of its exposure to publicity in July 1975, Amal was still evolving, and hence possessed too few trained combatants.[135] Third, the extent of Amal's involvement was bound to be inconsequential due to the nominal nature of al-Sadr's alliance with the leftist Lebanese National Movement, and his strained relationship with its leader, Kamal Jumblatt. For one thing, the Amal leader was averse to the latter's revolutionary agenda, which actively sought to overturn the Maronite-dominated confessional regime and replace it with a secular socialist republic.[136]

From Defiance to Disaster: Fadlallah and the Exodus from Nab'a

During the early phase of the war, the PLO managed to transform the portside slum districts of Karantina and Maslakh – which were strategically situated between Christian east Beirut and the Maronite hinterland to the north and east, and were home to some 30,000 residents and itinerant abattoir workers and stevedores (mostly Shi'a but including Syrian Kurds and Palestinians) – into a sniper's haven, from which Christian lines of communication and military convoys could be harassed.[137] A thorn in their side, the militiamen of the Christian right launched an assault on these localities in December 1975, and they were both eventually stormed, in January 1976. The ensuing massacres of hundreds of beleaguered defenders and defenceless civilians became known in Lebanese annals as Black Saturday.[138]

The indiscriminate killings and mass deportations of civilian survivors to west Beirut had the effect accelerating the momentum of militarisation of Shi'i enclaves within predominantly Christian eastern suburbs of Beirut. Unquestionably the most important of these locales, both strategically and demographically – with its 60,000–100,000 Shi'i residents – was Nab'a, which straddled the vital supply-line that connected east Beirut to the predominantly Christian suburbs of Sin el-Fil and Dekwaneh.[139]

With the exception of the Armenian-inhabited areas of central and northern Bourj Hammoud (which remained mainly neutral), Nab'a was bounded on three sides by hostile Maronite territory. What had hardened the resolve of the Shi'i residents of the district in defence of their enclave was the influence exerted by the radical Lebanese left and by the Palestinian organisations, with which the majority of the Shi'i youth were affiliated, or with which they sympathised. It was in recognition of the pivotal importance of that influence that the PLO, the Communists, the Ba'thists and the Syrian Social Nationalists had all established their regional headquarters in Nab'a. It was also in recognition of the significance of Nab'a's proximity to Tal al-Za'tar – the largest and most formidable Palestinian refugee camp and military compound in Lebanon – that the district's defence came under the general command of PLO military officers.[140]

Also mobilised were the small, dedicated minority of Islamists who coalesced around Fadlallah, and who were among the most active supporters of the Palestinian resistance movement.[141] While Fadlallah's relations with the Lebanese leftists was tense (stemming from their open aversion for religion) he had close contacts with the various Palestinian organisations, particularly Fatah. (Fadlallah, NBN Television interview, Part 2, 18 April 2004.) The extent to which these groups of Islamic activists in the defence of Nab'a acted under the direct influence of Fadlallah cannot be established with certainty, since his own recollections shed little light on the matter. The local Islamists, who had not yet formed themselves into a distinct, tightly structured organisation, had been bolstered significantly since 1974 by the entry into Lebanon of large numbers of Iraqi political fugitives – mostly members of Hizb al-Da'wa, many of whom were to undergo military training in the Palestinian camps during the war.[142]

Since late 1975, and particularly following the fall of the portside slum districts, the Christian right had imposed a partial blockade on Nab'a and Tal al-Za'tar, the two remaining Muslim-Palestinian strongholds in Beirut's eastern suburbs. The blockade was eased somewhat during a lull in the fighting in February 1976. The garrisons of both enclaves were subsequently reinvigorated during the major mountain offensive of the PLO-leftist-Muslim alliance in March 1976. However, with the full-scale Syrian military invasion of Lebanon in early June (ostensibly to avert the impending defeat of the Maronite militias, the partition of the country and the emergence of a Lebanese Muslim-Palestinian-dominated *de facto* state), the tide of the war shifted decisively against the PLO-Muslim coalition. As a result, on 22 June 1976 a total blockade was imposed on Nab'a and Tal al-Za'tar by the revitalised Maronite militias.[143]

Much weaker in its defences than Tal al-Za'tar, Nab'a was more vulnerable to a prolonged siege.[144] Much hardship was endured by the beleaguered civilian population of Nab'a as it struggled to cope with the effects of the siege, as well as the almost incessant and indiscriminate shelling. The precariousness of the situation was heightened by the existence of only one hospital in a district inhabited by approximately 100,000 people. The residents' ordeal was compounded by severe shortages of food and water, as well as medical supplies. With the increased sense of despair and helplessness in the face of hunger and death, the earlier enthusiasm and support for the Palestinian garrison by the Shi'i inhabitants, particularly among the older generation, began to wane. Desperate to save themselves and their families from imminent starvation or slaughter at the hands of the besiegers, a large proportion of Nab'a's population had already fled the quarter at the onset of the siege, hastily taking their meagre possessions with them.[145] Those fleeing the carnage and destruction in Nab'a had to risk sniper fire and artillery barrages to reach the relative safety of checkpoints manned first by the PLO, and then by the Christian Lebanese Forces.[146]

Still, a substantial but rapidly dwindling segment of Nab'a's population elected to remain in the quarter and endure the siege, either to protect their property or to join the resistance. Among those who chose to defy the siege and the movement towards exodus was Sayyid Fadlallah. From his recollections we learn that he lived through the ordeal of the period until he was compelled to leave the quarter at the outset of the siege, which coincided with the fall of the portside slum districts of Maslakh and Karantina, in January 1976. During that critical period, Fadlallah used his official status as the representaive of Ayatullah al-Ko'ie in Lebanon and hence a collector of religious tithes and donations to help financially the most desperate among Nab'a's beleaguered residents. Conscious of the inability of Nab'a's solitary hospital to cope with the ever increasing flow of wounded, Fadlallah attempted to ease the pressure by turning the Islamic Centre which he headed into a makeshift hospital and a tempoarary morgue. (Fadlallah, NBN Television interview, Part 2, 18 April 2004.) When he eventually decided to leave Nab'a it was because we are informed that he had to perform some social duties in South Lebanon, but he does not elaborate on the nature of those tasks, nor recall the specific circumstances that unfolded prior to his departure. In any case, he did not remain long in the south, as he deemed it to be his moral duty to return with his family to Nab'a to shore up the morale of its beleaguered residents. Despite the advice of friends and colleagues who believed the quarter was on the verge of being overrun by the Christian Phalangists, Fadlallah, convinced that was not the case, managed to return to the quarter, at great risk to himself and his family, at the height of the siege. Ironically, not long after he had returned to his residence, Fadlallah fell seriously ill, losing some 30kg in weight. He attributes the dramatic loss of weight to the physical strain and psychological stress emanting from his wartime ordeal. Fadlallah recounts how Nab'a was subjected throughout the siege to heavy shelling, forcing the frightened residents to seek shelter in the basements of residential buildings, how residents had to endure months without electricity and running water, with acute shortages in food and medical supplies, and described the overwhelming sense helplessness in the face of the wailing wounded, the weeping orphans, and grieving widows. (Fadlallah, NBN Television interview, Part 2, 18 April 2004.) With his life in jeopardy, Fadlallah felt compelled to leave for a second and final time. In doing so he was forced to traverse numerous checkpoints before returning again to Bint Jbail in the south.[147]

Though his roving *Da'wa* activities, and normal teaching sessions were disrupted by the intense fighting, Fadlallah continued to deliver his weekly sermon to Friday prayer worshippers, which dealt in parts with the worsening security situation. He would repeatedly warn the faithful to avoid undertaking the perilous journey from Nab'a to West Beirut, due to the numerous road blocks manned by rival armed militias. (Fadlallah, NBN Television interview, Part 2, 18 April 2004.) Yet, it was to intellectual writing that Fadlallah devoted most of his time. Indeed, it was those trying times that proved one of the most fertile periods for his intellectual output. He completed three seminal works during the siege and bombardment of the quarter. Published after the war, the books were to significantly enhance Fadlallah's intellectual stature, and gain him recognition as an influential Islamist theoretician.

The first, *al-Islam wa Muntiq al-Quwwah* (Islam and the Logic of Power), although was completed on 25 May 1976, had originally been the title of a lecture delivered in Nab'a. It was written by candlelight, 'during times of intermittent fighting and heavy indiscriminate shelling of the quarter'. He recorded these words, he said, 'so that [the siege and its conditions] may be remembered'.[148] The work was an exposition of the theory and praxis of power in Islam, and a critique of the Western conception of its nature and dynamics. In it, Fadlallah sets forth the juridical foundation and ethical guidelines of power, and delineates a scheme for the empowerment of the Shi'i community, on the basis of a reinvigorated Islamic identity and vision. He underscores the importance, and the means, by which to generate and deploy diverse varieties of power. For Fadlallah, the creation or acquisition of power was an indispensable element in sustaining a vibrant and influential Islamic entity, both locally and internationally. As for the use of force to achieve particular ends, he perceived it not as a distinct Islamic hallmark, but as a legitimate, and at times necessary, recourse in order to combat aggression and oppression.

Six weeks after completing this treatise, Fadlallah wrote a second work – original but less renowned. Entitled *al-Hiwar fil Qur'an* (Dialogue in the Qur'an*)*, the book is a systematic study of the nature and foundations of dialogue in the Qur'an. In it, he affirms the centrality of dialogue in Islam by attempting to demonstrate that the Qur'an is essentially a book of dialogue and discourse, and that a central value of the Qur'an is freedom of inquiry and debate. Ironically, Fadlallah's work on dialogue – among Muslims, between Muslims and adherents of other faiths, and between Muslims and atheists – was completed on 15 July 1976, at the height of the siege of Nab'a. Against a backdrop of fanaticism and violence, Fadlallah emerges as a man of moderation and tolerance. He narrates that he has developed extensive relations with local Christian leaders and major figures of political parties, and in his capacity as a religious leader had exerted a moderating influence on local Muslim residents, apparently dissuading them from engaging with their Christian Maronite rivals in tit-for-tat abductions and killings of civilians on the basis of confessional identity.[149]

Entitled *Khutuwat 'ala Tariq al-Islam* (Steps along the Path of Islam), Fadlallah's final work was written, like the others, at the height of the siege of Nab'a, with a postscript added in September 1977. In it, Fadlallah sets forth guiding principles and a practical agenda, and expounds the key issues and challenges, for Islamists engaging in religious–political activism. He sought to guide the public discourse and behaviour of Islamic activists by delineating legitimate and practicable methods of propagating Islamism. For Fadlallah, the Islamist transformation of the status quo is a gradual process that entails cohesive organisation and careful planning, and involves a certain flexibility with respect to methodology, as determined by the fluidity of the operational environment.[150]

The Fall of Nab'a and its Consequences

Although Fadlallah had left a few days before the seizure, on 6 August 1976, of Nab'a by the Phalangists, a significant number of residents opted to remain in the beleaguered quarter.[151] That the remaining residents of the quarter and its fighters were able to hold out can be attributed to the neutrality of the Armenian-inhabited sectors of Bourj Hammoud, which lay to the north of Nab'a. Christian Orthodox in persuasion, the Armenians steadfastly refused to enter into military alliance with the Maronite right, restricting their military activity to the organisation of local self-defence. As a consequence, the encirclement of Nab'a was incomplete, as the Armenians had opened to their neighbours a lifeline to food, medical and even arms supplies, as well permitting the transit of rightist forces. It was only towards the end of the siege, when that neutrality was abandoned, that the Armenians, who were provoked by the militias of the Maronite right and by PLO splinter groups, clashed with the Shi'a of Nab'a.[152]

As the situation deteriorated, al-Sadr entered into secret negotiations with the leader of the Kata'ib (Christian Phalange), Amin Gemayyel, the future president of Lebanon. Deeming the Shi'i defenders to be too few and ill-equipped to stave off a major onslaught by the enemy, al-Sadr believed that the fall of Nab'a was inevitable and imminent, and feared mass slaughter and wholesale evictions of its remaining residents. The negotiations with his adversary led to a secret agreement that included, on the one hand, the voluntary and peaceful evacuation of Shi'i residents, and, on the other, the forceful eviction of the Palestinian minority. Fadlallah was unaware of the deal to relinquish control of the quarter; so too was the defending garrison, which resisted the Kata'ib assault for another two days before being overwhelmed. In a clear snub to al-Sadr, Gemayyel reneged on his earlier pledge, and as a result the triumphant Lebanese Forces proceeded to uproot the local residents by force – Shi'a and Palestinians alike – subjecting the properties in the district to two days of looting and destruction.[153]

With the fall of the Nab'a enclave, which in turn had accelerated the subjugation of Tal al-Za'tar, with its 30,000 Palestinian-Shi'i inhabitants, the hitherto heterogeneous confessional pockets in Beirut's eastern suburbs were now systematically 'cleansed', paving the way for the de facto partition of Greater Beirut.[154] For the tens of thousands of displaced residents of Nab'a, the message could not have been clearer: a re-established Shi'i community in the emptied quarter would not be countenanced by a hostile Maronite population. For Fadlallah, the fall of Nab'a was devastating: the fruits of the diligent labour of a decade were now lost, his intensive grass-roots activities and institutional network crippled, his nascent circle of young dedicated Islamists dispersed, and the long-established local Shi'i community displaced.

Fadlallah was never to return to Nab'a, despite an offer, at the end of the war, by the Lebanese president Amin Gemayyel. According to Fadlallah, Gemayyel attempted to contact him by phone with an offer to relinquish control of the *Sayyid*'s cherished institutions. An embittered Fadlallah, did not respond to the gesture, perceiving it to be motivated by cynical political gain. In any case, as far as Fadlallah was concerned, 'no demand or offer – no matter how genuine – could redeem what they [the Christian Phalange] had inflicted.'[155]

As for al-Sadr, his role in the incalculable fall-out from Nab'a resulted in irreparable damage to his status and credibility. Despite explanations for his motives and vigorous denials, by many displaced Shi'a and Palestinians he was perceived to have colluded with an implacable enemy. He was accused of duplicity – and for the most disaffected, perfidy. On the one hand, he had publicly exhorted his followers in mid-1975 to bear arms against the enemy; yet, on the other hand, he had kept the local community and its leaders in the dark while he concluded a deal with the forces of the Maronite right.[156] As the author of an agreement that ultimately rested on assurances that were subsequently dishonoured by Amin Gemayyel, al-Sadr was assailed for what was seen to be the ignominious sacrificing of the strategic enclave.[157]

In contrast to many of his clerical colleagues, and in keeping with his strict protocol of avoiding personal diatribes against members of the 'ulama community, Fadlallah was reticent, publicly at least, on the controversial role of al-Sadr in the Nab'a episode. Fadlallah has stated on several occasions that there were mutual agreements, as well as disagreements and disappointments, with al-Sadr; it is certainly possible that the Nab'a debacle was the most contentious issue to have arisen between the two clerics.

In the aftermath of Nab'a, Fadlallah was forced to resettle, until the summer of 1976, in his ancestral village of 'Aynata, in the district of Bint Jbail in the extreme south, where he joined thousands of other displaced residents from the fallen enclave.[158] Untouched at this stage by the ravages of the civil war, and unlike many of his uprooted coreligionists, he had recourse to the patronage of his father, Ayatollah Sayyid Abdul Ra'uf, and his mother's powerful Bazzi clan. But given the town's proximity to the northern Israeli border, Bint Jbail was always going to be in a perpetual state of tension and insecurity, due to cross-border Palestinian guerrilla raids and Israeli military incursions and bombardments. In any event, Fadlallah's stay in the provincial town was short-lived. Within twelve weeks of his arrival in Bint Jbail – barely enough time to consolidate himself and re-gather his fragmented constituency – the security situation on the border had deteriorated rapidly.

Following its failed strategy of co-opting the Shi'i border villagers against the PLO and the Lebanese National Movement, Israel established, trained and equipped a proxy Christian militia, with the aim of creating a Christian satellite-buffer entity in the south, and thus pressuring the local Shi'is either into cooperating with it, or facing displacement.[159] Thus, to implement their anti-PLO strategy, the Israelis launched an offensive on 16 October 1976 which lasted until 30 March 1977, that resulted in the occupation of a swathe of mainly Shi'i villages (mostly in the Bint Jbail district).[160] Streaming ahead of the advancing Israeli army and its surrogate Lebanese militia were thousands of Shi'a, many of whom were refugees from Nab'a. Among those who joined the exodus from the embattled south to the relative tranquillity of Beirut was Fadlallah. Their general destination was the predominantly Shi'i inhabited al-dahiyyah al-janubiyyah li-Beirut (the Southern suburbs of Beirut), and for Fadlallah the depressed, crowded neighbourhood of B'ir al-'Abd. While there he began in earnest to preach from the pulpit of the Imam Rida Mosque.[161] With the generous financial contributions of wealthy Shi'i expatriates, the structure was enlarged to cater for the burgeoning number of worshippers, among whom Fadlallah was able carefully to nurture a coterie of dedicated Islamists.

In a development that enhanced his status and augmented his influence, Fadlallah was designated in the latter part of 1976 the official *wakil*, or representative, of Ayatollah Sayyid Abul Qasim al-Kho'ie, the world's pre-eminent Shi'i *Marja'*, who succeeded the late Ayatollah Sayyid Muhsin al-Hakim in 1970, in the Shi'i holy city of Najaf. The appointment conferred on Fadlallah the privilege and responsibility of being the authorised intermediary of Sayyid al-Kho'ie, and his official representative in Lebanon.[162] It gave Fadlallah the exclusive right, on behalf of his superior, to collect religious taxes (*zakat* and *khums*) and donations, to disseminate his juridical rulings and opinions, answer queries of religious laypersons in the light of al-Kho'ie's legal extrapolations, stipulate guidelines and precepts, and forward the more difficult or unprecedented issues to be tackled by the *Marja'* himself.

Though overshadowed, throughout this period, by al-Sadr's towering figure, highly publicised and assertive reformist agenda, and populist charismatic leadership style, nevertheless, by the mid-1970s, Fadlallah had become a prominent cleric. Yet he managed to attain that status while prudently maintaining a lower public profile and a less assertive political role than his more celebrated and influential peer.

That Fadlallah was appointed over his more senior and celebrated colleague, al-Sadr, is significant in that the appointment represented recognition at the highest levels in Najaf's 'ulama establishment of the reversal in their respective public appeal and personal stature. Indeed, whereas, in the immediate pre-war period, al- Sadr was at the peak of his popularity, by the end of the conflict his influence had waned considerably, ebbing to its lowest point (in his otherwise illustrious career), from which he was never fully to recover. Fadlallah, on the other hand – both despite and because of his ordeal in Nab'a and his scholarly literature – saw his influence and status rise significantly in the immediate wake of the civil war.

During his residence in Nab'a prior to the outbreak of the civil war, then, Sayyid Fadlallah operated in a cosmopolitan yet segmented mileu, characterised by Beirut's confessional diversity and political volatility – conditions that were perceived as conducive to spawning indigenous Islamist activity. Moreover, in organising themselves the Islamists, under Fadlallah's stewardship, capitalised on Lebanon's open and vibrant political culture. It is apparent, too, that despite his Islamist outlook and radical agenda, Fadlallah's approach was informed less by ideology or dogma than by an objective reading and practical response to the fluidity of the changing circumstances.

The massive dislocation that accompanied the fall of Nab'a, as devastating and tragic as it was for Fadlallah and his followers, proved a major, albeit temporary setback. As we have seen, he was to recover from the Nab'a disaster by resettling in the southern suburbs of Beirut, and rebuilding the various institutions he had earlier established in the now depopulated quarter. It was here, among the solidly Shi'i, mostly displaced and disaffected, inhabitants that Fadlallah set about creating a communal niche among the area's large, downtrodden proletariat; and it was here, among this reservoir of discontent, that his theology of liberation found deep resonance. Finally, despite the crucible of wartime Nab'a, Fadlallah's Islamist experience and credentials were to survive those trying times. His philosophy and programme of Islamist activism were to find fertile new ground among the radicalised and religious young generation of educated Shi'is, who in time were to transform much of the southern suburbs into a bastion of the Shi'i Islamist movement.

Yet, while Fadlallah's stature and clout were definitely growing, in sharp contrast to the experience of al-Sadr, it was the unfolding of a sequence of major developments during the following few years that would prove to be decisive in propelling him on to the path of pre-eminence, and catapulting the nascent Islamist movement towards ascendancy.

FIVE

The Rise of Sayyid Fadlallah and the Antecedents of Lebanon's Shi'i Islamism, 1977–1982

The period between late 1976 and mid-1982 – that is, from the end of the first phase of the Lebanese civil war (1975–76) to the eve of the second Israeli military invasion and occupation of Lebanon – saw a devastated and fragmented country whose central authority had all but collapsed, and whose national army had splintered along confessional fault-lines, begin the slow, tenuous road to recovery under Syrian overlordship. But Syria's military and political tutelage ensured that Lebanon, in its vital rebuilding and reconciliation process, would be economically, politically and militarily dependent on its powerful neighbour.

For the Shi'a, Lebanon's largest confessional community – underprivileged and, thanks to the populist, reformist leadership of Sayyid Musa al-Sadr, now politicised – this period witnessed momentous developments. Locally, these included Israel's first large-scale invasion, and subsequent occupation, of South Lebanon in March 1978; the disappearance of Sayyid al-Sadr in August 1978; and the resurgence of Amal and subsequent fall-out with the PLO and leftists. Regionally, the Islamic Revolution in Iran in January–February 1979 had profound ramifications for Lebanon's Shi'a (as well as for their coreligionists in other Arab countries). Regionally, the Iraqi Ba'thist regime's systematic suppression of the indigenous Shi'i Islamist movement between 1977 and

1980, culminating in the execution of its foremost Shi'i scholar-activist, Ayatollah Sayyid Baqir al-Sadr, and the outbreak of the Iran–Iraq war, had far-reaching repercussions for the Shi'i activists of the Amal movement and exiled affiliates of Hizb al-Da'wa. For Fadlallah, the events of these years, despite their varying importance, were constitutive factors in the turbulent milieu that would simultaneously propel and shape his crucial, low-key rebuilding process. It will be recalled from the previous chapter that in July 1976, at the height of the civil war, Fadlallah, along with his constituency, had been forcibly displaced from Beirut's beleaguered north-eastern quarter of Nab'a, and that he had found refuge among the powerful al-Bizzi clan (to which his mother belonged) in the southern town of Bint Jbail, before finally relocating to the capital's southern suburbs. In resettling in Beirut, not only did he manage to reconsolidate his position and enhance his influence – thanks to the resumption of a vigorous and extensive programme of teaching, lecturing and itinerant missionary work, the rebuilding and diffusion of his diverse network of communal institutions, and the reconstitution and expansion of his hitherto dispersed following; he was able to do so in a relatively short period, and in a highly volatile environment.

Fadlallah in Southern Beirut

In the summer of 1976, Fadlallah left the southern town of Bint Jbail, an area prone to Palestinian fedayeen operations and Israeli military incursions. His destination: al-Ghubayri, in Beirut's predominantly Shi'i southern suburbs.[1] In moving to this area, Fadlallah indicated that a return to his former residence was unfeasible – even dangerous. As described in the previous chapter, the right-wing Maronite Phalangists had in early July 1976 laid siege to Nab'a, before overrunning its defences and emptying it of nearly all of its approximately 100,000 Shi'i residents, who were supplanted by Maronite civilians from surrounding eastern suburbs.[2] By sharp contrast, al-Ghubairi, the most northern of Beirut's densely populated southern suburbs, with its preponderant Shi'i populace, provided Fadlallah with a sense of relative security, and with it a real incentive to restructure and enlarge his institutional and social networks.

Admittedly, Fadlallah did not need to rebuild completely the institutions he had abandoned in Nab'a, as these were relocated in the southern suburbs. As mentioned in the previous chapter, at the heart of this infrastructure were al-Ma'had al-Shar'i al-Islami (The Islamic Legal Institute, founded and headed by Fadlallah), and Usrat al-Ta'akhi (The Fraternal Society). Following its shift to Bi'ir al-Abd, in the southern suburbs, the society re-established its *husainiyya*, and opened a religious bookstore and a clinic. No sooner had Fadlallah taken up residence in Beirut's south than his religious students, teaching colleagues, seminary graduates and Islamist activists joined him.[3] Not surprisingly, the nuclei around which this body congregated were the Islamic Legal Institute (where Fadlallah gave advanced lessons on the principles and dynamics of Islamic Shi'i jurisprudence, and associated dialectics and modern *ijtihad)* and the Imam Rida mosque, where he led congregational prayers, delivered the Friday religious–political sermon, and established regular study circles. The functional significance of the institute and the mosque cannot be overemphasised, since they played a crucial part in Fadlallah's medium-term strategy of engendering a cohesive yet inclusive, vibrant Islamic microcosmic society.

Although Fadlallah's institution-building activities in this period were focused in the southern suburbs, they were not entirely restricted to Greater Beirut. He actively supported and periodically taught at Hawzat al-Imam al-Muntazar (a Shi'i religious-ideological seminary, established in 1978 in the eastern city of Baalbek).[4] Under the stewardship of Sayyid Musawi – a young Lebanese scholar-activist who had completed his education in Najaf, in Iraq, and would later serve as Secretary General of Hizbullah – the seminary became a focal point for activist students and young 'ulama, many of whom, like himself, had been forced to flee Iraq in the face of a crackdown launched in 1977 by the Ba'thist regime against dissidents and activists. Musawi was instrumental in motivating these exiled students to resume their studies, and to benefit from the erudition of both Fadlallah and Sayyid Musa al-Sadr.[5]

Later still, in late 1979, the seminary acquired fame as the headquarters of a contingent of Iranian Islamic Revolutionary Guards that had been dispatched to Lebanon by Ayatollah Khomeini, ostensibly to engage the Israeli army in the south. More immediately, their mission was to embark on the indoctrination of young members of the Shi'i community of Lebanon's Bekaa Valley, as well as providing them with irregular military training.[6] As we shall see, the Guards were instrumental in inculcating the religious fervour and ideological ardour that would, by 1982, drive radicalised Shi'i militants to launch an armed struggle – initially against the Israeli invading and occupying army, and subsequently, in 1983–84, against the foreign presence of the Multi- National Force.

Fadlallah did not confine his pursuits to teaching, organising and writing, but as a continuation of his work in the pre-civil-war period, included charitable and social welfare activities. Indeed, by 1978 – the year that saw the foundation of Jam'iyyat al-Mabarrat al-Khayriyyah (The Society for

Benevolent Charity) – Fadlallah's philanthropy coexisted with his well-known intellectual and political activities. Besides its affiliated mosque, the Society, thanks to its orphanage and boarding school, catered for the pressing needs of some of the most underprivileged and vulnerable segments of society – namely orphans, widows, the destitute and the physically disabled.[7] A number of intertwining factors contributed to the founding of the Society and its affiliate institutions. First, Fadlallah's childhood memories of financial hardship and deprivation, together with his personal experiences of living and mingling among the most underprivileged and impoverished residents – in Najaf and then in Nab'a – ensured that he would have a natural empathy and concern for those segments of society. Second, he had lived through the civil war in Beirut, and thus had experienced first-hand the indiscriminate loss of life, the wholesale destruction and looting of property, the maiming and wounding of civilians, and the deep psychological traumas this had caused. For Fadlallah it was the poor and underprivileged who suffered most, and as an ardent advocate of the social and political liberation of the impoverished and downtrodden, he felt obliged to ameliorate their plight.

Fadlallah's appointment in 1976 as the official *wakil* (personal representative) in Lebanon of Grand Ayatollah Sayyid Abu al-Qasim al-Kho'ie (his former mentor in Najaf) enabled that commitment to translate into reality. For, by virtue of that privileged office, Fadlallah was now afforded the authority of not only representing and disseminating the juridical opinions and rulings of the Shi'i world's pre-eminent living religious authority, but also of collecting and dispensing, in his name, substantial monetary donations (*sadaqat*) and prescribed religious dues (*al-khums* and *al-zakat*). The large charitable institution that he founded and formally directed served that end.

The year that saw the establishment of the charitable society also witnessed the formation of al-Ittihad al-Lubnani lil-Talibah al-Muslimeen (The Lebanese Federation of Muslim Students) – although Fadlallah did not hold any official role in relation to the latter organisation. Yet, from the time of its inception by graduates of the Arab University of Beirut, the figure of Fadlallah has loomed large over the organisation.[8] In a recent interview, he openly acknowledges the extent of that influence, affirming that from the outset he had 'encouraged and supported the setting up of the federation', with the object of countering the diffusion of secular ideas on academic campuses by promoting the Islamist paradigm.[9] The idea behind the creation of the federation seems to have originated from Fadlallah's own early experience in intellectual activism against the spread of secular ideologies, and of Communism in particular, in republican Iraq, which saw him play an informal, supporting role in the Najaf-based Jama'at al-Ulama (Society of Scholars) and a leading contributory role in the *al-Adwa'* magazine.

The Student Federation employed a variety of means to disseminate its ideas, ranging from the organisation of periodical conferences and seminars to weekly lecture series and regular discussion circles in the federation's own hall and reading room, in Beirut's southern suburb of al-Ghubayri.[10] Not surprisingly, Fadlallah was a regular and prominent speaker in those forums. The principal medium of propagation of its Islamist ideology to a general readership was the bi-monthly *al-Muntalaq* journal. Again, Fadlallah, through his series of intellectual articles on Islamic activism, was an indispensable contributor, raising the profile of the Federation's mouthpiece to a religiously educated Muslim audience. Indeed, by the early 1980s, owing to his sophisticated writings and lucid lectures, Fadlallah had earned recognition from secular academic institutions. Illustrative of this widening appeal were two lectures he gave as guest speaker in the Assembly Hall of the American University of Beirut, the bastion of secular higher learning in Lebanon.[11]

Fadlallah's gradual rise in stature and influence in the period following the end of the civil war contrasted with the definite waning of that of Sayyid al-Sadr. This was largely due to his role in relinquishing Nab'a to the Maronite Phalange militia in July 1976. Though al-Sadr never recovered his pre-war clout and prestige, he remained, until his mysterious disappearance in August 1978, the most important religious–political figure in the Shi'i community. Before considering the circumstances surrounding the sudden demise of al-Sadr, it is necessary to examine briefly the first large-scale Israeli invasion of Lebanon.

The 1978 Israeli Invasion and its Aftermath

The formal termination of the 1975–76 civil war brought a relative and tenuous calm to Beirut and its environs, Mount Lebanon, and the north – areas where fighting had been concentrated. By contrast, the region south of the port-city of Sidon had largely escaped the civil strife. However, with the cessation of conflict in the north, owing to the intervention of the Syrian army, fighting flared in South Lebanon, which lay outside the sphere of Syrian military control. Frequent and restricted armed clashes erupted between Palestinian guerrillas in alliance with leftist militiamen affiliated to the Lebanese National Movement (LNM), and Israel and its surrogate Christian rightist militias. This low-threshold conflict persisted throughout 1977 and early 1978, and was characterised by intermittent Palestinian cross-border raids and shelling of northern Israeli settlements, on the one hand, and Israeli ground incursions and aerial bombardment, on the other. Caught in the middle between the attacks and counter-attacks, between the overbearing presence of fedayeen bases and roving guerilla units affiliated to the PLO, on the one hand, and the indiscriminate punitive reprisals of the Israeli Defence Forces, on the other, were the hapless Shi'i villagers who comprised the bulk of the south's population.

On 11 March 1978, a Palestinian commando squad based in Lebanon mounted a surprise, sea-borne assault on the Haifa–Tel Aviv Highway. A commuter bus travelling on the route was intercepted and a number of passengers were slain.[12] Israel's response came three days later. Israel launched a full-scale invasion of South Lebanon, code-named 'Operation Litani'. Overwhelmed by the size and scope of the invasion, consisting of between 25,000 and 28,000 troops, and preceded by an intense bombing and artillery campaign, the several thousand Palestinian fedayeen effected a tactical withdrawal from forward positions. As a consequence the Israelis, in conjunction with their local proxy Christian militia, occupied (with the exception of the port of Tyre and its surrounds) the whole region south of the Litani River, which comprised 20 per cent of Lebanon's total area. Almost 100 villages were partially or totally destroyed, and close to 300,000 predominantly Shi'i residents were displaced.[13] Until May 1978, there was a constant, though limited, stream of displaced residents; but in the wake of the invasion and occupation, that restricted flow turned into an unprecedented exodus, as villages and towns in the region lost half of their inhabitants.[14] The dislocated Shi'i citizens fled northwards, settling primarily in the densely populated and depressed southern suburbs of Beirut.

A major consequence of the 1978 invasion was the alienation and polarisation between the Shi'i community – and in particular the Amal movement – and the PLO. The Shi'i villagers of the south resented the swift disengagement of the Palestinian guerrillas before the advancing Israeli army, whose invasion, it was perceived, they had provoked. These residents found themselves completely defenceless in the face of the Israeli juggernaut. Thus, abandoned by the PLO, the Shi'i residents now turned to the emerging Amal movement for protection. Those needs were met by the formation, under the supervision of Amal, of rudimentary village-based self-defence militias. Not unexpectedly, tension arose as pro-Amal villages barred the re-entry of PLO fighters in the wake of the withdrawal of Israeli troops.[15] As for Amal, which was marginalised during the civil war and whose influence was moribund in its wake, the net result of the exodus and the PLO disengagement was a reinvigorated movement, which saw its renewed strength exerted in the south, at the expense of the Lebanese left and the PLO.

Notwithstanding Fadlallah's uncompromising anti-Israeli and anti-Zionist rhetoric in his writings and lectures throughout the 1970s, scant information is available that would shed light on his public posture and activities during and in the immediate aftermath of the Israeli invasion.[16] As for the response of Sayyid al-Sadr, it came in an interview published on 24 March 1978 in an Arabic newspaper, in which he castigated the Arab states for their callous inaction in the face of 'blatant' Israeli aggression and abject apathy towards the plight of the citizens and Palestinian refugees of South Lebanon. This was followed by a tour of several Arab states with the aim of enlightening his hosts as to the gravity of the situation on the ground, and with the hope of spurring them into action.[17]

Sayyid al-Sadr's Disappearance and its Repercussions

Following visits to Saudi Arabia, Kuwait and Algeria, where he held talks with senior government officials on the current situation in South Lebanon and on national reconciliation, Sayyid al-Sadr travelled on 25 August 1978, with two aides, to Libya, apparently at the invitation of Colonel Muammar al-Qaddafi. Although the precise sequence of events that unfolded has not been established, it is known that some time after his scheduled meeting with the Libyan leader, all contacts with concerned Shi'i circles in Lebanon were broken. Ever since his disappearance, speculation has been rife as to al-Sadr's fate. According to one view, the Imam was kidnapped and is currently languishing in a secret location in the Libyan desert; according to another widely accepted view, he was murdered.[18] For their part, the Libyans have consistently denied any accusation of their involvement in the Imam's demise, claiming that he left Libya on a flight to Italy – a claim that, in its turn, has been strenuously denied by the Italian Government. Thus, the fate of Sayyid al-Sadr has never been satisfactorily resolved, as no trace of him has ever been found. In keeping with the Shi'i tradition of the Hidden Imam, the mystery surrounding the disappearance of their local charismatic Imam imbued al- Sadr with a supernatural and messianic dimension, instilling in the Shi'i community a belief in his continued existence, and in turn galvanising the community behind its leader, whose return is anxiously awaited.

More prosaically, the disappearance of al-Sadr had far-reaching ramifications for the future leadership of Lebanon's Shi'a. As the most influential spokesman and charismatic leader of the community at large, and the undisputed leader of both Amal and the Supreme Islamic Shi'i Council, his sudden demise created a religious and political vacuum, which rival Shi'i factions strove to fill. The disappearance of Sayyid al-Sadr accentuated the divergent tendencies within

Amal, and highlighted the underlying tension between Amal and the Shi'i Council. Henceforth, the two bodies would be headed by two separate leaders – the former by Shaykh Muhammad Mahdi Shams al-Din, a *mujtahid* and colleague of Fadlallah, but who as Vice-Chairman of the Council lacked the clout and charisma of his predecessor; and the latter by Hussein al-Husseini, a parliamentary deputy belonging to an eminent Shi'i family from the Bekaa valley.[19]

Rivalry for ascendancy among the two groups was heightened following the ascension to the leadership of Amal on 4 April 1980 of Nabih Berri. Under Berri, a professional lawyer and expatriate entrepreneur, Amal supplanted al-Sadr's Harakat Mahrumeen. Berri steered the organisation away from the orbit of the Supreme Islamic Council, and towards political and military assertiveness vis-à-vis the Palestinians and the LNM. Indeed, Amal's resurgence in the wake of the civil war was facilitated, among other things, by the decline of the leftist LNM (to which most Shi'i activists had previously been attracted), which was further weakened by the assassination in March 1977 of its premier spokesman, Kamal Jumblatt; by the alienation from the PLO of the Shi'i residents of South Lebanon; by the disappearance of al-Sadr; and last but not least, by the Islamic Revolution in Iran.[20] The impact of the Iranian Revolution will be assessed later. At this point, it is helpful to consider the correlation between the sudden demise of al-Sadr and the progressive rise of Fadlallah, in the context of the mutual relationship between al-Da'wa and Amal during the 1970s.

Fadlallah, Hizb al-Da'wa and Amal

There is no doubt that the disappearance of al-Sadr created a vacuum that facilitated the ascent of Fadlallah; had al-Sadr not disappeared, it would have been more difficult for Fadlallah to challenge the agenda of his colleague. The fact that the majority of Lebanon's Hizb al-Da'wa affiliates, whose numbers were bolstered during the course of the 1970s by comrades fleeing state repression in Iraq, looked to Fadlallah for religious–ideological guidance, raises the question of the nature of the relationship that existed between the Sayyid and the party.[21] Not unlike his links with Hizbullah, Fadlallah's association with al-Da'wa throughout the 1970s and early 1980s was, until the amalgamation of the two organisations in 1982, simultaneously informal and close. According to the Iraqi author of a monograph on Hizb al-Da'wa, Fadlallah had withdrawn from the party during the early 1980s.[22] This is a problematic claim, since there is no evidence to indicate that he is or ever was an organisational affiliate of al-Da'wa; his name does not appear among the list of activists who either founded or joined the Party. By contrast, there is no doubt that Fadlallah's late colleague, Sayyid Baqer al-Sadr, was one of the founding members of al-Da'wa. Fadlallah himself has consistently refuted assertions made by journalists of his having formal ties to al-Da'wa or any other organisation.[23] Despite the difficulty in understanding the exact nature of Fadlallah's relationship with both al-Da'wa and, later, Hizbullah, one can say definitively that he was and still is looked upon by affiliates of both Islamist groups as a leading – if not the pre-eminent – theoretician, guide and strategist of contemporary Shi'i Islamic activism. In this respect, al-Khurasani is correct in stating that Fadlallah's views and ideas found strong resonance among Hizb al-Da'wa's rank and file.[24]

As was noted in the previous chapter, there were marked differences in the respective approaches of Sayyids Musa al-Sadr and Fadlallah. In his quest for the gradual socio-economic advancement and for greater political and administrative representation of the Shi'i community, commensurate with its demographic weight, al-Sadr actively sought to mobilise a broad cross-section of his disenfranchised constituency. In contrast to this populist and loosely organised movement, Fadlallah pursued a strategy of rigorous religious–ideological indoctrination, with the careful nurturing of a select group of dedicated young cadres. Leadership of the Islamic movement was confined to this select coterie of 'enlightened' and committed Islamists. By comparison, the leadership of al-Sadr's mass-based Movement of the Deprived, with its diverse membership ranging from secular leftists to religious radicals, emerged from the ranks of prominent activists not necessarily affiliated to Islamist-oriented circles.[25]

What concerns us in this chapter, however, are the repercussions of these two contrasting strategies of social and political activism for the consequent relationship between Harakat al-Mahrumeen (after the civil war Harakat Amal), on the one hand, and Hizb al-Da'wa, on the other. Despite the common Shi'i identity of the two organisations' rank and file, Amal's heterogeneous membership, both in respect to religious identity and ideological outlook, contrasted with the pronounced Islamist orientation of al-Da'wa. This dissimilarity is further accentuated by the contrast between the ideological uniformity and organisational coherence of al-Da'wa, and the loose organisational structure, diverse membership and factional splits that characterised Amal.[26] As creations of al-Sadr, who was an advocate of confessional pluralism and political reformism, the Movement of the Deprived and its successor, Amal, strove for the socio-economic and political advancement of their Shi'i constituency within the constitutional – and institutional – parameters of the Lebanese state. As we have seen, al-Sadr was committed to the preservation of the diverse confessional make-up and political pluralism of Lebanon. Consequently, he was prepared to forge a working relationship with the dominant Maronite Christian community.

For the Lebanese branch of al-Da'wa, on the other hand, the Maronite domination of the country's state institutions over the numerically superior Muslim communities was unsustainable and unpalatable, as it was deemed to be contrary to the classical theory of Muslim governance.[27] In conformity with its Iraqi parent organisation, the Da'wa Party in Lebanon espoused a long-term revolutionary agenda, which sought a comprehensive transformation of society and politics through a strategy of discreet, non-violent subversion and gradual reform.

Aware of Harakat al-Mahrumeen's inherent 'deficiency' and vulnerability – a product of its amorphous structure and ideological vagueness – yet mindful of the wider appeal of al-Sadr among Lebanon's Shi'a, al-Da'wa strategists refrained from openly challenging the movement's continued existence, and from publicly undermining the legitimacy of al-Sadr's populist leadership and reformist agenda. Instead, al-Da'wa opted to discreetly infiltrate the Movement of the Deprived (and subsequently Amal) with senior party activists, some of whom would later become prominent figures in Hizbullah.[28]

Sources differ as to who was the architect of al-Da'wa's policy of infiltrating Amal. Fadlallah's exact role in the process is uncertain. In a recent interview, he dismissed out of hand suggestions that he was behind al-Da'wa's infiltration of Amal.[29] But one can speculate that it would have been inconceivable, in the light of the considerable influence he wields amongst the party's rank and file, for Fadlallah not to have been privy to such an important decision.[30] Working their way into influential positions in Amal, the infiltrated al-Da'wa operatives caught al-Sadr off-guard. Indeed, by the time the Imam became aware of this strategic move, al-Da'wa affiliates had consolidated their positions in the movement, compelling al-Sadr to accept these developments as a fait accompli. As a result, al-Sadr entered into a modus vivendi with al-Da'wa affiliates, whereby the former would concentrate on political and paramilitary activities while the latter would focus on Islamist cadre indoctrination and public religious–ideological dissemination.[31]

In this way, al-Da'wa succeeded in diffusing its influence gradually within Amal – a process that accelerated following the disappearance of al-Sadr and the election of Shaykh Shams al-Din as president of the Higher Islamic Shi'i Council.[32] The Islamic Revolution in Iran, and the resulting crackdown on Shi'i Islamic activists by the ruling Ba'th Party in Iraq, further strengthened the clout of the Islamist circle within Amal, invigorating the campaign of radical Islamisation. The two organisations began to work closely towards common objectives, principally relating to Iraqi targets in Beirut. Following the execution of Sayyid Baqer al-Sadr in April 1980, the Lebanese branch of al-Daʿwa was dissolved (apparently at the behest of the Iranian Revolutionary leadership). As a result, many erstwhile party affiliates followed their comrades in joining Amal, all the while maintaining their distinct ideological character and collective identity.[33]

The Iranian Revolution and its Impact on Lebanon's Shiʿa

'Then came the earthquake.'[34] This was Fadlallah's graphic description of the revolutionary upheaval in Iran that culminated, with the flight of Shah Muhammad Reza on 16 January 1979, in the fall of the Pahlavi dynasty and of the monarchy; the return of Imam Khomeini from exile in Paris to Iran on 1 February 1979; and, finally, following a referendum on 26 March 1979, the ushering in of an Islamic republic. The mass euphoria that greeted the Imam upon his arrival in Iran resonated far beyond the country's borders, precipitating a similar outpouring of emotion by Shiʿi communities throughout the Muslim world. The large Shiʿi community of Lebanon was one of the most profoundly affected by events in Iran. The defiance of a revered elderly Ayatollah; his prolonged Islamic struggle against the Shah and his increasingly repressive regime; and finally his triumph as leader of a popular Islamic and nationalist oppositional movement representing a broad cross-section of Iranian society against one of the most formidable states in the Middle East – these events captivated and energised Lebanon's Shiʿi activists and young religious scholars. Nearly all Shiʿa, and indeed many Sunnis, took pride in the extraordinary achievements of the Imam and his supporters, and many young activists began to fervently advocate the emulation of the revolutionary experience of their coreligionists in Iran.[35]

While the revolutionary ferment emanating from Iran inspired many of the disaffected and underprivileged Shiʿis of Lebanon with a sense of identity and power, the implications for Amal were mixed. On the one hand, revolutionary Iran was perceived by the movement as a whole as an invaluable asset – a dynamic and potent Shiʿi ally in the region; on the other hand, it substantially widened the rift between activists affiliated to Amal. With the Islamic Revolution, the evolving divergence in the movement headed by Nabih Berri between Islamist radicals and nationalist secular reformers deepened, with growth in the ranks and a surge in the assertiveness of Islamist activists and ardent supporters of revolutionary Iran. Although, in the early days of the Revolution, Amal was permitted to open a political office in Teheran, relations soon became cool. A number of related factors contributed to this state of affairs. The forging of relations between Iran and Libya following Iraq's invasion of Iran dismayed Lebanon's Shi'a, since it occurred despite the disappearance of their Imam, Sayyid Musa al-Sadr, in Libya. Disquiet was also caused by what was perceived to be the systematic purging of the movement's allies from key positions in Iranian state institutions – namely Mustapha Chamran (a key organisational and paramilitary leader of Amal), Sadeq Qotbzadeh and Ibrahim Yazdi – and by the ascension of Nabih Berri, a secular reformist, to the head of Amal in April 1980.[36] But arguably the most important of these concerns relates to the nascent Islamic Republic's foreign policy on Israel and the Palestinian armed struggle in South Lebanon.

The pursuit of an Islamic crusade against Israel – a persistent theme in Khomeini's early revolutionary discourse on imperialism and Zionism – was an integral element of his radical Islamic world-view and self-proclaimed mission in the region. Central to this policy was the Iranian strategy of bolstering Palestinian resistance, and indeed expanding the scope of the low-intensity irregular armed struggle against the Jewish state by launching a multinational jihad, spearheaded by the Islamic Republic's Revolutionary Guards in concert with local Shi'i paramilitary auxiliaries. That such a prodigious struggle would be launched from South Lebanon, and would consequently be in direct conflict with the interests of the Amal movement and the long-suffering local Shi'i populace, mattered little in Iran's grand scheme. Towards this grandiose end, the Islamic Republic severed economic, diplomatic and military ties with Israel, and handed its embassy in Teheran to the PLO.[37] This was followed by the announcement by the revolutionary regime of its plan to raise a standing army of 20 million volunteers to liberate Palestine.[38] As a first step, the Islamic Republic mobilised a force of 10,000 Revolutionary Guard 'volunteers' to fight Israel. The first contingents, comprising between 500 and 1,000 personnel, were despatched to eastern Lebanon. Their mission: to buttress the PLO, indoctrinate local Shi'i residents and supervise the military training of young activists.[39]

Almost simultaneously with the dispatch of the expeditionary force, Imam Khomeini proclaimed on 9 December 1979 the inauguration of International Quds Day. The annual event is celebrated by mass street processions, both in Iran and in mainly Shi'i-populated parts of Lebanon, in which Israel and globally domineering powers (*al-Istikbar al-'Alami* – the preferred Islamist term for imperialism) are denounced, and the commitment to the liberation of Palestine is reaffirmed. By invoking the emotive cause of 'occupied Palestine', Iran and its supporters among the activist 'ulama in Lebanon (Fadlallah included) sought to heighten the level of public awareness of the central importance of Palestine. By branding the issue of Palestine into the popular psyche, it was hoped that there would emerge among Lebanon's Shi'i a mass movement that would strive for the recovery of the Holy Land.[40]

If the long-term goal of Iran, through International Quds Day, was to buttress the ties between Lebanon's Shi'i community and the Palestinian resistance, it was in the short term undermined by the simmering tensions between Amal and the PLO. As we have seen, in the wake of the 1978 Israeli invasion of South Lebanon, Amal had opposed any move by armed Palestinian groups to re-establish their vacated or demolished military strongholds, in or near to villages – far from intensifying their guerrilla war with Israel, which would have invited massive retaliation from the Jewish state, with civilians, as always, bearing the brunt of such escalation in the conflict. It was in the context of these mounting tensions and irreconcilable interests that, in February–March 1980 (only two months after the inauguration of Quds Day and the arrival of Iranian Revolutionary Guards in Lebanon), fierce battles in Beirut and South Lebanon erupted between Amal and Fatah, as a result of a power vacuum created by the redeployment of Syrian troops in Beirut.[41]

To Islamists like Fadlallah, who had consistently preached the need for Sunni–Shi'i unity and for Lebanese solidarity with the Palestinian resistance against Israel, the frequent clashes between Amal and the PLO must have been disconcerting indeed. The internecine conflict not only ran counter to all that Fadlallah stood for, but its persistence threatened to undermine Iran's promising ecumenical and revolutionary agenda for Lebanon; an Iran that encapsulated the long-held Islamist values and aspirations of Sayyid Fadlallah. In March 1980 and July 1981, Fadlallah gave two lectures on the necessity of maintaining resistance to Israel. In the first of these, he underscored the importance of patriotism and self-reliance as pre-requisites for the liberation of South Lebanon. In an undated Friday sermon from that period, Fadlallah not only lamented the continuing Muslim (Amal–Palestinian) infighting that was being abetted by neo-imperial powers, but expressed dismay at how grave the situation had become. An increasing number of Shi'i Muslims were of the view that the Palestinians (through their armed struggle), rather than Israel, were at the root of the problem of the south, and were thus the chief source of misery for its inhabitants.[42]

Revolutionary Iran and Fadlallah's Islamism

From a cursory look at his speeches, lectures and writings, it is clear that Sayyid Fadlallah was from the outset a fervent supporter of the Islamic Revolution, and subsequently of the Islamic Republic, as well as an avid admirer of Khomeini. In outlining the radical Islamic paradigm expounded by Khomeini and assessing its implications for Fadlallah, two points ought to be considered: the first relates to Fadlallah's writings and speeches before the 1979 Revolution, and the second to the apolitical stance of Sayyid Abul Qasem al-Kho'ie (Fadlallah's former mentor, and a supreme Shi'i religious–juridical authority) and its implications for his representative in Lebanon.

In his now renowned Najaf juridical lectures of 1969–70, Khomeini expounded on the revolutionary theory of the General Governance of the Jurist (*Wilayat al-Faqih al-'Ammah*). The concept of clerical rulership was based on a radical reinterpretation of the classical Shi'i theory which had traditionally invested Shi'i jurists with the authority of settling legal disputes, collecting religious taxes, implementing statutory penalties (*al- hudud*) and administering the finances of minors and the intellectually impaired. In Khomeini's model, senior 'ulama and *fuqaha'* (scholars and jurists) were now invested with much wider powers, including the conduct of Friday congregational prayer, the undertaking of jihad, overseeing the process of individual rectitude and social conformity, and, most importantly, responsibility for government. This augmented jurisdiction, approximating the near-absolute authority of the infallible Imam or his deputy, was deemed necessary if the 'ulama were to become the vanguard of mass mobilisation and the harbingers of radical change in the social and political spheres. Khomeini justified the contention that only a government headed by senior jurists – 'the trustees of the prophets' – was legitimate on the grounds that in an Islamic regime governance is based solely on the shari'ah, and that therefore only Muslim jurists possess the necessary competence and integrity to supervise government and state affairs.[43]

It is not surprising that Fadlallah had since 1979 espoused the revolutionary theory of *Wilayat al-Faqih*, given that he had for two decades been a staunch proponent of the Islamist *weltanschauung*, despite the fact that Khomeini's theory of *Wilayat al-Faqih* had not been unanimously accepted by Shi'i jurisconsults in Iran, Iraq and Lebanon.[44] In Iraq, the most eminent Shi'i luminary who did not subscribe to Khomeini's theory was Grand Ayatollah Sayyid al-Kho'ie, who succeeded Grand Ayatollah Sayyid Muhsin al-Hakim in 1970 as the Shi'i world's pre-eminent *marja'*. According to Fadlallah, who had studied under al-Kho'ie and now represented him as *wakil al-shar'i* in Lebanon, his former mentor upheld the traditional, restricted view of the institution, and thus did not regard the establishment of an Islamic state in the absence of the Imam al-Mahdi as falling within the purview of the duties of the religious jurist.[45] Despite his capacity as the official representative of al-Kho'ie, and despite the latter's overtly quietist and generally apolitical leadership, Fadlallah had no hesitation – as a committed political activist and a *mujtahid* in his own right – in espousing the radical theory of *Wilayat al-Faqih*, and recognising Khomeini's revolutionary leadership. For Fadlallah, this parallel relationship did not necessarily pose a contradiction in allegiance, for each represented separate spheres of supreme authority: Sayyid al-Kho'ie in religious–juridical matters, Imam Khomeini in political leadership and organisation.

In his influential 1976 monograph, *al-Islam wa Muntiq al-Quwwa* (Islam and the Logic of Power), Fadlallah defined Islam as both 'religion and state' (*din wa dawlah*), and upheld Islam as a complete and comprehensive mode of existence regulating the temporal and spiritual dimensions, and the private and public spheres of life.[46] Yet, unquestionably, this conceptualisation of Islam as an holistic, comprehensive and unique paradigm is not unique to Fadlallah; it was coined by pioneering Sunni Islamists during the 1930s and 1940s – namely Sayyid Abu al-'Ala' al-Mawdudi (1903–79) and Hasan al-Banna (1906–49), crystallising in the 1950s into systematic theory in the writings of Sayyid Qutb (1906–65) and Taqi al-Din al-Nabahani (1909–77). Fadlallah, along with Sayyid Muhammad Baqer al-Sadr, and to a lesser extent Shaykh Muhammad Mahdi Shams al-Din, was among the first Shi'i 'ulama, under the influence of these figures, to propound Islam as an all-embracing political and ideological programme.

While, owing to the precedence given to individual and societal reform during this period, he did not set forth the specific character and functions of the modern Islamic state as expounded by Khomeini, Fadlallah was favourably disposed towards the concept of *Wilayat al-Faqih*. As scholar-activists, both men reinterpreted the functional meaning of distinctive quietist elements of Shi'ism – namely the traditional socio-religious practice of *taqiyya* (the recourse to dissimulation while under duress) and the axiomatic doctrine of *intizar* (waiting for the return of al-Mahdi, the Twelfth Shi'i Imam believed to be in indefinite occultation since 874 AH).

Detailed discussion of the political implications of this revisionist interpretation is outside the scope of this chapter. But in deeming the use of *taqiyya* to have encouraged prolonged acquiescence, Fadlallah (like Khomeini and Ali Shari'ati) regarded it as an exceptional rather than a normal requirement of the faith. Similarly, the belief in the Hidden Imam – the supreme and only legitimate religious–political leader of the Shi'i community – has traditionally justified the rejection, until his return, of all temporal Muslim authority, and with it of involvement in the establishment of an Islamic state. Again, rejecting the traditional Shi'i aversion to engagement in political affairs (with its concomitant metaphysical resignation) Fadlallah and Khomeini alike argued forcefully that messianic anticipation need not necessarily imply passivity, nor preclude Islamist political activism as an important precursor to the reappearance of the Rightly Guided Imam and the eventual establishment of global Islamic sovereignty. That the waiting period is indefinite makes it all the more imperative to meet the vital interests and immediate needs of society by establishing a 'genuine' Islamic state that would be able, through its institutions, to establish order and ensure social and economic progress, as well as dispense justice among its citizenry through the wholesale implementation of the shari'ah.[47]

In an important lecture delivered in 1978, and most probably influenced by the backdrop of the intensifying civil unrest in Iran, Fadlallah posed a key question: 'Does Islam have a tendency towards revolution or reform, and which of these do we select?' His answer: Islam sanctions *both* gradual segmented reform and comprehensive radical change.[48] As to which of these activists should pursue, Fadlallah is ambivalent yet pragmatic, saying that the pursuit of either course is ultimately predicated on the questions of practicability and likely consequences, necessitating a close examination of specific circumstances.[49] On the other hand, he shows his preference by espousing a distinctively syncretic, complementary approach, whereby both strategies – reform and revolution – might, as desirable or necessary, be pursued simultaneously or sequentially.[50]

The exercise of correlating the two paths reflected a conscious attempt to take into account the momentous developments unfolding in Iran – that is, the juxtaposition of peaceful methodical reform of the individual and society adopted by *al-Ikhwan al-Muslimeen* and Hizb al-Da'wa with the mass revolutionary upheaval against the state pursued by Khomeini. Realising that the process of comprehensive change may not always be fulfilled through revolution, due to institutional and international constraints, Fadlallah deemed it necessary to embark on a course of reform that would pass through sequential phases. He rejected the argument that by focusing on the reform of the individual, the more vital goal of transforming the political realm is undermined or deferred into the remote future.[51] In this respect, Fadlallah's thinking differed from Sayyid Musa al-Sadr's strategy of confessional mass politics, as well as from revolutionary movements like Fedayeen e-Islam (the defunct Iranian Shi'i Islamist organisation of the 1940s and 1950s), Jordan's Hizb al- Tahrir al-Islami, and Egypt's Munazammat al-Jihad, which strove to effect radical change by toppling the system of government.

That Fadlallah was among the earliest and most eminent Lebanese supporters of the Islamic Revolution is clear from his speeches, writings and activities. Along with his colleague Shaykh Shams al-Din, he featured prominently in consecutive anniversaries of the Islamic Revolution.[52] In 1980, he made his first visit to revolutionary Iran, and until the mid-1990s he was a regular visitor to the Islamic Republic, meeting and forging close ties with Khomeini and his successor Ayatollah Khamanei, as well as with Hujjtul-Islam Rafsanjani.[53]

Before 1982, Fadlallah had written three articles on the Revolution.[54] His first two, both appearing in the intellectual–activist journal *al-Muntalaq*, are important for the insight they provide into his interpretation of the Revolution. While clearly sympathetic, Fadlallah registered some concerns and hopes in his close observation of the tumultuous events that unfolded during its first anniversary. Firstly, he praised the Islamic Revolution as the embodiment of the aspirations of Islamic activists at the time, and he lauded Khomeini for his command of it – and for his rejection of the western democratic model, on the grounds that it was incompatible with the Islamic doctrine of divine sovereignty in general, and with *Wilayat al-Faqih* in particular. Second, he expressed his concern, in the light of the contending ideological and political forces striving for supremacy – from liberal democrats, secular nationalists, communists and militant leftists, to religious conservatives and radical Islamists – at the lack of solidarity between the latter two groups, as well as on the questions of ideological coherence and policy direction. Third, he identified the emerging dichotomy between those Islamists propounding 'revolution in one country' and those advocating the 'export' of the Revolution abroad. It is instructive that he took an unambiguous stance in the debate. Localising the Revolution for the sake of consolidation, he argued, would inevitably compromise its original global mission and undermine its dynamism, since both its mission and character would be reshaped by geopolitical and national factors.[55] In other words, such a course would subordinate the Islamist ideology of the Revolution to the interests and national character of Iran.

For Sayyid Fadlallah, like other Islamists like al-Banna, Qutb, al-Nabahani and al-Qaradawi, Islamic missionary work would not cease with the establishment of the Islamic state; on the contrary, the Islamic state would in turn become a potent vehicle for the Islamisation of neighbouring countries. Fadlallah gave no indication here – or indeed in any other article written during the early years of the Revolution – whether the project of political Islamisation should include Lebanon. A plausible explanation for this omission is that until 1985 the Islamist movement's political discourse and social composition were still evolving. The position of Shaykh Shams al-Din, by contrast, was unmistakable. While declaring his support for the establishment of Islamic regimes in Muslim-majority states like Iran, he did not deem the Iranian model to be suitable for a multi-confessional country like Lebanon. On the process of Islamic dissemination, Fadlallah made the unequivocal point that it is an incumbent duty on the individual, as much as it is on the state and society more broadly, stressing that the global mission of the Revolution is necessarily gradual, requiring the marshalling of all indigenous 'intellectual, political, social and military forces'.[56]

Holding the Islamic Revolution to be an authentic and comprehensive alternative to the 'godless' institutions and ideologies of modernity, Fadlallah concluded by expressing his desire to see the Revolution succeed along the path of its original mission, while simultaneously exhorting his brethren to do their utmost to ensure that the Islamic Republic would remain a catalyst for Islamic resurgence throughout the world – a driving force for Islamic liberation movements fighting to shrug off the 'yoke of infidel imperialism'. Finally, in an effort to foil what he described as the concerted and sinister attempts of the counter-revolutionary and anti-Islamic imperialists to undermine the Revolution and its global mission, Fadlallah made an impassioned plea to Islamic activists outside Iran to put aside whatever theoretical or confessional disagreements they might have with the revolutionary leadership, and embrace the Islamic Revolution.[57]

Some seven months later, Fadlallah followed with another article on the Revolution, in which he gave an analytical interpretation of the events surrounding the seizure, on 4 November 1979, of the United States embassy in Teheran. Proceeding from where he had left off in the previous piece, Fadlallah underscored the mutual hostility existing between the United States and the Islamic Republic, on account of their diametrically opposed interests and world-views. Proceeding from the widely-held view that a potent and ambitious Revolutionary Iran posed a serious threat to the vital regional and international interests of Western powers – particularly those of the United States – he wrote that a concerted and wide-ranging campaign had been mounted to destabilise the regime in Iran.[58]

Against this background, Fadlallah presented a revealing account of the seizure of the American embassy by Iranian revolutionary students on 4 November 1979, and the hostage-taking of its personnel. Refuting the suggestion that the series of events that culminated in the takeover of the embassy had unfolded spontaneously, through the independent enterprise of a group of anti-American students, Fadlallah was inclined to believe that the students' actions were pre-planned and discreetly orchestrated by senior 'ulama circles in government, with a view to consolidating the independence of the Revolution. Morover, despite (or perhaps because of) the ensuing ostracising of Iran in the Arab and Western worlds, and the imposition of sanctions by the United States and its allies, Fadlallah came out in support of the government's handling of the crisis. Contrary to what the critics of the hostage-taking incident believed, Fadlallah maintained, controversially, that the whole episode did not severely blemish the image of the Revolution or undermine its interests in the Muslim world. On the contrary, far from succumbing to mounting international pressure, the regime remained defiant and steadfast. For Fadlallah, the failure of the secret American rescue mission on 24 April 1980 only served to vindicate that defiance and justify a continued confrontational posture against the United States.[59]

In Sayyid Fadlallah's analysis, the upshot of the whole hostage drama and ensuing confrontation was clear. Iran had demonstrated to Muslim and Third World countries that it was possible to free their nations from the 'shackles' of foreign domination and economic exploitation, and that it was possible to shake the image of American invincibility. Moreover, Iran's defiantly independent foreign policy stance, encapsulated in the slogan 'Neither East nor West, but Islamic Republic', was seen by many Islamists as a viable alternative to the prevailing geopolitical order. For Fadlallah, the Iranian experience helped to dispel the popular perception of indigenous inferiority in relation to Western supremacy. Interestingly, in Fadlallah's eyes, the overriding significance of the Islamic regime in Iran did not lie in the imposition of a shari'ah-based penal code for a whole spectrum of legal offences, but rather in bringing about – as developed by Frantz Fanon in his theories of psychological oppression and liberation – 'the deliverance of the human will from a state of submission to iniquitous, aggressive, or infidel power, and the transformation of that liberated will-power into a practical, positive program dictated by a comprehensive reading of the Islamic shari'ah, in its economic, political and social dimensions'.[60] The Islamic Revolution, in Fadlallah's Fanonist analysis, provided the dynamism necessary for the awakening and rebellion of the hitherto subjugated collective indigenous spirit against its conditions of resignation, enfeeblement and subservience.

To the extent that Fadlallah is a staunch supporter of the Islamic Republic of Iran, he is a vehement opponent of the Ba'thist regime in Iraq, which, at the time of the publication of his article, had all but suppressed its largely Shi'i Islamist oppositional movement, and was on the point of invading its hostile neighbour.

Ba'thist Iraq's Repression of Shi'i Islamists and the Demise of Sayyid Baqer al-Sadr

A detailed account of the Iraqi regime's crackdown on its Islamist dissidents is beyond the scope of this chapter. What follows is an outline of the major phases in the history of that campaign, and a brief examination of its repercussions for Lebanon. The regime's clampdown on Shi'i political activism began soon after the ascension of the Ba'th Party to power in 1968, particularly following the death in 1970 of the Shi'i world's foremost *marja'* and patron of the Shi'i Islamist movement, Grand Ayatollah Sayyid Muhsin al- Hakim.[61] In 1972, the regime's security forces detained the Islamist movement's foremost theoretician and scholar, Sayyid Baqer al-Sadr. However, al-Sadr's deteriorating health, coupled with mass protests against the detention, forced his early release. Two years later, he was again arrested and detained briefly. This action was part of a major government crackdown on the Shi'i Islamist opposition, in which apparently hundreds of activists were rounded up, and five senior members of Hizb al-Da'wa were executed.[62]

As a direct result of the intensifying repression, Sayyid al-Sadr decreed that it was henceforth forbidden for his religious students and junior *'ulama* followers to be affiliated to Hizb al-Da'wa.[63] The decision, which sparked immediate controversy within activist circles, was calculated to stave off the decimation of Hizb al-Da'wa, and to ensure the survival of the religious seminaries.[64] In 1977, violent clashes occurred between state security forces and Shi'i mourners, following an attempt by the latter to block the path of traditional mass procession, which had started in Najaf and reached the outskirts of Karbala. Scores of Shi'i devotees were arrested, as was Sayyid al-Sadr, who was interrogated and pressured to express his support for the regime and its policies, but apparently refused to cooperate.[65]

The Iranian Revolution of January–February 1979 inspired and energised Shi'i Islamists in Iraq, just as it invigorated their coreligionists in Lebanon. It also emboldened Sayyid al-Sadr, who hastened to pledge his allegiance to Khomeini.[66] Due to al-Sadr's stature, the Iranian media reciprocated by referring to him as the leader of the Iraqi oppositional Shi'i movement; a move that, as far as the Iraqi regime was concerned, highlighted the potential threat posed by the cleric to state authority over its Shi'i citizens – thus prompting his rearrest in June 1979. Several months following his release, al-Sadr, now under house arrest, confronted the regime head on: he issued a fatwa declaring membership of the Ba'th Party to be fundamentally at odds with the tenets of Islam. This precipitated a new phase of repression, marked by the arrest and execution of hundreds of Shi'i activists and the beginning of armed Islamist militancy. Since the mid-1970s, hundreds of al-Da'wa affiliates and sympathisers had sought refuge in Lebanon. While there, many fugitives prepared for the escalating armed confrontation with the regime by undergoing military training, initially in Palestinian camps run by Fatah, and then in bases belonging to Amal. al-Sadr responded by issuing a fatwa obliging Muslims to wage jihad against the regime.[67]

The decisive turning point in the struggle between the Iraqi regime and the Islamist Shi'i opposition headed by Sayyid al-Sadr came on 1 April 1980, when an abortive attempt was made on the life of a senior government minister, Tariq Aziz. Although the attack was mounted by Munazzamat al-'Amal al-Islami (The Islamic Action Organisation, founded in the 1960s by Sayyid Hasan al-Shirazi), rather than Hizb al-Da'wa (which looked to al-Sadr for guidance), the incident gave the regime the pretext to eliminate al-Sadr, delivering a body-blow to the Islamist movement. Second, the regime embarked on widespread executions of Islamist detainees and mass deportations of Shi'i activists. In the third and final phase, on 5 April 1980 the security forces apprehended al-Sadr, who was taken to Baghdad. Despite clamorous appeals for clemency from intellectual and religious circles within Iraq, and from other countries in the region, al-Sadr and his sister Bint al-Huda (a leading Islamic activist) were executed on the 8 April.[68]

With the execution of Sayyid al-Sadr, Shi'i scholarly circles lost one of their most outstanding minds and figures of religious jurisprudence. The Shi'i Islamist movement, it lost its foremost ideologist and strategist. His untimely demise deprived the Iraqi Islamist opposition of its one unifying figure. With his execution, the party he founded and guided was decimated, its underground cellular network uncovered and eliminated. For Sayyid Fadlallah, the execution of al-Sadr was particularly distressing, as he lost a close friend and colleague; as young, aspiring religious scholars they had studied together, shared the same Islamist vision, and collaborated in the 1950s and 1960s on nurturing and guiding the Shi'i Islamist movement in Iraq. In memory of al-Sadr, Fadlallah wrote several articles reflecting on his legacy, and composed poems eulogising his late colleague.[69] Finally, with the demise of al-Sadr, Fadlallah became the most important intellectual guide for al-Da'wa affiliates in Lebanon.

The Repercussions on Lebanon's Shi'a of al-Sadr's Execution and the Iran–Iraq War

As news of the detention and execution of Sayyid Baqer al-Sadr resonated throughout Lebanon, its large Shi'i community became galvanised in its condemnation of Iraq's Ba'thist regime. The Shi'i residents of Beirut's southern suburbs manifested their indignation over the killing by staging large-scale street demonstrations and a mass strike, affecting businesses, schools and public buildings. The strike soon spread to west Beirut, the Bekaa Valley and the south. On the same day a bomb, apparently planted by pro-Iraqi activists, destroyed an Iranian Airlines Office in Beirut.[70] The following day saw the outbreak of fierce street fighting between Amal and pro-Iraqi Ba'thists. This last incident marked the beginning of a proxy war that pitted pro-Iranian Amal and al-Da'wa against pro-Iraqi Lebanese Ba'thists, the Palestinain Arab Liberation Front, and Lebanese communists.[71] The tit-for-tat cycle of militia violence – set to escalate following the Iraqi invasion of Iran in September 1980 – was characterised by wave and counter-wave of bombings, abductions, assassinations, and street clashes.

The full-scale Iraqi invasion of Iran in September triggered a regional conflagration that polarised not only the Arab countries of the Middle East and North Africa – with Syria and Libya siding with Iran and the Gulf states, Jordan and Egypt backing Iraq – but also sharpened the polarisation between contending political and paramilitary organisations in Lebanon. The tension, stemming from conflicting worldviews and interests, which had undermined relations between Iran's Islamic regime and the Amal Movement, had eased considerably following the execution of Sayyid al-Sadr and the Iraqi invasion. At the same time, relations with the PLO, which were beginning to cool due to the organisation's unilateral initiative in mediating in the American Embassy crisis in Teheran, had become strained by September. By the spring of 1981, those relations became hostile as the PLO abandoned its neutrality and aligned with Iraq.[72] As a direct consequence of this realignment, not only was the 'proxy war' in Lebanon intensified, but was expanded to include a new player in the equation: the PLO, which now sided with its ALF faction against Amal. It will be recalled that Amal and the PLO had been at loggerheads since 1978, engaging in intermittent fighting that became more frequent and intense during the course of 1981 and 1982.[73]

In November 1980, an attempt was made to assassinate Sayyid Fadlallah, who was driving his car through Ghubayri, in Beirut's southern suburbs, when it was fired on by gunmen who apparently failed to hit the vehicle, with

Fadlallah escaping unharmed.[74] In the Friday sermon given that week, he told the faithful of his unrelenting resolve to pursue his Islamist, activist agenda. Nevertheless, a small group of full-time bodyguards and part-time volunteers would henceforth accompany him wherever he went. This was the first of several attempts on his life during the early 1980s. Fadlallah states that three or four more assassination attempts took place between 1980 and 1982.[75] On the second occasion an attempt was made to storm his apartment. It was foiled by his bodyguards, one of whom was killed in the ensuing firefight. The third attempt involved the aiming of a rocket at his bedroom. It missed, instead striking an apartment on a lower floor.

The repeated attacks on Fadlallah highlighted the vulnerability of his residence in al-Ghubayri, in the vicinity of the armed Palestinian camps of Sabra and Shatila. Hence his decision to relocate to the more secure Islamist, and later Hizbullah, stronghold of B'ir al-'Abd, in the heart of Beirut's southern suburbs. The fact that he was among the most strident Islamist opponents of Iraq's ruling Ba'th Party, as well as wielding considerable influence among the cadres and leaders of Hizb al-Da'wa, the premier Iraqi Islamist opposition organisation, naturally made him a prominent target for Iraqi secret agents or pro-Iraqi Ba'thists in Lebanon. As early as November 1979, the Iraqi authorities imposed a ban on the publication and circulation of his influential books on Islamic activism.[76]

But he was not the only Shi'i scholar-activist to be marked for elimination, since there were other dissident Shi'i 'ulama at the forefront of the struggle against the Iraqi Ba'th regime and its supporters in Lebanon. Indeed, from the pattern of successful and abortive assassination attempts on a number of dissident Shi'i 'ulama, there is reason to believe that the incidents were part of a concerted campaign to eradicate their considerable influence on the Iraqi Islamist oppositional movement operating from abroad. In late 1979, Shaykh Ali Kaurani was shot and critically wounded.[77] On 3 May 1980, unidentified gunmen assassinated Sayyid Hasan al-Shirazi, another colleague of Fadlallah.[78] Ten days later, an attempt was made on the life of Shaykh Muhammad Farhat, General Director of the Higher Islamic Shi'i Council.[79]

The Lebanese branch al-Da'wa responded to the Iraqi Ba'thist campaign against the 'ulama by launching major attacks against Iraqi personnel and interests in Lebanon. In late 1981, following the assassination of a senior al-Da'wa activist in the United Arab Emirates, party operatives retaliated by striking down the chief of the Lebanese branch of the Ba'th Party. On 15 December 1981, a multi-storey building that housed the Iraqi Embassy in West Beirut was completely destroyed, resulting in the deaths of sixty-one employees, including the Iraqi Ambassador to Lebanon.[80] More significant than the fact that Hizb al-Da'wa claimed responsibility for the crime was the unprecedented nature of the operation: a vehicle laden with high explosives was driven suicidally into the embassy building. Two years later, this tactic was employed by Islamic Jihad, with even deadlier results, against the Multi-National Force stationed in Beirut.

Yet while al-Da'wa, at times in concert with Amal, was gradually reducing the influence of the Lebanese Ba'thists in West Beirut, Amal was locked in fierce battles with Lebanese Communist groups for control of the streets of Beirut's southern suburbs, in Fadlallah's 'backyard'. On 21 August 1981, Fadlallah's al-Imam Rida mosque in Bi'ir al-'Abd was damaged by shelling, apparently by Lebanese Communist Party militiamen. Denouncing the indiscriminate shelling and bitter in-fighting between Amal and the leftists, and between Amal and Palestinian factions, an angry Fadlallah declared that the real conflict ought to be exercised through intellectual debate, and that military operations ought to be directed against the 'Zionist enemy'.[81]

Since the early 1960s, Fadlallah has preached the message of ecumenical unity and political solidarity; the former between Sunnis and Shi'a, and the latter between Islamists and Arab nationalists. To the extent that Fadlallah's message of unity denoted broad concord, amicability and cooperation, rather than genuine fusion or coalescence, it did have the desired impact on Islamists and religious scholars of both denominations. Yet, despite the fact that Fadlallah dealt with the issues of unity and division in his lectures and sermons with greater frequency and urgency, this exhortation to close ranks found little resonance among the combatants of Amal and the PLO, or of the loose alliance of nationalist and leftist organisations, who fought each other with increasing ferocity. Nor did he have much success during these years in bringing about a discernible shift in primordial antipathies and deep-seated suspicions that have shaped the separate denominational identities of ordinary Sunnis and Shi'a. In any event, by June 1982 the 'Zionist nemesis', against which Fadlallah was endeavouring to unite and channel the energies of the myriad feuding parties and warring militias, had mustered its forces to embark on a massive invasion of its northern neighbour. The Israeli military juggernaut now swept all before it, as its armoured units reached and encircled West Beirut and its southern suburbs.

In accounting, then, for the sustained rise of Fadlallah during this period, it is evident that there is a correlation between his steady ascent and the major developments studied in this chapter – namely, the disappearance of Sayyid Musa al-Sadr, the Islamic Revolution in Iran, the execution of Sayyid Baqer al-Sadr, and the flight of Hizb al-Da'wa activists to Lebanon. Yet, as important as these events were to that process, of equal if not greater significance were elements intrinsic to Fadlallah: his persona, his programme, his achievements.

Fadlallah saw his influence gradually expand, thanks to several factors: his published books and written articles (principally as a regular contributor to *al-Muntalaq*); his charismatic and sophisticated oratory (in the form of sermons and lectures); his specialised religious, juridical, ideological and ethical lessons; and his institutional activities. And in the same way, relying on his resolve and dexterity, and on the challenges and opportunities brought about by developments during the following years, Fadlallah managed, despite the adversity of the times, to continue his ascendancy.

From the cauldron of the southern suburbs, and from his mosque pulpit, Fadlallah now projected this ardour, erudition and power of oratory, calling on the disaffected faithful to resist the foreign occupiers and rise up against their oppressors. In short, the following years would see, simultaneously, the meteoric rise of Hizbullah and the catapulting of Fadlallah from a cleric – little known beyond activist Islamist and religious scholarly circles – to the status of a major religious–political figure and leading intellectual on the national and regional scenes.

SIX

The Ascent of Sayyid Fadlallah and the Quest for an Islamic Order in Civil War Lebanon, 1982–1988

Spanning the period from June 1982 to July 1988, this chapter opens with the second Israeli invasion and occupation of Lebanon and closes with the battle for the Shi'i southern suburbs of Beirut and the termination of the Iran–Iraq war. The massive invasion and three-month siege and bombardment of Beirut, apart from its huge human and material toll, marked a new chapter in Lebanon's contemporary political history, as highlighted by such developments as the evolution of an amorphous Lebanese Shi'i Islamist resistance movement (the forerunner of Hizbullah), the dislodgement of PLO fighters from the south and their evacuation from west Beirut, the massacres of Palestinians in the slums of Sabra and Shatila, and the deployment of an American-led Multi-National Force. The battle for Beirut and the densely populated southern slums, pitting fighters affiliated to Hizbullah against co-religionist militiamen belonging to the rival Amal movement, ended in a resounding military victory for the former, and signalled a definite shift in the balance of power between the two movements.

A detailed account of the course and consequences of the Israeli invasion; the labyrinthine hostage saga; the convoluted militia war for control of west Beirut; the protracted Amal–PLO conflict in southern Beirut – these lie outside the scope of this chapter. Accordingly, these and other events will in general be looked at briefly, where they provide a contextual background for understanding the major forces shaping the turbulent milieu of that period. Nevertheless, the specific dimensions of a number of developments – thought to be pertinent to the study of the meteoric rise of Fadlallah and the evolution of his thought – will be closely examined. In addition to an effort to locate Fadlallah's role in Lebanon's shifting landscape, I will attempt to establish the extent to which he, as the pre-eminent Shi'i scholar activist, has been a harbinger of developments relating to the Lebanese Islamist movement; and, as a locus of religious–juridical authority and spiritual charisma, an influential agent of change.

Here I will try to relate Fadlallah's political views and activity during this period to a number of arguments already alluded to: that Fadlallah, as an Islamist theoretician and activist, is a pragmatic radical; that throughout his activist career, first in Iraq and then in Lebanon, Fadlallah assumed the role of mentor and guide to Islamist cadres, but without assuming a formal organisational position within Hizb al-Da'wa and Hizbullah; that his influence and ascent can be only partly accounted for by his informal association with Hizbullah.

It will be demonstrated that, despite his unofficial ties to Hizbullah, but because of his affinity with and influence on the Islamist movement, there is a correlation between his rapid ascent as an internationally recognised Islamist ideologue and activist, and the rise of Hizbullah as a major ideological and militant patriotic force in foreign-occupied and strife-ridden Lebanon. By virtue of his patriarchal role in relation to Hizbullah – whose clandestine offshoots are believed to have effected a series of devastating assaults on American, French and Israeli military and intelligence facilities, and to have seized western hostages during this period – Fadlallah was catapulted from the position of being a relatively unknown luminary outside Islamist and Shi'i circles, to that of a pre-eminent ideologue of militant Islamism in Lebanon. As a measure of his sudden public prominence in 1983, Fadlallah subsequently became a media celebrity, whose interviews were much sought after by correspondents reporting for Lebanese, Arab and Western newspapers. While there is no doubt that the militant exploits of Hizbullah and its offshoots contributed significantly (more by default than design) to raising Fadlallah's regional and international profile, his rapidly rising stature and influence were not solely due (as has been suggested by some scholars, such as Kramer) to Hizbullah's dramatic rise.[1]

On the contrary, it will be shown that his standing has owed more to his ability to inspire and guide the rank and file of Hizbullah and other Islamist groups, while remaining outside the structural framework of the movement, and thereby assuming the role of a patriarchal authority on religious jurisprudence, political ideology and strategic thinking. This has enabled him to be viewed as an enlightened sage occupying the high moral ground, transcending the parochial interests, partisan feuds and factional polemics commonly associated with ideological political organisations. It will also be argued that as an astute pragmatist – his radical outlook notwithstanding – Fadlallah showed himself to be less an unquestioning follower of Ayatollah Khomeini and avid proponent of Iran's assertive foreign policy towards Lebanon, than an independent Islamist thinker pursuing an activist agenda informed by the dynamics and particularities of civil war Lebanon. Indeed, Fadlallah demonstrated a capacity to inform and influence the Iranian decision-making process with regard to Lebanon.

The Israeli Invasion and its Consequences

The immediate catalyst for the Israeli invasion of Lebanon, on 6 June 1982, was the shooting and serious wounding of the Israeli ambassador to Britain.[2] On 6 June 1982, Israel launched a three-pronged invasion of Lebanon, code-named 'Operation Peace for Galilee', in which the Israeli Defence Force subjected the whole of Southern Lebanon to massive air, land and sea bombardment. Overwhelmed by the scale and ferocity of the invasion, the PLO garrisons stationed in the south began a hasty retreat towards Beirut and the northern Bekaa, where they planned to regroup. The strategic objectives of the invasion were manifold: the destruction of the PLO's military capacity and physical infrastructure; the dispersion of Palestinian refugees from camps in Lebanon; the undermining of the PLO as a credible organisation representing Palestinian nationalist aspirations; and the creation of a new political order in Lebanon through the installation of a pro-Israeli Maronite regime in Beirut.[3] To achieve these ambitious goals, Israeli army columns penetrated much further than in the 1978 invasion, heading for the Lebanese capital, driving before them the Palestinian guerrillas, and pushing back the forward positions of units of the Syrian army. On reaching the eastern outskirts of Beirut, the advancing Israelis linked up with the right-wing Maronite Phalangists based in the east of the capital, whereupon a siege was clamped around west Beirut and its southern suburbs.

According to Israeli military accounts, upon the invasion of South Lebanon the local Shi'a population, who had long suffered from the perpetual cycle of Palestinian commando raids and Israeli military strikes, were receptive to the IDF. They were ostensibly viewed as liberators from PLO oppression and domination – a view supposedly propagated by southern Shi'i clerics. Such an account of the reaction of southern Shi'i villagers is problematic, as it does not evoke the attitude of the majority of the community. While many southern Shi'a were, indeed, relieved to see the PLO fedayeen dislodged from their midst, 'what they had not been able to do themselves', ostentatious scenes of joy at the arrival of the army of 'liberation' were limited occurrences. Indeed, apart from a few Shi'i villages where the Israelis were well received, and limited cases of collaboration with the IDF, the attitude of the bulk of Shi'i southerners was one of indifference. Those villagers who initially welcomed the Israeli invasion did so on the mistaken assumption that Israel would quickly withdraw upon the eviction of the PLO from Lebanon.[4]

Except for a limited engagement with the Israelis by Amal militiamen fighting alongside Palestinian guerrillas defending a refugee camp near the port of Tyre, Amal remained neutral during the initial months of the invasion, mirroring the general indifference of the local Shi'i populace.[5] As was mentioned in the previous chapter, Amal's relations with the PLO had been frosty since the first Israeli invasion of April 1978, and at times openly hostile. Friction produced by fedayeen raids against Israel, and the latter's 'punitive' counter-strikes against mainly Shi'a villages and towns, led to frequent and intense armed clashes between the two parties.

In contrast to the stance of Amal fighters in southern Lebanon, their comrades in south Beirut fought alongside the PLO against the besieging Israeli army. Thus, when a column of Israeli armour and infantry reached Khalde on the southern outskirts of Beirut on 9 June, and attempted to advance on the international airport and the Palestinian encampments, they were halted by a combined force of PLO guerrillas, Amal militiamen and armed Shi'i Islamist students. A few days later, an amphibious armoured unit landed at the beach-front suburb of Ouzai, and proceeded along the coastal road before it too was repulsed by another combined Shi'i force. The successive failure of Israeli attempts to break through the capital's southern perimeter at Khalde had the effect of shoring up the flagging spirit of Beirut's besieged population and its garrison, while the tenacity of the frontline defenders demonstrated that the IDF was not invincible.[6]

The active participation of young Shi'i militiamen in the defence of the capital can be attributed to their solidarity with the Palestinian cause, dictated no doubt by the common threat posed by the intense and indiscriminate bombing of Beirut's west and southern suburbs, as well as the blockade of food and severing of electricity and water supplies affecting those areas.[7] Thus, unlike the polarisation that characterised Palestinian–Shi'i relations in South

Lebanon on the eve of the Israeli invasion, the three Palestinian camps in South Beirut included a large number of displaced Shi'a residents and were ringed by the densely populated Shi'i slums to the south. This 'belt of wretchedness', as it had been known since the outbreak of the civil war, was subject to the heaviest aerial, artillery and seaborne bombardment during the three-month Israeli siege.[8] This common hardship and spatial proximity yielded a feeling of mutual fortitude and defiance against the Israeli onslaught. The feeling of comradeship among the slum dwellers was reinforced by the preaching of Shi'i Islamist-oriented 'ulama, the most prominent of whom was Sayyid Fadlallah.

Fadlallah and the Evolution of the Islamic Resistance Movement

The timing, speed and scale of the Israeli invasion took Fadlallah – like most of his compatriots – by complete surprise. To his dismay, the Israeli army was able to sweep relentlessly northwards to reach the southern gates of an Arab capital in just three days. But such a grand sweep would not have been possible, argued an incensed Fadlallah, without the prior consent and backing of the United States, and the tacit approval of some Arab states. In any case, he watched the advance of the IDF from distant Teheran, where two months earlier, along with a large delegation of Lebanese religious scholars and activists, he had arrived to take part in an international conference for Islamic and Third World liberation movements on the 'Day of *Mustad'afeen* (the Downtrodden)'.[9]

Prior to attending the conference, Fadlallah was interviewed by the editor of an Iranian Islamist magazine, during which he voiced his admiration for the Iranian people and their achievements, their solidarity, steadfastness and fortitude. Later, in a speech on the occasion of the 'Day of the Downtrodden', Fadlallah lauded the Revolution and praised the leadership of Khomeini for, among other things, encapsulating the organic unity between Iranians and Lebanese Muslims, the bonds of which were manifested in the common struggle waged against Western 'imperialism' and Zionism. Further, as an expression of that solidarity, Fadlallah declared that an eventual Iranian military triumph over Iraq would be considered a regional victory by their Lebanese, principally, Shi'i brethren.[10]

Having suddenly heard of the invasion of their country, Fadlallah and his colleagues issued a statement condemning the Israeli aggression and exhorting the Lebanese populace to close ranks with the Palestinians and repel the aggressor. Given the gravity of the rapidly unfolding events, Fadlallah and his associates decided to hasten back to Lebanon so as to organise and direct local cells of resistance to Israeli occupation from the southern suburbs of Beirut and the Syrian-controlled zone of the Bekaa Valley. To that end, the Iranian leaders initiated two important developments. Prior to their departure, the Iranians persuaded their Lebanese guests, who comprised both Shi'i and Sunni 'ulama, to form the nucleus of an ecumenical association of activist 'ulama (Tajammu' al-'ulama al-Muslimeen), in which Fadlallah, thanks to his long-standing ecumenical views, was to play a leading role. The association, which at its foundational meeting included twenty religious activist scholars, later served as a front organisation for Hizbullah; it strove to inculcate the idea of the necessity of Sunni–Shi'i concord and solidarity, as well as to function as a vanguard for mobilising mass resistance to the Israelis.[11]

The second initiative was the decision to despatch a contingent of Iranian Revolutionary Guards to organise Islamist resistance cells among young Lebanese Shi'i activists. Coinciding with the battle for south Beirut, and arriving with Syrian assent, the first contingents of Guards in the Bekaa Valley belonged to a logistical and reconnaissance unit. These leading elements were later followed by the main body, which comprised several thousand Guards. They soon made Baalbek's main mosque a venue for religious inculcation and ideological indoctrination. Having been infused with religious revolutionary fervour, young local Shi'i recruits underwent military training at camps administered by the Revolutionary Guards. Among the first batch of trainees, numbering 180 individuals, was Sayyid Abbas al-Musawi, one of the founding figures of Hizbullah. In this way, over the course of the following weeks, hundreds of Lebanese Shi'i cadres, having completed intensive military training and indoctrination, were despatched to the frontlines near Beirut to fight, and ultimately drive the Israeli army of occupation out of Lebanon. While the larger body of Iranians consolidated their grip in Baalbek and surrounding villages, another group took up combat positions in support of Palestinian guerrillas, leftist militiamen and Syrian regulars, in the Shouf mountains overlooking Beirut. In addition to their military and ideological activities, the Guards toured surrounding villages, and set about providing essential social services (such as schools, clinics and pharmacies) in officially neglected rural towns and villages.[12] The Guards were to play a crucial role during the embryonic phases of Hizbullah, which will be examined below.

At the same time that Iran's Revolutionary Guards were arriving in eastern Lebanon, Fadlallah was making his way back, by the overland route, to Beirut, whose western and southern suburbs were being besieged and bombed by the Israelis and their Phalangist allies. On the eastern outskirts of the capital, the vehicle in which he was travelling was halted by a roadblock set up by an armed group belonging to the Kata'ib (Christian Phalange). After searching and finding Iranian-published material in the car (thereby damning him as a Khomeini protégé) the militiamen kidnapped Fadlallah and his eldest son, Ali, and drove them to a Phalangist office in the eastern suburb of al-Hazmiyah, for interrogation and detention. His incarceration in a cellar, however, would be brief; he was released after three hours, following the mediation of influential political figures. Years later, reminiscing over his first and only personal experience as a hostage, Fadlallah manifested a deep aversion towards all that hostage-taking stands for, and expressed empathy for those innocent people who have had their humanity taken away from them in such a way.[13] Fadlallah's position on the taking of western hostages in Lebanon by Islamic militant groups will be investigated later in this chapter.

With his release, Fadlallah made his way to the besieged western sector of the capital, whence he proceeded to his home quarter of B'ir al-Abd. Here, in an Islamist stronghold, close to the heavily bombed large Palestinian refugee camp of Bourj al-Barajnah, Fadlallah turned his mosque into a rostrum of caustic anti-Israeli rhetoric, and a focal point for the mobilisation of young Shi'i faithful for resistance against the Israeli army.[14]

On 16 July 1982, at the height of the Israeli siege and bombing of the capital, Fadlallah delivered a speech on the occasion of International Quds (Jerusalem) Day, an Iranian initiative designed to forge broad Muslim solidarity with the Palestinian cause. In what was to mark the beginning of his public anti-Israeli activism, Fadlallah lamented the orientation of Lebanese and Palestinian nationalist organisations towards Arab regimes with a view to solving their internal problems. That those states were viewed as having the backing of the great powers was based on the mistaken assumption that they were independent allies, when in fact – according to Fadlallah – they were the dependent surrogates of those powers. The upshot of this was clear: the Palestinians and Lebanese must rely on their own latent resources and willpower to determine their destinies. Underscoring the importance of the populace in bringing about radical change – and precluding, by inference, the validity of the notion of the elitist vanguard as the putative harbinger of revolution – Fadlallah asserted that revolutionism denotes the forging of genuine bonds with the masses, by nurturing a sense of comradeship with ordinary people. Accordingly, revolutionary action, for Fadlallah, involved inciting this innate collective 'spontaneity, this simplicity, and purity'.[15] Fadlallah would later develop a more systematic theory of revolutionary activism that would expound the dialectical dynamics of vanguard- versus community-instituted metamorphosis.

In stiffening the resolve of the Islamist defenders, Fadlallah – who had since the 1970s assumed an implacable position on Israeli 'expansionism' – became a mass agitator par excellence, and a stalwart of local resistance. It should be noted that, important as Fadlallah's role was in this regard, there were other clerics, both Shi'i and Sunni, who played an important part in the resistance cause in other parts of Beirut. At the forefront were the twenty middle- and junior-ranking 'ulama, loosely organised in the newly formed Tajammu al-'ulama al-Muslimeen. During the siege, some of these Islamist-minded activists took an active part in the resistance, while others sought to infuse the city's defenders with religious–patriotic ardour.[16]

The Splintering of the Amal Movement and the Formation of Hizbullah

As stated in the previous chapter, Amal had, since its inception, lacked organisational cohesion and ideological coherence, and thus the potential for internal fissuring was 'always latent'.[17] From the outset, Islamists, at the behest of Fadlallah, infiltrated the loosely structured movement with a view to transforming it from within. While two events associated with the Amal Movement and its leader Nabih Berri, in mid and late June 1982, were to act as catalysts for the formation of Islamic Amal, and the subsequent emergence of Hizbullah, the roots of the movement's internal split can be traced to the period preceding the second Israeli invasion. A widening rift within Amal's leadership became apparent during the movement's Fourth Congress, in March 1982.

Challenging Nabih Berri's secular and reformist orientation was a nascent radical Islamist wing.[18] Headed by Hussein al-Musawi, a schoolteacher and co-founder of the Amal movement, the faction aspired to restructuring Lebanon's political system in the image of Iran's Islamic republic. Paying homage to Imam Khomeini, and advocating the 'exportation' of the Islamic Revolution abroad, Amal's Islamists submitted a draft proposal that drew heavily on the Iranian model. The proposed agenda was rejected by the movement's dominant secular wing, led by Berri.[19] Propelling this polarisation towards an acrimonious split was, firstly, Berri's controversial decision in mid-June to halt Amal's armed resistance to the Israeli army besieging Beirut, on account of the overwhelming firepower of the Israelis, which rendered further resistance futile.[20]

The second factor accounting for the splitting of Amal was Berri's highly controversial decision to participate in the tripartite Hay'at al-Inqath al-

Watani (Committee for National Salvation). The Committee, headed by the Lebanese president, was convened on 20 July 1982.[21] The fact that such a high-level meeting was held at the height of the Israeli siege of Beirut roused the ire of Shiʿi Islamists, both within and outside Amal. This, together with the Committee's announcement of a ceasefire with Israel, was seen as tantamount to sanctioning the Israeli invasion and occupation, thereby rendering the body as no more than an instrument of American-Israeli strategic designs on Lebanon. The rejectionists denounced Berri's 'ignominious' involvement and declared their resolve to continue the armed resistance against the Israeli occupation.[22] With the active encouragement of Iran, al-Musawi, together with his 500 followers in Amal, withdrew to the ancient eastern city of Baalbek, from which Islamic Revolutionary Guards had recently been deployed.[23] Lying in the vicinity and overlooking Baalbek, the barracks became the military headquarters of the Guards, and a major training compound for young Shiʿi activists. The base would later serve as a springboard for Shiʿi commando squads sent on operations against Israeli and Western targets in Lebanon.[24]

In designating his breakaway group as 'Islamic Amal', al-Musawi did not regard himself as founding a rival movement to the parent Harakat Amal. On the contrary, in so far as the Committee was perceived as a vehicle for consecrating 'American-Israeli-Kata'ib [Phalangist] hegemony', Islamic Amal was viewed by its founder as a genuine corrective movement, in the context of Amal's deviationist path and 'Berri's betrayal of the legacy of Imam Musa al-Sadr and of the *umma*'.[25]

Besides those erstwhile radical Amal affiliates who coalesced around Hussein al-Musawi, there was another group of disaffected activists, consisting of independent Islamists who had merged with local radical groupings that sprang up in the southern suburbs of Beirut and the Bekaa, or had come under the influence of activist Shiʿi 'ulama like Fadlallah.[26] This loose collection of staunchly pro-Iranian and vehemently anti-Israeli Islamist Shiʿi formations was to represent the autonomous groupings of Hizbullah. Following the formation of Hizbullah, Fadlallah exhorted the significant number of disaffected Islamists affiliated to Amal to remain in the movement and seek to transform it from within.[27]

The appellation 'Hizbullah' is derived from two Qur'anic verses, denoting a generic party of believers, as opposed to *Hizb al-Shaytan*, the party of Satan. Lacking, at least in its early stages, a well-defined leadership, mature organisational structure, official membership, and detailed agenda, the 'Party of God', rather than being a conventional political party, was more an umbrella movement for a constellation of mainly Shiʿi Islamist groups sympathetic or loyal to Iran, and geared mainly towards fighting and expelling Israel from

Lebanon.[28] Unlike Amal's disparate mass following, with its multifarious political and ideological positions precariously united by the charismatic leadership of Musa al-Sadr and his legacy, the various groups that comprised Hizbullah were tied to one another by a common philosophical and political agenda.

It is difficult to establish from party sources the precise date when the movement was founded. The first two years of its development were dictated by secrecy, marked by the careful non-disclosure of its series of dramatic paramilitary and 'self-martyring' operations, and the identity of its leadership.[29]

Hizbullah seems to have come into being in late June or early July 1982, simultaneous with the founding of Islamic Amal in the Bekaa. While the movement arose with the active encouragement of Iran's revolutionary clerical leadership, and was given much impetus by the deployment of Iranian Revolutionary Guards and the presence of training facilities in the Bekaa, it is wrong simply to regard Hizbullah as Iran's creation – the tool of its foreign policy in Lebanon.[30] In the opinion of Abu Khalil, Hizbullah's emergence was the consequence of the 'convergence of Lebanese Shi'i interests with Iranian foreign policy priorities'. According to Sayyid Hasan Nasrallah, one of the earliest affiliates and current General Secretary of Hizbullah, the movement arose purely as a local, spontaneous initiative spawned by extraordinary local conditions in the wake of Israel's invasion and occupation. It emerged as an organisationally amorphous and rudimentary constellation of primarily Shi'i Islamist activist cells dedicated to fighting the Israeli army of occupation. In other words, Hizbullah's raison d'être was resistance against Israeli occupation. But there is little doubt that, as depicted in an official Hizbullah publication commemorating one of its martyred leaders, the movement arose and operated under the overall 'direction of Imam Khomeini and the guidance of his ideology, outlook and agenda'.[31]

At its inception Hizbullah comprised a loose aggregation of the following groups: the Lebanese branch of Hizb al-Da'wa al-Islami, al-Ittihadi al-Lubnani lil Talabah al-Muslimeen, Tajammu' al-'ulama al-Muslimeen, and Harakat al-Amal Islamiyya.[32] The last two, as mentioned above, emerged following Israel's June invasion of Lebanon, while the first two predated the 1979 Islamic Revolution. It will be recalled that Fadlallah was revered by the affiliates of the first two groups as a juridical authority and ideological guide. But whereas Hizb al-Da'wa in Lebanon dissolved itself as an independent entity soon after the execution of Ayatollah Sayyid Baqir al-Sadr in April 1980, with its members thereafter joining Amal, many ex-Da'wa members assumed senior positions in Amal, and later became the founding fathers and senior members of Hizbullah.[33] As to why these activist Islamist clerics opted to establish or join a new organisation rather than revive the recently defunct branch of al-Da'wa, the reasons lay in the organisation's secretive character, regimented strategy, and centralised structure. By contrast, Hizbullah was intended to evolve into a more open, socially and politically interactive movement, with a decentralised structure rendering it more capable of adapting to changing conditions, and of resisting governmental control and repression.[34]

Apart from Berri's conciliatory posture towards the minority Lebanese Maronite government, the founding figures in Hizbullah found Amal to be too secular, too reformist, and too nationalist a movement to be a suitable vehicle for the dissemination of the ideas of armed struggle against Israeli occupation and the Western military presence, and of radical socio-political change and pan-Islamism. As a formation that considers itself a mass movement of the Muslim faithful, rather than a strict political party, Hizbullah sees itself as an organic part of the world-wide Muslim *umma*, with a self-appointed vanguard role among the community of believers – both in Lebanon and beyond. Though its manifesto was not published until 1985, Hizbullah envisioned itself from the outset as a vanguard guiding the masses, organising their ranks, and spurring them to armed resistance and revolutionary activism. In this schematic process, the nominal or quietist Muslim is gradually transformed into a religiously observant and politically active individual. In common with the gradualist strategy first formulated and adopted by the Egyptian Muslim Brethren, the reform of the individual would set in process the transformation of society, which would, in turn, serve as a precursor to the establishment of an Islamic state. Its pan-Islamist vision essentially revolves around the spatial and political integration of the sprawling but disparate *umma* into a single super-state governed by the *wilayat al-faqih* regime headed by Imam Khomeini.[35] To underpin this pan-Islamist stance, and through the services of its affiliated body, the Association of Muslim 'ulama, Hizbullah was at the forefront of the Muslim ecumenical movement in Lebanon, of which Fadlallah was a chief proponent. Hence, the effort to develop denominational religious affinities and to forge political solidarity among Muslim Lebanese activists and clerics was crucial to Hizbullah's strategy of combating and overcoming the forces of western imperialism, 'Zionist expansionism', and Maronite hegemony.

Fadlallah and the Formation of Hizbullah: Ambivalence and Symbiosis

Since 1983, the year that marked the commencement of suicide operations against American and Israeli targets in Lebanon, perhaps the most often repeated question raised by Lebanese and foreign journalists interviewing Fadlallah has been that of his putative ties to Hizbullah. As a patriarchal figure who has proudly affirmed his nurturing role in relation to the generic Islamist movements in Lebanon and Iraq, Fadlallah has categorically and consistently denied all assertions that he is, or at any stage has been, the leader, mentor or spiritual guide of Hizbullah, or any particular Islamist group, and insisted that his teaching and writings are formulated to address the Islamist movement in general, in local and regional settings, rather than a specific group within it.[36]

But the question remains: how can one account for the media portrayal of Fadlallah as being synonymous with Hizbullah? Two related factors have contributed to that oversimplified view: the first is Fadlallah's undeniable influence among Hizbullah's rank and file; and the second stems from the absence, in its early phase, of public leadership figures within the movement.[37] Yet Fadlallah was unmistakably the most influential and articulate Islamist cleric in Lebanese Shi'i Islamist circles, and here lies the correlation between the movement and its guide. More pertinent to our inquiry than attempting to delineate the precise contours of the nexus between Fadlallah and Hizbullah, given the intricacies and fluidity of that relationship, is to establish and account for the influence of Fadlallah on Hizbullah's agenda, strategy and activities during this period. For all his influence, it is telling that the movement's cadres and leaders do not owe their allegiance to Sayyid Fadlallah; they are beholden to Iran's supreme leader, the late Imam Khomeini, and his successor Ayatollah Khamanei. As I hope will become evident, while Fadlallah has often been consulted by senior figures of Hizbullah, his views are not always adopted, nor have his instructions invariably been heeded.[38]

In relation to the question of his role in the formation of Hizbullah, sources close to Fadlallah credit him with encouraging the use of the name. Furthermore, in 1976, in 'Islam and the Logic of Power', Fadlallah had expounded the Qur'anic concept of generic 'hizbullah' in contradistinction to *hizb al-Shaytan* – literally 'the Party of Satan'. Refuting the basic assumption underlying the conservative view that organised social and political activism based on the model of the modern party structure is inherently divisive, Fadlallah argued that party affiliation need not be contrary to the corporate interests and aspirations of the *umma* as a whole. This endeavour – the first systematic attempt among Shi'i activist 'ulama – to reconcile seemingly divergent tendencies is premised on the view that 'the Party of God' mentioned in the Qur'an is an organic, generic body, whose fluid terms of action include all committed adherents of Islam in perpetual and multifaceted confrontation with the forces of 'irreligion, corruption and oppression'.[39]

Islamic political organisation thus provides a crucial vehicle for Islamist activism and an essential bulwark against the then growing influence of secular parties. Put simply, herein lies the religious and ideological rationale for the formation of Hizbullah, as well as other Islamist parties such as al-Da'wa and Jama'at al-Ikhwan al-Muslimoun. Fadlallah's exposition of the theory of 'hizbullah' and with its dialectical ramifications was later elaborated in a series of articles appearing during the 1980s in the Islamist intellectual magazine, *al-Muntalaq*. In those articles, Fadlallah propounded the idea of a well organised vanguard party apparatus. Affiliation to the movement would not consist of formal membership restricted to a select few, but would be open to the religious adhering public.[40] According to this conception, as a vanguard Hizbullah is a pragmatic and dynamic entity mobilising all segments of the community.

While it is difficult to establish the precise role played by Fadlallah in the founding of Hizbullah, it is clear that he was instrumental in inducing the Lebanese branch of al-Da'wa to merge into the nascent body of Hizbullah.[41] It will be recalled that, since Hizb al-Da'wa's inception in 1958 in Iraq, Fadlallah has had close informal ties with the party.[42] As a pre-eminent Islamist ideologue and strategist, Fadlallah is credited with devising Hizbullah's social and political agenda, based on periodised and gradualist schema, and has been responsible for formulating the guiding principles of the party's long- and short-term goals.[43]

Fadlallah prudently established his roles as jurisconsult and theoretician in a manner that would not lead him to be recognised as a formal supervisory figure, since his worldview and agenda transcended those of Hizbullah. A formal leadership role within the organisation would have risked delimiting his otherwise growing authority and influence, which since the early 1980s were directed at building a sizeable niche of followers who were not necessarily affiliates of Hizbullah, al-Da'wa or Amal. Furthermore, in keeping with his ecumenical outlook and commitment to universal Islam, Fadlallah actively sought to build a following among Sunni Islamists.[44]

There is a second consideration that would have dissuaded Fadlallah from becoming the formal oracle of Hizbullah: security. To be narrowly identified with Hizbullah would invariably place him in the position of incurring responsibility for major decisions taken by Hizbullah's leaders, and for operations embarked upon by its affiliates. Given the militancy of Hizbullah, Fadlallah would be a prime target for criticism, kidnapping, or even assassination. Thus, for Fadlallah, ever the pragmatist, any benefits that might have issued from such a leadership role would be outweighed by the potential risks. In opting for an extra-organisational role of general guidance, Fadlallah had by default distanced himself from the secret decision-making process in the party's highest echelons. As mentioned above, a crucial outcome of this arrangement was that Fadlallah held no veto over Hizbullah's decisions, nor was his advice binding on a movement that was ultimately beholden to Iran. The mutually beneficial or quasi-symbiotic relationship between Fadlallah and Hizbullah was unmistakable: the ayatollah's sermons, lectures and declarations were regularly published in the party's official organ, *al-'Ahd*; many, if not most, of those who regularly attended Friday congregational prayers and listened to the weekly mosque sermon were Hizbullah affiliates and sympathisers; Hizbullah paramilitaries manned checkpoints on streets leading to Fadlallah's high rise residence and mosque, in the Bi'r al-Abd quarter; and finally, his personal bodyguards, professionally trained in armed escort and protective duties, were drawn from the ranks of Hizbullah.

Fadlallah's close informal relationship with Hizbullah raises an intriguing question: to what extent did Fadlallah owe his growing prestige and influence to the rapid rise of that Islamist movement? On the one hand, one can certainly say that a close correlation existed between the dramatic ascent of Hizbullah and the contemporaneous rise in Fadlallah's public profile and stature, both at home and abroad. On the other hand, his rise in status and authority was not wholly contingent on the emergence of that movement. Gradually, through the course of the 1980s, Fadlallah's cross-sectional appeal, recognised scholarship, independent political stance towards Iran, and financial independence, ensured that, contrary to the contention of Martin Kramer, his 'fortunes and fate' were not 'inseparable from those of Hizbullah'.[45]

Fadlallah and the 17 May Agreement

The American-brokered Lebanese-Israeli negotiations that preceded the 17 May Agreement in 1983 represented a turning point in Fadlallah's political career. In particular, the event served as a catalyst for mass protests against the secret liaisons in which Fadlallah had played a pivotal role. The assassination of Phalangist leader and president-elect, Bashir Gemayel in a bombing of party headquarters in east Beirut, and the subsequent massacre between 16 and 18

September 1982 of hundreds of Palestinian refugees in the Sabra and Shatila slums by Israeli-backed Maronite Phalangists, provoked an international and domestic Israeli outcry. Consequently, Israel was forced in mid-December 1982 to pull its troops out of west Beirut, but only after reaching an agreement with Lebanon's newly elected president, Amin Gemayel. The proposed Accord committed Israel to withdrawing its troops from Lebanon, while binding the two countries into a mutual security arrangement and normalisation of relations.[46]

Though never ratified, the secret Accord made the withdrawal of the Israeli army from Lebanon contingent on the withdrawal of Syrian troops. Moreover, restrictions were placed on the number of Lebanese troops to be deployed along the southern border, and in an oblique reference to Syria, both parties agreed to prevent entry into, 'deployment in, or passage through [Lebanese] territory … by military forces … of any state hostile to the other party'. The Accord, however, was stillborn, as it rested on the approval of a hostile Syria, which considered it 'a deal of capitulation', and ignited the indignation of the Lebanese oppositional parties, whose leaders denounced it as treacherous and humiliating.[47]

For Fadlallah, who had consistently rejected the legitimacy of the state of Israel, the deal was an abomination that had to be annulled by popular protest. To that end Fadlallah was instrumental, in concert with his activist colleagues in the 'ulama Association, in transforming 'his' mosque in Bi'r al-Abd into a focal point for dissent and a rallying point for street demonstrations. On 17 May 1983, marking the impending signing of the Accord, a militant campaign was launched with a mosque sit-in, involving Fadlallah and a group of Islamist activist 'ulama. Before a large congregation of the faithful, Fadlallah and his colleagues denounced the Accord.[48] To Fadlallah, it was inconceivable that the Lebanese government would countenance a deal with a state that was 'devoid of legitimacy' and had embarked on a destructive invasion of the country. In concluding a security arrangement with Israel, Fadlallah said his government was rewarding Israeli aggression by conferring legitimacy on the 'Zionist' state, and conversely delegitimising the indigenous civil and armed resistance to Israel's military occupation of close to half of Lebanon. Following the conclusion of prayers, Fadlallah led a street procession of a few hundred followers, who denounced President Amin Gemayel as a traitor. The mass protest turned violent when the procession encountered a contingent of security forces who had set up a cordon to block their path, and proceeded to break up the march. In the altercations that ensued, one unarmed youth was shot and killed. While secular reformist figures of Amal, namely Nabih Berri and Shaykh Qabalan, reproached the activist league of 'ulama associated with

Fadlallah for what had happened, Fadlallah and his colleagues intensified their diatribes against a regime seen to be fully committed to crushing all public opposition to the 17 May Agreement.[49]

As the central authorities subsequently intensified their campaign of house raids and mass arrests of suspects tied to the burgeoning oppositional Islamist movement in the Shiʿi southern suburbs, Fadlallah's reputation as a major thorn in the government's side was enhanced. Equally, as Fadlallah's anti-government speeches came to feature prominently in Islamist revolutionary discourse, so too did his appeal grow among the increasingly disaffected and predominantly Shiʿi youth. Fadlallah did not limit his opposition to the policies of the Beirut government to fiery sermons and impassioned speeches; rather, he continued to organise and lead mass anti-government and anti-Israeli sit-ins and rallies. For example, during the conduct of formal Lebanese–Israeli negotiations in autumn 1984 under UN auspices, Fadlallah organised a large sit-in in his mosque, which was attended by senior religious dignitaries, middle-ranking activist clerics and Hizbullah figures.[50] The sit-in was followed by a mass street procession, in which protestors denounced the liaisons.

Though the 17 May Accord was not undone solely by his activism, nevertheless the militancy of Fadlallah and his fellow Islamist ʿulama provided the crucial spark for the launching of a major government crackdown against the predominantly Shiʿi opposition in the suburbs. This campaign precipitated in turn a Syrian-backed Amal Shiʿi and Druze counter-offensive that seriously emasculated the military power and political control of the central government, and ultimately led, on 5 March 1984, to the annulment of the 17 May Accord. In the wake of the Israeli withdrawal from the Shouf Mountains of central Lebanon in mid-September 1983, Jumblatt-led Druze fighters defeated the combined Phalangist Lebanese army units in the mountains above Beirut, while in west Beirut fierce clashes between Berri's Amal militiamen and the army led, on 6 February 1984, to the mutiny of the predominantly Shiʿi Sixth Brigade and its subsequent defection to the opposition camp. This development set in train a series of momentous events – namely, the collapse of central authority in the western sector of the capital, the withdrawal of the MNF from west and southern Beirut, the realignment of the precarious Gemayel administration away from Israel and towards Syria, and finally the formal abrogation of the 17 May Accord on 5 March 1984.

Fadlallah and the Suicide Bombings of MNF Facilities

If the 17 May Accord raised the public profile of Fadlallah on the local Lebanese scene, the dual bombings of the American Marine compound and the French Paratrooper barracks on 23 October 1983 catapulted him into the international limelight. The MNF, consisting of American, French and Italian peacekeeping units, were redeployed to west Beirut and the southern suburbs on 24 September 1982; that is, two weeks after the premature withdrawal of the original force.[51] Thus, the return of the MNF was apparently impelled by a sense of guilt – the feeling of indirect responsibility for the atrocity at the Palestinian camps. The ostensible mission of the 3,800 American, French and Italian troops was threefold: to serve as a buffer between the vacating Israelis and the militias of west Beirut, to reconcile the warring parties, and to bring about the withdrawal of Syrian and Israeli armies from Lebanon. The foreign peacekeepers were initially received warmly by many of Beirut's war-weary residents. The opposition militias and the Islamists were more circumspect, favouring a wait-and-see posture. Later, as the American and French contingents became increasingly embroiled in Lebanon's civil strife by propping up the tenuous power of the Gemayel regime, the attitude of the opposition movements became overtly hostile.

Emboldened by the presence of the MNF, the Lebanese government sent its army and security forces into west Beirut, where they proceeded to raid numerous residences, confiscating weapons, cordoning whole blocks, and detaining and interrogating scores of young Muslim men. The fact that only predominantly Muslim west Beirut was subjected to such a large-scale security operation – with Christian east Beirut allowed to remain an armed redoubt of the rightist Phalangists – only roused the resentment of the residents and militias of the western sector. To these people the army was no longer a national military formation but an extension of the Phalangists, and a tool of a minority Maronite administration. This resentment also extended to the American Marines, who not only equipped and trained the Lebanese army but also actively supported its operations.[52]

If one of the MNF's objectives was to induce the withdrawal of the Syrian and Israeli armies from Lebanon and uphold the 17 May Accords, Syria held diametrically opposed aims. Determined not to yield to US demands, Syria was equally committed to driving out the American and French contingents, wrecking the 17 May Accords and emasculating the central government. To that end, Syria unleashed its local Druze and Shi'a allies on the Lebanese army, the Phalangists and the MNF. The campaign against the American and French contingents of the MNF began in late 1982, with a series of drive-by shootings and intermittent sniping, and culminated in the devastating suicide bombings of the American Marine compound and French Paratrooper barracks on 23 October 1983.

The immediate background of the suicide bombings was the American decision – in response to President Gemayel's appeal for military assistance to relieve the hard-pressed Lebanese army – to use its massive naval fire-power against the positions of Druze irregulars above Beirut.[53] For their part, the French launched aerial bombing raids against suspected pro-Iranian training camps near Baalbek.[54] In intervening overtly on the side of Gemayal and his allies, the Americans and the French all but forfeited their supposedly impartial peacekeeping mission, and thus became – in the eyes of both the pro-Syrian secular and the pro-Iranian Islamist opposition – legitimate military targets.

Even before the double suicide bombing of the MNF, the seven-storey building that housed the American embassy in west Beirut had been destroyed by a suicide truck bomber on 18 April 1983. Among the sixty-three dead were seventeen Americans, who included senior CIA operatives. Al-Jihad al-Islami, a hitherto unknown group, claimed responsibility for the blast. Earlier, on 24 May 1982, the group, suspected of having links with Hizbullah, had also been responsible for the bombing of the French embassy only two weeks prior to the Israeli invasion. The blast left twelve dead and twenty-seven wounded. Following the relocation of the American embassy to Christian east Beirut, the organisation mounted another attack on 7 September 1984, using a suicide bomb-laden vehicle. The resulting explosion left twelve dead and fifty wounded.[55]

In another operation, in the early hours of 23 October 1983, a truck driver drove his 2,000kg TNT-laden vehicle into the Marine compound, adjacent to the international airport. The explosion devastated the reinforced multistorey structure, leaving 241 Marines dead and 75 wounded. It was the highest death toll suffered by the Marines in a single day since World War II. Barely twenty seconds later and four miles north, another suicide truck bomber rammed his vehicle with its lethal 300kg load into the nine-storey French Paratrooper compound. Fifty-eight French servicemen were killed and seventeen wounded – the biggest French military loss since the Algerian war.[56]

Shaken by the attacks, the Americans retaliated by using their big naval guns against Druze positions that overlooked the exposed, low-lying Marines, and together with the French conducted air raids against suspected Hizbullah and Iranian Revolutionary Guard camps and facilities. These punitive attacks proved ineffectual, as the demoralised Marines became more vulnerable to sudden suicide attacks and persistent firing on their positions from the adjacent southern suburbs, and from the hills above Beirut. Lacking the will to escalate dramatically the level of American military intervention in Lebanon, lest it slide deeper into the country's internal mire, and unwilling to sustain further casualties among its soldiers, the US administration evacuated its remaining 1,000 Marines to ships off-shore, on 26 February 1984.[57]

As mentioned above, Islamic Jihad claimed responsibility for the double attack, and demanded that all MNF personnel evacuate Lebanon or face further attacks.[58] Although Hizbullah leaders from the outset denied all links to the bombers or the Jihad organisation, they lauded the exploits of the two self-martyring operations. Hussein al-Musawi, for instance – leader of Islamic Amal, a sub-group of Hizbullah – while denying all responsibility, glorified the deeds of the bombers, who were seen as representing the downtrodden.[59] (Significantly, it was not until August 1985 that Hizbullah's central office issued a formal communiqué affirming the Islamist identity of the bombers, and upholding the view of the MNF as a legitimate military target.) Despite these denials, in a revealing interview with Robert Fisk, the late Hizbullah General Secretary, Sayyid Abbas al-Musawi, stated that the single greatest achievement of Hizbullah in the early 1980s was that 'by way of two martyrdom operations against the United States Marines and French Paratroopers, America and the multinational force were ousted from Lebanon'.[60]

Fadlallah's initial reaction to the suicide bombing of the MNF was more ambivalent and circumspect than that of some of Hizbullah's leading figures. On the one hand, he had been a staunch and vocal opponent of United States' policy towards Lebanon, and in particular opposed to the pro-government role of the American Marines in Beirut; but on the other, he had refrained from calling for the mounting of Islamist attacks on MNF facilities and personnel. As is clear from his statements in interviews referred to below, Fadlallah publicly endorsed the cause of the bombers, but was much more measured in his position on the legitimacy and utility of suicide or self-martyring operations. Fadlallah had refrained, both before and following the double bombing, from issuing a fatwa formally sanctioning the attacks, and his position on the legality and practicability of self-martyring operations was qualified and retrospective.[61]

The cautiousness of Fadlallah's support, in spite of his overt opposition to the role of the MNF, was dictated by several considerations. First, he feared that the bombings, with their huge casualty tolls, would not be left unavenged by the Americans and French, and would inadvertently serve the long-term goals of the western powers by providing a pretext for extending their presence, and deepening their control, in Lebanon. Second, from a legal perspective, Fadlallah had to grapple with the apparent contradiction between the explicit Islamic proscription of suicide and the undertaking of extraordinary paramilitary operations by self-professed Islamists against designated enemy targets. In an interview three weeks after the bombings of the MNF bases, Fadlallah explained that 'based on my personal interpretation of the shari'ah, I have reservations about resorting to suicide tactics in political activity'. The third factor accounting for Fadlallah's reservations may have been an anxiety about being unjustly held responsible, by virtue of his Islamist following and publicly anti-American posture.

Yet on the basis of information supplied by a branch of Lebanese intelligence linked to the Phalange Party, CIA investigating officers wrongly identified Fadlallah as both the most prominent leader of Hizbullah and the chief instigator of the bombing of the Marine barracks. On both counts, the evidence on which the allegations were based was flimsy. According to Phalangist sources, Fadlallah 'was in the Shi'i suburb adjacent to the US Marine compound the night of the attacks and [more seriously] gave his blessings to the [two suicide truck bombers]'. In his first interview with the Western press, only six days after the bombings, Fadlallah denied categorically all claims of his responsibility for the attacks. He said that he was baffled by the accusations of his involvement. He attacked the Christian Phalangists and Lebanese army intelligence for allegedly conspiring to undermine his growing influence and dent his reputation as a man of dialogue, adding apologetically that he was by nature 'a peaceful man, [who] harboured no grudges against either the US Marines or the French, and has always preached against violence'. He said that he had welcomed the arrival of the Marines the year before, because it resulted in the withdrawal of the Israelis from the airport. Yet in the same interview he prudently refrained from reaffirming his antipathy to the US Marines over their partisan role in the country's internal conflict. In another interview, in November 1983, Fadlallah said that he welcomed the Americans and French so long as they ended their 'aggressiveness' and reverted to the original terms of their mission.'[62]

This qualified receptiveness later changed to unmistakable hostility. As he said to the Iranian press in February 1984, he regarded the MNF as essentially an American-dominated NATO force that failed to realise its declared objectives.[63] Its intervention on the side of the Beirut government exacerbated, rather than defused, the volatile and intricate situation on the ground. Stating his position on suicide missions, Fadlallah rejected the view held by some Islamic activists that those who carry out such acts for religious reasons immediately ascend to paradise, adding, in an oblique reference to allegations that he had personally blessed the suicide duo, that neither he nor anyone else has been granted the authority to 'play God' in guaranteeing paradise to the bombers.[64]

The Attempted Assassination of Fadlallah and its Repercussions

Fadlallah's initial objections to self-martyring operations had undergone a discernible change by mid-1985, three months after his attempted assassination by a CIA-trained and Saudi-financed Lebanese counter-terrorist unit, and the launching of Israel's so-called 'Iron Fist' policy against the Lebanese resistance movement. On Friday 5 March 1985, a parked car packed with approximately 250kg of TNT was detonated some 50 metres from the eight-storey building that housed Fadlallah's apartment. The sheer force of the blast, timed to coincide with the dispersal of Muslim worshippers following the completion of Friday prayers at the nearby mosque, severely damaged four apartment blocks, showered debris over a 500-metre radius, killed between 80 and 105 people, and wounded another 200 to 275.[65] Despite the massive explosion, the bombers missed their prime target, Fadlallah, who was not in his apartment at the time of the bombing but in the nearby mosque, leading prayers for Muslim women and answering their queries.[66]

Emerging unscathed but shaken from the bomb attack, Fadlallah blamed the Americans, the Lebanese government and the Phalangists for their role in what became known as the B'ir al-Abd massacre. He exhorted the faithful to remain resolute in their confrontation with the forces of 'tyranny and neo-imperialism'. Fadlallah accused the CIA and the influential Saudi ambassador to the United States, Prince Bandar, of orchestrating and funding the bomb attack. The claim was not unfounded. For, according to the revelations of William Casey, then CIA Director, published posthumously in Bob Woodward's controversial book, *The Veil*, the CIA chief viewed Fadlallah as a menace to US interests in Lebanon for having allegedly masterminded the suicide bombings of American facilities in Beirut.[67] The Saudis, meanwhile, regarded Fadlallah as a thorn in their side, on account of his vocal support for revolutionary Iran and strident criticism of Saudi regional policy, and because of his alleged role in the kidnapping of the Saudi consul in Beirut.[68] This convergence of interests thus provided the basis for the secret quest for the elimination of their common foe. Following the abortive attempt to eliminate Fadlallah, Woodward, narrating the revelations of the Saudi ambassador, states that the Saudis switched to a more subtle tack to silence the Shi'i cleric: bribery. According to Prince Bandar's account, Fadlallah was approached to ascertain the possibility that, in return for $2 million, he would act as an 'early warning system for terrorist attacks on Saudi and American facilities'.[69] Fadlallah allegedly accepted the offer, so long as the payment was made in food, medicine and education expenses for the needy in the local community; he later completely denied the allegations.

In the face of the formidable military power of the United States and Israel, and in the absence of decisive conventional weapons in the possession of the Islamist resistance, Fadlallah now deemed it permissible and even obligatory to wage an unconventional war of self-defence. Lacking the means to confront the United States and Israel effectively, 'oppression impels the subjugated to discover new weapons and new vigour every day'. Accordingly, '[the resort to such] unconventional yet crude means for confronting the aggressor power cannot be viewed as terrorism. We deem this to be religiously licit warfare against the world's imperialist and domineering powers.' In such circumstances, in Fadlallah's view, 'there is no difference between dying with a pistol in your hand or exploding yourself'. A year earlier, in July 1984, in the same vein, Fadlallah had asked in a lecture: 'How is it possible to distinguish between setting out for battle certain you will die after slaying ten [enemy soldiers], and setting out to kill ten, whilst knowing you will die during the process?' Speaking some ten years after the bombings, Fadlallah rationalised the attacks on the Marines. 'When you consider the American role, you don't question the character of the American soldiers; when a country carries out actions which lead to the destruction of another country, it is natural that soldiers bear responsibility for those deeds, since they are its representatives.' Yet Fadlallah also underscored the importance of analysing the particular circumstances that were likely to determine the degree of success or failure, and the probable repercussions of each prospective self-martyring operation.[70]

Thus Fadlallah explained that 'self-martyring operations are not sanctioned unless they can shake the enemy'. He added that the believer cannot blow himself up unless the outcome will equal or exceed the loss of the martyring devotee, as self-martyring operations are not fatal accidents but legal actions governed by precepts which the faithful cannot transgress. While the spectacularly successful operations of the early 1980s had fulfilled the criteria set by Fadlallah, subsequent operations, primarily against Israeli targets in the south, tended to yield a diminishing number of casualties; and as a result such operations became far less common. As Israelis tightened security measures around their forces and facilities, with a consequent decline in the rate of suicide attacks, Fadlallah argued in such circumstances the 'life of the self-martyring person is not worth the expected outcome.'[71]

Israel and the Islamist Resistance in the South

As recounted above, during the Israeli siege and bombardment of west Beirut and the southern suburbs between June and August 1982, small bands of loosely organised Islamic activists, many of whom were inspired by the Iranian Revolution and incited by Fadlallah, played a prominent role in defending the southern approaches of the Lebanese capital from the advancing Israeli army. Although the Israelis would later withdraw – first from west Beirut, in late September 1982, in the wake of the Sabra and Shatila massacres, and in late August from the Shouf – the gradual retreat was occasioned largely by the mounting of armed resistance by Lebanese nationalist and leftist militias. During the first two years of Israeli occupation, Hizbullah and allied Islamist fighting groups were in a crucial phase of evolution. Yet despite the dominance of the secular nationalist movement, squads of Islamists, operating under the pseudonym of Islamic Jihad, carried out a series of suicide-bombing attacks on the Israeli military.[72] In the first such attack, on 14 November 1982, a massive explosion caused by a 200kg bomb-laden vehicle almost completely demolished the Israeli military headquarters in the southern port of Tyre, and left some 400 fatalities.[73]

Beginning with limited, unco-ordinated attacks on Israeli targets, the armed struggle for the liberation of the south had by mid-1984 come to be dominated by Shi'i fighters affiliated to either Amal or Hizbullah. The marked shift in attitude towards Israeli occupation among the south's largest confessional community, the Shi'a, was a crucial factor in propelling first Amal and then Hizbullah to the forefront of the resistance. It will be recalled that many Shi'a villagers, having suffered from the PLO–Israeli conflict in the south, were indifferent toward the invasion, as they mistakenly believed that the Israeli army would withdraw as soon as the PLO guerrillas had been evicted from Lebanon. However, once it became evident that Israel had no intention of leaving Lebanon, that mood changed to resentment. However, it was an incident in the southern market town of Nabatiyah that transformed this latent ill-feeling into open hostility, and marked the beginning of popular participation in the wider resistance movement.

On 16 October 1983 an Israeli patrol drove into a mass Shi'i *'Ashoura* procession mourning the martyrdom of Imam Hussein, the Prophet's grandson, on the plain of Karbala', in southern Iraq, in 681 AD. Shooting indiscriminately to clear a path through the 50,000-strong crowd, the Israeli military servicemen killed several Shi'i mourners and wounded scores of others. In the maelstrom that followed, a number of Israeli vehicles were set upon and set ablaze by the angry crowd.[74] The incident had immediate and far-reaching repercussions. Shi'i religious and political leaders denounced Israel, and all Lebanese Shi'i collaborators.

The role played by the Shi'i 'ulama in the resistance against Israel now became crucial. Mosque pulpits and *Husseiniyat* rostrums became the foci of civil agitation, mass mobilisation and recruitment, and clandestine organisation.[75] The religious centres became staging points for sit-ins, street demonstration, and armed attacks. The more senior 'ulama, such as Shaykh Shams al-Din, issued binding juridical–religious edicts, calling for the ostracising of collaborators and the pursuit of all forms of civil resistance, including the boycotting of Israeli goods and the organisation of general strikes.[76]

Indicative of the prominent role played by the 'ulama was the activist career of Shaykh Raghib Harb, from the southern front-line village of Jibshit, locus of Islamic revolutionary ferment and resistance activity. As mentioned in the preceding chapters, the young Islamist *'alim* had been a student of Fadlallah, and was one of the most virulent opponents of Israel's occupation of the South. He swiftly attained prominence through his uncompromising sermons and his organisational ability. As a result of that militancy, Shaykh Harb was abducted in early March by Israeli security forces.

The detention of the popular Shaykh triggered a furore among the Shi'a, both lay and clerical, and a series of country-wide sit-ins took place in protest. The most prominent of these sit-ins was that organised on 20 October 1984 by Fadlallah in the B'ir al-Abd mosque, in the southern suburbs, where a sizeable group of Shi'i and Sunni 'ulama had attended before leading a large procession of followers along the streets of the quarter. The assassination of Shaykh Harb by Israeli-hired gunmen on 16 February 1984 triggered a storm of popular indignation, and gave further impetus to the Islamist Shi'i wing of the armed struggle. In the following two weeks, Fadlallah featured prominently in commemorative ceremonies in Beirut, organised by the activist ecumenical league of clerics (Tajammu al-'ulama al-Muslimeen) in Beirut and in Bekaa, organised by Hizbullah.[77] Shaykh Harb was the first Shi'i *'alim* to be martyred in the cause of liberation, but several other middle-aged activist clerics and young religious students, who had also received their religious education under Fadlallah, would meet a similar fate.[78]

The more desperate and harsh the Israeli campaign to suppress the resistance, culminating in Israel's notoriously harsh Iron Fist policy, the greater the enmity toward Israel and the resolve to intensify the armed struggle against the occupation. A centrepiece of Israel's 'counter-insurgency' strategy was the policy of collective punishment. Designed to emasculate the growing resistance movement, the punitive measures – including raids on villages, the ransacking and demolition of houses, the setting of crops ablaze, and mass arrests and interrogations of young Shi'i suspects – had the net effect of invigorating and expanding the armed struggle against the occupation. The failure from August 1983 of Israel's campaign against the resistance led to a series of staged withdrawals southwards, ending in June 1985 with the redeployment of a much-reduced Israeli force along a narrow strip abutting the Israeli–Lebanese border. Originally carved out in 1978, and manned by surrogate, mainly Christian militias commanded by the former Lebanese army Major Sa'ad Haddad, the unilaterally declared security zone was subsequently policed by Israel's proxy, the South Lebanese Army, headed by Antoine Lahad, a former major-general.[79]

For Fadlallah, the retreat of Israel to the southern extremity of Lebanon did not herald the decline of resistance against Israeli occupation. On the contrary, the success of the Islamic resistance movement vindicated, in Shi'i eyes, the righteousness of its cause, and highlighted the need to continue and intensify the armed struggle until the complete liberation of South Lebanon. Yet, in Fadlallah's pan-Islamist view, the armed struggle against Israel in Lebanon was not an end in itself – a mere localised patriotic war of liberation – but a revolutionary means to expand a sacred struggle into Israel/Palestine itself.[80] It will be recalled that Fadlallah, like other Islamists, regarded Israel as anathema: an illegitimate expansionist entity built on the ruins of pre-1948 Palestine, and the eviction of its Arab population. Fadlallah now called forcibly for the pursuit of holy struggle against Israel, instilling the idea among the young Islamic Hizbullah activists that their armed struggle stemmed not merely from the occupation of southern Lebanon, but more importantly from the Israeli occupation of Palestine.

In a systematic and effective attempt to invoke religious motivation, Fadlallah forcibly argued that fighting the Israeli occupation was as sacred a duty as performing prayers; since the worshipper is impelled to refrain from all reprehensible acts or conditions, then it follows that he is duty-bound to fight all forms of abomination and injustice, most notably Israeli aggression and oppression. Similarly, Fadlallah sought to mobilise the thousands of young Shi'i devotees who engage in the traditional ritual self-flagellation during the annual *'Ashoura* ceremony. He persuaded many of his co-religionists to refrain from inflicting self-injury, and to emulate the revolt of their bereaved hero Imam Hussein by fighting the enemy on the battlefield. What many Lebanese failed to realise, argued Fadlallah in a lecture in early 1985, was that Israel, as a forward base of 'Western imperialism' in the region, was bent on territorial expansionism and political and economic domination of the Middle East. So long as Israel remained a regional power, the political stability, unity and development of Lebanon and the Arab world in general would be seriously undermined.[81] Hence, the confrontation with Israel transcended the issue of recovering Lebanon's southern territory; it encapsulated an existential and epic struggle, and represented a fundamental clash of destinies.

Even in the event of Israel being recognised by the PLO, the Arab regimes and the entire world, Fadlallah declared that in his eyes Israel would remain illegitimate and had no right to exist as a nation-state because what God had ordained could not be contradicted: namely, that theft and usurpation are illicit.[82] Fadlallah's radical solution: the return of all Palestinian refugees to Palestine, and the emigration of the non-indigenous Jewish settlers, who had arrived in Palestine following the displacement of the Palestinian inhabitants.[83] Thus, for Fadlallah and his Islamist followers, as long as the displaced Palestinians were deprived of their national homeland, Israel's state of illegality would never change.[84] In contradistinction to Hizbullah, Amal's participation in the resistance movement was dictated primarily by Israel's occupation of South Lebanon, and it had no desire to extend the conflict across the border.

Fadlallah saw the Lebanese resistance as a precursor for Islamising and revolutionising the patriotic struggle, both locally and globally. The resistance would instil in the Shi'i populace the ethos of revolt and independence, bringing about radical transformation of the status quo in Lebanon, and ensuring the inheritance of that spirit by successive generations. The resistance movement in Lebanon was viewed by Fadlallah as an integral part of the wider liberation struggle against 'Western neo-imperialism': 'We wish not only to be an Islamic resistance in the south but also in the Islamic and *mustada'feen* (downtrodden) peoples of the Third World.' Proceeding from the premise that freedom is indivisible, Fadlallah stressed that Lebanese Islamists are just as committed to the liberation of downtrodden non-Muslims as they are to the emancipation of subjugated Muslims. As a corollary to this tenet of Islamic liberation theology, Fadlallah postulated that the furthering and strengthening of the cause of liberation in any part of the less developed world is bound to invigorate the cause of freedom elsewhere in the Third World. Fadlallah sought to project Islamic resistance as a viable example of activism to Third World nations under foreign domination and local injustice. Herein lay Fadlallah's endeavour to internationalise the Lebanese resistance, so that it would become the rallying point for activists, Muslims and non-Muslims alike, in the Third World.[85] Central to this success, according to Fadlallah, was the endeavour to pool the resources and coordinate the activities of the various nationalist, leftist and Islamist groups fighting Israel. Thus, in mid-November 1984, Fadlallah received a delegation of the Lebanese Communist Party. The meeting centred on the need to intensify the resistance and forge closer ties between Islamic, leftist and nationalist movements, and the methods of doing so.[86]

In declaring in March 1985 that 'We [Islamists] must plan for a future in which Israel will not be present', Fadlallah was expressing a long-standing and implacable antipathy towards the state of Israel that reflected the aspirations of a committed radical activist. Conversely, as a realist and pragmatist, Fadlallah was under no illusions in relation to the fact that the defeat of the formidable 'Zionist entity' could only come about through careful, long-term strategic planning, based on the supple adjustment to changing circumstances. Ironically, the feasibility of such a goal was vindicated by the achievement of the European Zionist movement, which, thanks to its strategic planning, resources and commitment over a period of fifty years, saw the establishment of a Jewish national state in the 'Promised Land' in 1948. Thus, while Islamists like Fadlallah envisioned the liberation of Palestine, in practice the outcome of the struggle would depend on the nature of future circumstances. At present, and for the foreseeable future, the 'objective circumstances' governing the political equation in the region were not conducive to the liberation of Palestine.[87]

As a means of preparing the revolutionary ground for the decisive confrontation with Israel, Fadlallah and his Islamists strove to radicalise the masses of the Arab and Muslim worlds by engendering a populist, rejectionist *hala*, or condition, averse to any compromise with the Jewish state. Accordingly, Fadlallah did not envisage the current Arab regimes having any role in the liberation struggle; it was a 'noble' cause that had been cynically appropriated by these states and turned into empty slogans for public consumption with a view to bolstering their own problematic legitimacy. He asserted that the Arab states, despite their supposed commitment to Palestine as expressed in official rhetoric, had insidiously conspired against the Palestinians and their resistance, with the overriding concern being not how to liberate Palestine but how to free themselves from the 'unbearable burden' that is Palestine.[88]

Amal–PLO Conflict

If Fadlallah expressed lamentation about the status of the Palestinian cause in the recent policies of Arab states in the region, such as Jordan and Syria, he looked on with consternation as fierce clashes broke out between Syrian-backed Amal and the PLO in May 1985. In what became known as the 'War of the Camps', the conflict that began with Amal's protracted siege and bombardment of Beirut's three Palestinian camps subsequently expanded to engulf the Palestinian camps of South Lebanon, and continued with varying degrees of intensity until January 1988. Amal's offensive was precipitated by the rearmament of the Palestinian camps and the return from exile of fedayeen guerrillas from abroad. The renewal of guerrilla activity and the rebuilding of military infrastructure conflicted with Amal's recent ascendancy in west Beirut and the southern suburbs, and posed a potential impediment to Syria's overlordship in Lebanon. Amal's full-scale assault on the camps, and the high casualty toll among their civilian occupants, resulted in the rallying of the otherwise warring Palestinian factions behind Arafat's Fatah organisation, as well as their tacit backing of Jumblatt's mainly Druze PSP.[89]

Though officially neutral in what was viewed as an internecine war, Hizbullah tacitly supported the emasculation of its Shi'i rival, particularly during the latter phases of the conflict, in order to establish its own supremacy in the South. With the focus of fighting, as of April 1986, having shifted to the camps in the South, and fearing that a successful Amal military pacification of the South would substantially inhibit, if not close, the Islamc resistance's access to Israel's 'buffer' zone, Hizbullah began to align itself with the PLO.[90] Thanks to Fadlallah, who was largely responsible for infusing Hizbullah with an ideological commitment to the Palestinian cause, the Shi'i Islamist movement viewed the ongoing war as an international conspiracy against Muslim unity in the region.

Only two weeks after the eruption of the War of the Camps, Fadlallah issued a fatwa forbidding a continuation of the bloodletting. However, apart from the withdrawal of a significant minority of religiously inclined Amal affiliates, the fighting continued unabated. Six weeks later, Fadlallah managed to initiate a ceasefire between the two antagonists; but the truce proved short-lived, as fighting resumed three days later. In a Friday *khutbah* in mid-1985, Fadlallah admonished the feuding parties that those who genuinely sought to liberate Palestine would refrain from being embroiled in an internal war of attrition, the ultimate aim of which was to 'liquidate' the Palestinian cause. More immediately, Fadlallah claimed that, thanks to this internecine war, Israel had indefinitely suspended its withdrawal from Lebanon.[91] Although he objected to Arafat's leadership and liaisons with the Americans to bring pressure to bear on Israel, Fadlallah could not countenance any justification for the launching of attacks on defenceless Palestinian refugees.[92] Moreover, as a longstanding champion of the Palestinian resistance, Fadlallah opposed Amal's principal demand for the disarmament of the camps, asserting that they were entitled to be armed to defend themselves and fight Israel to recover Palestine. Yet Fadlallah stressed that he was only for the deployment of Palestinian men and material provided they were directed against Israel and its proxy militias.[93]

His opposition to the Amal–PLO war raises the question of the extent to which Fadlallah was successful in his efforts to limit the debilitating effects of the conflict. Fadlallah made a sustained effort to dispel the general Shi'i image of Palestinians as bogeymen, stressing that while this attitude, stemming from the domineering behaviour of the fedayeen in the pre-1982 period, may have been true of many Palestinian fighters, the image in no way represented Palestinians in general, most of whom were innocent, decent people.[94] That many Shi'a unaffiliated to Hizbullah were not prepared to support Amal's war against the Palestinians can be attributed in part to Fadlallah's speeches and sermons. More obvious was Fadlallah's success in keeping Hizbullah and allied Islamists largely out of the conflict.

Besides the capture of the small camp of Sabra, Amal failed in its campaign against the PLO. Not only was Amal weakened by internal divisions and exhausted by its repeated military assaults against the well defended camps; it was further sapped by its involvement, since the latter half of 1985, in a second front – in west Beirut, against the combined militias of the Druze PSP and the Lebanese Communist Party.[95] With its struggle against the leftists on the streets of west Beirut all but collapsing, Amal was eventually saved from complete defeat by the redeployment of Syrian troops in February 1987. Amal's weakness invigorated Hizbullah as a serious contender for the leadership of Lebanon's Shi'a. The re-entry of some 7,000 Syrian troops into west Beirut would mark the apogee of Hizbullah's expansion in the capital.

Internal Shi'i Conflict and the Western Hostages

On 24 February – that is, three days after the redeployment of Syrian troops – an incident took place that would mark the nadir of Syrian–Hizbullah relations. During an attempt to expand their zone of control in west Beirut, the Syrians were impeded in the Basta quarter, where a major Hizbullah base was located. Hizbullah fighters refused to accede to Syrian demands to disarm, and in the altercation that followed 23 Hizbullah cadres were pursued, shot and killed by a Syrian regular unit.[96]

The Syrians considered Hizbullah's presence in west Beirut as too independent and assertive, consequently posing a potential threat to their control. Although the confrontation confirmed Syrian mastery over the capital, and conversely represented a clear setback to Hizbullah's expansion into west Beirut, the Islamist movement maintained an active, albeit diminished presence. Fadlallah, however, took a different view: the mere closure of Hizbullah offices in west Beirut did not represent a major blow to the movement. He proceeded to explain that Hizbullah was a mass-based movement with a broad, amorphous following, rendering it very difficult, if not impossible, for any adversarial local or regional power to contain or eliminate it. Following the seizure of their headquarters in west Beirut, a large number of Hizbullah fighters withdrew to the southern suburbs. Many of these fighters, however, returned later to west Beirut, at the behest of Fadlallah.[97]

The killings provoked sharp condemnation by Iranian and Hizbullah leaders, who declared their emphatic rejection of any Syrian attempt to disarm the Islamist movement or expand the security operation to the southern suburbs. As a measure of the depth of anti-Syrian sentiment, some 50,000 Shi'a poured onto the streets of the southern suburbs, chanting anti-Syrian slogans in unison. Senior Iranian figures called for punishment of the perpetrators, while some Hizbullah leaders called for revenge.[98] For his part, Fadlallah depicted the shootings as 'premeditated killings' and 'a massacre'.[99]

While Fadlallah called for the trial of the Syrian soldiers, he astutely avoided publicly criticising the Syrian regime or its security plan for Beirut. Six days after the incident, in a Friday sermon in Teheran, Fadlallah issued a warning to the Syrians that in clamping down on Hizbullah they were not merely rousing the hostility of an ordinary political party but antagonising the whole *umma*.[100] Careful to avoid having his position misconstrued as a spur to anti-Syrian action by incensed Shi'i Islamists, Fadlallah maintained that the tragedy constituted an aberration from an otherwise effective peacekeeping mission, though he did not see any need for the security plan to be expanded to include the relatively calm southern suburbs.[101] In the end, major confrontation was only averted through intense Iranian–Syrian negotiations.[102]

No sooner had the hostilities between Amal and the PLO ended than a new conflict erupted, this time pitting Shi'i against Shi'i. The fratricidal war between Amal and Hizbullah was the culmination of heightening tension between the two rival movements contending for supremacy in the South; and it also reflected a fundamental divergence over the issue of Palestinian disarmament. Even before the War of the Camps, relations between the two movements had been strained on account of the wave of bombings, in 1984 and 1985, of bars and liquor-serving restaurants by Islamic activists linked to Hizbullah, and by the wave of kidnappings by Islamic Jihad of Westerners suspected to have loose ties to Hizbullah. With the fall of west Beirut to the Amal movement in the wake of the insurrection on 4 February 1984, the Islamic measures imposed by the Shi'i 'upstarts' posed a direct challenge to the authority of the secular-minded Nabih Berri and his reformist movement. As a result of Amal's attempts to curtail the activities of Hizbullah, clashes erupted between the rival groups, ending with the former overrunning the positions of the latter. Interviewed at the height of the anti-liquor campaign, Fadlallah explained that while there might be justification for devout Muslim individuals to smash liquor bottles, there was no legal basis for the wanton destruction of property. In another interview a week later, Fadlallah said that wilful damage of private property and injury of innocent bystanders was impermissible. In a speech delivered in December 1984, Fadlallah condemned the bombing of leisure centres and bars, lest they blemish the image of Islam.[103]

Since the first spate of kidnappings by the shadowy al-Jihad al-Islami, Fadlallah had disavowed any role in the abductions or knowledge of the captors. From the outset, Fadlallah had rejected the legitimacy and utility of kidnapping. He pointed out that there was no justification in Islam for the kidnapping of innocents, nor did he see any 'righteousness in any acts of that kind'. He might sympathise, Fadlallah added, with the motives or cause of the kidnappers or hijackers, but that did not denote an endorsement of the means pursued. Alluding to the seizure of Western journalists, academics, doctors and religious leaders, Fadlallah stressed that those professionals 'cannot be held responsible for the actions of their government'. Still, Fadlallah's stature among the Shi'i Islamist ranks made him the focus of Western media attention, and of several attempts (by such high-profile personalities as Terry Anderson, the Associated Press correspondent, Terry Waite, the special envoy of the Archbishop of Canterbury, and Giandomenico Picco, the UN hostage mediator) to solicit his services to mediate an end to the hostage crisis.[104] Yet, for all his attempts to bring about the release of the hostages, Fadlallah only succeeded in highlighting his own limited leverage over the captors and their patrons.

In apparent retaliation for the kidnapping of an American colonel serving with UNIFIL in south Lebanon, Amal launched a full-scale assault on Hizbullah strongholds in the south on 4 April 1988.[105] Caught unprepared by the swift and concerted attack, Hizbullah combatants lost the battle in three days of heavy fighting.[106] To consolidate its grip on the newly captured territory, Amal began deporting many Hizbullah fighters and cadres to the Bekaa valley. One month after its defeat in the south, Hizbullah launched a fierce counter-offensive against its rival, this time in the heavily populated southern suburbs of Beirut. Racked by poor discipline and defections, and infiltrated by Islamists, Amal saw its militiamen dislodged from all but two quarters.[107] The ferocious fighting, which gave Hizbullah some 90 per cent of the largely devastated suburbs, claimed the lives of 500 people, mostly civilians, and injured another 2,000.[108]

Living in the Hizbullah stronghold of B'ir al-Abd, Fadlallah was appalled by the extent of the destruction, with both sides using heavy weapons in densely populated slums; and he was distressed by the enormous casualty toll, the polarisation of neighbourhoods, and even the splintering of families along factional lines. Not for the first time, his home became a target of both concentrated shelling and a ground assault by Amal militiamen.[109] The eruption and continuation of the Hizbullah–Amal conflict was a personal setback for Fadlallah and a major blow to his efforts to avert systematic fratricide. The continuation, and indeed escalation, of the war threatened to unravel all that Fadlallah had so vigorously striven for – the solidarity of Muslim, and particularly Shi'i ranks, and confrontation with Israel. While in the War of the Camps he had managed with some success to prevent the spread of fighting from embroiling the Lebanese Islamist movement, the Shi'i–Shi'i war seriously threatened to tear asunder the very fabric of Fadlallah's own constituency.

From the outset, Fadlallah strove diligently but with limited success to bring the conflict to an end.[110] In the first Friday sermon delivered since the start of the conflict, Fadlallah 'exhorted all fighters to disobey combat orders issued by their commanders, to defect from their fighting units and to isolate their leaders'. Underscoring the absolute illegality of fratricide, Fadlallah made use of his credentials as *mujtahid* and ayatollah to insist that 'it is impermissible from the Islamic legal standpoint for a believer to bear arms against another believer, as the fate of [both] the killer and killed will be [an abode] in hell'. It is significant that Fadlallah did not issue a formal fatwa forbidding Amal–Hizbullah fratricide, citing as justification the possibility of it being misconstrued or misappropriated by either party. At the height of the battle for the slums, Fadlallah refuted as baseless the rumours that he had issued a fatwa permitting the slaying of Amal fighters. Fadlallah linked the allegation to the intelligence services, as part of their insidious campaign to discredit him. Later, as the conflict raged through the streets of the southern suburbs, *al-Dahyah*, Fadlallah challenged the warring parties to resolve their differences and turn their fury against Israel – the only beneficiary of the continued bloodletting. He told his audience that the nature of the petty and internecine conflict meant that there could be no triumph for either party, implying that victory could only be clinched by confronting Israel.[111] The severity of the fighting, despite energetic efforts to resolve it, once again served to underline the limits of Fadlallah's influence over Hizbullah. The fact that the war was finally brought to a conclusion through Iranian diplomacy demonstrated that, in the final analysis, Hizbullah's leadership was beholden to Iran's paramount leader, Ayatollah Khomeini.

Intermittent clashes between the two groups in the suburbs continued until an agreement was finally reached, in late May 1988, allowing the entry of Syrian peacekeepers. Contrary to Western expectations, the entry of 1,500 or so Syrian soldiers did not lead to a clampdown on Hizbullah, or to the release of the Western hostages. On the contrary, Hizbullah affiliates, in accordance with the Iranian-brokered arrangement, were permitted to keep their arms – as long as they were stored at home or used in combat against the Israelis in the south; and the movement was allowed to keep its newly conquered territory.[112]

In the wake of the termination of Hizbullah–Amal hostilities, and the entry of Syrian security forces into the suburbs, Fadlallah maintained in an interview that he had advised Hizbullah of the necessity of dialogue with their ideological and political opponents. The strategy was aimed at ensuring that Hizbullah did not become marginalised but remained an important feature of the political and ideological landscape of Lebanon. Through such openness and accommodation, Fadlallah sought to dispel the common perception of Hizbullah as an extremist and terrorist organisation.[113]

Fadlallah and the Debate over an Islamic State in Lebanon

Besides the discord over the scale and nature of the armed struggle against Israel's occupation of South Lebanon, one of the most contentious issues in Lebanese intellectual and political circles in the 1980s was the call for the establishment of an Islamic republic in Lebanon. Though promoted by the country's Islamist movement, the advocates of an Islamic polity differed over its feasibility and the best method of its achievement. Among the proponents of the theory of an Islamic state, Fadlallah was arguably the most sophisticated and lucid. He forcibly argued that Muslims, being adherents of a faith that encapsulates a distinct ideology with its own political tenets and institutions, should be entitled to propound the idea of an Islamic state as a major plank in contemporary political agenda; to re-introduce it as an important issue of intellectual debate between Muslims and Christians, and between Muslims themselves; and to propagate the idea among the public until it became a familiar, if not universally supported concept.[114] But, as a realist, Fadlallah stated that at present and for the foreseeable future an Islamic polity in Lebanon was an impracticable aspiration. His assessment was based on Lebanon's multi-confessional composition, the distaste of non-Islamists, and the hostility of regional powers – namely Israel and Syria.

Until 1983 the philosophical concept and the juridical imperative of an Islamic state had been delineated at the theoretical level in the broad context of Islamic activism, as expounded in a number of treatises.[115] Though doubtless important for the emergence of Fadlallah as an eminent Islamist intellectual, Fadlallah's evolving discourse on Islamic governance and activism was relatively unknown outside Shiʿi Islamist circles. Following the spectacular suicide bombings of American, French and Israeli targets in Lebanon, Fadlallah adroitly used his sudden exposure to the local and foreign media to set forth the Islamist vision of – and quest for – an Islamic state.

Deeming the repeated, strident calls made by Hizbullah activists and Iranian leaders for the immediate establishment of an Islamic government in Lebanon to be premature, Fadlallah advocated a gradualist strategy that included crucial preparatory and transitory phases. Essentially, this would entail creating the necessary conditions on the ground, based on a campaign of public education, gradually to erode the prevailing sentiment of opposition to such a state. As a first step to that end, Fadlallah opined during an annual festivity marking the success of the Islamic Revolution in Iran that the 'strategic goal of the Islamic movement in Lebanon is to eliminate the current confessionalist system of government; a goal shared by many secular-minded Lebanese, including nominal Christians'.[116]

Fadlallah's pragmatism – as much a reflection of realism as an independent mentality – placed him at loggerheads with some senior Iranian clerical figures, including Khomeini's designated deputy, Ayatollah Ali Muntazeri. Thus, while denying that the Iranian leaders were contemplating an Islamic republic in Lebanon, Fadlallah acknowledged that 'some Iranian scholars and some officials were perhaps not fully aware of the situation in Lebanon. We told them that Lebanon was different [from Iran]; that we do not have sufficient and necessary conditions for an Islamic Republic …' Indeed, a year earlier Fadlallah had expressed this view on the issue, stating in more than one interview that in the present circumstances the necessary pre-conditions for the emergence of an Islamic state were non-existent, and (in still another interview) that 'the person who does not consider the existing constraints on the scene is indulging in idealism or fantasy'. Instead, in line with other Muslim religious and political leaders, Fadlallah for now underscored the need to effect a redistribution of power away from the traditional configuration of Maronite minority rule, with a view to establishing a non-confessional democratic state. Though a staunch supporter of Iran's Islamic Revolution, Fadlallah had calculated that the possibility in Lebanon of a national religious upheaval similar to that of 1978–79 in Iran was very remote, owing to the country's heterogeneous population and regional opposition. Rather than violent, radical change, Fadlallah thus advocated peaceful infiltration of selected institutions within society. Only if and when the predominant majority of Lebanon's citizens voted in favour of an Islamic state, combined with conducive political circumstances in the region, could an Islamic government be installed.[117]

To allay the deep-seated apprehensions of Lebanon's large and powerful

Christian community, Fadlallah endeavoured to demonstrate the inclusivist character of Islam's political enterprise, arguing that it did not fundamentally conflict with – much less negate – Christianity, and that Islam's paradigm was irreconcilable with modern secular ideologies, particularly Marxism. He predicated his view on the basis of Islam's organic fusion of religious faith and political power. By contrast, in Christianity, Fadlallah argued – contentiously – that church and state were separate, and that its adherents were not enjoined to establish God's temporal kingdom. As a corollary, Fadlallah advanced the somewhat unconvincing argument that, with Christianity being oriented towards the nurturing of individual faith and social morality, Christians ought not to have problems integrating as citizens of an Islamic state, unlike within a Marxist or communist regime.[118] Fadlallah's premise that Christians would prefer to live in an Islamic state than an irreligious Marxist state rested on the erroneous assumption that Lebanon's Christians were religiously minded and receptive to their Muslim compatriots, rather than being confessionalist or secular in orientation. The second mistaken assumption underlying Fadlallah's views was that, to the extent that Christians are prepared to live in a communist or liberal state, they could be equally if not more willing to live in an Islamic–humanist state.

For the majority of Christian religious and political leaders who were not swayed by his reasoning, Fadlallah tried to justify the case for an Islamic political ideology by drawing on two analogies. First, just as Christian evangelists were committed to proselytising the non-Christian world, so too Muslim activists, impelled by their faith's global mission, sought to Islamise the non-Muslim world. Second, drawing a comparison between the Comintern, which theoretically subordinated the myriad national communist parties to the international apparatus based in Moscow, and pan-Islamism, which tied many local Islamist groups to the revolutionary Islamic regime in Iran, Fadlallah asked why Lebanon's Christian leaders tolerated trans-nationalist organisations (the Lebanese Communist Party, and pan-Arab nationalist groups) but not Islamist groups operating in the country. Citing Islam's historical and religiously enshrined recognition and institutional protection of *Ahl al-Kitab* (People of the Book – namely Jews and Christians), Fadlallah asked rhetorically, 'of the two, which poses a greater threat to Christianity [in Lebanon], an Islamic government or a Marxist regime? Surely a country that prides itself on religious freedom and political pluralism ought to give every citizen the right to propound his view and strive to transform it into reality, so long as it is not effected through coercion.' Yet, he told his readers, in contrast to the licensed socialist and communist parties, none of the Islamist parties active in a country that prided itself on individual freedom and political pluralism (in the 1980s) was legalised.[119]

The period between late August and mid-September 1986 saw a flurry of declarations and petitions in favour of an Islamic republic, ostensibly signed by local residents of the largely Shi'i villages, hamlets and urban quarters of Beirut. Alarmed that the publications signalled the start of a concerted drive by Islamists to install an Islamic regime in Lebanon, Fadlallah tried to reassure the Christians that 'we are not preparing to establish an Islamic republic ... all these petitions and cables do not represent the [mainstream] Islamic movement'. Denying all links with the group orchestrating the campaign (the small, radical Islamic Movement in Lebanon), Fadlallah declared that petitions would not give rise to an Islamic state, as it necessitated the existence of objective preconditions and a long preparatory phase of public awareness. Both were deemed to be absent from prevailing conditions in Lebanon. Fadlallah added that while he was committed, for the foreseeable future, to seeing Lebanon's Muslims live in peaceful co-existence with the Christians, he was equally committed to an equitable power-sharing arrangement that reflected the demographics of the two confessional communities. In common with nearly all Sunni, Shi'i and Druze religious and political figures, Fadlallah actively opposed the continued existence of a Maronite-dominated administration. But in calling for the ousting of the Gemayel minority administration, Fadlallah was non-committal as to the form of government he desired in its place. His vision of the new republic was rather vague, but included the requirements that it be deconfessionalised and truly representative, and independent of foreign influence and Israeli control.[120]

Earlier Fadlallah's pragmatism and openness towards Christians was demonstrated in Hizbullah's manifesto, 'Open Letter to the Downtrodden' (*al-Risalah al-Maftuha li al-Mustad'afeen*), published in February 1985. The manifesto was issued on the first anniversary of the assassination of Shaykh Raghib Harb, a fiery orator and vehement opponent of Israeli occupation. It also came one month after Israel had announced its decision to pull out the bulk of its troops from much of Lebanon and deploy a small garrison in its unilaterally declared security 'buffer zone'. The proclamation also marked the first year since the unceremonious pulling out of the MNF from Beirut, and the subsequent abrogation of the 17 May 1983 Accord. The Open Letter was distinguished by its stress on 'America as the cause of all afflictions and the source of all malice', and by the unequivocal declaration of total obedience to Khomeini, considered the ruling jurist (*waliyatu al-faqih*) and paramount leader (*qa'id*) of the universal Muslim *umma*. The ideological and political implications of this allegiance were clear: Khomeini's authority was not confined by political geography, as it encompassed the entire Muslim world. Fadlallah was instrumental in inserting a passage that enshrined the citizens' right to choose the form of government they desired. Three months after the promulgation of the manifesto, Fadlallah claimed he had persuaded senior Iranian government leaders into forgoing the revolutionary course and accepting a democratic path for Lebanon's restive Muslim majority. Thanks to the indelible imprint of Fadlallah's pragmatism, militant Hizbullah leaders such as Shaykh Subhi al-Tufayli now issued public statements upholding democracy as a mechanism for exercising political rights, while enunciating their preference for Islamic rule.[121]

Fadlallah had been expounding his views on Islamist political participation in democratic institutions in a series of articles appearing in the period between 1984 and 1986 in the bimonthly Islamic student journal, *al-Muntalaq*. After analysing the various options for invigorating the cause of Islamist activism, and deeming the Iranian-inspired path of revolutionary upheaval, advocated by a group of doctrinaire radicals, inappropriate to the Lebanese setting, Fadlallah advocated a strategy of systematic and gradual societal reform. To generate support for his insistence that the notion of an Islamic regime was not advocated as something to be forcibly imposed, but merely as a theoretical idea to be debated, Fadlallah led an Islamist initiative for a sustained intellectual dialogue between Muslim and Christian religious scholars. In time, objective and rigorous talks were envisaged to lead to a more profound understanding of Muslim–Christian sentiments and aspirations, resulting in a more congenial climate for relationship-building and a greater willingness for cooperation on issues of common concern. Thus, informed discussion and subtle persuasion would gradually dispel misconceptions and misapprehensions pertaining to Islamists and their agenda, eroding the large if not dominant domestic opposition to Islamic governance. With the majority of the citizenry now swayed in favour of a civil Islamic state, Islamists would be voted into government, either through a referendum or democratic elections.[122]

As a measure of the Herculean task that lay ahead in Fadlallah's quest for Islamic primacy in Lebanon, influential figures within the Shi'i community opposed the very notion of an Islamic state in their country. While Fadlallah's respected colleague, and leader of the Supreme Islamic Shi'i Council, Shaykh Mahdi Shams al-Din, was lukewarm about the idea, having advocated *al-Dimuqratiyah al-Ta'adudiyah* (an ambiguous system literally denoting 'Numeric Democracy', which he had formulated himself), his deputy, and Shi'i mufti, Shaykh Abdul-Amir Qabalan, rejected unequivocally any suggestions of an Islamic state. He was of the firm belief that such a state would further fracture rather than integrate the various communities comprising Lebanon's fragile heterogeneity. Nabih Berri, leader of the powerful Amal movement, opposed the establishment of an Islamic regime in the country, on the basis that Islamic radicalism would by default bolster the Maronite right, by providing the necessary pretext to establish a counter-Christian statelet.[123]

It is revealing that a survey conducted in early February 1986 by a group of Lebanese Muslim students on the question of an Islamic state in Lebanon yielded a list of 63 predominantly junior and middle-ranking Shi'i and Sunni 'ulama who, to varying degrees, expressed their support for such a polity.[124] Among the prominent signatories who gave their qualified endorsement were Fadlallah and Shaykh Shams al-Din. But equally prominent, by their absence, were Shaykh Hasan Khalid and Shaykh Qabalan, the highest state-appointed Sunni and Shi'i muftis.

In mid-March 1986, a Beirut daily newspaper reported that a preliminary proposal for an Islamic constitution in Lebanon (*Mashrou al-Dustour al-Islami fi Lubnan*) had been drafted, under Iranian aegis, by a coterie of Lebanese Shi'i and Sunni scholars and activists, reportedly including Fadlallah and Shams al-Din. The drawing up of the constitution apparently took place in Teheran, where an annual three-day international Islamic conference had been convened, and at the end of which the Lebanese delegation proceeded to the residence of Imam Khomeini, where discussions centred on the issue of the constitution. Khomeini apparently impressed on his guests the imperative of a new Islamic constitution for the Lebanese Republic, to replace the existing one immediately following the future declaration of the Islamic state.[125] Five days of intense discussions resulted in the endorsement of the preliminary draft of the proposed constitution, following recommendations made by Shams al-Din. Details on the role of Fadlallah in the whole process are ambiguous.

According to Carre, Fadlallah played a prominent part in devising the legal document, which carried his signature. In private correspondence, Fadlallah stated emphatically that the report was fallacious in its entirety. Be that as it may, one development that did occur during that extraordinary gathering was Khomeini's conferring of ayatollah status on the then *hujtul-islam* (literally, 'proof of Islam'), Fadlallah. This elevation now entitled him as a senior *mujtahid* to issue fatwas and become a juridical authority, a source of emulation for lay Shi'a in Lebanon and elsewhere. With this promotion, Fadlallah was now on a par with his colleague Shams al-Din, who had earlier been designated as an ayatollah. In time Fadlallah would overshadow his colleague in influence, if not scholarly authority.[126]

In early November 1987 leaflets began to circulate in Beirut streets carrying portraits of Fadlallah, together with those of three other activist 'ulama nominated for the presidency of the Republic.[127] The leaflets, whose contents had been given headline coverage by all Lebanese newspapers, were signed and issued by the Islamic Movement in Lebanon, a Bekaa-based grouping of staunchly pro-Khomeini middle- and junior-ranked 'ulama and lay Shi'i activists.[128] The movement, founded in the late 1970s, was headed by the Sayyid Sadeq al-Musawi.[129] Although there is no indication that Fadlallah had given his consent to the presidential campaign, his attitude to the issue was ambivalent. On the one hand, while his official spokesmen denied any links to the group behind the leaflets, saying that the unofficial nomination did not trouble him, on the other hand another newspaper reported that the publication was depicted as propaganda aimed at public incitement. By contrast, Fadlallah stated in an interview that while he did not approve of the inclusion of his candidature, he did perceive it as a means to challenge popular perception that the president must be a Maronite Christian.[130]

In contrast to a minority of Shi'i Islamic activists, who as staunch Khomeinists called for the immediate installation of an Islamic state modelled on Iran, the majority affiliated to Hizbullah – though espousing the Islamic state as an axiomatic ideological tenet – envisioned the realisation of that goal in the distant future. The leaders of Hizbullah gave precedence to the pursuit of armed struggle against the Israeli occupation of South Lebanon over the establishment of an Islamic regime.[131] Again, this ordering of priorities can be attributed to Fadlallah's influence. As a realist, Fadlallah correctly judged that with the majority of Lebanon's citizens, both Muslim and Christian, averse to the very notion of an Islamic state, any serious attempt to bring it about would be profoundly divisive, as well as detrimental to the more pressing goal of intensifying the resistance campaign.

Thus, for Fadlallah and his followers, the quest for an Islamic government in Lebanon was held in abeyance until favourable local and regional conditions prevailed. Regionally, the proponents of an Islamic state in Lebanon predicated the pursuit of that venture on the long-anticipated Iranian military breakthrough in its war of attrition with its neighbour, with the consequent collapse of the Ba'thist regime and the installation of an Islamic state in Iraq. According to Hizbullah's scenario, this metamorphosis would usher in a sequence of revolutionary upheavals in the adjoining Arab states, including Lebanon.[132] Issuing from these momentous changes would be the formation of a pan-Islamic dominion vehemently hostile to Israel. The ensuing confrontation with the Jewish state would result in the liberation of Palestine. Thus, if Fadlallah and Hizbullah leaders viewed the expulsion or withdrawal of Israeli troops from South Lebanon as a major step along the path towards Jerusalem, a decisive Iranian military victory over Iraq would be crucial to the prospects of the future jihad.

The End of the Iran–Iraq War

In early 1987, Iran launched a massive land offensive along the southern sector of the Iraqi front, aimed at capturing the important port city of Basra. In an interview in March 1987, Fadlallah expressed cautious optimism of an imminent Iranian breakthrough, believing that Iran possessed the military capacity to achieve that strategic goal. Thus, when on 14 July 1988 Khomeini reluctantly announced his war-weary country's readiness to accept a UN resolution for a truce, Fadlallah, who had in the preceding weeks confidently talked of Iran's unremitting fortitude and ardour in the face of US naval intervention against it, was startled by the momentous decision. Realising that the likelihood of an Iranian victory had all but disappeared, Fadlallah would later explain the acceptance of the ceasefire by citing American intervention in the conflict, the Iraqi deployment of chemical and biological weapons, and the launching of long-range missiles against major cities in Iran, combined with international isolation and Western sanctions. Fadlallah interpreted Khomeini's decision as a tactical move, signifying a temporary cessation of hostilities rather than a permanent settlement, adding that it was a 'calculated, courageous and intelligent' tactic that thwarted American designs on Iran, and protected the Islamic regime from an orchestrated counter-revolution.[133]

If the inconclusive termination of the Iran–Iraq war was a serious setback to the pan-Islamist cause against Israel, it was somewhat compensated for by the eruption in the neighbouring Palestinian territories of the Intifada (uprising) at the end of 1987. Fadlallah and fellow Lebanese Islamists saw in the Intifada a mass spontaneous Islamic uprising that constituted a potential precursor to a 'revolution that would convulse the enemy', and radically transform the future landscape of the region.[134] For Fadlallah the Intifada was particularly appealing and promising, because it was a genuine resistance movement sustained by mass spontaneity and propelled by Islamic sentiment that fed on a deep sense of deprivation and resentment. The populist movement was not instigated or controlled by the secular PLO; and herein lay, in Fadlallah's analysis, the potential threat to the Arab regimes, and the challenge to the credibility of the official rhetoric of solidarity with the Palestinian cause.[135]

As an international liberationist with a globalist outlook, Fadlallah insisted on the indivisibility and interdependence of liberation movements, since – notwithstanding their particular differences – they originated from a shared aspiration for freedom from oppression and foreign occupation. Accordingly, the Islamic resistance movement, spearheaded by Hizbullah in South Lebanon and the Palestinian uprising, and led by Hamas and Islamic Jihad in the Israeli-occupied territories, could only complement and reinforce each other. In this holistic perspective of universal activism, 'every position of power automatically provides the other position with new vigour'.[136]

Combined with his advocacy of a theory of Islamic liberation, and in addition to being a champion of inter-religious dialogue, Fadlallah has since the mid-1980s been a vocal proponent of Muslim–Christian political solidarity.[137] Invoking shared religious and moral values, Fadlallah appealed to Christian activists in Lebanon to forge a united front with their Muslim compatriots to combat their common enemy: Western imperialism, condemned for 'persecuting Christians as well as Muslims in the world'.[138]

As a contextual matrix for cultivating and sustaining the embryonic inter-religious solidarity against foreign hegemony and injustice, Fadlallah coined in June 1988 the concept of *Dawlat al-Insan* (literally, the 'state of man'). Perhaps surprisingly, the concept did not at the time arouse public controversy in the media. In advocating the theory for the first time during a Friday sermon, Fadlallah assured the faithful that the notion of *Dawlat al-Insan* was not intended as a substitute for but as a forerunner to an Islamic state. 'We advocate Islam', Fadlallah reaffirmed, 'but in the event that circumstances would not allow Islam to be in governance, then let us advocate *Dawlat al-Insan*.' Fadlallah conceived the proposed polity as a state that fostered the humane attributes of all Lebanese citizens – one that was founded on common human values such as dignity, social justice, economic equity, political empowerment, and freedom from foreign subjugation and influence. The official end of the fifteen-year Lebanese civil war two years later provided Fadlallah with the necessary impetus to work effectively towards making his Islamist vision an emerging reality.

It is evident from this discussion that the rapid ascent of Fadlallah onto the political scene at both national and regional levels closely mirrored the meteoric rise of Hizbullah during the course of the 1980s. It is also evident that at no stage during the evolution and crystallisation of Hizbullah did Fadlallah develop formal ties with the Shi'i Islamist movement – this despite the fact that Fadlallah, owing to his eminence as a religious scholar and jurisconsult as well as to his distinction as a leading activist and charismatic orator, exerted from the outset a major influence on Hizbullah's rank and file. As a result of his fiery political sermons, delivered from the pulpit of his mosque that overflowed with young devotees, and due to his dialectical writings on Islamist ideology and activism, Fadlallah was instrumental in orientating and nurturing the emerging Shi'i Islamist movement in the country into a major militant force fiercely opposed to American influence and Israeli occupation. True to his radical credentials, Fadlallah was arguably the most influential activist *'alim* to have inculcated a whole generation of young, predominantly but not exclusively Lebanese Shi'a, with the tenets of Islamic praxis. Conversely, for all his considerable authority and populist appeal, and in spite of his best endeavours, Fadlallah's inability to engender a lasting cessation of armed hostilities – initially between Amal and the PLO, and subsequently between Amal and Hizbullah – or to bring about the release of the western hostages in Lebanon, only served to underscore the limitations of that influence among the multifarious factions that constituted the Shi'i Islamist movement.

From the outset, while a staunch supporter of Iran's Islamic Revolution, of Khomeini's regime of clerical rule, as well as of the protracted war against Iraq, unlike the leaders of Hizbullah, Fadlallah established himself as an independent thinker and actor, rather than a mere disseminator of Khomeinist ideology or mouthpiece of Iran's revolutionary agenda in Lebanon. Despite his strident opposition to the continued Maronite domination of Lebanese politics and his unswerving hostility towards Israel, Fadlallah emerged as a prominent figure of Islamist openness to patriotic activists of other persuasions, a vocal advocate of inter-faith dialogue, and a proponent of an inclusivist liberation movement founded on Muslim–Christian solidarity.

The underlying theme of this chapter has been Fadlallah's emergence as a political pragmatist, rational thinker and radical visionary. His political realism and adaptability served the Islamist cause to which he has dedicated his life. Fadlallah's radicalism was manifest in his espousal of an Islamist *weltanschauung* and political ideology. It was specifically shown by his advocacy of an Islamic polity in Lebanon as an ideal, though distant goal. It was also reflected in his consistently strident opposition to Israel's occupation of South Lebanon, his implacable hostility towards both the 'Zionist' state and American 'neo-imperialism' in the region. At the same time, Fadlallah's pragmatism was borne out in his realistic reading of changing political circumstances, and his assessment of the opportunities and constraints yielded by a fluid operational environment. His practical approach to realising his goals was and remains a strategy based on the 'transformation of reality through the mechanisms that exist therein' [*taghyeer al-waqi bi adawaat al-waqa'*]. It is perhaps this tendency towards realism and malleability that has set Fadlallah apart from a large number of other Islamist activists.

Though consistently championing the right of Islamists to advance the notion of an Islamic state, as well as upholding the right of their opponents to debate the issue in intellectual and religious circles, Fadlallah was instrumental from the 1980s in swaying Hizbullah away from emulating Iran's revolutionary path to power. As will be borne out in the following chapter, he effectively impressed on the Lebanese Islamists the need to integrate into the country's democratic – albeit confessionalist – regime, and thereby gradually bring about the reform of state and societal institutions. For Fadlallah the realist, the onset and implications of the winds of change in reshaping the political landscape in Lebanon and the region in general indicated that the post-war era would yield new opportunities, as well as pose new challenges to which Lebanon's burgeoning Islamist movement would have to adjust if it was to continue to be a potent force in Lebanese society.

seven

Islamist Pragmatism and Accommodation in Post-Civil War Lebanon

The years between 1989 and 1996 saw a period of momentous local and regional change, beginning with the ratification of the Ta'if Accords, which itself foreshadowed the formal end, in 1990, of the fifteen-year Lebanese civil war. The twilight of the war era was marked by the quelling of General Aoun's military rebellion, and the termination of the long-running inter-Shi'i conflict between Amal and Hizbullah, while the onset of the shattered country's post-war experience saw the restoration of Beirut's central authority following the dissolution of Lebanon's numerous armed militias. In 1992, for the first time since the early 1970s, Lebanon had its first parliamentary elections, in which, unexpectedly, the country's Islamist parties, led by Hizbullah, performed impressively. Finally, in the years following the end of Amal–Hizbullah hostilities, a marked escalation took place in the guerrilla campaign waged by the Lebanese Islamic resistance against the Israeli military garrisons and their local Lebanese proxy army in occupied South Lebanon. The escalating hostilities culminated, in July 1993 and again in April 1996, in Israel's massive military onslaughts on southern Lebanon.

Regionally, the period saw the death of revolutionary Iran's founder and paramount leader, Imam Khomeini, and a consequent shift away from revolutionary idealism to pragmatic realpolitik in the Islamic Republic's foreign policy. In August 1990, Iraq invaded and occupied Kuwait, which subsequently led to the former's defeat in the 1991 Gulf War. This in turn precipitated the outbreak of the Kurdish and Shi'i insurrections in the northern and southern parts of Iraq, respectively. The resounding triumph of the military might and diplomatic clout of the United States, and the dramatic unravelling of the Soviet Union, heralded the evolution of America's proclaimed New World Order. A major consequence of American pre-eminence was transformation of the Arab–Israeli conflict, demonstrated with the inauguration of the Madrid Peace Conference and the subsequent Oslo Accords.

Important as these developments were in shaping, to varying degrees, the geopolitical landscape of the Middle East, a detailed account of these events is beyond the scope and purpose of this chapter. Instead, an attempt will be made to focus on those events that have had major repercussions for the discourse and activism of Sayyid Fadlallah and Lebanon's Islamist movements. As will become apparent, there is a close correlation between, on the one hand, the national and regional developments as well as the corresponding shift from the militant course pursued by Lebanon's Shi'i Islamists during the 1980s (one based on confrontation and radical transformation of the status quo through revolutionary upheaval), and the path of accommodation and gradualist reform, as followed in the post-civil war order of the 1990s, on the other. This chapter will enquire into how Fadlallah read and responded to those changes on local and regional levels, and how he in turn influenced the pragmatic tendency of Islamist political activism in post-war Lebanon.

The 1990s saw Fadlallah become the premier Lebanese Shi'i jurisconsult – the foremost Islamist activist–theoretician, media celebrity (whose image and interviews have appeared regularly in Lebanese dailies) and popular mosque Imam. It will be demonstrated that Fadlallah's prominence and influence were as much a product of his pragmatic radicalism as of his jurisprudential–scholastic authority. Beside his role as preacher, jurist, writer and mentor, Fadlallah became a leading Islamist theoretician and strategist; an Islamic ecumenist; a theologian of empowerment and liberation; an acclaimed inter-religious debater and dialectician, political analyst and activist; a spokesman for the downtrodden and wretched among the Shi'i masses; and, last but not least, a vehemently anti-imperialist and anti-Zionist campaigner.

While it is not the purpose of this chapter to examine in depth each of those roles, selective treatment of Fadlallah's capacities and functions will be necessary, in so far as this enhances our understanding of the dynamics of his authority and the calculus of his decision-making and public behaviour. This in turn raises the important question of the extent and the ways in which

Fadlallah has influenced the political choices and activist behaviour of the primarily Shi'i but also Sunni Islamist movements in Lebanon. An attempt will be made to explain, in the context of Fadlallah's pragmatic radicalism, the metamorphosis of the Lebanese Islamist movement – particularly Hizbullah – from a revolutionary paramilitary organisation into a loyal oppositional parliamentary party. I will establish the importance of Fadlallah's rational Islamist thought and pragmatic approach towards both reading and interacting with the world, and then of that nexus for our understanding of the underlying continuity between radical vision and strategic thought, on the one hand, and pragmatic and principled activism, on the other.

The Ta'if Accords and Islamist Reaction

In the summer of 1989, a large delegation of Lebanese parliamentarians met in the Saudi resort city of Ta'if. The aim of the meeting, convened jointly by Saudi Arabia and Syria, and with American backing, was to bring about an end to the fourteen-year civil war. The discussions, directed by the regional patrons, centred on amending the Lebanese constitution – diminishing the authority of the Maronite president and augmenting the jurisdictional powers of the Sunni prime minister and Ṣhi'i speaker of parliament. The delegates at the conference passed a number of resolutions, chief of which related to the reunification of the shattered country and the re-invigoration of its central authority, the restoration of state institutions, the dissolution of the myriad armed militias, and the state-wide deployment of military and security forces. The eventual agreement, though endorsed by a majority of the country's established and reformist-minded political and religious leaders, was sharply criticised by the Islamists, and denounced by the Maronite right, centred on renegade General Michel Aoun.[1]

Viewing the Accords as a patchy, ad hoc and superficial attempt at redressing the imbalance of power within the confessionally structured regime, Hizbullah's initial reaction was to reject the resolutions, calling instead for substantive reform and radical change of the whole political system.[2] This position on the Accords essentially mirrored that of Fadlallah, who had asserted that the agreement was inherently flawed because it failed to rectify the acute imbalance in the confessional make-up of governmental and bureaucratic posts.[3] He believed that it would not lead to genuine national reconciliation, as the Accords essentially served to consecrate the existing confessionalist and discriminatory political regime.[4] Contending that the Ta'if agreement encapsulated more the will of the international community – particularly of the United States – and less that of Lebanon's citizenry, Fadlallah called for a national referendum to discover the type of constitution his compatriots aspired to.[5] Notwithstanding the serious shortcomings of the Accords – as publicly aired by Hizbullah – the movement's leadership subsequently endorsed them, albeit reluctantly. Thus, unlike General Aoun, who had launched a 'war of liberation' against the Syrian army stationed in Lebanon, and had embarked on an open confrontation with the Beirut authorities, Hizbullah's leaders elected not to wage a military or civil campaign to wreck the Accords.

Hizbullah's acceptance of the Ta'if Accords can be attributed to the major changes in the local and regional situation – a confluence of circumstances that saw the death of Imam Khomeini in July 1989, and the gradual progression, under the stewardship of Hashemi Rafsanjani, the Speaker of the Iranian Parliament, towards a pragmatic Iranian foreign policy approach; the dissolution of the Soviet Union in 1991; the Iraqi invasion of Kuwait in August 1990; the ensuing regional realignment ahead of the 1991 Gulf War; and the subsequent Madrid Arab–Israeli Peace Conference in November 1991. Syria now became a key Arab participant, both in the American-led international military campaign against arch-rival Ba'thist Iraq, and in the American-sponsored forum for negotiations on settling the Arab–Israeli conflict. Syria's tilt away from the Soviet Union – and its successor state, Russia – and towards the US, and its advocacy of a 'just, comprehensive and lasting' peace agreement with the Jewish state, had profound repercussions for Lebanon. As the undisputed powerbroker in Lebanon, and principal overseer and undertaker of the Ta'if Accords, Syria resolved the principal outstanding security and military issues in Lebanon: namely, the fratricidal Amal–Hizbullah feud, Michel Aoun's military insurrection (styled by him a 'War of Liberation'), and the negotiated release of the Western hostages.

Solutions, in 1991, to the two most intractable issues – the ending of inter-Shi'i fratricide, and the release of Western captives – were brought about by Syrian and Iranian mediation.[6] With the rapid changes unfolding on the international scene, especially in the wake of the 1991 Gulf War, the two regional allies successfully used their respective leverage over the two warring parties – Hizbullah and Amal – to terminate their feud. Fadlallah, as set out in the previous chapter, was from the outset a prominent figure in the intricate negotiations towards a solution. Out of principle he had objected both to the taking of hostages and to the merciless inter-Shi'i blood-letting. As a measure of the gravity with which he viewed these armed hostilities, Fadlallah held talks in January 1989 with his estranged colleague, Shaykh Muhammad Mahdi Shams al-Din, who had close relations with Amal.[7] However, owing to significant differences in opinion on how to effect a truce and bring about a lasting cessation of hostilities, and despite broad agreement on the need to terminate the fighting, the meeting failed to yield a specific, practical mechanism to resolve the conflict and address its roots.[8]

Thus, despite Fadlallah's stature and authority within Islamist circles, and despite his prominent role in negotiations and mediation efforts pertaining to hostages and the Shi'i war, the fact that he failed to resolve both underscored simultaneously the limitations of that influence and the preponderant international and regional dimensions of the most intractable aspects of the conflict. During his meeting in 1987 with the representative of the Archbishop of Canterbury, Terry Waite, Fadlallah told his guest that the issue was very complicated, and that he had done his utmost to bring about the release of the captives, but to no avail, and finally came to realise that he was not a suitable mediator. A year later, Fadlallah played host to another important dignitary, UN hostage mediator, Giandomenico Picco, whom he advised to talk directly to the captors, 'as they were the only people who could help, and that guidance for this came only from Iran'.[9] While welcoming the March 1991 Hizbullah–Amal accord, viewing it as opening the way to co-operation on issues of mutual concern – namely, ending both the Israeli military presence in the unilaterally declared security zone in the South, and the continued Maronite political domination of the country – he did not perceive it as a precursor to a united political or paramilitary front.[10]

Informed by his close and objective reading of a changing reality, Fadlallah impressed on the Islamist resistance movement the necessity of altering its public posture and of reaching a modus vivendi with the post-war central authority. Exigency and realpolitik had dictated that it would be impracticable – indeed perilous – to campaign actively and overtly against the Taif Accords, as it would unmistakably mean a purposeful move to undermine the authority of the Lebanese government, as well as posing an open challenge to Syria's power and interests in Lebanon. From the early 1990s, Syria actively supported the Beirut government's quest to extend its authority by quelling the military rebellion led by renegade anti-Syrian General Michel Aoun, as well as by ensuring the physical disbanding of the myriad armed formations that operated within Greater Beirut.

At Fadlallah's behest, Hizbullah's leaders came to the realisation that, if the movement was to escape the impending fate of other armed Lebanese militias and organisations – namely dissolution, as stipulated by the Accords – it would be vital that it avoid arousing Syrian displeasure. With crucial Syrian backing, and with Fadlallah strenuously calling on the Lebanese government to exempt the Islamic Resistance, the armed wing of Hizbullah, from its general drive towards militia disbandment, the Islamist movement was permitted to continue to function in its distinct and unique capacity as a legitimate paramilitary movement of patriotic Islamic resistance against Israeli occupation in the South. Fadullah argued that so long as Israel occupied Lebanese territory, and given that the Lebanese army had not crystallised into a cohesive national institution, the patriotic resistance movement should be allowed to continue.[11]

Fadlallah's opposition to the Second Republic enshrined under Ta'if can be explained in the light of his long-standing call for the overhaul of the Lebanese political regime. As late as 1988, Fadlallah had reiterated, in an interview with a Lebanese daily, his commitment to bringing down the existing Maronite regime and supplanting it with a de-confessionalised system of government.[12] Still, in another interview accusing the ruling political establishment of being subservient and pandering to the Western powers, he called on the populace to remove it.[13] Yet in speaking out against the Maronite Christian monopoly of power, Fadlallah was not the only strident voice: he was joined by other prominent reformist figures and religious leaders, including Shaykh Shams al-Din, Shaykh Qabalan, Shaykh Khalid, and by political militia leaders such as Jumblatt and Berri.[14] Like other oppositional leaders, he viewed the current regime as anachronistic and regressive – an insidious legacy of French colonialism, originally imposed on the Lebanese by the French, and subsequently perpetuated by the Americans to consecrate Maronite domination.[15]

Dawlat al-Insan: Fadlallah's Alternative Vision for Post-war Lebanon

From 198, as we have already seen, Fadlallah had propounded the novel, hybrid notion of *Dawlat al-Insan* (literally, the human state). Such a polity would be based on the non-confessionalist democratic institutional mechanisms of electoral representation and public accountability, religious inclusivism, and social and economic justice. Fadlallah's political paradigm did not embody a specific form of structure of governance, nor the means by which to bring about the desired regime. Instead, Fadlallah had advocated a referendum in order to determine the system of government desired by the Lebanese electorate.[16]

Hizbullah, which had openly called for the dismantling of the Lebanese regime soon after the signing of the Accords, had by the winter of 1990 entered into a series of alternately open and discrete liaisons with government officials.[17] The contacts involved discussions on the future composition and policy orientation of the prospective government, and explored the possibility of

Hizbullah accepting ministerial portfolios.[18] Following a careful consideration of the government's offer, Hizbullah's leaders decided against the venture, deeming the incumbent government to be a managerial administration rather than one of national reconciliation. Hizbullah perceived the government to be intrinsically incapable of realising the movement's goals – namely, meeting the pressing needs of the neglected southerners, prosecuting the war of liberation against Israel, and ending the Lebanese army's traditional subordination to the Maronite political establishment.[19]

Hizbullah's decision to enter and then exit the round of talks with government officials seemm to have been influenced by Fadlallah, who had no objection, from an Islamic jurisprudential standpoint, to Islamists forming part of the country's government, so long as the Islamic interest was served by such an arrangement.[20] In 1990, Fadlallah had not deemed the incumbent administration to have met this primary criterion for a coalition government, and consequently advised the Islamists against the venture.[21]

As stated earlier, Fadlallah's *Dawlat al-Insan*, a novel, inclusivist institutional concept, was propounded for the first time in early June 1988. Reaffirming his commitment to Islam as a political ideology and existential paradigm, Fadlallah stated: 'We advocate Islam, but if [the present] situation is not conducive to propelling Islam to a position of governance, then we propound the state of Man.'[22] The nexus between the planned Islamic polity and such an 'interim entity' was clear in Fadlallah's exhortation that Islamists 'ought to activate all the elements … with a view to setting up the State of Man as a precursor to the removal of the impediments … along the path towards establishing an Islamic state'.[23] Amid an atmosphere of criticism and suspicion even within Islamist circles, Fadlallah endeavoured to explain the concept in a manner that would reassure his fellow activists and placate the fears of both non-Islamist secularists and Christians. To the former, Fadlallah explained that *Dawlat al-Insan* was proposed as an interim arrangement – a transient phase in the quest for the Islamic state.[24] For the latter, Fadlallah envisioned an entity founded on individual liberty, political pluralism and a de-confessionalised power structure.[25]

Rebutting the more dogmatic Islamists, who viewed the notion of a generic religious rather than a particularistic Islamic polity with misgivings, or even dismay, seeing it as a compromise on the cardinal goal of attaining an Islamic state, Fadlallah argued forcefully that in view of the impracticability of establishing and sustaining an Islamic regime in the present circumstances in Lebanon, a prolonged preparatory phase would be inevitable.[26] To that end, Fadlallah employed a gradualist strategy to educate the populace about the virtue of such a polity – a task that would require a concerted attempt to break down deep-seated stereotypes and exclusivist mentalities relating to confessional allegiances.[27]

The fact that Fadlallah sheds little light on the specific mechanics of the proposed *Dawlat al-Insan* may be due to the fact that his conjured entity was, as it remains, a preliminary schema, inviting – or so he hoped – substantive debate among the country's intellectuals, religious clerics and political activists. What is clear is that Fadlallah's proposed entity, though founded on values of justice, freedom and dialogue, was essentially an institutional mechanism or structure born of expediency, not principle. The transparency of that expediency was borne out in an interview with Fadlallah in early 1989, in which he stated that

> the propounding of *Dawlat al-Insan* was a tactical matter on the level of practical modality through which we aspire to bring down many of the practical and psychological barriers that may otherwise impede or prevent the activation of the Islamic scheme in a practical manner acceptable to the populace. And as far as that which we have propounded in connection to gradualist mechanisms, we advocate a periodisational schema that would finally realise the Islamic state.[28]

So long as an Islamic polity was unattainable in Lebanon, Islamists should therefore strive towards a de-confessionalised democratic regime.

Here it is worth briefly comparing the political agenda and vision of Fadlallah with that of his colleague, Shaykh Muhammad Mahdi Shams al-Din, who, until his death in 2001, headed the Supreme Islamic Shi'i Council in Lebanon. Although both clerics had consistently called for the dismantling of the confessionalised Lebanese political system, and both wanted a more modern, open and representative democratic regime, their views on the future role of such a democratic state in the overall Islamist political agenda were very different. Whereas Shams al-Din was a vocal advocate of *al-dimouqratiyya al-adadiyya* (numerical, as opposed to confessionally based, democracy) as a permanent replacement for the existing system of government, which served as a viable alternative to the maximalist conception of an Islamic state. Fadlallah, on the other hand, had always regarded the proposed *Dawlat al-Insan* not as an end in itself, but rather as a means to bringing about a more open and promising political milieu, enabling Lebanese Islamists to operate freely and effectively.[29]

With Fadlallah stating emphatically that '*Dawlat al-Insan* is one of the [available] means to an Islamic state, when some of the major impediments are [eventually] removed', it was not surprising that this proposed interim state held little appeal for a largely sceptical and secular-minded Christian community.[30] Fadlallah's proposal has been received largely with passive indifference, and in some cases with open rejection. Yet, at least for the first few years since being proposed, *Dawlat al-Insan* found little resonance even with in Islamist circles. The more doctrinaire Islamists questioned the legitimacy and practicability of Fadlallah's vague, hybrid political entity.

However, by the mid-1990s, as a measure of Fadlallah's growing influence among Lebanon's Sunni Islamists, no less important an activist leader than Shaykh Faysal al-Mawlawi, the General Secretary of the Lebanese al-Jama'ah al-Islamiyya, had both espoused the concept and borrowed the term of *Dawlat al-Insan*. In accounting for the conceptual basis of the state, al-Mawlawi, a judge, had argued that if Islamic state aspired to in Lebanon could not be attained, then Islamic activists should be directed towards establishing *Dawlat al-Insan*.[31] Again like Fadlallah, al-Mawlawi envisioned the state as a generic entity that would enshrine such supposedly commonly held values as justice, freedom, morality and religiosity.[32] In the light of Lebanon's heterogeneous confessional composition and regional power balance, *Dawlat al-Insan* was advanced as a substitute for the current regime and as a precursor to the Islamic state.[33] An ecumenical Islamist, Fadlallah had, throughout the 1980s and 1990s, developed close ties with the leaders of Sunni Islamist groups in Lebanon – namely al-Jama'ah al-Islamiyya and Harakat al-Tawheed al-Islamiyya.

For all the ambiguity and controversy surrounding Fadlallah's *Dawlat al-Insan*, it is clear that he always advocated it as a forerunner to a future Islamic regime. To the extent that Fadlallah has always been a resolute believer in an Islamic state, he is a radical, committed to fundamentally transforming the status quo.[34] Similarly, to the extent that he was and is presently endeavouring to 'activate the notion [of *Dawlat al-Insan*] in a realistic manner … so that it represents a certain flexibility on a practical level', Fadlallah was and remains a pragmatist, and a principled political accommodationist.[35]

The 1992 Parliamentary Elections and the 'Lebanonisation' of the Islamist Movement

If Fadlallah had limited success in promoting *Dawlat al-Insan*, the same cannot be said with respect to Islamist participation in the Lebanese parliamentary elections – the first since 1972. Fadlallah's influence was pivotal in propelling the Islamists along the newly charted democratic path. As mentioned in the previous chapter, Fadlallah had sanctioned, as early as the mid-1980s, the pursuit of gradual reform through the agency of democratic state institutions. However, the fact that Fadlallah's exposition of Islamist institutional integration unfolded at the height of the Lebanese civil war ensured that the idea of accommodation with the state remained unappealing to the majority of Islamists. Fadlallah's polemical advocacy of reform from within was largely confined to intellectual debates with Islamic activists associated with *al-Muntalaq*, a bi-monthly journal issued by the Lebanese Muslim Student Association.[36] In a revealing article published in this Islamist periodical in 1986, Fadlallah argued that '[if] revolution at present cannot be realised, then reformation becomes obligatory; and in the event of the revolution being postponed Islamic activists ought to strive to create an Islamic societal milieu ... that would ultimately pave the way to revolutionary change'.[37]

The post-war years ushered in a new era, symbolised among other things by reinvigorated state institutions, providing a legitimate and lively forum for political and ideological debate; conditions that, in turn, were to provide Fadlallah's reformist, accommodationist ideas with vital impetus for expansion, as well as accord them particular relevance and practicality. The official entry of the Islamists into Lebanon's parliamentary politics heralded what came to be dubbed the 'Lebanonisation' of the country's Islamist movement. The expression was first coined by Fadlallah in mid-1988.[38] For Fadlallah, it referred to those Islamists operating in Lebanon who were 'cognisant of the manifold characteristics of Lebanon with a view to formulating their methods, means and strategies in ways that conform to Lebanese reality...'.[39] Fadlallah defined 'Lebanonisation' as a process that 'examines the prevailing circumstances in Lebanon and formulates the strategy within that framework, making allowances for Lebanon's particular circumstances, its confessional sensitivities, its perception of its environment'.[40] He conceived the process as involving transformation of the status quo by means of realpolitik, based on what is possible to achieve. By 'Lebanese reality', Fadlallah was alluding to the distinctive heterogeneous make-up of the country, its quasi-democratic institutions and general post-war political conditions, to which Islamists were compelled to adjust in order to further their own agenda. He stressed the paramount importance of tailoring the Islamist political agenda to suit the Lebanese milieu, so that Islamists were able to advance sound and realistic solutions to Lebanon's intricate problems.[41]

In this way, Islamist ideological, political and organisational activities in Lebanon inevitably differed from their cognates in other countries, where different sensitivities and problems existed. A key element in Islamist calculus in the Lebanese setting was the country's traditionally dominant and now restive Christian Maronite community. Their disquiet stemmed from unfavourable demographic trends (a high Muslim birth rate and low rate of emigration) and from the heightened level of Muslim political agitation, especially from the Shi'i movements of Hizbullah and Amal. As in the case of *Dawlat al-Insan*, Fadlallah exhorted his fellow Islamists to take into account the particular sentiments of the country's Christians by trying to devise specific mechanisms that would effectively address those concerns and allay their deep-seated fears.[42]

Somewhat ambivalently, Fadlallah maintained that he was not advocating the domestication or coopting of the Islamist movement by the Lebanese government. He drew an important distinction between acknowledging the juridical legitimacy of the regime and coming to a modus vivendi with it.[43] By operating within the existing political system, Islamists strove to reform the governmental structure and to become a potent political force in influencing government decision-making and policy orientation.[44] While advising Islamists to be vigilant against unwittingly becoming the pawns of the 'neo-imperialist' game-plan, Fadlallah underscored the distinction between being outside such a game and being a proactive force in reality.[45] For Fadlallah and the majority of Lebanon's Islamists, the parliamentary experiment did not compromise the Islamist political agenda, as the existing arena had opened up new 'horizons that would enable them to draw nearer to their interim objectives along the path to their strategic goals'.[46]

In theorising the integration of the Islamist movement into a parliamentary democracy, Fadlallah contended that 'the means by which to transform society, politically, is by no means confined to revolution, but rather it may be possible to effect that [metamorphosis] through the existing institutions in political reality…'[47] Fadlallah revealed that he had 'propounded this view at a time when the Islamist circle in general was uneasy with such propositions because they were regarded as non-revolutionary'.[48] Fadlallah did not regard Islamist entry into parliamentary institutions as a retreat from the original radical or revolutionary path he had embarked on. This was so, he argued, because, 'in motion, revolutionism (*al-thawriyya*) does not necessarily embody impulsive discourse, nor represent violence-laden slogans.'[49] Instead, revolutionism, in Fadlallah's view, is that which commits the activist to working inexorably in order to attain his strategic target(s).[50]

At the same time, the genuine revolutionary is necessarily a realist, demonstrating resolve, prudence and adroitness in the quest to reach his target by 'operating within the parameters of the objective circumstances; conditions whereunder the activist may be impelled to substitute the pursuit of one method in this [current] phase for another, or to alter one means with another'.[51] Similarly, the revolutionary is one who is ready and able to exploit all opportunities that may bring him closer to his goals, and assist him in overcoming the barriers that prevent him from reaching those goals.[52] Thus, whatever path is followed or mode of operation adopted, in the final analysis, 'all roads lead to Rome'.[53] What is evident here is a nexus between radicalism and realism, a commitment to a radical agenda geared towards gradual revolutionary transformation of the status quo, while being informed and guided by both a realist outlook and Islamic worldview.

In this theoretical context, Fadlallah did not regard the entry of the Islamist movement into state institutions – namely the parliament – as necessarily entailing recognition of the regime or endorsement of its policies. Instead, Fadlallah perceived it as a means by which organised domestic political opposition might bring about the reform of the regime, its structure, institutions, laws and policies.[54] Post-war Lebanon provided Islamists with an opportunity to organise themselves into an effective parliamentary force of opposition to the ruling establishment, and to reinvigorate Islam as an ideological paradigm and way of life with supposedly sound solutions to complex and multifarious societal problems. While the revolutionary Islamist movement was transformed in Lebanon into a mass movement with a domestic and national reform agenda, Hizbullah and al-Jama' al-Islamiyya could not divorce themselves from Islam's universalist identity and global mission.

For Fadlallah, the 1992 parliamentary elections provided the Islamists with an opportunity to establish a foothold within the parliamentary system, with a view to expanding their influence in society and fortifying their leverage on public policy. As important as the elections were for the restoration of democratic institutions in Lebanon's political life, Fadlallah remained as committed as he had been a decade earlier to bringing about the desired transformation – albeit, on this occasion, gradually, legitimately, and from within the existing system.[55] For Fadlallah, participation in the democratic institutions was thus essentially a strategic choice: a democratic, pluralistic milieu, in contrast to a dictatorship, was conducive to the 'dissemination and rejuvenation of Islamism, and helps to further the cause of Islam or secure total control by the will of the majority'. He stressed, however, that this favourable view of democracy 'ought not be construed as recognition by Islamists of democratic rule, either in thought or practice. [Instead, it essentially represented] an accommodation to reality and to the liberties accorded to the Islamic movement – alongside the non-Islamic movement – to contest one another.'[56] A minority of doctrinaire Shi'i Islamists in Lebanon, however, did not subscribe to this view. This dogmatic group, led by Shaykh Subhi al-Tufayli, the former General Secretary of Hizbullah, stridently opposed the Islamist participation in the parliamentary elections, lest they become integrated into the very Maronite-dominated political system the movement had consistently denounced.[57]

Although one cannot establish a Marxist antecedent to Fadlallah's strategic thinking, there is a noticeable similarity in the shift in strategy from one of the revolutionary overthrow of the political system to one of reforming the regime from within, and between the influential communist and leftist parties of democratic western Europe and the Islamist movements in quasi-democratic states in the Arab world, such as Jordan, post-war Lebanon and pre-civil war Algeria. It is clear that Fadlallah was to some extent influenced, if not inspired, by the communist experience in the West, given his repeated references, whenever he is impelled to justify the legalisation and secular tolerance of Islamist movements espousing reform agendas (cited in the previous chapter), to the legitimation of reformist Marxist movements in the West.

Securing twelve seats (eight Islamist deputies and four aligned leftists), Hizbullah emerged as the 'strongest and the most cohesive and disciplined bloc' in the 128-member parliament.[58] The strong performance of the Islamists in general, and of Hizbullah in particular, came, in the words of Fadlallah, 'as a shock to those who had branded them as extremists', who supposedly existed on the margins of society, and purportedly lacked popular support.[59] Hizbullah's impressive performance was attributed to its popularity and success as a resistance movement, and to its extensive and effective social service network.[60] For Fadlallah, the successful venture of the Islamists into Lebanese parliamentary politics had vindicated their pragmatism, as well as his own realism and 'objectivity', which stood in sharp contrast to the foreign portrayal of them as dogmatic revolutionaries.[61] The Christian Maronites had boycotted the elections out of opposition to the Syrian political and military domination of the country, anticipating the election results to be predetermined in favour of pro-Syrian candidates. Yet, had the Maronites participated in the election, the results would have varied marginally with regard to the pro-Islamist Shi'i electorates.

While there was the potential risk for parliamentary Islamists of being co-opted by the regime, thereby compromising their credentials and tarnishing their populist image, Fadlallah deemed that to be a remote possibility, which in any case was outweighed by the benefits to be accrued by operating from within the system.[62] Some doctrinaire Islamists, such as Shaykh Subhi al-Tufayli and Sayyid Sadeq Musawi, held the view that, as licensed parties with parliamentary representation, Hizbullah and al-Jama'a would function as loyal parties opposing the policies of the government, instead of opposing the regime itself, thus conferring legitimacy on the incumbent government.[63]

Fadlallah, who rejected this claim, argued that since radical change through revolutionary upheaval was not a feasible course at present, and given that the transformation of the political structure and culture could be achieved other than by armed struggle and violent revolution, then it logically followed that when an opportunity arose enabling the gradual transformation of the incumbent regime through the existing institutions of the state, activists should seize it to further their agenda.[64] Nevertheless, realising the inherent constraints in the present system, Fadlallah maintained that, although integrated Islamists may well not be able to effect the intended radical change, they certainly could bring about significant changes in the spheres of legislation, and of public and foreign policy. Ultimately, Islamists would have to work hard over a prolonged period in order to build sufficient public confidence and forge a cross-confessional national following before they would be in a position to govern in their own right.

Mindful of the importance of alliance-building for Hizbullah's venture into the parliamentary arena, and for its potential as a shaping force in Lebanese politics, Fadlallah had urged Lebanese Islamists to build bridges with other parties and movements.[65] Hence the rapprochement between Hizbullah and its erstwhile warring foe, Amal, and the thawing of relations with its formerly implacable adversary, the right-wing Phalange Party, al-Kata'ib. Hizbullah's impressive showing in the 1992 and 1996 parliamentary elections was achieved on the back of tactical alliances based on a list of joint candidates from Amal, the Syrian Ba'thists, Communists and Syrian National Socialists.[66] That Hizbullah had heeded Fadlallah's advice underscored the deference he was accorded, and the degree of influence he wielded over the movement's leadership during this period. Fadlallah's authority and guidance notwithstanding, the leverage of Iran under the leadership of President Rafsanjani should not be underestimated, as it rivalled, and in time surpassed, that of Fadlallah. That ought not to be surprising, in view of Hizbullah's religious–juridical allegiance and ideological subservience to Iran's supreme leader and ruling jurisconsult, Ayatollah Ali Khamanei.

As to the question of reconciling Hizbullah's armed resistance against the Israelis with the party's internal reform programme, Fadlallah asserted that he had perceived no fundamental conflict between the two activities, contending that Islamists had entered the state parliament in order to pursue the 'armed liberation struggle from an advanced position'.[67] Fadlallah argued (not without reason, as we shall see) that Hizbullah's entry into parliament had not compromised the movement's cardinal mission. On the contrary, the Islamic Resistance, the armed wing of Hizbullah, had without interruption continued to mount guerrilla attacks against the Israeli army and its surrogate

SLA in occupied South Lebanon.[68] Indeed, despite Hizbullah's emergence as an oppositional parliamentary party, and its involvement in Lebanon's intricate domestic affairs, not only was the Islamist movement able to sustain its level of armed resistance in the occupied south, but in the years after the 1992 parliamentary elections there had been an appreciable increase in the number of guerrilla operations mounted by Islamic Resistance against Israeli military targets inside Lebanon (ending with the expulsion of Israeli forces in May 2000).[69]

The 1991 Madrid Conference, the Peace Process, and the Islamist Response

Triumphant in its coalition war against Iraq in early 1991, the United States proclaimed the dawn of a 'New World Order', a new age of globalised order – political, economic and military – under the aegis of the United Nations. The successful international intervention in Kuwait was from that point projected as a model of the future, robust free-world response to regional 'bullies'. Like other Islamist and secular critics of the new age, Fadlallah viewed the New World Order as a euphemism for American global hegemony, to which the rest of the world ought to submit; a world where America, in the wake of the fall of the Soviet Union, would function as a self-appointed global policeman, with Israel as its regional deputy.[70] Thus, for Fadlallah and other activists, the New World Order did not represent the will of the international community, but instead encapsulated the designs of the United States.[71] Alluding to the disintegration of Yugoslavia and the conflicts in the Caucasus, Fadlallah asserted that, far from ushering in an age of order and stability, the world was now beset by myriad local and regional conflicts. Those crises, ostensibly fuelled by primordial ethnic and religious animosities, had not elicited the same response from the United States as that of the 1991 Gulf War.[72] While envisioning the same fate for America as that of the USSR (implosion owing to deep-seated and irreversible societal and economic malaise), Fadlallah predicted a bleak future for the Arabs: 'just as America had obliterated the Red Indians, so too would the Arabs be dispossessed and forcibly displaced'.[73] And yet, to avoid a melancholic state of fatal resignation, Fadlallah attempted to reassure the faithful of a future where the international balance of power would inevitably shift from the West, and the United States in particular, to the Islamic *umma*, with its vast material and human resources. Fadlallah reasoned that, just as 'power is not the eternal destiny of the powerful', so too, 'weakness is not the eternal destiny of the feeble' and disinherited.[74]

As an intrinsic part of its grand vision for a New World Order, the United States pursued in earnest a settlement, if not a resolution, of the Middle East's oldest and most pivotal conflict. To that end, the Madrid Peace Conference was convened by the administration of George Bush Sr. on 30 October 1991. The participants in the conference included senior government delegates from Israel and the adjoining Arab states. In line with other Islamists, and in continuity with his long-standing, immutably hostile stance towards Israel, Fadlallah immediately denounced the conference.[75] He declared emphatically that neither this nor other international or regional conventions could – from an Islamic standpoint – confer legitimacy on Israel as an independent political entity.[76] This stance was predicated on the assumption that no nation has the right to build a national state on the debris of another pre-existing state – namely, pre-1948 Palestine. He reiterated his argument that the acquisition and seizure of national land, and the forcible eviction and displacement of its Arab inhabitants, could not be countenanced from an Islamic standpoint, legally or constitutionally.

For Fadlallah, his stance on Israel is immutable and axiomatic: 'We as adhering Muslims do not acknowledge any negotiations, nor abide by any treaty or peace accord effected by any Arab or Muslim entity with Israel.'[77] Fadlallah stridently opposed the conference and the ensuing peace process, firstly because, like other Islamists in Lebanon, he viewed Israel as anathema – an illegitimate, abominable entity – for having emerged as a national Jewish homeland at the expense of the majority indigenous Palestinian Arabs.[78] And secondly – with the Soviet Union on the threshold of dissolution, and with a militarily triumphant America heralding in the wake of the 1991 Gulf War the dawning of a new era, one of whose vital pivots was the permanent settlement of the Arab–Israeli conflict – Fadlallah looked on with dismay and resentment as American regional and global hegemony became invigorated, seemingly without challenge.

Thus, even in the period leading up to the conference, when James Baker, the American Secretary of State, had been warning the Arab leaders of the incalculable consequences of not seizing the unique opportunity to join the peace process, Fadlallah had been exhorting the Arabs to undermine actively the upcoming conference of 'perfidy'.[79] In his efforts to woo the Arab heads of state to attend the conference and conduct face-to-face negotiations with Israel, Baker embarked on a vigorous round of shuttle diplomacy. During eight successive tours to the region in preparation for the conference, Baker visited Jordan, Egypt, Syria, Lebanon, Israel and Saudi Arabia.[80] Making his stance on the whole issue unambiguous, Fadlallah declared that while he was not opposed to peace as such, he categorically denounced the current peace process as an ignominious capitulation, deeming it to be overtly discriminatory and profoundly unjust.[81] As a measure of his defiance of the peace agreement, Fadlallah declared emphatically that Islamists would stand against any peace treaty, even if they were to remain the sole voice of rejection.[82] In view of the deep-seated hostility of Islamists towards successive American administrations, due largely to the strategic alliance of that country with Israel, and given that it was the Americans who had engineered and sponsored the Madrid Peace Conference, it was not surprising that Fadlallah and his fellow Islamists emerged as the harshest critics of the American peace initiative.[83]

Despite – or perhaps because of – the fact that the peace process was packaged by the Americans as being in the best long-term interests of both Israel and the Arab states, Fadlallah found it objectionable that, given the vital relationship between the United States and Israel, the whole process was designed to apply maximum pressure on the Arab states to come to the negotiating table, precisely when they were seriously emasculated and fractured by the 1991 Gulf War.[84] On the other hand, the same process was putatively aimed at fortifying an already militarily and demographically strengthened Israel, and consequently sustaining Israel's regional superiority on the back of what was expected to be an expanded and more robust economy. In Fadlallah's view, the peace process served Israeli strategic interests insofar as it allowed the Jewish state to penetrate the whole region – politically, culturally and economically – which would not have been possible under conditions of war. It would allow the Israelis, on the one hand, to exploit the vast Arab market of cheap unskilled and semi-skilled labour, as well as the natural resources of the region, and on the other, to revitalise and expand its otherwise moribund and stagnant economy, by securing unfettered access to Arab consumer markets for its produce and manufactured products.[85] For this reason, having concluded that the intended peace was a vital Israeli and American interest, Fadlallah attempted unsuccessfully to reassure the Arabs that they wouldn't be losing a thing if they did not enter into the negotiations. And with such a peace initiative weighted in favour of Israeli interests, Fadlallah simultaneously endeavoured to warn the Palestinian leadership against attending the conference, believing it would not secure anything of significance except limited autonomy, and fearing that it would lead them to forfeit their inalienable national rights, thereby sacrificing the sacred Palestinian cause.[86]

Besides his firm moral and religious–legal convictions with regard to Israel and the peace process, Fadlallah objected to the Arabs' participation out of geopolitical and strategic realism. Fadlallah observed on the eve of the conference that the Arab states in general, and the dispirited and enfeebled

Palestinian leadership in particular, were negotiating with their seemingly united adversary from a position of weakness.[87] In embarking on that path, Fadlallah argued, the Arab delegates had erred seriously in their judgement. The six separate Arab negotiating parties were much more vulnerable than Israel to American-induced pressure to make further concessions, while Israel could and would afford to remain intransigent on those issues deemed fundamental to its national security.[88] Besides the stark imbalance in the strength, resolve and purpose of the negotiating parties – especially between the Israelis and Palestinians – Fadlallah expressed his concern that, while Arafat and the PLO had publicly renounced the course of armed struggle for the liberation of Palestine and recognised Israel's pre-1967 borders, Israel had apparently failed to meet any of the preconditions stipulated by the Palestinian leadership before attending the talks. Included among these were: a halt to Israeli settlement construction in the occupied territories, permission for the Palestinian negotiating team to include dignitaries from East Jerusalem and the diaspora, and official Israeli recognition of the Palestinian right to self-determination. Hence, as a scholar–activist who had since the mid-1970s been developing ideas on the logic and relevance of power in social, political and international relations for his Islamist followers, Fadlallah had a few words of advice for Arafat: negotiate from a position of strength, if not parity, and avoid rushing headlong into talks with Israel until the preconditions for negotiations stipulated by the Palestinian side are met.[89]

Thus, while Fadlallah was (as he remains) staunchly opposed to any negotiation with the State of Israel that does not explicitly guarantee the return of all Palestinians living in exile to reclaim their properties inside Israel and thereby supplant the large Jewish population that originated from outside British Mandatory Palestine, he is endowed with sufficient political acumen to realise that such an aspiration was, at least for the foreseeable future, unattainable – if not irrational. Despite his radical and remote vision for a post-Israeli entity, Fadlallah – in his readiness to adjust to rapid and momentous change, to accommodate a shifting landscape, and even to coexist with an unsavoury or imposed reality – displayed adroit political pragmatism and a firm grasp of realpolitik. In other words, while Fadlallah has, ever since his return to his ancestral country in the mid-1960s, consistently advocated the idealist, maximalist Islamist position on Israel's existence as an independent Jewish national homeland, as the peace process gained momentum he expressed strong criticism of specific facets of the Arab–Israeli negotiations. There was as a discernible shift in Fadlallah's discourse away from the radical utopian rhetoric of total and uncompromising rejection of Israel's legitimacy, towards an effort at highlighting and redressing the procedural, organisational and timing problems relating to the terms on which the peace process was being negotiated.

Fadlallah, Hizbullah and the Gaza–Jericho Agreement

While the Madrid Conference did not produce a breakthrough, the unprecedented official face-to-face negotiations set the ground for further intense negotiations under American and, to a lesser extent, European mediation. The talks culminated in the secret Oslo Accords, and were followed by the Gaza–Jericho Agreement. The principal characteristics of the Gaza–Jericho Accords, signed in September 1993, were: the PLO's formal recognition of Israel's existence as an independent sovereign national state within its pre-1967 borders; the formal renunciation by the PLO of armed struggle for the liberation of Palestine or parts thereof; and, in return, Israel's acknowledgment of the negotiating authority of the PLO.

It will be recalled from the previous chapter that Arafat and the PLO, at an extraordinary meeting convened in Algiers in 1988, took the decision to endorse UN Resolution 242, which enshrined the right of a Palestinian national state to exist alongside Israel. Fadlallah, encapsulating the general Islamist position, rejected such a truncated entity, since his aspiration was for a state that would encompass the whole of Palestine. Not surprisingly then, Fadlallah viewed the declaration as a capitulation – or at best an unwarranted and hastily initiated concession.[90]

For Fadlallah and fellow Islamists, what was particularly unsavoury about the Accords was that the PLO had taken the unilateral and unthinkable decision of formally relinquishing all territorial rights to pre-1967 Palestine, including West Jerusalem, considered to be historically and religiously inalienable national land.[91] An incensed Fadlallah exclaimed that the so-called peace process was an abomination.[92] Fadlallah saw deep flaws in the Accords, particularly in relation to limited self-rule in the separated occupied territories, linked together by a single road under Israeli control.[93] The autonomous territories were shorn of real sovereignty, with only limited authority related to the administration of civil matters such as health, education, policing and internal security, infrastructure and local government affairs.[94] In effect, Fadlallah asserted, the Palestinian entity would function as a tributary or dependency of Israel. The second major inference drawn by Fadlallah from the agreement was that, by officially renouncing the armed struggle against Israel, the PLO leadership had put itself at odds with the rejectionist Palestinian organisations, as well as the militant Islamist groups – namely Hamas and al-Jihad al-Islami. By committing himself to establishing a semi-autonomous state coexisting with and heavily dependent on Israel, Yasser Arafat was obliged to suppress all civil and organised violence against Israel, its citizens and national interests.[95] Accordingly, those young Palestinians participating in the Intifada, which had begun in late 1987, would be deemed by the nascent Palestinian Authority to have engaged in an illegal activity, and would thus be subject to arrest, detention and prosecution.[96]

Only a year after its eruption, Fadlallah projected that the Intifada was a revolutionary uprising, a portent for the future that liberation could not be realised by negotiation but only by a protracted struggle that might take fifty years to complete.[97] The Intifada had manifested an indomitable spirit of defiance and fortitude. The Palestinians had finally managed to break the psychological inhibitions of fear, feebleness and inferiority. Consequently, they had been instilled with a new fighting vigour that had given rise to a new, hardened individual prepared to challenge the former state of resignation to Israeli oppression and subjugation.[98]

In keeping with his strategy of spurring mass agitation against the Gaza–Jericho Agreement, Fadlallah exhorted the Lebanese people to protest against the Accords on the streets, with a view to discouraging the Lebanese Government from entering into negotiations with Israel.[99] Thus, on 13 September 1993, a mass street demonstration, organised by Hizbullah and consisting of tens of thousands of protestors, took place in the densely populated Shi'i suburbs of Beirut.[100] The Lebanese government, which had earlier banned all street protests, viewed the procession as an open challenge to its central authority, and thus ordered the deployment of military and security personnel to block and break up the march. In the ensuing confrontation, the security forces opened fire on the unarmed protestors, killing thirteen and wounding scores of others. Fadlallah, together with the Hizbullah leaders, bitterly denounced the government for its heavy-handedness, accusing it of perpetrating a cold-blooded and premeditated massacre, and demanded its immediate resignation.[101] Despite the fierce diatribes against prime minister Rafiq al-Hariri by the Shi'i Islamists, who held him personally responsible for the incident, the frosty relations between the government and the Islamist opposition began to warm in the wake of an Israeli aerial strike on a Hizbullah training compound in the Bekaa Valley in June 1994, which killed twenty trainees.[102] As a good-will gesture the government issued a formal decree declaring the fallen to be 'martyrs of Lebanon'.[103] The government initiative towards reconciliation was given further impetus in 1995, when it officially recognised those who were killed protesting against the Gaza–Jericho Agreement as patriotic martyrs.[104] Full normalisation of relations came about in the wake of Israel's second military onslaught on South Lebanon (code-named the 'Grapes of Wrath') in April 1996.

Fadlallah, the Peace Process and the 'Lebanonisation' of the Islamic Resistance

Months before the signing of the Oslo Accords and the Gaza–Jericho Agreement, Fadlallah, despite his implacable hostility towards the Jewish state, acknowledged that 'Israel has now become an undisputed fact on the ground … whether we like or not.'[105] But this realistic assessment did not equate to fatalistic resignation. To exist alongside such an unfavourable reality should be read neither as acquiescing to Israel as a permanent reality, nor conferring legitimacy upon it.[106] Instead, with the formal recognition of Israel by the Arab states, and a concomitant peace, likely prospects in the near future, Fadlallah felt the need to adjust the tactics that had been pursued by the Islamist movement in relation to Israel, with emphasis on the liberation of South Lebanon.[107] While he foresaw restrictions on the Islamic Resistance's freedom of movement in the wake of the Accords, he was of the view that those constraints could be overcome if tactics could be developed to suit the new realities on the ground.[108] Yet for all his manifest adaptability, in the period immediately after the Gaza–Jericho Accords Fadlallah had remained consistent in his hard-line posture towards Israel, regarding the very idea of negotiation with it while its forces continued to occupy parts of Lebanon as unthinkable, and viewing armed resistance as the only path that would lead to the liberation of South Lebanon.[109]

In a situation in which a Lebanese government might enter into a peace treaty with Israel once occupied Lebanese territory had been evacuated, Fadlallah advocated the transformation of the Islamic resistance movement from an armed struggle for the liberation of Palestine to one of anti-Israel cultural, civil and political agitation, combined with a boycott of Israeli commodities. In an interview in December 1992, Fadlallah clearly spelt out his position on the issue: 'If the [Arab] regimes must make peace [with Israel], the populace ought not [to] follow suit, should not purchase Israeli products, and should not receive any Israeli tourists.'[110]

In July 1993, Israel launched a massive aerial and sea bombardment of southern Lebanon. Code-named 'Operation Accountability', the week-long assault, which came in response to intensified Hizbullah raids against Israeli and its SLA surrogate's military installations and personnel, left 130 civilians dead, and caused large-scale devastation and the displacement of tens of thousands of town-dwellers and villagers, who streamed northwards to the relative safety of Beirut and its environs.[111] Hizbullah retaliated by lobbing Katyusha rockets from mobile launchers into northern Israel. To prevent the conflict from expanding and embroiling Syria in a regional conflagration, the Americans brokered a ceasefire that eventually became a memorandum of understanding. Hizbullah pledged not to launch military attacks against targets inside Israel, as long as Israel refrained from initiating military strikes against civilian targets inside Lebanon.[112] The unwritten understanding of 1993, and then the April 1996 written agreement, marked a watershed in Hizbullah's armed struggle against Israel, in that they marked a mutual understanding with respect to the parameters of the protracted low-intensity conflict in South Lebanon.[113] Above all, the two understandings marked the localisation of Lebanon's Islamic Resistance. For the first time, these agreements bestowed international recognition on the Islamic Resistance as a legitimate movement of armed struggle against foreign occupation. For its part, in reaching a deal with Israel about the 'rules of combat', Hizbullah had conferred de facto recognition of Israel as a fait accompli.[114]

As in the case of Hizbullah's participation and success in the 1992 parliamentary elections, the transformation of the Islamist resistance movement from one pursuing an open-ended pan-Islamic existential struggle to the pursuit of a local, patriotic liberation movement, whose objectives were restricted to freeing South Lebanon from foreign occupation, was guided by Fadlallah. It was Fadlallah, it will be recalled, who had called for the 'Lebanonisation' of the country's Islamist movement. This shift away from revolutionary rhetoric to pragmatic politics was officially confirmed by Shaykh Hasan Nasrallah, Hizbullah's General Secretary, who had declared in a television interview on 2 May 1996 that 'the scope of military operations of the Islamic resistance is limited to the liberation of occupied Lebanese territory and the halting of the armed struggle once that objective is attained'.[115] Still, the venture of the 'liberation' of Palestine was temporarily suspended, not cancelled permanently. Given its inherent limitations, both local and regional, the epic struggle for Palestine's 'liberation' would be not abandoned, but held in abeyance until there emerged a regional Arab–Islamic military front capable of maintaining sustained military engagement with Israel.[116]

Asked in an interview in 1996 whether the armed Islamist resistance to Israel would cease in the event of Israeli military withdrawal from South Lebanon, Fadlallah would neither confirm nor deny the suggestion. Instead, he found it prudent to keep the enemy guessing as to Hizbullah's real intentions, adding that if the path to armed struggle was impeded, then a search would be made for 'a thousand other avenues to perpetuate the struggle'. As far as Fadlallah was concerned, the liberation of the South would represent the realisation of the Islamist movement's principal short-term goal.[117] This position contrasted sharply with that of Fadlallah's colleague, Shaykh Shams al-Din, who had boldly issued a fatwa that forbade the unilateral fighting of Israel by the Lebanese resistance following any future Israeli withdrawal from Lebanon.[118] Fadlallah's implacable hostility towards Israel derives less from the Jewish cultural–religious identity of the country than with his perception of gross injustice in relation to the mass dispossession of Palestinians.[119] Thus, what is crucial in Fadlallah's militant discourse on Israel is not the question of conflict between Islam and Judaism, since the State of Israel was not a religious autocracy, headed by orthodox rabbis and governed by the Torah. Rather, the key issue of contention is one of injustice, epitomised by the antithesis between Israeli 'usurpation' and Palestinian disinheritance. Thus, for Fadlallah, even in the inconceivable situation in which the Jewish citizens of Israel were to profess Islam, his stance on the illegitimacy of Israel would not change. He would call on the recent Muslim converts of Jewish origin to leave 'occupied Palestine' en masse, so as to allow the return of Palestinian refugees to the country.[120]

Closely associated with the mission to evict Israel from South Lebanon was Fadlallah's exhortation of Islamists to forge links with local leftist and Arab nationalist forces opposed to foreign occupation in the South. The quest for alliance-building stemmed from a desire to broaden the strategic ties of the Islamist movement, as much as from Fadlallah's long-espoused philosophy of empowerment and liberation from neo-imperialism. Although not fully specified by him, Fadlallah's vision for cooperation between liberation movements was broadly as follows: a loose, ecumenical and universal alliance, or front, of Third World liberation movements, comprising both religiously based Islamist and Catholic liberation and revolutionary groupings, and secular-oriented movements, whether Arab nationalist, Marxist or socialist. Fadlallah saw that a common thread uniting all of these movements was the struggle against Western 'neo-imperialism' – a patriotic, sacred and just cause fought to end foreign subjugation and exploitation.[121] This priority did not constitute a new development in Fadlallah's pragmatic activism. Instead, it clearly reflected a continuity with his earliest Islamist intellectual and ideological activism, starting in Iraq during the 1950s and mid-1960s.

In contrast to his clear moderation and pragmatism on the issues of an Islamic state in Lebanon and of the integration of the Islamist movement into Lebanese political life, Fadlallah was maintained a hardline stance on resistance to Israeli occupation, and in his hostility towards the existence of the 'Zionist' state. If being resolutely committed to combating and terminating Israeli occupation – exclaimed Fadlallah proudly – was perceived in the Western media as a radical and extremist stance, then so be it. On the other hand, if moderation implied any tendency to acquiesce to the status quo and submit to foreign occupation, then he was no moderate.[122]

Ascent to the Marja'iyya

Despite the considerable authority wielded by Fadlallah and the profound reverence in which he was held by Hizbullah affiliates, as shown by his influence on the course of the Islamist movement in post-war Lebanon, relations between Lebanon's foremost Shi'i scholar-activist and the movement's leadership became strained following the *'alim*'s ascent to the *marja'iyya* in 1995. The rift in relations mirrored that of the position of Iran's clerical ruling establishment on the international office of *Marja' al-Taqlid*, the pre-eminent source of religious–legal emulation for Shi'i laymen. A divergence of opinion arose between Fadlallah and Ayatollah Khamanei, Khomeini's successor as Iran's paramount leader (*Wali al-Faqih*), as to who should succeed first the Grand Ayatullah Sayyid Abu al-Qasem al-Kho'ie (Fadlallah's former mentor), and then his short-lived successor, Grand Ayatullah Sayyid Rida Gulpegani in 1993.[123] While Fadlallah nominated another Iraqi *mujtahid* based in Najaf, Sayyid Ali al-Sistani, as pre-eminent jurisconsult, Khamanei backed the nomination of Ayatollah Sayyid Mohammad al-Araki, an Iranian[124] – a position echoed by Hizbullah, led by Sayyid Hasan Nasrallah, and under the firm influence of Iran. With the death of the 107-year-old Iranian jurist, Fadlallah found himself at odds with Hizbullah's leaders, who immediately declared their allegiance to Khamanei, who now combined the traditionally separate leadership roles of *Wilayat al-Faqih* and *Marja' al-Taqlid*.[125]

Thus, when his followers and students in Lebanon began to address him as *al-Marja'*, following the publication of his juridical treatise in March/April 1995, Fadlallah was perceived by the clerical associates and followers of Khamanei, including Hizbullah, to be challenging the authority and credentials of the sole and supreme *marja'*.[126] For his part, Fadlallah dismissed all suggestions published in the media of rivalry and conflict between Khamanei and himself, revealing that his candidacy was thrust upon him by his followers, and that he was motivated purely by apolitical, intellectual concerns. He also asserted that, historically, there always been more than one *marja'* at any one time, each having his distinct body of followers.[127]

Ever since assuming the role of *marja'*, Fadlallah has vocally advocated the modernisation and institutionalisation of *al-marja'iyya*. The institution was envisaged by Fadlallah as a hierarchical institution, not dissimilar to the papacy, headed by the chief jurisconsult, and aided by an able and accountable team of researchers and experts in a wide range of fields.[128] Such a collegial arrangement would enable the various specialist departments to keep abreast of rapid changes and important developments by giving timely and informed advice and recommendations to the head of the establishment.[129] This in turn, Fadlallah hoped – as had his former colleague Sayyid Baqer al-Sadr when he propounded *al-Marja'iyya al-Rashidah* (the rightly guided *marja'iyya*) – would ensure that an enlightened *marja'iyya* would remain relevant to the lives of the Shi'i faithful.[130] The concurrent activity of Khomeini and al-Kho'ie, both widely recognised pre-eminent jurisconsults, was a more recent example of the model *marja'iyya*.

It is indicative of the seriousness of the fall-out from the deepening controversy that Fadlallah became the target of a systematic campaign of criticism.[131] His opponents, both in Lebanon and in Iran, distributed pamphlets in Beirut's southern suburbs calling on the Shi'i faithful to halt the spread of Fadlallah's *fitna*, or sedition.[132] The alleged 'sedition' related to Fadlallah's tentative attempt in 1993 to revise a traditional and widely accepted Shi'i historical narrative pertaining to Fatima, the beloved daughter of the Prophet Muhammad and wife of Imam Ali. Fadlallah, during question time at one of his regular religious lessons for women, had boldly challenged the veracity of the evidence in the account relating to the putative mistreatment of Fatima by Umar bin al-Khattab, the second 'Rightly Guided Khalif'.[133] Fadlallah's reinterpretation of the subject caused a furore in Iranian religious circles, where he was publicly denounced and even accused of heresy. Conservative '*ulama* in Iran began to censor Fadlallah's works; his books were taken off the shelves of bookshops in Beirut, and mosque Imams exhorted believers to ostracise him.[134]

Traditionalist scholars in Lebanon and Iran were further angered by Fadlallah's polemical stance on self-flagellation, regularly performed as a central feature of the annual ceremony that sees its climax on the tenth day (*'Ashoura*) of the holy month of *Muharram*, and commemorates the slaying of Imam Hussein, the Prophet's grandson and, according to Shi'i belief, the third infallible Imam. Fadlallah had declared that the ritual was culturally reactionary, socially backward, and, from a shari'ah standpoint, illegitimate.[135] Rather than perpetrating pointless and inhumane acts of self-harm, Fadlallah challenged and implored those who were sincere in their love of Husayn to emulate the exploits of the Imam by shedding their blood on the battlefield while combatting the forces of injustice and oppression – an allusion to Israeli occupation.[136]

By the late 1990s, Fadlallah seemed to have weathered the storm over the *marja'iyya*, and had recovered fully from the serious blows he had received to his public authority. Fadlallah's recovery was the product of an indomitable spirit, combined with acumen and erudition. Fadlallah's *marja'iyya* came to be associated with openness, rationality and modernity, and thus, for the ever-growing educated, aspiring Shi'i middle and lower-middle class, his edicts and guidelines seemed to be relevant to their concerns and aspirations. With Fadlallah's growing appeal and influence, frosty relations with the Iranian ruling establishment began to thaw. The thawing process was much quicker in Lebanon, as Hizbullah put aside its differences over the leadership issue and regularly solicited the advice and guidance of Fadlallah. That Hizbullah's General Secretary, and some of his most senior subordinates, are regularly present among the thousands of believers who attend Fadlallah's Friday sermon and congregational prayer; that the eminent figures of that Islamist movement frequent well-attended venues where Fadlallah delivers topical lectures; that a large segment of those devotees who pray behind Fadlallah, listen to his sermons, and attend his lessons, are either Hizbullah cadres or sympathisers – all of these facts serve to illustrate the close relations between the mentor and his protégés.

It was to Fadlallah's credit that he had overseen, and to a large degree engineered, the transformation of the Shi'i Islamist movement from a small, secretive, doctrinaire, exclusivist and highly militant organisation into an open, mass-based, pragmatic, yet principled and influential social and political movement – an influential force in the Lebanese political mainstream, and the primary patriotic force of resistance to Israeli military occupation. Fadlallah was instrumental in guiding Lebanon's Islamists away from impulsive, revolutionary rhetoric, ideological rigidity and ossification, towardsa reformist gradualism supported by pragmatic, dispassionate activism. As in the case of the democratic experiment of the Islamic Salvation Front in Algeria in 1989–91, Hizbullah's venture into Lebanon's parliamentary politics marked a new phase in the strategic course of Islamism. While it is too early to give a definitive assessment of Hizbullah's parliamentary experience, the party's performance in the 1990s demonstrated that Islamists could operate competently in an open, competitive political forum, engaging politically and ideologically with rival and formerly hostile political forces, and entering into cooperation with the previously despised political establishment. The values and vision of Ismamism have provided an underlying constant in this process of accommodation, adaptation and acculturation.

Fadlallah demonstrated his adeptness at reading and responding to political developments and analysing their repercussions for the Islamist movement in Lebanon. Furthermore, as a trained senior jurisconsult, Fadlallah has been a leading exponent of *al-fiqh al-haraki* – literally, dynamic jurisprudence – in contemporary Islamist praxis. Islamist theoreticians and strategists like Fadlallah are prepared, whether dictated by opportunity or necessity, to alter, suspend or abandon their tactics. In such a situation, where there is a dynamic interplay between Islamic textual interpretation and social and political praxis, Islamists may quite readily adopt a gradualist strategy of reformist change including a series of sequential phases – especially when the goal of the radical transformation of the social and political sphere is thought to be out of reach.

By the same token, that which is normatively proscribed may under certain circumstances become permissible, and vice versa. In this way, though the post-war government and state political institutions were deemed theoretically to be illegitimate, the opportunities offered by an open, multi-party, representative quasi-democracy meant that there were considerable potential benefits to be gained by a participatory, integrationist Islamist movement, which thus becomes a permissible vehicle of activism. In engineering this transition, Fadlallah sought to ensure that Islam would remain a major influential force in Lebanon's political arena, as well as becoming a potentially significant factor in regional and international spheres. In approaching this objective, though Fadlallah regarded the propounding of an Islamic republic in Lebanon as an unfeasible objective in the short term, he thought it sensible and necessary to activate the Islamic political and ideological paradigm in the local setting. Such a quest would 'signify and demonstrate that Islam is not a confessional phenomenon, but instead represents an ideological condition active in political reality, with a potential of agitating the whole political reality with its notions'.[137]

Similarly, in imploring his compatriots and brethren to wage an unrelenting armed struggle against the Israeli occupation of South Lebanon, Fadlallah encapsulated a consistent, principled position on Israel, one of long-standing implacable hostility to the very existence of the state of Israel. For Fadlallah and fellow Islamists the continued Israeli occupation of Arab territories seized in the 1967 Six-Day War was thus merely a symptom of what had long been viewed as the Jewish state's 'Zionist colonial settler' character. Israel's establishment; the concomitant expulsion and displacement of Palestinians; its subsequent territorial expansionism into adjoining Arab states; its strategic military and political alliance with the United States; its inexorable drive for political and economic dominance and military and technological superiority in the Middle East – all have served to vindicate the deep-seated antipathy felt by Islamists towards Israel. This sentiment, shared by Fadlallah, was borne out of a radical Islamist *weltanschuung* and activist, liberationist agenda predicated on an existential political and ideological struggle against Western cultural dominance (real or perceived), American 'neo-imperialism', and oppressive, or at the very least unrepresentative, pro-Western Arab regimes.

EIGHT

Fadlallah's Legacy: Lebanon, Iraq and Beyond

We have seen, throughout Fadlallah's career, the dynamic interplay between radicalism and pragmatism, and between activism and intellectualism. During the latter part of his career, and since the late 1990s in particular, Fadlallah has cemented his status as a rationalist religious scholar, modernist intellectual, and pragmatic Islamic activist. Those three key strands are manifest in the changing nature of his leadership and the diversification of his roles – that of a reformist Shi'i *marja'* receptive to the challenges of modernity, yet also an intellectual Islamist shaping contemporary discussion on the regional and international scenes; that of ecumenist seeking to transcend the historical and doctrinal schism between Sunnism and Shi'ism, combined with that of a Shi'i scholar who affirms the validity and authenticity of his denomination as the true inheritor of Islam.

And yet Fadlallah has not ceased being a radical. To the extent he remains staunchly anti-Israeli and anti-Zionist, he remains a radical; to the extent that he has persistently objected to successive US-sponsored peace initiatives to resolve the Palestinian-Israeli conflict – form the Oslo Accords to Wye River, Camp David II, and ending with Road Map – he remains a radical; to the extent that he calls for the return of all Palestinian refugees to Israel proper, and the departure of Jewish immigrants from Palestine, he remains a radical; to the extent that he firmly believes in the illegitimacy of the Jewish state bent on dominating the region, he remains, unquestionably, a radical; to the extent he has been a strident supporter of the Palestinian Intifada, and an ardent advocate of suicide operations against Israeli targets, he remains a radical; and a to the extent that he maintains warm relations with militant Palestinian organisations such as Jihad and Hamas, whose leaders regard him highly for his political analysis and strategic thinking, he remains a radical. And finally, to the extent that he has avowedly opposed American foreign policy in the region and actively engaged in raising public awareness of US plans over the years – particularly in the post-9/11 era – Fadlallah remains a radical.

This chapter will examine how Fadlallah responded to key events and developments since 1997, starting with the momentous Iranian presidential election, through to the evacuation of Israeli troops from southern Lebanon in 2000, and ending with the cataclysmic events of 11 September 2001, and the subsequent US invasion and occupation of first Afghanistan, then Iraq.

On 23 May 1997, Dr Mohammad Khatami, a moderate religious scholar, contested the presidential elections by running on a populist–reformist platform. With a 77 per cent turnout, the former minister of Culture and Islamic Guidance won 70 per cent of the 29 million votes cast.[1] The vast majority of voters were young Iranians, who comprised the bulk of the country's estimated population of over 70 million. Due largely to his modernist views and reformist agenda, advocating the rule of law, individual liberty and Islamic democracy, Sayyid Khatami appealed to intellectuals, academics, university students, artists, women, bureaucrats, and even young 'ulama.[2] He managed to repeat that impressive performance in 2001.

In July 1999, Iran was rocked by serious urban unrest. At the heart of the disturbances were student demonstrations that swept a number of cities. Frustrated by the slow pace of the legal and social reforms instituted by Khatami, who was stymied by the powerful conservative-controlled state institutions, the university students demanded the lifting of press censorship and called for individual freedoms.[3] Among those who closely watched these events unfold was Fadlallah, who correctly described the student protest movement as representing a broad spectrum, from secular leftists, nationalists and modernising Islamists to rightists. What welded these disparate elements together was a vague vision of progressive change.[4]

Fadllallah praises Khatami for handling the crisis prudently, despite his walking a tightrope between the reformers and the conservatives. As the student disturbances came to be punctuated by riots, violence and arson, Khatami, having decided to 'ride the wave of protests', began to distance himself from the students. For the young, aspiring and discontented Iranians who had voted en masse to elect Khatami, as head of state, with genuine hopes of reform, the perceived vacillation and inability of the President to break the hold of the conservative opposition on the levers of power was particularly disappointing and demoralizing.[5]

Fadlallah informs us how, during a meeting with the president, he pointed out the need to recognise an important fact: that Iran's youth had little or no affinity with the 1979 Revolution, as they had not experienced its events first-hand, and many of them were thus now restless, with a tendency to question many aspects of the current order.[6] In his assessment, the current traditional-minded *hawza* is inherently incapable of responding to the needs of the young generation of frustrated and aspiring Iranians. He concludes by stating that, if we want the new generation to be receptive to an Islam characterised by openness, than a genuine effort must be made to answer satisfactorily all of their concerns and fulfil their aspirations.[7]

It is not surprising to find Fadlallah – a modernist and progressive Islamic thinker himself – sharing many of the key views espoused by Khatami. It was his accession to the *marja'iyya* in 1995 that provided Fadlallah with the institutional framework and juridical authority to develop a new body of religious–legal judgements based on rational interpretation of the canonical texts. From this point, as we will see below, Fadlallah was to embark on an influential yet controversial project involving the reinterpretation of accepted notions, historical sources, and doctrinal and legal positions.

We have already explored the sequence of events that followed the death in 1992 of Grand Ayatollah Abul Qasem al-Kho'ie, who since 1970 held the status of the world's pre-eminent *marja' li al-taqleed*. He was succeeded first by Grand Ayatollah Muhammad Reza Golpayegani, who died in 1993, and then by Grand Ayatollah Araki, who died 1994. The origins of the disagreement between Fadlallah and the pro-Khamanei camp can be traced to the period immediately after the death of al-Kho'ie; Fadlallah supported the candidacy of the Najaf-based al-Araki, while Khamanaei, along with the Hizbullah leadership, backed the Iranian Golpayegani.

Fadlallah subscribes to the view of a pluralist *maraj'aiyya* (*al-Marja'iyya al-Ta'adudiyya*). He points to the existence of Lebanese *maraje'* throughout the history of the country, such as the late Sayyid Muhsin al-Amin (d. 1953), who had an independent following and was not beholden to either Najaf or Qom. In more recent times, particularly following the death of al-Kho'ie, at least four independent *maraje'*, arose in Iran: Sistani (Najaf), Rohani (Qom), Khamanei (Tehran) and Shirazi (Qom).[8] Fadlallah's view of the *marja'iyya* should be seen in the wider context of intellectual continuity, based in part on his deeply held predilection towards 'diversity (of religious and intellectual currents) within unity (of Islam)'. There are both advantages and disadvantages in having several independent religious authorities, says Fadlallah. One of the benefits is that pluralism provides for a richness of thought, and a variety of streams or juridical currents, through the exercise of *ijtihad* (independent legal reasoning). It gives Shi'i laypersons the opportunity to choose the most suitable jurisconsult, according to his erudition, the effectiveness of his social skills, his piety, integrity, and leadership qualities. By contrast, the disadvantages lie in the danger of this respected and tolerated diversity degenerating into partisanship and personal sensitivities, which might deprive the Shi'i community of unity.[9] Naturally, Fadlallah's espousal of a pluralist *marja'iyya* is to be expected, in defence of his own public nomination to the leadership; a rationale for his candidacy was vital in order to gain recognition from other 'ulama and to attract a wide following – especially in light of the controversy that surrounded his timing and motives. In Fadlallah's words, 'to the extent to which the *marja'* adheres to Islam and strives for the higher interest of the public, his involvement in political affairs becomes manifest by means of criticism of various political plans and means of monitoring and scrutinising political reality'. At the same time, he stresses that it is very important that the *marja'* not be biased towards one particular organised group, by being a member – much less a leader – of an organisation.[10] To be a party member, Fadlallah argues, would render him subject or subservient to the organisation's decrees, which he would be obliged to abide by, thereby surrendering the *marja'iyya* as an independent source of authority.

In an oblique reference to Hizbullah and Hizb al-Da'wa, Fadlallah does make a provision for the *marja'* to assume the role of overseeing the direction and activities of an Islamist organisation or movement, and in certain cases he may support that particular formation that embodies the views of the *marja'*.[11] It is ironic that Fadlallah who has consistently denied all claims of his being the 'spiritual leader' of Hizbullah – denials that have proved to be justified – has never been able to completely dispel the media and public perception of his being a partisan of the 'Party of God'. The single most oft-repeated question asked by Lebanese, Arab and western journalists interviewing Fadlallah since the early 1980s has been the nature of his relationship with Hizbullah.

Fadlallah has departed from the traditional view, holding that the *marja'* should be the most learned (*al-'alim*) in Islamic *fiqh wa usouluhu*. The traditionalists – the elder *mujtahids* in Iran and Iraq – objected on those grounds to Sayyid Khamanaei to becoming *marja'*. Instead of espousing *al-Marj'aiyya al-Mutlaqa* (the absolutist *marja'iyya*) embodied in Khamanei, Fadlallah advocates the notion of *al-Marja'iyya al-Shamila* – that is, the comprehensive *marja'iyya*, an all-embracing institution that would be committed and capable of addressing the pressing and complex needs of society. Furthermore, he envisages a *marja'iyya*, as manifested in his own leadership, that would be ecumenical in orientation, providing sound guidance not just to the Shi'i faithful but to Muslims in general. Such an institution would interact with modernity while simultaneously providing an Islamic perspective on all contemporary issues.[12]

In contradistinction to traditional *marja'iyya*, Fadlallah calls for a reformed, modern institution, embodying an elaborate organisational structure with diverse functions. The envisaged institution would incorporate specialised departments, such as scientific, technical and medical committees, whose primary responsibilities would be to assist the *marja'* through the gathering and analysis of data and the writing of reports. Since becoming *marja'* in the mid-1990s, Fadlallah's influence has grown exponentially. Thanks to the annual tithe, *al-khums* and regular *sadaqat*, and to his erudition and influence, Fadlallah has been able to build up an impressive country-wide network of agencies, serving the diverse needs of his community. The departments include: al-Maktab al-Alaqaat al-Kharijiyya (Bureau of External Relations), Maktab al-Istifsar (Bureau of Enquiries), Maktab al-Istifta' (Bureau of Fatwa Elicitation), Maktab al-'Ilami (Bureau of Information), Maktab al-Shar'i (Legal Bureau), and Maktab al-Alaaat al-Ijtima'iyya (Bureau of Social Relations). Through these offices, Fadlallah's representatives handle legal (*shar'i*) queries, provide financial assistance to the poor, housing for the homeless, and specialist accommodation and training programmes for orphans and children with disabilities.

Again, in contrast to the majority of the Shi'i jurisisconsults, Fadlallah does not deem the *marja'iyya* to be an office exclusively for males. Observing his own espousal of that view some twenty years ago, Fadlallah argues that there is no Islamic legal basis to support the traditionally accepted view of male exclusiveness. Rather, the reasons for this restriction can be found in social norms and traditional attitudes. Recognising the controversy of his position, Fadlallah cites the names of two contemporary senior *mujtahids* with similar viewpoints: the late Sayyid Muhsin al-Hakim (d. 1970) and Sayyid Muhsin al-Amin (d. 1953).[13]

We have seen how, ever since becoming a *marja'* in 1996, Fadlallah has been subjected to a vociferous campaign of criticism waged by powerful conservative *maraje'*. The war waged by conservative clerical circles in the Shi'i world against Fadlallah's *marja'iyya* has seen his excommunication, the banning of his books and audiovisual material, and calls for his assassination. Indeed, four years ago a serious attempt was made on Fadlallah's life while he was delivering the Friday sermon at Masjid al-Imamayn, in Harait Hraik. Asked about the identity and motives of the culprit, Fadlallah replied that he was unable to shed any light on these questions, as he had eluded capture by the security forces. Fadlallah now tends to downplay the incident, describing the would-be assassin as an individual with a juvenile mentality. In the eyes of Fadlallah's critics, he is guilty of radically reinterpreting accepted Shi'i tenets, traditional rituals and historical narratives, and has been accused of trying to overturn Shi'i religious dogma and imposing Sunni doctrine in its place. Detractors pointing to his close links with Sunni scholars and activists, and to his long-standing and staunch advocacy of ecumenism. For being a rational modernist thinker, Fadlallah has been accused of being too influenced by western philosophical thought, particularly modernism and secularism.[14]

Fadlallah has no illusions as to why he has become a source of controversy. Indeed, he proudly states that he has 'endeavoured to be free in interpreting history and independent-minded in understanding Islam'.[15] He has countered his critics by affirming that he is entitled as a scholar and jurist to re-examine the Shi'i textual sources, and reinterpret historical narrative, just as his celebrated predecessors had done before him. For Fadlallah, the scholarly views and legal opinions of any *marja'*, no matter how illustrious or pre-eminent, are articulated by fallible mortals, and consequently should not be above scrutiny and evaluation by his contemporaries and successors.

In his own defence, Fadlallah holds that his detractors have essentially failed to read his writings closely and objectively enough, and have consequently misunderstood the nature of his *ijtihad*. He asserts that there is nothing new in his writings; he is not the first *mujtahid*, nor will he be the last, to review selective historical events, religious rituals and doctrinal tenets. As a case in point, he mentions his late colleague, Sayyid Baqer al-Sadr, who, along with other reformers, was accused by the conservatives of deviation from 'orthodoxy'. Paradoxically, Fadlallah tries to rebut the assertion that he has diverged from Shi'ism by dismissing the accepted notion that the *ijma'* of the 'ulama, held by both Sunnis and Shi'a, is a binding source of Islamic law.[16]

Fadlallah has issued a number of bold, controversial edicts, ranging from such religious matters as determining the beginning and end of the ninth lunar month of Ramadan, social attitudes and relations (such as the purity of *Ahl al-Kitab* [The people of the Book, i.e. Jews and Christians]), and scientific–ethical issues, most notably human cloning.

In relation to Ramadan, Fadlallah declared that, with the tremendous advances in astronomical observation, it is possible to calculate precisely, months ahead, the date and time of the moon's birth and possible sighting (weather permitting), rendering the traditional mechanism of human sighting of the moon redundant. He argues – and correctly so – that the old method of determining the start and end of Ramadan is prone to human error.[17] While he is not the first to advocate such a method among either Shi'i or Sunni scholars, he is the most prominent figure to publicly and forcefully promote it. This clear break with tradition has raised the ire of the conservative Shi'i 'ulama. Furthermore, unlike his late colleague, Shaykh Mahdi Shams al-Din, Fadlallah has again exercised his independence from Iran, by stipulating the requirement that Muslims in Lebanon follow the local timeframe, which varies from that of Iran.

On the highly controversial issue of cloning, Fadlallah has come out in favour of the process. Much criticised for the 'hasty' sanctioning of cloning, Fadlallah was the first Shi'i *'alim* to give his qualified support. Certain guidelines informed by Islamic Law and ethical concerns need to be met. Among the Sunnis, al-Qaradawi and al-Zuhayli were among the first scholars to legitimise the technique, subject to strict criteria.[18]

Fadlallah's ascension to the *marja'iyya* marked a watershed in the relationship between the pre-eminent Shi'i cleric and Hizbullah. The affinity and intimacy that had for so long characterised the relationship between Fadlallah, the theoretician and jurist, and Hizbullah, the Islamist resistance movement and parliamentary political party, had given way to estrangement and frostiness. The rift was initiated and maintained by some of Iran's senior conservative clergy. Initially, elements within Iran's clerical leadership waged a campaign to undermine Fadlallah's *marja'iyya*. However, to put an end to speculation that attacks on Fadlallah's authority had the tacit approval of Iran's supreme leader, Ayatollah Khamenei personally intervened on Fadlallah's side, calling for a halt to public recriminations. More recently, the Iranian Cultural Advisor, Muhammad Mahdi Taskhir, publicly lauded Fadlallah for his credentials and defended him against his opponents.[19]

Such has been the extent of the impact on his relationship with Iran's conservative religious establishment that Fadlallah has, since becoming a *marja'* refrained from travelling to Iran, consistently declining repeated invitations from Iranian officials and from independent reform-minded 'ulama, as well as from his supporters (mainly seminary students in Qom) to visit the country, citing time constraints resulting from his increased responsibilities as a *marja'*, as well as security concerns. Following the publicising of a series of controversial edicts and revisionist readings of historical narrative and religious dogma, Fadlallah has been subject to a concerted campaign of criticism, his books in some quarters have been taken off the shelves, his erudition challenged, his loyalty to Shi'ism questioned, and his life threatened; he has been labelled by some powerful conservatives a heretic and an apostate, pandering to Sunni, even Wahhabi–Salafi, sentiment.[20]

Although Fadlallah has invariably been held in high esteem, and was referred to for guidance, it was to Iran's paramount leader – first Khomeini, then Khamenei – that Hizbullah's ultimate allegiance has always been owed. But it would be wrong to see the ties as having been completely severed. Fadlallah's Friday sermons are still listened to by a significant number of Hizbullah cadres. The party's deputy General Secretary, Shaykh Na'im Qasim, frequently visits Fadlallah at his residence in Harat Hraik for consultations. The fact that their relationship remains close can be traced to their long-standing ties, harking back to Qasem's pre-Hizbullah days, when he was an active member of Hizb al-Da'wa, and like many of his peers in Lebanon looked to Fadlallah for ideological and juridical guidance.

In May 2000 Israel, under newly elected prime minister Ehud Barak, ended its eighteen-year military occupation of southern Lebanon. Since 1985, Hizbullah's armed wing, al-Muqawamah al-Islamiyyah (Islamic Resistance) has emerged as the most potent organised paramilitary group waging a guerrilla war against the regular units of the occupying Israeli military and their Lebanese auxiliaries (the South Lebanese Army). In the face of an increasingly sophisticated, disciplined and determined foe, the Israeli military seemed incapable of halting – much less reversing – the mounting losses among its ranks, or of stopping the climbing rate of defections and infiltrations among its SLA allies. Calculating that the continued occupation of South Lebanon would be militarily unsustainable and politically untenable, Barak, in keeping with his pre-election pledge, effected the unconditional withdrawal of the IDF (Israeli Defence Forces) from its northern neighbour.

At the time of the retreat of the Israeli army, relations between Fadlallah and Hizbullah had begun to improve, and in its immediate aftermath the ties were all but cemented as Fadlallah heaped praise on Hizbullah's armed wing, Islamic Resistance, and extolled its exploits.[21]

Basking in the 'glory' of unprecedented triumph, where the Lebanese Shi'i Islamist movement he helped to engender has been able to achieve what no Arab state has managed to realize, a jubilant Fadlallah declared that this is the first time in the long history of the Arab-Israeli conflict that Israel has been forced to retreat by military force from occupied Arab territory.[22]

The withdrawal of Israeli military forces from all but a narrow, albeit strategic, strip of the Shebaa farms district, straddling the border with Syria, did not mean the end of Lebanese resistance. On the contrary, Fadlallah declared that 'the battle for liberation has not ended; in fact, it has only just begun'. Accordingly, he affirmed the right of the Lebanese to resume the fight until the liberation of the remaining occupied highlands. To that end, Fadlallah has from the outset stoutly upheld Hizbullah's right to hold on to its weapons, and to resist calls form certain government officials to disband the paramilitary organisation. Indeed, Fadlallah and Hizbullah have remained publicly committed to the realisation of their grand goal – the liberation of Jerusalem – although acknowledging that this quest would necessitate a concerted multilateral effort.[23]

Underlining Fadllallah's argument in favour of a continued military role for Hizbullah in the wake of Israeli withdrawal is a deeply held belief that Israel, despite its vital role in the precarious, ongoing peace process, which had been set in motion in 1993 by the Oslo Accords, was not genuinely interested in a just and comprehensive peace agreement with the Palestinians and the Arab states. History has taught the Arabs, according to Fadlallah, that negotiations might lead to a settlement, but not to a just, lasting peace. The problem, as he sees it, is that Israel, with the unswerving support of the United States and, to a lesser extent, Europe, is committed to maintaining its military–technological superiority over the Arabs, and to expanding its power in the region. It is worth pointing out here that at the height of the peace process – which witnessed, on the one hand, steady progress between Israel and the PLO and between Israel and Syria, and on the other hand a breakthrough between Israel and Jordan, with the signing of a peace treaty – Hizbullah not only continued its integration into Lebanon's political institutions, but prepared itself for a possible settlement between Israel and the regimes of its Arab neighbours.[24] Just as Fadlallah had influenced the 'Lebanonisation' of Hizbullah, so too he impressed on the Shi'i Islamist movement the imperative, by campaigning from within state institutions, of retarding, if not preventing, the normalisation of relations between Israel and Lebanon.

Just as the Islamist-dominated armed resistance to Israeli occupation in Lebanon had directly inspired the first Intifada, which erupted in December 1987, so too the liberation of all South Lebanon stimulated the second Intifada, in October 2000. The impressive achievement of Hizbullah in Lebanon spurred Palestinians – particularly those activists among them associated with Hamas and Islamic Jihad – to launch a protracted campaign of civil disturbance and armed insurrection. To the dispirited Arabs, and to the Palestinians in particular, Hizbullah's success shattered the myth of Israeli invincibility, and demonstrated the vulnerability of Israel's military and the fragility of its public opinion.[25]

In common with other Islamists, Fadlallah views the conflict between the Israelis and Palestinians as an unequal conflict, a David-versus-Goliath struggle, in which Israel possesses the most advanced weaponry, while the Palestinians have only stones and small arms. In such a total war, the hard-pressed weaker party is compelled to go beyond conventional means in its war in order to defend itself. The fact of the matter, according to Fadlallah, is that 'Those Palestinians who carried operations inside the "green line" [Israel proper] had targeted Israeli [national] security, and not the Israeli civilians per se.'[26] On the question of the recent phenomenon of female suicide bombers, Fadlallah says that 'self-martyring' is not incumbent on them, but that it is permissible for women to undertake such operations. Fadlallah goes further, glorifying the Palestinian women who 'self-martyr' themselves as 'heroines who will produce a new history'. Islam, he adds, does not specify a particular method by which to carry out jihad, of which 'self-martyring' is the highest form.[27]

Voicing Arab and Muslim public opinion, Fadlallah regards America as bearing full responsibility for what is happening and has happened in Palestine. Successive American administrations have been committed to ensuring Israel's national security, and have given Israel unfettered access to the latest in American military technology, while American military supplies and technology transfers have been crucial to making Israel the pre-eminent military and political power in the region.[28]

The uprising in the Palestinian territories, and its ensuing wave of violence, were soon overshadowed by the cataclysmic events of 11 September 2001. Fadlallah was one of the first Islamic scholars to publicly condemn the coordinated terrorist attacks on that day. Six days after the assaults, Fadlallah, speaking in his first interview, deemed the hijacking of the passenger airliners and their steering into the World Trade Center and the Pentagon to be illegitimate from an Islamic standpoint. Islam prohibits the holding, terrorising and killing of innocent civilians, even though their government may be perceived to be hostile in its policy towards the Muslim world. Islam, Fadlallah argued, does not sanction offensive martial jihad. Citing a relevant Qur'anic verse – 'No person should bear responsibility for a crime committed by another' (no matter how close they may happen to be) – Fadlallah argued that it would be unlawful to impose on American civilians – be they passengers, merchants, visitors, or otherwise – responsibility for the policies of their government. Accordingly, Fadlallah states that, unlike the 'self-martyring' operations carried out by Palestinian Hamas and Islamic Jihad against 'illegitimate occupiers of Palestine' (namely Israeli residents, settlers and military personnel), the 9/11 attacks constituted a suicidal operation.[29]

Five weeks after the 9/11 attacks, Fadlallah expressed the hope that this cataclysmic convulsion would present an opportunity for the Americans to reconsider the impact of their foreign policies. He gave the advice that, if the United States truly wishes to lead the world, than it ought to base its foreign policy on love, not subjugation. Fadlallah explained that 'The roots of the events of September 11 lie in the nature of American foreign policy.' For the peoples of the Third World in general, and the Middle East in particular, the outcome of those policies has been 'subjugation, injustice, despair – conditions which have spawned deep-seated feelings of animosity' towards the United States. Grievances stemmed, on the one hand, from the United States' hostility towards Iran, Iraq, Libya, Sudan and Syria, all of which were branded as sponsors of terrorism, with the first three subjected to sanctions, and on the other hand from America's open and unconditional support of Israel.[30]

If Fadlallah unequivocally condemned the 9/11 attacks, and publicly sympathised with the victims – a sentiment that did not extend to the US administration – that sympathy, on the eve of the aerial bombing of Afghanistan, had been replaced by an unmistaken antipathy for the United States and open solidarity with the Afghan people who had been oppressed under the Taliban regime – a stance that saw its crystallisation, on the eve of the unilateral war on Iraq, in his open exhortation of believers to wage jihad against the Anglo-American invasion force.

Accounting for the bin Laden phenomenon, Fadlallah attempts to situate the al-Qa'eda leader in a historical context. He observes that, since the 1950s, the Arabs have been searching for a hero or saviour, a figure who embodies the sentiments and aspirations of the Arab nation and Muslim *umma*. Through his exploits attacking US interests, bin Laden, for large sections of disenfranchised and disaffected Muslim and Arab youth, had come to fulfil the long-sought yearning for a champion of the Arab–Muslim cause. Bin Laden's declaration of jihad against the so-called Christian Crusader and Jewish Zionist alliance, led by the United States, and the subsequent al-Qa'eda suicide bombings of US embassies in Nairobi and Dar es-Salaam, aroused much expectation, even eagerness, among many Muslims to see an inevitable climactic showdown. The crescendo came on 11 September 2001. In this way, bin Laden was able to garner support throughout the Muslim world. According to Fadlallah, the reaction of many Muslims to the 9/11 attacks was one of jubilation at seeing the stunning images of American landmarks being hit, of the US leadership going underground, and of confusion and disorientation in decision making.[31]

Fadlallah makes the reasonable observation that, despite the magnitude of the 9/11 attacks, and despite all the vigour and vitality manifested by al-Qa'eda, bin Laden and his associates had calculated, unrealistically, that the defeat of the US was possible and imminent through such a terrorist strike, just as it had been possible to triumph over the USSR. The analogy was flawed, largely because the ten-year resistance to the Russians in Afghanistan was a global campaign, in which the US played a covert but crucial role, as did Saudi Arabia and Pakistan.[32]

In explaining the strategic response of the United States following the shock and outrage of the 9/11 attacks, Fadlallah mentions their devastating psychological impact, convulsing as they did the American sense of complacency in their homeland, and a sense of immunity from international terrorism. Thus, for Fadlallah and indeed for other Islamists, the American self-declared 'War on Terror' emanated, on the one hand, from an immediate need to restore national pride and international prestige, and on the other, from a long-held desire to expand its influence worldwide, and dominate the affairs and resources of the Middle East and Central Asia. Thus, for Fadlallah the true driving force of US foreign policy has little to do with the much-publicised mission of spreading the values of justice and freedom throughout the world, but everything to do with preserving and advancing America's interests.[33]

In the same vein, Fadlallah, in a live interview on MBC Satellite Television on 28 December 2001, expressed the view that the terrorist attacks gave the United States the opportunity to expand globally, and with that the ability to realise its strategic plans, which would not have been possible in peacetime. Furthermore, the attacks had restricted the freedoms of Islamic activists operating in the west. As part of the pretext of fighting terrorism, Islamist oppositional movements were now subsumed within the rhetoric of this global campaign.[34]

For the proclaimed 'war on terror' was problematic from conceptual and practical standpoints. First, the term is too broad and ambiguous; second, it is subjective and politically laden (including such militant groups as Hamas and Hizbullah, and states like Iran, but not Israel); third, its duration is indefinite, and its reach global; and finally, the relationship between the states participating in the campaign to eradicate terrorism is not a partnership of equals, but rather a reluctant alliance of dominant powers and subservient states.

The American media, according to Fadlallah, has managed to make bin Laden larger than life so that victory over him, when it eventually comes, will be proportionate to his supposed threat. Fadlallah concludes by stating that 'the Islamists, if they indeed had carried out [the September 11 attacks], managed, unwittingly, to advance the [long-term strategic interests] of the Americans'. Ironically, despite – or perhaps because of – bin Laden's extremist attempts to destroy America, 'such has been the importance', Fadlallah asserted, 'of the service that bin Laden provided that had the Americans expended billions of dollars' they would not have attained the position and influence that they wield in the world in general, and the Middle East and Central Asia in particular.[35]

For Islamist movements, the challenge in the wake of 9/11 is unmistakably serious: Islamic activists, lamented Fadlallah, have not risen to the level of that challenge. Why have Islamists not 'worked on presenting Islam to the contemporary individual in a new language that is distinct from the traditional modes of expression'? He added that Islamists had become absorbed in either political or jihadist pursuits, and had consequently drifted away from the 'all-encompassing Islamic wordview'. As to what ought to be done to remedy the situation, Fadlallah speaks broadly of the need for integrated Islamic action, which would entail Islamic scholars and Islamic movements liaising together with a view to formulating a complete, holistic plan, under which martial jihad would constitute one form of *Da'wa*, just as political activity would form an integral part of the Islamic struggle. Finally, he underscores the importance of maximising the benefits emanating from the changes in the international sphere, in order to propound Islam in a spirit is concordant with those changes.[36]

The events of 9/11 and the American war on global Islamic terrorism had a clear impact on the Palestinian-Israeli conflict. Israel joined the war on terror by having Hamas and Islamic Jihad recognised by Western countries as 'terror' organisations for their suicide attacks on civilians. The biggest loser from 9/11 was the Palestinian cause, since the US managed to portray the Palestinian resistance as 'terrorism'. For Fadlallah, there is no similarity between the terrorist attacks perpetrated by al-Qa'eda and the 'self-martyring' operations carried out by Hamas and Islamic Jihad, among others. Reiterating his earlier position on 9/11, Fadlallah argued that the element of armed aggression against civilians in peacetime, or at least not under conditions of formal war, from a shari'ah standpoint, is forbidden. By contrast, in Palestine every Jew, as an occupier of Palestinian property, is a legitimate target. Highlighting Israel's use of the most technologically advanced weaponry, and underscoring the grossly uneven struggle in Palestine, Fadlallah legitimises the Palestinians' employment of whatever is within their means to undermine Israel's national security, just as the Jewish state has perpetually undermined the security of the occupied territories.[37]

In March 2002 the Sharon government took the public decision to move against Yasser Arafat and his Palestinian National Authority in Ramallah. Arafat was blamed for the increase in the number of suicide attacks on Israelis by Palestinian militants. In the eyes of the Israelis, Arafat was either unable or unwilling to crack down on those militants, and was therefore no longer a fitting partner in peace negotiations. Consequently Sharon branded Arafat an enemy, and publicly called for his assassination or deportation. Henceforth, PNA administrative buildings in Ramallah were systematically demolished, including all but a few rooms where the beleaguered Palestinian leader was holed up in his crumbling headquarters. If the tragic events of 11 September and the subsequent war on terrorism provided a conducive backdrop against which Sharon could launch his campaign to marginalise, or even eliminate, his long-time nemesis, the strong protestations of the European Union and the Arab League seemed to have compel Sharon to retreat from capturing or killing Arafat. In that context, asked what advice he would give to the besieged Palestinian Chairman, Fadlallah replied emphatically: 'Presently, there is no voice other than the voice of confronting the Israeli enemy with all that you possess.'[38]

In the couple of weeks following 11 September, President Bush geared his country towards a global war on an unconventional and amorphous enemy. The first vital front in that war was Afghanistan, where the Taliban regime had given sanctuary to the prime suspects of the 9/11 attacks. In assessing the factors that contributed to the American-led bombardment and subsequent invasion of Afghanistan in October 2001, Fadlallah stated correctly that under the Taliban the country was a haven for extremists and 'terrorists'. It was a ready target, he said, since the Americans had foreknowledge of the intentions of the Taliban's leaders: that they would refuse to accede to US requests to handover bin Laden and his associates. He subscribes to the now commonly held view that, as a movement, the Taliban was essentially the creation of the Pakistani intelligence agency (ISI), which operated with the tacit approval of the US. In the end, the Taliban were toppled because they had 'rebelled against their masters in Washington'. The targeting of the Taliban by a punitive American campaign was especially necessary in the light of the need to mollify the growing American domestic sentiment in the wake of the 9/11 attacks.[39]

Fadlallah strongly opposed the war on the Taliban, even though he stridently objected to the movement's forceful imposition of its rigid and ultra-traditionalist version of Islam, manifested in the oppression of women and persecution of minorities. His stance was based largely on legal considerations. He contended that the US had no constitutional or legal jurisdiction to demand the handing over of suspects involved in the 9/11 attacks for trial in the US, arguing that under international civil law they should be tried by the host country. Similarly, under international law the US had no jurisdiction to declare war on Afghanistan, on account of the Taliban's refusal to hand over those accused of planning and ordering the attacks. Furthermore, the US had crucially failed, at that early stage, to furnish hard evidence of the culpability of the suspects, as demanded by the Taliban. Fadlallah concluded that, just as there was no legal 'justification for the bombings that occurred in the United States, so too there is no justification for the war', which, consequently, was deemed to be 'a war of aggression'.[40]

Not content with publicly opposing the Bush administration's decision to invade Afghanistan, Fadlallah issued a fatwa – and was among the few senior Shi'i 'ulama to do so – in which he explicitly forbade Muslims from assisting the Americans in any manner, in the event of an invasion of any Muslim country. Fadlallah called on Muslims not to assist the United States and its allies in 'striking at a Muslim people, such as the Afghans, who are a dislocated and malnourished people, as the United States is flexing its muscles against this wretched people'.

Fadlallah faults the many commentators and analysts who had predicted that the Taliban would remain steadfast in the face of an American invasion, that they would prosecute an effective resistance campaign, and that eventually the US, like the former Soviet Union, would find itself in a quagmire. The crucial distinguishing factor between the Soviet and American invasions was the crucial role played by the anti-Taliban Northern Alliance in launching a land offensive under American air cover, and the concomitant withdrawal of Pakistani logistical and military support for their erstwhile surrogates in Kabul. The US also had the active support of its NATO allies (through the agency of the special forces). The net result was a swift Taliban collapse.[41]

Assessing the fall-out from the war against the Taliban and al-Qa'eda in Afghanistan, Fadlallah warns that the conditions of subjugation and humiliation imposed on Afghans, together with the deployment of overwhelming military force, will breed a new generation of hardened terrorists. In other words, the manner in which the US and its allies were conducting the air war and land invasion of Afghanistan will not deliver a body-blow to international terrorism; rather, it will spread it throughout the world.[42]

On the eve of the war on Iraq, Fadlallah called for a boycott of American merchandise as a protest against US foreign policy. To that end, he issued a fatwa prohibiting all dealings in American goods. Significantly, this was not the first time that Fadlallah has issued a religious–legal decree banning the import of American items; as mentioned earlier, he had issued a similar fatwa in the mid-1990s. Nor is he the only *'alim* who called for the boycott of American goods. Qaradawi, who shares many of Fadlallah's views on a variety of key issues, and with whom he has good relations, also joined his friend in such action. In Fadlallah's view, and indeed that of other activist scholars, if all the Muslim world's religious jurists could issue similar binding edicts collectively, they would have such devastating impact on American corporations that it would exert enormous pressure on the US administration to change its policies. Joint action among the 'ulama and public receptiveness to the boycotting of US goods would be a much more effective strategy for mobilising popular action and harming the economy of the US than issuing a fatwa calling for jihad and merely designed for public consumption.[43]

Unfortunately, in the absence of independent research on the subject, it is difficult to gauge the success or otherwise of the fatwa. Fadlallah claims that, on a local and regional scale, his fatwa has found popular resonance, especially among his followers, and has led to an appreciable drop in the import and consumption of US goods, particularly dispensable and substitutable soft drinks, such as Coca-Cola and Pepsi.

Fadlallah objected strongly to any role played by the Iraqi opposition in collaboration with the American-led alliance in the impeding invasion of Iraq in order to bring down Saddam Hussein. He anchored his opposition on the experience of Afghanistan, where he argued that the US employed the Northern Alliance, which was the main opposition force to the Taliban, as a symbolic formation. Similarly, in Iraq, Fadlallah predicted, the US would in effect deploy the Iraqi opposition as surrogates of its own administration in the country. As in Afghanistan, in a post-Ba'th Iraq, the pro-US Iraqi opposition to Saddam would become a mere appendage of the power of America and its allies.[44]

To Fadlallah's dismay, some Iraqi Shi'i Islamist opposition figures, such as Sayyid Muhammad Bahr al-'Ulum, head of the London-based Independent Islamic Movement in Iraq, and those affiliated with the formerly Iranian-based Supreme Council for Islamic Revolution in Iraq, had sent a delegation to hold talks with American officials, and discussed organisational readiness for the impending invasion. However, it is wrong to assume that the posture of the Iranian-created SCIR in Iraq was representative of other Shi'i Islamist groups. In that context, Fadlallah cites the case of al-Da'wa, the largest and oldest Shi'i Islamist group, whose leaders defer to Fadlallah. Fadlallah did not believe that the US would defend the Iraqi people if they were to 'rise up and overthrow the regime, since America is not a philanthropic society, and because it seeks to dominate absolutely the oil reserves and their utilisation in Iraq and the region as a whole'. He contended that the Iraqi opposition in exile was deceived by the US administration in believing that the only effective way to get rid of Saddam Hussein was to collaborate with the United States. It is inconceivable 'to establish a democratic system of government with the help of a superpower that dispenses with democracy when dealing with nations'.[45]

While Fadlallah's opposition to the holding of elections in the shadow of American occupation is shared by the more activist 'ulama-led groups, such as those headed by Sayyid Ahmad al-Hasani al-Baghdadi, Shaykh Jawwad al-Khalisi (a former student of Fadlallah) and Sayyid Muqtada al-Sadr, it is totally at odds with the position adopted by Iraq's recognised Shi'i *maraje'*.[46]

Unquestionably, the most outspoken and influential of this coterie of elderly jurisconsults has been Ayatollah al-'Uzma Sayyid Ali Sistani, based in Najaf. Sistani, who before the overthrow of the Ba'thist regime had been an apolitical recluse, had come out forcefully in favour of nationwide democratic elections to be held on schedule, in spite of the increasingly deadly insurgency, and most recently has exhorted the Shi'i multitude to cast their ballots on election day, and called on the various competing Shi'i political groups to forge a broad, common front. As a measure of al-Sistani's influence, his appeal has been heeded by the key Shi'i formations (with the exception of al-Sadr's movement), principally al-Da'wa and al-Majlis. It seems ironic that al-Da'wa's leaders have decided not to boycott the coming elections, against the advice of their unofficial guide, Fadlallah. Yet this is not untypical of al-Da'wa's pattern of behaviour, especially in light of its fluctuating relationship with a line of former guides or *maraje'*, from Sayyid Baqer al-Sadr through to al-Kazem al-Ha'eri, and ending with al-Asifi.[47]

To give his position legal weight and resonance, Fadlallah issued a fatwa prohibiting co-operation, in all its forms, with the Americans and their western allies. Fadlallah's alternative strategy to bring down Saddam was based on the forlorn quest to unify the disparate oppositional forces. To that end, he issued an edict in which he declared that it was legitimate for Islamists to co-operate with secularists for the object of overthrowing the Ba'th regime. Fadlallah's fatwa could be understood as a means by which to make Muslims recognise impending dangers, and to raise public awareness of the gravity of the situation and of the true motives which apparently belie the public claim of the US that they are seeking actively to remove the brutal dictatorship of Saddam Hussein.[48]

Fadlallah dismissed the US's publicly declared aim of toppling Saddam Hussein, among other reasons, because of his being the 'world's worst dictator'. For it was the US, Fadlallah argued, that was instrumental in preserving the Ba'th regime, as shown by its overt support for Iraq during its eight-year war with Iran, and by its public neutrality vis-à-vis the serious insurrections in the Kurdish north and Shi'i south of the country, following the invasion of Kuwait. Having sided with and supported Saddam Hussein's war with Iran, and having allowed his regime to survive by allowing the brutal suppression of the Shi'i and Kurdish insurrections that broke out in southern and northern Iraq, respectively, following the eviction of Iraqi forces from Kuwait in January–February 1991, the US was not committed to toppling the Ba'ath regime despite the sanctions imposed on the country, Fadlallah argued, as it was Iraqi citizens and not the regime that suffered. For Fadlallah it was clear that America was not remotely concerned about how tyrannical the regime was, or the extent to which Iraqi people were suffering under the sanctions;

rather, it was solely concerned with how to preserve its vital interests.[49]

American reasons for favouring the continuity of the Saddam regime, as interpreted by Fadlallah, were several: the US benefited from the instability in the region caused by Saddam Hussein's regime; it benefited from the pressures it was able to bring to bear on the precarious Gulf States; and earlier, during the first Gulf War, the US needed the services of Iraq in order to emasculate Iran. Finally, Fadlallah refers to what is now well known regarding the neutrality of the US in the run-up to the Iraqi invasion of Kuwait in August 1990: a stance that emboldened Saddam Hussein to attack his southern neighbour. Thus, in Fadlallah's analysis the only reason why the United States chose now to remove Saddam Hussein was that he had exhausted his usefulness to the Americans, and thus the time had come to replace him with another more compliant strongman. Thus, the US had no intention of replacing Saddam Hussein's dictatorial regime with a representative democratic government. Rather, the US was planning to control the economy and political capacity of Iraq, to monopolise investment ventures in the country, to control its markets, and perhaps to transform Iraq into a base from which it could exert pressure on other states in the region, making them more benign in their foreign policies. Among those countries that America was, and still is planning to contain and destabilise are Syria and Iran. Saudi Arabia, he predicted, would also be pressured into making concessions, by clamping down on its radical Islamists and militants, opening up its society and reforming its absolute monarchical rule.[50]

Fadlallah then proceeds to enumerate what he perceives as America's ulterior motives in invading Iraq. The first of these was to gain complete control of Iraq's oil, including exploration, production, refining, marketing, pricing and distribution. Given that oil is the mainstay of the modern world economy, it follows that by gaining control of the world's second-largest deposit, and one of the cheapest to extract, the US would be in a strong position to dictate the economies of rival regional powers, such as Japan, China and Western Europe, with the aim of ensuring US global supremacy for the foreseeable future. Other objectives were to hold sway over the Gulf States, to contain Iran, and to strengthen Israel. While Fadlallah reiterates his position on the need to overthrow Saddam and the ruling Ba'th party, he does not believe that America's campaign was aimed at demolishing the regime per se, but rather at destroying Iraq as a country. Moreover, he exhorted the Muslim populace, especially in the Arab world, 'to change their incumbent regimes, or to resolve their problems from within' – that is, without foreign intervention.[51]

Fadlallah argued that assisting the Americans and their allies would thus entail striking the Iraqi people, because 'we believe that the Iraqi people will be hit in order to gain control of all its capacities and transform them into a people living on the margins of American policy, and on the sidelines of Israeli policy.'[52] Assessing the gravity of the implications stemming from the American invasion of Iraq, Fadlallah sombrely expressed the view that 'the [present] phase is one of the most critical periods that the *Umma* has experienced in its history'.[53]

Three years into America's global war on terror, and its stated quest to implant democracy in Iraq following the invasion of the country, as a first step to spreading it to other countries in the region, Fadlallah claims that 'If the United States is advocating political reform in the Muslim world, then we should call on it to reform its foreign, security and economic policies so that it may become friendly to other nations, instead of being an enemy of them.' He warns that

> if the US was to persist in its cycle of violence, occupation and antagonism towards Muslim and Arab issues, and continue supporting Israel, then the conditions might engender more than one September 11. The various downtrodden peoples may submit for a long time to pressure, but beware of a powerful backlash upon their reawakening.[54]

In a recent interview with the *al-Hayat* newspaper, Fadlallah stated clearly where he stood in relation to the current insurgency in Iraq. 'We are with the resistance against the US occupation of Iraq, regardless of whether that occupation is open [and direct] or is cloaked in an Iraqi thin shroud, and irrespective of whether the resistance is peaceful or military in nature,' stressing that there is a simultaneous need for both forms of resistance. As far as Fadlallah was concerned, the current tumult and instability were caused by the presence of the Allied troops and their operations, and not by the resistance. Thus, for Fadlallah non-violence is a practicable strategy that would lead to the end of the occupation. In so far as he approves of peaceful means to resisting and forcing the withdrawal of coalition troops from Iraq, Fadlallah envisages it as something more substantial and profound than mere declarations denouncing the occupation and calling for its end; rather, such a strategy should entail a total civil boycott of the Americans and of the Iraqi Provisional Government, and of its successor, the Iraqi Interim Government, both of which he deems illegitimate.[55]

Yet, as a realist with a close understanding of the nature and course of the military conflict in Iraq, Fadlallah dismisses the view voiced increasingly in journalistic and political circles, both in the Arab world and in the west, that America is currently in a quagmire in Iraq. He contends that any analogy with the past American military experience in Vietnam is misplaced. Fadlallah is convinced that Iraq will not be America's second Vietnam, since the nature of that country, the character of its people, and the regional and international circumstances that surrounded the Vietnam War – especially the role of the former USSR, which was a superpower at that time – were totally different from those currently existing in Iraq. In Fadlallah's view, American military forces may be bogged down in 'Iraqi mud', but they will not be sunk in a quagmire. Asked to expand on the difference between the two, Fadlallah responds: 'Swamps have a watery extension, whereas on muddy ground movement is complicated [but not paralysed].' However, that should not be misconstrued to mean that America will not be forced to withdraw from Iraq. On the contrary, the military entanglement of American forces in the long term might force their withdrawal. As a case in point, Fadlallah refers to the experience of the MNF in Lebanon in 1983, when the compounds of both the American marines and the French paratroopers were targeted and destroyed by two explosive-laden trucks.[56] The suicide bombing of the barracks, and the resultant high casualties among the marines, who suffered 241 fatalities, led immediately to withdrawal of the remaining American forces from Lebanon.

Tracing the contours of Fadlallah's informal relationship with Shi'i groups in post-Saddam Iraq reveals his influence, to varying degrees, within three separate groups: al-Da'wa, the leaders of which have affinity with Fadlallah, and in some cases defer to him for guidance; Muqtada al-Sadr's movement (both Muqtada and Fadlallah share a deep-seated loathing for American foreign policy and its occupation of Iraq, and senior clerical associates of al-Sadr had in the pre-invasion period liasied with Fadlallah and studied under him, many of them still showing deference to their former teacher); and finally, Jawad al-Khalisi, head of the smallest of these groups, and also a former protégé of Fadlallah and scholar–activist – an outspoken opponent of Americans and the Interim Government.

Apart from Hizb al-Da'wa, there are two other, albeit loosely organised, Islamist and vehemently anti-American movements that are ideologically and politically close to Fadlallah: al-Harakah al-Islamiyya fil Iraq (Islamic Movement in Iraq) and al-Tayyar al-Sadri. The smaller of the two, the Islamic Movement is headed by a former student of Fadlallah, Shaykh Jawad al-Khalisi (b. Najaf, 1938), a middle-ranking Shi'i scholar based in Baghdad. In common with Fadlallah, al-Khalisi has from the outset been a strident opponent of the Anglo-American invasion and occupation of Iraq, and a proponent of religious rapprochement and political solidarity between Sunnis and Shi'a. Among the most prominently active Shi'i 'ulama, al-Khalisi has maintained close relations with Hay'at 'Ulama al-Muslimeen fil Iraq, the largest and most influential umbrella group of Sunni 'ulama opposed to the occupation.[57]

As indicated by its name, al-Sadr's movement is led by a young militant Shi'i cleric, Sayyid Muqtada al-Sadr, the youngest surviving son of the late Ayatollah Muhammad Sadeq al-Sadr, who was assassinated together with his older sons by a suspected Ba'thist hit squad in 1999.[58] In April 2004, and again in August, al-Sadr's armed but poorly trained militia, called Jaysh al-Mahdi (Mahdi Army) clashed with American, British and other allied troops in Baghdad's Sadr City, Najaf, Kufa, Basra, and other southern cities. Though denying claims of having links with al-Sadr's movement, Fadlallah does express his open support for the movement, in so far as it is confronting militarily the 'Anglo-American occupation' and defending the sacred shrines of Najaf. At the height of the battle for Najaf, Fadlallah called on his fellow Muslims in Iraq to rally behind the armed resistance movement led by Muqtada al-Sadr, urging them to demand an end to the American occupation. As far as Fadlallah is concerned, the source of Iraq's deep-seated problems is unambiguous: it is the very presence and behaviour of American troops and 'those Iraqis working under them'. While he does not deny that there may have been certain weaknesses evinced by the movement, those elements are outweighed by what he sees as the movement's stalwartness and defiance. In any case, Fadlallah asserts that he is not in a position to assess the performance of the movement, but is in a position to stress the importance of 'confronting the occupation'.[59]

While denying the existence of ties between himself and al-Sadr's movement, Fadlallah concedes that many of al-Sadr's supporters respect or revere him – particularly the young clerical leaders of the movement, many of whom, we learn, attended Fadlallah's weekly Saturday Islamic study circle (*hawza*) held every week in Damascus.[60]

On the question of the future political role of Shi'i and Sunni Islamist movements, Fadlallah stresses that there is an American resolve to prevent those Islamists who espouse a political agenda that encompasses the state from assuming any positions of power, because the United States is striving to make Iraq a secular state with an 'Islamic flavour'. In defence of this claim, Fadlallah cites the significant number of Islamists who were initially appointed to influential posts in the Provisional Government – so much so that that it appeared that Iraq would be transformed into an Islamic state modelled on Iran. By sharp contrast, in the present Interim Government the majority of the ministers are non-Islamists. Indeed, Islamists have been sidelined in the new, reshuffled administration. Fadlallah therefore concludes that, unless the Islamists – both Sunni and Shi'a – forge a dynamic, united Islamic front capable of asserting their presence, he personally doubts that Islamists will loom large in the future government.[61]

Since the mid-1950s, when he embarked on his scholastic Islamist career, Fadlallah has emerged as an independent, unaffiliated thinker and activist. It is in large part because of this that one is able to discern a cluster of interrelated and subsuming intellectual traits – namely, pragmatic radicalism, radical reformism, rational scholasticism and intellectual humanism.

How does Fadlallah reconcile these seemingly contradictory, divergent mentalities – the mind of the *faqih/marja'* in contradistinction to that of the intellectual? Essential to an understanding of his ability to bridge this dichotomy is his critical revisionism, his dynamic reformist *fiqh*, his humanism and ecumenism, and his rationalism. Fadlallah, in his writings and lectures, repeatedly underscores the central role of *al-'aql* (reason) and *'aqlaniyya* (rationalism) in interpreting and reinterpreting the textual sources of Islam, in critically re-examining historical sources, and in revising historical narratives. In Shi'i Islam, *al-'aql* is regarded as the fourth source of Islamic law, in place of *qiyas*, as espoused by Sunnism.

The second major strand in Fadlallah's thought is his universalist world-view – an outlook that is antithetical to *'asabiyya* (zealous partisanship or tribal loyalty), and averse to confessional identity and sectarian allegiance. In this he shares common ground with such Arab intellectuals as the late Edward Said, and with such Islamist religious scholars as Shaykh Yusuf al-Qaradawi and Shaykh Hasan al-Saffar.

How does Fadlallah assume and reconcile the distinct and somewhat conflicting identities of, on the one hand, the Shi'i *marja'*, advancing the welfare and interests of the Shi'i minority, and on the other, the Islamic ecumenist, advocating Sunni–Shi'i concord and solidarity? The question is symptomatic of broader issues of multiple loyalties and identities – Shi'i confessionalism, nationalism and Islamic universalism (*umma*).

Thus, for Fadlallah, in contrast to Olivier Roy, the failure of Islamists outside Iran to win and retain power does not necessarily denote ideological bankruptcy and inherent structural flaws. Rather, an explanation lies in what he sees as the stark imbalance of power that manifested itself following the fall of the USSR, when the west launched a systematic campaign against radical Islamic movements around the world.[62] Fusing Shi'i messianic utopianism with radical Islamist activism, Fadlallah stresses the need for Muslims to 'establish a just state here and there, and espouse the cause of justice in the world, by supporting all the causes of justice in the face of iniquity in the world'.[63]

That Fadlallah's endeavours and influence will be profound and enduring for Lebanon's Shi'a in particular, and, more generally, for the Shi'a in the Arab world and Islamists at large, is beyond doubt. In responding to the challenges of modernism and globalisation, Fadlallah has succeeded in articulating Islam as an energising and liberating ideological and cultural force, with a global civilisational and humanist mission As a scholar–activist leader with a radical vision, infused with a pragmatic reading of ever-changing reality and a rationalist interpretation of religious tradition and scriptural sources, Fadlallah's message will continue to resonate and give meaning and immediacy to the lives of Shi'i devotees and Islamists who form part of changing Muslim societies in an increasingly globalised world.

As a Qur'anic liberationist thinker, Fadlallah will continue to contribute towards and shape the nature of evolving contemporary Islamist discourse, and as a strategist and theoretician will continue for the foreseeable future to have a major influence in charting the course of Islamic activists in Lebanon, Iraq and the wider Shi'i Arab world, as well as Islamists in general in the Middle East, thereby making a clear contribution towards ensuring that Islamists, both radical and reformist, remain a potent force shaping the Muslim world, and world politics in general.

For Fadlallah, the future of the Islamist movements in the Arab world seems secure, and although in the wake of 9/11 they may have been 'emasculated here and contained there, [he doubts] that anyone could bring about their demise'.[64] Given Fadlallah's own status within a number of key Islamist movements, his resources, resolve and pragmatism, there is little doubt that Fadlallah will continue to be a major influential figure in charting a course for Islamic activists that will ensure that Islamism – both reformist and revolutionary – will remain a potent ideological, political and social force in Muslim societies.

Fadlallah will continue to be among the leading Islamist scholars who strive for the forging of a unified front of Sunni and Shi'i activists; he will continue to be among the foremost activist–scholars insisting on the need for the regeneration of Islamic dynamism and the strategic reformulation of future action; he will continue to be among the most prominent advocates of pragmatism and accommodation. As the foremost theologian of Islamic liberation, Fadlallah is unflinching in the belief that America's power is not absolute or infinite; in fact it is waning. Conversely he holds an unshakable conviction that the present *umma*, despite its myriad and profound problems, has the dynamic capacity and potential preparedness to change its current state, through self-empowerment and self-redemption. With the benefit of the enlightened guidance of oracles like himself, Fadlallah envisages educated and devout Muslims, individually and collectively, becoming less pugnacious, impulsive-driven, reactive and apologetic, and more rational, resolute, principled and proactive; less concerned about the criticisms by the West, and more motivated by the pursuit of their own interests. In the true tradition of liberation theology, Fadlallah exhorts believers to take back the initiative, and to deal – from a unitary, holistic Islamic world-view – with all of the contemporary issues that relate to women's rights, pluralism, democracy, individual liberties, human rights, and much else besides.[65]

Fadlallah emerged in the early 1980s from relative obscurity, unknown outside Shi'i clerical circles and Islamic activist networks, to become, by the late 1990s, a *marja'* with an international following – one of the Shi'i world's most influential yet controversial religious scholars and jurisconsults. As a corollary, his role and image have seen major transformations from those of a one-dimensional partisan – eschewing publicity, engaged in religious teaching and writing, and in the Islamist indoctrination of future cadres of Hizb al-Da'wa and Hizbullah – to contribute to the profile of an eminent rational Islamic intellectual and media celebrity in the Arab world, where he is renowned as a sophisticated thinker and accomplished debater. Similarly, he has risen from being a theoretician for radical Islamist groups to become a globally recognised dialogist and ecumenist. He has stamped his authority within an expanding niche of Shi'i faithful in the Arab Gulf, Iraq and the West. He is revered by the members and leaders of Hizb al-Da'wa, Hizbullah, al-Sadr's movement, and al-Harakah al-Islamiyya al-Iraqiyya, and is respected by Sunni activists and scholars associated with al-Ikhwan al-Muslimeen.

While the future trajectory of Fadlallah's influence is difficult to predict with precision, it is almost certain that his authority will continue to expand, both in the Middle East and in Western countries. Since the late 1990s, Fadlallah has emerged as the foremost Shi'i authority in Lebanon, and one of the Arab world's pre-eminent Islamist thinkers. Fadlallah has been able to expand his following steadily in strife-torn Iraq. In the next few years, we will probably see Fadlallah's politically activist and modernist *marja'iyya* providing an alternative, and thus posing a serious challenge to the traditionalist religious leadership of Ayatollah Ali al-Sistani. It is thus in Iraq – a crucible of Shi'ism – that the outcome of this contest of wills and of visions will be decided, with all its concomitant ramifications for the future course of Shi'a Islam, and the orientation of its adherents in the Middle East and the world at large. For Fadlallah, just as Iraq had shaped his past and influenced his character and career, it will also have a significant, perhaps defining role in determining the scope and constraints of his authority – and, in conjunction with Lebanon, will shape his legacy.

Conclusion

In arguing that Fadlallah is essentially a pragmatic radical Islamist, I have attempted to reveal the complexity of his background and character, the multi-dimensional nature of his interests, and the multifaceted nature of his influence. He is a committed Islamist, but a rational intellectual; a radical reformer and a pragmatic activist; a liberationist and a realist; a confrontationist and accommodationist; a non-conformist modernist and a scrupulous Islamic scholar; a calculating political analyst and a principled player; a poet and a jurisconsult; a philosopher and a philanthropist; an orator and a theoretician; a dedicated ecumenist and a devout Shi'i; a partisan and a humanist.

An attempt has been made to analyse Sayyid Fadlallah's multifaceted role in society and politics by examining the interplay between two complex and continuously evolving backgrounds: his professional and activist career, and the religious–cultural, ideological and political settings of Iraq, Iran and Lebanon. The course of Fadlallah's Islamist career, the development of his intellectual writings, and the continuity of his political activism were shaped, on the one hand, by traditional Shi'i religious scholasticism and Islamic ideological radicalism, and, on the other, by political tumult and confessional ferment. Those forces defined crucial periods in the history of modern Iraq and Lebanon, and moulded their complex and changing milieux. Hence, the background and nature of Fadlallah's emergence as an Islamist intellectual-activist provides insight into the evolution of Shi'i Islamist movements like Hizb al-Da'wa in Iraq and Hizbullah in Lebanon, and illustrates the extent to which the Islamist leaders and their organised activist followers can be conditioned by fluid local settings.

Since leaving Iraq, his country of birth, in 1966 to settle permanently in Lebanon, his ancestral homeland, Fadlallah has seen his authority expand rather than diminish among Hizbullah members who used to belong to Hizb al-Da'wa, among existing party cadres in Iraq, Iran, other Gulf states, and among Shi'i émigré communities in Europe. Fadlallah's authority among al-Da'wa activists increased in the wake of the summary execution of his colleague and foremost party theoretician, Sayyid Baqir al-Sadr, following the publication of his monographic and periodical Islamist writings throughout the 1980s, and as a consequence of his status, since the mid-1990s, as one of the Shi'i world's premier jurisconsults and scholars.

I have shown that Fadlallah has at no stage been the officially recognised mentor or patron of Hizbullah or Hizb al-Da'wa. He has been able to assume the role of a leading (but not the only) mentor and guide to these two Shi'i Islamist groups without holding a formal position within them, or even maintaining formal organisational ties to them. It has been shown that Fadlallah's speeches, sermons and writings provided a source of inspiration for the formation of Hizbullah, and that due to his portrayal in the media as the 'leader' of Hizbullah, Fadlallah's rapid rise in the 1980s as an internationally recognised Islamist ideologue and activist had paralleled the publicised exploits of the militant Shi'i Islamist movement in Lebanon during that period. Yet it is also clear that Fadlallah's emergence as one of the world's pre-eminent figures of Islamism would have occurred even without his informal relationship with Hizb al-Da'wa and Hizbullah, and that, consequently, his influence and ascendancy on the public political and intellectual scene can only be partly explained by the nature and scope of that relationship.

Despite the separation – and more recently divergence – between Fadlallah and Hizbullah, his intellectual role in relation to Hizbullah was crucial, particularly during the 1980s and early 1990s. In guiding the Lebanese Shi'i Islamist movement during its evolving phase, and in steering Hizbullah through the hazards of the civil war, Fadlallah left an indelible mark on the party. He was instrumental in encouraging Hizbullah to reconcile with its rival, Amal, and with its opponents in the Christian Maronite rightist party, al-Kata'ib. Even more striking was Fadlallah's role in persuading the Hizbullah leadership to integrate their Islamist party with the reformed democratic political order of post-civil war Lebanon. Thus, Fadlallah managed to shift Hizbullah away from its idealist revolutionary quest for an Islamic republic, modelled on the Iranian regime of *Wilayat al-Faqih*, towards a position that embraced gradualist change through legitimate reform.

Fadlallah's imprint on contemporary Islamist intellectual and political discourse is unmistakable. In Islamist circles, Fadlallah is recognised as a distinguished exponent of the 'dynamic *fiqh*', or modernist system of jurisprudence, predicated on the continuous process of textual reinterpretation and contextual re-reading. The practical implication of this has been a fluid definition, in the light of changing circumstances, of the parameters of what is religiously and legally enjoined and what is permissible. This schema is crucial to our understanding of Fadlallah's legal and political justification for the participatory role of Lebanon's Islamists in the country's post-war political institutions, as well as of the strategic moves he deemed necessary to achieve it.

Fadlallah was the first Islamist scholar in Lebanon to seize the opportunity to encourage Hizbullah and – as a measure of his influence among Sunni Islamist groups – al-Jama'ah al-Islamiyya, to participate in the country's first parliamentary elections since the start of the civil war. In advancing the integration of the Islamists into the very system that, a decade earlier, he had attacked and actively sought to overturn, Fadlallah, recalling the approach of Gramsci, advocated the integration of movements espousing radical change, with a view to consolidating a base within the prevailing regime which might eventually become a legitimate force of gradual transformation within state institutions. This realist–pragmatic disposition was reflected in his gift for adjusting his tactics in line with the shifting political scene, and consistently with the dynamics of socio-cultural change. Thus, in contrast to his immutably radical world-view, the tactics and strategies employed by Fadlallah were predicated on a careful assessment of the varying constraints and opportunities thrown up by changing realities.

Though Fadlallah was inspired by the Islamic revolution in Iran, expressing admiration for the leadership of Imam Khomeini and adopting some of his conceptual terminology, ultimately derived from the Qur'an (such as *al-mustakbiroun* [the arrogant] *wa al-mustad'ifoun* [the downtrodden]), his deference did not translate into acquiescence. Fadlallah was quite able to maintain his financial, intellectual and political independence. His espousal of Khomeini's general or supreme governance of the jurist (*wilayat al-faqih al-'ammah al-mutlaqah*) was not unqualified; he argued in favour of checks and balances in the form of a powerful consultative body of experts (*Majlis al-Khubara'*). He did not share Iran's enthusiasm for a mirror Islamic regime in Lebanon, and differed with the Iranian leadership on the issue of Western hostages, as well as on the protracted armed conflict between Amal and Hizbullah. Finally, he has more recently fallen out with Iran's powerful clerical establishment over his elevation to the pre-eminent position of *Marja' al-Taqlid*, over his revisionist interpretation of Shi'i historical events and venerated figures, and over his modernist social and cultural views.

As an influential theoretician, Fadlallah has made a major contribution to Islamist intellectual and political thought by systematically addressing the issues of democracy, Islamic governance and political legitimacy, the nature and processes of change, and the interplay between tradition and modernity. Witnessing the unfolding, during the course of the last two decades of the twentieth century, of the unprecedentedly rapid, complex and profound changes in international political, social and cultural affairs, technology and science, Fadlallah felt impelled by his function as jurist, mentor and theoretician to be abreast of such momentous developments in order to address them effectively, and chart for the Islamist movement a new path in post-war Lebanon, guiding it in the post-modern and increasingly globalised world.

To the extent that Fadlallah's Islamist discourse addresses the key issues of modernity (secularism, pluralism, democracy, scientific and technological progress, and cultural Westernisation), and the question of how to deal rationally and legitimately with its challenges and opportunities, it is of a modernist stripe. As a pragmatic activist and rational thinker, Fadlallah is less opposed to modernism than to Westernisation. He rejects certain Western values and institutions of modernity, and, more specifically, rejects the postulates that underlie Western secular epistemology, with its pronounced anti-traditionalism. Finally, he rejects the materialist foundation and hegemonic tendency of Western modernity. Fadlallah's repudiation of the notion that the Western model of modernity is the only desirable and legitimate modernising paradigm for contemporary Muslim societies is a position shared by other Islamist thinkers and scholars, such as Baqir al-Sadr, Sayyid Qutb, Hasan al-Turabi, Rashid al-Ghanoushi and Yousuf al-Qaradawi.

What distinguishes Fadlallah's radical discourse from those of other Islamists is a more focused critique of Western modernity, with particular attention paid to the pattern of political, economic and cultural hegemony of the Western powers in general, and to that of the United States in particular. This theme permeates his writings and speeches, and therein lies the key to understanding Fadlallah's concern with Muslim/Third World empowerment and liberation. Fundamentally, for Fadlallah, liberationism is inseparable from Islamism. Illustrative of the inextricable nature of that nexus is Fadlallah's statement that the central goal of Islamist activists is the transformation of the 'Muslim psyche', which is presently characterised by 'acquiescence to domineering and hegemonic [Western] power'.[1]

Despite the adaptive shifts in Fadlallah's priorities and tactics in line with the shifting landscape, there remains a continuity in the constitutive elements underlining his thought: Islamic rationalism, universalism, ecumenicalism and liberationism, or activism. Reminiscent of Fanonist theory on the psychology of oppression and liberation, Fadlallah advocated Muslim–Christian solidarity in the face of injustice and tyranny, the championing of Third World issues of dependency, foreign domination and economic exploitation, expanding on the themes of the empowerment and dynamism needed to overcome the inferiority complex, inertia, fatalism and resignation endemic in the region and beyond. Fadlallah argued that there was no perpetual, predestined weakness or strength; that human enfeeblement was not divinely predestined; and that the downtrodden, by overcoming the psychological conditions of fear, paralysis, disorientation and self-contempt, could challenge and erode the previously unassailable power of their subjugators and oppressors. The potency of those ideas was illustrated most patently in Lebanon, where Islamist radical ideology and sophisticated irregular warfare saw the military evacuation of the American Marines in early 1984, and, through a sustained military campaign of attrition, ended in the complete withdrawal of the Israeli army from South Lebanon in mid-2000.

Fadlallah also parts company with other Islamists – particularly those activists associated with al-Ikhwan al-Muslimeen and Hizb al-Tahrir al-Islami – in not subscribing to a method of societal change that is dictated by the Prophet Muhammad's two-phase struggle against Arab pagans in seventh-century Arabia. Fadlallah rejected the prevailing view that underscored the legitimacy and necessity of rigidly pursuing two or three sequential phases: individual moral rectitude and credal indoctrination, communal reform, and finally regime transformation. Instead, and in keeping with his pragmatist mode of thinking, he argued that just as the Prophet's missionary course was shaped by the imposing circumstances of that age, so too the contemporary Islamists must be flexible in determining whatever phases are deemed necessary along the path of change envisaged in the light of changing contemporary reality.

The milieux that evolved in post-civil war Lebanon, and post-1991 Gulf War Arab-Israeli peace process posed challenges for Fadlallah's Islamist, liberationist agenda. A rational thinker, realist reader, and pragmatic activist, Fadlallah fine-tuned his intellectual and political discourse to accommodate those momentous developments. On a practical level, Fadlallah engineered the reconciliation of the radical Islamist movement with the Lebanese regime; its integration into state institutions; the forging of closer ties between Sunni and Shi'i Islamist movements; and a rapprochement between Islamists and their erstwhile political foes – namely secular leftists and Maronite rightists.

As I have argued, Fadlallah's radical vision and ideology were matched by a preference for pragmatic politics, based on a realistic reading of the balance of power, and of evolving trends. Necessarily included in this equation was an accurate assessment of current and future Islamist capabilities. On the basis of this assessment, and in a regional environment shifting towards Arab-Israeli military disengagement and political settlement, the pursuit of unilateral armed struggle by Hizbullah against Israel proper, and launched from liberated South Lebanon, should be suspended. The military campaign against Israel would be resumed in the event of the development of a more favourable regional situation.

Until and beyond that point, Fadlallah – the liberation theologian and champion of the downtrodden – can be expected to continue his strident rhetorical sermons and speeches against Israel and its occupation of Arab territories, and against America and its regional order in the Middle East. As an Islamist theoretician and scholar-activist, he will maintain his pivotal roles in indoctrinating coteries of would-be Islamic activists, training young students in reformist religious *fiqh* and activist Islamist thought, and providing religious–juridical guidance to a growing body of followers drawn from a cross-section of Shi'i devotees in Lebanon and beyond. He will also continue to provide guidance to cadres, and liaise with the leaders, of Lebanon's Islamist movements, of both Sunni and Shi'i persuasions.

APPENDIX

The Twelver Shi'i 'Ulama: Context and Consequences

The Shi'i 'ulama, or religious scholars, have, at various stages, played an assertive role in the modern political history of Iran and, to a lesser extent, that of Iraq and Lebanon. In the case of Iran, the Shi'i 'ulama played pivotal roles in the Tobacco Rebellion of 1891–92, the Constitutional Revolution of 1906–9, the oil nationalisation movement of the late 1940s and early 1950s, the violent disturbances of 1963 against the Shah's 'White Revolution', and, most significantly, the Islamic Revolution of 1978–79. With regard to Iraq, the Shi'i 'ulama were at the forefront of the indigenous resistance to the British invasion and occupation of Iraq in World War I, and were instrumental in inciting and leading a major insurrection in 1920–21 against British rule. In 1958, a circle of politically disposed Shi'i activist scholars founded an Islamist revolutionary party (Hizb al-Da'wa al-Islamiyya), which subsequently, during the course of the late 1970s and early 1980s, constituted the most serious organised internal political challenge to the Ba'thist regime in Iraq. In Lebanon, a group of militant Shi'i 'ulama, who were inspired by the ideological and rhetorical discourse of Sayyid Fadlallah, and by the revolutionary Islamic paradigm of Ayatollah Khumaini, founded – in the immediate wake of the 1982 Israeli invasion of Lebanon – Hizbullah ('Party of God). During the course of the 1980s and 1990s Hizbullah became the largest and most potent Islamist movement in the country.

Whether in the form of mass revolutionary upheaval in Iran, semi-clandestine Islamist dissent and militancy in Iraq, or armed Islamic resistance in Lebanon, the groups of politically active Shi'i 'ulama who assumed those (as well as other) roles were unquestionably of the highest significance. Among the key questions that will be addressed in this survey are the following. First, what are the doctrinal and juridical bases of the authority of the Shi'i 'ulama? Second, how can we account for the processes by which the Shi'i 'ulama have been able to enhance their power and influence in Iranian society, during the Safavid and Qajar dynastic reigns? Third, to what extent can we attribute the ascent of the autonomous power and status of the Shi'i 'ulama to the distinctive doctrinal, juridical and institutional characteristics of Twelver Shi'ism? Fourth, how can we explain the historical vicissitudes of 'ulama–state relations?

Scholarly Views of the Character and Authority of the Shi'i 'Ulama

Before attempting to set forth the doctrinal–juridical foundations of Shi'i 'ulama authority, it would be useful to set out the central arguments and observations that will underpin the discussion in this appendix.

While it is generally accepted by Western scholars of Islam that it is erroneous to equate the Muslim 'ulama with the Christian clergy – rightly observing among the former the absence of both divine intermediaries between God and the faithful, on the one hand, a specialised priesthood consecrating sacred rituals, on the other – nevertheless it is commonly, but wrongly, assumed that the 'ulama historically constituted a homogeneous, cohesive class.[1]

Recent academic studies have shown that, while the 'ulama have historically formed a distinct professional status group, they do not now, and did not in the past, constitute a monolithic or coherent body. Members of the 'ulama were differentiated by their diverse occupational backgrounds and social status. They were drawn from virtually every stratum of society, and thus comprised a heterogeneous body, insofar as social origins and affiliations were concerned. Among their number were members of the nobility, traditional landowners, merchants and petty bourgeoisie (namely artisans and craftsmen). Combined with this division based on occupation and status was an elaborate hierarchical structure that evolved during the second millennium, and assumed its definite form in early-twentieth-century Iran. The 'ulama were classified into several categories based on rank: namely, Ayatollah al-'azam (grand Ayatollah), who acted as pre-eminent Shi'i scholarly-juridical authorities; Ayatollahs, or senior professional scholars and jurists; and hujatul-Islam (proof of Islam), who were middle-ranking 'ulama.

Furthermore, as a group of religious scholars and jurists, the 'ulama and *fuqaha'* have never formed a self-contained, detached elite, interacting only with one another. On the contrary, the religious–juridical elite always interacted with all segments of society. The influence of their public behaviour and thought was indeed pervasive. Yet it would be wrong to assume that the 'ulama were immune from various influences that emanated from their relationships with certain socio-economic groups in society.[2]

A corollary of this is that, historically speaking, the public activities of the 'ulama did not comprise a uniform or consistent pattern of behaviour in relation to the state. The attitude and praxis of the Shi'i 'ulama with regard to the temporal power varied, in large and small ways, so that they encompassed the whole range of conceivable positions on the political spectrum. It would be useful to begin the discussion of the question of 'ulama authority with a brief and selective survey of the relevant canonical literature, as embodied in the Qur'an and *hadith*, which are regarded by both Sunni and Shi'i Muslims as the cardinal textual sources of Islam.[3] Sunni and Shi'i 'ulama also concur over the doctrinal justification for their eminence and various important roles in society, roles that include teaching, preaching, counselling, administration, legislation, arbitration and reconciliation.

A number of Qur'anic verses are frequently cited to uphold the pivotal roles of the 'ulama, including: 'Allah will elevate in degrees those among you who believe, and those who have been granted knowledge'; 'It is those who have knowledge among his servants that truly fear God'; 'If a contingent from every expedition remained behind they could devote themselves to studies in religion'; 'Oh, you who believe! Obey God, and obey the Apostle and those in authority among you.' In addition to these verses are the following relevant *hadiths*, attributed the Prophet Muhammad: 'The 'ulama are the heirs of the Prophets'; 'When the Day of Judgement arrives, God will gather all the people and the blood of the martyrs, and the ink used by the scholars will be weighed on the scales. The pens of the scholars will be given preference over the blood of the martyrs'; 'To think for an hour about knowledge is better than forty years of worship.'[4]

There is broad unanimity among members of both Sunni and Shi'i denominations that these canonical references can be adduced to affirm the supreme status and responsibility of the 'ulama, since they are believed to be invested with the authority of the 'authentic' faith and sacred law, in the face of perceived heresy, corruption and innovation.

Despite this interdenominational concord, the Shi'i 'ulama have diverged from their Sunni counterparts on the important question of interpretation. A case in point is that of the differing readings of the Qur'anic verse cited above in which God enjoins the faithful to obey those vested with authority. The classical Sunni Qur'anic commentators had interpreted this verse in a generic way, to denote the divinely ordained duty to obey the 'ulama, the Muslim rulers and their installed governors, as well as their appointed military commanders.[5] The Shi'i exegetes, by contrast, have invariably understood it to denote an obligation to render unquestionable obedience to the Twelve infallible Imams, who succeeded one other by heredity. In recent times there has been a clear tendency to assert a traditionally strict interpretation of the verse, with contemporary Shi'i scholars such as Fadlallah maintaining that 'those in authority' refers not merely to the Twelve Imams, but also to their delegated religious scholars and jurisconsults.[6]

While both Sunnis and Shi'is profess Islam's fundamental tenets of belief – the doctrines of monotheism, prophethood, and the hereafter – it is the confessional doctrine of the Imamah that sets apart the latter from the former. To understand the Shi'i theory of the Imamah and its implications for the concepts of temporal and sacred authority, it is necessary to provide a brief exposition of the origins and evolution of Shi'ism.

The Genesis and Evolution of Twelver Shi'ism

Shi'i Islam has its origins in the controversy around the pivotal question of the religious–political succession to the Prophet Muhammad, whose death in AD 632 left the nascent Islamic community divided over who should assume the mantle of vicegerent leadership. Two divergent views arose, which subsequently developed into mutually exclusive theories. The first, which became associated with the Sunni majority, held that the Prophet had not explicitly nominated a successor, nor established a consistent or clear set of guiding principles and mechanisms for determining the person most entitled to the office of paramount leader of the ummah. Instead, according to this view, the crucial question of succession was purposefully left for the community of believers or their representatives to consult one other (or exercise *shura*) with a view to selecting a *khalifa* from among their number. In effect, the Sunni theory of religious–political authority, as embodied by the institution of the *khilafa*, was founded on the processes of *shura* (among dignitaries in the community, principally the 'ulama, and between them and the Islamic ruler), and *ijma'* (consensus). In theory, the legitimacy of the *khalifa* was derived from his personal conformity to, and public application of, the shari'ah, and failure to govern in accordance with the shar'iah would render the *khalifa* illegitimate, thereby ending his right to continued allegiance on the part of his subjects.[7]

While the principle of governance in accordance with the shari'ah is also shared by the Shi'a, they differ from their Sunni co-religionists in that they consider the succession process of the Imam (or supreme religious–political leader) of the ummah to be subject to divine designation (or *nass*), rather than community-based consultation and election. Upon this premise, 'Ali bin Abi Talib, the Prophet's cousin and son-in-law, was the only legitimate successor to the Apostle. Shi'at Ali (the partisans of 'Ali, as they became known), believed, accordingly, that the accession of Abu Bakr (the Prophet's earliest companion and father-in-law) and his two successors, 'Umar and 'Uthman, had deprived 'Ali, wilfully or by default, of what had rightfully belonged to him, and they were thus viewed as usurpers.[8]

To underpin the theory of the legitimacy of 'Ali's claim to the *khilafa* (caliphate) or *Imamah*, Shi'i scholars have cited what they regard as incontrovertible textual proof, attesting to the Divine and Prophetic designation of 'Ali and his hereditary line of succession. Verse 3 of Chapter 5, believed to be among the final revealed verses of the Qur'an, affirms God's 'perfection' of Islam. To the Shi'a, this verse is of the utmost importance, as it was revealed in the immediate wake of the Prophet's purported designation of 'Ali as Imam and *khalifa* (caliph). According to Shi'i sources, that designation had taken place on 10 March, AD 632, at a site known as Ghadir Khum, where the Prophet was believed to have proclaimed: 'He whose master (*mawlah)* I am, 'Ali is his master.'[9]

Thus, crucially for the Shi'a, the verse signifying that Islam had assumed its final, complete and immutable form was predicated on the Prophet's public nomination of 'Ali as his divinely ordained successor. It would be inconceivable, in the Shi'i view, for God, given his grace and wisdom, to have allowed the passing away of his greatest and final Prophet without having designated a successor. A corollary of this theory is the view that, without a legitimate successor to the Prophet, in the form of an uninterrupted line of Imams, drawn from the Apostle's household and progeny, Muhammad's mission of guiding humanity, of upholding the sacred law, and of preserving the true faith, would have been critically jeopardised.[10]

The pivotal significance of the Imams in Twelver Shi'i creed can be understood from a tradition attributed to the Fifth Imam, Muhammad al-Baqer, that 'the world could never exist for a moment without a *hujja*', or proof from God. Like the Prophets before them, the Imams are revered as impeccable guides of humankind, and are believed to be endowed with divinely ordained and near-absolute religious–political authority. However, unlike the Prophets, the Imams are not believed to have been bearers of new revelations or laws from God. Notwithstanding their extraordinary knowledge and authority, the Imams, according to Shi'i doctrine, cannot abrogate, amend or add to the revealed core of the shari'ah. Still, they are believed to be infallible, their lives exemplary, and their guidance and instructions binding on the faithful. By sharp contrast, the ummah is, for the Sunnis, inherently inerrant.[11]

Despite their venerated status and extensive authority, the Twelve Imams, as a group, were unable, owing to the unfavourable course of political events, to translate their religious–juridical legitimacy into concrete rule. Indeed, only the first three Imams – namely 'Ali and his two sons Hasan and Hussein – had engaged in political affairs by actively exercising, with varying degrees of success, their right to govern. The only Imam to accede to the *khilafa*, following the assassination of 'Uthman (the third 'Rightly Guided' *khalifa*), was 'Ali. Beset by serious and persistent dissent, arising from the slaying of his predecessor, 'Ali (who ruled between 656 and 661 AD, from the Iraqi town of Kufa) became embroiled in a protracted, sanguinary conflict with his chief rival, Mu'awiyya, the governor of Syria.[12] In 661, while attending congregational prayers, 'Ali was fatally stabbed by a bitter opponent affiliated with *al-Khawaraj* ('the seceders'), a radical breakaway group.

The Martyrdom of Imam Hussein and its Consequences

Believing that legitimate leadership had passed to him, Hasan was pre-empted from succeeding his father by Mu'awiyya, who also laid claim to the *khilafa*. Wishing to avoid an internecine war over the leadership issue, Hasan acceded to a negotiated settlement which stipulated his right to succeed Mu'awiyya to power upon the latter's death. That undertaking, however, was not fulfilled by Mu'awiyya, who opted to nominate his son, Yazid, as his successor. This, and the subsequent rule of oppression by ibn Ziyad, the infamous governor of Iraq, prompted Hasan's younger brother, Hussein, who had heard impassioned pleas for deliverance from the disaffected Kufan populace, to challenge ibn Ziyad's power and bring about an end to tyranny.[13]

Committed to realising that revolutionary aspiration, the Prophet's grandson, along with a contingent of family members and some seventy-two armed followers, set out in 680 AD upon a fateful journey from Mecca to Kufa. But the small band of insurgents was intercepted by a force of several thousand mounted government soldiers on the plains of Karbala, north of Kufa, and a tense stand-off ensued, with periodic skirmishes. Besieged and cut off from outside help, Hussein's beleaguered camp was systematically overwhelmed by the much stronger and larger government force. His small band of armed retainers were cut down, and nearly all of his family members and relatives, and finally Hussein himself, were slain, their bodies decapitated, and the heads mounted on spears and paraded through the streets of Kufa.[14] The date was 'Ashoura, on 10 Muharram 61 AH (10 October 680 AD).

To this day, the martyrdom of Imam Hussein is the most commemorated event on the Shi'i calendar. During the first ten days of Muharram, the first Islamic month, the Shi'a everywhere participate in a profound outpouring of grief and lamentation over the tragedy of Hussein. The communal emotion reaches a climax on 10 Muharram, when the event, known as *Ta'ziyya,* is re-enacted, with elaborate passion plays that traditionally included the sanguinary, ritualistic drama of self-flagellation.[15]

The tragic struggle and martyrdom of Imam Hussein had momentous consequences. His legacy came to be immortalised in the Shi'i ethos and embedded in the Shi'i psyche; an epic historical event was transformed into metahistory. Hussein became in the process a legendary figure who epitomised the perpetual human struggle between good and evil, justice and iniquity, altruism and selfishness, piety and ungodliness, moral idealism and material expediency. For contemporary Shi'i Islamist activists, Hussein's quest for Islamic justice and freedom was the ideal revolutionary paradigm for the faithful to emulate.

In a sense, the model of Hasan and the story of Hussein's struggle came to represent two divergent sides of Shi'ism – activism and quietism. The Imam's martyrdom proved to be a watershed insofar as it decisively defined the future course of action of succeeding Imams in relation to the state. Henceforth, all of Hussein's successors elected, in the face of largely unfavourable circumstances, not to exercise their full religious–political authority, lest it provoke the suspicion and hostility of the Umayyad and Abbasid monarchs. The remaining seven Shi'i Imams – particularly the fifth and sixth, Muhamamd al-Baqer and Ja'far al-Sadiq – disavowed public claims to the *Imamah,* and in fact eschewed political involvement altogether. The Imams adopted a policy of accommodation with the state, a practice that entailed political acquiescence and de facto recognition of the Sunni rulers whom they theoretically viewed as usurpers.[16]

To justify this major reorientation from the pursuit of political militancy and Islamic armed struggle, as exemplified by the exploits of Imam Hussein, to that of apolitical quietism and acquiescence, Imam Ja'far al-Sadiq (AD 700–765) is credited with having formulated the Shi'i practice of *taqiyya* (prudent or tactical dissimulation).[17] Historically, the practice of *taqiyya* permitted – indeed obliged – the aggrieved, persecuted Shi'i minority, under threatening or inhospitable conditions, to conceal its true identity and assume the public behaviour of the Sunni majority. Consequently, the legitimate recourse to tactical dissimulation in times of duress became a distinguishing characteristic of Shi'i Islam.

The Occultation of the Twelfth Imam

The evolution of the quietist–activist dichotomy in Shi'i tradition was given further impetus by the development of the doctrine of al-Mahdi al-Muntazar ('the Awaited Rightly Guided One'). The Shi'i messianic notion of the Mahdi as the saviour of humanity in a pre-apocalyptic utopian age of universal justice and equity had profound implications for the subsequent theory of 'ulama authority, and consequently for the patterns of clerical–political behaviour. According to traditional Shi'i sources, the Eleventh Imam, Hasan al-'Askari, died in early AD 874, allegedly, like his predecessors, from poisoning. The death of al-'Askari precipitated a crisis over the continuity of the *Imamah*, as it was held by a Shi'a minority that the Imam had died without a surviving male heir. The Shi'i majority, however, who later comprised the mainstream Twelver denomination of Shi'ism, held that al-Askari did indeed leave a son, named Muhammad. The Twelver Shi'i accounts relate that the Twelfth Imam, Abul Qasim Muhammad ibn Hasan, was compelled, under constant fear for his life from a hostile Abbasid government, to go into hiding.[18]

The last Imam is believed to have concealed himself from all but a few of his celebrated followers, who belonged to eminent families and who successively acted as his authoritative agents (*wukula'*) or deputies (*nuwwab*). The first vicegerent of the living hidden Imam appeared in AD 872, and the last died in AD 940, thus ending the period known as the Lesser Occultation (*al-Ghaybah al-Sughra*) of the Twelfth Imam. Henceforth, all contacts between the Hidden Imam and his trusted representative were severed. This initiated a long period, known as the *Ghaybah al-Kubrah*, that would end only with the final reappearance of the *Mahdi*, who would preside over a global Islamic order.[19]

In accordance with the Shi'i doctrine of the necessity of an uninterrupted line of divinely inspired guides, the theory of the vicegerency of the Hidden Imam served to maintain the supreme locus of divine authority in a supposedly living but absent Imam. It also provided an important basis for the conferment of part of that authority on the four successive representatives. This authority, as will be shown later, was claimed to have been subsequently invested in the 'ulama. Facilitated by the apolitical aloofness of the Tenth and Eleventh

Imams (al-Hadi and al-Hasan al-Askari, respectively) in Samarra, north of Baghdad, during the reign of the Abbasid rulers, the role of the *wakil* was expanded into the spheres of jurisprudence and the compilation of the *hadith* of the Prophet, and the *akhbar* (sayings) of the Imams. This process gained momentum with the establishment of Dar al-Wukala' ('the Agents' Abode') around the time of the death of the Eleventh Imam.[20]

It was symptomatic of the considerable rise in the authority of the *wakil* that by the time the last of the Imam's representatives had exercised his authority, it was commonly held that his utterances were in fact the words of the Imam himself. For the *wakil* was supposedly the sole individual capable of gaining access to the Imam, either by visions or revelatory intuition (*kashf*). Concurrent with the enhancement of the *wakil*'s authority was a corresponding expansion of the roles of the 'ulama, the elevation of their status, and the strengthening of their independence; and central, in turn, to the process of enhanced 'ulama authority was the formulation of a theory that essentially posited the devolution of the Twelfth Imam's prerogatives onto the senior 'ulama. The office of *Wikala* or *al-Niyaba al-Khassah* (special deputyship), which assumed prominence during the Lesser Occultation, was replaced during the Greater Occultation by *al-Niyaba al-'Ammah* (general deputyship) of the senior religious jurists (*fuqaha'*). To justify the devolution of authority onto the 'General Deputyship' of the 'ulama, a key directive was cited, attributed to the Twelfth Imam, instructing his disciples that, 'As far as new emerging cases are concerned, refer them to the transmitter of our statements; for they are my "proof" (*hujja)* unto you, and I am God's Proof unto them.'[21]

Although this institutional mechanism served to buttress the juridico-religious authority of the 'ulama and enhance their status, it is clear that in the period prior to the establishment of the Shi'i Safavid dynasty in Iran (AD 940–1500), 'the 'ulama functioned as individuals rather than as a corporate body'. The fact that the Twelver Shi'i 'ulama lacked a clerical hierarchical structure, but preserved considerable independence from state control and influence, can be attributed to several factors, the most consequential of which, prior to 1501 AD, were the absence of a powerful, centralised Shi'i state and the dispersion of the 'ulama in the major Shi'i urban centres in the Middle East.[22]

During this period, the majority of the 'ulama tended to disavow politics and shun all association with temporal power, advocating a quietist line. There were a few notable exceptions to that rule, such as al-Sharif al-Murtada (d. 1044), who held that involvement in governmental affairs was lawful. al-Murtada was credited with defining the circumstances in which a Shi'i jurist might accept a post from an illegitimate or usurper regime. He asserted that, in holding office, the Shi'i jurist must not allow himself to be led 'into anything which would not have been necessary for him if he had not accepted [public] office, while through the office he is enabled to order what is proper and prohibit what is reprehensible. Thus it is obligatory that he seeks to attain that through the office.'[23]

The significance of al-Murtada's theory on the legitimacy of holding government office was that, while the Twelfth Imam possessed fundamental inherent legitimacy, a just Shi'i ruler could acquire 'derivative functional legitimacy'.[24] Moreover, it is instructive that the stipulations and guidelines set forth by al-Murtada were generally endorsed by later Shi'i authorities. The elaboration and unanimous acceptance of the axiomatic theory of the devolution of religious–juridical authority to the 'ulama ensured that the Shi'i religious scholars and jurists would refrain from conceding *de jure* legitimacy to any temporal power, irrespective of official religious persuasion.

The Institutionalisation of the Shi'i 'Ulama under the Safavids

Despite this dominant tendency, and insofar as the passive and prolonged wait for the eschatological return of the Twelfth Imam sanctioned – encouraged, even – the tacit approval of secular or temporal government, there was during the Safavid era a perceptible trend among a sizeable segment of the Shi'i 'ulama towards countenancing de facto recognition of temporal power. The Safavid state – which was founded in AD 1501, and whose first monarch, Shah Ismail I, claimed descent from the Eighth Imam, Musa al-Kazim, and ruled as the vicegerent of the Hidden Imam – was the first avowedly Shi'i dynasty to disseminate and enforce Shi'ism in Iran AD systematically.[25]

The momentous religious–political developments that unfolded during the emergence and consolidation of the Shi'i Safavid polity brought about a marked change in clerical–state relations. Unlike their predecessors from the pre-Safavid era, the majority of the Shi'i – particularly Iranian – 'ulama were no longer averse to involvement in political affairs, nor hostile to the unprecedented and explicitly Twelver Shi'i state and its religious establishment. Indeed, a kind of symbiotic relationship developed between the Shi'i 'ulama and the Safavid rulers, which arose from a sense of mutual dependence. The Iranian sovereigns required the quasi-legitimacy that only the 'ulama could offer, as well as the active co-operation of the 'ulama in proselytising the Shi'i faith among their subjects; while the 'ulama, for their part, needed a powerful regime committed to protecting and advancing the cause of Shi'ism.[26]

The pre-eminent scholarly cleric, who held the highest religious–juridical office in sixteenth-century Safavid Iran, was Shaykh Ali al-Karaki (d. 1534). In his capacity as the '*Mujatahid* of the Age,' and as the self-designated deputy of the Hidden Imam, Shaykh al-Karaki issued several important edicts that have had far-reaching consequences. In conformity with al-Sharif al-Murtada's legal and political views on accepting government office, Shaykh al-Karaki ruled that it was permissible for the 'ulama to occupy certain public posts, and that it was legal to receive a stipend from technically illegitimate rulers. The second ruling that was issued by al-Karaki was unprecedented. It stipulated the requirement of performing the hitherto suspended Friday congregational prayers during the Occultation of the Twelfth Imam. Henceforth, the Shi'i 'ulama – in line with their Sunni counterparts, who have consistently observed the socio-religious ritual – assumed a new influential function: that of delivering religious sermons and leading prayers in mosques. al-Karaki also ruled against emulating the *ijtihad* of a deceased *mujtahid*. Although the formal espousal of *ijtihad* was accredited to the celebrated Shi'i scholar of the fourteenth century, 'Allamah al-Hilli, whose work provided the basis for strengthening the juridical authority of the 'ulama, it was al-Karaki's edict that decisively augmented that authority. He had laid down that it was incumbent upon the lay faithful to imitate the most erudite living jurist.[27]

Another important development that augmented the power of the 'ulama was the clerical appropriation of authority over the collection and dispensation of *al-zakat* (alms) and *al-khums* (tithe).[28] These two fiscal institutions constituted a substantial source of income for the 'ulama, who consequently became financially independent of state patronage. This trend, which gained momentum during the late Safavid and succeeding Qajar eras, contrasted strikingly with the integrated, salaried Sunni clerisy of the Ottoman Empire.

Although constituting a small minority within the 'ulama community, the strident oppositional attitude that characterised the group is significant. Among the few eminent 'ulama who were staunchly traditionalist in outlook were Shaykh Ibrahim al-Qatifi (d. AD 1539) and Shaykh Muhammad Baqer al-Sabzavari (d. AD 1679). They opposed the enhancement of clerical authority based on the theory of the deputyship of the Hidden Imam, refuted the legality of Friday congregational prayer, objected to the key role played by the Shi'i 'ulama in assuming control over the collection and dispensation of *al-zakat* and *al-khums*, and sharply criticised the articulated theory of *ijtihad*. Most of all, these conservative purists attacked the so-called court jurists for compromising the primacy of Islam and the integrity of the 'ulama. As justification for the two jurists' inimical attitude towards the state-integrated *mujtahids*, they cited the following *hadith* attributed to the Prophet Muahammad: 'The *fuqaha'* are the trustees of the prophets … so long as they do not follow the sultan [or temporal ruler].'[29]

The dispute between reformers and conservatives revolved fundamentally around the pivotal concept of *ijtihad.* It was the most contentious issue in the seventeenth-century scholarly conflict between the *Usuli* (rationalist) and *Akhbari* (traditionalist) schools of legal thought. The *Akhbari* 'ulama rejected outright the legitimacy of *ijtihad*, citing the existence of the Hidden Imam, whose authority they believed to be infallible and absolute. In their view, Islamic Shi'i jurisprudence essentially involved the extrapolation of principles and rulings directly from verses of the Qur'an and the *hadiths* of the Prophet and the Imams. By contrast, the *Usuli* scholars, in addition to the Qur'an and the *hadith*, deemed the principles of *ijma'* (consensus) and *aql* (reason) to be the sources of the shari'ah. It was the employment of rigorous intellectual reasoning in the *Usuli* methodological approach that had furnished it with a more rationalist foundation for responding to evolving situations and complex issues.[30]

Whereas the *Akhbaris* regarded all Shi'a Muslims – laymen and experts alike – to be bound by the instructions and teachings of the Imams, the *Usulis* advocated the division of the Shi'i faithful into two distinct categories: a professional religious–juridical elite qualified to exercise *ijtihad* (known as *al-mujtahidun* – sing. *mujtahid*), and a general community of lay devotees (*al-muqallidun* – sing. *muqallid*), who are deemed to be obliged to choose and emulate a particular *mujtahid* (preferably the most senior jurist) in all aspects of his rulings.[31]

Moreover, unlike their *Akhbari* rivals, the proponents of *Usulism*, on the one hand, stipulated the incumbent duty of exercising *ijtihad* upon the senior jurists during the absence of the Twelfth Imam, and, on the other, prohibited the emulation of a deceased *mujtahid.* Although, as mentioned above, the rationale for, and legal methodology of, *ijtihad*, was propounded by Allamah al-Hilli, in the twelfth century, and while the binary *mujtahid/muqallid* classification was developed by Shaykh al-Karaki and his successors, the eventual triumph of *Usulism* was largely the accomplishment of its foremost exponent, Shaykh Agha Muhammad Baqer Bihbahani (d. 1792/3).[32]

In addition to contributing to the general elevation of the Shi'i 'ulama, the enhancement of their authority, and expansion of their influence, the definitive triumph of the *Usuli* school of religious–legal thought had two specific consequences. First, the victory of *Usulism* led to 'the enhanced status of the Shi'i theological school complexes (*hawzat al-'ilmiyya*)', as the only centres offering the comprehensive acquisition of this kind of scholastic learning. Consequently, significant impetus was given to the establishment of a 'more centralised ecclesiastical network'. The second consequence was the emergence of pre-eminent religious–juridical authorities who had mastered all the relevant religious sciences, and upon whom was conferred the title *Maraje' al-Taqlid* (sing. *Marja' al-Taqlid*), or 'Sources of Emulation'. The jurist considered to be the most eminent among the elite of *mujtahids* was known as *Marja' al-Taqlid al-Mutlaq* ('Supreme Source of Emulation').[33]

'Ulama–state Relations under the Qajar Dynasty

Contemporary with the undisputed triumph of *Usulism* was the advent of the Qajar dynasty to power. Unlike the Safavid rulers, the Qajar monarchs did not claim descent from the Shi'i Imams, as they belonged to a Turkoman tribe, and thus could not claim to be ruling as the temporal deputies of the Hidden Imam; to have done so would have led inevitably to a clash with the powerful 'ulama establishment, whose representatives regarded themselves as the deputies of the Hidden Imam.[34]

Despite the fact that the Qajar sovereigns claimed to rule in the capacity of God's vicegerents, their quasi-legitimacy was contingent on the validating authority of the 'ulama, who viewed the Qajar Shahs as possessing functional legitimacy, their authority resting primarily on the degree to which those monarchs governed in accordance with the shari'ah and effectively defended the territory of the state from external threats. Though a significant number of 'ulama co-operated with the Qajar state, and held various important religious, juridical and teaching posts within it, nevertheless the religious scholars and jurists, as a group, and in contradistinction to their clerical predecessors under the Safavids, 'stood over and against the state', and resisted government attempts to integrate them into the regime.[35]

The determinants of the expanded autonomy and enhanced influence of the Shi'i 'ulama can be traced to the intricate processes that unfolded during the Safavid era, when major religious institutional reforms were embarked upon, resulting in both an increased diversification of roles played by the 'ulama and a significant expansion of the authority and influence of the more senior Shi'i clerics and jurists.

Alongside with this complex set of changes was the decisive consolidation of Shi'i Islam among the majority of Iran's erstwhile Sunni inhabitants. Though Shi'ism was the espoused persuasion of the Safavid monarchs, it was the 'ulama (many of whom had immigrated to Iran from Arab countries) who played a pivotal role in bringing about that metamorphosis. This confessional transformation was, in turn, crucial in buttressing the ties between the 'ulama and the Shi'i faithful.

The 'ulama's discernible progress towards authority within the state began in earnest in late-seventeenth-century Iran, when the integrating power of the centre had gradually started to wane. Thus, with the final disintegration of the Safavid Empire in 1722, a void was created which was to some extent filled by the 'ulama, who in the process assumed a multiplicity of roles formally associated with the state.[36]

The fortifying centrifugal forces (represented by the powerful frontier tribal confederations, the warring Ottoman Turks, and the invading Afghans) that shaped the milieu of the interregnum period between the demise of the Safavid dynasty and the rise of Qajar kingdom, were in turn perpetuated by the decentralised nature of the ruling administrative regime. This situation was simultaneously conditioned by, and gave impetus to, the consolidation of local power bases in society, of which the firmly established 'ulama network was a major, if not preponderant element.[37]

This unmistakable trend towards an elaborate, secure and autonomous 'ulama power structure did not by itself translate into a state of mutual hostility between the state and the clerics. Though 'ulama–state relations generally oscillated between cordiality and uneasiness, a marked deterioration in those relations became increasingly apparent during the course of the nineteenth century.[38] The principal sources of tension in those relations were, broadly, two-fold: inexorable external pressures and state responses, on the one hand, and internal governmental reforms and 'ulama responses, on the other.

With regard to the former, the 'ulama became increasingly antagonistic towards the central authority as it failed to halt growing foreign political and military and economic encroachment on the country. Much to the dismay of the 'ulama, Iran fell increasingly under the geopolitical and economic influence of rival imperial 'infidel' powers – namely Britain and Russia. Thus, when the modernising Qajar monarch, Nasir al-Din Shah, granted in 1891 a state licence to a British company to monopolise the sale and distribution of tobacco in Iran, a certain Mirza Hasan al-Shirazi (then the foremost Shi'i religious authority) issued a fatwa that prohibited the consumption of tobacco. Confronted with a popular insurrection led by a large segment of the 'ulama, who perceived the tobacco licence as a threat to Islam and to Iranian proto-nationalist interests, the regime was compelled to repeal the deeply unpopular tobacco concession. The Shi'i Iranian 'ulama, while not taking a uniform stance on this contentious issue, had nevertheless demonstrated the magnitude of their power and influence in society.[39]

The other important source of tension in clerical–state relations under the

Qajar dynasty during the nineteenth century emanated from various reformist government policies aimed at centralising and partially secularising the Islamic system of education, the shari'ah-based judiciary, and the traditional fiscal regime. The unprecedented attempt at reforming these three key sectors, which were traditionally monopolised by the 'ulama, had engendered a virulent clerical reaction. Viewing these initiatives as posing a real threat to their sustained autonomy, and by extension to their power and leverage in society, the 'ulama began, not surprisingly, to agitate against the perceived injustice.[40]

In tenaciously defending their inherent authority and vested interests (and those of other traditional socio-economic groups such as the landowning gentry), the 'ulama did not, however, aim to create radical change in the status quo.[41] Nevertheless, the much detested policy of centralisation, and accordingly arbitrary nature of government decision-making, did precipitate an inexorable trend towards constitutional reform, which gathered considerable momentum at the turn of the twentieth century.

This historical overview of the evolutionary course and institutional development of Twelver Shi'ism has revealed the complex processes that have give definitive shape to its distinctive traits, of which the most salient are the ritual mourning of the slain Imam Hussein and the eschatological awaiting of the return of the Twelfth Imam. The different readings of these two intrinsic confessional themes, depending on the socio-political milieu of the interpreter, have given rise to two divergent yet valid trends in Shi'i Islam: namely, political activism and apolitical quietism.

The basis and historical ascendancy of the institutional authority, autonomic power, and generally anti-state orientation of the 'ulama can be attributed largely to the distinctive nature of Twelver Shi'i religious–political doctrine and legal theory. But the full impact of the assertive religious–political behaviour of such contemporary activist 'ulama as Khomeini, Baqer al-Sadr and Fadlallah, who have actively advocated the radical transformation of current Muslim societies and polities, cannot be satisfactorily understood without considering the causes and consequences of the profound socio-cultural, economic and political changes that have taken place in those societies in modern times.

Notes

Introduction

1. Fadlallah, *al-Mudannas wal Muqaddas*, p. 46; www.islamonline.net/Arabic/famous/2004/08/article02d.shtml.
2. For the portrayal of Fadlallah as 'Hizbullah's spiritual leader', see foreword, and also: *Washington Post*, 30 October 1983, p. 29; *Middle East*, July 1989, p. 13; *Time*, no. 134, 9 October 1989; *Jerusalem Report*, 20 October 1994, p. 11; *Time*, 15 January 1996, p. 26; J. Miller, 'The Charismatic Islamists', *Middle East Lectures*, no. 2, 1997, pp. 39–46; *al-Sharq al-Awsat*, 1 October 1998, p. 5.
3. www.bayynat.org; *al-Nahar*, (Australian ed.), 18 May 2000, p. 14.
4. M. H. Fadlallah, *Bayyinat* (Explications), no. 98 (27 August 2000).
5. *Ibid.*
6. 'Quelques mots-clés de Muhammad Husayn Fadlallah' [Some notes on Fadlallah], *Revue Française de Science Politique*, vol. 37, no. 4 (August 1987), pp. 478–501; 'La révolution islamique selon Muhammad Husayn Fadlallah', [Revolution according to Fadlallah] *Orient*, vol. 29, no.1 (March 1988), pp. 68–84. These two articles, along with other individual studies, were republished in a monograph entitled: *L'Utopie islamique dans l'Orient arabe* (Paris: Presses de la Fondation Nationale des Sciences Politiques, 1991). Carré followed up these studies with a four-page biographical account of Fadlallah, 'Fadlallah, Muhammad Husayn', in J. L. Esposito, *The Oxford Encyclopedia of the Modern Islamic World*, 2 vols (New York: Oxford University Press, 1995), vol. 2, pp. 453–6.
7. I. Abu Rabi, *Intellectual Origins of the Islamic Resurgence in the Modern World* (New York: State University of New York Press, 1996), Chapter 7; M. Kramer, 'The Oracle of Hizbullah: Muhammad Husayn Fadlallah', in R. S. Appleby (ed.) *Spokesmen for the Despised* (Chicago: University of Chicago Press, 1997), Chapter 2. Kramer's chapter comprises over eighty pages (including endnotes), with extensive referencing to Arabic source materials, particularly journalistic interviews. Kramer has written the first, rather terse, biographical profile of Fadlallah: 'Muhammad Husayn Fadlallah', *Orient*, vol. 26, no. 2 (June 1985), pp. 147–9.

8. M. Mallat, *Shi'i Thought from the South of Lebanon* (Oxford: Centre for Lebanese Studies, 1988).

Chapter One

1. W. J. U. Nazmi, *al-Juthour al-Siyasiyya wa al-Fikriyya wa al-Ijtima'iyya li al-Haraka al-Qawmiyya al-'Arabiyya (al-Istiqlaliyya) fi al-'Iraq* [The political, intellectual and social roots of the (independent) Arab nationalist movement of Iraq] (Beirut: Markaz al-Wahadah al-Arabiyya, 1986), p. 31.
2. P. Marr, *The Modern History of Iraq* (Boulder: Westview Press, 1991), p. 2.
3. Y. Nakash, *The Shi'is of Iraq* (Princeton: Princeton University Press, 1994), p. 13; P.-J. Luizard, *La Formation de l'Irak Contemporain* (Paris: Edition du CNRS, 1991), p. 41; H. Batatu, *The Old Social Classes and Revolutionary Movements of Iraq* (London: Saqi Books, 2004), p. 40; P. Sluglett, *Britain in Iraq* (London: Ithaca University Press, 1976), p. 300; Sluglett, *op. cit.*, p. 300; Batatu, *op. cit.*, p. 40; Batatu, *op. cit.*, p. 40 ; Nazmi, *op. cit.*, p. 35.
4. Batatu, *op. cit.*, p. 37; A. H. al-Rahimi, *Ta'rikh al-Haraka al-Islamiyya fi al-'Iraq* [History of the Islamic movement in Iraq] (Beirut: al-Dar al-Alamiyya, 1985), p. 30; A. A. Shikara, *Iraqi Politics 1921–1941* (London: n.p., 1987), p. 17.
5. A. al-Qazzaz, 'The Power Elite in Iraq', *The Muslim World*, vol. 61 (1971), p. 277; Marr, *op. cit.*, p. 7; Batatu, *op. cit.*, p. 17; al-Qazzaz, *op. cit.*, p. 271 ; Marr, *op. cit.*, p. 7.
6. D. Fromkin, *A Peace to End All Peace* (London: Penguin, 1989), p. 109; M. E. Yapp, *The Making of the Modern Middle East* (London: Longman, 1987), p. 266.
7. A. al-Nafisi, *Dawr al-Shi'a fi Tatawwur al-'Iraq al-Siyasi al-Hadith* [Role of the Shi'a in the modern political development of Iraq] (Beirut: Dar al-Nahar, 1973), pp. 87–9; *Ibid.*, p. 84; Nakash, *op. cit.*, pp. 60–1; D. Silverfarb, *Britain's Informal Empire in the Middle East* (New York: Oxford University Press, 1986), p. 4.
8. Silverfarb, *op. cit.*, p. 3.
9. *Ibid.*
10. Fromkin, *op. cit.*, pp. 97–8, 104–5; Luizard, *op. cit.*, p. 320; *Ibid.*, pp. 109–10; Luizard, *op. cit.*, p. 319; al-Rahimi, *op. cit.*, pp. 163–4; W. Ende, 'Iraq in World War One', in R. Peters (ed.), *Proceedings of the Ninth Congress of the Union Europeenne des Arabisants es Islamisants* (Leiden: Brill, 1981), p. 66.
11. Among those Shi'i jurists who had issued or endorsed the fatwa of jihad, or actively organized local civil or armed resistance against the British expeditionary force, were Shaykh Muhammad Taqi al-Shirazi, Shaikh Muhammad Kazem al-Yazdi, Shaikh Mahdi al-Khalisi, Shaikh al-Shari'ah Isfahani, and Shaikh Muhammad S. Habibi. Luizard, *op. cit.*, p. 324; al-Rahimi, *op. cit.*, pp. 163–4; A. H. al-Rahimi, *Fatawa al-'Ulama al-Shi'a bi al-Jihad difa'un 'un al-Dawlah al-'Uthmaniyya'*, [Edicts by the Shi'i 'ulama on jihad in defence of the Ottoman state], *al-Thaqafah al-Islamiyya* [Islamic Culture], no. 22, 1989, pp. 181–3.
12. Ende, *op. cit.*, p. 65; Luizard, *op. cit.*, pp. 320–4; S. G. Haim, 'Shi'ite Clerics and Politics', *Israel Oriental Studies*, vol. 10 (1980), p. 165.
13. Fromkin, *op. cit.*, pp. 104–5. Also see J. B. Glubb, *A Short History of the Arab Peoples* (London: Hodder & Stoughton, 1969), p. 273.
14. Fromkin, *op. cit.*, pp. 114–15.
15. Glubb, *op. cit.*, pp. 273–5. I. Shbaru (ed.), *Thawrat al-Arab did al-Atrak* [The Arab

Revolt against the Turks] (Beirut: Dar al-Tadamun, 1993), pp. 60–4, 162–3. A. A. Duri, *The Historical Formation of the Arab Nation* (London: Croom Helm, 1987), p. 303.

16. Fromkin, *op. cit.*, pp. 98–9; Glubb, *op. cit.*, p. 213; J. C. Hurewitz, *Diplomacy in the Near and Middle East*, vol. II (Gerrards Cross: Archive Editions, 1987), p. 13.
17. For Kitchener's reply see Glubb, *op. cit.*, p. 273; R. Peters, *Islam and Colonialism* (The Hague: Mouton, 1979), pp. 90–3.
18. Glubb, *op. cit.*, p. 275 ; W. Laqueur and B. Rubin (eds), *The Israeli-Arab Reader* (New York: Penguin, 1984), pp. 15–16.
19. Laqueur and Rubin, *op. cit.*, p. 16; Fromkin, *op. cit.*, pp. 148–9, 183.
20. Fromkin, *op. cit.*, p. 179; Laqueur and Rubin, *op. cit.*, p. 16; Hurewitz, *op. cit.*, p. 15; Fromkin, *op. cit.*, p. 179; Laqueur and Rubin, *op. cit.*, p. 16.
21. Fromkin, *op. cit.*, p. 183; Luizard, *op. cit.*, p. 343; S. H. Longrigg, *Iraq* (London: n.p., 1953), p. 114; Luizard, *op. cit.*, p. 343; Longrigg, *op. cit.*, p. 114.
22. Fromkin, *op. cit.*, p. 222; J. L. Bacharach, *A Middle East Studies Handbook* (Cambridge: Cambridge University Press, 1984), p. 65.
23. Bacharach, *op. cit.*, p. 65; Shbaru, *op. cit.*, pp. 21–2; Glubb, *op. cit.*, p. 278; Bacharach, *op. cit.*, p. 65.
24. Bacharach, *op. cit.*, p. 65; Fromkin, *op. cit.*, pp. 200–1; Luizard, *op. cit.*, pp. 320, 338–9; Fromkin, *op. cit.*, p. 202; Luizard, *op. cit.*, pp. 339–40; Luizard, *op. cit.*, p. 343; Bacharach, *op. cit.*, p. 65.
25. Shbaru, *op. cit.*,p. 22; E. Penrose, *Iraq* (London: Benn, 1978), p. 33; Hurewitz, *op. cit.*, pp. 18–19; Laqueur and Rubin, *op. cit.*, pp. 12–13.
26. Hurewitz, *op. cit.*, p. 19; Yapp, *op. cit.*, p. 277;
27. Penrose, *op. cit.*, p. 33; Longrigg, *op. cit.*, p. 115.
28. H. Shubbur, *Tarikh al-'Iraq al-Siyyasi* [The political history of Iraq] (Beirut: Dar al-Turath al-'Arabi, 1989) , pp. 36, 73–4; A. al-Bahadli, 'Jam'iyyat al-Nahda al-Islamiyya', [The Islamic Renaissance Society], *al-Muntalaq*, nos. 94, 95, September 1992, p. 142.
29. Bahadli, *op. cit.*, p. 154; Shubbur, *op. cit.*, pp. 36–7; Bahadli, *op. cit.*, pp. 150–1; Shubbur, *op. cit.*, pp. 39–40; Bahadli, *op. cit.*, pp. 151–2; Shubbur, *op. cit.*, p. 41; Shubbur, *op. cit.*, p. 74.
30. *Ibid.*, pp. 24–5, 42; E. Tauber, *The Formation of Modern Syria and Iraq* (London: Frank Cass, 1994), p. 279; Shubbur, *op. cit.*, pp. 279–80.
31. Shubbur, *op. cit.*, p. 25; Tauber, *op. cit.*, pp. 279–80.
32. Among the most outstanding figures associated with al-'Ahd was Nuri al-Sa'id, who first became Prime Minister in 1930, and thereafter presided over no less than 14 cabinet formations. Shubbur, *op. cit.*, p. 25; M. Basri, *'Alaamun Siyasiyya fi al-'Iraq al-Hadith* [Political figures of modern Iraq] (London: Riyad al-Rayyes, 1987), p. 130.
33. Shubbur, *op. cit.*, pp. 43–4; Tauber, *op. cit.*, p. 281. Shubbur, *op. cit.*, pp. 51–2; Tauber, *op. cit.*, p. 284.
34. Nazmi, *op. cit.*, pp. 26, 336; Shubbur, *op. cit.*, pp. 54–5; Tauber, *op. cit.*, p. 286; Nazmi, *op. cit.*, p. 335; Shubbur, *op. cit.*, p. 55; Tauber, *op. cit.*, p. 287; Shubbur, *op. cit.*, pp. 54–5; Tauber, *op. cit.*, p. 287; I*bid.*, pp. 295–8, 304; Shubbur, *op. cit.*, pp. 68–70.
35. Longrigg, *op. cit.*, pp. 114–15; Penrose, *op. cit.*, p. 36.
36. Nazmi, *op. cit.*, p. 298; Nafisi, *op. cit.*, p. 117; Nafisi, *op. cit.*, p. 127; Nakash, *op. cit.*, pp. 62–3; Nazmi, *op. cit.*, p. 304.
37. Nafisi, *op. cit.*, pp. 127, 129; Nakash, *op. cit.*, pp. 63–4; H. al-Amin, 'al-Thawra al-

Iraqiyya al-Kubra', [The great Iraqi Revolt] *al-Thaqfa al-Islamiyya*, no.22 (1989), pp. 196–7, 201–2; Nazmi, *op. cit.*, p. 308; Nakash, *op. cit.*, p. 65.

38. Batatu, *op. cit.*, pp. 77, 86–8; D. Pool, 'From Elite to Class', *International Journal of Middle East Studies*, vol. 12, no. 3 (1980), pp. 304–41; Batatu, *op. cit.*, p. 94; Marr, *op. cit.*, p. 32; Pool, *op. cit.*, pp. 340–41; Batatu, *op. cit.*, pp. 88–9; Marr, *op. cit.*, p. 32; Pool, *op. cit.*, p. 342; Marr, *op. cit.*, p. 32; Batatu, *op. cit.*, p. 95.
39. Marr, *op. cit.*, p. 32; Batatu, *op. cit.*, pp. 84, 98; Batatu, *op. cit.*, pp. 96–7; Batatu, *op. cit.*, p. 82; Nakash, *op. cit.*, p. 71.
40. Longrigg, *op. cit.*, p. 115; Luizard, *op. cit.*, pp. 385–6; Marr, *op. cit.*, p. 32; Marr, *op. cit.*, p. 33; Luizard, *op. cit.*, pp. 386–7; M. Jacobsen, 'Only by the Sword, British Counter-Insurgency in Iraq', *Small Wars and Insurgencies*, vol. 2, no. 2 (1991), p. 323.
41. A. Vinogradov, 'The 1920 Revolt in Iraq Reconsidered', *International Journal of Middle East Studies*, vol. 3, no. 2 (1972), pp. 123–4; Marr, *op. cit.*, p. 33; Vinogradov, *op. cit.*, p. 125; Batatu, *op. cit.*, p. 23.
42. al-Nafisi, *op. cit.*, p. 144; al-Rahimi, *op. cit.*, pp. 223–8 ; Haim, *op. cit.*, p. 165; S. al-Hasani, *Dawr al-'Ulama al-Shi'a fi Muwajihat al-Isti'mar* [Role of the Shi'i 'ulama in confronting imperialism] (Beirut: al-Ghadir, 1995), pp. 236–42.
43. al-Nafisi, *op. cit.*, p. 144; al-Nazmi, *op. cit.*, pp. 394–5; al-Amin, *op. cit.*, p. 210; Tauber, *op. cit.*, p. 294; al-Amin, *op. cit.*, p. 201; Haim, *op. cit.*, p. 165.
44. L. Lukitz, *Iraq* (London: Frank Cass, 1994), p. 61; Nakash, *op. cit.*, pp. 296–8; Sluglett, *op. cit.*, p. 303.
45. Nakash, *op. cit.*, pp. 75–7.
46. Nakash, *op. cit.*, pp. 296–8; Sluglett, *op. cit.*, p. 303.; Marr, *op. cit.*, p. 35.
47. *Ibid.*, p. 36 ; A. A. Shikara, *Iraqi Politics* (London: n.p., 1987), p. 30; M. M. al-Adhami, 'The Elections of the Constituent Assembly in Iraq, 1922–4,' in A. Kelidar (ed.), *The Integration of Modern Iraq* (London: Croom Helm, 1979), p. 16; Longrigg, *op. cit.*, p. 141.
48. Shikara, *op. cit.*, pp. 38–9; al-Adhami, *op. cit.*, p. 16; Longrigg, *op. cit.*, p. 141; al-Adhami, *op. cit.*, p. 16; Shikara, *op. cit.*, p. 39; al-Adhami, *op. cit.*, p. 17.
49. al-Adhami, *op. cit.*, p. 17; *Ibid.*, p. 15; Marr, *op. cit.*, p. 38.
50. Marr, *op. cit.*, p. 38.
51. al-Rahimi, *op. cit.*, pp. 246–7; Marr, *op. cit.*, pp. 43–4; Shikara, *op. cit.*, p. 44; al-Rahimi, *op. cit.*, pp. 247–8; al-Rahimi, *op. cit.*, pp. 248–51; al-Adhami, *op. cit.*, p. 19; Longrigg, *op. cit.*, p. 140.
52. Nakash, *op. cit.*, pp. 81–2; al-Adhami, *op. cit.*, p. 21; Longrigg, *op. cit.*, p. 140; Shikara, *op. cit.*, pp. 46–7; al-Rahimi, *op. cit.*, p. 281; Nakash, *op. cit.*, p. 82; al-Adhami, *op. cit.*, p. 21; Nakash, *op. cit.*, pp. 83–4; al-Rahimi, *op. cit.*, pp. 282–3; P. Martin, 'Les Chiites d'Irak', *Peuples Mediterraneens*, vol. 40 (1987), p. 162.
53. al-Adhami, *op. cit.*, p. 24.
54. Marr, *op. cit.*, p. 39.
55. Lukitz, *op. cit.*, p. 62; Shikara, *op. cit.*, p. 19.
56. R. Simon, 'Iraq', in F. Tachau (ed.), *Political Parties of the Middle East and North Africa* (London: Mansell, 1994), p. 176; Marr, *op. cit.*, pp. 46, 50.
57. *Ibid.*, p. 51; Shubbur, *op. cit.*, pp. 130–1; Nakash, *op. cit.*, p.118; Shubbur, *op. cit.*, pp. 129–30; Simon, *op. cit.*, p. 177.
58. Batatu, *op. cit.*, pp. 96–7; M. Farouk-Sluglett and P. Sluglett, 'The Transformation of Land Tenure and Rural Social Structures in Central and Southern Iraq', *International Journal of Middle Eastern Studies*, vol. 15 (1983), pp. 491–502; Batatu, *op. cit.*, 96–7; Lukitz, *op. cit.*, pp. 56–7.

59. *Ibid.*, p. 500; Lukitz, *op. cit.*, p. 56; Farouk-Sluglett and Sluglett, *op. cit.*, p. 500; Lukitz, *op. cit.*, p. 56; Lukitz, *op. cit.*, pp. 54–5.
60. Farouk-Sluglett and Sluglett, *op. cit.*, p. 501; Marr, *op. cit.*, p. 50; al-Qazzaz, *op. cit.*, pp. 271–2.

Chapter Two

1. C. Mallat, *The Renewal of Islamic Law* (Cambridge: CUP, 1993), p. 19.
2. A.H. al-Bahadli, 'Najaf al-Ashraf', *Noor al-Islam*, nos. 31, 32 (Sept.-Oct. 1992), p. 76; C. E. Bosworth, 'al-Nadjaf', in: C. E. Bosworth, E. Van Donzel et al. (eds), *The Encyclopaedia of Islam*, vol. 6 (Leiden: E. J. Brill, new edn 1992), p. 859; Srour, *al-'Allamah Fadlallah*, pp. 26–7; S. Mervin, 'La Quete du Savior a Nagaf', *Studia Islamica*, vol. 81, no.1, 1995, pp. 177.
3. Karabala is believed by the Shi'a to be the burial site of the martyred Imam Hussein, the son of Ali. Kazimayn contains the shrine of Musa al-Kazim, the Seventh Imam, while Samarra is believed to be site where the Twelfth Imam, Muhammad al-Mahdi, disappeared in AD 874, and went into indefinite *ghayba* occultation. Luizard, *La Formation de l'Irak*, pp. 143–53.
4. Y. Nakash, *The Shi'is of Iraq* (Princeton : Princeton University Press, 1994), pp. 256–7.
5. al-Bahadli, *op. cit.*, pp. 89–90 ; Nakash, *op. cit.*, pp. 18, 188; Nakash, *op. cit.*, p. 186; Luizard, *op. cit.*, pp. 143–4 ; M. al-Ghawri, 'al-Hawaza al-'Ilmiyya al-Diniyya fi Najaf al-Ashraf,' *al-Thaqafa al-Islamiyya*, no. 28 (Dec.-Jan. 1989–90), pp. 105–7.
6. Nakash, *op. cit.*, pp. 199–200. Those measures included mandatory registration, special transit passes and burial permits.
7. A. H. al-Bahadli, *al-Hawaza al-'Ilmiyya fi Najaf* (Beirut: Dar al-Zahra', 1993), p. 70; al-Ghawri, *op. cit.*, pp. 157–8, 57–8; al-Bahadli, 'Najaf ,' p. 30; al-Bahadli, *al-Hawza*, pp. 70, 98.
8. al-Bahadli, 'Najaf,' pp. 85–6; Nakash, *op. cit.*, pp. 244–5; F. Jamali, 'The Theological College of Najaf,' *The Mulsim World*, vol. 50, no.1 (1960), p. 16; Jamali, *op. cit.*, p. 16; al-Bahadli, 'Najaf', pp. 45–7; al-Bahadli, *al-Hawza*, pp. 133–4; A. A. Sachedina, 'al-Khums', *Journal of Near Eastern Studies*, vol. 39, no. 4 (1980), p. 276; N. Calder, 'Khums in Imami Shi'i Jurisprudence,' *Bulletin of the School of Oriental and African Studies*, vol. 45 (1982), p. 39.
9. The manifold purposes of *al-khums* distribution can be subsumed under one of the following categories: religious propagation, education and social welfare; Sachedina, *op. cit.*, pp. 284–7; A. A. Sachedina, *The Just Ruler in Shi'ite Islam* (Oxford: OUP, 1988), pp. 238, 244–5; Luizard, *op. cit.*, p. 155.
10. Sachedina, 'al-Khums', pp. 287–8; Calder, *op. cit.*, pp. 39–40; al-Bahadli, *al-Hawza*, pp. 134–5; Luizard, *op. cit.*, p. 155; Calder, 'Zakat', pp. 468, 478–80.
11. Calder, 'Zakat', p. 480; Sachedina, *The Just Ruler*, p. 245; Luizard, *op. cit.*, p. 156.
12. Nakash, *op. cit.*, p. 245; Jamali, *op. cit.*, pp. 18–19; Mallat, *op. cit.*, p. 40; Mervin, *op. cit.*, pp. 177–8.
13. Nakash, *op. cit.*, p. 245; al-Bahadli, *al-Hawza*, pp. 279–80; Jamali, *op. cit.*, pp. 18–19; Mervin, *op. cit.*, pp. 179–80.
14. Mallat, *op. cit.*, p. 141; al-Bahadli, *al-Hawza*, pp. 102, 274; Mervin, *op. cit.*, pp. 181–2; al-Bahadli, *al-Hawza*, pp. 284–5; Nakash, *op. cit.*, p. 245; Jamali, *op. cit.*, p. 29; Mallat, *op. cit.*, p. 41; Nakash, *op. cit.*, p. 245.

15. al-Bahadli, *al-Hawza*, p. 285; Mervin, *op. cit.*, p. 183; Mallat, *op. cit.*, p. 42–3. *Ijtihad* refers to the process embarked upon by the *mujtahid* to issue a religious–legal judgement through the reinterpretation of certain textual sources, based on the extrapolated principles of the Shari'ah, and in response to the legal and social queries of the faithful and the challenges of modern times.
16. Mervin, *op. cit.*, pp.174–5; Jamali, *op. cit.*, p. 22; Srour, *op. cit.*, p. 27; Nakash, *op. cit.*, p. 244.
17. al-Bahadli, *al-Hawza*, pp. 70, 118 ; Nakash, *op. cit.*, p. 245; Jamali, *op. cit.*, p. 15; Martin, 'Les Chi'ites d'Irak', p. 161; Nakash, *op. cit.*, pp. 257–9.
18. *Ibid.*, p. 255; Jamali, *op. cit.*, p. 22.
19. *Ibid.*, pp. 21–2; Nakash, *op. cit.*, pp. 251–5.
20. al-Bahadli, *al-Hawza*, p. 347; *ibid.*, pp. 315–22.
21. *Ibid.*, pp. 317–18; Nakash, *op. cit.*, pp. 263–8; al-Bahadli, *al-Hawza*, pp. 315–23.
22. The most renowned of these Iraqi poets who hailed from, or studied in, Najaf were Muhammad Mahdi al-Jawahiri, Muhammad Rida al-Shabibi, Muhammad Sa'id Najafi and Ahmad Safi Najafi. S.K. Jayyusi, *Trends and Movements in Modern Arabic Poetry*, vol.1 (Leiden: E.J. Brill, 1977), p. 18; al-Hulou and al-Faqih *As'ilah wa Rudoud*, p. 24; Soeid, *al-Islam wa Filistin*, p. 45.
23. al-Bahadli, 'Najaf', p. 91; Jayyusi, *op. cit.*, p. 176.
24. *Ibid.*, p. 203.
25. Nakash, *op. cit.*, pp. 257–61; *ibid.*, p. 201.
26. *Ibid.*, p. 172.
27. Ende, 'The Flagellations', pp. 21–3 ; J.S. Jad'oun, 'al-Sha'ir al-Husainiyya bayn al-Asalah wa al-Tajdid' [The *husainiyya* ritual between authenticity and renewal] *al-'Irafan*, nos 9–10, vol. 77 (Nov.-Dec. 1993), pp. 17–23. A detailed account of the life and works of Sayyid Muhsin al-Amin can be found in M. Shari'ati (ed.), *al-Muslih al-Islami al-Sayyid Muhsin al-Amin fi Zikrahu al-Sanawiyya al-Arba'een* [The Islamic Reformer, al-Sayyid Muhsin al-Amin in his fortieth anniversary] (Damascus: The Cultural Centre of the Islamic Republic of Iran, 1992). The monograph is a collection of papers delivered in Damascus in 1992. Among the contributors were Sayyid Fadlallah and Shaykh Shams al-Din.
28. Nakash, *op. cit.*, pp. 160–1.
29. Najaf's celebrated *fuqaha'*, led by *Shaykh* Muhammad Kashif al-Ghita', were content to assume a secondary role to that of the tribal *shaykhs*, restricting their opposition to the regime to voicing the greivances and aspirations of the largely impoverished and marginalised *Shi'a* constituency. Nakash, *op. cit.*, pp. 160-61; Marr, *The History of Iraq*, pp. 62-64.
30. Kramer, 'Fadlallah,' p. 147; Carré, 'Fadlallah, p. 453; al-Hulou, *op. cit.*, p.10; Srour, *op. cit.*, p. 19; Hammoud, *al-Wajh al-Akhar*, p. 21; Y.M. 'Amru, *'ulama 'Araftuhum,'* [Scholars I Knew], *al-'Irfan*, vol. 79, nos. 7-8 (October 1995), p. 96 ; '*al-Rahil al-Kabir Ayatollah al-Sayyid Abdul al-Ra'uf Fadlallah,*' [The great deceased …], *al-Muntalaq*, no. 27, February 1985, p. 89; Hammoud, *op. cit.*, p. 121 ; Srour, *op. cit.*, p. 19; Momen, *An Introduction to Shi'i Islam* (New Haven: Yale University Press, 1985), pp. 271-72; al-Hulou, *op. cit.*, p. 10; 'Amru, *op. cit.*, p. 96 ; '*al-Rahil al-Kabir,*' *op. cit.*, p. 89 ; M. H. al-Amini, '*Aal Fadlallah,*' [The Fadlallah familiy], *al-Murshid*, nos. 3-4 (1995), p. 208.
31. *al-Rahil al-Kabir, op. cit.*, p. 89; *'Amru, op. cit.*, p. 97.
32. *al-Rahil al-Kabir, op. cit.*, p. 90; *'Amru*, op. cit., p. 97.

33. al-Amini, *op. cit.*, p. 209–11; *'Amru, op. cit.*, p. 97; *'Amru, op. cit.*, p. 98 ; *al-Rahil al-Kabir, op. cit.*, p. 90; *'Amru, op. cit.*, p. 98.
34. al-Amini, *op. cit.*, p. 209; Srour, *op. cit.*, pp. 26–7; Mervin, *op. cit.*, pp. 175, 177; F. Musa, *al-Shaykh Muhammad Mahdi Shams al-Din* (Beirut: Dar al-Hadi, 1993), p. 31–4; al-Hulou, *op. cit.*, p. 11; Mallat, *op. cit.*, p. 8; Srour, *op. cit.*, p. 37; *al-Rahil al-Kabir, op. cit.*, pp. 92, 95–6.
35. Srour, *op. cit.*, pp. 59–60.
36. Srour, *op. cit.*, pp. 23–5; al-Hulou, *op. cit.*, p. 17; Jad'oun, *op. cit.*, pp. 18–23.
37. al-Hulou, *op. cit.*, pp. 11–12; al-Hasani, *Sira' al-Iradat*, p. 123; Srour, *op. cit.*, p. 25.
38. Srour, *op. cit.*, p. 26; al-Hulou, *op. cit.*, pp. 12–13; al-Hasani, *op. cit.*, pp. 123–4; M. B. al-Sadr, *Buhouth Islamiyya* [Islamic Treatises] (Beirut: al-Dar al-Islamiyya, 1991), pp. 16–17; M. al-Husseini, *al-Imam al-Shahid Muhammad Baqer al-Sadr* [The Martyred Imam M. B. al-Sadr] (Beirut: Dar al-Furat, 1989), p. 57; Srour, *op. cit.*, p. 49.
39. al-Hulou, *op. cit.*, pp. 14–15; al-Hasani, *op. cit.*, p. 124; Srour, *op. cit.*, p. 28.
40. The earlier dates are cited in: al-Hulou, *op.cit.*, p. 15; *Maraya al-Ahdath*, [The Reflections of Events], a videotaped interview with Fadlallah by the Beirut-based al-Manar TV Station in January 1995. The latter dates are cited in al-Hasani, *op. cit.*, p. 124; Srour, *op. cit.*, p. 28.
41. al-Hulou, *op. cit.*, pp. 13–14; al-Suwayd, *op. cit.*, p. 6; Hammoud, *op. cit.*, p. 23; J. Brugman, *An Introduction to the History of Modern Arabic Literature in Egypt* (London: E.J.Brill, 1984), pp. 273–4.
42. al-Hasani, *op. cit.*, p. 124; al-Suwayd, *op. cit.*, p. 5; Srour, *op.cit* ., p. 28; al-Hulou, *op. cit.*, p. 14.
43. Fadlallah's poetic output was a significant contribution to the tradition of poetic writing among the Shi'i 'ulama of Iraq. Of the Shi'i poets among the 'ulama, the most distinguished in modern times, were Sayyid Muhammad Sa'eed al-Habubi, Shaykh Muhammad Hussein al-Kashif al-Ghita', al-Murtada and al-Rida. M. H. Fadlallah, *Ya Zilal al-Islam* [Oh! The Shadows of Islam] (Beirut: Dar al-Ta'aruf, 1985), p. 17.
44. al-Hasani, *op. cit.*, p. 125.
45. al-Hasani, *op. cit.*, p. 125; Jayyusi, *op. cit.*, p. 203; al-Hulou, *op. cit.*, p. 24; al-Suwayd, *op. cit.*, p. 5; Hammoud, *op. cit.*, pp. 21–2; M.M. Badawi, *A Critical Introduction to Modern Arab Poetry* (Cambridge: CUP, 1975), p. 250; *ibid.*, pp. 253, 255; Marr, *op. cit.*, p. 150.
46. Hammoud, *op. cit.*, p. 21; M. H. Fadlallah, *'Ala Shati' al-Wujdan* [On the Shores of Passion] (London: Riyyad al-Rayyes, 1990), p. 11; Brugman, *op. cit.*, pp. 38–9; Badawi, *op. cit.*, pp. 62–5.
47. Srour, *op. cit.*, p. 34; al-Hulou, *op. cit.*, p. 25; al-Hasani, *op. cit.*, pp125–6.
48. *Ibid*; Srour, *op. cit.*, p. 49.
49. 'Amru, *op. cit.*, p. 98; *al-Rahil al-Kabir, op. cit.*, p. 90; al-Suwayd, *op. cit.*, p. 1; Srour, *op. cit.*, p. 33; al-Amini, *op. cit.*, p. 210; al-Hasani, *op. cit.*, p. 126; A. A. al-Muntafaki, *Jami' al-Suwar li al-'Ulama wa al-Udaba wa al-Kuttab* [A Photo Collection of Scholars and Writers] (Beirut: Dar al-Muwaddah, 1993), pp. 18, 112, 182.
50. al-Hasani, *op. cit.*, p. 126; al-Bahadli, *al-Hawza al-'Ilmiyya*, p. 285; al-Jamali, *op. cit.*, p. 28; Srour, *op. cit.*, p. 43; Kramer, *op. cit.*, p. 147.
51. al-Hasani, *op. cit.*, pp. 126–7; Srour, *op. cit.*, pp. 49–50; al-Suwayd, *op. cit.*, pp. 8–9; Marr, *op. cit.*, pp. 76–82; M. Khadduri, *Independent Iraq* (Oxford: OUP, 1960), pp. 124–5; M. Farouk-Sluglett and P. Sluglett, 'The Social Classes and the Origins of the Revolution', in R. A. Fernia and W. R. Louis (eds), *The Iraqi Revolution of 1958*

(London: I.B. Tauris, 1991), pp. 124–5 ; H. Batatu, *The Old Social Classes and the Revolutionary Movements of Iraq* (London: Saqi Books, 2004), pp. 337–8.

52. Marr, *op. cit.*, pp. 102–3; Khadduri, *op. cit.*, pp. 262–8; H. Shubbur, *al-'Amal al-Hizbi fi al-'Iraq* [Party Activity in Iraq] (Beirut: Dar al-Turath al-Arabi, 1989), p. 192; I. M. Husseini, *The Moslem Brethren* (Beirut: Khayat College Co-operatives, 1956), p. 184; Batatu, *op. cit.*, pp. 545–50ff; al-Suwayd, *op. cit.*, pp. 6–7, 9.
53. College students and teachers were at the forefront of the mass protests. Batatu, *op. cit.*, pp. 550–7; Khadduri, *op. cit.*, pp. 267–70; Farouk-Sluglett, *op. cit.*, p. 127.
54. Batatu, *op. cit.*, p. 545; Khadduri, *op. cit.*, p. 267; Marr, *op. cit.*, p. 104.
55. Farouk-Sluglett, *op. cit.*, p. 128; Marr, *op. cit.*, p. 106; Khadduri, *op. cit.*, pp. 273–4.
56. Fadlallah wrote another poem on Palestine in 1953 in which he lamented the plight of the Palestinians and the forlorn cause of Palestine. M. H. Fadlallah, *Qasa'id lil-Islam wa al-Hayat* [Short Poems for Islam] (Beirut: al-Mu'assash al-Jam'iyyeh li al-Dirasat wa al-Nashr, 1984), pp. 138–9; al-Hulou, *op. cit.*, p. 14; al-Suwayd, *op. cit.*, p.5; Srour, *op. cit.*, p. 28.
57. al-Suwayd, *op. cit.*, p. 8.
58. Khadduri, *op. cit.*, pp. 274–5; Marr, *op. cit.*, p. 109; al-Suwayd, *op. cit.*, p. 9.
59. Marr, *op. cit.*, p. 112; Farouk-Sluglett, *op. cit.*, p. 129; Shubbur, *op. cit.*, pp. 192, 231; al-Suwayd, *op. cit.*, p. 7; Srour, *op. cit.*, p. 53 ; Hammoud, *op. cit.*, pp. 24-25 ; al-Suwayd, *op. cit.*, p. 7.
60. Srour, *op. cit.*, pp. 29, 53; al-Hulou, *op. cit.*, p. 21; Hammoud, *op. cit.*, p. 24; al-Hulou, *op. cit.*, p. 21; Srour, *op. cit.*, p. 29; al-Suwayd, *op. cit.*, pp. 9, 10. Fanon was the author of the influential activist work, *The Wretched of the Earth*, while Freire authored *Pedagogy of the Oppressed*. al-Hulou, *op. cit.*, p. 126; 'Personal correspondence with Sayyid Fadlallah', 31 May 1999.
61. Srour, *op. cit.*, p. 54; 'Amru, *op. cit.*, p. 99.
62. I*bid.* During his stay in Bint Jbail, South Lebanon, Fadlallah wrote a number of political poems. One of these, entitled 'We will rise up', was composed in August 1956, in the heyday of Nasser's regime. Fadlallah, swept up in the pan-Arab fervour of the period, proclaimed the certainty of an Arab revolution against subjugation, iniquity and humiliation; one which would reclaim Arab rights, and regain their national pride and dignity. Fadlallah, *Qasa'id lil Islam*, pp. 148–9.
63. Khadduri, *op. cit.*, p. 348; Farouk-Sluglett, *op. cit.*, p. 130; Marr, *op. cit.*, pp. 118–19.
64. al-Suwayd, *op. cit.*, p. 8. As a measure of his early enthusiasm for Nasser's radical policies, Fadlallah wrote on 7 September 1956 a three-page poetic piece in which he lauded the nationalisation of the Suez Canal. Fadlallah, *Qasa'id lil Islam wal Hayat*, pp. 150–2.
65. Shubbur, *op. cit.*, p. 193; Marr, *op. cit.*, pp. 119–20; Batatu, *op. cit.*, pp. 750–1.
66. Batatu, *op. cit.*, pp. 752–4; Martin, *op. cit.*, p. 150.
67. al-Suwayd, *op. cit.*, p. 7.

Chapter Three

1. Batatu, *The Old Social Classes*, p.783; U. Dann, *Iraq under Qassem* (New York: Praeger, 1969), p.20. Born in 1914, into a poor humble family of mixed Sunni-Shi'i descent, residing in the working-class quarter of west Baghdad, Qasem had graduated from military college in 1936, and distinguished himself as a serving officer in Palestine in 1948.

2. M. Khadduri, *Republican Iraq* (Oxford: Oxford University Press, 1969), p. 1; M. Farouk-Sluglett and P. Sluglett, *Iraq Since 1958* (New York: St. Martin's Press, 1990), pp. 47, 57; Marr, *Modern History of Iraq*, pp. 153–4; Farouk-Sluglett, *op. cit.*, p. 57; Khadduri, *op. cit.*, pp. 26–7.
3. *Ibid.*, pp. 6–7; Marr, *op. cit.*, p. 154; Murdan, *op. cit.*, pp. 25–7; Khadduri, *op. cit.*, p. 2; Marr, *op. cit.*, p. 153; Khadduri, *op. cit.*, p. 2.
4. F. Ibrahim, *al-Ta'ifiyya al-Siyasiyya fil Watan al-Arabi* [Political confessionalism in the Arab world] (Cairo: Maktabat Madbouli, 1996), p. 206.
5. Farouk-Sluglett, *op. cit.*, p. 50; Khadduri, *op. cit.*, p. 2; Farouk-Sluglett, *op. cit.*, p. 50; Khadduri, *op. cit.*, p. 2; Batatu, *op. cit.*, p. 766; *ibid.*; Khadduri, *op. cit.*, p. 2; Batatu, *op. cit.*, p. 766; Khadduri, *op. cit.*, p. 14.
6. Batatu, *op. cit.*, p. 758; R. Simon, 'Iraq', in F. Tachau (ed.) *Political Parties of the Middle East and North Africa* (London: Mansell, 1994), p. 182; Batatu, *op. cit.*, p. 762–3.
7. *Ibid.*; Khadduri, *op. cit.*, p. 7; *ibid.*; E. Picard, *Lebanon* (London: Holmes & Meier, 1996), p. 74; Marr, *op. cit.*, p. 155; *ibid.*, p. 156; Batatu, *op. cit.*, pp. 797–9.
8. Batatu, *op. cit.*, pp. 797–8; Marr, *op. cit.*, p. 156; *ibid.*, p. 50; Dann, *op. cit.*, p. 33; Khadduri, *op. cit.*, pp. 51–2.
9. Marr, *op. cit.*, p.158; Khadduri, *op. cit.*, pp .64–5; Farouk-Sluglett, *op. cit.*, p. 50. Qasem oversaw the promulgation of a provisional constitution, which affirmed the republican character of the state, recognised Islam as the country's official religion, and affirmed Iraq as an integral part of the Arab world. In foreign policy, the ruling clique brought about the dissolution of the Hashemite federal pact between Iraq and Jordan, the suspension of the government's representation in the Baghdad Pact, and the closure of the British military bases.
10. Fadlallah, *Qasa'id lil-Islam*, pp.144–5; *ibid.*, p.140.
11. Fadlallah, 'Taqdim' [Introduction], in M. B. al-Sadr, *Risalatuna* [Our Message], (Beirut: al-Dar al-Islamiyya, 1981), pp. 11–12; A. I. al-Siraj, *al-Imam Muhsin al-Hakim* (Beirut: Dar al-Zahra, 1993), pp. 214–16.
12. Farouk-Sluglett, *op. cit.*, pp. 52–3; *ibid.*, p. 51; *ibid.*, pp. 56–7; Khadduri, *op. cit.*, pp. 86–7; Marr, *op. cit.*, p. 159; Khadduri, *op. cit.*, p. 87.
13. The origins of the Iraqi Communist Party can be traced to an Iraqi student, Hussein al-Rahhal, who in 1924 established the first Marxist study circle in Iraq. The first organised communist cells were formed in the southern Iraqi cities of Basra and al-Nasiriyya in 1927 and 1928, followed by Baghdad in 1933. Alarmed by the rapid growth of the party, in late 1948 the old regime launched a major crackdown on the movement. While the party was emasculated by the mass detention of its members, and by the internal dissension and decimation of its leadership, it recovered gradually during the early 1950s to become indisputably the largest and most powerful political opposition force in Iraq. Batatu, *op. cit.*, pp. 393, 404-406, 414–15, 567; S. al-Khurasan, *Safahat min Tarikh al-Harakah al-Shuyou'iyah fi al-Iraq* [Pages from the History of the Communist Movement in Iraq] (Beirut: Dar al-Furat, 1993), pp. 17–19, 69–71, 393, 414–15.
14. Batatu, *op. cit.*, p.475.
15. *Ibid*, pp. 476, 478, 480.
16. *Ibid.*, p. 480; H. Batatu, 'Iraq's Underground Shi'a Movements', *Middle East Journal*, vol. 35, no. 4 (August 1981), p. 586.
17. *Ibid*; Jamali, 'Theological Coleges', p. 15; Batatu, 'Iraq's Underground', p. 586; A. Baram, 'Two Roads to Shi'ite Fundamentalism in Iraq', in M. E. Martin and R. S.

Appleby, *Accounting for Fundamentalisms* (Chicago: University of Chicago Press, 1994), p. 535.

18. Ibrahim, *op. cit.*, p. 232; Shubbur, *Tarikh al-Iraq*, vol. 2: *al-Tahharuk al-Islami*, p. 312; Ibrahim, *op. cit.*, pp. 214–19; Shubbur, *op. cit.*, pp. 351–2.
19. S. al-Askari, *al-Harakah al-Islamiyyah al-Mu'sairah fi al-Iraq* [The Contemporary Islamic Movement in Iraq], *al-Fikr al-Jadid*, no. 4 (December 1992), p. 225.
20. Nakash, *The Shi'is of Iraq*, p. 255; al-Askari, *op. cit.*, p. 225.
21. Batatu, 'Iraq's Underground', pp. 189–90.
22. *Ibid.*, p. 190; al-Bahadli, *al-Hawza al-'Ilmiyyah*, p. 130, n. 2; Batatu, 'Iraq's Underground', p.190.
23. Shubbur, *op. cit.*, p. 383; Ibrahim, *op. cit.*, p. 222; Shubbur, *op. cit.*, pp. 371–2; Ibrahim, *op. cit.*, p. 222; Batatu, *The Old Social Classes*, p. 694; Shubbur, *op. cit.*, pp. 378–80; Ibrahim, *op. cit.*, p. 222.
24. Ibrahim, *op. cit.*, pp. 202, 208.
25. *Ibid.*, pp. 201, 218.
26. Batatu, *op. cit.*, pp. 650, 699; Ibrahim, *op. cit.*, p. 218.
27. Batatu, *The Old Social Classes*, p. 752; R. Soeterik, *The Islamic Movement of Iraq* (Amsterdam: Stichting MERA, 1991), p. 7; Batatu, *op. cit.*, p. 858; M. H. Fadlallah, *al-Diyar*, 11 January 1992, p. 3.
28. al-Bahadli, *op. cit.*, pp. 312–13, 316–17, 321–2; al-'Askari, *op. cit.*, p. 226.
29. al-Bahadli, *op. cit.*, p. 323; al-'Askari, *op. cit.*, pp. 226, 233.
30. H. Shubbur, *al-'Amal al-Hizbi fi al-Iraq* [Party activity in Iraq] (Beirut: Dar al-Turath al-Arabi, 1989), p. 255; M. al-Nizari, *Abdul Sahib Dakhil* (Beirut: Dar al-Furat, 1990), p. 22; Shubbur, *op. cit.*, p. 255.
31. *Ibid.*; Shubbur, *al-Taharruk al-Islami*, pp. 367, 368; al-Nizari, *op. cit.*, p. 22.
32. J. al-Quzwaini, 'Ishkaliyyat al-Fuqaha wa al-Dawlah wa bidayat al-Harakah al-Islamiyyah fi al-Iraq' [The Problem of the Jurists and the State and the Origins of the Islamic Movement in Iraq], *al-Fikr al-Jadid*, no. 2 (June 1992), p. 250; Shubbur, *al-'Amal al-Hizbi*, p. 254; al-Askari, *op. cit.*, p. 233; al-Mu'min, *Sanawat al-Jamr*, p. 25.
33. Shubbur, *op. cit.*, p. 254; al-khatib Ibn Najaf, *Tarikh al-Harakah al-Islamiyyah al-Mu'asirah fi al-Iraq* [History of the Contemporary Islamic Movement in Iraq] (Beirut: Dar al-Muqadisi, 1982), p. 39; al-Mu'min, *op. cit.*, p. 25. The latter of the two booklets was most likely an Islamist response to an influential nationalist publication: *Min Wahy al-Qawmi*.
34. al-Askari, *op. cit.*, p. 233; Shubbur, *op. cit.*, p. 254.
35. al-Askari, *op. cit.*, p. 234; Shubbur, *op. cit.*, p. 254.
36. Ibn Najaf, *op. cit.*, p. 39; al-Mu'min, *op. cit.*, p. 26; Ibn Najaf, *op. cit.*, p. 39; al-Mu'min, *op. cit.*, p. 26; Ibn Najaf, *op. cit.*, p. 39; al-Mu'min, *op. cit.*, p.26.
37. Shubbur, *op. cit.*, p. 252; al-Mu'min, *op. cit.*, pp. 23–4; Husaini, I. M., *The Moslem Brethren*, p. 84; T. H. al-Azami, 'The Emergence of the Contemporary Islamic Revival in Iraq', *Middle East Affairs Journal*, vol. 3, nos 1 & 2 (Winter–Spring 1997), p.128; al-Azami, *op. cit.*, p. 129.
38. al-Azami, *op. cit.*, p. 131; al-Mu'min, *op. cit.*, p. 24.
39. *Ibid*; Shubbur, *al-Taharruk al-Islami*, p. 364; al-Azami, *op. cit.*, p.131.
40. *Ibid.*, p. 132; Shubbur, *al-Taharruk al-Islami*, p. 363.
41. al-Askari, *op. cit.*, p. 234; al-Mu'min, *op. cit.*, p. 24; Shubbur, *al-Amal al-Hizbi*, p. 253; T. D. al-Nabahani, *al-Dawlah al-Islamiyyah* [The Islamic State](Jerusalem, 1953), pp. 182, 191–2; T. D. al-Nabahani, *al-Takattul al-Hizbi* [The Islamic Bloc] (Jerusalem, 1953), pp. 6–7, 53–6.

42. al-Mu'min, *op. cit.*, p. 24; *ibid.*, p. 25; S. Taji-Farouki, *A Fundamental Quest* (London: Grey Seal, 1996), pp. 90–102; al-Nabahani, *al-Takkattul al-Hizbi*, pp. 36–46.
43. al-Mu'min, *op. cit.*, p. 25; al-Mu'min, *op. cit.*, p. 24; Shubbur, *al-'Amal al-Hizbi*, p. 254.
44. 'Personal Interview with Sayyid Fadlallah', (Beirut, 7 March 1996); Dann, *op. cit.*, p. 303; al-Mu'min, *op. cit.*, pp. 24, 114. According to al-Mu'min, the most prominent figure among Shi'i members of Hizb al-Tahrir was Shaykh Aref al-Basri, who was born in 1937 and held a Masters degree from Baghdad University. He left the party in early 1958 to join Hizb al-Da'wa, where he rose through the ranks to become a member of its leadership council.
45. 'Personal Interview', *op. cit.*; al-Mu'min, *op. cit.*, p. 49; Shubbur, *al-Taharruk al-Islami*, p. 365.
46. Abu Ali, *al-Harakah al-Islamiyyah fi al-Iraq* [The Islamic Movement in Iraq] (Beirut: Mu'assasat al-Jihad, 1985), pp. 136–7.
47. *Ibid.*, p. 137.
48. M. H. Fadlallah, 'Taqdim,' [Introduction] in M. al-Husayni, *al-Imam al-Shahid Sayyid Muhammad Baqer al-Sadr* [The martyred Imam, Sayyid M. B. al-Sadr] (Beirut: Dar al-Furat, 1989), pp. 6–7; Ibrahim, *op. cit.*, p. 247.
49. al-Mu'min, *op. cit.*, pp. 30–1; Fadlallah, 'Taqdim', *al-Imam al-Shahid*, p. 5; Fadlallah, 'Taqdim', *Risalatuna*, pp. 10–11; Ibrahim, *op. cit.*, p. 245; al-Mu'min, *op. cit.*, pp. 30–1.
50. al-Husaini, *op. cit.*, pp. 48–9; C. Mallat, *The Renewal of Islamic Law* (Cambridge: Cambridge University Press, 1993), p. 8; C. Mallat, 'Muhammad Baqer al-Sadr', in A. Rahnema (ed.), *Pioneers of Islamic Revival* (London: Zed Books, 1994), p. 258; 'al-Marja al-Shahid Ayatullah al-Sayyid Muhammad Baqer al-Sadr', *al-Muntalaq*, no. 10 (*Sha'ban* 1400 AH, 1980), p. 15.
51. Mallat, *The Renewal*, p. 8; M. B. al-Sadr, *Buhuth Islamiyyah* [Islamic Studies] (Beirut: Dar al-Zahra', 1991), p. 14; al-Husaini, *op. cit.*, pp. 32–4, 56; Mallat, *The Renewal*, p. 8; al-Husaini, *op. cit.*, pp. 57–8; Mallat, *The Renewal*, p. 9; G. Hasan, *al-Shahid al-Sadr* [al-Sadr, the Martyr] (Teheran: Ministry of Islamic Guidance, 1401 AH), pp. 6–7; al-Husaini, *op. cit.*, pp. 62–3; Hasan, *op. cit.*, p. 8; Mallat, *The Renewal*, p. 9; al-Husaini, *op. cit.*, pp. 62–3; Mallat, *The Renewal*, p. 9; Hasan, *op. cit.*, p. 8; A. L. al-Khafaji, *al-Shahid al-Sadr* (Beirut: Dar al-Ma'alim lil Matbu'at, n.d.), pp. 49–50; Ja'far, *op. cit.*, p. 513, notes 35, 36; Hasan, *op. cit.*, p. 17; al-'Askari, *op. cit.*, p. 234.
52. *Ibid.*, p. 235; Fadlallah, 'Taqdim', in: *al-Imam al-Shahid*, p. 6; al-'Askari, *op. cit.*, pp. 234–5.
53. Fadlallah, 'Taqdim', *Risalatuna*, p. 17; al-'Askari, *op. cit.*, p. 233; Fadlallah, 'Taqdim', *Risalatuna*, pp. 10–11, 17.
54. Shubbur, *al-'Amal al-Hizbi*, pp. 255–6; Ja'far, *op. cit.*, p. 511, note 18; S. al-'Askari, 'al-Imam al-Sadr wa Dawrruhu fi al-Sira' al-Siyyasi fi al-Iraq', [The Imam al-Sadr and his role in the Political Conflict in Iraq], in *Muhammad Baqer al-Sadr* (London: Dar al-Islam, 1996), p. 525; Ja'far, *op. cit.*, p. 511, note 18; Wiley, *The Islamic Movement*, p. 32.
55. Baram, *op. cit.*, p. 533; *al-Jihad*, 24 November 1986, p. 1, cited in Wiley, *op. cit.*, p. 32; Batatu, *op. cit.*, p. 578; Farouk-Sluglett, *op. cit.*, p. 195.
56. A. R. Hasan, 'al-Imam al-Shahid Muhammad Baqer al-Sadr', *al-Fikr al-Jadid*, no. 6 (July 1993), p. 324, note 8; Fadlallah, *ạl-Diyar*, 11 January 1992, p. 12.
57. al-Mu'min, *op. cit.*, p. 32; al-Husaini, *op. cit.*, p. 229; al-'Askari, *op. cit.*, p. 235; al-

Husaini, *op. cit.*, p. 87; al-Mu'min, *op. cit.*, p. 34; al-Quzwaini, *op. cit.*, p. 252.

58. al-Mu'min, *op. cit.*, p. 32; A. R. Hasan, *op. cit.*, p. 324; al-Mu'min, *op. cit.*, p. 32.
59. *Ibid.*; A. R. Hasan, *op. cit.*, pp. 322–3.
60. For instance, al-Quzwaini, *op. cit.*, p. 251, mentions the names of three founding members: Sayyid al-Sadr, Sayyid al-Rifai'i and Sayyid al-Hakim; Mu'min, *op. cit.*, p. 32 and al-Askari, 'Imam al-Sadr', p. 525, do not disclose the identities of the remaining four activists; and finally, the list of names of party affiliates as provided by Ibrahim, *op. cit.*, p. 187, contrasts with that of al-Husaini, *op. cit.*, p. 244.
61. A. R. Hasan, *op. cit.*, pp. 323–4, notes 7 and 8; al-'Askari, *op. cit.*, p. 235; al-Husaini, *op. cit.*, p. 244.
62. *al-Jihad*, no. 184 (April 1981), pp. 22–6, cited by H. al-Batatu, 'Shi'i Organisations in Iraq', in J. R. I. Cole and N. R. Keddie, *Shi'ism and Social Protest* (New York: Yale University Press, 1986), p. 192; T. M. Aziz, 'The Role of Muhammad Baqer al-Sadr in Shi'i Political Activism in Iraq', *International Journal of Middle Eastern Studies*, vol. 25, no. 2 (May 1993), p. 209.
63. Fadlallah, *al-Jihad*, no. 233 (4 Sha'ban 1406 AH), cited in al-Husaini, *op. cit.*, p. 229; al-'Askari, *al-Harakah al-Islamiyyah*, p. 237; Ja'far, *op. cit.*, p. 472; Aziz, *op. cit.*, p. 209.
64. Fadlallah, 'Shahid al-Islam al-Sayyid Baqer al-Sadr fi Dawrihi al-Islami al-Fa'il' [The Martyr of Islam, al-Sayyid Baqer al-Sadr in Influential Islamic Role], *al-Wahdah al-Islamiyyah*, no. 3, 13 April 1984, p. 32.
65. Fadlallah, 'Taqdim', in al-Husaini, *Imam al-Shahid*, p. 7; al-Husaini, 'al-Imam al-Sadr', in *Muhammad Baqer al-Sadr*, p.88; al-Quzwaini, *op. cit.*, p. 252; A. R. Hasan, *op. cit.*, pp. 332–3.
66. Fadlallah, 'Taqdim', in al-Husaini, *Imam al-Shahid*, p.7; al-Husaini, *Imam al-Sadr*, p. 88.
67. Fadlallah, *al-Safir*, 31 April 1987; Fadlallah, *al-Diyar*, 11 January 1992.
68. al-Mu'min, *op. cit.*, p. 32; author's correspondence with Shaykh Ali al-Shihimi', 10 May 1997; Surrour, *al-'Allamah Fadlallah*, pp. 49–50; Suwaid, *al-Islam wa Filistin*, pp. 8–9; 'Maraya al-Ahdath', [The Mirrors of Events (televised interview)] *al-Manar*, 20 January 1995; author's correspondence, 10 May 1997; Baram, *op. cit.*, p. 555; al-Mu'min, *op. cit.*, p. 33.
69. Personal correspondence with Sayyid Fadlallah, 31 October 1997.
70. al-Siraj, *op. cit.*, pp. 197–201.
71. Fadlallah, 'Taqdim', al-Husayni, *al-Imam al-Shahid*, p. 6.
72. al-'Askari, 'al-Harakah al-Islamiyyah', p. 237; al-'Askari, 'Imam al-Sadr', p. 527.
73. al-'Askari, 'al-Harakah al-Islamiyyah', p. 237; al-Husaini, *al-Imam al-Shahid*, p. 226; al-'Askari, 'al-Harakah al-Islamiyyah', p. 237; al-Husaini, *al-Imam al-Shahid*, p. 226.
74. M. B. al-Sadr, *Ahl al-Bayt* [The (Prophet's) Household] (Beirut: Dar al-Ta'arif li al-Matbu'at, n.d.), p. 128; M. B. al-Sadr, *al-Islam Yaqud al-Hayat* [Islam Guides Life] (Teheran: Ministry of Islamic Guidance, 1403 AH), p. 175.
75. Fadlallah, 'Taqdim', al-Husaini, *al-Imam al-Shahid*, p. 7.
76. al-Mu'min, *op. cit.*, pp. 33–4; S. al-'Askari, 'Nizam al-Hukm fi Birnamaj al-Harakah al-Islamiyyah' [The system of government in the programme of the Islamic movement], *al-Fikr al-Jadid*, no. 7 (November 1993), pp. 287–8; al-Nizari, *op. cit.*, pp. 142–3.
77. *Ibid.*, pp. 149–51.
78. *Ibid.*, p. 152.
79. al-'Askari, 'Nizam al-Hukm', p. 288; al-Sadr, 'Kayfa Nad'u al-Nass', cited by al-Husaini, *al-Imam al-Shahid*, pp. 361–2.

80. al-Nizari, *op. cit.*, pp. 152, 154; T. D. al-Nabahani, *al-Khilafa* (Jerusalem: no publisher, 1953), pp. 3–4.
81. al-Husaini, *al-Imam al-Shahid*, p. 343; M. H. Fadlallah, 'Azamat al-Insan fi al-Tashri'at Ghayr al-Islamiyyah', *Qadayana 'ala Daw' al-Islam* [Our Affairs in the Light of Islam] (Beirut: Dar al-Zahra, 6th edn, 1985), p. 105; Fadlallah, *Qadayana*, p. 105; al-Husaini, *al-Imam al-Shahid*, p. 343.
82. al-Husaini, *al-Imam al-Shahid*, p. 343.
83. *Ibid.*, pp. 343–4.
84. *Ibid.*, pp. 350–1.
85. *Ibid.*, p. 349.
86. al-Nizari, *op. cit.*, p. 154.
87. al-'Askari, 'Nizam al-Hukm', p. 289; al-Mu'min, *op. cit.*, pp. 36–7; al-'Askari, 'Nizam al-Hukm', pp. 288–9; al-Mu'min, *op. cit.*, p. 37; al-Nizari, *op. cit.*, p. 288; al-Mu'min, *op. cit.*, p.37; al-'Askari, *op. cit.*, p. 288; al-Mu'min, *op. cit.*, p. 37; al-'Askari, *op. cit.*, p. 288.
88. Wiley, *op. cit.*, pp. 32–3; Baram, *op. cit.*, p. 534; al-Nizari, *op. cit.*, p. 124; Ja'far, *op. cit.*, p. 472; Baram, *op. cit.*, p. 534.
89. Baram, *op. cit.*, p. 535; al-Nizari, *op. cit.*, p. 124; Baram, *op. cit.*, p. 534.
90. Wiley, *op. cit.*, p. 108; *ibid*; Ibrahim, *op. cit.*, p. 280, f.n. 47; al-Mu'min, *op. cit.*, p. 34; Wiley, *op. cit.*, p. 85; al-Mu'min, *op. cit.*, p. 34; al-Husaini, *al-Imam al-Shahid*, p. 231; Baram, *op. cit.*, p. 538; Baram, *op. cit.*, p. 540.
91. al-Quzwaini, *op. cit.*, p. 253.
92. al-'Askari, 'al-Harakah al-Islamiyyah', pp. 230–1, 236.
93. Ibrahim, *op. cit.*, p. 240; al-Mu'min., *op. cit.*, pp. 32–3; Ibrahim, *op. cit.*, pp. 24–5.
94. Baram, *op. cit.*, pp. 255, 540–1.
95. al-Mu'min, *op. cit.*, pp. 35–6.
96. Fadlallah, 'Taqdim', *Risalatuna*, pp. 11–13; Wiley, *op. cit.*, p. 108; Ja'far, *op. cit.*, p. 469.
97. al-'Askari, *al-Harakah al-Islamiyyah*, p. 238; al-'Azami, *op. cit.*, p. 134.
98. Fadlallah, *al-Diyar*, p. 3.
99. Dann, *op. cit.*, p. 96; Batatu, *op. cit.*, p. 827; Farouk-Sluglett, *op. cit.*, pp. 56–7; Batatu, *op. cit.*, pp. 821–2; al-Khurasan, *op. cit.*, p. 54.
100. al-Khurasan, *op. cit.*, pp. 59–61; Khadduri, *op. cit.*, p. 117; al-Khrasan, *op. cit.*, pp. 87–8; Khadduri, *op. cit.*, p. 120; Farouk-Sluglett, *op. cit.*, p. 56.
101. al-Khurasan, *op. cit.*, p. 88; Batatu, *op. cit.*, pp. 828, 849; Farouk-Sluglett, *op. cit.*, p. 62; Dann, *op. cit.*, p. 118; Batatu, *op. cit.*, pp. 849, 875.
102. Farouk-Sluglett, *op. cit.*, pp. 59–60; Dann, *op. cit.*, pp. 79–80; Murdan, *op. cit.*, pp. 50, 60–3; Khadduri, *op. cit.*, p. 99; Farouk-Sluglett, *op. cit.*, p. 60; Murdan, *op. cit.*, pp. 61, 69.
103. Batatu, *op. cit.*, p. 858; Khadduri, *op. cit.*, p. 121; Batatu, *op. cit.*, p. 858, 998; Khadduri, *op. cit.*, p. 118; Batatu, *op. cit.*, pp. 858, 894; Dann, *op. cit.*, p. 125; Farouk-Sluglett, *op. cit.*, p. 63.
104. Batatu, *op. cit.*, p. 188; Fadlallah, 'Taqdim', *al-Imam al-Shahid*, p. 5; Ja'far, *al-Hayat al-Siyyasiyyah*, p. 468; Fadlallah, 'Taqdim', *al-Imam al-Shahid*, p. 6.
105. Ja'far, *al-Hayat al-Siyyasiyyah*, p. 468; Ibrahim, *op. cit.*, p. 250.
106. P. Martin, 'Une Grande Figure de l'Islamisme en Iraq', *Les Cahiers de l'Orient*, nos. 8–9 (1987–88), p. 123, cites 1959 as the year of its founding; ibn Najaf, *op. cit.*, p. 16, mentions late 1958; al-Husaini, *al-Imam al-Shahid* and *al-Imam al-Sadr* cite 1958 and

1959, respectively; al-Sarraj, *op. cit.*, p.116, cites September 1958; al-'Askari, *al-Imam al-Sadr*, p. 528, cites 1959; al-Mu'min, *op. cit.*, p.45, asserts that it was founded some eighteen months after the founding of Hizb al-Da'wa. Baram, *op. cit.*, p. 545, states that the society was set up a few months after the establishment of Hizb al-Da'wa.

107. Fadlallah, 'Taqdim', *Risalatuna*, pp. 15–16; al-Husaini, *al-Imam al-Shahid*, pp. 243–4; al-Quzwaini, *op. cit.*, p. 251; Ibn Najaf, *op. cit.*, p. 66; Fadlallah, 'Taqdim', *Risalatuna*, p. 16; al-Husaini, *al-Imam al-Sadr*, p. 92; al-Mu'min, *op. cit.*, p. 45; Ibn Najaf, *op. cit.*, p. 45; al-Husaini, *al-Imam al-Shahid*, pp. 374–5; al-Siraj, *op. cit.*, p. 118.
108. al-Mu'min, *op. cit.*, p. 45; Martin, *op. cit.*, p. 123; Wiley, *op. cit.*, pp. 83, 157, erroneously asserts (as it is based on a mistaken reading of C. Mallat, 'Religious Militancy in Contemporary Iraq', *Third World Quarterly*, vol. 10, no., 2 April 1988) that Fadlallah was a member of Jama'at al-Ulama.
109. al-Mu'min, *op. cit.*, p. 45; Martin, *op. cit.*, p. 123; al-Husaini, *al-Imam al-Shahid*, p. 244; al-Husaini, *al-Imam al-Sadr*, p. 92.
110. al-Mu'min, *op. cit.*, p. 47; Ibn Najafi, *op. cit.*, pp. 34–6; Baram, *op. cit.*, p. 545; al-Mu'min, *op. cit.*, pp. 47, 67; Baram, *op. cit.*, p. 545; al-Mu'min, *op. cit.*, p. 67; Baram, *op. cit.*, p. 545; Ibn Najafi, *op. cit.*, pp. 75–7.
111. Ibrahim, *op. cit.*, p. 250; 'Aziz, *op. cit.*, p. 209; 'Aziz, *op. cit.*, p. 209; Martin, *op. cit.*, p. 123; al-Mu'min, *op. cit.*, p. 47; Ibn Najaf, *op. cit.*, pp. 78–82.
112. *Ibid.*, pp. 21–3, 26; al-Mu'min, *op. cit.*, p. 41.
113. Ibn Najaf, *op. cit.*, p. 20; al-Mu'min, *op. cit.*, p. 42; Ibn Najaf, *op. cit.*, pp. 18, 20.
114. al-Husaini, *al-Imam al-Shahid*, pp. 129–31; Fadlallah, 'Taqdim', *al-Imam al-Shahid*, p. 5; M. B. Sadr, *Falsafatuna* (Beirut: Dar al-Ta'arif, 1986), pp. 11–12; al-Husaini, *al-Imam al-Shahid*, p. 134; Hasan, *op. cit.*, p. 17; Fadlallah, 'Taqdim', *al-Imam al-Shahid*, p. 5.
115. al-'Askari, *al-Harakah al-Islamiyyah*, p. 238; Mallat, *The Renewal of Islamic Law*, p. 11.
116. al-Sadr, *Falsafatuna*, pp. 183–93; Ja'far, *al-Harakah al-Islamiyyah*, p. 470; G. al-Shabundar, 'al-Tahawwullat al-Fikriyyah wa al-Siyasiyyah fi al-Iraq Khilal al-Qarnayn al-Akhirayn', *al-Fikr al-Jadid*, no.1 (January 1992), pp. 306–7.
117. al-Sadr, *Falsafatuna*, pp. 24–5, 28–31; Ja'far, *al-Hayat al-Siyyasiyyah*, p. 470; al-Sadr, *Falsafatuna*, p. 12; Mallat, *The Renewal of Islamic Law*, p. 11.
118. Murdan, *op. cit.*, pp. 69–70; Dann, *op. cit.*, p. 165; Batatu, *op. cit.*, p. 871, 872–3; Dann, *op. cit.*, p. 179; Farouk-Sluglett, *op. cit.*, p. 67; Batatu, *op. cit.*, pp. 888–9; Khadduri, *op. cit.*, pp. 106–11; al-Mu'min, *op. cit.*, pp. 39–40, 48; al-'Azami, *op. cit.*, p. 134; *Middle East Record, 1960* (London: Weidenfeld & Nicolson, 1960), p. 250.
119. al-Siraj, *op. cit.*, pp. 218–19.
120. Dann, *op. cit.*, pp. 144, 328; Wiley, *op. cit.*, p. 34; *Middle East Record, 1961* (London: Weidenfeld & Nicolson, 1961), p. 278; H. al-'Alawi, *al-Shi'ah wa al-Dawlah al-Qawmiyyah fi al-Iraq* (Qom: Dar al-Thaqafah, 1990), p. 210; Ibrahim, *op. cit.*, p. 250; al-Mu'min, *op. cit.*, p. 50.
121. Farouk-Sluglett, *op. cit.*, p. 71; Dann, *op. cit.*, p. 223; Batatu, *op. cit.*, p. 912; Batatu, *op. cit.*, pp. 922–3, 926–9; Dann, *op. cit.*, p. 223; Batatu, *op. cit.*, pp. 922–3.
122. Farouk-Sluglett, *op. cit.*, p. 71; Batatu, *op. cit.*, p. 923; Dann, *op. cit.*, pp. 224, 226; Farouk-Sluglett, *op. cit.*, pp. 75–6.
123. *Ibid.*, p. 83.
124. Wiley, *op. cit.*, pp. 38, 108; al-'Askari, *al-Harakah al-Islamiyyah*, pp. 237–8.
125. Batatu, *op. cit.*, p. 723; Khadduri, *op. cit.*, p. 115; Batatu, *op. cit.*, pp. 730–1.

126. *Ibid.*, pp. 742–3; Ibrahim, *op. cit.*, p. 214; Batatu, *op. cit.*, pp. 742, 748, 1,010; Ibrahim, *op. cit.*, p. 215.
127. Marr, *op. cit.*, pp. 163–4; Khadduri, *op. cit.*, p. 127; Dann, *op. cit.*, p. 255; Marr, *op. cit.*, p. 164; Dann, *op. cit.*, p. 251; Batatu, *op. cit.*, p. 931.
128. M. Dann, 'Licenced Parties in Qasem's Iraq', *Asian and African Studies*, no. 3 (1967), pp. 1–33; Wiley, *op. cit.*, p. 36; Khadduri, *op. cit.*, p. 141; Dann, *Iraq*, pp. 302–3; al-Mu'min, *op. cit.*, p. 48; *Middle East Record, 1960*, p. 250; Dann, *Iraq*, p. 303; Dann, 'Licenced Parties', p. 31; *Middle East Record, 1960*, p. 250; al-Mu'min, *op. cit.*, p. 49; Dann, 'Licenced Parties', p. 29.
129. al-Mu'min, *op. cit.*, p. 49; Wiley, *op. cit.*, p. 36; al-Mu'min, *op. cit.*, p. 49; Wiley, *op. cit.*, p. 36; al-Alawi, *op. cit.*, p. 213; Dann, 'Licenced Parties', p. 28; al-Alawi, *op. cit.*, pp. 211–12; al-Mu'min, *op. cit.*, p. 49; Wiley, *op. cit.*, p. 36.
130. Dann, 'Licenced Parties', p. 29; al-Mu'min, *op. cit.*, p. 49; Khadduri, *op. cit.*, p. 146; al-Mu'min, *op. cit.*, p. 49; Dann, 'Licenced Parties', p. 29; al-Siraj, *op. cit.*, p. 320, note 26; 225–7; Khadduri, *op. cit.*, p. 146; Batatu, *op. cit.*, p. 954; Martin, *Les Chiites d'Irak*, p. 164; Soeterik, *op. cit.*, p. 14.
131. al-Siraj, *op. cit.*, p. 224; al-Mu'min, *op. cit.*, p. 39; Dann, *Iraq*, p. 110; al-Mu'min, *op. cit.*, p. 39; al-Alawi, *op. cit.*, p. 215; al-Siraj, *op. cit.*, pp. 224–5.
132. al-'Alawi, *op. cit.*, p. 214; al-Mu'min, *op. cit.*, p. 43; al-Siraj, *op. cit.*, p. 225; Ibn Najaf, *op. cit.*, pp. 14–15; Batatu, *op. cit.*, p. 954; Ibrahim, *op. cit.*, pp. 251–2; al-'Alawi, *op. cit.*, p. 215; Dann, *Iraq*, p. 303.
133. *Middle East Record, 1960*, p. 250; Dann, *op. cit.*, pp. 145, 328; 'Aziz, *op. cit.*, p. 209; al-Siraj, *op. cit.*, pp. 222, 228.
134. *Middle East Record, 1960*, p. 249; al-Mu'min, *op. cit.*, p. 49; *Middle East Record, 1960*, p. 249; Khadduri, *op. cit.*, p. 146.
135. Dann, 'Licenced Parties', p. 30; *Middle East Record, 1960*, p. 249; Khadduri, *op. cit.*, p. 146.
136. al-Mu'min, *op. cit.*, p. 49; *Middle East Record, 1960*, p. 249; Khadduri, *op. cit.*, p. 146; Dann, 'Licenced Parties', pp. 30–1; *Middle East Record, 1961*, p. 273; Dann, 'Licenced Parties', p. 31.
137. Surrour, *op. cit.*, p. 49; Ibn Najaf, *op. cit.*, pp. 28–9.
138. M. B. al-Sadr, *Iqtisaduna* (Beirut: Dar al-Ta'aruf, 1991); al-Husaini, *al-Imam al-Shahid*, pp. 163–9; Mallat, *The Renewal of Islamic Law*, pp. 111–12, 142–3; al-Sadr, *Iqtisaduna*, pp. 37–47; al-Husaini, *al-Imam al-Shahid*, pp. 159–62; Mallat, *The Renewal of Islamic Law*, pp. 116–23, 146–8; Fadlallah, *al-Diyar*, p. 4.
139. M. H. Fadlallah, *Uslub al-Da'wa fi al-Qur'an* (Beirut: Dar al-Malak, 5th edn, 1994), p. 9. In the second edition of the above work, Fadlallah states that there existed at the time a pressing need for such expositions as his own, since there had previously been no book available dealing systematically and objectively with the subject.
140. *Ibid.*, pp. 34–6, 385.
141. *Ibid.*, pp. 87–9, 96–8, 110–13. According to an Islamic periodical, Shaw had asserted, during discussion with a certain Shaykh Abdul 'Alim al-Saddiqi, that 'Islam had spread by the sword'. *al-Muslimoon*, no. 12, 1383 AH, p. 147. Cited in Fadlallah, *Usloub al-Da'wa*, p. 88.
142. *Ibid.*, pp. 14, 18–20, 23, 26, 45–9.
143. *Ibid.*, pp. 91–6, 99–100, 109. Fadlallah's conception of jihad as an instrument of *Da'wa* was congruent with the view expounded by other Islamist 'ulama of this period. One of those influential scholars was Ayatollah Murtada Mutahhari. In the early 1960s,

around the same time that Fadlallah wrote the above-mentioned work, Mutahhari delivered a series of lectures in Iran on the subject which were compiled into a booklet. In it, Mutahhari stated that if a regime sets up a barrier to the call of truth, it is then permissible to fight against it until that obstacle is removed. In common with Fadlallah, Mutahhari classified this form of jihad as defensive. M. Mutahhari, *Jihad: The Holy War Idea and its Legitimacy in the Quran* (Tehran, Islamic Propagation Organisation, 1981), p. 63.

144. *Ibid.*, pp. 88–92, 94–100, 102–4.
145. *Ibid.*, pp. 69–71, 114. Sayyid Qutb was the radical theoretician of Egypt's al-Ikhwan al-Muslimun and author of the influential multi-volume commentary on the Qur'an, whose first edition was published in the late 1950s.
146. Mallat, 'Religious Militancy', p. 707.
147. *Ibid.*, pp. 707–14. al-Sadr's first work, entitled *Fadak fi al-Tarikh* [Fadak in history], written in 1955, was sharply particularistic. It dealt with the sensitive issue of the right of Fatima, daughter of the Prophet and wife of Imam Ali, to a bequest following the death of the Prophet.
148. al-Mu'min, *op. cit.*, p. 47; A. R. Hasan, *op. cit.*, p. 291; M. B. al-Nasiri, 'al-Tahhurruk al-Islami al-Mu'asir fi al-Iraq' (The Contemporary Islamic Movement in Iraq) *al-Fikr al-Jadid*, no.2 (June 1992), p. 40. Sources are at variance as to the precise date on which the first issue of *al-Adwa'* was published. According to Ali al-Mu'min and Muhammad Baqer al-Nasiri, the journal was launched in 1959. This contrasts with the date of 10 June 1960 cited by Muhammad al-Husayni. This inconsitency can be attributed to the fact that the sources may have been based either on the commencement of *al-Adwa'* as a fortnightly unregistered pamphlet, or on its subsequent publication as a legalised monthly periodical.
149. Surrour, *op. cit.*, p. 49; al-Husaini, *al-Imam al-Shahid* p. 249; Ibn Najafi, *op. cit.*, pp. 28–9; Fadlallah, 'Taqdim', *al-Imam al-Shahid*, p. 6; al-Husaini, *al-Imam al-Shahid*, pp. 249, 252; A. R. Hasan, *op. cit.*, p. 325, note 10; Surrour, *op. cit.*, p. 49; 'Maraya al-Ahdath'.
150. Fadlallah's first three editorials, in chronological order, were the following: 'Min Wahy al-Ghadir', [From the inspiration of Ghadir]; 'Islamuna Taharrur' [Our Islam is liberation; originally written in 1956]; and "Indama Yuktabu Tarikh al-Hadarah' [When the history of civilisation is written; published in June 1960]. The first editorial was a piece of prose, while the other two were poetic compositions. Fadlallah, *Qasa'id lil-Islam*, pp. 91–4; Fadlallah, *al-Mashrou' al-Hadari*, p. 58.
151. M. H. Fadlallah, *Qadayana 'ala Daw' al-Islam* [Our Affairs in the Light of Islam] (Beirut: Dar al-Zahra, 6th edn, 1985), pp. 16–18. The monograph, which by 1985 had reached its sixth enlarged edition, includes new chapters of speeches and lectures delivered by Fadlallah at various occasions during the 1970s in Lebanon.
152. Mallat, 'Muhammad Baqer al-Sadr', p. 254; Mallat, *The Renewal of Islamic Law*, p. 16; Fadlallah, 'Taqdim', *Risalatuna*, pp. 9–19; A. R. Hasan, *op. cit.* ., p. 325, note 10.
153. I. Fadlallah, *op. cit.*, p. 57; al-Mu'min, *op. cit.*, p. 47; Abu Ali, *al-Harakah al-Islamiyya fi al-Iraq*, p. 58.
154. The work was first published in Beirut in 1980, and then expanded and reprinted in 1991. M. H. Fadlallah, *Afaq Islamiyya* [Islamic horizons] (Beirut: Dar al-Zahra, 2nd. edn, 1991); pp. 15–19, 20–59.
155. Fadlallah, *Qadayana*, pp. 102–4, 101–10. The above-cited article appeared in *al-Adwa'* in 1964.

156. *Ibid.*, p. 105. The key verb *yahkumu* can be rendered as either 'judge' or 'govern', with Islamists insisting on the latter.
157. *Ibid.*, pp. 239–40.
158. *Ibid.*, p. 242.
159. *Ibid.*, pp. 21–31. The article is entitled 'al-'Amal Awwalun' (Action First).
160. *Ibid.*, p. 30
161. *Ibid.*, pp. 26, 31.
162. al-Sadr, *Risalatuna*, p. 21.
163. *Ibid.*, p. 24.
164. In those editorials, al-Sadr underscored the intrinsic importance of *Da'wa* activity in Islam, highlighted the intimate relationship between thought and sentiment, conceived Islam as an ideology, and underscored the centrality of unity in Islam. al-Sadr, *Risalatuna*, pp. 27–61.
165. The poems in the latter work were essentially personal, emotive compositions that vividly reflected the aspiring *'alim's* restless youth and inquisitive mind in his quest for meaning in a turbulent age (Fadlallah, *'Ala Shati' al-Wujdan*). In his composition entitled *'Uodu il al-Islam* (Return to Islam), which was published in 1960 in *al-Adwa'*, Fadlallah stated that his purpose in writing this poetic piece was as a response to those who contended that the role of religion 'has lapsed and its goals have outlived their purpose, and who [presumably an allusion to communists] assert that religion had lived [vibrantly] for a designated period in history but that with time it has become antiquated. What have we accomplished from [emulating Western] civilisation?' Fadlallah's emphatic answer: we have lost our true identity and proper sense of purpose. He concludes by exhorting wayward and sceptical Muslims to return wholeheartedly to Islam. Fadlallah, *Qasa'id*, pp. 107–8.
166. Martin, 'Une Grande Figure', p. 123.
167. Mallat, *The Renewal of Islamic Law*, p. 9. In a poetic composition entitled *Alimu al-Dajjij* (The World of Clamour), published in *al-Adwa'* on 20 February 1960, Fadlulah criticised those [presumably conservative apolitical] 'circles who have raised unwarranted suspicions about the motives and goals' of Islamic activists and sought to dicredit their mission. He reaffirmed that the 'noble struggle for the sake of the faith will continue, in spite of the forces of darkness positioned on our path. Their rancour and bitterness will not, regardless of how much suffering and torment we endure, affect our determination to fulfil our divinely enjoined mission...' Fadlallah, *Qasa'id*, p. 87.
168. Ja'far, *op. cit.*, p. 473; al-Husaini, *al-Imam al-Shahid*, pp. 251–2; al-'Askari, 'al-Harakah al-Islamiyyah', p. 243.
169. al-Husaini, *al-Imam al-Shahid*, pp. 251–2. Another factor that soured relations between the conservatives and the radicals was the publication in *al-Adwa'* in 1961 of a letter by Sayyid al-Hakim who, at the behest of Shaykh Mahmud Shaltut (the rector of Cairo's celebrated al-Azhar University), corresponded with his Iranian counterpart, Sayyid Muhammad Behbihani, who maintained close ties to the royal court, in which he deplored the Shah's recent resolve to establish formal diplomatic relations with Israel, and exhorted the latter to exert pressure on the Iranian monarch to change his decision (*ibid.*, al-Askari, 'al-Harakah al-Islamiyya', pp. 242–3).
170. al-Siraj, *op. cit.*, pp. 118–20; Fadlallah, 'Shahid al-Islam', p. 32; M. H. Fadlallah, *Ma' al-Hikmah fi Khatt al-Islam* (Beirut: al-Dar al-Islamiyyah, 1985), p. 186; Fadlallah, 'Taqdim', *Risalatuna*, pp. 16–17.
171. *Ibid.*, pp. 186–7; Fadlallah, 'Taqdim', *Risalatuna*, pp. 16–17. The first drafts of

Risalatuna were examined and commented on by al-Sadr prior to its publication. According to Fadlulah, following the resignation of his colleague, *Kalimatuna* (the second editorial) replaced *Risalatuna* as the leading article in *al-Adwa'*, which Fadlallah continued to write until 1966.

172. Fadlallah, 'Taqdim', *Risalatuna*, p. 17; Fadlallah, 'Taqdim', *al-Imam al-Shahid*, p. 7; Fadlallah, 'Shahid al-Islam', p. 32.
173. al-Nizari, *op. cit.*, pp. 36–8, 40–1; al-Mu'min, *op. cit.*, p. 52; al-Husaini, 'al-Imam al-Sadr', p. 89; Aziz, *op. cit.*, p. 210; Ja'far, *op. cit.*, p. 474; al-Nizari, *op. cit.*, p. 37; Ibrahim, *op. cit.*, p. 300; Aziz, *op. cit.*, p. 210.
174. al-Nizari, *op. cit.*, p. 41; al-Mu'min, *op. cit.*, p. 52; al-Nizari, *op. cit.*, pp. 32–44, 161–2; Ibrahim, *op. cit.*, p. 244; Ibrahim, *op. cit.*, p. 280, note 59; al-Nizari, *op. cit.*, pp. 42–6; Wiley, *op. cit.*, p. 108; Ibrahim, *op. cit.*, p. 300; al-Mu'min, *op. cit.*, p. 52; Wiley, *op. cit.*, pp. 110–11.
175. Batatu, *op. cit.*, pp. 942, 945-46, 965; Dann, *op. cit.*, p. 289; Batatu, *op. cit.*, p. 951; Dann, *op. cit.*, p. 289; Batatu, *op. cit.*, p. 951; Dann, *op. cit.*, p. 289.
176. Dann, *op. cit.*, p. 362; Marr, *op. cit.*, p. 183; Dann, *op. cit.*, pp. 363, 368–71; Batatu, *op. cit.*, pp. 974–82; Marr, *op. cit.*, p. 185; Khadduri, *op. cit.*, pp. 191–5. The president himself was arrested, tried by a kangaroo court, and promptly executed.
177. Batatu, *op. cit.*, p. 983; Ibrahim, *op. cit.*, p. 257; Martin, *Les Chi'ites d'Irak*, p. 153; Batatu, *op. cit.*, p. 983; Ibrahim, *op. cit.*, p. 257.
178. Batatu, *op. cit.*, pp. 987–8; Khadduri, *op. cit.*, p. 198; Farouk-Sluglett, *op. cit.*, pp. 85–6.
179. al-Siraj, *op. cit.*, p. 229; Aziz, *op. cit.*, p. 211; al-Siraj, *op. cit.*, p. 229.
180. *Ibid*; al-Mu'min, *op. cit.*, pp. 59–60; Ibrahim, *op. cit.*, p. 292; al-Mu'min, *op. cit.*, p. 59; Wiley, *op. cit.*, p. 39.
181. Batatu, *op. cit.*, pp. 1,017–24; Khadduri, *op. cit.*, pp. 201–4; Farouk-Sluglett, *op. cit.*, pp. 91–3.
182. Batatu, *op. cit.*, pp. 1,030–1; Khadduri, *op. cit.*, p. 215; Farouk-Sluglett, *op. cit.*, p. 93. Between November 1963 and February 1964, senior Ba'thist officials, both civilian and military, were eased out of power through subtle demotions and transfers.
183. Batatu, *op. cit.*, p. 1,031.
184. Khadduri, *op. cit.*, pp. 220–2, 234; Batatu, *op. cit.*, p. 1,031.
185. Batatu, *op. cit.*, pp. 1,028–9; Khadduri, *op. cit.*, p. 221; al-Mu'min, *op. cit.*, p. 61; A. Baram, 'The Radical Shi'ite Opposition Movements in Iraq', in E. Sivan and M. Friedman (eds), *Religious Radicalism and Politics in the Middle East* (Albany: State University of New York Press, 1990), p. 137.
186. Wiley, *op. cit.*, pp. 40–1; Ja'far, *op. cit.*, p. 476; Ibrahim, *op. cit.*, p. 295.
187. Ibn Najaf, *op. cit.*, pp. 82, 85–6; Ibrahim, *op. cit.*, p. 296; al-'Alawi, *op. cit.*, p. 225.
188. al-Mu'min, *op. cit.*, p. 61; al-Siraj, *op. cit.*, p. 239; al-Mu'min, *op. cit.*, p. 62; al-Siraj, *op. cit.*, pp. 239–40; Ja'far, *op. cit.*, p. 476.
189. Ibrahim, *op. cit.*, p. 504; al-Nizari, *op. cit.*, pp. 43–4; Ibrahim, *op. cit.*, p. 293; Wiley, *op. cit.*, pp. 108, 110.
190. *Ibid.*, p. 40; al-Nizari, *op. cit.*, pp. 43–4; Wiley, *op. cit.*, pp. 40–1; Ja'far, *op. cit.*, p. 476.
191. Ja'far, *op. cit.*, p. 476; Baram, 'Two Roads', pp. 546–7; al-Bahadli, *op. cit.*, p. 342; Ibn Najaf, *op. cit.*, pp. 79–80.
192. Aziz, *op. cit.*, pp. 210–11; al-Bahadli, *op. cit.*, pp. 342–3; Ibn Najaf, *op. cit.*, p. 57; Aziz, *op. cit.*, p. 210; al-Bahadli, *op. cit.*, pp. 343–7.

193. al-Mu'min, *op. cit.*, p. 66; al-Nizari, *op. cit.*, p. 87; Wiley, *op. cit.*, p. 40.
194. Fadlallah, *Afaq Islamiyyah*, pp. 28–43.
195. *Ibid*, pp. 33–5.
196. *Ibid.*, pp. 38, 40–43.
197. *Ibid.*, pp. 218–24.
198. al-Mu'min, *op. cit.*, p. 67; Ja'far, *op. cit.*, p. 67; al-Mu'min, *op. cit.*, p. 67; Ja'far, *op. cit.*, p. 512, note 34; Ibn Najaf, *op. cit.*, p. 8.
199. Baram, 'Two Roads', p. 36; S. al-Hadidi, *al-Tahhaddi al-Kabir* (The Great Challenge) (London: Dar al-Rafid, 1994), p. 46.
200. Baram, 'The Radical *Shi'ite*', p. 36; Wiley, *op. cit.*, pp. 37, 78, 83; al-Hadi, *op. cit.*, p. 46; al-Mu'min, *op. cit.*, p.223; A. Baram, 'From Radicalism to Radical Pragmatism', J. Piscatori (ed.), *Islamic Fundamentalism and the Gulf Crisis* (Chicago: American Academy of Arts and Sciences, 1991), p. 36. While sources close to Hizb al-Da'wa adamantly deny that its off-shoot organisation had existed in the 1960s, members of the organisation assert that it was formed in the early 1960s, and that until the mid-1970s, when it began its armed struggle against the ruling Ba'th Party, it had focused on clandestine organisational and political activity. Be that as it may, there is strong reason to believe that the organisation did exist in the 1960s, although with a restricted, localised membership and influence. Moreover, during the formative phase of its development, the Islamic Action Organisation had not yet assumed the character of a well structured, cohesive political entity. Far from it – the organisation represented a coalescence of like-minded young scholar–activists, grouped loosely around the founding and guiding figure of Sayyid Muhammad al-Shirazi.
201. M. al-Allousi, *Likay la Yatakarrar al-Khata* (So the the Error is not Repeated) (n.pl.: n.p., 1991), p. 173.
202. *Ibid.*, pp. 172–4.
203. The article's title was based on an oft-quoted Prophetic *hadith*: 'Whoseoever does not concern himself with the affairs of Muslims is not a Muslim.' (Fadlallah, *Afaq Islamiyya*, pp. 68–9.)
204. *Ibid.*, pp. 68–9, 84–5.
205. *Ibid.*, pp. 87–8.
206. M. A. Montazam, *Life and Times of Ayatollah Khomeini* (London: Anglo-European Publishers, 1994), pp. 153–4; S. Akhavi, *Religion and Politics in Contemporary Iran* (Albany: State University of New York Press, 1986), pp. 94–5.
207. S. R. Khomeini, *Islam and Revolution* (Berkeley: Mizan Press, 1981), p. 17; Akhavi, *op. cit.*, p. 98; Montazam, *op. cit.*, p. 150; Khomeini, *op. cit.*, p. 18; Montazam, *op. cit.*, pp. 154–5; Akhavi, *op. cit.*, p. 98; Montazam, *op. cit.*, pp. 154–5; Floor, 'The Revolutionary Character', pp. 92–3; Khomeini, *op. cit.*, p.18; Montazam, *op. cit.*, p. 56; Akhavi, *op. cit.*, p. 104.
208. H. al-Dujaili, *al-Fuqaha' Hukkam 'ala al-Muluk* ('Judges preside over the kings' – Beirut: Dar al-Adwa', 1991), p. 230; H. Algar, 'The Oppositional Role of the 'Ulama in Twentieth-Century Iran', in N. Keddie (ed.), *Scholars, Sufis, and Saints* (Berkeley: University of Califonia Press, 1972), p. 249.
209. Algar, *op. cit.*, p. 249; H. Dabashi, 'By What Authority?', *Social Compass*, vol. 36, no. 4 (1989), p. 515.
210. al-Husaini, *op. cit.*, p. 263; Wiley, *op. cit.*, p. 41; al-Mu'min, *op. cit.*, pp. 78–80; al-Husaini, *al-Imam al-Shahid*, pp. 262–3.
211. Ibrahim, *op. cit.*, p. 370; Dabashi, *op. cit.*, pp. 513–14; E. Abrahmian, *Khomeinism* (Berkeley: University of California Press, 1993), p. 22.

212. al-Mu'min, *op. cit.*, p. 65; D. Brumberg, 'Khomeini's Legacy', in R. S. Appleby (ed.), *Spokesmen for the Despised* (Chicago: University of Chicago Press, 1997), p. 30.
213. al-Husaini, *al-Imam al-Shahid*, pp. 261–2; 'Ayatollah al-Sadr', *al-Muntalaq*, no. 10 (July 1979), p. 33; Mallat, *The Renewal of Islamic Law*, p. 51; A. Taheri, *The Spirit of Allah* (London: Hutchinson, 1985), p. 161; Khadduri, *op. cit.*, p. 262; Marr, *op. cit.*, pp. 196–7.
214. 'Personal Interview', 6 March 1996.
215. H. Dabashi, *Theology of Discontent* (New York: New York University Press, 1991), p. 430.
216. Kramer, 'The Oracle of Hizbullah', p. 90; Fadlallah, *al-'Ahd*, no. 425, 14 August 1992.
217. Kramer, *op. cit.*, pp. 90–1.
218. Surrour, *op. cit.*, p. 45; 'author's correspondence with Shaykh Ali Shimie', 10 May 1997.
219. *Ibid.*
220. His successor, Major-General Abdul Rahman 'Aref, was a more congenial and less politically adroit and rigorous leader than his deceased brother. The second 'Aref regime tolerated a whole constellation of political movements, released communist and Ba'thist prisoners, and granted unprecedented freedom for all aspects of political and organisational activitiy. Taking advantage of the political openness and effeverescence was the Islamist movement, with its manifold organisational constituents, which experienced, until the ascension of the Ba'th Party to power in July 1968, an appreciable heightening of its influence and expansion in its membership, as well as a significant broadening of the scope of its activities. Batatu, *op. cit.*, p. 1,063; Marr, *op. cit.*, p. 97; al-Mu'min, *op. cit.*, pp. 67–73; al-Bahadli, *op. cit.*, pp. 398–400.

Chapter Four

1. M. Halawi, *A Lebanon Defied* (Boulder: Westview Press, 1992), p. 50. According to demographic data published by the *al-Nahar* newspaper in April 1956 there were approximately 251,000 Shi'a, comprising some 17.8 per cent of Lebanon's population, making them the third-largest community after the Maronites and the Sunni*s*. However, by 1975 the Shi'a had doubled their share of the country's population, forming the largest confessional community.
2. According to A. R. Norton, by all indices the Shi'ia were the most disadvantaged confessional community in the country. Data for 1971, for instance, indicated that the average Shi'i family's income was 4,500 Lebanese pounds, in comparison with the national average of 6,250 Lebanese pounds, and that they were the most poorly educated; only 50 per cent had schooling, compared to 70 per cent nationwide. Based on government statistics for 1974, South Lebanon, which contained 20 per cent of the country's population, the bulk of its residents being Shi'a, received a mere 0.7 per cent of the state budget. A. R. Norton, 'Harakat Amal', in E. E. Azar et al. (eds), *The Emergence of New Lebanon* (New York: Praeger, 1984), pp. 163–4.
3. Halawi, *op. cit.*, p. 90.
4. W. Shararah, *Dawlat Hizb al-Allah* [The State of the 'Party of God'] (Beirut: Dar al-Nahar, 1997), pp. 23–9, 42; M. J. Mughniyyah, *al-Wadaw al-Hadar fi Jabal 'Amil, 1946-1966* [The Current Situation in Jabal 'Amil] (Sidon: Matba'at al-'Irfan, n.d.), pp. 58–9.

5. Halawi, *op. cit.*, pp. 83–7; A. R. Norton, Amal *and the Shi'a* (Austin: University of Texas Press, 1988), p. 15.
6. The PLO used South Lebanon as a major staging point for the launching of fedayeen operations against enemy personnel and installations inside Israel – incursions which regularly precipitated Israeli military attacks on guerilla and (mostly Shi'i) civilian targets, resulting in a constant stream of internal refugees fleeing to the relative safety of the north. A fuller discussion of the impact of the Palestinian resistance movement on the Shi'i community will be presented later in the chapter.
7. *Ibid.*, pp. 51–2, 68. Between 1960 and 1970, the agricultural sector shrank from 20 per cent to less than 9 per cent, while the proportion of the country's active population working in agriculture had diminished substantially, from 48.9 per cent in 1959 to 17 per cent in 1974. As a result, between 1960 and 1971, approximately half of Lebanon's Shi'i residents had migrated from the south and the Bekaa and settled in Beirut. According to data provided by Norton (*Amal*, p. 23), by 1974 40 per cent of the predominantly Shi'i inhabitants of the south and 25 per cent of the population of the Bekaa had migrated, principally to Beirut.
8. Halawi, *op. cit.*, p. 74; Norton, *Amal*, p.23.
9. I. M. al-Sadr, *Minbar wa Mihrab* [Pulpit and niche] (Beirut: Dar al-Hawra',1987), p. 187; H. Fadlallah, *Fikr al-Imam Musa al-Sadr al-Siyyasi wa al-Islahi* [The political and reformist thought of Imam Musa al-Sadr] (Beirut: Dar al-Hadi, 1997), p. 35; A. R. Norton, 'Musa al-Sadr', in A. Rahnema (ed.) *Pioneers of Islamic Revival* (London: Zed Books, 1994), p. 195; F. Ajami, *The Vanished Imam* (Ithaca: Cornell University Press, 1986), p. 32. H. Fadlallah, *op. cit.*, pp. 34–5; Ajami, *op. cit.*, p. 34.
10. al-Sadr, *op. cit.*, p. 187; H. Fadlallah, *op. cit.*, pp. 34–5; Ajami, *op. cit.*, pp. 33–4. Sayyid al-Sadr's great-grandfather, Sayyid Saalah Sharaf al-Din al-Sadr, was born in the village of Shahour in 1710, and became a notable *'alim* in the Tyre district. He was subsequently, due to Ottoman persecution, forced to flee with his family to Iraq, and settled in Najaf, where his sons embarked on traditional religious study. One of his sons, Sayyid Sadr al-Din, who had attained the rank of *mujtahid*, later migrated to Iran. Of his five sons, all of whom were to become 'ulama, the most distinguished was Sayyid Isma'il al-Sadr (Sayyid al-Sadr's grandfather), who was born in Isfahan, and studied and taught in Najaf, where he rose through the ranks of the 'ulama establishment to become the *Marja' al-Taqlid al-Mutlaq* (the supreme source of juridical emulation) for the Shi'i faithful. He died in 1919. He fathered four sons, again all religious scholars, including Sayyid al-Sadr's father, Sayyid Sadr al-Din, who was to migrate to Iran, where he took up residence in Qom and taught in its seminaries, until his death in 1953 or 1954.
11. H. Fadlallah, *op. cit.*, p. 35; H. M. Gharbieh, 'Political Awareness of the Shi'ites in Lebanon' (Durham: PhD, 1996), p.138; H. Fadlallah, *op. cit.*, pp. 35–6; Halawi, *op. cit.*, p. 126; H. Fadlallah, *op. cit.*, p. 36; Halawi, *op. cit.*, p. 126; Gharbieh, *op. cit.*, p. 139; S. Shapira, 'The Imam Musa al-Sadr', *The Jerusalem Quarterly* 44 (Fall 1987), p. 123; H. Fadlallah, *op. cit.*, p. 36; Ajami, *op. cit.*, p. 45; Norton, 'Musa al-Sadr', p. 195.
12. *al-Diyar*, 12 January 1992; *al-Sharq al-Awsat*, May–June 1996; *Magazine* (1595) 27 February 1988.
13. H. Fadlallah, *op. cit.*, pp. 36–7; Ajami, *op. cit.*, pp. 42–3; Halawi, *op. cit.*, p. 121; *al-Shira'*, *al-Harakat al-Islamiyyah fi Lubnan* [The Islamic Movements in Lebanon] (Beirut: no publisher, n.d.), p. 30; Ajami, *op. cit.*, p. 44; Shapira, *op. cit.*, p. 123; Gharbieh, *op. cit.*, pp. 139–44; Norton, 'Musa al-Sadr', pp. 195–6; Ajami, *op. cit.*, p. 45.

14. Gharbieh, *op. cit.*, pp. 143–4.
15. Ajami, *op. cit.*, p. 87; Halawi, *op. cit.*, p. 61.
16. Ajami, *op. cit.*, p. 86.
17. Halawi, *op. cit.*, p. 135; al-Sadr, *op. cit.*, p.10; al-Sadr, *op. cit.*, pp. 10–13.
18. Halawi, *op. cit.*, p. 136. The society was also responsible for organising religious festivals and cultural carnivals, as well as administering the community's *waqf* (inalienable charitable foundations), and managing the affairs of mosques and *husaiyniyyat*; al-Sadr, *op. cit.*, p. 13.
19. H. Fadlallah, *op. cit.*, p. 117; al-Sadr, *op. cit.*, p. 13; Halawi, *op. cit.*, p. 136; al-Sadr, *op. cit.*, p. 13; Halawi, *op. cit.*, p. 136; Shapira, *op. cit.*, p. 124.
20. Halawi, *op. cit.*, p. 136; al-Sadr, *op. cit.*, pp. 37–51, 59; Halawi, *op. cit.*, p. 137.
21. S. Nasr, 'Les Formes de Regroupement Traditionnel dans la Societe de Beyrouth', in S. Nasr (ed.), *L'Espace Social de la Ville Arabe* (Paris: Maisonneuve et Larouse, 1979), pp. 155–6 [henceforth cited as S. Nasr, 'Les Formes']; S. Husseini, 'La Redistribution des Communautes Chi'ite et Sunnite dans le Grande-Beyrouth', in M. F. Davie (ed.), *Beyrouth: Regards Croises* (Tours: URBAMA, 1997), p. 210.
22. Eight localities make up the eastern suburbs of Beirut: Bourj Hammoud, Sin el-Fil, Dekouneh, Mkalles, Baochriye, Jdeidah, Fanar and Zalqa. S. Nasr and M. Nasr, 'Morphologie Sociale de la Banlieue-Est de Beyrouth', *Maghreb-Machrek*, no. 73 (July–September 1976) [henceforth cited as S. Nasr, 'Morphologie'], p. 78.
23. S. Nasr, 'Morphologie', pp. 81–2; al-Husseini, *op. cit.*, p. 210; S. Nasr 'Les Formes', p. 151. After the Shi'a, the next-largest community were the Maronites, who numbered 74,000 and accounted for 25 per cent of the total population, followed by the Armenians, numbering between 55,000 and 70,000 individuals.
24. Bourj Hammoud straddles the vital road link between Christian east Beirut and the Maronite hinterland. It was bounded on the east by the Beirut river, on the south and south-west by Sin el Fil and Dekouanah, on the west by Jdaideh and Baouchriye, and on the north by the Mediterranean Sea.
25. J. Suad, 'Politicisation of Religious Sects in Bourj Hammoud' (Columbia University: PhD, 1975), pp. 43, 46. Situated 5km east of Beirut CBD [Central Business District], Bourj Hammoud was at the onset of World War One a swampy farming locality, where cultivated land was owned by Maronites, the predominant local residents, who numbered between 1,000 and 2,000 persons.
26. *Ibid.*, pp. 46, 62, 64. The second wave of refugees began in 1937, precipitated by the French transfer of the former Ottoman province of Alexandretta to Republican Turkey, while the third wave occurred in the aftermath of the Palestine War.
27. Nasr, 'Morphologie', p. 82; Joseph, *op. cit.*, p. 106. Sources cited by the latter put the number of Shi'i residents in the locality in the early 1970s anywhere between 40,000 and 80,000. The Armenians comprised the second-largest community, with 40,000 members, or 30 per cent of Bourj Hammoud's population.
28. *Ibid.*, p. 80.
29. Suad, *op. cit.*, p. 106; S. Nasr, 'Beyrouth et le Conflit Libanaise', in G. Mutin and J. Metral (eds), *Politiques Urbaines dans le Monde Arabe* (Lyon: Maison de l'Orient Mediterranean, 1984), p. 296. The author estimates the number of Shi'i residents in the quarter in the mid-1970s as 65,000. According to A. Rieck, Nab'a's pre-war population was 100,000 – Rieck, *Die Schiiten und der Kampf um den Libanon* (Hamburg: Deuttsches Orient-Institut, 1989), p. 219.
30. Nasr, 'Morphologie', p. 78; Suad, *op. cit.*, p. 104; Suad, *op. cit.*, p. 107; *ibid.*, pp. 46, 107.

31. *Ibid.*, p. 74–5. Traditionally skilled craftsmen, Armenians had, during this period, dominated the country's lucrative leather manufacturing enterprise, as well as all but monopolising the jewellery industry.
32. T. Hanf, *Co-existence in Wartime Lebanon* (London: I. B. Tauris, 1993), pp. 201–2; Nasr, 'Morphologie', p. 85; Suad, *op. cit.*, pp. 110, 179; Hanf, *op. cit.*, p. 201.
33. *Ibid.*, pp. 201–2; H. Fadlallah, *al-Khiyar al-Akhar* [The Other Option] (Beirut: Dar al-Hadi, 1994), p. 84; Nasr, 'Morphologie', p. 80; Suad, *op. cit.*, p. 106.
34. Suad, *op. cit.*, p. 106; Hanf, *op. cit.*, p. 201.
35. Shararah, *op. cit.*, p. 86, p. 98 note 1; M. H. Fadlallah [interview], *al-Sayyaad* , May 1986.
36. Shararah, *op. cit.*, p. 98, note 1; Fadlallah, *al-Sayyaad.* Under the patronage of Muhammad Husayn's father, Sayyid Abdul Ra'uf Fadlallah, who had returned to settle in Lebanon in 1955, an Islamic centre was built, which overtime comprised a *husayniyyah*, a mosque and a general library; Fadlallah, NBN Television interview, part 2, 18 April 2004.
37. Shararah, *op. cit.,* p. 98, note 1. In accordance with Shi'i legal tradition, as a Sayyid (one who can trace his lineage to the Prophet Muhammad through his Aliid household), Fadlallah was entitled to receive a tithe; that is, half of *al-khums.*
38. Fadlallah, *al-Sayyaad.*
39. H. Srour, *al-'Allamah Fadlallah wa Tahaddi al-Mumnu'* [The most learned, Fadlallah and the forbidden defiance] (Beirut: Dar al-Malaak, 1992), p.69. According to Fadlallah's recollections, Nab'a was completely devoid of medical clinics, schools and general municipal services.
40. Suad, *op. cit.*, p. 108; A. H. Schbley, 'Religious Resurgence and Religious Terrorism', (PhD, University of North Texas, 1988), p. 108; Suad, *op. cit.*, pp. 107–8, 237.
41. *Ibid.*, pp. 108–9.
42. Shararah, *op. cit.*, p. 89; H. Fadlallah, *op. cit.*, p. 84; Srour, *op. cit.*, p. 56.
43. *Ibid.*, pp. 54, 56.
44. *Ibid.*, p. 55.
45. H. Sabra, "An al-Sahwa al-Islamiyyah fi Lubnan' [On the Islamic Awakening in Lebanon], in *Nadwat al-'Alam al-Thalith, al-Harakat al-Islamiyyah al-Mu'asirah fi al-Watan al-'Arabi* (Beirut: Markaz Dirasat al-Wahdah al-Islamiyyah, 1987), p. 172.
46. Shararah, *op. cit.*, p. 71; Srour, *op. cit.*, p. 55; H. Fadlallah, *op. cit.*, p. 38.
47. Srour, *op. cit.*, p. 55; M. H. Fadlallah, televised interview, *al-Manar* station, 2 Janary 1995; H. Fadlallah, *op. cit.*, p. 38; S. Shapira, 'The Origins of Hizbullah', *Jerusalem Quarterly*, no. 46 (1988), pp. 117, 128–9.
48. Shararah, *op. cit.*, pp. 87–8.
49. *Ibid.*; Shapira, *op. cit.*, pp. 116, 126–7; Shararah, *op. cit.*, p. 87; Shapira, *op. cit.*, pp. 126–7; Rieck, *op. cit.*, p. 605.
50. Shararah, *op. cit.*, pp. 72, 77. According to Suad (*op. cit.*, pp. 237–8), the mosque was poorly attended even during congregational prayer; Ajami, *op. cit.*, p. 214.
51. Srour, *op. cit.*, p. 56.
52. Rieck, *op. cit.*, p. 219; S. Nasr and M. Nasr, *op. cit.*, p. 82. In the two most populous Maronite suburbs of Sin el-Fil and Dekouanah, Shi'i residents constituted sizeable minorities, amounting to 25.6 per cent and 18.3 per cent of their respective populations.
53. Srour, *op. cit.*, pp. 55, 61.
54. *Ibid.*, pp. 55, 61–3.

55. Even prior to 1970–1, when an armed insurrection by Palestinian resistance organisations based in Jordan was crushed by King Hussein's regular army, resulting in the eviction of thousands of Palestinian fighters from camps in the kingdom and their relocation to South Lebanon, armed border clashes had taken place in South Lebanon. What commenced with the Palestinian shelling of a kibbutz inside Israel, and was soon answered by retaliatory Israeli shelling, had by May expanded to involve artillery exchanges between units of the Lebanese and Israeli armies. On 14 June 1968 a South Lebanese village was shelled by Israeli gunners, leaving fifty-six civilians wounded. The skirmishes foreshadowed a marked escalation in the conflict. In early May 1970, an Israeli force of 2,000 ground troops and 100 tanks invaded south Lebanon in pursuit of Palestinian guerrillas. The incursion resulted in the deaths of nine Lebanese civilians and the wounding of nineteen others. The town of Bint Jbail and its hinterland were in the process occupied for thirty-six hours, resulting in the displacement of between 15,000 and 30,000 villagers. Later that month, Israeli forces retaliated against a Palestinian attack on an Israeli bus by once again shelling border villages, leaving twenty civilians dead and forty others wounded. By the end of May, 50,000 southerners – mostly Shi'a – were forced to flee from thirty villages. Halawi, *op. cit.*, pp. 143–4; Hanf, *op. cit.*, pp. 164–8; R. Brynen, *Sanctuary and Survival* (London: Pinter, 1990), pp. 56, 59.
56. Srour, *op. cit.*, pp. 62–3; M. H. Fadlallah, *Mafahim Islamiyya 'Ammah* [General Islamic Concepts] (Beirut: Dar al-Zahra', 1991), p. 9.
57. Fadlallah, *Mafahim*, pp. 7–10.
58. *Ibid.*, pp. 9–10.
59. Fadlallah, *Qadayana 'ala Daw' al-Islam*, pp. 296–8, 302–4.
60. *Ibid.*, pp. 305–7.
61. Fadlallah, *Mafahim*, pp. 14–16, 36.
62. *Ibid.*, pp. 43–5.
63. *Ibid.*, pp. 46–7. To substantiate that theory, Fadlallah cites Chapter 65, Verse 6 of the Qur'an.
64. *Ibid.*, pp. 47–51.
65. *Ibid.* pp. 47–51, 356–7.
66. *Ibid.*, pp. 257–60.
67. *Ibid.*, pp. 103–4.
68. *Ibid.*, p. 104.
69. *Ibid.*
70. *Ibid.*, pp. 112–13. He quotes Chapter Three, Verses 97–100.
71. *Ibid.* He cites Chapter Three, Verses 138–39.
72. *Ibid.*, pp. 107–14.
73. *Ibid.*, pp. 111–12.
74. Karl Marx held that 'Religion is ... the imaginary reality. Thus the struggle against religion is indirectly the struggle against that world whose spiritual aroma is religion ... Religion is the opium of the people. The real happiness of the people requires the abolition of religion, which is their illusionary happiness.' Statement quoted by L. Kolakowski, *Main Currents of Marxism. 1: The Founders* (Oxford: Oxford University Press, 1981), pp. 128–9.
75. Fadlallah, *Mafahim*, pp. 246–7.
76. *Ibid.*, pp. 247–8. According to Engels, 'the first gods arose through the personification of natural forces and, as religion developed, assumed more and more an extra-mundane form'. Quoted by Kolakowski, *op. cit.*, p. 398.

77. Fadlallah, *Mafahim*, pp. 252–6.
78. Fadlallah, *al-Diyyar*, 12 January 1992; Fadlallah interview, NBN Television, part 3, 25 April 2004; Gharbieh, *op. cit.*, p. 151. Born in 1904 in the village of Tayr Dibba in the district of Tyre, Shaykh Mughniyyah, who was orphaned at the age of ten, was forced to live in severe poverty. Penniless and destitute, he journeyed on foot to Beirut, where he survived precariously on street hawking. In 1925 he travelled to Najaf to pursue religious learning. After eleven years of study he returned to Lebanon in 1936, where, following the death of his brother, he became imam of the mosque in the South Lebanese village of Ma'rakah. In 1948 or 1949 he was appointed judge at the Higher *Ja'fari* Shi'i Court in Beirut, and subsequently assumed the post of President of the court; a position which he held until 1956, when he was forced to resign owing to pressure brought to bear on the Prime Minister by the Shi'i parliamentarians aligned to the feudal lords, who accused the cleric of being a communist. A. H. Mughniyyah (ed.), *Tajarab Muhammad Jawwad Mughniyyah* [The Experiences of Muhammad Jawad Mughniyyah] (Beirut: Dar al-Jawwad, 1980), pp. 23–8, 36, 81, 99, 105; Gharbieh, *op. cit.*, pp. 147–8; Mallat, *Shi'i Thought*, pp. 16–18.
79. Gharbieh, *op. cit.*, p. 148; Mallat, *op. cit.*, pp. 16–17; Srour, *op. cit.*, pp. 62–3.
80. Gharbieh, *op. cit.*, p. 151. The delegation comprised Sayyid al-Hakim's two sons, al-Mahdi and al-Hadi, as well as Muhammad Bahr al-Uloum, a respected *'alim.*
81. *Ibid.* There were other 'ulama who voiced their opposition to Sayyid al-Sadr; but Shaykh Mughniyyah was the most vociferous and relentless.
82. *Ibid.*; *al-Diyyar*, *op. cit.*; Gharbieh, *op. cit.*, p. 151; Fadlallah, *al-Diyyar*.
83. *al-Shira'*, *op. cit.*, p. 32; al-Sadr, *op. cit.*, pp. 87–92;
84. *al-Shira'*, *op. cit.*, p. 53. Until the official establishment of the Higher Islamic Shi'i Council in 1969, matters pertaining to Shi'i personal status, religious education and administration of *waqf* (charitable foundations) were administered by the Majlis al-Islami al-Shari' al-'Ala' (Supreme Official Islamic Council), which was presided over by the Mufti of the Republic; Gharbieh, *op. cit.*, p. 185; Halawi, op. cit., p. 138. During the mid-1950s, three separate attempts were made to establish a Shi'i council; all, for different reasons, were unsuccessful (Halawi, *op. cit.*, p. 139).
85. Gharbieh, *op. cit.*, p. 185.
86. Halawi, *op. cit.*, pp. 140–1; Shapira, *op. cit.*, p. 127; *al-Shira'*, *op. cit.*, p. 56; Ajami, *op. cit.*, p. 114.
87. Ajami, *op. cit.*, p. 117. On the other end of the spectrum, the pan-Arabists viewed the Council as a scheme devised by foreign regional powers – namely Iran – with the aim of exploiting the body in order to further its national interests among the Shi'a of Lebanon, at the expense of Egypt under President Nasser (Srour, *op. cit.*, p. 57).
88. *al-Shira'*, *op. cit.*, p. 57; Srour, *op. cit.*, pp. 57–8.
89. *Ibid.*, p. 58; *al-Diyyar*, 12 January 1992; Fadlallah, al-Manar Television interview, 2 January 1995.
90. Ajami, *op. cit.*, p. 117. According to *al-Shira'* and Halawi, of the original 115 members of the council's juridical organ, only fifty-eight attended the convention, of whom fifty-one voted; *al-Shira'*, *op. cit.*, p. 59; Halawi, *op. cit.*, p. 142. According to the latter source, the low turnout of legislative members stemmed from Sayyid al-Sadr's refusal to heed their call to postpone the election.
91. Srour, *op. cit.*, p. 58; *al-Diyyar*, *op. cit.* Shaykh Shams al-Din was born in Najaf in 1936 into a Shi'i Lebanese 'ulama family. At the age of ten, Shaykh Shams al-Din was left to pursue his studies in al-Najaf by his father, Shaykh Abdulkarim. Like Fadlallah, he

endured much hardship during his childhood and youth, and studied under Najaf's foremost religious scholars and jurists, Sayyid Muhsin al-Hakim and Sayyid Abul-Qasim al-Kho'ie. During the mid-1950s he forged close ties with Sayyid Musa al-Sadr, and later on made a significant intellectual contribution, along with Fadlallah, to the nascent Shi'i Islamist movement in Iraq. He moved and settled in Lebanon in 1969. In 1975, he reluctantly accepted Sayyid al-Sadr's request to run for the vice-presidency of the Higher Islamic Shi'i Council. Thanks to al-Sadr's strong support, he was elected uncontested. F. Musa, *al-Shaykh Muhammad Mahdi Shams al-Din* (Beirut: Dar al-Huda, 1993), pp. 30–49.

92. Srour, *op. cit.*, p. 58.
93. *al-Shira'*, *op. cit.*, p. 33. On 29 March 1975, the executive committee voted overwhelmingly to extend the tenure of the incumbent president until the retirement age of 65.
94. Ajami, *op. cit.*, p. 114; Gharbieh, *op. cit.*, p. 183; Ajami, *op. cit.*, p. 117; Shapira, *op. cit.*, p. 126.
95. Gharbieh, *op. cit.*, p. 187; Ajami, *op. cit.*, p. 117. Traditionally, in the Shi'i world the title was reserved for the Twelve infallible leaders, who were members of the Prophet's Household (*Ahl al-Bayt*).
96. Srour, *op. cit.*, p. 57; H. Fadlallah, *al-Khiyar al-Akhar*, pp. 84–5.
97. Fadlallah, *Afaq Islamiyyah*, pp. 88–9; Norton, *Amal*, p. 41; R. Sayegh, *Too Many Enemies* (London: Zed Books, 1994), p. 167.
98. M. H. Fadlallah [interview], *al-Afkar*, 29 October 1984; Ajami, *op. cit.*, pp. 88–9.
99. Fadlallah, *al-Khiyar*, p. 84; M. H. Fadlallah [interview], *al-Sayyad*, 8 April 1986; Fadlallah, *al-Khiyar*, p. 84; Fadlallah, *al-Sayyad.*
100. Sayyid al-Hakim, who was based in Najaf, permitted – and under certain circumstances enjoined – Shi'i Muslims to join the PLO, and contribute their religious dues and donations to further their cause, 'deemed to be among the most virtuous of deeds and most important of religious duties'. al-Siraj, *al-Imam Muhsin al-Hakim*, pp. 288–92. It was after this official sanction that Sayyid al-Sadr organised a political function, on 17 December 1968, at Beirut International Hotel during the holy Muslim month of Ramadan. The venue was attended by Palestinian resistance leaders, as well as Lebanese political and religious personalities. al-Sadr called for Lebanese solidarity with the Palestinians, and the active participation of citizens in the liberation struggle. He finally called on those present to donate generously to the Palestinian cause. al-Sadr, *op. cit.*, p. 136.
101. Hanf, *op. cit.*, pp. 167–8. In May 1970, Israeli troops invaded South Lebanon, driving Shi'i refugees before their advance, and withdrew only after building fortifications in the area.
102. Brynen, *op. cit.*, p. 51; E. Hagopian and S. Farsoun, *South Lebanon* (Detroit: AAUG, 1978), pp. 15–16; E. Picard, *Lebanon: A Shattered Country* (London: Holmes & Meier, 1996), p. 86; *ibid.*, p. 168; Brynen, *op. cit.*, p. 64.
103. Brynen, *op. cit.*, p. 67. Between 1968 and 1974, about 150,000 Lebanese citizens (one-third of the south's population) had become displaced by the conflict.
104. Ajami, *op. cit.*, p. 162; Norton, *Amal*, p. 43.
105. Brynen, *op. cit.*, p. 47. Despite the dislocation and destruction associated with the conflict, the popularity of the Palestinian movement remained high. According to a 1971 study of Lebanese student attitudes towards the Palestinian armed struggle, the strongest support was among Shi'a, followed by Sunnis. H. Barakat, 'Social Factors

Influencing Attitudes of University Students in Lebanon Towards the Palestinian Resistance Movement', *Journal of Palestine Studies*, vol. 1, no. 1 (Autumn 1971), p. 112.

106. al-Sadr, *op. cit.*, pp. 140, 201, 216; Brynen, *op. cit.*, p. 67; *al-Shira'*, *op. cit.*, p. 34; Gharbieh, *op. cit.*, p. 196.
107. *al-Shira'*, *op. cit.*, p. 35; Halawi, *op. cit.*, p. 144; Gharbieh, *op. cit.*, p. 198. At the height of the strike, al-Sadr addressed a crowd of 50,000 of his followers who had converged on the headquarters of the Supreme Islamic Shi'i Council, in al-Hazimiyya, a south-eastern suburb of Beirut.
108. *al-Shira'*, *op. cit.*, p. 35; Gharbieh, *op. cit.*, p. 199; Norton, 'Harakat Amal', p. 170.
109. Fadlallah, *Mafahim*, p. 135.
110. *Ibid.*, pp. 135–6. Despite al-Sadr's personal misgivings regarding the adverse impact of the Palestinian armed struggle on the security and development of South Lebanon, he regarded Israel as an illegitimate and racist entity. al-Sadr, *op. cit.*, pp. 136–7.
111. Fadlallah, *Mafahim*, p. 135.
112. *Ibid.*, pp. 135–6. Fadlallah's message about the inextricably linked destinies of South Lebanese Palestine would have appealed to the large numbers of young, radicalised Shi'a who joined the Palestinian resistance movement in the 1960s and 1970s; Kramer, 'The Oracle of *Hizbullah*', p. 96.
113. The lecture was delivered four months after an Israeli cross-border incursion. For a period of thirty-six hours the invading force occupied a swathe of small towns and villages in South Lebanon, including Bint Jbail.
114. Fadlallah, *Mafahim*, p. 127–2
115. *Ibid.*, p. 130.
116. *Ibid.*, p. 131.
117. *Ibid.*, p. 135.
118. At a speech delivered on 17 February 1974 to a crowd of 7,000 Shi'a in Bekaa, al-Sadr highlighted the enduring significance of Karbala' by skilfully linking the epic drama of the struggle and martyrdom of Imam Hussein to the present-day ordeal of the Shi'i community's struggle for justice and progress. Halawi, *op. cit.*, pp. 182–3.
119. *Ibid.*, p. 184; Ajami, *op. cit.*, p. 145.
120. Shapira, *op. cit.*, p. 131; *al-Shira'*, *op. cit.*, p. 36. It was two weeks after al-Sadr's landmark speech and mass rally in Baalbek, that Fadlallah and Shaykh Shamsiddin issued a joint statement addressed to the Lebanese government and published in the country's reputed *al-Nahar* newspaper. The two clerics explicitly criticised the government's failure to improve the 'unparalleled wretched' conditions experienced by the majority of Shi'i Muslims, and expressed their unequivocal support for al-Sadr's reformist agenda. *al-Nahar*, 29 March 1974.
121. Ajami, *op. cit.*, pp. 147–8; Halawi, *op. cit.*, pp. 191–2.
122. Norton, *op. cit.*, p. 147; Gharbieh, *op. cit.*, p. 208; *al-Shira'*, *op. cit.*, pp. 36–7; Halawi, *op. cit.*, p. 156.
123. G. Tueni, *Bu'asa' wa Muhrumin wa – Musallahun* [Wretched, deprived and – armed] *al-Nahar*, 18 March 1974.
124. Shapira, *op. cit.*, p. 132.
125. The incident in the Maronite south-eastern suburb of 'Ayn al-Rummna on 13 April 1975, in which between twenty-seven and thirty Palestinians were ambushed and massacred while riding on a bus that crossed the district, was the catalyst to the war, leading directly to four days of fierce fighting, and causing between 250 and 350

fatalities. T. Petran, *The Struggle Over Lebanon* (New York: Monthly Review Press, 1987), p. 166; R. Fisk, *Pity the Nation* (Oxford: OUP, 1990), p. 78; Picard, *op. cit.*, p. 105. The Lebanese National Movement was formed in 1969 by Kamal Jumblatt, the political chief of the Druze community and leader of the Progressive Socialist Party. Besides this party, among the organisations that were affiliated to the umbrella Lebanese National Movement were: the Lebanese Communist Party, the Organisation For Communist Action, the Syrian Social Nationalist Party, the Independent Nasserites, the Ba'th Arab Socialist Party, and the Movement of the Deprived. The platform of the Movement was embodied in three cardinal planks: first, solidarity with the PLO and support for the Palestinian resistance movement in general; second, the upholding of Lebanon's integral Arab character; and third, the reform of the confessional political system. F. Sharuru, *al-Ahzab wal Tanzimat wal Quwah al-Siyyasiyyah fi Lubnan* [The parties, organisations and political forces in Lebanon] (Beirut: Dar al-Masirah, 1981), p. 19.

126. K. Salibi, *Crossroads to the Civil War* (Delmar: Caravan Books, 1976), pp. 99, 104, 116; Srour, *op. cit.*, pp. 69–70.

127. Salibi, *op. cit.*, p. 111; *al-Shira'*, *op. cit.*, p. 41; Gharbieh, *op. cit.*, p. 214; Ajami, *op. cit.*, p. 166; Halawi, *op. cit.*, p. 206.

128. al-Sadr was forced to travel to the war-affected zones in eastern Lebanon, where he was instrumental in persuading the Muslim–leftist militiamen (who included local Shi'a) to lift their siege of Christian villages in the area. Gharbieh, *op. cit.*, pp. 214–15; *al-Shira'*, *op. cit.*, pp. 41–2.

129. The incident, which took place on the 6 July 1975, involved the accidental explosion of a landmine during military training undertaken by several hundred cadets affiliated to the nascent Amal movement, and under the direction of Palestinian Fatah officers. The mishap took the lives of between thirty-five and forty Shi'i trainees, and wounded another 100. *al-Shira'*, *op. cit.*, pp. 62, 65; Gharbieh, *op. cit.*, p. 215; Salibi, *op. cit.*, p. 119; A. Laurent and A. Basbous, *Guerres Secretes au Liban* (Paris: Gallimard, 1987), p. 236. The precise date of Amal's founding is unknown, but according to Gharbieh it was formed immediately after Israel's assault on, and destruction of, the village of Kfar Shubba, in South Lebanon, on 21 March 1975. In a statement that foreshadowed the movement's establishment, he declared that 'military training has become a duty'. Gharbieh, *op. cit.*, p. 218. He asserted that, in the absence of an effective deterrent presence on the part of the Lebanese army in the south, it had consequently become the duty of the county's citizens to form a patriotic resistance militia to repel Israeli military incursions. *al-Shira'*, *op. cit.*, p. 38.

130. Shapira, *op. cit.*, p. 135; *al-Shira'*, *op. cit.*, p. 38; Halawi, *op. cit.*, p. 206; Ajami, *op. cit.*, p. 168; Gharbieh, *op. cit.*, pp. 216–17.

131. Laurent, *op. cit.*, p. 144; Shapira, *op. cit.*, pp. 134–5. The most prominent Iranian opponents of the Shah who entered Lebanon in 1972 were Mustapha Chamran, a pivotal organisational figure in the Movement of the Deprived, who later served, in the wake of the Iranian Revolution, as the Islamic Republic's first Minister of Defence; and Abbas Zamani (known as Abu Sharif), the future chief of Operations for the Iranian Revolutionary Guards. The two, together with a young militant Iranian Cleric, Shaykh Mahmud Muntazeri, oversaw the military training of Iranian revolutionaries, Iraqi Islamists (who from the onset of state repression in 1974 sought refuge in Lebanon), and local Shi'i activists, in camps run by the Fatah faction of the PLO (Laurent, *op. cit.*, pp. 235–7); Shapira, *op. cit.*, p. 135; Theroux, *op. cit.*, p. 36; Shararah, *op. cit.*, p. 41.

132. Laurent, *op. cit.*, p. 45. The author's assertion is based on information contained in J. Buob and S. Haeri, 'Comment Khomeyni veut Conquérir le Monde', *L'Express*, 6–12 July, 1984. It will be recalled from the preceding chapter that Fadlallah's public opposition to the Shah began as early as 1963, when he collaborated with al-Sadr on the drafting of a petition addressed to the Iranian monarch, protesting against his government's detention of Ayatollah Khomeini for his diatribes against the regime. Despite his intermittent criticism of the Shah's policies, the definite rupture in al-Sadr's otherwise friendly relationship with the monarch came in October 1973. Shapira, *op. cit.*, p. 141; A. R. Norton, 'Shi'ism and Social Protest in Lebanon', in Cole and Keddie (eds), *Shi'ism*, p. 163; Laurent, *op. cit.*, p. 238.
133. Ajami, *op. cit.*, p. 169; Shapira, *op. cit.*, p. 136; Norton, 'Shi'ism and Social Protest', p. 164; Gharbieh, *op. cit.*, pp. 216–17.
134. Norton, 'Harakat Amal', p. 171. The principal groups to which Shi'a were attracted included: the Lebanese Communist Party, the pro-Syrian Ba'th Party, the Syrian Social Nationalist party, and the Iraqi-backed Arab Liberation Front. Roughly half of the Communist Party members, and 40 per cent of its sympathisers, were Shi'a. Petran, *op. cit.*, p. 403, note 12.
135. Shapira, *op. cit.*, p. 136. Estimates of Amal's numerical strength varied between 800 – estimated by Sayegh, *op. cit.*, p. 117 and B.J. Odeh, *Lebanon: Dynamics of Conflict* (London: Zed Books, 1985), p. 215 – and 1,500, mentioned by A. R. Norton, 'A Counterintuitive Perspective on the Shi'a of Lebanon', in H. Amirahmadi and N. Entessar (eds), *Reconstruction and Regional Diplomacy in the Persian Gulf* (London: Routledge, 1992), p. 53.
136. Shapira, *op. cit.*, pp. 136–7; Ajami, *op. cit.*, p. 172; Gharbieh, *op. cit.*, pp. 237–9. Sayyid al-Sadr reproached Jumblatt for prolonging what he perceived to be a forlorn conflict. He also sarcastically accused Jumblatt of being prepared to 'fight the Christians to the last Shi'ite'. Theroux, *op. cit.*, p. 39. The formal split between the two leaders came on 9 June 1976, when he publicly called on Syria to intervene with military force to end the war – a move that was vehemently opposed by Jumblatt.
137. Petran, *op. cit.*, pp. 187–8; J. Randal, *The Tragedy of Lebanon* (London: The Hogarth Press, 1983), pp. 88–9.
138. *al-Shira'*, *op. cit.*, p. 43; Srour, *op. cit.*, p. 71. According to *al-Shira'* (*op. cit.*, p. 71), 300 were killed, with another 1,000 wounded, while Hanf (*op. cit.*, p. 211) puts the death toll at 100.
139. Petran, *op. cit.*, p. 166; Salibi, *op. cit.*, pp. 150–1.
140. Shararah, *op. cit.*, pp. 76–7; Shapira, *op. cit.*, p. 138; Shsrarah, *op. cit.*, pp. 72–3; Goria, *op. cit.*, p. 184; A. R. Norton, 'The Origins and Resurgence of *Amal*', in M. Kramer (ed.), *Shi'ism, Resistance and Revolution* (Boulder: Westview Press, 1987), p. 216; Salibi, *op. cit.*, p. 150.
141. Shararah, *op. cit.*, p. 168.
142. On the authority of Amir Taheri (the author of *The Spirit of Allah*), Shararah states that some 700 cadres of the Da'wa Party underwent military training in Lebanon in 1976 (Shararah, *op. cit.*, p. 109, note 13). This was corroborated by a former student of Fadlallah, known by the pseudonym Shaykh Hasan, who stated that, by virtue of his close ties to Hizb al-Da'wa, he had personally supervised the military training of approximately 400 Shi'i youth in the al-Nabatiyya district of South Lebanon; Shararah, *op. cit.*, p. 91.
143. Rieck, *op. cit.*, p. 220.

144. Tal al-Za'tar was a fortified military camp with an elaborate network of underground tunnels and bunkers, ammunition depots and factories, and whose approaches were protected by heavy gun emplacements and land mines, making it almost impregnable to military assault (*ibid*).
145. *Ibid*; Norton, 'Origins', pp. 216–17, note 11; Srour, *op. cit.*, p. 70; Rieck, *op. cit.*, p. 220.
146. Srour, *op. cit.*, pp. 70–1. According to Fadlallah, one of the more notorious for frequent killings and abductions was the Syrian checkpoint manned by Christian militiamen, and straddling the frontline connecting eastern and western sectors of Beirut.
147. *Ibid.*, p. 71; Fadlallah [interview] *al-Afkar*, 29 October 1984.
148. M. H. Fadlallah, *al-Islam wa Muntiq al-Quwwah* [Islam and the Logic of Power] (Beirut: al-Mu'assash al-Jamiyyah lil-Dirasat wal-Nashr, third edition, 1985), p. 9.
149. M. H. Fadlallah, *al-Hiwar fi al-Qur'an* [Dialogue in the Qur'an] (Beirut: Dar al-Ta'aruf, fifth edition, 1987), pp. 5–12; M. H. Fadlallah, *al-Afkar* [interview], 29 October 1984.
150. M. H. Fadlallah, *Khutuwat 'ala Tariq al-Islam* [Steps along the path of Islam] (Beirut: Dar al-Ta'aruf, fifth edition, 1986); *ibid.*, pp. 9–12, 397–8; *ibid.*, pp. 9–15, 208, 393–6.
151. *Ibid.* After surviving a tight siege for six months, Tal al-Za'tar's resistance was finally broken on the 12 August 1976 (six days after the fall of Nab'a), due to a major thrust launched by Christian units of the regular army and the various militias of the Maronite right. Petran, *op. cit.*, pp. 207–9; Rieck, *op. cit.*, p. 221. The storming of the camp ensued in arguably the largest massacre of the war; an estimated 2,500–3,000 Palestinian and Shi'i died. Rieck, *op. cit.*, p. 221; Khalidi, *op. cit.*, p. 61; Odeh, *op. cit.*, p. 179.
152. Rieck, *op. cit.*, p. 220–1.
153. Theroux, *op. cit.*, p. 39; C. Glass, *Tribes without Flags* (New York: The Atlantic Monthly Press, 1990), p. 381; Srour, *op. cit.*, p. 71; Petran, *op. cit.*, pp. 208–9.
154. Srour, *op. cit.*, p. 71.
155. Fadlallah, *al-Afkar*. Sources vary as to the total number Shi'i residents uprooted from Nab'a. Fadlallah, Ajami and Beydoun cite 250,000–300,000, 100,000–200,000, and 100,000, respectively. M. H. Fadlallah, *al-Usbu' al-Arabi* [interview] no. 1,337, 27 May 1985; Ajami, *op. cit.*, p. 172; A. Baydoun, 'Bint-Jbeil', *Maghreb–Machreq*, no. 125 (July–September 1989), p. 78. Cobban also gives a figure of 100,000; H. Cobban, 'The Growth of Shi'i Power in Lebanon and its Implications for the Future', in Cole and Keddie (eds), *op. cit.*, p. 143.
156. Shapira, *op. cit.*, p. 138; Ajami, *op. cit.*, p. 117.
157. al-Sadr was accused of seeking to ensure safe passage for his own community, while callously leaving the Palestinians to their fate. The Lebanese National Movement and the PLO castigated him over his decision to relinquish control of Nab'a, because it paved the way for the subjugation of Tal al-Za'tar and the subsequent massacres of camp survivors. Theroux, *op. cit.*, pp. 39–40; Sayegh, *op. cit.*, p. 172; Norton, 'Harakat Amal', p. 172. Among the Shi'i community, the groundswell of disaffection towards al-Sadr came to the fore at a mass rally in Baalbek, to where many of Nab'a's displaced residents had relocated. The assembly, which took place several days after the fall of the district, was organised by a staunch critic of al-Sadr, Shaykh Suleyman al-Yahfufi, the Shi'i Mufti of Baalbek, who denounced him for his complicity to the disaster. Shapira, *op. cit.*, p. 138.

158. The influx swelled Bint Jbail's population to 13,000. Many of those displaced found refuge in the homes of relatives and friends, doubling or trebling the number of households in the process. Still, many others were forced to sleep out in the open, while another 200 families were sheltered in the town's schools, which were closed during the summer vacation. Baydoun, *op. cit.*, p. 78.
159. Hagopian, *op. cit.*, pp. 27–9.
160. *Ibid.*, p. 29. On 24 February 1977, Bint Jbail was attacked by the Israeli-backed Christian auxillary force. Although the assault was repulsed by the defending Palestinian guerrillas and leftist militiamen, the town was subjected from afar to prolonged shelling.
161. Kramer, *op. cit.*, p. 99.
162. *Ibid.*, p. 100; Ajami, *op. cit.*, p. 214; Kramer, *op. cit.*, p. 100; Ajami, *op. cit.*, p. 216.

Chapter Five

1. Srour, *al-'Allamah Fadlallah*, pp.87–8; Fadlallah, *al-Mushrou' al-Hadari*, pp. 211 (note 2), 233.
2. According to Fadlallah, several years after the fall of Nab'a, Amin Gemayyal, head of the Christian Phalange Party, and future president of Lebanon, attempted to speak to Fadlallah by phone with a view to persuading him to return to Nab'a and reclaim his institutional buildings. But an embittered Fadlallah, who was not at home at the time, declined to return his call. *al-Afkar*, 29 October 1984.
3. Shararah, *Dawlat Hizbullah*, p.129.
4. The seminary was founded by one the founders and leaders of Hizbullah, Sayyid Abbas Musawi (1952–92); al-Wahdah al-'Ilamiyyah al-Markaziyyah li-Hizbullah (ed.), *Amir al-Thakirah* [The Prince of Memory] (Beirut: Munshurat al-Wala', 1993), p. 32.
5. al-Wahdah al-'Ilamiyyah li Hizbullah (ed.), *Midad wa Dima'* [Exemplar and blood] (Beirut: no publisher, n.d.), p. 32–3.
6. *Ibid.*, p. 33.
7. *Jam'iyyat al-Mabarrat al-Khairiyyah, Biyout al-Birr* (Beirut: no publisher, n.d.), pp. 4–6. Fadlallah's first charitable institution was founded in the name of Imam al-Kho'ie, whose juridical authority Fadlallah represented in Lebanon. In its first year the society's school had 275 enrolled students. *al-Muntalaq*, no. 3, Ramadan 1398 AH, p. 113.
8. Shapira, 'The Origins of Hizbullah', pp. 126–7. As an indication of Fadlallah's influence over the federation, one can cite the cases of prominent student activists who pursued university education in science and engineering whist also attending religious–juridical classes run by Fadlallah at the Islamic Legal Institute (al-Ma'had al-Shar'i); Shararah, *op. cit.*, pp. 88–9.
9. *al-Diyya* [Lebanese daily], republished in *al-Bayynat*, no. 160, p. 2; www.bayynat.org./lb/bayynat.160.html.
10. Kramer, 'The Oracle of Hizbullah', p. 104.
11. The first lecture, entitled 'The Role of Women in Society', was delivered on 15 May 1981; the second, on 29 April 1982, was given at a conference entitled 'Women in Islam,' where he shared the podium with Rabab al-Sadr, the sister of Sayyid Musa al-Sadr, *al-Nahar* [Lebanese daily], 29 April 1982, cited in *Chronology of Religion and Politics in Lebanon*, CEMAM Reports, Special Issue, 1982, (Beirut: Dar el-Machreq, 1985), p.21; M. H. Fadlallah, *Dawr al-Mar'ah al-Risali*, (Beirut: Religious Students in the American University, n.d.).
12. I. Rabinovich, 'The Problem of South Lebanon', in C. Legum (ed.), *Middle East*

Contemporary Survey, vol. 2, 1977–78 (New York: Holmes & Meier, 1979), p. 187; M. Kaurani, *al-Juthour al-Muqawamah al-Islamiyyah fi Jabal 'Amal* [The Roots of the Islamic Resisitance in Jabal 'Amil] (Beirut: Dar al-Wasilah, 1993), p. 359.

13. Kawrani, *op. cit.*, p. 359-62; F. Grimblat, '*La Communaute Chiite Libanaise et le Mouvement National Palestinien*,' *Guerres Mondiales et Conflicts Contemporains*, no. 151 (1988), p.79; Rabinovich, *op. cit.*, p. 188; Norton, *Amal*, p. 49; Norton, '*Harakat Amal*,' p. 113.
14. Israel's occupation of the south lasted three months before a phased withdrawal was completed on 13 June 1978; Rabinovich, *op. cit.*, p. 188. On April 1979, a buffer zone, manned by United Nations Peacekeeping Force in Lebanon (UNIFIL) was created north of what became known as 'Haddad Land,' in reference to formerly Israeli-occupied land under the control of pro-Israeli Saad Haddad, an erstwhile Lebanese army Major. Grimblat, *op. cit.*, p. 79 .
15. Norton, *Amal and the Shi'a*, pp. 50-51.
16. In mid 1978, some two months after the Israeli invasion of Lebanon, an interview with Sayyid Fadlallah was published in the 'Voice of Muslim Youth Magazine,' put out by the Islamic Cultural Committee, based in al-Ghubayri, in the southern suburbs of Beirut. Interestingly, the interview, entitled 'Peace in Islam,' did not touch on recent momentous events but, in response to questions relating to Islamic view of peace and Muslim-Christian relations, Sayyid Fadlallah proceeded to delineate the determinants of Islamic world-view, outlining the fundamental principles on which Islamic theory of peaceful relations with non-Muslim communities are based. Fadlallah, *Mafahim Islamiyyah 'Ammah*, pp. 557-569
17. Kawrani, *op. cit.*, p. 367; H. Sharaf al-Din, *al-Imam al-Sayyid Musa al-Sadr* (Beirut: Dar al-Arqam, 1996), p. 149.
18. Ajami, *The Vanished Imam*, p. 180–3; Norton, 'Harakat Amal', p. 114; Norton, *Amal*, p. 52; Sharaf al-Din, *op. cit.*, pp. 150–1.
19. A. R. Norton, 'Origins and Resurgence of Amal', in M. Kramer (ed.), *Shi'ism, Resistance and Revolution* (Boulder: Westview Press, 1987), p. 215; Y. Gorzalez-Quipno, 'Les Interpretations d'un Rite', *Maghreb-Machrek*, no. 115 (January–March 1987), pp. 16–17.
20. Norton, 'Origins', p. 215; M. Deeb, 'Shi'a Militant Movements', *Third World Quarterly*, vol. 10, no. 2 (April 1988), p. 686; S. Kassir, 'L'affirmation des Chiites Libanais', *Le Monde Diplomatique* (May 1985), p. 12.
21. Since the seizure of power in Iraq by the Ba'th Party, the young Shi'i emigrés and exiles, comprising religious activist students and 'ulama, arrived in Lebanon over a period of ten years. While the majority were affiliates or sympathisers of the al-Da'wa Party, and coalesced around Fadlallah, a minority of Shi'i dissidents were affiliated to a rival radical Islamist group, Munazammat al-'Amal al-Islami (Islamic Action Organisation). The activists of the latter group gathered around Ayatollah Sayyid Hasan al-Shirazi, one of the founders and premier theoreticians of the organisation, who, after fleeing Iraq in 1969, had resided, until his assassination in 1980, in Beirut and Damascus.
22. al-Khurasan, *Hizb al-Da'wa al-Islamiyyah*, p. 418.
23. Fadlallah cited the lack of 'objective circumstances' on the ground as a reason for not becoming a formal member of the party; author's correspondence, 31 October 1997. As to the claim, made by al-Khurasan, that he was a one-time senior affiliate, Fadlallah has stated in recent correspondence that the assertion is inaccurate; author's correspondence with Sayyid Fadlallah, 16 and 19 November 1999.

24. al-Khurasan, *op. cit.*, pp. 388, 418. As a measure of that informal influence, Fadlallah was, with a number senior figures of al-Da'wa, instrumental in democratising the party's central leadership council, by involving members in the election process.
25. Fadlallah, *al-Khiyar al-Akhar*, p. 85.
26. al-Khurasan, *op. cit.*, p. 489.
27. Rieck, *Die Schiiten und der Kampf*, p. 327.
28. al-Khurasan, *op. cit.*, p. 489; Rieck, *op. cit.*, p. 327. Among those al-Da'wa affliates who later joined and assumed leadership roles in Hizbullah were: Shaykh Muhammad Isma'il al-Khaliq, Shaykh Ali al-Kawrani, Shaykh Subhi al-Tufayli, Shaykh Na'im Qassem and Shaykh Hassan Nasrallah; Ranstorp, *Hizb'Allah*, p. 37; al-Khurasan, *op. cit.*, pp. 216, 342.
29. M. H. Fadlallah, interview with *al-Diyyar* (a Lebanese daily), republished online at www.bayynat.org.lb/bayynat160.html.
30. According to Shapira, *op. cit.*, p. 118; Sabra, *Un al-Sahwa al-Islamiyya*, p. 172, the strategy of infiltration was the idea of Sayyid Baqer al-Sadr, the pre-eminent Iraqi theoretician of al-Da'wa, who had apparently taken the secret decision during his visit and brief stay in Lebanon in 1969.
31. al-Khurasan, *op. cit.*, p. 489.
32. *Ibid.* As previously mentioned, during his lengthy stay in Iraq in the 1950s and 1960s, Shaykh Shams al-Din had been a student colleague of Fadlallah, with whom he collaborated in editing the intellectual-activist periodical *al-Adwa'* (the Lights), and had close informal ties with the al-Da'wa Party.
33. *Ibid.* Rieck, *op. cit.*, p. 327; Shapira, *op. cit.*, p. 118.
34. M. H. Fadlallah, 'l-Thawrah al-Islamiyyah fi Iran bayn al-Takhtit al-Maddi wal-Isnad al-Ilahi'[The Islamic Revolution in Iran between material planning and divine support] *al-Muntalaq*, no. 10, *Sha'ban*, 1400 AH (June–July 1980), p. 7.
35. Sunni supporters of the Revolution in Lebanon were represented by young religious–political activists affiliated to al-Jama'ah al-Islamiyyah (The Islamic Group), as well as by middle-ranking independent activist 'ulama. Outside Lebanon, support for the Revolution came from Egyptian, Jordanian, Syrian and Palestinian Muslim Brethren (and their radical off-shoots), as well as from a number of prominent Islamist intellectuals – namely Sayyid Abul 'Ala' al-Mawdudi, founder and leader of Pakistan's *Jamaat e-Islami*, Shaykh Rashid al-Ghannoushi, leader of the Tunisian *Harakat al-Ittijah al-Islami*, Shaykh Abdul Salam Yasin, and Shaykh Hasan al-Turabi; A. Khamahyar, *Iran wa al-Ikhwan al-Muslimeen* (Beirut: Markaz al-Dirasaat al-Istiratijiyyah wa al-Buhouth wa al-Tawtheeq, 1997), pp. 229–42.
36. M. Kramer, 'Redeeming Jerusalem', in D. Menashri (ed.), *The Iranian Revolution and the Muslim World* (Boulder: Westview Press, 1990) pp. 109, 114; Shapira, *op. cit.*, pp. 119–20.
37. I. Rabinovich, 'Lebanon', in C. Legum (ed.), *Middle East Contemporary Survey*, vol. 4 (1979–80) (New York: Holmes and Meier, 1981), p. 619; C. P. Ioannides, 'The PLO and the Iranian Revolution', *American-Arab Affairs*, no. 10 (Fall 1984), pp. 89–90, 102; Grimblat, *op. cit.*, p. 80. During the 1970s, the PLO provided sanctuary, logistical advice and military training to Iranian dissidents, both Islamist and leftist.
38. Ioannides, *op. cit.*, p. 90.
39. Grimblat, *op. cit.*, p. 80; A. Rieck, 'Abschied vom 'Revolutionsexport'?', *Beitrage zur Konfliktforschung*, vol.2 0, no. 2 (1990), p. 85. According to Hikmat Shehabi, a Lebanese journalist, most of the Iranian 'volunteers' were among the several thousand

Iranian dissidents who underwent military training in PLO camps in the Bekaa Valley. J. Miller, *God has Ninety-Nine Names* (New York: Simon & Schuster, 1996) p. 282.

40. *al-Imam fi Muwajihat al-Sahyouniyya* [The Imam in confrontation with Zionism] (Teheran: Markaz al-'Ilam, 1403 AH) pp. 92–5; Fadlallah, *Min Ajal al-Islam*, pp. 95–101.
41. Rabinovich, 'Lebanon', *MECS*, vol. 4, p. 619. The following month saw fighting between the belligerents, in Beirut and fifteen South Lebanese villages, rage for a week (13–20 April), causing the deaths of at least 100 fighters and civilians. On 30 May 1980, another clash with the Arab Liberation Front (a pro-Iraqi Palestinian group affiliated to the PLO) and elements of the Lebanese National Movement in South Lebanon left twenty-seven combatants dead, before a tenuous truce came into effect. Grimblat, *op. cit.*, p. 83.
42. *al-Muntalaq*, no. 10, (*Sha'ban*, 1400 AH) p.90; *al-Muntalaq*, no. 13 (*Rabi al-Thani*, 1401 AH), p.101; Fadlallah, *Min Ajal al-Islam*, p. 189.
43. F. Ibrahim, *al-Faqih wa al-Dawlah* [The Jurist and the State] (Beirut: Dar al-kunouz al-Adabiyyah, 1999) pp. 227–82; A. B. Sachedina, *The Just Ruler in Shi'ite Islam* (Oxford: Oxford University Press, 1988), p. 216; M. Momen, 'Authority and Opposition in Twelver Shi'ism', in R. M. Burrell (ed.), *Islamic Fundamentalism* (London: Royal Asiatic Society, 1989), pp. 64–5; S. Scmidtke, 'Modern Modifications of the Shi'i Doctrine of the Expectation of the Mahdi', *Orient*, vol. 25, no. 3 (1987), p. 405; Khomeini, *Islam and Revolution*, pp. 78–80.
44. Among those senior jurists who opposed the absolute authority of the governing *faqih* were two Iranian Grand Ayatollahs – Sayyids Shari'at Madari and Gulbigani – while in Lebanon the most outspoken critic was Shaykh Muhammad Jawad Mughniyyah. Ibrahim, *op. cit.*, p. 284; C. Mallat, *Shi'i Thought*, pp. 21–5.
45. As Fadlallah explains, Sayyid al-Kho'ie had strong reservations, from a juridical standpoint, regarding the legitimacy of an Islamic state, whose establishment – as in the case of Revolutionary Iran – is preceded by, or ensues in, 'the shedding of blood'. *al-Diyyar* [newspaper], republished over the Internet in the *al-Bayynat* weekly series, no. 149, 24 September 1999.
46. Fadlallah, *al-Islam wa Muntiq al-Quwwa*, p. 234.
47. Fadlallah, *al-Quwwa*, p. 246; Ibrahim, *op. cit.*, pp. 279–80; H. Enayat, *Modern Islamic Political Thought* (London: Macmillan, 1982), pp. 25–6; Sachedina, *op. cit.*, pp. 5–6, 90–2; Fadlallah, *al-Islam wa Muntiq al-Quwwa*, pp. 236–7.
48. Fadlallah, *Mafaheem Islamiyyah 'Ammah*, pp. 467–77.
49. *Ibid.*, pp. 477–8. In another lecture, delivered on 17 January 1981, entitled 'The Islamic Programme in this Century', Fadlallah is somewhat more blunt in his position: 'We side with reformism so long as it is a step in the direction of transformation.' Fadlallah, *Afaq Islamiyyah*, p. 292.
50. M. H. Fadlallah, *Mafahim*, pp. 477–80.
51. *Ibid*, pp. 478–9.
52. To mark the occasion, both, Fadlallah and Shaykh Shams al-Din delivered special sermons to their respective religious followers after Friday congregational prayer. In 1981 and 1982 anniversaries of the Islamic Revolution, the clerics were invited by the University of Beirut and the Lebanese University, respectively, to deliver lectures before a student audience. *al-Muntalaq*, no. 9, (April 1980), p. 94; *al-Muntalaq*, no. 14, pp. 105–6; *al-Nahar*, 14 February 1982, p. 7.
53. Srour, *op. cit.*, pp., 108–9; H. Fadlallah, *op. cit.*, p. 86. Sayyid Fadlallah narrates that

his friendship with the present leader of the Islamic Republic, Ayatollah Ali Khamanei, is an old one, originating in the mid-1960s. It was developed during the last years of Sayyid Fadlallah's stay in Najaf when, following his completion of his higher religious and juridical studies, he embarked on his first visit to Iran. It was during his tour of Mashad that he met Khamanei, who was then a religious student and Islamic activist. Follow-up visits took place in the 1970s, made possible through the arrangements of his brother, Sayyid Jawad Fadlallah (d. 1975), who was pursuing his seminary studies in Najaf. H. Fadlallah, *op. cit.*, p. 86; Srour, *op. cit.*, p. 108.

54. These are: *al-Thawrah al-Islamiyyah fi Iran: Ta'ammulat min al-Dakhil* [The Islamic Revolution in Iran: Reflections from Within], *al-Muntalaq*, no. 8 (February–March 1980), pp. 6–17; *al-Thawrah al-Islamiyyah: Durous wa 'Ibar* [The Islamic Revolution: Lessons and Implications], *al-Hikma*, no. 8 (January 1981), republished in M. H. Fadlallah, *Ma al-Hikma fi Khatt al-Islam* [Considering Wisdom in the Path of Islam] (Beirut: Mu'assasat al-Wafa', 1985), pp. 141–68.
55. M. H. Fadlallah, *al-Thawrah al-Islamiyyah fi Iran: Ta'ammulat min al-Dakhil*, p. 12–16.
56. *Ibid.*, p.16; *al-Safir* [Lebanese daily newspaper], 9 February 1979, reprinted in M. Shams, and H. Marji (eds), *al-Jamhouriyyah al-Islamiyyah fi Lubnan* [The Islamic Republic in Lebanon], vol. 1 (Beirut: al-Wakalah al-Sharqiyyah li al-Tawzi', 1989) pp. 16–17, 61–2.
57. *Ibid.*, p. 17.
58. According to Fadlallah, a malicious strategy based on the dissemination of misinformation was employed by the American administration to malign the image of the Revolution and discredit its leaders. As part of that conspiracy, Fadlallah asserts that the neo-imperial powers secretly fostered the outbreak of ethnic secessionist revolts and urban leftist insurgencies, and fanned dissension within the leadership hierarchy with a view to weakening and eventually overthrowing the regime. Fadlallah, *al-Thawrah al-Islamiyyah fi Iran bayna al-Takhteet al-Maddi*, pp. 7–8.
59. *Ibid.*, p.9–10.
60. *Ibid.*, p. 12.
61. In 1969, the regime detained its first prominent Islamist dissidents – Sayyid Hasan al-Shirazi and Shaykh Abdul Aziz al-Badri. The former, a Shi'i *'alim* from the holy city of Karbala', was released in 1970; the latter, a Sunni *'alim* from Baghdad, died under torture. al-Mu'min, *Sanawat al-Jamr*, p. 232.
62. *Ibid.*, p. 114; Hasan, *al-Shahid al-Sadr* , pp. 55–6; al-Mu'min, *op. cit.*, p. 116; Hasan, *op. cit.*, p. 56.
63. al-Mu'min, *op. cit.*, pp. 124–5; Hasan, *op. cit.*, p.56.
64. al-Mu'min, *op. cit.*, p. 125. The crackdown on Islamist-oriented students and activists forced hundreds of their detained colleagues to flee abroad, principally to Iran, Lebanon and the Gulf states.
65. Ibrahim, *al-Ta'ifiyyah wa al-Siyyasitya*, p. 369; Hasan, *op. cit.*, pp. 58–9.
66. In his letter, addressed to Imam Khomeini, Sayyid al-Sadr is quoted to have said: 'We look forward to more decisive victories, and we place all our resources at the service of your exalted entity', al-Mu'min, *op. cit.*, p. 147; Hasan, *op. cit.*, pp.59–60. Moreover, not only did he endorse Khomeini's *Wilayat al-Faqih*, but had earlier devised a preliminary outline of the prospective constitution of the Islamic Republic; B. al-Sadr, *Lamha Fiqhiyyah Tamhidiyyah 'un Mashrou' Dustour al-Jumhouriyyah al-Islamiyyah fi Iran* [A Preliminary Jurisprudential Outline of the Proposed Constitution of the

Islamic Republic of Iran] (Teheran: External Propagation Section, n.d.) pp.12–13.

67. Ibrahim, *op. cit.*, p. 373–4; al-Mu'min, *op. cit.*, p.162; al-Khurasani, *op. cit.*, pp. 339, 361, 489; Shararah, *op. cit.*, p.109.
68. Ibrahim, *op. cit.*, pp.374–5; A. Babakhan, *l'Irak, 1970–1990* (Paris: no publisher, 1994), p. 92. First, it promulgated a decree outlawing *al-Da'wa*, making affiliation to the party or its splinter groups punishable by death. Babakhan, *op. cit.*, p. 92; Hasan, *op. cit.*, p. 60; Ibrahim, *op. cit.*, p. 375; al-Khurasan, *op. cit.*, p. 379.
69. The first of these appeared in early 1981, on the first anniversary of Sayyid al-Sadr, as an article in the journal *al-Hikma*, which was later republished in a book cited above, *Ma'al Hikma fi Khatt al-Islam*.
70. *al-Muntalaq*, no. 10, pp. 91–2. On 24 of May, Shaykh Shams al-Din, who heads the Higher Islamic Shi'i Council, announced three days of public mourning for Sayyid al-Sadr.
71. In May 1980, for instance, intense clashes erupted between Amal militiamen and fighters belonging to the ALF, backed by elements of the Iraqi Ba'th Party. The seriousness of the fighting prompted the return of Syrian army units to areas in Beirut engulfed by the conflict, but not before Amal fighters had wrested control of the ALF's offices in West Beirut, set ablaze the premises of the pro-Iraqi paper *al-Muharrer*, and bombed the offices of the Iraqi News Agency. After a brief interlude in which a fragile truce was negotiated, fighting resumed, and a spate of assassinations began. Rabinovich, 'Lebanon', *Middle East Contemporary Survey*, vol. 4, pp. 604, 606, 619; *al-Muntalaq*, no. 13, p. 102.
72. Ioannides, *op. cit.*; pp. 97–102.
73. In April 1982, for example, fighting broke out between the two groups in the slum quarters of Beirut's southern periphery, and in sixteen southern villages. Norton, *Amal and the Shi'a*, p. 68.
74. *al-Muntalaq*, *op. cit.*, no. 13, p. 99; Srour, *op. cit.*, p. 87; Shapira, *op. cit.*, p. 118. Following that attempt, Fadlallah received a personal visit at his home from the Speaker of Iran's Parliament, Shaykh Ali Akbar Rafsanjani, who had arrived in Lebanon on 26 November 1981, to liaise with senior Shi'i religious and political figures. *al-Muntalaq*, *op. cit.*, no. 13, p. 99; Kramer, 'The Oracle of Hizbullah,' p. 104.
75. R. Wright, *Sacred Rage* (New York: Simon & Schuster, 1986) p. 96; Fadlallah, *Min Ajl al-Islam*, pp. 175–89.
76. Srour, *op. cit.*, p.87; M. al-Qubaysi, *Lamha Mawjizah min Hayat al-Marja' Ayatullah al-Uzma al-Sayyid Muhammad Husayn Fadlallah* [A Brief Glimpse from the Life of Sayyid Fadlallah], www.bayynat,org.lb; al-Khurasan, *op. cit.*, p. 649.
77. Shaykh al-Kawrani, who subsequently recovered from his wounds and later moved to the relative safety of Teheran, was a senior figure in the Lebanese branch of Hizb al-Da'wa. al-Khurasani, *op. cit.*, pp. 316–17.
78. Sayyid al-Shirazi, who headed Jami'yyat al-'Ulama al-Shi'a (The Society of Shi'i 'Ulama) and co-founded Munazzamat al-'Amal al-Islami (The Islamic Action Organisation) was born in 1937 and educated in the Iraqi holy city of Karbala'. He was detained and interrogated for his oppositional activities in 1969, but released the following year. al-Mu'min, *op. cit.*, p. 232; A. Baram, 'The Radical Shi'ite Opposition Movements in Iraq', in A. E. Sivan and M. E. Friedman, (eds) *Religious Radicalism*, p. 97; T. al-Shaykh, *'Un al Iraq wal Harakah al-Islamiyyah* [On Iraq and thc Islamic Movement] (London: al-Safa, 1988) p. 192.
79. *al-Muntalaq*, *op. cit.*, no. 10, p. 93.

80. *al-Khurasan*, *op. cit.*, p. 361.
81. *al-Muntalaq*, no. 17 (*Muharram* 1402 AH/October 1981) p. 107.

Chapter Six

1. M. Kramer, 'The Oracle of Hizbullah' in: R. Scott Appleby (ed.), *Spokesmen for the Despised* (Chicago: University of Chicago Press, 1997), p. 107.
2. The attack, which was carried out by Abu Nidal, the leader of a breakaway faction of the PLO, followed an escalation in Palestinian fedayeen cross-border raids and Israeli artillery shelling and air strikes against PLO headquarters in south Beirut; R. Brynen, *Sanctuary and Survival* (London: Pinter, 1990), pp. 149–50, 157; Z. Schiff & E. Ya'ari, *Israel's Lebanon War* (New York: Simon & Schuster, 1984.), p. 109.
3. K. E. Shulze, *Israel's Covert Diplomacy in Lebanon* (London: Macmillan, 1997), p. 127.
4. S. M. Katz, *Guards Without Frontiers* (London: Arms & Armour Press, 1990), p. 123; Schiff, *op. cit.*, p. 134; F. Ajami, *The Vanished Imam*, p. 114; Norton, *Amal and the Shi'a*, p. 86; Hanf, *Coexistence in Wartime Lebanon*, p. 279; Norton, *op. cit.*, p. 86.
5. Schiff, *op. cit.*, p. 134.
6. J. Stork, 'The War for the Camps', *MERIP Report*, vol. 15, no. 5 (June 1985), p. 5; Norton, *op. cit.*, p. 86; Fadlallah, *Harb al-Iradat*, p. 55; al-Kourani, *al-Juthour al-Tarikhiyyah*, p. 387; R. A. Gabriel, *Operation Peace for Galilee* (New York: Hill & Wong, 1984), p. 154; *al-Safir*, 10 June 1982, p. 6; Kurani, *op. cit.*, p. 387; Khalidi, *op. cit.*, p. 54; Fisk, *Pity the Nation*, pp. 228, 255.
7. Though the Israeli blockade and bombing blitz of the capital impacted severely on civilians – a strategy designed to pressure the PLO into evacuating Beirut – the hardship and relentless attacks had the effect of hardening the attitude of west Beirut's residents towards Israel. William Stewart, *Time*, 16 August 1982; N. Chomsky, *The Fateful Triangle* (Cambridge, MA: South End Press, second edn, 1999), p. 218.
8. Khalidi, *op. cit.*, p. 133; Fisk, *op. cit.*, pp. 255–6. Two weeks of fighting around the southern gateway suburbs in June 1982 left 518 killed and 619 wounded, a large number of whom were Palestinian and Shi'a guerrillas.
9. Srour, *al-'Allamah Fadlallah*, p. 75–8; Fadlallah, *al-Khiyar al-Akhar*, p. 87.
10. *Sawt al-Wahdah al-Islamiyyah* [The voice of Islamic Unity], no. 31 (30 April 1982), p. 26; *Risalat al-Thawrah al-Islamiyyah* [The message of the Islamic Revolution], July–August 1982, p. 31.
11. H. Fadlallah, *op. cit.*, p. 132; A. Khazem, *Tajammu al-Ulama al-Muslimeen* [The Association of the Muslim 'Ulama], www.al-wahdaalislamiyia.org, pp. 4–5.
12. S. Shapira, 'The Origins of Hizbullah,' *Jerusalem Quarterly*, no. 46 (1988), p. 123; H. Fadlallah, *al-Khiyar al-Akhar*, pp. 14–15, 57–8; H. Fadlallah, *Harb al-Iradat*, pp. 57–8; Gabriel, *op. cit.*, p. 111.
13. Srour, *op. cit.*, pp. 75–6; H. Fadlallah, *al-Khiyar al-Akhar*, p. 87.
14. Due to its proximity to Palestinian guerrilla strongholds in the southern suburbs, B'ir al-Abd was one of the most heavily bombed Shi'i quarters; Fisk, *op. cit.*, p. 256; M. Bashour, *Beirut* (Beirut: Mu'assasat Dar al-Kitab al-Hadeeth, 1984), p. 41.
15. Fadlallah, *Min Ajl al-Islam*, p. 98–101.
16. A. Khazem, *op. cit.*, p. 4; Shapira, *op. cit.*, p. 126. Among the senior clerics, the most prominent in their opposition included the Sunni mufti of Lebanon, Shaykh Hasan Khalid, the Sunni Arabist Shaykh Abdul Hafiz Qasim, Shaykh Shams al-Din, the then

vice-president of the Supreme Muslim Shi'i Council, and the Shi'i mufti, Shaykh Abdul Amir Qabalan. The latter two issued fatwas forbidding the faithful from maintaining any contacts with the enemy. Bashour, *op. cit.*, p. 41; CEMAM Reports, *op. cit.*, 32–3.

17. Norton, *op. cit.*, p. 87.
18. M. Deeb, *Militant Islamic Movements in Lebanon* (Washington, DC: Georgetown University, 1986), p. 2.
19. The internal division was settled, albeit temporarily, with the election of Hussein al-Musawi as Vice-President; H. Fadlallah, *Harb al-Iradat*, p. 64.
20. Chomsky, *op. cit.*, pp. 247–8. According to an Israeli military reporter, at the height of the Israeli siege, in return for Amal being allowed to keep to its arms, Berri offered the Israelis unfettered access across their lines to mount assaults on the Palestinian camps in the capital; Schiff, *op. cit.*, p. 206.
21. Apart from the President and Nabih Berri, the Committee comprised Bashir Gemayel (Phalangist leader), Walid Jumblatt (Druze leader), Shafiq al-Wazzan (Prime Minister). Jumblatt subsequently withdrew from the Committee; *al-Safir*, 21 June 1982; H. Fadlallah, *al-Khiyar al-Akhar*, p. 31.
22. H. Fadlallah, *al-Khiyar al-Akhar*, p. 31; H. Fadlallah, *Harb al-Iradat*, p. 63.
23. According to one academic source, the opponents of Berri's unilateral decision had referred matters to the Iranian ambassador to Syria, Ali Akabar Mohtashami, who ruled in favour of the rejectionists. As'ad Abu Khalil, 'The Ideology and Practice of Hizbullah', *Middle Eastern Studies*, vol. 27, no. 3 (July 1991), p. 391. Liaising closely with al-Musawi's group, the Revolutionary Guards seized Shaykh Abdallah barracks, which since 1976 had been abandoned by the Lebanese army. CEMAM Reports, *op. cit.*, p. 39; Con Coughlin, *Hostage* (London: Warner Books, 1992), p. 105.
24. Coughlin, *op. cit.*, p. 105.
25. CEMAM Reports, *op. cit.*, p. 33; Deeb, *op. cit.*, p. 8. According al-Musawi, during Amal's first congress in Tyre in 1976 Sayyid Musa al-Sadr defined the Islamic identity of the Movement, declaring that Amal was an Islamic movement and its ideology was Qur'anic Islam, *al-Shira*, *al-Harakat al-Islamiyya fi Lubnan*, p. 222.
26. H. Fadlallah, *Harb al-Iradat*, p. 64.
27. M. Kramer, *Hezbollah's Vision of the West* (Washington, DC: The Washington Institute for Near East Policy, 1989), p. 20. Questioned about his role, and no doubt mindful of repercussions that might flow from any acknowledgment of it, Fadlallah gave an ambiguous, non-committal answer; author's correspondence with Sayyid Fadlallah, 1 September 1999.
28. al-Shira', *op. cit.*, p. 22; A. Kurani, *Tariqatu Hizbillah fil 'Amal al-Islami* [Hizbullah's approach towards Islamic activism] (Beirut: al-Mu'assasah al-'Amaliyyah, 1406 AH [1985 CE]), p. 11.
29. It was only in 1984 that the movement began to issue communiqués through its official spokesman, Sayyid Ibrahim al-Amin – the only position, prior to 1988, to be made public within Hizbullah's leadership structure.
30. This view is held by Shapira, Israeli scholar of Hizbullah, who contends that the movement was essentially formed under an Iranian aegis to serve Iranian foreign interests. Shapira, *op. cit.*, p. 402.
31. Abu Khalil, *op. cit.*, p. 391; H. Nasrallah Interview, *The Middle East Insight*, May–August 1996, p. 38; H. Nasrallah Interview, *Wilayat Hizbullah* [Hizbullah's authority] *al-Hawadeth*, 19 March 1999, p. 18; *al-Wahdah al-'Ilamiyyah al-Markaziyyah li-*

Hizbullah, Amir al-Thakira [The prince of memory] (Beirut: Munshourat al-Walaa', 1993), p. 37.

32. Islamic Amal, not unlike Tajammu al-'ulama, is both a distinct and integral part of Hizbullah; H. al-Musawi, Interview, *Kayhan al-Arabi*, 27 August 1985, p. 2; Shapira, *op. cit.*, p. 125.
33. Among the senior figures of the Lebanese Da'wa Party who rose to prominence in Hizbullah were: Shaykh Ali Kurani, Sayyid Ibrahim al-Amin (former Amal representative in Teheran), Shaykh Subhi al-Tufayli (b. 1948), Sayyid Hasan Nasrallah (b. 1959, enrolled at the age of ten in Fadlallah's Islamic *Shari'i* Institute in Nab'a), Shaykh Na'im Qasem and Muhammad Ra'ad; *al-Shira*, 27 September 1993; Shapira, *op. cit.*, p. 125; al-Khurasan, *Hizb al-Da'wa al-Islamiyyah*, p. 216; A. Khoury, 'Hezbollah', *Arabies*, December 1992, p. 21.
34. Kurani, *op. cit.*, pp. 123–4.
35. H. al-Musawi interview, *Kayhan al-Arabi*, 29 August 1985, p. 11; *al-Shira', op. cit.*, pp. 148, 161–2.
36. Despite his consistent denials, Fadlallah had since 1983 been 'identified in Lebanon and abroad as the mentor of Hizbullah', *Monday Morning*, 15 October 1984. Countering the claim that he is the patron of Hizbullah, Fadlallah asserts emphatically that if he were such a leader he would acknowledge it. Fadlallah interview, *al-Afkar*, 29 October 1984.
37. This explanation is also consistent with Fadlallah's own account – namely that Hizbullah in its early years was a headless movement, at least publicly, while he himself, due to his activities, was seen to wield considerable clout within the movement. Interview with Fadlallah, *al-Bayrak*, 15 October 1984.
38. That from the beginning Hizbullah's leadership gave their unswerving allegiance to Khomeini is clear from statements made Sayyid Hasan Nasrallah and Sayyid Ibrahim al-Amin: 'We must obey *al-Wali al-Faqih* (governing jurisconsult); disagreement with him is not permitted'; and 'We do not derive our political decision-making from anyone save *wali al-faqih*' *al-'Ahad*, 24 April 1987; *al-Shira'*, *al-Harakat*, p. 48, respectively.
39. H. Fadlallah, *al-Khiyar al-Akhar*, p. 87; Fadlallah, *al-Islam wa Muntiq al-Quwwa*, pp. 246–7.
40. M. H. Fadlallah, 'Mun al-thi yaqoud 'amaliyat al-taghyeer? Hizbullah or ummat Hizbullah' ['Who should institute the process of change? 'Hizbullah or the nation of the Party ?'] *al-Muntalaq*, no. 31, October 1986, p. 105.
41. H. Fadlallah, *al-Khiyar al-Akhar*, p. 87.
42. In an interview with a western reporter, a senior member of *al-Da'wa* stated that Fadlallah provides general 'direction and spiritual guidance', without maintaining formal links with the party. R. Wright, *Sacred Rage* (New York: Simon & Schuster, 1986), p. 92.
43. H. Fadlallah, *al-Khiyar al-Akhar*, p. 81.
44. Fadlallah had forged close ties with the leaders of the main Sunni Islamist movements in Lebanon – namely Harakat Tawhid al-Islami, founded and led by the late Shaykh Saeed Sha'ban, and al-Jama'ah al-Islamiyyah, founded and led by Fathi Yakan.
45. Kramer, 'Oracle of Hizbullah', p. 107.
46. Schiff, *op. cit.*, p. 291.
47. Fisk, *op. cit.*, p. 482; 'The Saga of May 17th,' *Washington Report on Middle East Affairs*, 20 February 1984, pp. 1–2; Schiff, *op. cit.*, p. 297.
48. 'Hiwar al-Umr' [Dialogue of a lifetime], televised interview, February 1999; H. Fadlallah, *al-Khiyar al-Akhar*, p. 47.

49. M. H. Fadlallah, *al-Muqawamah, al-Islamiyyah* [The Islamic resistance] (Beirut: Lajnat Masjid al-Imam Rida, second edn, 1986), pp. 54–5; 'Hiwar al-Umr', *op. cit.*; H. Fadlallah, *al-Khiyar al-Akhar*, pp. 47–50; CEMAM Reports, Chronology of Religion and Politics in Lebanon, 1983 (Beirut: CEMAM, 1985), p. 28; Khazem, *op. cit.*, p. 5.
50. H. Fadlallah, *al-Khiyar al-Akhar*, pp. 51–3.
51. The force deployed earlier, on 25 August 1982, oversaw the evacuation of PLO guerrillas from Beirut, and was commissioned to safeguard the now defenceless Palestinian refugee camps. However, the premature withdrawal from Lebanon, the assassination four days later of the pro-Israeli president-elect and Phalangist leader, Bashir Gemayel, and the entry of Israeli troops and Phalangist allies into west Beirut and the Palestinian camps, led to the infamous Sabra and Shatila massacre of 16–18 September 1982. According to Thomas Friedman, 'at least a quarter, and possibly many more [of those slain, variously estimated at between 800 and 2,000 camp dwellers] were Lebanese Shi'ite Moslems'. Chomsky, *op. cit.*, p. 370.
52. Fisk, *op. cit.*, pp. 453, 462.
53. *Ibid.*, pp. 504–5; S. Abu Diyeh, *Dirasah Tahliliyyah fi al-'Amaliyyat al-Istishhadiyyah fi Janoub Lubnan* [An analytical study of self-martyring operations in south Lebanon] (Amman: al-Mataba' al-Ta'awaniyyah, 1986), pp. 36–7; *The Times*, 3 October 1983.
54. Petran, *The Struggle over Lebanon*, p. 330.
55. Abu Diyyeh, *op. cit.*, p. 31; Fisk, *op. cit.*, pp. 480–1; *Washington Report*, 24 April 1983; Abu Diyyeh, *op. cit.*, pp. 34, 48.
56. Fisk, *op. cit.*, p. 512; Wright, *op. cit.*, pp. 70–1; Abu Diyyeh, *op. cit.*, p. 38; Wright, *op. cit.*, p. 72; Abu Diyyeh, *op. cit.*, p. 39; Fisk, *op. cit.*, p. 512.
57. Schiff, *op. cit.*, p. 299; CEMAM Reports, 1983, p. 57; BBC, *States of Terror* (television documentary), 1994.
58. Wright, *op. cit.*, p. 73. In April 1983, Jihad al-Islami had also claimed responsibility for the suicide bombing of the American embassy in west Beirut.
59. ABC television documentary, *Hostage*, 1999. In another interview, al-Musawi elaborated this position by declaring that 'we [Hizbullah] support them fully and we bow our heads to the greatness of their work', H. al-Musawi, *Kayhan al-Arabi*, 29 July 1986.
60. *Kayhan al-Arabi*, 22 August 1985, p. 2; Fisk, *The Independent on Sunday*, 21 April 1996.
61. Interview with Fadlallah, *al-Mustaqbal*, 6 July 1985. Interviewed some fifteen months after the suicide bombings, Fadlallah stated that 'I have not issued any fatwa since the commencement of these operations.'
62. *al-Khalij*, 14 November 1983; *Washington Post*, 28 October 1983, A25; *The Washington Report*, 30 October 1983, A29; Wright, *op. cit.*, p. 92.
63. Interview with Fadlallah, *Kayhan al-Arabi*, 22 February 1984. Immediately following the MNF withdrawal from Lebanon in early February, Fadlallah led a large delegation of 'ulama to Iran, where talks were held with Khomeini and Rafsanjani on the latest developments in Lebanon and the current situation of the Islamist movement in the country.
64. *Ibid.* In another interview, Fadlallah disclaimed all responsibility for the attacks on the grounds that as an Islamist he does not condone the use of violence in oppositional political campaigns; violence could only be sanctioned by 'ulama-approved jihad campaigns. Interview with Fadlallah, *Iqra'*, 17 November 1983.
65. B. Woodward, *The Veil* (London: Simon & Schuster, 1987), p. 397; M. H. Fadlallah, *Min Ajl al-Islam*, p. 142.

66. Fadlallah, *Min Ajl al-Islam*, pp. 142, 154. Five of Fadlallah's bodyguards were killed in the blast. 'Aftershocks in Beirut', *al-Shira'*, 18 March 1985, vol. 125, pp. 30–3.
67. *Ibid.*, pp. 149–50; Woodward, *op. cit.*, p. 396.
68. *Ibid.*, pp. 395–6. According to a report in the *Washington Post*, the bombing was carried out by mercenaries hired by senior figures in a Maronite-dominated Lebanese army intelligence unit, which had discreetly undergone counter-terrorist training and assistance by the CIA. 'Blackmail in Beirut', *Time*, vol. 125, 27 May 1985, p. 36.
69. Woodward, *op. cit.*, p. 397.
70. Interview with Fadlallah, *al-Ittihad*, 7 June 1985; interview with Fadlallah, *Kayhan al-Arabi*, 14 November 1985; interview with Fadlallah, *Middle East Insight*, June/July 1985, p. 11; Fadlallah, *al-Muqawamah*, p. 50; Interview with Fadlallah, 'States of Terror', television documentary, 1994; interview with Fadlallah, *Politique Internationale*, no. 29, Autumn 1985, p. 268.
71. Fadlallah, *al-Nahar*, 14 May 1985; interview with Fadlallah, *Monday Morning*, 16 December 1985.
72. About a year prior to the twin suicide attacks on the MNF, a hitherto unknown Islamist group, *al-Kifah al-Islami*, claimed responsibility for the suicide bombing of the IDF headquarters in the southern port of Tyre. Abu Diyyeh, *op. cit.*, p. 28.
73. Abu Diyyeh, *op. cit.*, pp. 27–8.
74. *al-Safir*, 10 October 1983; Petran, *op. cit.*, p. 323.
75. Three months after the Nabatiyyeh incident, a truck bomber affiliated to Islamic Jihad slammed his vehicle into Israeli military headquarters in Tyre, the second such attack. On this occasion, the attack killed twenty-eight Israelis and severely wounded dozens of others. Abu Diyyeh, *op. cit.*, pp. 46–7; Katz, *op. cit.*, pp. 125–7.
76. Markaz al-Dirasaat wa al-Tawfiq, *al-Muqawamah fi al-Khitab al-Fiqhi al-Siyasi lisamahat al-Imam al-Shaykh Muhammad Mahdi Shams al-Din* [Resistance in the juridico-political discourse of Shaykh Shams al-Din] (Beirut: al-Mu'assasat al-Duwaliyyah, 1997), p. 115; Petran, *op. cit.*, p. 322. Fadlallah, for his part, 'exhorted the southerners to pursue the Israelis in every place and with every means at their disposal'. *al-Safir*, *op. cit.*
77. Petran, *op. cit.*, p. 322; H. Fadlallah, *Harb al-Iradat*, p. 99. The Shaykh was released the following month; *Midad wa Dima* [Ink and blood] (Beirut: al-Wahdah al-'Ilamiyya li Hizbullah, n.d.), p. 150; *al-Muntalaq*, May 1984, p. 131.
78. One of those Shi'i 'ulama who was assassinated by Israeli agents (in 1988) for his resistance activities was Shaykh Ali Kurayem. Like his more distinguished predecessor, Shaykh Kurayem hailed from South Lebanon and had been a former student of Fadlallah, having graduated in the early 1970s from the Nab'a-based Islamic *Shari'i* Institute that was founded and headed by his mentor. *Midad wa Dima'*, pp. 171, 176.
79. 'Israel and South Lebanon', *Washington Report on Middle East Affairs*, 5 March 1984, p. 4; B. Morris, *Israel's Secret Wars* (New York: Grove Weidenfield, 1991), p. 394; Petran, *op. cit.*, p. 323; Scot Macleod, 'No Peace for Galilee Now', *The Nation*, 23 February 1985, vol. 240, p. 203; Brynen, *op. cit.*, p. 184. The Haddad militia and the SLA were armed, trained and financed by Israel.
80. M. H. Fadlallah, 'Reflexions sur la Resistance,' *Revue d'êtudes Palestiniennes*, no. 16 (Summer 1985), p. 42; *al-'Ahd*, no. 1, June 1984.
81. Fadlallah, *al-Muqawamah al-Islamiyyah*, pp. 45–6; *al-Nahar*, 27 September 1985; Fadlallah, *Min Ajl al-Islam*, pp. 196–7.

82. *Ibid.*, p. 121; interview with Fadlallah, *al-Safir*, 19 November 1986; interview with Fadlallah, *Middle East Insight*, June/July 1985, p. 18.
83. Interview with Fadlallah, *Middle East Insight*, June/July 1985, p. 13; interview with Fadlallah, *Middle East Insight*, vol. 5, no. 6 (1988), p. 5.
84. Fadlallah, *al-Muqawamah*, pp. 53–4.
85. Fadlallah declared in mid-1985: 'We feel that Muslims and non-Muslims, who are fighting for the sake of freedom, are obliged to confront Israel's existence ... by eradicating it as an entity from the region.' *al-Liwa*, 9 April 1985; Fadlallah, *al-Muqawamah*, p. 99.
86. *Ibid.*, p. 69; Fadlallah's declaration came in a speech delivered on 2 July 1984; Fadlallah, *al-Muqawamah*, p. 83; *ibid.*, pp. 15, 60; *CEMAM Report*, 1984, p. 60.
87. *CEMAM Report*, 1985, p. 22; *CEMAM Reports, 1985*, p. 22; interview with Fadlallah, *al-Amal*, 27 May 1987; interview with Fadlallah, *Journal of Palestine Studies*, vol. 14, no. 4, p. 166; interview with Fadlallah, *al-Nahar al-Arabi wa al-Duwali*, 24 January 1985.
88. Interview with Fadlallah, *al-Ufuq*, 10 January 1985; Fadlallah, *Min Ajl al-Islam*, p. 63; Fadlallah, *Min Ajl al-Islam*, pp. 62, 65; interview with Fadlallah, *al-Anwar*, 18 November 1986.
89. As'ad Abu Khalil, 'The Palestinian-Shi'ite War in Lebanon', *Third World Affairs* (1988), pp. 84–5; F. Grimblat, 'Le Communaute Chiite Libanaise et le Mouvement National Palestinien' *Guerres Mondiales et Conflits Contemporains*, no. 151 (1988), p. 87; J. Stork, 'The War of the Camps', MERIP, vol. 15, no. 5 (June 1985), p. 7.
90. Stork, *op. cit.*, p. 7; G. Usher, 'Hizbullah, Syria, and the Lebanese Elections', *Journal of Palestine Studies*, vol. 26, no. 2 (Winter 1997), p. 63; A. Ehteshamiand R. A. Hinnebusch, *Syria and Iran* (London: Routledge, 1997), p. 131.
91. *al-Liwa*, 6 April 1985; interview with Fadlallah, *Kayhan al-Arabi*, 23 May 1985, p. 16; *CEMAM Report*, 1985, p. 31; interview with Fadlallah, *al-Anwar*, 18 November 1986; interview with Fadlallah, *al-Nahar*, 8 June 1985; interview with Fadlallah, *al-Nahar*, 8 June 1985.
92. Fadlallah had declared that no harm must befall the Palestinian civilians stranded in the camps. Interview with Fadlallah, *al-Safir*, 19 November 1986.
93. Interview with Fadlallah, *Al'Alam*, 22 July 1985; interview with Fadlallah, *al-Hawadet*, 13 February 1987. Fadlallah did however share Amal's opposition to any attempt by a reinvigorated PLO to re-establish their unofficial pre-1982 state-within-a-state in Lebanon.
94. Fadlallah, *Min Ajl al-Islam*, p. 273.
95. Brynen, *op. cit.*, p. 190.
96. *Kayhan al-Arabi*, 12 March 1987; Shararah, *op. cit.*, p. 360.
97. *al-Bayrak*, 6 March 1987.
98. *Ibid*; *al-Nahar*, 26 February 1987; Ehteshemi, *op. cit.*, p. 133; H. Fadlallah, *al-Khiyar al-Akhar*, *op. cit.*, p. 145.
99. Interview with Fadlallah, *al-Bayrak*, 6 March 1987. He reminded the Syrians of the pivotal role played by Hizbullah in forcing the MNF from Beirut and the Israelis from most of Lebanon. Interview with Fadlallah, *Kayhan al-Arabi*, 28 February 1987.
100. *Kayhan al-Arabi*, 28 February 1987.
101. *al-Bayrak*, *op. cit.* Fadlallah added diplomatically: 'We might have dissimilar views on the current political situation, or differences with the ideological line of Syrian policy, and we might have our reservations regarding certain things, but we do not feel that the present phase justifies any conflict between us and the Syrians at this stage.'

102. H. Fadlallah, *al-Khiyar*, p. 145. Henceforth Hizbullah, under Fadlallah's pragmatic stewardship, will avoid at all costs openly challenging Syrian policy on, or control of, Lebanon. Shararah, *op. cit.*, p. 362.
103. The hostages were held in Hizbullah-controlled territory; Coughlin, *op. cit.*, pp. 108–9; interview with Fadlallah, *al-Safir*, 29 May 1984; interview with Fadlallah, *al-Afkar*, 4 June 1984; interview with Fadlallah, *al-Safir*, 10 December 1984.
104. *The Washington Post*, April 1986, C5; British Channel 4 documentary, 1999, *Hostage*; Coughlin, Hostage, pp. 162, 347; *al-Bayrak*, 6 March 1987; *al-Nahar al-Arabi wa al Duwali*, 9–15 February 1987.
105. Although Hizbullah denied any involvement in the kidnapping of Colonel Higgens – who was accused by Fadlallah, on the authority of a report appearing in the *Washington Post*, of espionage – Amal believed that he was being held in a Hizbullah-controlled area. M. H. Fadlallah, *al-Jum'ah* [Friday (sermons)] (Beirut: Dar al-Malaak, 1996), p. 93.
106. W. Harris, 'Lebanon,' *Middle East Contemporary Survey*, vol. 12 (Boulder: Westview Press, 1990), p. 630.
107. It will be recalled that, on the advice of Fadlallah, Hizbullah had since the mid-1970s been systematically infiltrating the ranks of Amal.
108. Harris, *op. cit.*, 631.
109. Fadlallah, *al-Jum'ah*, pp. 242, 248.
110. *Ibid.* p. 226. During the first phase of the conflict, in the South, Fadlallah maintained that he was instrumental in bringing the feuding parties to the negotiating table, as well as formulating the guiding principles that brought the conflict to the brink of resolution, before it flared anew in Beirut's southern suburbs.
111. *Ibid.*, p. 92; *al-Anwar*, 27 February 1988; *al-Shira'*, 6 June 1988; *al-Liwa*, 9 April 1988; Fadlallah, *al-Jum'ah*, pp. 227–8.
112. *Economist*, 4 June 1988, p. 41.
113. Interview with Fadlallah, *al-Diyar*, 29 May 1988.
114. Interview with Fadallah, 'L'Islam Imperial,' *Politique Internationale*, no. 29 (August 1985), p. 266; interview with Fadlallah, *al-Shira*, 16 July 1984.
115. In his seminal work, entitled, *Islam and the Logic of Power*, written in 1976, Fadlallah stipulated that it is imperative for Muslims to form an Islamic vanguard committed to transforming nominal Muslim states that have deviated from the Islamic paradigm, and dedicated to overturning the 'regime of unbelievers'. Fadlallah, *al-Islam wa Muntiq al-Quuwwa*, pp. 250–1.
116. Interview with Fadlallah, *al-Usbou al-Arabi*, 24 December 1984; *al-Nahar*, 3 February 1986.
117. Interview with Fadlallah, *Middle East Insight*, June/July 1985; interview with Fadlallah, *al-Safir*, 29 May 1984; *Magazine*, 5 May 1984; interview with Fadlallah, *al-Nahar al-Arabi wa al-Duwali*, 26 August 1984; interview with Fadlallah, *Kayhan al-Arabi*, 22 February 1984; *Middle East Insight*, June/July 1985, p. 15.
118. Interview with Fadlallah, *Sabah al-Khayr*, 5 March 1988; interview with Fadlallah, *al-Minbar*, April 1986; *Sabah al-Khayr*, 5 March 1988; *al-Minbar*, April 1986.
119. Fadlallah, 'al-Unf wal-Islam', *al-Safir*, 20 March 1986; interview with Fadlallah, *al-Safir*, 23 March 1985; interview with Fadlallah, *al-Safir*, 23 May 1988; Fadlallah, 'al-Unf wal-Islam,' *al-Safir*, 20 March 1986; Fadlallah, *Min Ajl al-Islam*, p. 163.
120. Shams and Marji, *al-Jumhouriyya al-Islamiyya fi Lubnan*, pp. 1,281–302; *al-Nahar*, 16 September 1986; *al-Ahad*, October 1985.

121. Norton, *Hizballah of Lebanon*, p. 12; H. Fadlallah, *al-Khiyar al-Akhar*, pp. 35–37, 189–90; *al-Shira'*, *al-Harakatal-Islamiyyah*, p. 148; *al-Hawadeth*, 24 May 1985; *Kayhan al-Arabi*, 22 August 1985.
122. *al-Nahar*, 7 April 1985; Fadlallah, *Min Ajl al-Islam*, p. 163; interview with Fadlallah, *al-Shira'*, 16 July 1984; Fadlallah, *Min Ajl al-Islam*, p. 163; Kramer, 'Redeeming Jerusalem,' p. 124.
123. *al-Nahar*, 22 and 23 March 1986.
124. *Kayhan al-Arabi*, 8 February 1986.
125. *al-Safir*, 15 March 1986.
126. Author's Correspondence with Fadlallah, 22 April 2000; *al-Safir*, 15 March 1986.
127. *al-Safir*, 11 November 1987; *al-Anwar*, 3 November 1987. Three other personalities were: Shaykh Shams al-Din, Sayyid Sadeq Mausawi, and Shaykh Saeed Sha'ban. The first two were Sh''i, while the last was a Sunni cleric.
128. *al-Bayraq*, 3 November 1987; *Teheran Times*, 3 November 1987.
129. Beginning with the public distribution of leaflets and petitions in 1977, al-Musawi was the first Shi'i activist *'alim* in Lebanon to openly agitate for an Islamic state in Lebanon. Interview with S. Sadeq al-Musawi, *al-Shira'*, 20 June 1988, cited in *al-Jumhouriyya al-Islamiyya fi Lubnan*, pp. 971, 979.
130. *al-Masirah*, 7 November 1987; *al-Safir*, 7 November 1987; interview with Fadlallah, *al-Anwar*, 9 November 1987.
131. *al-Shira'*, *al-Harakat al-Islamiyyah*, p. 226; *Kayhan al-Arabi*, 22 and 29 August 1985.
132. *Ibid.*, pp. 160–1, 226–7.
133. Interview with Fadlallah, *al-Nahar al-Arabi wa al-Duwali*, 9–15 February 1987; Fadlallah, *al-Juma'*, p. 417; interview with Fadlallah, *al-Ra'i*, 5 September 1988; *al-Ra'i*, 5 September 1988; interview with Fadlallah, *al-Mustaqbal*, 30 July 1988; interview with Fadlallah, *al-'Ahd*, 23 July 1988.
134. *al-Nahar*, 19 December 1987; interview with Fadlallah, *al-Haqiqah*, 21 December 1987.
135. Fadlallah, *al-Jum'ah*, pp. 45, 60.
136. *Ibid.*, p. 61.
137. Fadlallah's public call for scholastic inter-religious dialogue, launched formally in late 1986, was cordially received by Christian clerics. Thus began a series of serious and congenial discussions between Fadlallah and moderate Christian clergymen – exchanges that have continued to the present day. S. al-Hasani, *Sira' al-Iradat* [The contest of wills] (Beirut: Dar al-Malaak, second edn, 1995), p. 134.
138. *Ibid.*, p. 133.

Chapter Seven

1. At a conference on 5 November 1989, the participating Islamist Lebanese groups passed resolutions condemning the Accords for perpetuating the unjust status quo; A. M. Shams and H. Murji, *al-Jumhouriyya al-Islamiyya fi Lubnan* [The Islamic Republic in Lebanon] (Beirut: al-Wakala al-Sharqiyya li al-Tawzi', nd.), vol. 3, pp. 758–9.
2. T. al-Madani, 'Harakat Amal wa Hizbullah fi Lubnan', in J. Baaroot et al. (eds) *al-Ahzaab wal Harakaat wal Jama'aat al-Islamiyya* [The Islamic parties, movements and groups], 2 vols (Damascus: The Arabic Centre for Strategic Studies, 2000), vol. 2, p. 493; Fadlallah, *al-Khiyar al-Akhar*, p. 108. At its fifth annual meeting, convened in August 1989 by the movement's external relations body, Hizbullah issued a statement

calling for the demolition of the Lebanese regime from its roots (*al-Safeer*, 16 August 1989). This implacable hostility towards the Lebanese regime can be attributed to Hizbullah's ideological stance, encapsulated in the movement's manifesto, published in 1985 as an Open Letter.

3. Interview with Fadlallah, *al-Nahar*, 4 December 1989.
4. Interview with Fadlallah, *al-Nahar*, 4 October, 1989.
5. Interview with Fadlallah, *al-Nahar*, 14 July 1990. In another interview, Fadlallah proclaimed that the parliamentary deputies who were present at Ta'if and signed the Accords were essentially agents of regional powers, rather than representatives of local constituencies (*al-Safir*, 5 October 1989).
6. The end of the Iran–Iraq war in June 1988, the death of Khomeini in 1989, and the ascent of Rafsanjani to the republic's presidency brought about a marked change in the Iranian posture on the hostage issue. The new Iranian leadership now gave precedence to the rebuilding of the country's devastated infrastructure and economy. In this new context, for a cash-strapped Iran the continued holding of the Westerners was no longer an asset to Iranian foreign objectives. In particular, by bringing about the release of the hostages, Iran hoped to retrieve its overseas financial assets, frozen by the United States. A. A. R. Norton, *Hizballah of Lebanon* (New York: Council on Foreign Relations, 1999), p. 19.
7. Interview with *al-Hayat*, 20 January 1989; *al-Shira'*, 23 January 1989.
8. Interview with Fadlallah, *al-Shira'*, 23 January 1989.
9. Interview with Fadlallah, *al-Bayrak*, 6 March 1987; *al-Hawadeth*, 13 February 1987; *Hostage*, ABC documentary, 1999. Fadlallah declared unambiguously that there was neither Islamic legal justification nor moral righteousness in the kidnapping of innocents. *Washington Post*, 16 April 1986. 'It is forbidden to kidnap or kill an innocent person because one has a score to settle with a head of state.' AFP (Beirut), 15 March 1987, in Martin Kramer, 'The Moral Logic of Hizbullah', in Walter Reich (ed.), *Origins of Terrorism* (Cambridge: Cambridge University Press, 1990), p. 154. Western hostages 'cannot be held responsible for the actions of their government'. *Washington Post*, 16 April 1986.
10. *al-Hawadeth*, 29 March 1991.
11. M. H. Fadlallah, *Iradat al-Quwwa* [The Will of Power] (Beirut: *Dar al-Malaak*, 2000) p. 147; Madani, *op. cit.*, p. 493; G. Izzi, *Hizbullah min al-Hilm al-Aydiyoulouji ila al-Waqi'iyyah al-Siyasiyyah*, [Hizbullah from ideological vision to political realism] (Kuwait: al-Qurtas, 1998), p. 77. For Fadlallah, the call to disarm Hizbullah was tantamount to forfeiting the fight against Israel (*al-Duwaliyya*, 25 August 1993).
12. *al-Liwa*, 17 December 1988.
13. *Ibid.*
14. *al-Safeer*, 22 April 1989; *al-Sharq*, 22 April 1989.
15. *al-Nahar*, 22 April 1989.
16. *al-Nahar*, 3 October 1989.
17. Fadlallah, *al-Khiyaar al-Akhar*, p. 117. In Hizbullah's 'Open Letter' or manifesto, enunciated in 1985, the party unequivocally rejected the Lebanese political entity, and denounced its system of government as an extension of the Western 'neo-imperial' order, and an integral part of the geopolitical realm that 'is hostile to Islam'. The whole structure was depicted as oppressive and unjust in its foundations: 'Any attempt to reform or patch up the prevailing regime will be in vain, as its decrepit state is beyond repair, and therefore the only viable and necessary prescription for this malady is to transform the whole political regime from its roots.'

18. *Ibid.*
19. *Ibid.*
20. *al-Aalem*, 22 December 1990, p. 22.
21. *Ibid.*
22. *al-Wadah al-Islamiyya*, 14 October 1988, p. 40.
23. *Ibid.*, p. 42.
24. *al-'Ahd*, 1 March 1989.
25. *Ibid.*
26. *Ibid.*
27. *Ibid.*
28. *Ibid.* The chief impediment to Fadlallah's agenda for Islamic governance was undoubtedly confessionalism; it was seen to be divisive and exclusivist.
29. *al-'Ahd*, 1 March 1989.
30. *al-Wahdah al-Islamiyya*, 26 January 1989.
31. Questions from *al-Nahar* (www.mawlawi.net).
32. *Ibid.*
33. *Ibid.*
34. Asked by his interviewer whether the advocated *Dawlat al-Insan* was intended to supplant the original advocacy of an Islamic regime, Fadlallah's reply was emphatic: 'Since 40 years ago until the present, I have not retreated, nor will I ever, from [disseminating] this slogan of the Islamic state.' *al-Wahdah al-Islamiyya*, 26 January 1989, p. 13.
35. *Ibid.*
36. Fadlallah expounded on the issue of Islamist-instituted reform and institutional integration in a series of insightful articles that analysed the strategies pursued and challenges faced by Islamic political activists. The first of these studies on the subject, which appeared in the Islamist periodical *al-Muntalaq*, to which Fadlallah was a regular and eminent contributor, was published in April 1984. Those articles were later republished in his influential book, *al-Harakah al-Islamiyya* [The Islamic movement].
37. M. H. Fadlallah, *Kayfa Nuwaajah Qadiyat al-Taghyeer fil Ummah* [How do we face the issue of change in the *umma*?] *al-Muntalaq*, no. 27 (Febraury 1985), p. 31.
38. *al-Shira'*, 6 June 1988, cited in Fadlallah, *Umara' wa Qaba'il*, p. 107.
39. Swayd, *Islam wa Filisteen*, p. 80.
40. M. Hussein Fadlallah, 'Islamic Unity and Change', *Journal of Palestine Studies*, vol. 25, no. 1 (Autumn 1995), p. 67.
41. *Ibid.*, p. 76.
42. *Ibid.*, pp. 77–8.
43. *al-Nahar*, 22 July 1992.
44. *al-Shira'*, 6 June 1988.
45. *al-Wahadah al-Islamiyya*, 21 July 1988, p. 38.
46. *al-Nahar*, 22 July 1992.
47. *al-Diyar*, 30 September 1992.
48. *Ibid.*
49. *Ibid.*
50. *Ibid.*
51. *Ibid.*
52. *Ibid.*
53. *Ibid.*

54. *Ibid.*
55. *al-Anwar*, 16 October 1994.
56. M. H. Fadlallah, 'Qira'ah Islamiyya Sari'ah li Mafhoumay al-Hurriyah wal Dimouqratiyyah fil Janib al-Fikri al-Hadari' [A brief Islamic reading of the notions of freedom and democracy in civilisational thought] *al-Muntalaq*, no. 65 (April 1990), p. 18.
57. Shaykh al-Tufayli exhorted his followers in Bekaa to boycott the elections and even to destroy ballot boxes. He even considered severing ties with the movement he had helped to form, and establishing his own party, *Ansar Allah* (Partisans of God), Nizar A. Hamzeh, 'Lebanon's Hizbullah', *Third World Quarterly*, vol. 14, no. 2 (1993) p. 324.
58. M. Chartouni-Dubarry, 'Hizbullah: From Militia to Political Party', in R. Hollis and N. Shehadi (eds), *Lebanon on Hold* (Oxford: Centre of Lebanese Studies, 1996), p. 61.
59. *al-Nahar*, 16 September 1992.
60. M. Ranstorp, 'The Strategy and Tactics of Hizbullah's Current "Lebanonisation" Process', *Mediterranean Politics*, vol. 3, no. 1 (Summer 1998), p. 123. Hizbullah's parliamentary performance was repeated in the 1996 elections. Since 1992, Hizbullah has operated as Lebanon's premier opposition party to the administration of Prime Minister Rafiq al-Hariri. It has focused its energies on governmental policies, in particular highlighting government negligence, corruption and nepotism, and addressing the issue of the management of state funding to alleviate poverty, reconstruct the devastated South, generate employment, and establish social services for outlying regions of the country. Mats Warn, 'Staying the Course', (MA thesis, 1994), Chapter 4, p. 9 (www.AlMashriq.org).
61. *Ibid.*
62. Fadlallah, *al-Harakah al-Islamiyya*, p. 40
63. *al-Anwar*, 16 October 1994.
64. *Ibid.*
65. Shrarah, *Dawlat Hizbullah*, p. 370.
66. *Ibid.*
67. *al-Diyar*, 20 September 1992, *op. cit.*, p. 266
68. *Ibid.*
69. According to data published by the movement's Research and Documentation Office, the total number of operations conducted by Hizbullah's Islamic Resistance Movement in the five years prior to the 1992 parliamentary elections was 614. This contrasted sharply with the 2,374 operations during the five years from 1992 and 1996, inclusive (Izzi, *op. cit.*, p. 47).
70. Fadlallah, *Iradat al-Quwwa*, pp. 161, 301.
71. Srour, *al-Allamah Fadlallah*, pp. 143–4.
72. *Ibid.*
73. *Ibid.*, p. 145; Fadlallah, *Iradat al-Quwwa*, p. 136.
74. *al-Nahar*, 19 October 1987.
75. One such prominent Islamist, albeit of Sunni persuasion, was Fathi Yakan, founder and theoretician of Lebanon's *al-Jama' al-Islamiyya*. Yakan's views, both on Israel and on parliamentary elections, are almost indistinguishable from those of Fadlallah. Fathi Yakan, *al-Qadiyyah al-Filistiniyya min Munzoor Islami* [The Palestinian issue from an Islamic perspective] (Beirut: *al-Mu'assasah al-Risalah*, 1995) and Yakan, *Adwa' 'ala al-Tajribah al-Niyabiyya al-Islamiyya fi Lubnan* [Insights into the Islamic parliamentary experiment in Lebanon] (Beirut: *Mu'assasat al-Risalah*, 1996).

76. Fadlallah, *Iraadat al-Quwwa*, p. 186.
77. *Ibid.*, p. 305.
78. *Ibid.*, p. 188.
79. *Ibid.*, p. 195
80. W. Quandt, *Peace Process* (Berkeley: University of California Press, 1993), pp. 396–404.
81. Fadlallah, *Iradat al-Quwwa*, p. 195.
82. *al-Diyar*, 30 September 1992, in *al-Hiwaraat*, p. 268.
83. Space does not permit a detailed treatment of the subject. Suffice to say that the Islamists – despite the multiplicity of organisational groups they belong to, such as Hizbullah, al-Jama'a al-Islamiyya, Harakat al-Tawheed, and al-Tajammu al-'Ulama – were all at one in their uncompromising position on direct negotiations, much less a peace agreement, with Israel.
84. Srour, *op. cit.*, p. 129. By bringing a settlement or a resolution to the intractable Arab-Israeli conflict, the US sought both to reorder the geopolitical landscape in the wake of the dissolution of the Soviet Union, and to underpin its own strategic interests by pacifying so-called rejectionist states and nationalist and Islamist movements opposed to American tutelage and peace with Israel.
85. Srour, *op. cit.*, pp. 129–30; Fadlallah, *Hiwaraat,* p. 446.
86. *Ibid.*, p. 211; Fadlallah, *Hiwaraat*, p. 447.
87. S. al-Hasani, *al-Islamiyoun wa al-Tahaddiyat al-Mu'asirah* [The Islamists and contemporary challenges] (Beirut: *Dar al-Malaak*, 1995), p. 67.
88. *Ibid.*; *Sawt al-Fayha'*, 31 October 1991; Fadlallah, *Iraadat al-Quwwa*; pp. 213–14.
89. *Ibid.* p. 213.
90. *al-Nahar*, 14 November 1988; *al-'Ahd*, 18 November 1988.
91. Fadlallah, *Iradat al-Quwwa*, p. 360.
92. *Ibid.*, p. 377.
93. Fadlallah, *Iradat al-Quwwa*, p. 361.
94. *Ibid.*
95. *Ibid.*, p. 361.
96. *Ibid.*
97. *al-Wahdah al-Islamiyya*, 16 December 1988, p. 49.
98. *Ibid*, p. 23.
99. *Kayhan al-Arabi*, 18 September 1993.
100. Izzi, *op. cit.*, pp. 79–80.
101. Fadlallah, *Iradat al-Quwwa*, pp. 382, 387. Fadlallah accused the government of perpetrating the killings so as to suppress all populist movements opposed to US interests in the region, and thereby vindicate its pro-US stance (*Kayhan al-Arabi*, 18 September 1993).
102. Izzi, *op. cit.*, p. 80.
103. *Ibid.*
104. *Ibid.*
105. Interview, *Monday Morning*, 1 February 1993.
106. Fadlallah underscored the distinction between 'coexisting separately with falsehood' (Israel) and conferring legitimacy, formally, on the 'Zionist' state (*al-Safeer*, 19 June 1995, in *Hiwaraat*, p. 314).
107. *Shu'un al-Awsat*, September 1993, p. 8.
108. *Nida' al-Watan*, 18 August 1993.

109. Fadlallah, *Iradat al-Quwwa*, p. 438.
110. *Shu'oun al-Awsat*, 14 December 1992.
111. Jaber, *Hezbollah*, pp. 167, 172; Fadlallah, *Harb al-Iradat*, pp. 160–1.
112. Madani, *op. cit.*, p. 495; Fadlallah, *Harb al-Iradat*, p. 166.
113. Like the previous offensive, the massive seventeen-day air, sea and land assault on South Lebanon was aimed at eliminating Hizbullah's military capacity to launch attacks on northern Israel. The Israeli operation, code-named 'Grapes of Wrath', caused over 200,000 southerners to flee their homes, and led to 200 Lebanese fatalities, including the villagers who were killed while sheltering in the United Nations base in the village of Qana. The Qana massacre, as it became known, precipitated frenetic American shuttle mediation that eventually led to a truce. Jaber, *op. cit.*, p. 202; Fadlallah, *Harb al-Iradat*, pp. 192–3; Ranstorp, *op. cit.*, p. 103; Augustus R. Norton, 'Walking between Raindrops', *Mediterranean Quarterly*, vol. 3, no. 1 (Summer 1999), p. 96.
114. H. Mazahim, 'Hizbullah wa Ishkaliyat al-Tawfeeq bayna al-Aydiyoulijiyya wal Waqi'', [Hizbullah and the problem of reconciling ideology and reality] *Sh'oun al-Awsat*, no. 59 (January–February 1997), p. 67.
115. Madani, *op. cit.*, p. 495. The declaration was revealing, given that it marked the first time that a Hizbullah leader had openly delimited the operational extent of the Islamic movement's liberation struggle.
116. *Ibid.*, p. 493.
117. *al-Ahd*, 8 December 1995; *al-Najwa*, 19 February 1996; *al-Safeer*, 21 June 1995.
118. *al-Ahd*, 8 December 1995.
119. *al-Hawadeth*, 18 August 1995.
120. M. H., Fadlallah, 'al-Harakat al-Islamiyya al-Arabiyya wa Ishkaliyat al-Taswiyya wa al-Tatbi' [The Islamic Arab movements and the problem of settlement and normalisation], in *al-Harakat al-Islamiyya fi Muwajihat al-Taswiyya* [The Islamic movements in opposition to the (Arab–Israeli) settlement] (Beirut: Markaz al-Dirasat al-Istiratijiyya wal Buhouth, 1995), p. 141; Fadlallah, *Majallat al-Fath*, no. 313, 16 April 1994, cited in Z. Ghazawi, *al-Mu'assasah al-Diniyya al-Islamiyya wal Kiyan al-Sahyouni* [The Islamic religious institution and the 'Zionist entity'] (Beirut: *Ghadir*, 1996), pp. 225–6, note 2.
121. *Dunya al-Arab*, no.70 (September 1990), in Fadlallah, *Hiwaraat fil Fikr*, pp. 134–5.
122. *al-Diyar*, 5 May 1995.
123. *al-Shira'*, 10 January 1994.
124. *al-Wasat*, 24 January 1994
125. Izzi, *op. cit.*, p. 85.
126. *Ibid.*, p. 86; *al-Wasat*, *op. cit.*
127. *al-Hawadeth*, 4 March 1994.
128. *al-Bilad*, 26 September 1992, p. 46.
129. *al-Watan al-Arabi*, 28 January 1994.
130. *al-Bilad*, *op. cit.* Fadlallah articulated his views in detail in his recent book, al-Hasani (ed.), *al-Ma'alem al-Jadidah* .
131. Izzi, *op. cit.*, p. 86.
132. *Ibid.*, *al-Watan al-Arabi*, 7 January 1994.
133. *Ibid.* For more details, see: S. Rosny, 'The Tragedy of Fatema al-Zahra in the Debate of two Shiite Theologians in Lebanon', in: R. Brunner and W. Ende (eds), *The Twelver Shia in Modern Times* (Leiden: E. J. Brill, 2001), pp. 207–19. For sympathetic expositions of Fadlallah's views on the subject, see: J. S. al-Bahrani, *Marja'iyyat al-marhala wa*

Ghibar al-Taghyeer: Dirasah 'Amaliyya Tawdihiyya li ba'ad al-Turuhat al-Fikriyya wa al-Fiqhiyya wa al-Tarikhiyya li Samahat Ayatullah al-'Uzma al-Sayyid Muhammad Husayn Fadlallah (Beirut: Dar al-Amir, 1998); M. al-Husayni, *Hawamesh Naqdiyya, Dirasa fi kitab Ma'sat al-Zahra'* (Beirut: Mu'assasat al-'Aref, 1997); N. Noor al-Din, *Ma'sat Kitab al-Ma'sat* (Beirut: Dar al-Rasoul al-Akram, 1997).

134. *Ibid.*, *al-Watan al-Arabi*, 7 January 1994.
135. *al-Watan al-Arabi*, 11 November 1997.
136. *Ibid.*
137. Interview with *al-Jihad* paper, 15 February 1988, cited in al-Hasani, *Sira' al-Iraadaat*, p. 99.

Chapter Eight

1. B. Baktiari, 'Iran's new President', *Middle East Insight*, November-December 1997, p. 17.
2. *Ibid.*; M. Mehran, 'Political Reform and Education in Iran', *Comparative Education*, vol. 39, no. 3, August 2003, p. 1.
3. See http://news.bbc.co.uk/2/hi/middle_east/3879535.stm.
4. *al-Nahar*, 7 October 1999.
5. *Ibid.*
6. Fadlallah omits to mention where and when that meeting took place. Fadlallah, *Ittijiahaat wa 'alaam*, p. 59.
7. *Ibid.*
8. F. Abdul-Jabar, 'The Genesis and Development of Marja'ism versus the State', in Abdul-Jabar, ed., *Ayatollahs, Sufis and Ideologues* (London: Saqi Books, 2002), p. 86.
9. 'Tawa'ef Lubnan,' documentary series, al-Arabiyya Satellite Television, 2003.
10. Fadlallah, *Ittijahaat wa' 'alaam*, pp. 32, 63–4.
11. *Ibid.*, p. 73.
12. *Ibid.*, p. 59; Fadlallah, 'al-Marja'iyya: al-Waqe' wal Muqtada', in Fadlallah et al. (eds), *Araa' fil Marja'iyya al-Shi'iyya* (Beirut: Dar al-Rawdah, 1994), p. 113.
13. *Ibid.*, pp. 34, 38.
14. For details of the background and polemics of Fadlallah's marja'iyya, as recounted by a conservative cleric, see Muhammad Baqer al-Safi, *Fitnat Fadlallah* (n.pl.: n.pub., 1997); *al-Watan al-Arabi*, 12 April 2000; interview with Fadlallah, 'Kalam al-Nass', LBC Television, 11 May 2000; Fadlallah, *Ittijahaat wa 'ilaam*, p. 133.
15. Fadlallah, *al-Mudannas wal Muqaddas* (Beirut: Riad al-Rayyes, 2003), p. 379.
16. Fadlallah, *Ittijahat wa 'ilaam*, (Beirut: Dar al-Malak, n.d.), p.134
17. A 'Question and Answer' session with Fadlallah, 6 March 1996, recorded on videotape and in the possession of the author.
18. Fadlallah, 'al-Istinsakh wa al-Din', in Abdul Wahid 'Ilwani (ed.) *al-Istinsakh: Jadal al-'Ilm wa al-Din wa al-Akhlaq* (Damascus: Dar al-Fikr, 1997), pp. 99–101; Wahbah al-Zuhayli, 'al-Istinsakh', in A. W. 'Alwani, *op.cit.* pp. 115–32; 'Istinsakh al-Bashar wa Ra'i al-Qaradawi fih', *al-Rayah*, 30 December 2002, www.qaradawi.net.
19. 'Tafasil al-Khilaf bayna Fadlallah wa Hizbullah', *al-Watan al-Arabi*, No. 889, 7 January 1994, pp. 34–5; unpublished internal document, dated 14 October 1997; LBC interview, *op. cit.*
20. LBC interview, *op. cit.*; al-Safi, *op. cit.*; *al-Watan al-Arabi*, op.cit., pp. 32–5.
21. Interview with Fadlallah, *Monday Morning*, 26 June 2000.

22. Interview with Fadlallah, LBC Satellite Television, 11 May 2000.
23. Interview with Fadlallah, *Monday Morning*, 26 June 2000, www.bayynet.net; Interview with Fadlallah, Maftooh, NTV Satellite Television, n.d., in *al-Muddannas*, p. 230; interview with Fadlallah, *Monday Morning*, E. Zisser, 'Hizballah' in: B. Rubin, Revolutionaries and Reformers (Albany: State University of new York Press, 2003), p. 100.
24. Interview with Fadlallah, NTV Satellite Television, n.d., op.cit; pp. 229–30; interview with Fadlallah, *Monday Morning*, 26 June 2000; Zisser, *op. cit.*, p. 95.
25. T.'Itrisi, 'Hizbullah wa Tahrir al-Janoub', *Shu'un al-Awsat*, nos 96–7 (June–July 2000), pp. 4–7; M. al-Sayyid Sa'id, 'al-'Aam wal Khass fi al-Tajribah al-Nidaliyyah li Hizbullah', *Sutour*, no. 58 (September 2001), p. 25; Ahmad Mansour, 'Hizbullah kama yarahu al-Share' al-Suri', *op. cit.*, pp. 26–9.
26. Interview with Fadlallah, MBC, 28 December 2001.
27. Interview with Fadlallah, MBC Satellite Television, 28 December 2001, in Fadlallah, al-Mudannas, p. 192; interview with Fadlallah, al-hiwar al-Maftooh, al-Jazeera, 30 March 2002, in al-Muddannas, p. 213.
28. Interview with Fadlallah, al-Jazeera, 30 March 2002, p. 208.
29. *al-Liwa'*, 17 September 2001; *al-Safir*, 29 December 2001; *al-Liwa*, 17 September 2001.
30. *al-khalij*, 26 October 2001; *al-Liwa'*, 17 September 2001.
31. *al-Safir*, 29 December 2001.
32. *Ibid.*
33. *al-Liwa*, 17 September 2001; Lebanon Television, interview with Fadlallah, 29 September 2001.
34. Fadlallah, *al-muqaddas wal mudannas*, p. 180; Fadlallah, *al-Mudannas*, p. 357.
35. *al-Safir*, 29 December 2004.
36. *al-Telegraph*, (Arabic tri-weekly newspaper), 26 November 2004, p. 11.
37. *al-Liwa'*, 9 September 2002; *al-Khalij*, 26 October 2001;
38. Interview with Fadlallah, al-Jazeera, 30 April 2002, in *al-Mudannas* p. 206.
39. *al-Safir*, 29 December 2001; *al-Diyar*, 22 October 2001.
40. *al-Diyar*, interview with Fadlallah, 22 October 2001.
41. *Ibid.*
42. *al-Khalij*, 26 October 2001.
43. Interview with Fadlallah, Hiwar Maftooh, 30 March 2002, in: Fadlallah *al-Mudannas*, p. 212.
44. Interview with Fadlallah, al-Daleel, June 2002, in *al-Mudannas*, p. 291.
45. www.ebaa.net/hewarat/index; *al-Liwa*, 9 September 2002; Interview with Fadlallah, Ikkaz, newspaper, n.d., in *al-Mudannas*, pp. 237–8.
46. Among ayatollahs – the second tier of 'ulama – who opposed the occupation was and remains Ayatollah Mahmoud al-Hasani (see www.alwihdah.com/view.asp?cat=1&id=1230).
47. *al-Watan al-Arabi*, no. 879, 7 July 1994, p. 35.
48. *Majllat Yaqatha*, 5 October 2002.
49. Interview with Fadlallah, *Ikaaz* newspaper, *op. cit.*, pp. 317–8.
50. *Ibid.*, pp. 317–9.
51. *Ibid.*, p. 237.
52. *Ibid.*
53. *Ibid.*

54. *al-Sharq al-Awsat*, 11 September 2004.
55. Fadlallah interview, *al-Hayat*, 3 September 2004.
56. *al-Hayat*, 3 September 2004.
57. See www.islamonline.net/Arabic/news//2004-01/article05.shtml. In August 2003, al-Khalisi attacked the Iraqi Provisional Government as a puppet administration, imposed on the country's citizens by the Americans. He declared that the 'only option open to Iraqis is resistance by all available means'. Earlier in April of that year, al-Khalisi called for a jihad against American military forces in Iraq. Headed by Dr. Shaykh Hareth al-Dari, the clerical body issued a fatwa in August prohibiting all Iraqis from joining the American military campaign to crush Muqtada al-Sadr's al-Mahdi Army.
58. For background information on the movement, see J. Cole, 'The United States and Shi'ite Religious Factions in Post-Ba'thist Iraq', *The Middle East Journal*, vol. 52, issue 4 (August 2003), pp. 1–16; Y. Nakash, 'The Shi'ites and the Future of Iraq', *Foreign Affairs*, July–August 2003, (www.foreignaffairs.org).
59. J. White and R. Philips, 'Sadrists Revolt Provides Lessons for Counterinsurgency in Iraq', *Janes Intelliegence Review*, August 2004, pp. 22–8; www.bayynat.org/www/Arabic/nachatat/bayan14082004.htm; *al-Hayat*, 3 September 2004.
60. *Ibid.*
61. Fadlallah interview, *al-Hayat*, 3 September 2004;
62. Fadlallah, *Ittijahaat wa i'lam*, pp. 185–6.
63. *al-Safir*, 29 December 2001.
64. Fadlallah, *al-Mudannas wal Muqadannas*, p. 62.
65. *al-Telegraph*, 26 November 2004.

Conclusion

1. M. H. Fadlallah, 'al-Sahwah al-Islamiyya, Ishkalat, mawaqif, wa tatalu'at' [The Islamic awakening: issues, standpoints, and aspirations] *al-Muntalaq*, no. 54 (May 1989), pp. 13–14.

Appendix

1. F. Khuri, 'The 'Ulama: A Comparative Study of Sunni and Shi'a Religious Officials', *Middle Eastern Studies*, vol. 23 (1987), p. 293.
2. Humphreys, *op. cit.*, p. 208; Moaddel, *op. cit.*, pp. 520–1; V. Martin, *Islam and Modernism* (London: I. B. Tauris, 1988), p. 15.
3. Where the two denominations differ is over the interpretation of particular verses that have doctrinal import or juridical significance. In addition, whereas for the Sunnis the *hadiths* comprise the utterances of the Prophet Muhammad, for the Shi'a they also include the authoritative sayings of the Twelve infallible Imams. In addition, each denomination has separate, mutually exclusive compilations of Prophetic *hadiths*, based on dissimilar chains of transmission.
4. *Qur'an*, ch. 58 v. 11, ch. 35 v. 28, ch. 9 v. 122; ch. 4, v. 59; A. A. al-Badri, *Al-Islam bayna al-'Ulama' wa al-Hukkam* [Islam between the scholars and the rulers] (Medina: Al-Maktabah al-'Ilmiyya, n.d.), p. 37; S. M. Sabzavari, *Islamic Political and Juristic Thought in Safavid Iran* (Glasgow: Royston Publishers, 1990), p. 39.
5. Ibn Kathir, *Mukhtasar Tafsir ibn Kathir* [Ibn Kathir's Abridged Commentary] (Beirut: Dar al-Ma'rifa, 1987), vol. 1, p. 207; M. J. Kister, 'Social and Religious Concepts of Authority in Islam', *Jerusalem Studies in Arabic and Islam*, vol. 18 (1994), pp. 98–9.

6. The only exception to this pattern of continuity was Hussein, the Third Imam, who succeeded through the eldest male offspring from among the progeny of 'Ali. S. A. Q. al-Kho'ie, *al-Bayan fi Tafsir al-Qur'an* [Rhetoric in the commentary on the Qur'an] (Beirut: Dar al-Zahra', 1992), p. 467; J. al-Mughniyya, *Al-Jawame' wa al-Fawariq bayna al-Sunna wa al-Shi'a* [Commonalities and differences between the Sunnis and Shi'a] (Beirut: Mu'assasat 'Izzedeen, 1994), p. 119; M. H. Fadlallah, *Min Wahy al-Qur'an* [From the revelation of the Qur'an] (Beirut: Dar al-Zahra', 1983), vol. 7, pp. 227–9.
7. H. Enayet, *Modern Islamic Political Thought* (London: Macmillan, 1982), p. 21; M. 'Imarah, *Al-Islam wa Falsafat al-Hukm* [Islam and the philosophy of governance] (Beirut: Al-Mu'assasah al-'Arabiyyah li al-Dirasat wa al-Nashr, 1977), p. 75; K. D. al-Sawi, *Tatawwur al-Fikr al-Siyasi ind Ahl al-Sunnah* [The development of Sunni political thought] (Amman: Dar al-Bashir, 1992), p. 38; Enayet, *op. cit.*, p. 5; M. Momen, *An Introduction to Shi'i Islam* (New Haven: Yale University Press, 1985), pp. 14–16; A. K. S. Lambton, *State and Government in Medieval Islam* (Oxford: Oxford University Press, 1981), pp. 10, 15, 18, 19; B. Lewis, 'Usurpers and Tyrants', in R. M. Savory and D. A. Agius (eds), *Logos Islamikos* (Toronto: Pontifical Institute of Medieval Studies, 1984), p. 259.
8. M. M. Shams al-Din, *Nizam al-Hukm wa al-Idarah fi al-Islam* [The system of government and administration in Islam] (Beirut: Al-Duwaliyya al-Mu'assasah, 1995), pp. 105–7; H. Hanafi, *Al-Turath wa al-Tajdid* [Heritage and renewal] (Beirut: Dar al-Tanwir, 1988), pp. 242–3; Shams al-Din, *op. cit.*, p. 388; Lambton, *op. cit.*, p. 222; Momen, *op. cit.*, pp. 19–21.
9. The verse referred to commences with the key words: 'Al-yawma akmaltu lakum deenakum…' ['Today I have perfected your religion …']. *Qur'an*, ch. 5, v. 3; F. I. Khuri, *Imams and Emirs* (London: Saqi Books, 1990), pp. 108–9; A. M. Subhi, *Nazariyat al-Imamah lida al-Shi'a Ithna 'Ashariyya* [Theory of the Imams in Twelver Shi'ism] (Beirut: Dar al-Nahdah al-Arabiyya, 1991); Fadlallah, *op. cit.*, vol. 8, pp. 40–2; Lambton, *op. cit.*, p. 221; Enayat, *op. cit.*, p. 4; H. Dabashi, *Authority in Islam* (New Brunswick: Transaction Books, 1993), pp. 98–9.
10. M. H. Tabataba'i, *Shi'a* (Qom: Ansariyan Publishers, 1981), p. 40; Enayat, *op. cit.*, pp. 4–5; Subhi, *op. cit.*, pp. 71–3; Tabatabai, *op. cit.*, pp. 174–5.
11. Momen, *op. cit.*, p. 148; W. Madelung, 'Authority in Twelver Shi'ism in the Absence of the Imam', in G. Makdisi et al. (eds), *La Notion d'Autorite au Moyen Age* (Paris: Presses Universitaires de France, 1982), p. 163; J. Mughniyya, *Al-Shi'a fi al-Mizan* [The Shi'a in the scales] (Beirut: Dar al-Tayyar al-Jadid, 1989), pp. 334–5; Madelung, *op. cit.*, p. 163; Subhi, *op. cit.*, p. 74; Mughniyya, *Al-Shi'a*, pp. 42–4; Madelung, *op. cit.*, p. 104. Sunni scholars have traditionally cited a *hadith* of the Prophet in support of that view: 'My community will never concur in error.' Mughniyya, *Al-Jawami'*, p. 86; Lambton, *op. cit.*, p. 15; Enayat, *op. cit.*, p. 21.
12. Subhi, *op. cit.*, pp. 349–50; Madelung, *op. cit.*, p. 165; Momen, *op. cit.*, pp. 24–5.
13. Subhi, *op. cit.*, pp. 313–2; Momen, *op. cit.*, pp. 26–8; Momen, *op. cit.*, pp. 28–30; Subhi, *op. cit.*, pp. 330–4.
14. Momen, *op. cit.*, p. 30; Y. Richard, *Shi'ite Islam* (Cambridge: Blackwell Publishers, 1995), pp. 27–8; Momen, *op. cit.*, p. 30; Richard, *op. cit.*, pp. 28–9; Momen, *op. cit.*, p. 30; Richard, *op. cit.*, pp. 28–9.
15. Momen, *op. cit.*, pp. 33, 240–3; Richard, *op. cit.*, pp. 30–2; Mughniyya, *Al-Shi'a* , pp. 396–7; Momen, *op. cit.*, pp. 240–3; W. Ende, 'The Flagellations of Muharram and the

Shi'ite 'Ulama', *Der Islam*, vol. 55 (1978), p. 20; Y. Nakash, 'An Attempt to Trace the Origin of the Rituals of '*Ashoura*', *Die Welt des Islams*, vol. 33 (1993), pp. 161–3.

16. Enayat, *op. cit.*, p. 181; Richard, *op. cit.*, pp. 29, 32; Subhi, *op. cit.*, pp. 349–50; Richard, *op. cit.*, p. 33; Madelung, *op. cit.*, p. 165; H. A. Hasan, *Al-Fikr al-Siyasi al-Shi'i* [Shi'i political thought] (Beirut: Dar al-'Alamiyya, 1988), pp. 270–3; Momen, *op. cit.*, pp. 35–8.
17. Momen, *op. cit.*, p. 39; Richard, *op. cit.*, p. 36.
18. Mughniyya, *Al-Shi'a*, p. 249; Momen, *op. cit.*, p. 44; M. Watt, 'The Significance of the Early Stages of Imami Shi'ism', in N. Keddie (ed.), *Religion and Politics in Iran* (New Haven: Yale University Press, 1983), p. 27; Momen, *op. cit.*, pp. 45, 59–60; S. A. Arjomand, *The Shadow of God and the Hidden Imam* (Chicago: University of Chicago Press, 1984), pp. 36, 40; Momen, *op. cit.*, pp. 45, 116; Richard, *op. cit.*, pp. 40–1; Mughniyya, *Al-Shi'a*, p. 252.
19. Momen, *op. cit.*, pp. 162–4; J. M. Hussain, *The Occultation of the Twelfth Imam* (New York: Methuen, 1986), pp. 79–84; Arjomand, *op. cit.*, pp. 40–3; Watt, *op. cit.*, pp. 27–2; Momen, *op. cit.*, pp. 162–4; Arjomand, *op. cit.*, pp. 40–2; Arjomand, *op. cit.*, pp. 43–4; Momen, *op. cit.*, pp. 164–5; Mughniyya, *Al-Shi'a*, pp. 252–3.
20. Hussain, *op. cit.*, pp. 81, 117; D. M. Maceon, 'Changes in Charismatic Authority in Qajar Shi'ism', in E. Bosworth and C. Hillenbrand (eds), *Qajar Iran* (Edinburgh: Edinburgh University Press, 1983), p. 153.
21. Hussain, *op. cit.*, p. 156; Mughniyya, *op. cit.*, pp. 252–3; Momen, *op. cit.*, p. 198; Madelung, *op. cit.*, p. 166; M. B. al-Sadr, *Buhouth Islamiyya* [Islamic Studies] (Beirut: Dar al-Zahra', 1991), pp. 99–100; Momen, *op. cit.*, p. 198; Madelung, *op. cit.*, p. 166.
22. Maceon, *op. cit.*, pp. 154, 156.
23. W. Madelung, 'A Treatise of the Sharif al-Murtada on the Legality of Working for the Government', *Bulletin of the School of Oriental and African Studies*, vol. 40, no. 3 (1980), pp. 26–7.
24. *Ibid.*, p. 30.
25. Watt, *op. cit.*, p. 30; N. Calder, 'Legitimacy and Accommodation in Safavid Iran', *Iran*, vol. 25 (1987), p. 102; Lambton, *op. cit.*, pp. 264, 266; Arjomand, *op. cit.*, pp. 105, 109–10.
26. Lambton, *op. cit.*, pp. 266–7.
27. *Ibid.*, pp. 267–8; S. A. Arjomand, 'The Clerical State and the Emergence of a Shi'ite Hierocracy in Safavid Iran', *Journal of the Economic and Social History of the Orient*, vol. 28 (1985), p. 189; Arjomand, 'The Clerical State', p. 189; Lambton, *op. cit.*, p. 273; Arjomand, 'The Clerical State', p. 189, 196–7; Momen, *op. cit.*, pp. 190–1.
28. A. J. Newman, 'Towards a Reconsideration of the Isfahan School of Philosophy', *Studia Iranica*, vol. 15 (1986), p. 191; N. Calder, 'Zakat in Imami Shi'i Jurisprudence', *Bulletin of the School of Oriental and African Studies*, vol. 45, no. 3 (1981), pp. 470–5.
29. Arjomand, 'The Clerical State', pp. 191–2; A. J. Newman, 'The Myth of the Classical Migration to Safawid Iran', *Die Welt des Islams*, vol. 33, no. 1 (1993), pp. 83–4; Sabzavari, *op. cit.*, pp. 28–30; Momen, *op. cit.*, p. 198.
30. *Ibid.*, p. 117; A. J. Newman, 'The Nature of the *Akhbari/Usuli* Dispute in late Safavid Iran', pt 1, *Bulletin of the School of Oriental and African Studies*, (1992), p. 22; J. R. I. Cole, 'Shi'i Clerics in Iraq and Iran, 1722–1780', *Iranian Studies*, vol. 18, no. 1 (1985), p. 13; Momen, *op. cit.*, p. 198; Newman, 'The Nature', p. 22; Cole, *op. cit.*, p. 13; Maceoin, *op. cit.*, p. 158; L. Binder, 'The Proofs of Islam', in G. Makdisi (ed.), *Arabic*

and Islamic Studies in Honor of Hamilton A. R. Gibb (Cambridge: Harvard University Press, 1965), p. 125.

31. Arjomand, *The Shadow*, p. 231; N. R. Keddie, 'The Roots of the 'Ulama's Power in Modern Iran', in N. R. Keddie (ed.), *Scholars, Saints and Sufis* (Berkeley: University of California Press, 1972), pp. 223–4; H. Algar, 'Shi'ism and Iran in the Eighteenth Century', in T. Naff and R. Owen (eds), *Studies in Eighteenth Century Islamic History* (Carbondale: n.p., 1977), p. 330.
32. Keddie, *op. cit.*, pp. 223–4; Algar, *op. cit.*, p. 300; Cole, *op. cit.*, p. 13; Algar, *op. cit.*, p. 300; Cole, *op. cit.*, pp. 20–3.
33. Maceoin, *op. cit.*, p. 159; A. K. Moussawi, 'The Establishment of the Position of *Marja'iyyat-I-Taqlid* in the Twelver Shi'i Community', *Iranian Studies*, vol. 18, no. 1 (Winter 1985), pp. 35–7.
34. Martin, *op. cit.*, pp. 22–3; A. K. S. Lambton, *Qajar Persia* (London: Tauris, 1987), p. 1.
35. Arjomand, *The Shadow*, p. 223; Martin, *op. cit.*, p. 32; Lambton, *Qajar Persia*, p. 29.
36. Martin, *op. cit.*, pp. 22–3; Keddie, *op. cit.*, pp. 22–3.
37. Keddie, *op. cit.*, pp. 213–4; Martin, *op. cit.*, pp. 22–3.
38. Arjomand, *The Shadow*, pp. 248–9; Algar, *op. cit.*, p. 300; Lambton, *Qajar Persia*, p. 198.
39. Keddie, *op. cit.*, pp. 214–15; Martin, *op. cit.*, p. 4; W. M. Floor, 'The Revolutionary Character of the Iranian 'Ulama', in N. R. Keddie (ed.), *Religion and Politics in Iran* (New Haven: Yale University Press, 1983), pp. 74–5; Martin, *op. cit.*, p. 4; H. Algar, *Religion and State in Iran* (Berkeley: University of California Press, 1969), pp. 213–24; Algar, *Religion*, p. 215; Martin, *op. cit.*, p. 4; Algar, *op. cit.*, pp. 213–14.
40. Floor, *op. cit.*, pp. 74–5; Arjomand, *The Shadow*, pp. 248–9; Lambton, *Qajar Persia*, p. 198; Floor, *op. cit.*, p. 75; Martin, *op. cit.*, p. 4; Lambton, *Qajar Persia*, pp. 30, 198.
41. Algar, *Religion*, p. 260.

Bibliography

1. Primary Sources

a. Arabic Books and Articles

Abd al-Jabbar, M.(ed.), *al-Mashrou' al-Hadari al-Islami, fi Hiwar ma' al-'Allama al-Sayyid Muhammad Husayn Fadlallah* [The Islamic civilizational scheme: a dialogue with *Sayyid* Fadlallah] (Beirut: Mu'asasat al-'Aref, 1991).

Ahmad, A. & al-Qadi, A. (ed.), *Dunya al-Shabab, fi Hiwar ma' Ayatullah al-Sayyid Muhammad Husayn Fadlallah* [The world of the youth: An interview with *Sayyid* Fadlallah] (Beirut: Mu'asasat al-'Aref, 1995).

Ahmad, A. & al-Qadi, A. (ed.), *Hiwar ma' Samahat Ayatullah al-'Uzma al-Sayyid Muhammad Husayn Fadlallah fi Fiqh al-Hayat* [An interview with *Sayyid* Fadlallah on the jurisprudence of life] (Beirut: Mu'asasat al-'Aref,1997).

al-Hasani, S. (ed.), *al-Ma'alem al-Jadidah li al-Marja'iyya al-Shi'iya: Dirasah wa Hiwar ma' Ayatullah al-Sayyid Muhammad Husayn Fadlallah* [The new signposts of the *Shi'i Marja'iyya*: A study on, and dialogue with, Sayyid Fadlallah] (Beirut: Dar al-Malaak,1993).

al-Hasani, S. (ed.), *al-Islamiyoun wa al-Tahadiyyat al-Mu'asirah: Mutarahaat Fikriyyah wa Siyasiyyah li Samahat Ayatullah al-'Uzma al-Sayyid Muhammad Husayn Fadlallah* [The Islamists and the contemporary challenges: Intellectual and political propositions of *Sayyid* Fadlallah] (Beirut: Dar al-Malaak, 1995).

al-Hasani, S. (ed.), *Siraa' al-Iradaat: Diraasah fi al-Fikr al-Haraki li Samahat Ayatullah Muhammad Husayn Fadlallah* [The contest of wills: A study on the activist thought of *Sayyid* Fadlallah] (Beirut: Dar al-Malaak,1995).

al-Holou, W. Y. & al-Faqih, I. (ed.), *As'ilah wa Rudoud min al-Qalb* [Questions and responses from the heart] (Beirut: Dar al-Malaak,1993).

al-Imam fi Muwajihat al-Sahyouniyya [*Imam* (Khomeini) in confrontation with Zionism] (Teheran: Markaz al-'Ilam, 1403 A. H. (1983/84).

al-Kho'ie, A. Q., *al-Bayan fi Tafsir al-Qur'an* [Rhetoric in the commentary of the *Qur'an*] (Beirut: Dar al-Zahra,1992).

al-Lahham, K. (ed.), *Qadaya Islamiyya Mu'asira: Hiwar ma' al-Sayyid Muhammad Husayn Fadlallah* [Contemporary Islamic issues: a dialogue with *Sayyid* Fadlallah] (Beirut: Dar al-Malaak, 1993).

al-Mausawi, S. (ed.), *Li al-Insan wa al-Hayat, Ayatullah al-'Uzma al-Sayyid Muhammad Husayn Fadlallah* [For the sake of man and life](Beirut: Dar al-Malaak, 1996).

al-Nabahani, T. D., *al-Dawla al-Islamiyya* [The Islamic state] (Jerusalem: n. p., 1953)

al-Nabahani, T. D., *al-Takattul al-Hizbi* [The partisan bloc] (Jerusalem: n.p., 1953).

al-Nabahani, T. D., *al-Khilafa* [The caliphate] (Jerusalem: n.p., 1953).

al-Qubaysi, M., '*Lamha Mawjizah min Hayat al-Marja' Ayatullah al-'Uzma al-Sayyid Muhammad Husayn Fadlallah,*' [A brief glimpse from the life of *Sayyid* Fadlallah], www.bayynat.org.lb.

al-Qur'an al-Karim [The Holy Qur'an].

al-Sadr, M. B., *Lamha Fiqhiyya Tamhidiyya 'un al-Mushrou' Dustour al-*

*Jumhouriyya al-Islamiyya fi Iran [*A preliminary jurisprudential outline of the proposed constitution of the Islamic Republic of Iran] (Teheran: External Propagation Section, n.d.).

al-Sadr, M. B., *al-Islam Yaqoud al-Hayat* [Islam guides life] (Teheran: Ministry of Islamic Guidance, 1403 AH/ 1983 AD).

al-Sadr, M., *Minbar wa Mirhab* [Pulpit and niche] (Beirut: Dar al-Hawra,' 1987).

al-Sadr, M. B., *Iqtisaduna* [Our economics](Beirut: Dar al-Ta'aruf, 1989).

al-Sadr, M. B., *Falsafatuna* [Our philosophy](Beirut: Dar al-Ta'aruf, 1991).

al-Sadr, M. B., *Buhouth Islamiyya* [Islamic Studies] (Beirut: Dar al-Zahra, 1991).

al-Sadr, M. B., *Ahl al-Bayt* [The (Prophet's) Household] (Beirut: Dar al-Ta'aruf, n.d.)

Bin Judou, G. (ed.), *Khitaab al-Islamiyeen wa al-Mustaqbal: Hiwaraat ma' Samahat Ayatullah al-Sayyid Muhammad Husayn Fadlallah* [The Islamists' discourse and the future: dialogues with Sayyid Fadlallah (Beirut: Dar al-Malaak, 1995).

Fadlallah, M. H., *Dawr al-Mar'ah al-Risali* [Role of the missionary woman]

(Beirut: Religious Students of the American University, n.d.).

Fadlallah, M. H., '*al-Thawra al-Islamiyya fi Iran: Ta'ammulat min al-Dakhil*' [The Islamic Revolution in Iran: Reflections from within], *al-Muntalaq*, no. 8 (February-March 1980), pp. 12–17.

Fadlallah, M. H., '*al-Thawra al-Islamiyya fi Iran bayna al-Takhtit al-Maaddi wa al-Isnad al-Ilaahi*' [The Islamic Revolution in Iran between material planning and divine support], *al-Muntalaq*, no.10 (*Sha'ban* 1400 A. H. [June–July 1980]), pp. 6–12.

Fadlallah, M. H., '*al-Thawra al-Islamiyya: Durous wa 'Ibar*' [The Islamic Revolution: Lessons and Implications], *al-Hikma*, no. 8 (January 1981), republished in: *Ma' al-Hikma fi Khatt al-Islam* [Considering wisdom in the path of Islam] (Beirut: Mu'assasat al-Wafa, 1985), pp. 141–168.

Fadlallah, M. H., '*Taqdim,*' [introduction], in: *Risalatuna* [Our Message] (Beirut: *al-Dar al-Islamiyya*, 1981).

Fadlallah, M. H., '*Shahid al-Islam al-Sayyid Muhammad Baqir al-Sadr fi dawrihi al-Islami* [The martyr of Islam, *al-Sayyid* Baqir al-Sadr in his influential Islamic role] *al-Wahada al-Islamiyya* , no. 3, 13 April 1984, pp. 31–34.
Fadlallah, M. H., *Qasa'id li al-Islam wa al-Hayat* [Short poems for Islam] (Beirut: al-Mu'asasah al-Jam'iyah li al-Dirasat wa al-Nashr, 1984).
Fadlallah, M. H., *Qadayana 'ala Daw' al-Islam* [Our Affairs in the light of Islam] (Beirut: Dar al-Zahra, 6th ed., 1985).
Fadlallah, M. H., *Ya Zilal al-Islam* [Oh ! the shadows of Islam] (Beirut: Dar al-Ta'aruf li al-Matbu'at, 2nd ed., 1985).
Fadlallah, M. H., *Ma'al-Hikma fi Khatt al-Islam* [Wisdom in the path of Islam] (Beirut: Mu'asasat al-Wafa,'1985).
Fadlallah, M. H., *al-Islam wa Muntiq al-Quwwa* [Islam and the logic of power] (Beirut: al-Mu'asasah al-Jam'iyah li al-Dirasat wa al-Nashr, 3rd ed., 1985).
Fadlallah, M. H., '*Mun thallathi yaqoudu 'amaliyyat al-Taghyeer fi al-Ummah, Hizb al-Ummah aw Hizbullah ?'* [Who should institute the process of change, the community's party or the party of God?], *al-Muntalaq*, no. 31 (Oct. 1986), pp. 4–16.
Fadlallah, M. H., *al-Muqawamah al-Islamiya, Afaq wa Tatalu'at* [The Islamic resistance, horizons and aspirations](Beirut: n.p., 2nd ed., 1986).
Fadlallah, M. H., *Khutawat 'ala Tariq al-Islam* [Steps along the path of Islam] (Beirut: Dar al-Ta'aruf, 5th Ed., 1986).
Fadlallah, M. H., *al-Hiwar fi al-Qur'an* [Dialogue in the *Qur'an*] (Beirut: Dar al-Ta'aruf, 5th ed., 1987).
Fadlallah, M. H., '*al-Sahwah al-Islamiyya*: *Ishkaliyat wa Mawaqif wa Tatallu'at'* [The Islamic Awakening: problems, standpoints and aspirations], *al-Muntalaq*, no. 54 (May 1989), pp. 4–15.
Fadlallah, M. H., *Min Ajl al-Islam* [For the sake of Islam](Beirut: Dar al-Ta'aruf, 1989).
Fadlallah, M. H., '*Taqdim*,' [introduction] in: al-Husayni, M., *al-Imam al-Shahid Sayyid Muhammad Baqir al-Sadr* [The martyred *Imam Sayyid* Baqir al-Sadr] (Beirut: Dar al-Furat, 1989).
Fadlallah, M. H.,'*Ala Shati' al- Wujdan* [On the shores of passion] (Beirut: Riyyad al-Rayyes, 1990).
Fadlallah, M. H., '*Qira'ah Islamiyya Saree'ah li Mafhoumay al-Huriyya wa al-Dimoqratiyya fi al-Janib al-Fikri al-Hadari*,' [A quick Islamic reading of the notions of freedom and democracy in civilizational thought], *al-Muntalaq*, no. 65 (April 1990), pp. 4–21.
Fadlallah, M. H., *Mafahim Islamiyya 'Ammah* [General Islamic Concepts] (Beirut: Dar al-Zahra', 2nd ed., 1991).
Fadlallah, M. H., *al-Harakah al-Islamiyyah, Humoum wa Qadaya* [The Islamic movement, concerns and issues](Qom: Muntada Jabil 'Amil, 2nd ed., 1991).
Fadlallah, M. H., *Afaq Islamiyyah* [The Islamic horizons](Beirut: *Dar al-Zahra*, 2nd ed., 1991).
Fadlallah, M. H., '*al-Marja'iyya: al-Waqe' wa al-Muqtada*,' [al-Marja'iyya: Reality

and necessity] in: Fadlallah, M. H. (et. al.) (eds.) *Araa' fi al-Marja'iyya al-Shi'iyya* [Views on the Shi'i marja'iyya] (Beirut: Dar al-Rawda, 1994), pp. 111–196.

Fadlallah, M. H., *Uslub al-Da'wa fi al- Qur'an* [Methodology of the (missionary) call in the *Qur'an*](Beirut: Dar al-Malak, 5th ed., 1994).

Fadlallah, M. H., *Fi Afaq al-Hiwar al-Islami al-Masihi* [Among the horizons of the Islamic-Christian dialogue](Beirut: Dar al-Malaak, 1994).

Fadlallah, M. H., *'al-Harakat al-Islamiyya al-Arabiyya wa Ishkaliyat al-Taswiyya wa al-Tatbee,'* in: *al-Harakat al-Islamiyya fi Muwajihat al-Taswiyya* [The Islamic movements in opposition to the (Arab-Israeli) settlement] (Beirut: Markaz al-Dirasaat al-Istiraatijiyya wa al-Buhouth, 1995), pp. 107– 126.

Fadlallah, M. H., *al-Juma'a: Minbar wa Mihrab* [Friday: pulpit and niche](Beirut: Dar al-Malaak, 1996).

Fadlallah, M. H., *'al-Insinsakh wa al-Din,'* [Cloning and Science] in: 'Ilwani, Abdul Wahid (ed.), *al-Istansakh: Jadal al-'Ilm wa al-Din wa al-Akhlaq* (Damascus: Dar al-Fikr, 1997), pp. 97–102.

Fadlallah, M. H., *Hiwaraat fi al-Fikr wa al-Siyyasa wa al-Ijtima'* [Dialogues in thought, politics and society] (Beirut: Dar al-Malaak, 1997).

Fadlallah, M. H., *al-Juma'a: al-Kalima wa al-Mawqef* [Friday: The word and the position] (Beirut: Dar al-Malaak, 1998).

Fadlallah, M. H., *Min Wahy al-Qur'an* [From the revelation of the *Qur'an*](Beirut: Dar al-Malak, 2nd ed., 1998), 24 vols.

Fadlallah, M. H., *Iradat al-Quwwa: Jihad al-Muqawama fi Khitab samahat Ayatullah al-'Uzma al-Sayyid Muhammad Husayn Fadlallah* [The will of power: The sacred struggle of the Resistance in the discourse of the eminent Grand Ayatullah Sayyid Muhammad Husayn Fadlallah] (Beirut: Dar al-Malaak, 2000).

Fadlallah, M. H., *Umara' wa Qaba'el: Khafaya wa Haqa'eq Lubnaniyya* [Princes and tribes: Lebanese facts and secrets] (Beirut: Dar Riyad al-Rayyes, 2001).

Fadlallah, M. H., *Ittijahaat wa 'Alaam: Hiwaraat fikriyya fi Shu'oun al-Marja'iyya wa al-Haraka al-Islamiyya* [Trends and luminaries: Intellectual dialogues on the affairs of al-marja'iyya and the Islamic movement] (Beirut: Dar al-Malaak, 2003).

Fadlallah, M.H., *al-Mudannas wa al-Muqaddas: America wa Raayat al-Irhab al-Duwali* [The Profane and the sacred: America and the banner of international terrorism] (Beirut: Dar Riyad al-Rayyes, 2003).

Hamiyyah, S. (ed.), *Dunya al-Mar'ah, Hiwar ma'a Ayatullah al-'Uzma al-Sayyid Muhammad Husayn Fadlallah* [The woman's world, a dialogue with *Sayyid* Fadlallah] (Beirut: Dar al-Malaak, 1997).

Hammoud, Z. (ed.) *al-Wajh al-Akhar lahum: Dirasat wa Hiwarat fi al-Sirah* [The other side to them: biographical and dialogic studies](Beirut: Dar al-Rasheed li al-'Uloum, 1993), pp. 15–70.

Ibn Kathir, *Makhtasar Tafsir ibn Kathir* [Ibn Kathir's Abridged *Qur'anic* Commentary] (Beirut: Dar al-Ma'rifa, 1987).

Risaalatuna [Our message (articles by *Sayyid* Baqir al-Sadr)(Beirut: al-Dar al-Islamiyya, 1981).

Srour, A. H., *al-'Allamah Fadlallah wa Tahaddi al-Mumnou'* [The learned Fadlallah and the forbidden defiance](Beirut: Dar al-Malaak, 1991).

Suwayd, M. (ed.), *al-Islam wa Filistin, Hiwar Shamil ma' al-Sayyid Muhammad Husayn Fadlallah* [Islam and Palestine: A comprehensive interview with *Sayyid* Fadlallah] (Beirut: Mu'asasat al-Dirasat al-Filistiniyya, 1995).

b. Author's Interviews and Correspondences with Fadlallah

Author's interview with Sayyid Fadlallah, 7 March 1996.
Author's correspondence with Shaykh Ali Shimie (Fadlallah's principal secretary), 10 May 1997.
Author's correspondence with Sayyid Fadlallah, 31 October 1997.
Author's correspondence with Sayyid Fadlallah, 31 May 1999.
Author's corresondence with Sayyid Fadlallah, 16 November 1999.
Author's correspondence with Sayyid Fadlallah, 19 November 1999.
Author's correspondence with Sayyid Fadlallah, 30–31 December 1999.
Author's correspondence with Sayyid Fadlallah, 18 January 2000.
Author's correspondence with Sayyid Fadlallah, 22 April 2000.
Author's correspondence with Sayyid Fadlallah, 5 May 2000.
Author's correspondence with Sayyid Fadlallah, 1 July 2000.

c. Western languages Primary Sources

Fadlallah, M. H., '*Réflexions sur la Résistance,*' *Revue d'études palestiniennes*, no. 16 (summer 1985), pp. 39–42.
Fadlallah, M. H., [interview]'*Entretien avec le Sheikh Mohamed Husayn Fadlallah,*' *Politique Internationale*, vol. 29 (August 1985), pp. 265–270.
Fadlallah, M. H., [interview]'The Future of the Islamic and National Resistance,' *Journal of Palestine Studies*, vol. 14, no. 4 (Summer 1985), pp. 164–166.
Fadlallah, M. H., 'Interview with *Shaikh* Mohammad Hussein Fadlallah,' *Middle East Insight*, vol. 4, no. 2 (1985), pp. 10–19.
Fadlallah, M. H., [interview] 'Islam and Violence in Political Reality,' *Middle East Insight*, vol. 4, nos. 4–5 (1986), pp. 4–13.
Fadlallah, M. H., 'To avoid a World War of Terror,' *Washington Post*, 6 April 1986.
Fadlallah, M. H., [interview] 'The Palestinians, the *Shi'a*, and South Lebanon,' *Journal of Palestine Studies*, vol. 16, no. 2 (winter 1987), pp. 3–10.
Fadlallah, M. H., [interview] 'The Islamic Resistance in Lebanon and the Palestinian Uprising,' *The Middle East Insight*, vol. 5, no. 6 (1988), pp. 4–12.
Fadlallah, M. H., [interview] 'An Islamic Perspective on the Lebanese Experience,' *Middle East Insight*, vol. 6, no. 1 (summer 1988), pp. 18–26.
Fadlallah, M. H., [interview]'Give Islamists their Right to Participate in Politics,' *Middle East Insight*, vol. 10, no. 6 (September–October 1994), pp. 18–22.
Fadlallah, M. H., [interview] 'Islamic Unity and Change,' *Journal of Palestine Studies*, vol. 25, no.1 (Autumn 1995), pp. 61–75.
Khomeini, I., *Islam and Revolution*, London: Kegan Paul International, 1985, *L'Express*, 6 July 1984.

Magazine, 5 May 1984; 27 February 1988.
Monday Morning, 15 October 1984; 16 December 1985; 1 February 1993.
Mutahari, M., *Jihad: The Holy War Idea and its Legitimacy in the Qur'an* (Teheran: Islamic Propagation Society, 1981).
Time, 16 August 1982; 27 May 1985.
The Washington Post, 18 October 1983; 30 October 1983; 16 April 1986.
Washington Report on Middle East Affairs, 24 April 1983; 20 February 1983.

d. Televised Interviews with Sayyid Fadlallah

al-Jazeera Satellite Television, 30 March 2002.
Lebanon Television, 29 September 2001.
LBC Satellite Television, 11 May 2000.
'*Hiwar al-'Umr*,' February 1999.
'Hostage,' British Channel 4 documentary, 1999.
'*Maraya al-Ahdath*,' [The reflections of events] (a video-taped interview by the Beirut-based *al-Manar* T.V. Station with Sayyid Fadlallah in January 1995).
'States of Terror,' BBC Television documentary, 1994.

2. Secondary Sources

a. Arabic Books and Articles

al-Amini, M. H., *Aal Fadlallah* [The Fadlallah family], *al-Murshid*, nos. (3–4), 1995), pp. 208–212.
al-Bahrani, J. S., *Ayatullah al-'Uzma al-Sayyid Muhammad Husayn Fadlallah wa Harakiyyat al-'Aql al-Ijtihadi lida Fuqaha' al-Shi'a al-Imamiyyah* [Fadlallah and the dynamics of independent legal reasoning in the mind of *Imami Shi'i* jurists] (Beirut: Dar al-Malaak, 1998).
al-Bahrani, J. S., *Marja'iyyat al-Marhala wa Ghibar al-Taghyeer: Dirasah 'Amaliyya Tawdihiyya li ba'ad al-Turuhat al-Fikriyya wa al-Fiqhiyya wa al-Tarikhiyya li Samahat Ayatullah al-'Uzma al-Sayyid Muhammad Husayn Fadlallah* [The *Shi'i* religio-legal establishment of the present juncture and the fallout from change: An explicatory account of some Fadlallah's intellectual, juridical and historical postualtes](Beirut: Dar al-Amir, 1998).
al-Husayni, M., *Hawamesh Naqdiyya, Dirasah fi Kitab Ma'sat al-Zahra'* [Critical footnotes, a study of the book: 'Tragedy of (Fatima) al-Zahra'](Beirut: Mu'asasat al-'Aref, 1997).
al-Husayni, M., *Mutarahat fi Qadaya Qur'aniyya, Dirasah fi Tafsir Min Wahy al-Qur'an* [Propositions relating to *Qur'anic* issues, a study of (Fadlallah's) exegesis] (Beirut: Dar al-Malaak, 2000).

al-Mausawi, Y., *Mulahazat 'ala Munhaj al-Sayyid Muhammad Husayn Fadlallah* [Comments on Fadlallah's methodology](Beirut: Dar al-Saddiqah, 1414 A. H. 1993/1994).

'al-Rahil al-Kabir Ayatullah al-Sayyid Abdul Ra'uf Fadlallah' [The deceased *Sayyid* Abdul Ra'uf Fadlallah], *al-Muntalaq*, no. 27, (February 1985), pp. 88–96.

al-Safi, Muhammad Baqer, *Fitnat Fadlallah* [Fadlallah's sedition] (n.pl.: n.pub., September 1997) (www.wthga.com)

'Amru, Y. M., *'Ulama 'Araftahum* [Scholars I knew], *al-'Irfan*, vol. 79, nos. 7–8 (Oct. 1995), pp. 96–197.

Nour al-Deen, N., *Ma'sat Kitab al-Ma'sat* [The tragedy of the Book of Tragedy] (Beirut: Dar al-Rasoul al-Akram, 1997).

Sham'oun, I., *Ayatullah al-Sayyid Muhammad Husayn Fadlallah, Da'iyat Hiwar – am Dhamiyyah !* [Fadlallah, a proponent of dialogue or an advocate of *Dhimmiya*, (or notion of protected non-Muslim subjects)](Beirut: Bisan li al-Nashr, 1995).

b. Unpublished Secondary Arabic Sources

Fadlallah, I., *'al-Mushrou' al-Hadari al-Islami fi Fikr Ayatullah Fadlallah,'* [The Islamic civilisational project in the thought of *Sayyid* Fadlallah] (Unpublished Masters thesis, Arts Faculty, The Lebanese University, 1999).

c. Other Secondary Arabic Sources

Abu Ali, *al-Haraka al-Islamiyya fi al-Iraq* [The Islamic movement in Iraq](Beirut: Mu'asasat al-Jihad, 1985).

Abu Diyyah, S., *Dirasah Tahliliyya fi al-'Amaliyyat al-Istishhadiyya fi Junoub Iraq* [An analytical study of self–martyring operations in South Lebanon](Amman: n.p., 1986).

al-Amin, H., *'al-Thawra al-Iraqiyya al-Kubra,'* [The great Iraqi revolt], *al-Thaqfa al-Islamiyya*, no. 22 (1989), pp. 190–202.

al-Alawi, H., *al-Shi'ah wa al-Dawlah al-Qawmiyya fi al-Iraq: 1914–1990* [The *Shi'a* and the nationlist state in Iraq] (Qom: Dar al-Thaqafah wa al-Nashr, n.d.)

al-Allousi, M., *Likay laa Yatakarrar al-Khata'* [So that the error is not repeated] (n.p.: n.p., 1991).

al-Askari, S., *'al-Haraka al-Islamiyya al-Mu'asira fi al-Iraq,'* [The contemporary Islamic movement in Iraq], *al-Fikr al-Jadid*, no.4 (Dec. 1992), pp. 221–248.

al-Askari, S., *'Nizam al-Hukm fi Birnamaj al-Haraka al-Islamiyya: Iraq Numouthajun'* [The system of government in the programme of the Islamic movement: The Iraqi model], *al-Fikr al-Jadid*, no. 7 (Nov. 1993), pp. 285–294.

al-Askari, S., *'al-Imam al-Sadr wa dawruhu fi al-Sira' al-Siyyasi fi al-Iraq'* [The *Imam* al-Sadr and his role in the political conflict in Iraq], in: *Muhammad Baqir al-Sadr* (London: Dar al-Salam, 1996), pp. 523–550.

al-Badri, A. A., *al-Islam bayna al-'Ulama wa al-Hukkam* [Islam between the scholars and rulers] (Medina: al-Maktabah al-Ilmiyya, n.d.).

al-Bahadli, A. A., *al-Najaf: Jami'atuha wa Dawruha al-Qiyadi* [al-Najaf: its seminary and leadership role](Beirut: *Mu'asasat al-Wafa',*1989).

al-Bahadli, A., '*Jam'iyyat al-Nahdah al-Islamiyya,*' [The Islamic Renaissance Society], *al-Muntalaq*, nos. 94–95, September 1992, pp. 142–154.

al-Bahadli, A., '*al-Najaf al-Ashraf,*' *Noor Islam*, no.s 31–32 (Sept.-Oct. 1992), pp. 75–91.

al-Bahadli, A. A., *al-Hawza al-'Ilmiyya fi al-Najaf* [The teaching seminaries of al-Najaf](Beirut: Dar al-Zahra, 1993).

al-Basri, M., *Alaamon Siyasiyya fi al-Iraq al-Hadith* [Political figures of modern Iraq] (London: Riyyad al-Rayyes, 1987).

al-Dujayli, H., *al-Fuqaha' Hukkam 'ala al-Mulouk* [Judges preside over kings] (Beirut: Dar al-Adwa', 1991).

al-Ghawri, M., '*al-Hawza al-'Ilmiyya al-Diniyya fi al-Najaf al-Ashraf,*' *al-Thaqafa al-Islamiyya*, no. 28 (December-January 1989–1990), pp. 105–168.

al-Hadidi, S., *al-Tahaddi al-Kabir* [The great challenge](London: Dar al-Rafid,1994).

al-Hasani, S., *Dawr Ulama al-Shi'a fi Muwajihat al-Isti'mar* [The Role of the *Shi'a 'Ulama* in confronting colonialism] (Beirut: al-Gahdir, 1995).

al-Husayni, M. M., *al-Imam al-Shahid al-Sayyid Muhammad Baqir al-Sadr: Dirasah fi Siratihi wa Munhajihi* [The martyred *Imam, Sayyid* Baqer al-Sadr: A study of his career and programme](Beirut: Dar al-Firat, 1989).

al-Husayni, M. S., *al-Khatamiyya: al-Muslaha bayna al-Din wa al-Huriyya* [al-Khatamiyya: The reconciliation between religion and liberty] (Beirut: Dar al-Jadid, 1999).

al-Khafaji, A. L., *al-Shahid al-Sadr* [al-Sadr, the martyr] (Beirut: Dar al-Ma'alim, n.d).

al-Khurasan, S., *Safahat min Tarikh al-Haraka al-Shiyou'iyyeh fi al-Iraq* [Pages from the history of the Communist Movement in Iraq] (Beirut: Dar al-Furat,1993).

al-Khurasan, S., *Hizb al-Da'wa al-Islamiyya: Haqa'iq wa Watha'iq, Fusoul min Tajribat al-Harakah al-Islamiyya fi al-Iraq* [The Islamic Call Party: facts and documents, chapters from the experience of the Islamic movement in Iraq](Beirut: al-Mu'asasah al-Arabiyya li al-Dirasat wa al-Buhouth al-Istiratijiyyeh, 1999).

al-Kaurani, A., *Tariqat Hizbullah fi al-'Amal al-Islami* [The Party of God's approach to Islamic activism](Beirut: al-Dar al-Islamiyya, 1406 A.H.).

al-Madani, T., '*Harakat Amal wa Hizbullah fi Lubnan,*' [The Amal Movement and Hizbullah in Lebanon] in: Baroot, J. (et. al.) (ed.), *al-Ahzab wa al-Harakaat wa al-Jama'at al-Islamiyya* [The Islamic parties, movements, and groups], 2 vols (Damascus: The Arabic Centre for Strategic Studies, 2000), pp. 395–528.

al-Mu'min, A., *Sanawat al-Jamr: Masirat al-Haraka al-Islamiyya fi al-Iraq* [The years of smouldering embers] (London: Dar al-Masira, 1993).

al-Muntafaki, A. A., *Jami' al-Suwar li al-'Ulama wa Udaba wa al-Kuttab* [A collection of portraits of scholars, literalists and writers] (Beirut: Dar al-Muwaddeh, 1993).

al-Nasiri, M. B., '*al-Taharruk al-Islami al-Mu'asir fi al-Iraq,*' [The contemporary Islamic movement in Iraq], *al-Fikr al-Jadid*, no. 2 (June 1992), pp. 34–55.

al-Nafisi, A., *Dawr al-Shi'a fi Tatawwur al-Iraq al-Siyasi al-Hadith* [The role of the *Shi'a* in the modern political development of Iraq](Beirut: Dar al-Nahar, 1973).
al-Nizari, M., *Abdul Sahib Dakhil wa Bidayat al-Haraka al-Islamiyya* [Abdul Sahib Dakhil and beginnings of the Islamic movement](Beirut: Dar al-Furat, 1990).
al-Quzwayni, J., '*Ishkaliyyat al-Fuqaha wa al-Dawla wa bidayat al-Haraka al-Islamiyya fi al-Iraq*,' [The problem of jurist-state relations and the origins of the Islamic movement in Iraq], *al-Fikr al-Jadid*, no.2 (June 1992), pp. 245–268.
al-Rahimi, A. H., *Ta'rikh al-Harakah al-Islamiyya fi al-Iraq: al-Juthour al-Fikriyya Wa al-Waqi' al-Tarikhi (1900–1924)* [History of the Islamic movement in Iraq, the intellectual roots and historical reality] (Beirut: al-Dar al-Alamiyya,1985).
al-Rahimi, A. H., '*Fatawa al-'Ulama al-Shi'a bi al-Jihad difa'un 'un al-Dawlah al-'Uthmaniyya*,' [Edicts by the *Shi'i 'ulama* on *jihad* in defence of the Ottoman state], *al-Thaqafah al-Islamiyya*, no. 22 (1989), pp. 89–181.
al-Sawi, K. D., *Tatawwur al-Fikr al-Siyasi 'ind Ahl al-Sunnah* [The development of *Sunni* political thought] (Amman: Dar al-Basheer, 1992).
al-Shaykh, T., *'Un al-Iraq wa al-Haraka al-Islamiyya* [On Iraq and the Islamic movement] (London: al-Safa,' 1988).
al-Shira, *al-Harakat al-Islamiyya fi Lubnan* [The Islamic movements of Lebanon] (Beirut: Dar al-Sannin, 1985)
al-Siraj, A. I., *al-Imam Muhsin al-Hakim,1889–1970* (Beirut: *Dar al-Zahra,* 1993).
al-Shabundar, G., '*al-Tahawulaat al-Fikriyya wa al-Siyasiyya fi al-Iraq khilal al-Qarnayn al-Akhirayn,'* [The intellectual and political transformations in Iraq during the last two centuries] *al-Fikr al-Jadid*, no.1 (January 1992), pp. 167–205.
al-Siraj, A. I., *al-Imam Muhsin al-Hakim* (Beirut: Dar al-Zahra, 1993).
al-Wahadah al-'Ilamiyya al-Markaziyya li Hizbullah, *Amiru al-Thakira: Siratu That, Siratu Ummah* [The prince of memory](Beirut: Munshurat al-Wala',1993).
al-Wahdah al-'Ilamiyya al-Markaziyya li Hizbullah (ed.), *Midad wa Dima'* [Exemplar and blood] (Beirut: n.p., n.d.).
Baroot, J. (et. al.) (ed.), *al-Ahzab wa al-Harakaat wa al-Jama'at al-Islamiyya* [The Islamic parties, movements, and groups], 2 vols.(Damascus: The Arabic Centre for Strategic Studies, 2000), pp. 395–528.
Bizri, D., *Dunya al-Deen wa al-Dawlah*: *al-Islamiyoun wa Iltibasaat Mushrou'uhum* [The world of religion and state: the Islamists and the ambiguity of their scheme] (Beirut: Dar al-Nahar, 1994).
Balqeez, A. I., *al-Muqawamah wa Tahrir Junoub Lubnan, Hizbullah min al-Hawza al-'Ilmiyya ila al-Jubha* [The resistance and the liberation of South, the 'Party of God' from the religious seminaries to the front] (Beirut: Markaz Dirasat al-Wahadah al-Arabiyya, 2000).
Bashour, M., *Beirut* (Beirut: Mu'assasat Dar al-Kitab al-Hadeeth,1984).
Fadlallah, H., *al-Khiyar al-Akhar, Hizbullah* [The other option] (Beirut: Dar al-Hadi, 1994).
Fadlallah, H., *Fikr al-Imam Musa al-Sadr al-Siyyasi wa al-Islah* [The political and reformist thought of *Imam* Musa al-Sadr] (Beirut: Dar al-Hadi, 1997).
Fadlallah, H., *Harb al-Iradaat: Sira' al-Muqawama wa al-Ihtilal al-Isra'ili fi Lubnan*

[The war of wills: the struggle of the resistance and the Israeli occupation of Lebanon] (Beirut: Dar al-Hadi, 1997).

Ghazawi, Z., *al-Mu'assasah al-Diniyya al-Islamiyya wa al-Kiyan al-Sahyouni* [The Islamic religious institution and the Zionist entity] (Beirut: Ghadir,1996).

Hanafi, H., *al-Turath wa al-Tajdid* [Heritage and renewal] (Beirut: Dar al-Tanwir, 1988).

Harb, R., *al-Minbar al-Muqawim, min Muhadarat al-Shahid al-Shaykh Raghib Harb* [The fighting pulpit, a selection of lectures by the martyr *Shaykh* Harb](Beirut: Dar al-Balagha,1988).

Hasan, A. R., '*al-Imam al-Shahid Muhammad Baqir al-Sadr*,' *al-Fikr al-Jadid*, no. 6 (July 1993), pp.259–285.

Hasan, G., *al-Shahid al-Sadr* [al-Sadr, the martyr] (Teheran: Ministry of Islamic Guidance, 1401 A.H.).

Hasan, H. A., *al-Fikr al-Siyasi al-Shi'i* [*Shi'i* political thought] (Beirut: al-Dar al-'Alamiyya,1988).

Ibn al-Najaf, K., *Tarikh al-Haraka al-Islamiyya al-Mu'asira fi al-Iraq* [The history of the contemporary Islamic movement in Iraq] (Beirut: Dar al-Muqadisi,1982).

Ibrahim, Farhad, *al-Ta'ifiyya wa al-Siyyasa fi al-'Alem al-Arabi, Numouthaj al-Shi'a fi al-Iraq* [Confessionalism and politics in Arab world, a case study of the *Shi'a* in Iraq](Cairo: Maktabat Madbouli, 1997).

Ibrahim, Fu'ad, *al-Faqih wa al-Dawlah, Tatawur al-Fikr al-Siyasi al-Shi'i* [The jurist and the state, the evolution of *Shi'i* political thought](Beirut: Dar al-Kunouz al-Adabiyya,1998).

Imarah, M., *al-Islam wal Falsafat al-Hukm* [Islam and the philosophy of governance] (Beirut: al-Mu'assasah al-Arabiyya li al-Dirasat wa al-Nashr,1977).

'Itrisi, T., '*Hizbullah wa Tahrir al-Janoub,*' [Hizbullah and the liberation of the South], *Shu'oun al-Awsat*, No. 96–97 (June-July 2000), pp. 4–5.

Izzi, G., *Hizbullah, min al-Hilm al-Aidiyolouji ila al-Waq'iyya al-Siyasiyya* [The 'Party of God' from ideological vision to political realism] (Kuwait: Dar al-Qartas, 1998).

Ja'far, M. A. A., '*al-Hayat al-Siyasiyya lil Imam al-Sadr*,' [The political life of *Imam* (Baqer) al-Sadr] in: *Muhammad Baqir al-Sadr: Dirasaat fi Hayatihi wa Fikrihi* (London: *Dar al-Islam*, 1996), pp. 463–519.

Jad'oun, J. S., '*al-Shaa'ir al-Husayniyya bayna al-Asalah wa al-Tajdid,*' [The *Husayniyya* rituals between authenticity and renewal], *al-'Irfan* , no.s 9 & 10, vol. 77 (Nov.-Dec. 1993), pp. 17–36.

Kaurani, M., *al-Juthour al-Tarikhiyya li al-Muqawama al-Islamiyya fi Jabal 'Amil* [The roots of the Islamic resistance in *Jabal 'Amil*, South Lebanon] (Beirut: Dar al-Wasila,1993).

Khamahyar, A., *Iran wa al-Ikhwan al-Muslimeen* [Iran and the Muslim Brethren] (Beirut: *Markaz al-Dirasaat al-Istiratijiyya wa al-Buhouth wa al-Tawtheeq*,1997).

Khazem, A., *Tajammu al-'Ulama al-Muslimeen fi Lubnan: Tajribah wa Numouthaj* [The Association of Muslim Scholars in Lebanon](Beirut: Dar al-Ghirbah, 1997).

Markaz al-Dirasat wa al-Tawtheeq, al-Muqawima fi al-Khitab al-Fiqhi al-Siyyasi li Samahat al-Imam al-Shaykh Muhammad Mahdi Shams al-Din [Resistance in the jurisprudential and political discourse of *Shaykh* Shams al-Din] (Beirut: al-Mu'assah al-Duwaliyya, 1997).

Mazaham, H., *'Hizbullah wa Ishkaliyyat al-Tawfeeq bayna al-Aydiyoulijiyya wa al-Waqi,'* [Hizbullah and the Problem of reconciling ideology and reality], *Shu'oun al-Awsat*, no. 59 (Jan.-Feb. 1997), pp. 61–68.

Mughniyya, A. H. (ed.), *Tajarab Muhammad Jawad Mughniyya* [The experiences of Muhammad Jawad Mughniyya] (Beirut: Dar al-Jawwad, 1980).

Mughniyya, J., *al-Wada' al-Hadar fi Jabal 'Amil, 1946–1966* [The current situation in Jabal 'Amil] (Sidon: Matba'at al-'Irfan, n.d.).

Mughniyya, J., *al-Shi'a fi al-Mizan* [The Shi'a in the scales] (Beirut: Dar al-Tayyar al-Jadid,1989).

Mughniyya, J., *al-Jawama' wa al-Fawariq bayna al-Sunna wa al-Shi'a* [Commonalities and differences between the Sunnis and Shi'a] (Beirut: Mu'assasat Izzideen, 1994).

Munsour, M., *'Hizbullah kama yarahu al-Share' al-Suri,'* [Hizbullah as viewed from the Syrian street] *Sutour* No.58 (September 2001), pp. 26–29.

Murdan, J. M., *Abdul Karim Qasim: al-bidaya wa al-suqout* [Abdul Karim Qasim: the rise and fall](n.p.: al-Maktaba al-Sharqiyya, n.d.).

Musa, F., *al-Shaykh Muhammad Mahdi Shams al-Din* (Beirut: Dar Hadi, 1993).

Nazimi, W. J. U., *al-Juthour al-Siyasiyya wa al-Fikriyya wa al-Ijtima'iyya li al-Haraka al-Qawmiyya al-Arabiyya (al-Istiqlaliyya) fi al-Iraq* [The political, intellectual and social roots of the (independent) Arab nationalist movement in Iraq] (Beirut: Markaz Dirasat al-Wahda al-Arabiyya, 3rd ed., 1986).

Ra'ouf, A., *al-'Amal al-Islami fi al-Iraq, bayna al-Marja'iyya wa al-Hizbiyya, Qira'ah Naqdiyya li Masirat Nisf Qarn, 1950–2000* [Islamic activism in Iraq, between the *Shi'i* religio-legal establishment and partisan organisation](Damascus: al-Markaz al-Iraqi li al-'Ilam wa al-Dirasat, 2000).

Sabra, H., *''Un al-Sahwa al-Islamiyya fi Lubnan,'* in: Nadwa, *al-Harakat al-Islamiyya al-Mu'asirah fi Watan al-Arabi* [On the Islamic awakening in Lebanon] (Beirut: Markaz Dirasat al-Wahda al-Arabiyya, 1987), pp. 163–185.

Sa'id, M. S., *'al-'aam wa al-khaas fi al-tajriba al-nidaliyya li Hizbullah,'* [The particular and the general with respect to the militant experience of Hizbullah], *Sutor*, No. 58, (September 2001), p. 25.

Shams, M., & Murji, H., *al-Jumhouriyya al-Islamiyya fi Lubnan* [The Islamic Republic in Lebanon] 3 vols. (Beirut: al-Wakala al-Sharqiyya li al-Tawzi,' 1989–1990).

Shams al-Din, M. M., *Nizam al-Hukm wa al-Idarah fi al-Islam* [The system of government and administration in Islam](Beirut: al-Mu'assasah al-Duwaliyya, 1995).

Sharara, W., *Dawlat Hizbullah* [Hizbullah' state](Beirut: Dar al-Nahar, 1996).

Sharaf al-Din, H., *al-Imam al-Sayyid Musa al-Sadr* (Beirut: Dar al-Arqam, 1996).

Shari'ati, M. (ed.), *al-Muslih al-Islami al-Sayyid Muhsin al-Amin* [The Islamic reformer, al-*Sayyid* Muhsin al-Amin] (Damascus: The Cultural Centre of the Islamic Repubic of Iran, 1992).

Sharuru, F., *al-Ahzab wa al-Tanzimat wa al-Quwwa al-Siyasiyya fi Lubnan* [The parties, organisations and political forces of Lebanon] (Beirut: Dar al-Masira, 1981).

Shburou, I. (ed.), *Thawrat al-Arab didd al-Atrak* [The Arab revolt against the Turks] (Beirut: Dar al-Tadamon, 1993).

Shubbur, H., *Tarikh al-Iraq al-Siyyasi,* [The political history of Iraq], vol. 1, *al-'Amal al-Hizbi fi al-Iraq, 1908–1958* [Party activity in Iraq] (Beirut: Dar al-Turath al-Arabi, 1989).

Shubbur, H., *Tarikh al-Iraq al-Siyyasi al-Mu'asir,* Vol.2, *al-Taharruk al-Islami, 1900 1957* [Political history of contemporary Iraq, The Islamic movement](Beirut: Dar al-Muntada li al-Nashr, 1990).

Subhi, A. M., *Nazariyat al-Imamah lida al-Shi'a al-Ithna al-Ashariyya* [The Imamite theory of the Twelver Shi'a] (Beirut: Dar al-Nahdah al-Arabiyya, 1991).

Yakan, F., *al-Qadiyya al-Filistiniyya min Munzoor al-Islami* [The Palestinian issue from an Islamic Perspective] (Beirut:Mu'assasah al-Risalah, 1995).

Yakan, F., *Adwa' 'ala al-Tajribah al-Niyabiyya al-Islamiyya fi Lubnan* [Insights into the Islamic parliamentary experiment in Lebanon] (Beirut: Mu'assasah al-Risalah, 1996).

Zu'aitar, M., *Nazrah ala Tarh al-Jumhouriyya al-Islamiyya fi Lubnan* (Beirut: al-Wakala al-Sharqiyya li al-Tawzi, 1988).

d. Secondary Western Sources on Fadlallah

Abu Rabi, I., *Intellectual Origins of the Islamic Resurgence in the Modern World* (New York: State University of New York, 1996), pp. 220–247.

Carre, O., ' *Quelques mots-clés de Muhammad Husayn Fadlallah,'* [Some notes on Fadlallah] *Revue Française de Sciences Politiques*, vol. 37, no. 4 (August 1987), pp. 478–501.

Carre, O., '*La Révolution Islamique selon Muhammad Husayn Fadlallah,*' [Islamic revolution according to Fadlullah] *Orient,* vol. 29, no.1 (March 1988), pp. 64–84.

Carre, O., *L'Utopie Islamique dans l'Orient Arabe* [Islamic utopianism in the Arab East] (Paris: *Presses de la Fondation Nationale des Sciences Politiques,* 1991).

Carre, O., 'Fadlullah, Muhammad Husayn,' in: Esposito, J. L. (ed.), *The Oxford Encyclopedia of the Modern Islamic World,* 2 vols. (New York: Oxford University Press, 1995), vol.2, pp. 453–456.

Kramer, M., 'Muhammad Husayn Fadlallah,' *Orient,* vol. 26, no. 2 (June 1985), pp. 147–149.

Kramer, M., 'The Oracle of Hizbullah: Sayyid Muhammad Husayn Fadlallah,' in: Appleby, R. S. (ed.) *Spokesmen for the Despised: Fundamentalist Leaders of the Middle East* (Chicago: University of Chicago Press, 1997), pp. 83–181.

Mallat, C., *Shi'i Thought from the South of Lebanon* (Oxford: Centre for Lebanese Studies, 1988).

Miller, J., 'Faces of Fundamentalism, Hassan al-Turabi and Muhammed Fadlallah,' *Foreign Affairs,* (November–December 1994), vol. 73, no. 6, pp. 123–142.

Rosiny, S. 'The Tragedy of Fatima al-Zahra in the debate of two Shi'ite Theologians in Lebanon,' in: Brunner, R. and Ende, W. (eds.), *The Twelver Shi'a in Modern Times: Religious Culture and Political History* (Leiden: Brill, 2001), pp. 207–219.

e. Other Published Secondary Western Sources

Abdul Jabar, F., 'The Genesis and Development of Marja'ism versus the State,' in: Abdul Jabar, F. (ed.) *Ayatollahs, Sufis and Ideologues* (London: Saqi Books, 2002), pp. 61–89.

Abrahmian, E., *Khomeinism* (Berkeley: University of California Press, 1993).

Abu Khalil, A., 'The Palestinian- Shi'ite War in Lebanon,' *Third World Affairs,* (1988), pp. 77–89.

Abu Khalil, A., 'The Ideology and Practice of Hizbullah,' *Middle Eastern Studies*, vol. 27, no. 3 (July 1991), pp. 390–403.

Ajami, F., *The Vanished Imam* (Ithaca: Cornell University Press, 1986).

al-Adhami, M. M., 'The Elections of the Constituent Assembly in Iraq, 1922–4,' in: Kelidar, A. (ed.), *The Integration of Modern Iraq* (London: Croom Helm, 1979).

Akhavi, S., *Religion and Politics in Contemporary Iran* (Albany: State University of New York Press, 1986).

al-Azami, T. H., 'The Emergence of the Contemporary Islamic Revival in Iraq,' *Middle East Affairs Journal*, vol. 3, nos. 1–2 (winter-spring), pp. 123–141.

Algar, H., *Religion and State in Iran* (Berkeley: University of California Press, 1969).

Algar, H., 'The Oppositional Role of the *'Ulama* in Twentieth-Century Iran,' in: Keddie, N. (ed.), *Scholars, Sufis, and Saints* (Berkeley: University of California Press, 1972), ch. 2.

Algar, H., 'Shi'ism and Iran in the Eighteenth Century,' in: Naff, T. & Owen, R. (eds.), *Studies in Eighteenth Century Islamic History* (Carbondale: n.p., 1977), pp. 288–302.

al-Qazzaz, A., 'The Power Elite in Iraq,' *The Muslim World*, vol. 61 (1971), pp. 267–83.

Appleby, R.S. (ed.), *Spokesmen for the Despised* (Chicago: University of Chicago Press, 1997).

Arjomand, S. A., *The Shadow of God and the Hidden Imam* (Chicago: University of Chicago Press, 1984).

Arjomand, S. A., 'The Clerical State and the Emergence of the Shi'ite Hierocracy in Safavid Iran,' *Journal of the Economic and Social History of the Orient*, vol. 28, (1985), pp. 169–219.

Aziz, T. M., 'The Role of Muhammad Baqer al-Sadr in Shi'i Political Activism in Iraq,' *International Journal of Middle Eastern Studies*, vol. 25, no.2 (May 1993), pp. 207–222.

Babakhan, A., *L'Irak, 1970–1990* (Paris: n.pub., 1994).

Bacharach, A., *A Middle East Studies Handbook* (Cambridge: Cambridge University Press, 1984).

Badawi, M. M., *A Critical Introduction to Modern Arab Poetry* (Cambridge: Cambridge University Press, 1975).

Bahram, Baktiari, 'Iran's New President,' *Middle East Insight*, (November-December 1997), pp. 16–23.

Baram, A., 'The Radical Shi'ite Opposition Movements in Iraq,' in: Sivan, E. & Friedman, M. (eds.), *Religious Radicalism and Politics in the Middle East* (Albany: State University of New York Press, 1990), pp. 95–126.

Barakat, H., 'Social Factors influencing Attitudes of University Students in Lebanon towards the Palestinian Resistance Movement,' *Journal of Palestine Studies*, vol.1 no.1 (Autumn 1971), pp. 87–112.

Baram, A., 'The Radical Shi'ite Opposition Movements in Iraq,' in: Sivan, E. & Friedman, M. E. (eds.)., *Religious Radicalism and Politics in the Middle East* (Albany: State University of New York Press, 1990), pp. 95–126.

Baram, A., 'From Radicalism to Radical Pragmatism,' in: Piscatori, J. (ed.), *Islamic Fundamentalism and the Gulf Crisis* (Chicago: American Academy of Arts and Sciences, 1991), pp. 28–51.

Baram, A., 'Two Roads to Revolutionary Shi'ite Fundamentalism in Iraq,' in: Martin, M. E. & Appleby, R.S. (eds.), *Accounting for Fundamentalisms* (Chicago: University of Chicago Press, 1994), pp. 531–588.

Batatu, H., *The Old Social Classes and Revolutionary Movements of Iraq* (London: Saqi Books, 2004).

Batatu, H., 'Iraq's Underground *Shi'a* Movements,' *Middle East Journal*, vol. 35, no. 4 (Autumn 1981), pp. 578–594.

Batatu, H., 'Shi'i Organizations in Iraq,' in: Cole, J. R. I. & Keddie, N. R. (eds.), *Shi'ism and Social Protest* (New York: Yale University Press, 1986), pp. 179–200.

Baydoun, A., 'Bint-Jbeil,' *Maghreb-Machrek*, no. 125 (July-Sept. 1989), pp. 69–81.

Binder, L., 'The Proofs of Islam,' in: Makdisi, G. (ed.), *Arabic and Islamic Studies in Honor of Hamilton A. R. Gibb* (Cambridge: Harvard University Press, 1965), pp. 118–140.

Bosworth, E. & Hillenbrand, C. (eds.), *Qajar Iran* (Edinburgh: Edinburgh University Press, 1983)

Bosworth, C. E., '*al-Nadjaf*,' in: Bosworth, C. E. (et. al.) (ed.), *The Encyclopaedia of Islam*, vol.6 (Leiden: E. J. Brill, new ed., 1992), p. 859.

Brugman, J., *An Introduction to the History of Modern Arabic Literature in Egypt* (London: E. J. Brill, 1984).

Brumberg, D., 'Khomeini's Legacy,' in: Appleby, R. S. (ed.), *Spokesmen for the Despised* (Chicago: University of Chicago Press, 1997), pp. 16–82.

Brynen, R., *Sanctuary and Survival* (London: Pinter, 1990).

Calder, N., '*Zakat* in Imami Shi'i Jurisprudence,' *Bulletin of the School of Oriental and African Studies*, vol. 45, no. 3 (1981), pp. 470–475.

Calder, N., '*Khums* in Imami Shi'i Jurisprudence,' *Bulletin of the School of Oriental and African Studies*, vol. 45 (1982), pp. 39–47.

Calder, N., 'Legitimacy and Accommodation in Safavid Iran,' *Iran*, vol. 25 (1987), pp. 91–105.

Chartouni-Dubarry, M., 'Hizbullah, from Militia to Political Party,' in: Hollis, R. & Shehadi, N. (eds.), *Lebanon on Hold* (Oxford: Centre of Lebanese Studies, 1996).

Chomsky, N., *The Fateful Triangle* (Cambridge, MA: South End Press, 2nd ed., 1999)

Chronology of Religion and Politics in Lebanon, CEMAM Reports, Special Issue, 1982, (Beirut: Dar el-Machreq, 1985).

Chronology of Religion and Politics in Lebanon, 1983 (Beirut: CEMAM, 1985).

Cole, J. R. I., 'Shi'i Clerics in Iraq and Iran, 1722–1780: The *Akhbari-Usuli* Controversy Reconsidered' *Iranian Studies*, vol. 18, no.1 (1985), pp. 3–34.

Cole, J. R.I., 'The United States and Shi'ite Religious Factions in Post-Ba'thist Iraq,' *The Middle East Journal* Vol. 57, No. 4 (Autumn 2003), pp. 1–16.

Cobban, H., ' The Growth of Shi'i Power in Lebanon and its Implications for the Future,' in: Cole, J. R. I. & Keddie, N. R. (eds.), *Shi'ism and Social Protest* (New Haven: Yale University Press, 1986), pp. 137–155.

Cole, J.R.I. & Keddie, N.R. (eds.) *Shi'ism and Social Protest* (New Haven: Yale University Press, 1986).

Coughlin, C., *Hostage* (London: Warner Bks., 1992).

Dabashi, H., 'By What Authority ?' *Social Compass*, vol. 36, no. 4 (1989), pp. 511–538.

Dabashi, H., *Theology and Discontent* (New York: New York University Press, 1991)

Dabashi, H., *Authority in Islam* (New Brunswick: Transaction Books, 1993).

Dann, U., 'Licensed Parties in Qasim's Iraq,' *Asian and African Studies*, no.3 (1967), pp. 1–33.

Dann, U., *Iraq under Qasem* (New York: Praeger, 1969).

Deeb, M., 'Shi'a Militant Movements,' *Third World Quarterly*, vol. 10, no.2 (April 1988), pp. 683–698.

Duri, A. A., *The Historical Formation of the Arab Nation* (London: Croom Helm, 1987).

Ehteshami, A. & Hinnebusch, R. A., *Syria and Iran* (London: Routledge, 1997).

Enayet, H., *Modern Islamic Political Thought* (London: Macmillan, 1982).

Ende, W., 'The Flagellations of Muharram and the Shi'ite 'Ulama,' *Der Islam*, vol. 55 (1978), pp. 19–36.

Ende, W., 'Iraq in World War One: The Turks, the Germans and the Shi'ite Mujtahids' Call for Jihad,' in: Peters, R. (ed.), *Proceedings of the Ninth Congress of the Union Europeene des Arabisants et Islamisants* (Leiden: Brill, 1981), pp. 57–71.

Euben, R. L., *Enemy in the Mirror, Islamic Fundamentalism in the Limits of Modern Rationalism* (Princeton: Princeton University Press, 1999).

Fernia, R.A. & Louis, W. R. (eds), *The Iraqi Revolution of 1958* (London: I. B. Tauris, 1991).

Fisk, R., *Pity the Nation* (Oxford: Oxford University Press, 1990).

Floor, W. M., 'The Revolutionary Character of the Iranian 'Ulama,' in: Keddie, N. R. (ed.), *Religion and Politics in Iran* (Berkeley: University of California Press, 1983), pp. 73–97.

Fromkin, D., *A Peace to End All Peace* (London: Penguin, 1989).

Gabriel, R. A., *Operation Peace for Galilee* (New York: Hill & Wong, 1984).

Glass, C., *Tribes without Flags* (New York: The Atlantic Monthly Press, 1990)

Glubb, J. B., *A Short History of the Arab Peoples* (London: Hodder & Stoughton, 1969).
Golnar, Mehran, 'Political Reform and Education in Iran,' *Comparative Education*, Vol. 39, No.3, (August 2003), pp. 311–329.
Gonzalez-Quipno, Y., ' *Les Interpretations d'un Rite: Celebrations de la Achoura au Liban*,' [The interpretations of a ritual: '*Ashoura* Celebrations in Libanon] *Maghreb-Machrek*, no. 115 (January-March 1987), pp. 5–28.
Grimblat, F., ' *La Communaute Chiite Libanaise et le Mouvement National Palestinien*,' [The Lebanese *Shi'i* community and the Palestinian national movement] *Guerres Mondiales et Conflicts Contemporains*, no. 151 (1988), pp. 71–91.
Hagopian, E. & Farsoun, S., *South Lebanon* (Detroit: A. A. U.G., 1978).
Haim, S. G., 'Shi'ite Clerics and Politics,' *Israel Oriental Studies*, vol. 10 (1980), pp. 165–172.
Halawi, M., *A Lebanon Defied: Musa al-Sadr and the 'Shi'a awakening' in Lebanon* (Boulder: Westview Press, 1992).
Hamzeh, N. A., 'Lebanon's Hizbullah: From Islamic Revolution to Parliamentary Accommodation,' *Third World Quarterly*, vol. 14, no. 2 (1993), pp. 321–337.
Humphreys, R. S., *Islamic History* (Princeton: Princeton University Press, 1991).
Hanf, T., *Coexistence in Wartime Lebanon* (London: I. B. Tauris, 1993).
Harris, W., ' Lebanon,' *Middle East Contemporary Survey*, vol. 12 (Boulder: Westview Press, 1990).
Hurewitz, J. C., *Diplomacy in the Near and Middle East*, vol. II (Gerrards Cross: Archive Editions, 1987).
Husayni, I. M., *The Moslem Brethren* (Beirut: Khayat College Co-operatives, 1956).
Hussain, J. M., *The Occultation of the Twelfth Imam* (New York: Methuen, 1986).
Husseini, S., '*La Redistribution des Communautés Chi'ite et Sunnite dans le Grand-Beyrouth*,' [The redistribution of Shi'i and Sunni communities in Greater Beirut], in: Davie, M. F. (ed), *Beyrouth: Regards Croises* (Tours: URBAMA, 1997), pp. 207–223.
Ioannides, C. P., ' The PLO and the Iranian Revolution,' *American-Arab Affairs*, no. 10 (Fall 1984), pp. 89–105.
Jaber, H., *Hezbollah* (New York: Columbia University Press, 1997).
Jacobsen, M., 'Only by the Sword: British Counter-Insurgency in Iraq,' *Small Wars and Insurgencies*, vol. 3, no. 2 (1991), pp. 323–363.
Jamali, F., 'The Theological College of Najaf,' *The Muslim World*, vol. 50, no. 1 (1960), p. 15–22.
Jayyusi, M., *Trends and Movements in Modern Arabic Poetry*, vol.1 (Leiden: E.J. Brill, 1977).
Kassir, ' *L'affirmation des Chiites Libanais*,' *Le Monde Diplomatique* (May 1985).
Katz, S. M., *Guards Without Frontiers* (London: Arms & Armour, 1990).
Keddie, N. R. (ed.), *Scholars, Saints and Sufis* (Berkeley: University of California Press, 1972).
Keddie, N. R., 'The Roots of the *'Ulama's* Power in Modern Iran,' in: Keddie, N. R. (ed), *Scholars, Saints and Sufis* (Berkeley: University of California Press, 1972).

Keddie, N. R. (ed), *Religion and Politics in Iran* (New Haven: Yale University Press, 1984).
Kelidar, A. (ed.), *The Integration of Modern Iraq* (London: Croom Helm, 1979).
Khadduri, M., *Independent Iraq* (Oxford: Oxford University Press, 1960).
Khadduri, M., *Republican Iraq* (Oxford: Oxford University Press, 1969).
Khalidi, W., *Conflict and Violence in Lebanon* (Cambridge: Centre for International Affairs, 1979).
Khalidi, W., *Under Siege* (Tel Aviv: Marachot Publishers, 1988).
Khory, A., '*Hezbollah: la Nébuleuse*,' *Arabies*, (Dec. 1992), pp. 12–21.
Khuri, F., 'The 'Ulama: A Comparative Study of Sunni and Shi'i Religious Officials,' *Middle Eastern Studies*, vol. 23 (1987), pp. 291–312.
Khuri, F., *Imams and Emirs* (London: Saqi Books, 1990).
Kister, M. J., 'Social and Religious Concepts of Authority of Authority in Islam,' *Jerusalem Studies in Arabic and Islam* vol. 18 (1994), pp. 84–127.
Kolakowski, L., *Main Currents of Marxism: 1 The Founders* (Oxford: Oxford University Press, 1981).
Kramer, M. (ed.), *Shi'ism, Resistance and Revolution* (New Haven: Yale University Press, 1986).
Kramer, M., *Hezbollah's Vision of the West* (Washington, D.C.: The Washington Institute for Near East Policy, 1989).
Kramer, M., 'Redeeming Jerusalem,' in: Menshari, D., (ed.), *The Iranian Revolution and the Muslim world* (Boulder: Westview Press, 1990), pp. 105–130.
Kramer, M., ' The Moral Logic of Hizbullah,' in: Reich, W. (ed.), *Origins of Terrorism* (Cambridge: Cambridge University Press, 1990), pp.131–157.
Lambton, A. K.S., *State and Government in Medieval Islam* (Oxford: Oxford University Press, 1981).
Lambton, A. K. S., *Qajar Iran* (London: Tauris, 1987).
Laqueur, W. & Rubin, B. (eds.), *The Israeli–Arab Reader* (New York: Penguin,1984)
Laurent, A. & Basbous, A., *Guerres Secretes au Liban* (Paris: Gallimard, 1987).
Lewis, B., 'Usurpers and Tyrants,' in: Savory, R. M. & Agius, D. A., (ed.), *Logos Islamikos* (Toronto: Pontifical Institute of Medieval Studies, 1984), pp. 259–267.
Longrigg, S. H., *Iraq* (London: n.p., 1953).
Luizard, P. J., *La Formation de l'Irak Contemporain* [The formation of contemporary Iraq] (Paris: Editions du CNRS, 1991).
Lukitz, L., *Iraq* (London: Frank Cass, 1994).
Maceon, D. M., 'Changes in Charismatic Authority in Qajar Shi'ism,' in: Bosworth, E. & Hillenbrand, C. (eds.), *Qajar Iran* (Edinburgh: Edinburgh University Press,
1983), pp. 148–176.
Macleod, S., 'No Peace for Galilee Now,' *The Nation*, vol. 240, 23 February 1985, p. 203.
Madelung, W., 'A Treatise of the Sharif al-Murtada on the Legality of Working for the Government,' *Bulletin of the School of Oriental and African Studies*, vol. 40, no. 3 (1980), pp. 18–31.

Madelung, W., 'Authority in Twelver Shi'ism in the Absence of the Imam,' in: Makdisi, G. (et al.) (eds.), *La Notion d'Autoritie au Moyen Age* (Paris: Presses Universitaires de France, 1982), pp. 163–173.

Makdisi, G. (ed.), *Arabic and Islamic Studies in Honor of Hamilton A.R. Gibb* (Cambridge: Harvard University Press, 1965)

Mallat, C., *Shi'i Thought from the South of Lebanon* (Oxford: Centre for Lebanese Studies, 1988)

Mallat, C., 'Religious Militancy in Contemporary Iraq,' *Third World Quaterly*, vol. 10, no. 2 (April 1988), pp. 699–729.

Mallat, C., *The Renewal of Islamic Law: Muhammad Baqer as-Sadr, Najaf and the Shi'i International* (Cambridge: Cambridge University Press, 1993).

Mallat, C., 'Muhammad Baqer al-Sadr,' in: Rahnema, A. (ed.), *Pioneers of Islamic Revival* (London: Zed Bks., 1994), pp. 251–272.

Marr, P., *The Modern History of Iraq* (Boulder: Westview Press, 1991).

Martin, M. E. & Appleby, R. S. (eds.), *Accounting for Fundamentalisms* (Chicago: University of Chicago Press, 1994).

Martin, P., '*Les Chiites d'Irak: Une Majorite Dominee a la Recherche de son Destin'* [The Shi'a of Iraq, a dominated majority in search of its destiny], *Peuples Mediterraneens*, vol. 40 (1987), pp. 127–169.

Martin, P., '*Une Grande Figure de l'Islamisme en Iraq*,' [A major figure of Islamism in Iraq] *Les Cahiers de l'Orient*, nos. 8–9 (1987–1988), pp. 117 -135.

Martin, V., *Islam and Modernism* (London: I. B. Tauris, 1988).

Menashri, D. (ed.), *The Iranian Revolution and the Muslim World* (Boulder: Westview Press, 1990).

Mervin, S., '*La Quete du Savior a Nagaf: les etudes religieuses chez les Chi'ites Imamites de la fin du xix siecle a 1960,'* [The quest for knowledge: the religious texts of the Imami Shi'a from the end of the 19th Century to 1960], *Studia Islamica*, vol. 81, no. 1 (1995), pp. 165–185.

Middle East Record, 1960 (London: Weidenfeld & Nicolson, 1960).

Middle East Record, 1961 (London: Weidenfeld & Nicolson, 1961).

Miller, J., *God has Ninety-Nine Names* (New York: Simon and Schuster, 1996).

Moaddel, M., 'The Shi'a 'Ulama and the State in Iran,' *Theory and Society*, vol. 15, no. 4 (1986), pp. 519–556.

Momen, M., *An Introduction to Shi'i Islam* (Oxford: Ronald, 1985).

Momen, M., 'Authority and Opposition in Twelver Shi'ism,' in: Burrell, R. M. (ed.), *Islamic Fundamentaism* (London: Royal Asiatic Society, 1989), pp. 48–66.

Montazam, M. A., *Life and Times of Ayatollah Khomeini* (London: Anglo-European Publishers, 1994).

Morris, B., *Israel's Secret Wars* (New York: Grove Weidenfield, 1991).

Moussawi, A. K., 'The Establishment of the Position of *Marja'iyyat–I-Taqlid* in the Twelver Shi'i Community,' *Iranian Studies*, vol. 18, no. 1 (Winter 1985), pp. 35–51.

Naff, T. & Owen, R. (eds.), *Studies in Eighteenth Century Islamic History* (Carbondale: n.p., 1977).

Nakash, Y., 'An Attempt to Trace the Origin of the Rituals of *Ashoura*,' *Die Welt des Islams*, vol. 33 (1993), pp. 161–181.

Nakash, Y., *The Shi'is of Iraq* (Princeton: Princeton University Press, 1994).

Nakash, Y., 'The Shi'ites and the Future of Iraq,' *Foreign Affairs*, (July 2003), www.Foreignaffairs.org

Nasr, S. & Nasr, M., '*Morphologie Sociale de la Banlieue-Est de Beyrouth*,' [The social morphology of Beirut's eastern suburbs] *Maghreb-Machrek*, no. 73 (July- Sept. 1976), pp. 78–90.

Nasr, S., '*Les Formes de Regroupement Traditionel dans la Société de Beyrouth*,' [The traditional forms of social regrouping in Beirut] in: Nasr, S. (ed.), *L'Espace Social de la Ville Arabe* (Paris: *Maisonneuve et Larose*, 1979), pp. 145–98.

Nasr, S., ' *Beyrouth et le Conflit Libanaise*,' [Beirut and the Lebanese conflict] in: Mutin, G. & Metral, J. (eds.), *Politiques Urbaines dans le Monde Arabe* (Lyon, *Maison de l'Orient Mediterraneen*, 1984), pp. 287–305.

Newman, A. J., 'Towards a Reconsideration of the Isfahan School of Philosophy,' *Studia Iranica*, vol. 15 (1986), pp. 165–199.

Newman, A. J., 'The Nature of the *Akhbari/Usuli* Dispute in late *Safawid* Iran,' *Bulletin of the School of Oriental and African Studies*, pt.1 (1992), pp. 22–51.

Newman, A. J., 'The Myth of the Classical Migration to *Safawid* Iran,' *Die Welt des Islams*, vol. 33 no. 1 (1993), pp. 66–112.

Norton, A. R., 'Harakat Amal,' in: Azar, E. E. (ed.) (et. al.), *The Emergence of New Lebanon* (New York: Praeger, 1984), pp. 162–204.

Norton, A. R., ' The Origins and Resurgence of Amal ,' in: Kramer, M. (ed.), *Shi'ism, Resistance and Revolution* (Boulder: Westview Press, 1987), pp. 203–218.

Norton, A. R., ' *Shi'ism* and Social Protest in Lebanon,' in: Cole, J. R. I. & Keddie, N. R. (eds.), *Shi'ism and Social Protest* (New Haven: Yale University Press, 1986), pp. 156–178.

Norton, A. R., *Amal and the Shi'a* (Austin: University of Texas Press, 1988).

Norton, A. R., ' A Countersensational Perspective on the *Shi'a* of Lebanon,' in: Amirahmadi, H. & Entessar, N. (eds.), *Reconstruction and Regional Diplomacy in the Persian Gulf* (London: Routledge, 1992), pp. 45–61.

Norton, A. R., ' Musa al-Sadr,' in: Rahnema, A. (ed.), *Pioneers of Islamic Revival* (London: Zed Books, 1994), pp. 184–207.

Norton, A. R., ' Walking between Raindrops,' *Mediterranean Quarterly*, vol. 3, no.1, (Summer 1999), pp. 81–102.

Norton, A. R., *Hizballah of Lebanon: Extremist Ideals versus Mundane Politics* (New York: Council on Foreign Relations, 1999).

Odeh, B. J., *Lebanon, Dynamics of Conflict* (London: Zed Books, 1985).

Penrose, E., *Iraq: International Relations and National Development* (London: Benn, 1978).

Peters, R., *Islam and Colonialism* (The Hague: Mouton, 1979).

Peters, R. (ed.), *Proceedings of the Ninth Congress of the Union Europeene des Arabisants et Islamisants* (Leiden: Brill, 1981).

Petran, T., *The Struggle over Lebanon* (New York: Monthly Review Press, 1987).

Picard, E., *Lebanon, A Shattered Country* (London: Holmes & Meire, 1996).

Pool, D., ' From Elite to Class,' *International Journal of the Middle East Studies*, vol. 12, no. 3 (1980), pp. 304–341

Quandt, W., *Peace Process* (Berkeley: University of California Press, 1993).

Rabinovich, I., 'The Problem of South Lebanon,' in: Legum, C. (ed.), *Middle East Contemporary Survey*, vol. 2, 1977–78 (New York: Holmes & Meire, 1979).

Rabinovich, I., ' Lebanon,' in: Legum, C. (ed.), *Middle East Contemporary Survey*, Vol. 4, *1979–80* (New York: Holmes & Meire, 1981).

Rahnema, A. (ed.), *Pioneers of Islamic Revival* (London: Zed Bks., 1994).

Randal, J., *The Tragedy of Lebanon* (London: The Hogarth Press, 1983).

Ranstorp, M., *Hizb'Allah in Lebanon* (London: Macmillan Press, 1997).

Ranstorp, M., 'The Strategy and Tactics of Hizbullah's Current 'Lebanonization' Process,' *Mediterranean Politics*, vol. 3, no. 1 (Summer 1998), pp. 103–136.

Richard, Y., *Shi'ite Islam* (Cambridge: Blackwell Publishers, 1995).

Rieck, A., *Die Schiiten und der Kampf um den Libanon* [The Shi'a and their struggle in Lebanon](Hamburg: Deutsches Orient-Institut, 1989).

Rieck, A., '*Abschied von 'Revolutionsexpor?*' [Farewell to the 'export of revolution'?] *Beitrage zur Konfliktforschung*, vol. 20, no.2 (1990), pp. 81–104.

Sabzavari, S. M., *Islamic Political and Juristic Thought in Safavid Iran* (Glasgow: Royston Publishers, 1990).

Sachedina, A. A., ' *al-Khums*: The Fifth in the Imami Shi'i Legal System,' *Journal of Near Eastern Studies*, vol. 39, no. 4 (1980), pp. 275–289.

Sachedina, A. A., *The Just Ruler in Shi'ite Islam* (Oxford: Oxford University Press, 1988).

Salibi, K., *Crossroads to the Civil War* (Delmar: Caravan Books, 1976).

Sayegh, R., *Too Many Enemies* (London: Zed Bks., 1994).

Schiff, Z. & Ya'ari, E., *Israel's Lebanon War* (New York: Simon & Schuster, 1984).

Schahgaldian, N. B., *The Classical Establishment in Iran* (Santa Monica: Rand, 1989).

Shakira, A. A., *Iraqi Politics* (London: n.p., 1987).

Shapira, S., ' The Imam Musa al-Sadr,' *The Jerusalem Quarterly*, no. 44 (Fall 1987), pp. 121–144.

Shapira, S., ' The Origins of Hizbullah,' *Jerusalem Quarterly*, no. 46 (1988), pp. 115–130.

Shulze, K. E., *Israel's Covert Diplomacy in Lebanon* (London: Macmillan, 1997).

Silverfarb, D., *Britain's Informal Empire in the Middle East* (New York: Oxford University Press, 1986).

Simon, R., ' Iraq,' in: Tachau, F. (ed.), *Political Parties of the Middle East and North Africa* (London: Mansell, 1994).

Sivan, E. & Friedman, M. (eds.), *Religious Radicalism and Politics in the Middle East* (Albany: State University of New York Press, 1990).

Sluglett, P., *Britain in Iraq* (London: Ithaca University Press, 1976).

Sluglett, M. F. & Sluglett, P., 'The Transformation of Land Tenure and Rural Social Structures in Central and Southern Iraq,' *International Journal of Middle East Studies*, vol. 15 (1983), pp. 491–502.

Sluglett, P. & Sluglett, M. F., *Iraq since 1958* (New York: St. Martin's Press, 1991).
Sluglett, P. & Sluglett, M. F., 'The Social Classes and the Origins of the Revolution,' in: Fernia, R. A. Louis, W. R. (eds.), *The Iraqi Revolution of 1958* (London: I. B. Tauris, 1991), pp. 118–141.
Soeterik, R., *The Islamic Movement of Iraq* (Amsterdam: Stichting MERA, 1991).
Stork, J., ' The War for the Camps,' *MERIP Reports*, vol. 15, no. 5 (June 1985), pp. 3–9.
Tabataba'i, M. H., *Shi'a* (Qom: Ansariyan Publishers, 1981).
Tachau, F. (ed.), *Political Parties of the Middle East and North Africa* (London: Mansell, 1994).
Taji-Farouki, S., *A Fundamental Quest* (London: Grey Seal, 1996).
Tauber, E., *The Formation of Modern Syria and Iraq* (London: Frank Cass, 1994).
Tayekh, Ray, 'Iran at the Crossroads,' *The Middle East Journal*, Vol. 57, No.1 (Winter 2003), pp. 42–52.
Theroux, P., *The Strange Disappearance of Imam Moussa Sadr* (London: Wedenfeld & Nicolson, 1987).
Usher, G., ' Hizbullah, Syria, and the Lebanese Elections,' *Journal of Palestine Studies*, vol. 26, no.2 (Winter 1997), pp. 59–67.
Vinogradov, A., ' The 1920 Revolt in Iraq Reconsidered,' *International Journal of Middle East Studies*, vol. 3, no. 2 (1972), pp. 123–139.
Watt, M., 'The Significance of the Early Stages of Imami Shi'ism,' in: Keddie, N. (ed.), *Religion and Politics in Iran* (New Haven: Yale University Press, 1984), pp. 21–32.
White, J. and Philips, R., 'Sadrist Revolt provides lessons for counter-insurgency in Iraq,' *Jane's Intelligence Review*, August 2004, pp. 22–28.
Wiley, J., *The Islamic Movement of Iraqi Shi'ites* (Boulder: Rienner, 1992).
Woodward, B., *The Veil* (London: Simon & Schuster, 1987).
Wright, R., *Sacred Rage* (New York: Simon & Schuster, 1986).
Yapp, M. E., *The Making of the Modern Middle East* (London: Longman, 1987).
Zisser, E., 'Hizballah: between Armed Struggle and Domestic Politics,' in: Rubin, B. (ed.), *Revolutionaries and Reformers: Contemporary Islamist Movements in the Middle East* (Albany: State University of New York Press, 2003), pp. 91–104.

f. Unpublished Secondary Western Sources

Gharbieh, H. M., ' Political Awareness of the Shi'ites in Lebanon,' (Durham: PhD, 1996).
Schbley, A. H., ' Religious Resurgence and Religious Terrorism: A Study of the Actions of the Shi'a Sectarian Movements in Lebanon' (PhD thesis, University of North Texas, 1988).
Suad, J., ' Politicization of Religious Sects in Bour Hammoud,' (PhD thesis, Columbia University, 1975).
Warn, M., ' Staying the Course,' (M.A. thesis, 1994), www.AlMashriq.org.

Index